ISBN 978-0-266-01800-1
PIBN 10960858

English
Français
Deutsche
Italiano
Español
Português

www.forgottenbooks.com

Mythology Photography **Fiction**
Fishing Christianity **Art** Cooking
Essays Buddhism Freemasonry
Medicine **Biology** Music **Ancient**
Egypt Evolution Carpentry Physics
Dance Geology **Mathematics** Fitness
Shakespeare **Folklore** Yoga Marketing
Confidence Immortality Biographies
Poetry **Psychology** Witchcraft
Electronics Chemistry History **Law**
Accounting **Philosophy** Anthropology
Alchemy Drama Quantum Mechanics
Atheism Sexual Health **Ancient History**
Entrepreneurship Languages Sport
Paleontology Needlework Islam
Metaphysics Investment Archaeology
Parenting Statistics Criminology
Motivational

EIGHTY-SIXTH

ANNUAL REPORT

OF

THE MOUNT SINAI HOSPITAL

OF THE

CITY OF NEW YORK

For the Year 1938

Act of Incorporation Filed February, 1852

CONTENTS

Extracts from the Constitution on Endowed Beds and Endowments

A Contribution of $2,500 to the General Fund of the Hospital, if accepted by the Board of Trustees, shall endow a Life Bed. Such contribution shall entitle the donor thereof, during his or her lifetime, to name a patient from time to time to use and occupy one bed in the general wards of the main Hospital, free of charge.

A Contribution of $3,500 to the General Fund of the Hospital, if accepted by the Board of Trustees, shall endow a Memorial Bed. Such contribution shall entitle the donor thereof, during his or her lifetime, to name a patient from time to time to use and occupy one bed in the main Hospital, free of charge. Such donor may bequeath that right to a successor appointed by the said donor in his or her last will and testament, or by any other instrument under seal. In the event of such successor being appointed, the rights hereinbefore mentioned shall continue for a period of not over fifty years from the date of such contribution—such period, however, not to end before ten years from the death of the donor.

A Contribution of $5,000 to the General Fund of the Hospital, if accepted by the Board of Trustees, shall endow a Perpetual Bed in the Children's Pavilion. Such contribution shall entitle the donor thereof, during his or her lifetime, to name a patient from time to time to use and occupy one bed in the wards of the Children's Pavilion, free of charge. Such donor may bequeath that right to a successor appointed by said donor in his or her last will and testament or by any other instrument under seal.

A Contribution of $7,500 to the General Fund of the Hospital, if accepted by the Board of Trustees, shall endow a Perpetual Bed, but where, under the provision of any will executed prior to March 20, 1921, the sum of $5,000 or more is bequeathed to the Hospital in payment of any Perpetual Bed, the Board of Trustees may, at their option, accept such sum in payment of such Perpetual Bed. Such contribution shall entitle the donor thereof, during his or her lifetime, to name a patient from time to time to use and occupy one bed in the general wards of the main Hospital, free of charge. Such donor may bequeath that right to a successor appointed by said donor in his or her last will and testament, or by any other instrument under seal.

When a corporation is the donor, the privilege shall expire at the end of twenty-five years from the date of such contribution.

Tablets to commemorate the endowment of Life and Memorial Beds shall be placed in designated areas, subject to the rules of the Hospital. Tablets for Life Beds shall be maintained during the life of the donor, tablets for Memorial Beds for a period not beyond fifty years from the date of their endowment, such period, however, not to end before ten years from the death of the donor. The endowment of a Perpetual Bed shall entitle the donor, or his legal representative, to have a tablet placed in the ward selected by him, or by them, or to have the endowment recorded on a tablet provided for that purpose in the corridor of the Hospital; such tablets shall be maintained in perpetuity.

A donor may change a Life Bed endowed by him or her to a Memorial Bed by making an additional contribution of $1,000, or to a Perpetual Bed by making an additional contribution of $5,000, or may change a Memorial Bed to a Perpetual Bed by making an additional contribution of $4,000.

No patient shall occupy a Life, Memorial or Perpetual Bed unless he shall comply with the current rules of the Hospital and be a proper subject for treatment according to its regulations.

An endowment for the establishing of any special fund may be accepted by a resolution of the Board of Trustees. Such fund may be created either for a special purpose, in which event the income therefrom shall be devoted to such purpose only, or under the name of one or more persons, in which event the income therefrom shall be devoted to the general purposes of the Hospital. Such endowment funds shall be kept by the Treasurer as special accounts. Contributions to existing funds may be made at any time, but no funds shall be created with an initial endowment of less than Ten Thousand Dollars.

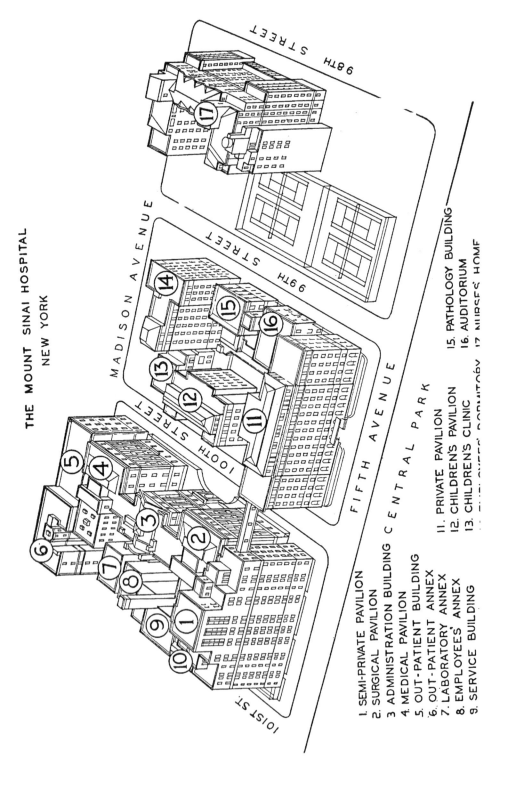

THE MOUNT SINAI HOSPITAL
NEW YORK

1. SEMI-PRIVATE PAVILION
2. SURGICAL PAVILION
3. ADMINISTRATION BUILDING
4. MEDICAL PAVILION
5. OUT-PATIENT BUILDING
6. OUT-PATIENT ANNEX
7. LABORATORY ANNEX
8. EMPLOYEES' ANNEX
9. SERVICE BUILDING

11. PRIVATE PAVILION
12. CHILDREN'S PAVILION
13. CHILDREN'S CLINIC

15. PATHOLOGY BUILDING
16. AUDITORIUM
17. NURSES' HOME

HISTORICAL NOTE

The Mount Sinai Hospital was organized and incorporated in 1852 for "benevolent, charitable and scientific purposes." The work of the Hospital was begun in a small private dwelling on 28th Street, between Seventh and Eighth Avenues, which accommodated 28 patients. The Hospital now has accommodations for 856 patients, including 18 beds in the receiving ward.

In 1871 the Hospital completed and occupied, at Lexington Avenue, 66th and 67th Streets, a building having a capacity of 200 beds.

The Dispensary, now known as the Out-Patient Department, was inaugurated in 1872.

The clinical departments first organized were those of medicine and surgery; a gynecologist was appointed in 1877.

Mount Sinai created precedents among the hospitals of New York by setting up a distinct pediatric service in 1878 and an otologic service in 1879; the latter was at first combined with, but in 1910 was separated from, ophthalmology and laryngology.

The Mount Sinai Training School for Nurses, in affiliation with the Hospital, was incorporated in March, 1881; the name of the school was changed in 1923 to The Mount Sinai Hospital School of Nursing.

In 1883 a committee was formed to develop a Medical Library.

In 1886 a district medical service was inaugurated.

Provision for the care of private patients was first made in 1886; an intermediate or "semi-private" ward was opened in 1904.

In 1893 a Pathological Department was established, and consultants in dermatology and neurology were appointed.

The corner stone of the group of ten hospital buildings occupying the block bounded by Fifth and Madison Avenues, 100th and 101st Streets, was laid May 22nd, 1901; the buildings were completed and occupied March 15th, 1904, when 500 beds became available for the care of the sick.

A Department of Dietetics was established in 1905.

A Social Service Department was inaugurated in 1906.

A Tuberculosis Clinic was organized in 1908.

The first of a series of "Fellowship" funds was created in 1908 to assist investigators engaged in scientific medical work.

The Hospital's first X-ray machine was installed in 1900. In 1910 a full-fledged Department of Radiology was formed and in 1924 the department was subdivided into separate branches for (a) radiography and (b) X-ray and radium therapy.

In 1910 the three-story Out-Patient Building, which had been completed in 1904 was altered to a five-story building, and the Nurses' Home was enlarged from a six-story to an eight-story building. At the same time new isolation wards were erected on the roof of the Medical Building.

A Dental Department was established for the benefit of in-patients in 1910; this work was extended to the Out-Patient Department in 1925.

An orthopedic surgeon and a physio-therapist were named in 1911.

Roof wards for outdoor treatment were erected on the Medical and Surgical Pavilions in 1912.

The Hospital in 1912 accepted a fund "for the advancement of preventive medicine." A "health class" for children was promptly established.

In 1913 the erection of seven additional buildings south of 100th Street was begun; four of these buildings were occupied in 1915, and three, namely, the Private Pavilion, the Children's Pavilion and the Auditorium, were completed in the spring of 1922. With these additions, the Hospital was able to care for 654 patients.

The first of a series of lectureship funds was established in 1913. These funds provide honoraria for distinguished visiting lecturers.

Electro-cardiography was instituted in 1915.

In 1917, Mount Sinai Hospital became a constituent member of the Federation for the Support of Jewish Philanthropic Societies, which was organized in that year.

Until 1917, tonsillectomies were performed in the Dispensary, often without anesthesia; in the year mentioned, a "tonsil and adenoid" ward, with a fully equipped operating room, was opened.

A Mount Sinai Hospital Unit, organized as a section of the Medical Department of the United States Army, was sent to France in 1918.

Post-Graduate medical instruction was formally organized in 1923, in affiliation with the College of Physicians and Surgeons of Columbia University.

A permanent fund for the support of medical research was inaugurated in 1925, prior to which research was precariously supported by occasional donations.

The construction of a new school and residence building for the School of Nursing, fronting on 98th Street, between Fifth and Madison Avenues, was begun in 1925 and completed in 1927; the residence accommodates 490 nurses.

The new Semi-Private Pavilion for the care of patients of moderate means was completed and opened to the public in 1931.

Group or cooperative special nursing was introduced for the first time in 1931.

A Consultation Service for ambulant out-patients of moderate means was organized in 1931.

Neuro-surgery was included in General Surgery until 1932, when a separate service was created.

The modernization of the Out-Patient Department Building was completed in 1933.

New facilities for cystoscopy were built and occupied in 1933.

In 1934, the vacant former laboratory on 101st Street, was renovated and restored to use, providing space for a number of exiled German scientists and others.

Renovation and modernization of the Medical and Surgical Pavilions, part of the group of 10 buildings built in 1901, was begun in 1935 and completed in 1936.

The Isolation Ward was rebuilt in 1936 and, with the approval of the Department of Health, became the first Isolation Unit in New York City to be made available for use of private patients.

The Clinical Photographic Department, on a volunteer basis for more than a score of years, was established on a full time basis in 1936.

The Research Foundation of The Mount Sinai Hospital was incorporated in 1936 "to conduct, promote, encourage, and assist investigation in the services and arts of hygiene, medicine, and surgery and allied subjects."

Renovation of the Administration Building—after more than 30 years of use—was undertaken in 1937 and completed in 1938, providing enlarged facilities for Physiotherapy, Hydrotherapy, Occupational Therapy, Dentistry and other diagnostic and therapeutic services. Improved classroom and amphitheatre facilities for postgraduate medical instruction were also provided.

STATISTICAL SUMMARY

Year	Patients Treated in Hospital	Hospital Days	Consultations in Out-Patient Department	Total Disbursements for all Maintenance and Non-Budgetary Purposes (Non-Capital)
1857	216	6,048*	None	$9,000.00
1860	297	8,316*	None	14,000.00
1870	663	18,564*	None	20,000.00
1880	1,474	43,164	9,922	44,376.10
1890	2,862	65,255	43,560	100,000.00
1900	3,145	75,113	86,431	135,272.00
1910	7,613	149,198	115,726	410,000.00
1920	9,548	146,841	173,682	899,704.97
1930	12,179	193,482	222,489	1,785,244.23
1937	16,348	228,744	327,068	2,295,183.58
1938	16,657	231,243	343,862	2,329,674.17

* Estimated.

PRESIDENT'S REPORT

In assuming the responsibilities of President of The Mount Sinai Hospital, I was keenly conscious of the fact that my task was doubly difficult because I succeeded Mr. George Blumenthal, whose brilliant leadership for a period of over twenty-seven years had set a standard that challenged comparison. My aim for the past year has been and will continue to be, as long as I hold office, to keep the reputation of the Hospital at the same high level, and to have it keep pace with the scientific progress which is making new records with amazing rapidity. Any success which is achieved in this direction, will be possible only because the Board of Trustees, the Medical Staff and the Administrative Staff of the Hospital give me their splendid support as in the past.

In practically all Departments there has been an increase in the service rendered in 1938 over 1937. The total number of patients treated in the Hospital was 16,657 in 1938 as against 16,348 in 1937. In the Private Pavilion there were 32,756 hospital days' care as against 33,191 in 1937 and in the Semi-Private Pavilion there was a slight increase, namely 42,487 hospital days' care in 1938 against 42,013 in 1937. The total number of hospital days' care established a new high record of 231,243.

In the Out-Patient Department where there was an average daily attendance of 181 physicians, another high mark of 343,862 consultations was established in comparison with 327,068 the previous year. The Consultation Service continued to attract large numbers and admitted 2,768 patients as against 2,658 in 1937.

Although no new construction of major importance was undertaken during the past year, there were a few changes and improvements which appeared to be necessary in order to maintain the high grade of service on which the Hospital prides itself. Among these, were the long delayed renovating of two floors of the Adolph Lewisohn Pathological Building, completion of the installation of self-leveling devices of the elevators of the Private, Children's, Surgical and Medical Pavilions, as well as of the Administration Building, making them safer for patients, the remodeling of the first floor of the Laboratory Annex for cancer work of Dr. Richard Lewisohn, paid for by special donations, and also of the old operating amphitheatre which can now be used for teaching as well as for operations. Several especially noisy areas throughout the Hospital were acoustically treated, resulting in greater comfort and efficiency. New flush elevator doors were installed in the Out-Patient Department replacing the old dangerous open iron doors.

We have for several years past been confronted with a problem of providing sufficient electric power to meet the growing demands of the Institution. Under the guidance of Mr. Mordecai, Chairman of the Building Committee, a plan was matured which will not only secure additional power, but will do so at a reduced cost and will provide for future growth. A contract for two 500 H.P. 350 K.W. Diesel-driven generators together with the necessary auxiliary equipment has been signed, one-half of the cost of which will be met by Federation.

We take pride in the loyalty of our Administrative Staff, evidenced not only by efficient work but by length of service, During the year, Gold Medals and gifts were presented to Miss Margaret Hynes, maid, and to Mr. Kalman Fuchs, orderly, on the completion of 26 and 25 years respectively of devoted service to the Hospital.

In keeping with the times, salaries and wages throughout the Institution have been increased during the year by $40,000, bringing the total increase since 1934 to $212,000. Much of this increase has been in the shape of restoration of cuts forced upon us by the depression following the year 1929.

Many interesting clinical developments have taken place in the wards of the Hospital, and these as well as the research work will be recorded elsewhere in the report by the President of the Medical Board.

Among the developments, mention might be made here of the following:

To meet the demand for a supply of blood for transfusions, when required very promptly in emergencies, a "Blood Bank" was established in the Hospital in May of 1938. Organized and maintained by the Laboratory of Hematology under the direction of Dr. Nathan Rosenthal, this procedure has thus far given good results and has been expanded to take care of cases other than emergencies, with satisfactory results, both medically and economically. This work is still being conducted on an experimental basis to determine its precise value in medicine.

10

In cooperation with the Department of Health and the Committee on Neighborhood Health Development, an experiment in the Intravenous Drip Method for rapid treatment of syphilis was successfully carried on under the direction of Dr. George Baehr by Doctors Harold T. Hyman, Louis Chargin and William Leifer. Six beds were assigned to this work, which, on the basis of results to date, offers great promise of real progress in the fight against this scourge. The support for this work has been supplied by a fund raised by the Committee on Neighborhood Health Development to which the New York Foundation and the Friedsam Foundation have generously contributed and which is administered by Dr. Walter Clarke, Consultant to the Department of Health.

New modern equipment as replacements was installed in the X-Ray Department from funds especially established for this purpose.

In the Physio-Therapy Department which had been moved to larger quarters early in the year, the treatment of disease by the use of heat, was further developed. To Dr. William Bierman, who heads this Department, the Hospital is also indebted for his generous gift of equipment for the new Physics Laboratory and for his help in securing the donation of a high tension static machine which was overhauled and installed in the Out-Patient Physio-Therapy Department. The official opening of our enlarged and newly equipped Department of Physio-Therapy was marked by the Spring Meeting of the Eastern Section of the American Congress of Physio-Therapy which met at the Hospital on April 13, 1938.

The Clinical Pathological Conferences which have for several years been taxing the capacity of the George Blumenthal Auditorium have under the able direction of Drs. Klemperer and Baehr continued to attract large numbers of men from within and without the walls of the Hospital, the average attendance having been over 300.

Teaching in the Post-Graduate Classes in affiliation with Columbia University continued and the courses were more popular than ever, with an attendance of 299 students.

Under the guidance of its editor, Dr. Joseph Globus, the Journal of The Mount Sinai Hospital has prospered and has attained the distinction of having its contents indexed in the Journal of the American Medical Association. Its circulation has increased 12% over 1937.

Honors have been conferred upon several of the members of our Medical Staff, among which I might mention that—Dr. Isidore Friesner was elected President of the American Otological Society and Dr. Bela Schick had awarded to him the Gold Medal of the New York Academy of Medicine and the Addingham Gold Medal by the William Hoffman Wood Trust of Leeds, England, for his outstanding accomplishment in medicine.

Lectures by distinguished members of the medical profession were given in the George Blumenthal Auditorium as follows:

Professor Juan Bacigalupo, University of Buenos Aires, South America: "The Life History of Fasciola Hepatica."

Dr. George White Pickering, University College Hospital Medical School, London: "The Problem of High Blood Pressure in Man" and "Headache."

Professor Walter Bradford Cannon, Harvard Medical School, delivered the William Henry Welch Lectures: "Some new aspects of Homeostasis"; "The Aging of Homeostatic Mechanisms."

Professor Einer Hammersten, The Carolingian Medical University, Stockholm, Sweden, delivered the Edward Gamaliel Janeway Lectures: "Duodenum and its Associates, The Important Hormonal Centrum"; "Cell Structure: Functions of Nucleic Acid."

Dr. Ludwik Gross of the Pasteur Institute, Paris, France: "Experimental Anti-Cancerous Immunity."

Clinics were held and lectures given by members of our Staff at the Hospital during the Annual Sessions of the American College of Physicians and of the American College of Surgeons.

As usual we took part in the Graduate Fortnight of the New York Academy of Medicine and members of our Medical Staff contributed clinics and lectures on the subject of "Diseases of the Blood" and "Blood Forming Organs."

It is with deep sorrow that we make record of the heavy toll that has been taken of members of the Board of Trustees and of the Medical Staff.

Mr. Joseph F. Cullman, Trustee since 1897 and Mr. Adolph Lewisohn, Trustee since 1898, passed away in August of 1938. Their service to the Hospital was very great, and record of our sense of loss is made in the resolutions on their death, which appear elsewhere in this report.

Of the Medical Staff, we have suffered irreparable losses in the death of Dr. Edwin Beer, Consulting Surgeon, Dr. Henry W. Berg, Physician to the Isolation Service and Dr. Walter L. Horn, Associate Otologist. Resolutions which were adopted by the Board of Trustees are printed in this Annual Report.

Mr. Alfred Loewenthal who had generously served as volunteer photographer for the Hospital for many years, was another good friend who was lost to us by death.

The community suffered a great loss in the death of Mr. Lawrence Marx, President of Federation, who had given of himself unsparingly in the interest of the general welfare. Resolution adopted by the Board of Trustees expressing their sentiments appears in this report.

Mr. Arthur H. Harlow, after ten years of devoted service, resigned as Secretary but continued as Trustee. Mrs. Arthur J. Cohen and Mr. Robert Lehman were elected Trustees.

At the annual meeting, at which Mr. George Blumenthal's resignation as President was regretfully accepted, he was elected President Emeritus, a position which had been created for the purpose. Mr. Waldemar Kops was elected First Vice-President, Mr. George B. Bernheim, Second Vice-President, Mr. Leo Gottlieb, Third Vice-President, Mr. Nelson I. Asiel, Treasurer, and Mr. Paul M. Rosenthal, Secretary.

Several changes in the Administrative Staff occurred during the year. Miss Adeline Wood, who had served as Supervising Dietitian since 1925, resigned, and her assistant, Miss Helen Somers, was appointed Acting Supervising Dietitian. To take the place of Dr. Mayer A. Green, who resigned as Assistant Director, Dr. Maxwell S. Frank was appointed. Dr. Milton L. Dryfus was appointed to the newly created position of Administrative Assistant.

During the year, retirements from active service and appointments to the Consulting Staff, included the late Dr. Edwin Beer and Dr. Israel Strauss, both of whom had given the Hospital devoted and outstandingly able service for more than thirty years.

The Board of Trustees presented them with appropriately inscribed desk sets as a mark of their appreciation, as was also done in the cases of Dr. Robert T. Frank and Dr. Richard Lewisohn, who had retired in the previous year.

The following changes have taken place in our Medical Staff:

RESIGNATIONS FROM THE MEDICAL STAFF

Dr. Moses Keschner................................Associate Neurologist
Dr. Joseph B. Stenbuck...........................Adjunct Surgeon
Dr. Carl Levenson ....Adjunct Physiotherapist

NEW APPOINTMENTS ON THE MEDICAL STAFF

Dr. Edwin Beer (Deceased) ....Consulting Surgeon
Dr. Israel Strauss ....Consulting Neurologist
Dr. Abraham Hyman ....Surgeon to Hospital
Dr. Israel S. Wechsler..........................Neurologist to Hospital
Dr. Joseph H. Globus ....Neuro-Pathologist
Dr. Leon Ginzburg ....Associate Surgeon
Dr. Leo Edelman ....Associate Surgeon
Dr. Richard M. Brickner........................Associate Neurologist
Dr. Abraham Kaplan ....Associate Neuro-Surgeon
Dr. Otto Marburg ....Associate Neuro-Pathologist
Dr. Sadao Otani ....*Associate Pathologist
Dr. Louis J. Soffer................................Adjunct Physician
Dr. Arthur R. Sohval.............................Adjunct Physician
Dr. Arthur H. Aufses.............................Adjunct Surgeon
Dr. Leonard J. Druckerman ....Adjunct Surgeon
Dr. H. Evans Leiter...............................Adjunct Surgeon
Dr. Judah Marmor ....Adjunct Neurologist
Dr. Benjamin H. Balser.........................Adjunct Neurologist
Dr. Leo Stone ....Adjunct Psychiatrist
Dr. Sidney W. Gross.............................Adjunct Neuro-Surgeon
Dr. Abou D. Pollack..............................*Assistant Pathologist
Dr. Alexander Kolin ....*Physicist

To commemorate the completion of Mr. George Blumenthal's 46 years of service as Trustee and 27 years as President as well as the 80th anniversary of his birthday, the Trustees tendered

---

* On full time.

him a banquet on April 7, 1938 at which a tablet which was subsequently installed in the Main Hall of the Administration Building, was unveiled. The inscription on the tablet reads as follows:

> "Erected on the occasion of the 80th birthday of George Blumenthal by his Fellow Trustees to record their grateful appreciation of his inspired leadership and unparalleled contribution to the development of this Institution during 46 years as Trustee and 27 years as President—April 7th, 1938."

We have been fortunate to receive during the year 1938 the following gifts and legacies:

DEDICATION OF BEDS

Children's Perpetual Bed:

In memory of Celia and Solomon Oppenheimer— Founded by provision in the will of Solomon Oppenheimer (excluding mortgage certificate of undetermined value) $3,857.62

Memorial Bed:

In memory of Levi and Sarah Goldenberg—Founded by provision in the will of their daughter, Helen B. Chaim 3,500.00

BEQUESTS

Estate of Edward J. King—Additional for the Edward J. and Jennie I. King Memorial Fund $113,212.77

Estate of Marco Fleishman—Additional for the Rosetta and Marco Fleishman Memorial Fund 38,464.70

Henry W. Putnam 50,000.00

Bettie Meierhoff (excluding mortgage certificate of undetermined value) 36,543.07

Harry J. D. Plaut 5,107.50

Charles S. Erlanger 5,000.00

Emanuel Felsenheld 1,250.00

Morris Drey 1,000.00

David J. Frankel 1,000.00

Sara T. Lowman 1,000.00

LEGACIES AND DONATIONS OF $500 AND MORE FOR
SPECIAL PURPOSES DURING YEAR 1938

Estate of Amelia Meyers $233,026.35

> For the alteration and dedication of the Laboratory Annex to be known as "The Abraham and Amelia Meyers Memorial" and for the support of research work carried on therein.

Estate of Charles Klingenstein—to be added to the Mr. and Mrs. Charles Klingenstein Fund for non-budgetary purposes 50,000.00

Estate of William N. Cohen—For the William N. Cohen Research Fund; income to be used for research work 25,000.00

Estate of William N. Cohen—to be added to the Etta C. Lorsch Memorial Fund; income to be disbursed by the Social Service Auxiliary for the special country care of children.. 10,000.00

Committee on Neighborhood Health Development— For Intravenous Drip Therapy Project.................... 8,625.33

David A. Schulte—For the Out-Patient Department Dental Clinic 8,000.00

Mr. and Mrs. George Blumenthal—For non-budgetary purposes 5,000.00

Blanche and Frank Wolf Foundation, Inc.—For Dr. Shwartzman's work in cancer research.............. 3,000.00

Mr. and Mrs. Steven J. Hirsch—In memory of his brother, Walter A. Hirsch—To be added to the Morris J. and Carrie Hirsch Fund.......................... 2,500.00

Dr. I. C. Rubin—For Dr. Hiram N. Vineberg Fund for Gynecology Research 2,400.00

The Friedsam Foundation, Inc.—For Ear, Nose and Throat Research 1,800.00

Mrs. Addie H. Homan—For the Isidor Hernsheim Fellowship in Chemistry 1,500.00

Mrs. Charles Klingenstein—To be added to the Charles Klingenstein Fellowship Fund 1,500.00

"A Friend"—For a Fellowship in Gynecology to commemorate the 75th Birthday of Dr. Joseph Brettauer 1,200.00

Eli Lilly Company—For Eli Lilly Fellowship	$1,200.00
Josiah Macy, Jr. Foundation—For studies on the secretion of a para-sympathetic substance under emotional stress	1,000.00
Mount Sinai Hospital Research Foundation, Inc.—For Venom Research	900.00
Dr. Ralph Colp—For Fellowship in Bacteriology	800.00
The Friedsam Foundation, Inc.—For special pediatric research on drug reactions	750.00
Josiah Macy, Jr. Foundation—For research on psychological and physiological aspects of angina pectoris	750.00
United Fruit Company—For studies on carbohydrate absorption	500.00
John Wyeth and Brother, Inc.—For the study of the continuous drip method in treating peptic ulcer	500.00

DONATIONS OF $500 AND MORE FOR SUPPORT OF CANCER RESEARCH WORK OF DR. RICHARD LEWISOHN

Mrs. Arthur Lehman	$2,500.00
New York Foundation	2,250.00
Mrs. Paul Gottheil—In memory of daughter, Elsie Gottheil Jaretzki	2,000.00
Ittleson Foundation	1,500.00
Frances and John L. Loeb Foundation	1,500.00
Sam A. Lewisohn	1,000.00
Mrs. Benjamin J. Buttenwieser	500.00
Mrs. Louis J. Grumbach	500.00
Frank Lewisohn	500.00
Miss Adelaide Reckford	500.00

LEGACIES AND DONATIONS OF $500 AND MORE FOR CARDIO-VASCULAR RESEARCH

Estate of Henry Esberg	$5,000.00
Mr. and Mrs. Frank Altschul	996.26
Mrs. Charles Altschul	500.00
Anonymous	500.00

LEGACIES AND DONATIONS OF $500 AND MORE TOWARD FELLOWSHIP FOR GASTRO-ENTEROLOGY RESEARCH

The Friedsam Foundation, Inc.	$2,500.00
Dr. Ralph Colp	500.00
Mrs. Clara Klingenstein	500.00
Dr. Percy Klingenstein	500.00
Estate of Louise King Reckford	500.00

LEGACIES AND DONATIONS OF $500 AND MORE FOR RESEARCH FUND

Mrs. Paul Gottheil—In memory of daughter, Elsie Gottheil Jaretzki	$3,000.00
Mrs. Levy Mayer—In memory of son-in-law Walter A. Hirsch	1,000.00
Estate of S. Morgan Barber	500.00

To Mrs. Kurt Semon we are again indebted for her assistance in providing for the horses so urgently needed for Dr. Shwartzman's work.

It is with a sense of deepest gratitude that we make acknowledgment of these generous gifts which have helped to make it possible for us to carry on the routine work of the Hospital on an increased scale and to continue some of the research work which will, we hope, make itself felt in the preventive and therapeutic advances, which make medical history.

The Associated Hospital Service has been making great strides during the past year. An increase in the number of patients and days' care of more than 120% is an indication of its growth. Although these admissions showed a loss to the Hospital, adjustments are being made which will, I hope, gradually eliminate such loss. The insurance feature of the system is sound and should be encouraged by the member hospitals even at a temporary sacrifice.

The Neustadter Convalescent Home which has cared for many of our convalescent women and children patients, decided to discontinue accepting children, inasmuch as there appears to be fairly ample provision for this class of cases, and instead to accept men convalescents. It is believed that this change of policy will meet a real need and it is greatly welcomed.

18

At the request of the Blythedale Home, the facilities of the Hospital were put at its disposal for the purpose of examining applicants for admission.

The Private and the Semi-Private Pavilions have functioned smoothly, and I am pleased to report that general satisfaction with these Services is constantly expressed. A number of portable air-conditioning machines were available to patients in the Private Pavilion during the past summer and were provided at a small additional fee. Eight-hour Nursing Service in the Private Pavilion continued on an optional basis and was availed of to the same extent as in the previous year, namely about 11%.

The expenditures for current purposes of the Hospital including the School of Nursing, the Social Service Department and the Ladies' Auxiliary in 1938 amounted to $2,329,674.17

Receipts applicable to current expenditures were 2,035,132.11

Leaving a net deficit of 294,542.06

Included in the Receipts are the following:

Received from Federation $545,256.10

Received through Federation on behalf of the Greater New York Fund 55,742.93

Total 600,999.03

From the United Hospital Fund—For the Hospital and the Social Service Auxiliary $88,813.09

From the City of New York—For custodians and part payment of cost of cases approved by the City 197,558.39

The deficit in 1938 amounted to $294,542 which added to other deficits since the depression years, beginning with 1930, has now reached a total of $1,544,505.

The deficit which has been incurred in 1938 is the largest in our history and has been due in great part to increased cost of salaries and wages and the shortening of working hours, in conformity with the times. Our rapidly dwindling funds available for meeting deficits cause us considerable anxiety, and unless a greater amount can be made available to us by Federation or directly through the generosity of our friends in the community, curtailment of our work may become a reality. We have steadfastly refused to lower our standards of service as we firmly believe that we are rendering a real service not only to those in our care but also to the community at large by consistently following this policy.

As in years past, we have had the sympathetic cooperation of Mayor LaGuardia, Comptroller McGoldrick and the Board of Estimate, as well as that of Commissioners Goldwater, Rice and Hodson, for all of which we are deeply appreciative.

It is difficult to find words which will adequately measure the debt of gratitude which has been placed upon us and the community by the unselfish devotion of the Medical Staff, which, under the leadership of Dr. Isidore Friesner, has again given of its time and effort without stint.

To the School of Nursing and its President, Hugo Blumenthal, to the Social Service Department and its leader, Mrs. Alfred A. Cook, to the Ladies' Auxiliary Society, headed by Mrs. Leopold Bernheimer, we likewise are grateful for this splendid accomplishment of the year, without which, the Hospital would of course have been unable to function. For the second successive year, The Mount Sinai Social Service Department was awarded the $1,000.00 prize by the United Hospital Fund for securing the largest number of individual contributions in its drive.

I wish also to express on behalf of the Board of Trustees the thanks to the Administrative Staff ably led by Dr. Joseph Turner, and seconded by his Assistants and Department Heads and to each and every individual worker in the Hospital, the School of Nursing and the Social Service Department for their faithful and efficient performance of their duties.

We have received splendid support from Federation, which, under the leadership of Mr. Walter Rothschild has completed a brilliant campaign under what appeared to be insurmountable handicaps.

To the United Hospital Fund and The Greater New York Fund, we likewise extend our expression of gratitude and admiration for their achievements.

Respectfully submitted,

LEO ARNSTEIN,

President.

RESOLUTION ON THE DEATH OF
MR. ADOLPH LEWISOHN

In the death of Adolph Lewisohn, on August 17, 1938, the country has lost one of its outstanding citizens who for many years had devoted a large part of his time, energy and means, with great success, to the improvement of its educational, civic and charitable institutions. The Mount Sinai Hospital has lost an interested, loyal and liberal Trustee who played an important part in the development of the Hospital, having personally made possible its original laboratory and later its present modern Lewisohn Laboratory Building.

The breadth of interest and wide sympathy which characterized Mr. Lewisohn's life are exemplified by the variety and magnitude of his philanthropic works. Of these, The Mount Sinai Hospital claimed a large share of his attention.

As a member of the Board of Trustees since 1898, he was interested in all aspects of the work of the Hospital, but his special interest was in its medical research, which led him to support most generously this phase of the Hospital's activities.

At a special meeting of the Board of Trustees of The Mount Sinai Hospital, it was unanimously resolved to make this formal record of the esteem in which Mr. Lewisohn was held by the Board and its sense of great loss in his death, and to present to his family an engrossed copy of this resolution.

LEO ARNSTEIN,
President

PAUL M. ROSENTHAL,
Secretary.

21

RESOLUTION ON THE DEATH OF
MR. JOSEPH F. CULLMAN

In the death of Joseph F. Cullman The Mount Sinai Hospital has suffered a real loss. For more than forty-one years he has faithfully served as Trustee, during which time he has given unsparingly of his time and his means.

As member of the Executive Committee and as Chairman of the Committee on Medical Instruction he has made a real contribution to the health work of the community. His wise counsel and his genial personality will be sadly missed by his co-Trustees who extend to his bereaved family their heartfelt sympathy.

In recognition of his outstanding services, the flag of the Hospital has been ordered flown at half-staff, and it was resolved to send an engrossed copy of these sentiments to the members of his family.

LEO ARNSTEIN,
President

PAUL M. ROSENTHAL,
Secretary.

RESOLUTION ON THE DEATH OF
DR. EDWIN BEER

The Board of Trustees of The Mount Sinai Hospital has learned with deep regret of the death of Dr. Edwin Beer, consulting surgeon to the Hospital and one of the most distinguished members of its staff. Dr. Beer was connected with the institution in various capacities for more than thirty years, having been attending surgeon for fifteen years until his appointment as consulting surgeon in 1937. During the period of his service on the staff of the Hospital Dr. Beer faithfully served its patients with untiring devotion and with great professional skill. His achievements in his field of surgery won for him an outstanding position in his profession. His passing is a sad loss to the Hospital and to the community.

To the members of his family we extend this expression of profound sympathy in this time of sorrow.

LEO ARNSTEIN,
President

PAUL. M. ROSENTHAL,
Secretary.

RESOLUTION ON THE DEATH OF
DR. LEOPOLD JACHES

The Board of Trustees of The Mount Sinai Hospital has learned with deep regret of the death of Dr. Leopold Jaches, who for more than thirty years has faithfully served this Institution in the capacity of radiologist to the Hospital. His outstanding services in his chosen field and his scientific attainments earned the respect and admiration of the medical world. His splendid character, lifelong devotion to duty and readiness to help others established a lasting memorial in the hearts of his friends and colleagues.

To his bereaved family the Board extends the assurance of its sincerest sympathy.

LEO ARNSTEIN,
President

PAUL M. ROSENTHAL,
Secretary.

RESOLUTION ON THE DEATH OF
DR. HENRY W. BERG

At the regular meeting of the Board of Trustees of The Mount Sinai Hospital, on January 10, 1939, announcement was made of the death of Dr. Henry W. Berg, whereupon the Board gave expression to its sense of loss in the following Minute:

In the death of Dr. Henry W. Berg, The Mount Sinai Hospital has lost a true friend, who for more than forty years, gave unstintingly of his time and skill to the patients in the wards of the Hospital, to whose care he was deeply devoted.

His thorough knowledge in the field of contagious diseases was always at the service of the Hospital, and he made a valuable educational contribution through his lectures on this subject in the School of Nursing.

The Board of Trustees of The Mount Sinai Hospital wishes to make record of its debt of gratitude for his skill and devotion, and to extend to Dr. Albert A. Berg its heartfelt sympathy in the great loss that he has sustained.

LEO ARNSTEIN,
President

PAUL M. ROSENTHAL,
Secretary.

RESOLUTION ON THE DEATH OF
MR. LAWRENCE MARX

The Board of Trustees of The Mount Sinai Hospital has learned with deep regret of the sudden death of Lawrence Marx.

For many years he has been one of the most effective workers in the raising of funds and during the past year has filled the office of President of Federation with distinction.

His forceful personality and devotion to this work combined to make him an outstanding figure in communal activity. He was interested in all phases of philanthropic endeavor and gave unstintingly of himself whenever called upon.

To his bereaved family we extend our most heartfelt sympathy.

LEO ARNSTEIN,
President

PAUL M. ROSENTHAL,
Secretary.

In Memoriam

FRANCES FISCHER
Employed 24 Years
PRIVATE PAVILION
Died May 12, 1938

MICHAEL SONEK
Employed 2½ Years
MAIN HALL
Died May 23, 1938

MIKE SOKA
Employed 15 Years
HOUSEKEEPING DEPARTMENT
Died July 2, 1938

RENA GROSSMAN
Employed 22 Years
SOCIAL SERVICE DEPARTMENT
Died Oct. 4, 1938

29

31

32

33

OFFICERS AND STANDING COMMITTEES OF THE MEDICAL BOARD FOR 1939

OFFICERS AND STANDING COMMITTEES OF THE MEDICAL BOARD FOR 1939

(Continued)

Committee on Radiology

RUDOLPH KRAMER, M.D...*Chairman*
WILLIAM BIERMAN, M.D.   *COLEMAN B. RABIN, M.D.
*HARRY A. GOLDBERG, D.D.S.   ISADORE ROSEN, M.D.

Committee on Out-Patient Department

JOHN H. GARLOCK, M.D...*Chairman*
*RICHARD M. BRICKNER, M.D.   ISADORE ROSEN, M.D.
*HENRY MINSKY, M.D.   *SAMUEL ROSEN, M.D.
*ELI MOSCHCOWITZ, M.D.   BELA SCHICK, M.D.
*ASHER WINKELSTEIN, M.D.

Committee on Nurses

BELA SCHICK, M.D...*Chairman*
*DAVID BECK, M.D.   ISIDOR C. RUBIN, M.D.

Committee on Records

ABRAHAM HYMAN, M.D...*Chairman*
*EDWARD B. GREENSPAN, M.D.   ROBERT K. LIPPMANN, M.D.
*PERCY KLINGENSTEIN, M.D.   *SOLOMON SILVER, M.D.

Committee on Cardiography

BERNARD S. OPPENHEIMER, M.D...*Chairman*
*ERNST P. BOAS, M.D.   *WILLIAM M. HITZIG, M.D.
*ARTHUR M. FISHBERG, M.D.   BELA SCHICK, M.D.

Committee on Social Service

ISRAEL S. WECHSLER, M.D...*Chairman*
*SAMUEL H. AVERBUCK, M.D.   *WILLIAM H. MENCHER, M.D.
*DAVID BECK, M.D.   *HERMAN SCHWARZ, M.D.

Dental Committee

RALPH COLP, M.D. ....*Chairman*
*CHARLES K. FRIEDBERG, M.D.   JACOB L. MAYBAUM, M.D.
RUDOLPH KRAMER, M.D.   *ARTHUR SOHVAL, M.D.
*ARTHUR S. W. TOUROFF, M.D.

---

* Not a member of the Medical Board.

OFFICERS AND STANDING COMMITTEES OF THE MEDICAL BOARD FOR 1939

(Continued)

Committee on Economy

HAROLD NEUHOF, M.D...*Chairman*
SAMUEL H. GEIST, M.D.   *HERBERT POLLACK, M.D.
*FREDERICK H. KING, M.D.   SETH SELIG, M.D.
*GORDON D. OPPENHEIMER, M.D.   *FREDERIC D. ZEMAN, M.D.

Committee on Pharmacy

*ERNST P. BOAS, M.D..*Chairman*
*MORRIS S. BENDER, M.D.   *DANIEL POLL, M.D.
*SAMUEL KARELITZ, M.D.   *IRVING R. ROTH, M.D.
                *LESTER R. TUCHMAN, M.D.

Committee on Dietetics

BELA SCHICK, M.D...*Chairman*
*BURRILL B. CROHN, M.D.   *HERBERT POLLACK, M.D.
*HERMAN LANDE, M.D.   *ASHER WINKELSTEIN, M.D.

Committee on Library

*ELI MOSCHCOWITZ, M.D..*Chairman*
WILLIAM BIERMAN, M.D.   *LEON GINZBURG, M.D.
*LEO EDELMAN, M.D.   *SYLVAN E. MOOLTEN, M.D.
                KAUFMAN SCHLIVEK, M.D.

Committee on Medical Publications

IRA COHEN, M.D. ....*Chairman*
*MURRAY H. BASS, M.D.   *REUBEN OTTENBERG, M.D.
SAMUEL H. GEIST, M.D.   *LOUIS J. SOFFER, M.D.
*SOL W. GINSBURG, M.D.   ISRAEL S. WECHSLER, M.D.

OFFICERS OF THE ASSOCIATION OF THE JUNIOR MEDICAL STAFF

FREDERIC D. ZEMAN, M.D..*Chairman*
MORRIS A. GOLDBERGER, M.D...............................*Vice-Chairman*
SOLOMON SILVER, M.D...*Secretary*
DAVID BECK, M.D.   } *Delegates to the Medical Board*
PERCY KLINGENSTEIN, M.D.   }

---

* Not a member of the Medical Board.

36

MEDICAL AND SURGICAL STAFF

(With changes up to April 30, 1939)

CONSULTING STAFF

Physicians

Emanuel Libman, M.D.   Morris Manges, M.D.

Alfred Meyer, M.D.

Pediatrician

Henry Heiman, M.D.

Neurologists

Bernard Sachs, M.D.   Israel Strauss, M.D.

Surgeons

Albert A. Berg, M.D.   Charles A. Elsberg, M.D.

*Edwin Beer, M.D.   Richard Lewisohn, M.D.

Howard Lilienthal, M.D.

Gynecologists

Joseph Brettauer, M.D.   Robert T. Frank, M.D.

Hiram N. Vineberg, M.D.

Otologists

Isidore Friesner, M.D.   Fred Whiting, M.D.

Ophthalmic Surgeons

Carl Koller, M.D.   Charles H. May, M.D.

Julius Wolff, M.D.

Orthopedist

Philip D. Wilson, M.D.

Physical Therapist

Heinrich F. Wolf, M.D.

Chemist

Samuel Bookman, Ph.D.

* Deceased.

37

MEDICAL AND SURGICAL STAFF

MEDICAL SERVICE
Physicians
George Baehr, M.D.   Bernard S. Oppenheimer, M.D.

Associate Physicians
David Beck, M.D.   Eli Moschcowitz, M.D.
Ernst P. Boas, M.D.   Reuben Ottenberg, M.D.
Harold T. Hyman, M.D.   Daniel Poll, M.D.

Associates in Medicine
Burrill B. Crohn, M.D.   Arthur M. Master, M.D.
Arthur M. Fishberg, M.D.   Coleman B. Rabin, M.D.
Joseph Harkavy, M.D.   Nathan Rosenthal, M.D.
Herman Lande, M.D.   Irving R. Roth, M.D.
Asher Winkelstein, M.D.

Adjunct Physicians
#Samuel H. Averbuck, M.D.   Frederick H. King, M.D.
#Solon S. Bernstein, M.D.   **S. S. Lichtman, M.D.
Emanuel Z. Epstein, M.D.   Sylvan E. Moolten, M.D.
#Philip Finkle, M.D.   Arthur Schifrin, M.D.
Charles K. Friedberg, M.D.   #Solomon Silver, M.D.
(a)Ben Friedman, M.D.   Louis J. Soffer, M.D.
Edward B. Greenspan, M.D.   Arthur R. Sohval, M.D.
William M. Hitzig, M.D.   Lester R. Tuchman, M.D.
Herman Hennell, M.D.   **Kaufman Wallach, M.D.
(For Chest Diseases)   #Harry Weiss, M.D.
Frederic D. Zeman, M.D.

Assistant Physicians
(In charge of Out-Patient Department Clinics)
Morris Blum, M.D.   Alfred Romanoff, M.D.

Assistants in Medicine
(Hospital or Out-Patient Department)
Harold A. Abel, M.D.   Hubert Mann, M.D.
Harold A. Abramson, M.D.   Herbert Pollack, M.D.

Senior Clinical Assistants
(Out-Patient Department)
Frank A. Bassen, M.D.   Herbert Lampert, M.D.
Kurt Berliner, M.D.   Jacob Liff, M.D.
N. W. Chaikin, M.D.   Harry S. Mackler, M.D.
Joseph Echtman, M.D.   Fred E. Maisel, M.D.
Sydney C. Feinberg, M.D.   Charles R. Messeloff, M.D.
Samuel A. Feldman, M.D.   P. N. Ortiz, M.D.
Isidore Fischer, M.D.   David Paley, M.D.
Elmer S. Gais, M.D.   Frank Pierson, M.D.
Emil Granet, M.D.   Philip Reichert, M.D.
Selian Hebald, M.D.   Joseph Reiss, M.D.
Abraham Jerskey, M.D.   Herman S. Roth, M.D.

For Special Service.
** Off Service.
(a) Appointed 1939.

MEDICAL AND SURGICAL STAFF

MEDICAL SERVICE—(Continued)

Senior Clinical Assistants (Continued)
(Out-Patient Department)

Robert V. Sager, M.D.
Isidore Schapiro, M.D.
Siegfried S. Schatten, M.D.
Morris T. Siegel, M.D.
David I. Singer, M.D.

Rose Spiegel, M.D.
Abraham Sternbach, M.D.
Peter Vogel, M.D.
Herman Zazeela, M.D.
Bernard M. Zussman, M.D.

Clinical Assistants
(Out-Patient Department)

Frederic S. Adler, M.D.
David Adlersberg, M..D.
Bernard H. Alberg, M.D.
Salvatore Amato, M.D.
John Amoruso, M.D.
Ludwig Anfanger, M.D.
Joseph Bandes, M.D.
Aaron Barcham, M.D.
Paul Barron, M.D.
Herbert Blau, M.D.
Perry Blumberg, M.D.
Jack Brandes, M.D.
Joseph Bronstein, M.D.
Paul N. Bulova, M.D.
Bension Calef, M.D.
Anne F. Casper, M.D.
Morris Chamurich, M.D.
George C. Cole, M.D.
Salvatore Contento, M.D.
Albert Cornell, M.D.
Simon Dack, M.D.
D. Alfred Dantes, M.D.
Max David, M.D.
Henry Dolger, M.D.
Morris L. Drazin, M.D.
Ernest F. Dupre, M.D.
Max Ellenberg, M.D.
Rudolph R. Ebert, M.D.
Alan Emanuel, M.D.
Kurt Esser, M.D.
Paul Fagin, M.D.
Henry Feibes, M.D.
A. Stuart Ferguson, M.D.
Betty Finkelstein, M.D.
Sylvan A. Frankenthaler, M.D.
Walter Fischbein, M.D.
I. E. Gerber, M.D.
Sidney L. Gottlieb, M.D.
Mayer A. Green, M.D.
Edward B. Grossman, M.D.
Arno D. Gurewitsch, M.D.

Herbert L. Gutstein, M.D.
Samuel A. Handelsman, M.D.
Joseph Herzstein, M.D.
Henry Horn, M.D.
Morris Hyman, M.D.
Harry L. Jaffe, M.D.
Saul W. Jarcho, M.D.
Abraham Jezer, M.D.
Friedrich Kach, M.D.
Edward Kahn, M.D.
Henry H. Kalter, M.D.
Daid Kastoff, M.D.
Harold W. Keschner, M.D.
Victor H. Kugel, M.D.
Morton Kulick, M.D.
Nicholas Langer, M.D.
Alan N. Leslie, M.D.
Sidney Levinson, M.D.
Aaron Levinsky, M.D.
Hyman Levy, M.D.
Richard Levy, M.D.
Frederick J. Lewy, M.D.
Adolph A. Lilien, M.D.
Walter Loewenberg, M.D.
Rafael A. Marin, M.D.
Sigmund H. May, M.D.
Milton Mendlowitz, M.D.
Martin Meyer, M.D.
Nathan Meyer, M.D.
Abraham Penner, M.D.
Arthur Post, M.D.
Irving Rapfogel, M.D.
Charles W. Rieber, M.D.
Randolph Rosenthal, M.D.
Harry W. Rothman, M.D.
Hyman J. Rubenstein, M.D.
Benjamin Rubin, M.D.
Norman A. Samuels, M.D.
Irving A. Sarot, M.D.
Maxwell Sayet, M.D.
Lydia Shapiro-Mindlin, M.D.

MEDICAL AND SURGICAL STAFF

MEDICAL SERVICE—(Continued)

Clinical Assistants (Continued)
(Out-Patient Department)

Gerhard Schauer, M.D.
Israel S. Schiller, M.D.
Siegfried Schoenfeld, M.D.
Sheppard Siegal, M.D.
Isidore Siegel, M.D.
Joseph I. Singer, M.D.
Irving Somach, M.D.
Eugene Somkin, M.D.
Morris F. Steinberg, M.D.

J. Edward Stern, M.D.
Milton H. Stillerman, M.D.
Louis Stix, M.D.
Oscar Tannenbaum, M.D.
Meyer Texon, M.D.
Charles Weisberg, M.D.
Victor Willner, M.D.
Morton W. Willis, M.D.
E. Gunther Wolff, M.D.

Harry Yarnis, M.D.

Volunteers

Henry Dolger, M.D.
Mayer A. Green, M.D.

Edward B. Grossman, M.D.
Eugene Somkin, M.D.

PEDIATRIC SERVICE

Pediatrician
Bela Schick, M.D.

Associate Pediatricians
Murray H. Bass, M.D.   Herman Schwarz, M.D.

Associate in Pediatrics
Ira S. Wile, M.D.

Adjunct Pediatricians

Bernard S. Denzer, M.D.
#Alfred E. Fischer, M.D.
George J. Ginandes, M.D.

Samuel Karelitz, M.D.
Jerome L. Kohn, M.D.
**Sara K. Welt, M.D.

Assistant Pediatricians
(In charge of Out-Patient Department Clinics)

U. Himmelstein, M.D.
M. Murray Peshkin, M.D.
William Rosenson, M.D.

Irving R. Roth, M.D.
Henry M. Weisman, M.D.
Harry O. Zamkin, M.D.

Assistants in Pediatrics
Margit Freund, M.D.   Anne Topper, M.D.

Senior Clinical Assistants
(Out-Patient Department)

Henry H. Blum, M.D.
Max Chidekel, M.D.
Harry J. Cohen, M.D.
Jacob Elitzak, M.D.

Gertrude Felshin, M.D.
A. H. Fineman, M.D.
Maurice Gelb, M.D.
Fred Glucksman, M.D.

For Special Service.
** Off Service.

PEDIATRIC SERVICE—(Continued)

Senior Clinical Assistants (Continued)
(Out-Patient Department)

Henry L. Greene, M.D.
Gertrude Greenstein, M.D.
Ferenc Grossman, M.D.
Maurice Grozin, M.D.
Harold Herman, M.D.
Jacob Hirsh, M.D.
Raphael Isaacs, M.D.
M. J. Karsh, M.D.
Sidney D. Leader, M.D.
Edward Lehman, M.D.
Harry S. Mackler, M.D.
Joseph Mayeroff, M.D.

William Messer, M.D.
Hanna Mulier, M.D.
Albert B. Newman, M.D.
Harry D. Pasachoff, M.D.
Gustave Salomon, M.D.
Joseph Schapiro, M.D.
William A. Schonfeld, M.D.
J. Schwarsbram, M.D.
Rose G. Spiegel, M.D.
Jacob Sugarman, M.D.
Anna Weintraub, M.D.
Carl Zelson, M.D.

Clinical Assistants
(Out-Patient Department)

John Bauer, M.D.
Arthur J. Berger, M.D.
Eugene Bernstein, M.D.
Victor Blass, M.D.
Sidney Blumenthal, M.D.
Harvey Brandon, M.D.
Joseph Bronstein, M.D.
Paul N. Bulova, M.D.
Samuel H. Dender, M.D.
Albert Dingmann, M.D.
Else R. Ebert, M.D.
Samuel Ehre, M.D.
Else Farmer, M.D.
Irving Feuer, M.D.
Mayer A. Green, M.D.
Franz H. Hanan, M.D.
Charles R. Hayman, M.D.
Lotte Heinemann, M.D.
Sylvia Heymann, M.D.
Walter Hirschfeld, M.D.
Wilfred C. Hulse, M.D.
Godel I. Hunter, M. D.
Dora Joelson, M.D.
Eva C. Kivelson, M.D.
Israel S. Klieger, M.D.
Arthur Lesser, M.D.

Richard Levy, M.D.
Walter Levy, M.D.
Bessie Metrick, M.D.
Ludwig Michaelis, M.D.
Morton R. Milsner, M.D.
Stephan Mussliner, M.D.
Arthur Nathan, M.D.
George Neuhaus, M.D.
William Neuland, M.D.
Antoine Noti, M.D.
Harry L. Orlov, M.D.
Jean Pakter, M.D.
Carl Pototsky, M.D.
Howard G. Rapaport, M.D.
Elwood Roodner, M.D.
Abraham I. Rosenstein, M.D.
Eugene H. Schwarz, M.D.
Adele Sicular, M.D.
Morris Sonberg, M.D.
Ernst Steinitz, M.D.
Fannie Stoll, M.D.
Herman Vollmer, M.D.
Fritz Weil, M.D.
Hans Weil, M.D.
Samuel B. Weiner, M.D.
Morton W. Willis, M.D.

Alexander Winter, M.D.

Volunteers

Sidney Blumenthal, M.D.
Sidney D. Leader, M.D.
Arthur Lesser, M.D.
Sidney H. Miller, M.D.

Howard G. Rapaport, M.D.
Freda Rath, M.D.
Rose G. Spiegel, M.D.
Samuel B. Weiner, M.D.

MEDICAL AND SURGICAL STAFF

NEUROLOGICAL SERVICE

Neurologist
Israel S. Wechsler, M.D.

Associate Neurologists
Joseph H. Globus, M.D. Richard M. Brickner, M.D.

Associate Psychiatrists
Clarence P. Oberndorf, M.D. Sandor Lorand, M.D.

Adjunct Neurologists
Benjamin H. Balser, M.D. Judah Marmor, M.D.
Morris B. Bender, M.D. William Needles, M.D.
Irving Bieber, M.D. Nathan Sa/itsky, M.D.
#Herman G. Selinsky, M.D.

Adjunct Psychiatrists
Arnold Eisendorfer, M.D. Albert Slutsky, M.D.
Sol W. Ginsburg, M.D. Leo Stone, M.D.

Assistants in Neurology
(Hospital or Out-Patient Department)
Joseph Salan, M.D. John Scharf, M.D.

Assistants in Psychiatry
(Hospital or Out-Patient Department)
Arpad Pauncz, M.D. E. Gordon Stoloff, M.D.

Clinical Assistants
(Out-Patient Department)
(Neurology)
David Beres, M.D. Leon M. Herbert, M.D.
Alfred Dannhauser, M.D. Jakob Leffkowitz, M.D.
Sidney Elpern, M.D. Viva Schatia, M.D.
Frank P. Eves, M.D. Sidney Tarachow, M.D.
David Gersten, M.D. Edgar C. Trautman, M.D.
Alexis Gottlieb, M.D. George Trefousse, M.D.

Senior Clinical Assistant
(Out-Patient Department)
(Psychiatry)
Harry I. Weinstock, M.D.

Clinical Assistants
(Out-Patient Department)
(Psychiatry)
Abraham Apter, M.D. Henry G. Grand, M.D.
George G. Arato, M.D. Emil A. Gutheil, M.D.
P. Goolker, M.D. Max Loeb, M.D.

Volunteer
Daniel E. Schneider, M.D.

Clinical Psychologist
Silas Cohen, M.A.

For Special Service.

MEDICAL AND SURGICAL STAFF

DERMATOLOGIAL SERVICE

Dermatologist
Isadore Rosen, M.D.

Associate Dermatologists
Louis Chargin, M.D.   Oscar L. Levin, M.D.

Adjunct Dermatologists
Samuel M. Peck, M.D.   Max Scheer, M.D.

Assistant Dermatologists
(In charge of Out-Patient Department Clinics)

Lewis A. Goldberger, M.D.   Henry Silver M.D.
Arthur Sayer, M.D.   Charles Wolf, M.D.

Assistant in Dermatology
(Hospital or Out-Patient Department)
Herbert Rosenfeld, M.D.

Senior Clinical Assistants
(Out-Patient Department)

D. B. Ballin, M.D.   H. J. Kohnstam, M.D.
Max Berkovsky, M.D.   William Leifer, M.D.
Eugene T. Bernstein, M.D.   Morris Raif, M.D.
Raphael Breakstone, M.D.   Sidney B. Rooff, M.D.
Julius Davis, M.D.   Joel Schweig, M.D.
Morris M. Estrin, M.D.   Harry Sherwood, M.D.
Philip S. Greenbaum, M.D.   Harry Slatkin, M.D.
H. C. Herrman, M.D.   Samuel Strumwasser, M.D.
Maurice Umansky, M.D.

Clinical Assistants
(Out-Patient Department)

Ernest Bass, M.D.   Adrian Neumann, M.D.
Alphons Breit, M.D.   Kermit E. Osserman, M.D.
Erich Buechler, M.D.   Samuel J. Rabinowitz, M.D.
Jacob Churg, M.D.   Ferd. Rosenberger, M.D.
Frank E. Cross, M.D.   Gdali Rubin, M.D.
Hirsch L. Gordon, M.D.   Richard Schindler, M.D.
Alfred Hess, M.D.   Abraham M. Skern, M.D.
David Kane, M.D.   Adolf Sternberg, M.D.
Murray L. Kaplun, M.D.   E. N. Winograd, M.D.
Morton Yohalem, M.D.

Arseno-Therapy Clinic
(Out-Patient Department)
Associate Dermatologist
Louis Chargin, M.D.

Senior Clinical Assistants
Harry Sherwood, M.D.   Maurice Umansky, M.D.

43

MEDICAL AND SURGICAL STAFF

SURGICAL SERVICE
Surgeons
Ralph Colp, M.D.

John H. Garlock, M.D.

Abraham Hyman, M.D.

Harold Neuhof, M.D.

Associate Surgeons
Leo Edelman, M.D.

Leon Ginzburg, M.D.

Percy Klingenstein, M.D.

Arthur S. W. Touroff, M.D.

Adjunct Surgeons
Ernest E. Arnheim, M.D.

Arthur H. Aufses, M.D.

Maurice M. Berck, M.D.

Leonard J. Druckerman, M.D.

Ameil Glass, M.D.

Samuel H. Klein, M.D.

H. Evans Leiter, M.D.

Sigmund Mage, M.D.

William H. Mencher, M.D.

Gordon D. Oppenheimer, M.D.

Myron A. Sallick, M.D.

#Samuel Silbert, M.D.

Moses Swick, M.D.

Assistant Surgeon
(In charge of Out-Patient Department Clinic)
Sylvan D. Manheim, M.D.

Senior Clinical Assistants
(Out-Patient Department)
Moses Benmosche, M.D.

Daniel Casten, M.D.

Benjamin Damsky, M.D.

Milton M. Eckert, M.D.

Norman L. Goldberg, M.D.

Aron Goldschmidt, M.D.

Sidney Grossman, M.D.

Sidney Hirsch, M.D.

Borris A. Kornblith, M.D.

Norman F. Laskey, M.D.

H. G. Rose, M.D.

Isidore Schapiro, M.D.

Ralph W. Watsky, M.D.

Herman Zazeela, M.D.

Clinical Assistants
(Out-Patient Department)
Meyer Abrahams, M.D.

Aaron Berger, M.D.

Harry Bergman, M.D.

Harry Bettauer, M.D.

William Braunstein, M.D.

Sydney Bressler, M.D.

Fishel Charlap, M.D.

Ralph Cohen, M.D.

Arthur Dallos, M.D.

Thomas W. Dixon, M.D.

Henry Doubilet, M.D.

Celia Ekelson, M.D.

Robert C. Elitzik, M.D.

Fritz Falk, M.D.

S. A. Frankenthaler, M.D.

Benjamin Glick, M.D.

Meyer L. Goldman, M.D.

Milton H. Goolde, M.D.

William Hayn, M.D.

S. Lawrence Kaman, M.D.

Abner Kurtin, M.D.

Mark J. Markham, M.D.

Helmuth Nathan, M.D.

Hellmuth Oppenheimer, M.D.

Henry Peskin, M.D.

Willy Perez, M.D.

Erich Plocki, M.D.

Aaron Prigot, M.D.

Irving R. Rachlin, M.D.

Benjamin Ritter, M.D.

Gustav Rosenburg, M.D.

Gerhard Sachs, M.D.

M. Salzberg, M.D.

Anna Samuelson, M.D.

Emil Schnebel, M.D.

Gabriel P. Seley, M.D.

Sigmund A. Siegel, M.D.

Richard Silberstein, M.D.

Arthur Simon, M.D.

Meyer M. Stone, M.D.

For Special Service.

MEDICAL AND SURGICAL STAFF

SURGICAL SERVICE—(Continued)

Clinical Assistants (Continued)
(Out-Patient Department)

Rudolph Strauss, M.D.

Joseph A. Tamerin, M.D.

Irwin P. Train, M.D.

Leonard J. Trilling, M.D.

Robert Turell, M.D.

Leonard Weinroth, M.D.

Erhardt Weltmann, M.D.

Eric Wohlauer, M.D.

Saul Zager, M.D.

Thomas S. Zimmer, M.D.

Volunteers

Henry Doubilet, M.D.

Edward E. Jemerin, M.D.

Irving A. Sarot, M.D.

Gabriel P. Seley, M.D.

Irwin P. Train, M.D.

NEURO-SURGICAL SERVICE

Neuro-Surgeon
Ira Cohen, M.D.

Associate Neuro-Surgeon
Abraham Kaplan, M.D.

Adjunct Neuro-Surgeon
Sidney W. Gross, M.D.

GENITO-URINARY DIVISION OF OUT-PATIENT DEPARTMENT OF SURGICAL SERVICE

Assistant Surgeons
(In charge of Out-Patient Department Clinic)

William Bisher, M.D.

Lewis T. Mann, M.D.

Jerome M. Ziegler, M.D.

Senior Clinical Assistants
(Out-Patient Department)

N. D. Benezra, M.D.

Jacob Birnbaum, M.D.

William L. Ferber, M.D.

Edward O. Finestone, M.D.

Abraham Firestone, M.D.

Joseph Haas, M.D.

Leo Jacoby, M.D.

Bernard D. Kulick, M.D.

Norman F. Lasky, M.D.

Clinical Assistants
(Out-Patient Department)

Robert H. Abrahamson, M.D.

Maurice Alden, M.D.

George F. Dayton, M.D.

Henry Feibes, M.D.

Frank E. Fink, M.D.

Joseph Garteff, M.D.

Paul E. Gutman, M.D.

Kurt A. Heinrich, M.D.

Harry D. Italiener, M.D.

Edward Jacobs, M.D.

Edward E. Jemerin, M.D.

Herman I. Kantor, M.D.

Bruno Mark, M.D.

Pasquale Montilli, M.D.

George E. Raskin, M.D.

Natale A. Sabatino, M.D.

David Schreiber, M.D.

MEDICAL AND SURGICAL STAFF

GYNECOLOGICAL SERVICE
Gynecologists
Samuel H. Geist, M.D.   Isidor C. Rubin, M.D.

Associate Gynecologists
Morris A. Goldberger, M.D.   Max D. Mayer, M.D.

Adjunct Gynecologists
Phineas Bernstein, M.D.   U. J. Salmon, M.D.
Joseph A. Gaines, M.D.   Seymour Wimpfheimer, M.D.

Assistant Gynecologists
(In charge of Out-Patient Department Clinics)
Morris Feresten, M.D.   Maurice E. Mintz, M.D.
Emanuel Klempner, M.D.   Frank Spielman, M.D.

Senior Clinical Assistants
(Out-Patient Department)
Siegfried F. Bauer, M.D.   Oscar Glassman, M.D.
Isabel Beck, M.D.   H. C. Herrman, M.D.
Samuel G. Berkow, M.D.   Samuel Hochman, M.D.
Gertrude Felshin, M.D.   Monroe A. Rosenbloom, M.D.
Leonard Zweibel, M.D.

Clinical Assistants
(Out-Patient Department)
Johanna N. Bulová, M.D.   William Nussbaum, M.D.
Arthur M. Davids, M.D.   Herbert Pollack, M.D.
Richard Fleischer, M.D.   James A. Rosen, M.D.
Eleanor B. Gutman, M.D.   Raymond W. Sass, M.D.
Maximilian Lewitter, M.D.   William A. Schonfeld, M.D.
Sello Leopold, M.D.   Abbey D. Seley, M.D.
H. Richard Mayer, M.D.   Paul Steinweg, M.D.
Herbert F. Newman, M.D.   Robert I. Walter, M.D.

OTOLOGICAL SERVICE
Otologist
Jacob L. Maybaum, M.D.

Associate Otologists
(a) Joseph G. Druss, M.D.   *Walter L. Horn, M.D.
Samuel Rosen, M.D.

Adjunct Otologists
Harry Rosenwasser, M.D.   Eugene R. Snyder, M.D.

(a) Appointed 1939.
* Deceased.

MEDICAL AND SURGICAL STAFF

LARYNGOLOGICAL SERVICE

Laryngologist
Rudolph Kramer, M.D.

Associate Laryngologists
Morris S. Bender, M.D.   Irving B. Goldman, M.D.

Adjunct Laryngologists
Joseph L. Goldman, M.D.   Louis Kleinfeld, M.D.
Max L. Som, M.D.

Assistant Oto-Laryngologist
(In charge of Out-Patient Department Clinic)
Harry D. Cohen, M.D.

Senior Clinical Assistants
(Out-Patient Department)
Julius Golembe, M.D.   William J. Hochbaum, M.D.
Morris F. Heller, M.D.   S. Mencher, M.D.

Clinical Assistants
(Out-Patient Department)
Adolph N. Abraham, M.D.   Bruno Griessmann, M.D.
Benjamin I. Allen, M.D.   Wm. F. Mayer-Hermann, M.D.
Lester L. Coleman, M.D.   Hans Meinrath, M.D.
Maurice R. Goodwin, M.D.   A. Harry Neffson, M.D.

OPHTHALMOLOGICAL SERVICE

Ophthalmic Surgeon
Kaufman Schlivek, M.D.

Associate Ophthalmic Surgeons
Robert K. Lambert, M.D.   Henry Minsky, M.D.

Adjunct Ophthalmic Surgeons
Joseph Laval, M.D.   David Wexler, M.D.

Assistant Ophthalmic Surgeons
(In charge of Out-Patient Department Clinics)
Murray A. Last, M.D.   Herman Ostrow, M.D.

Senior Clinical Assistants
(Out-Patient Department)
Edward J. Bassen, M.D.   M. Rosenbaum, M.D.
Bertha Gladstern, M.D.   Saul Miller, M.D.

MEDICAL AND SURGICAL STAFF

OPHTHALMOLOGICAL SERVICE—(Continued)

Clinical Assistants
(Out-Patient Department)

Philip L. Adalman, M.D.
Richard Baruch, M.D.
Eva C. Dienst, M.D.
Jacob Goldsmith, M.D.
Morris Greenberg, M.D.
Abraham L. Kornzweig, M.D.

Norbert Lewin, M.D.
Max Mannheimer, M.D.
Philip L. Masor, M.D.
Ernst L. Metzger, M.D.
David I. Mirow, M.D.
Meta Mueller, M.D.

Frederick H. Theodore, M.D.

Refractionists
(Out-Patient Department)

Bertha Gladstern, M.D.

M. Rosenbaum, M.D.

ORTHOPEDIC SERVICE

Orthopedists

(a) Robert K. Lippmann, M.D.

(a) Seth Selig, M.D.

Associate Orthopedist

**Edgar D. Oppenheimer, M.D.

Adjunct Orthopedists

Edgar M. Bick, M.D.

Albert J. Schein, M.D.

Senior Clinical Assistant
(Out-Patient Department)

Jacob Mandel, M.D.

Clinical Assistants
(Out-Patient Department)

Ernst Bettmann, M.D.
Max Kliger, M.D.
Heinz R. Landmann, M.D.

Herman S. Lieberman, M.D.
Rudolf Selig, M.D.
Stephan Wahl, M.D.

ISOLATION SERVICE

Physician

*Henry W. Berg, M.D.

Associate Physician

Benjamin Eliasoph, M.D.

(a) Appointed 1939.
* Deceased.
** Off Service.

MEDICAL AND SURGICAL STAFF

PHYSICAL THERAPY DEPARTMENT

Physical Therapist
William Bierman, M.D.

Adjunct Physical Therapists
***Carl L. Levenson, M.D.   Sidney Licht, M.D.

Assistant Physical Therapists
Erich Levy, M.D.   A. W. Schenker, M.D.

Clinical Assistant
(Out-Patient Department)
Alexander Hersh, M.D.

CARDIOGRAPHIC LABORATORY

Associate in Medicine
Arthur M. Master, M.D.

Assistant in Medicine
Hubert Mann, M.D.

Research Assistants
Simon Dack, M.D.   Abraham Jezer, M.D.
Harry L. Jaffe, M.D.   ***Mrs. Enid Tribe Oppenheimer

Volunteers
Rudolph Friedmann, M.D.   Richard S. Gubner, M.D.

THE LABORATORIES

Pathologist
Paul Klemperer, M.D.

Bacteriologist
Gregory Shwartzman, M.D.

Chemist
Harry H. Sobotka, Ph.D.

Neuro-pathologist
Joseph H. Globus, M.D.

Hematologist
Nathan Rosenthal, M.D.

Associate Neuro-pathologist
***Otto Marburg, M.D.

*** Resigned.

49

MEDICAL AND SURGICAL STAFF

THE LABORATORIES—(Continued)

Associate in Pathology
(b) George Baehr, M.D.

Associate in Surgical Pathology
(b) Samuel H. Geist, M.D.

Associate Pathologist
Sadao Otani, M.D.

Assistant Pathologist
Abou D. Pollack, M.D.

Assistant in Morbid Anatomy
Henry Horn, M.D.

Assistant in Bacteriology
Lewis H. Koplik, M.D.

Assistant Bacteriologist
Cecele Herschberger, B.S.

Assistant Chemist
Miriam Reiner, M.S.

SPECIAL LABORATORY APPOINTMENTS
Fellows
(1938-1939)

Arthur C. Allen, M.D............Moses Heinemen Fellowship
Edith Bloch, Ph.D...............Hernsheim Fellowship in Chemistry
Leonard Finkelstein, M.D.....Theodore Escherich Fellowship
Charles L. Fox, Jr., M.D......Moritz Rosenthal Fellowship
Ben Friedman, M.D............Richard and Ella Hunt Sutro Fellowship
Franklin Hollander, Ph. D...Fellowship in Gastro-enterology
Emanuel Klempner, M.D...Dr. Hiram N. Vineberg Fellowship
Leo Moschkowitz, M.D.......Eugene Meyer, Jr. Fellowship
Gerhard Schauer, M.D.......George Blumenthal, Jr. Fellowship
Robert I. Walter, M.D.......Dr. Joseph Brettauer Fellowship
Tobias Weinberg, M.D.......George Blumenthal, Jr. Fellowship
Joseph M. Zucker, M.D.....Charles Klingenstein Fellowship
(1939-1940)
Arthur C. Allen, M.D........George Blumenthal, Jr. Fellowship
Ben Friedman, M.D...........Lionel Sutro Fellowship
Mark G. Kanzer, M.D........Minnie Kastor Fellowship in Psychiatry
Joseph Pick, M.D...............Theodore Escherich Fellowship
Gabriel P. Seley, M.D........Dr. Ralph Colp Fellowship in Bacteriology
Eugene Somkin, M.D..........Charles Klingenstein Fellowship
Robert I. Walter, M.D.......Dr. Joseph Brettauer Fellowship
Edwin A. Weinstein, M.D....Dr. Isadore Abrahamson Memorial Fellowship
Joseph M. Zucker, M.D....Moritz Rosenthal Fellowship

(b) Until April 30, 1939.

MEDICAL AND SURGICAL STAFF

SPECIAL LABORATORY APPOINTMENTS—(Continued)

Research Assistants

BACTERIOLOGY

Norman Q. Brill, M.D.
Morris Greenberg, M.D.
Sheppard Siegal, M.D.

Joseph Pick, M.D.
Florence Sammis, M.D.

CHEMISTRY

David Adlersberg, M.D.
Joseph Bandes, M.D.
Lester Blum, M.D.
Albert Cornell, M.D.
Eugene Somkin, M.D.

Arthur M. Davids, M.D.
Edward B. Grossman, M.D.
Emanuel Klempner, M.D.
Arthur Post, M.D.

DERMATO-PATHOLOGY

(b)Emanuel Gahan, M.D.

Arthur Glick, M.D.

ENDOCRINOLOGY

Gertrude Felshin, M.D.

HEMATOLOGY

(b) Louis Wasserman, M.D.

MORBID ANATOMY

(b)William Antopol, M.D.
Alice I. Bernheim, M.D.
I. E. Gerber, M.D.
Abraham J. Gitlitz, M.D.

E. C. Holder, M.D.
Daniel Laszlo, M.D.
Rudolf Leuchtenberger, M.D.
Abraham Penner, M.D.

NEURO-PATHOLOGY

(b) Charles Schultz, M.D.

OPHTHALMO-PATHOLOGY

(b) Jacob Goldsmith, M.D.

SURGICAL PATHOLOGY

Joseph C. Ehrlich, M.D.

Michael L. Lewin, M.D.

THROMBO-ANGIITIS OBLITERANS

Norman F. Laskey, M.D.
Herman Zazeela, M.D.

Mae L. Friedlander, Ph.D.

Voluntary Assistants

BACTERIOLOGY

Corrado Ajo, M.D.

Baruch Paderski, M.D.

CHEMISTRY

(b)D. Alfred Dantes, M.D.
Baruch Paderski, M.D.

Henry Dolger, M.D.

DERMATO-PATHOLOGY

(b) Elizabeth Jagle, M.D.

HEMATOLOGY

Harold A. Abel, M.D.
Corrado Ajo, M.D.
Frank A. Bassen, M.D.

Pedro N. Ortiz, M.D.
Irving Somach, M.D.
Peter Vogel, M.D.

(b) Until April 30, 1939.

MEDICAL AND SURGICAL STAFF

SPECIAL LABORATORY APPOINTMENTS—(Continued)
Voluntary Assistants (Continued)

MORBID ANATOMY

Stephen Elek, M.D.
H. Gudemann, M.D.
Julian A. Jarman, M.D.

(b) Philip J. Kresky, M.D.
Morris F. Steinberg, M.D.
Tobias Weinberg, M.D.

Julius Wolfram, M.D.

NEURO-PATHOLOGY

(b) David Beres, M.D.
James McDonald, M.D.

Jacob H. Friedman, M.D.
Mark Gerstle, Jr., M.D.

(b) Leon M. Herbert, M.D.

OPHTHALMO-PATHOLOGY

Abraham L. Kornzweig, M.D.　　Murray A. Last, M.D.

OTO-PATHOLOGY

Benjamin I. Allen, M.D.　　Lester L. Coleman, M.D.

SURGICAL PATHOLOGY

(b) Arnold Bachman, M.D.
Max Ellenberg, M.D.
Herman L. Jacobius, M.D.

Borris A. Kornblith, M.D.
Abner Kurtin, M.D.
A. H. Neffson, M.D.

Max Schenck, M.D.

DEPARTMENT OF ROENTGENOLOGY AND RADIOTHERAPY

Radiologist

*Leopold Jaches, M.D.　　(a) Marcy L. Sussman, M.D.

Associate Radiologists

Arthur J. Bendick, M.D.　　Samuel J. Goldfarb, M.D.

Assistant Radiologists

Benjamin Copleman, M.D.　　Coleman B. Rabin, M.D.

Radiotherapist
William Harris, M.D.

Associate Radiotherapist
Albert Kean, M.D.

Assistant Radiotherapists

Myer E. Golan, M.D.
Samuel Richman, M.D.
Sidney M. Silverstone, M.D.

Seymour Wimpfheimer, M.D.
Charles Wolf, M.D.
Louis E. Zaretski, M.D.

---

* Deceased.
(a) Appointed 1939.
(b) Until April 30, 1939.

MEDICAL AND SURGICAL STAFF

DEPARTMENT OF ROENTGENOLOGY AND RADIOTHERAPY—(Continued)

Volunteer
Morris F. Steinberg, M.D.

Physicists
Carl B. Braestrup, B.Sc.　　　Alexander Kolin, Ph.D.

PHARMACOLOGY

Consultant
Charles L. Lieb, M.D.

DEPARTMENT OF ANESTHESIA

Visiting Anesthetists
William Branower, M.D.　　　Bernard H. Eliasberg, M.D.
Harry G. Goldman, M.D.

Anesthetists in Out-Patient Department
Sidney Grossman, M.D.　　　Barney Isaacson, M.D.

Resident Anesthetists
***Gladys Austin, R.N.　　　Thelma C. Darlington, R.N.
***E. E. Bair, R.N.　　　***Isabel M. Fairbank, R.N.
Fanny Bergmann, M.D.　　　***Evelyn Grabenhorst, R.N.
Florence Califano, R.N.　　　Helen Grabenhorst, R.N.
Evelyn T. Clerico, M.D.　　　***Helen F. MacManus, R.N.

DISTRICT SERVICE

Physicians
Abraham Jerskey, M.D.　　　Morris F. Steinberg, M.D.

ADMITTING SERVICE
Julius L. Weissberg, M.D.

ASSISTANT PHYSICIAN TO EMPLOYEES
D. Alfred Dantes, M.D.

(b) Until April 30, 1939.
*** Resigned.

53

MEDICAL AND SURGICAL STAFF

DENTAL DEPARTMENT
(Hospital and Out-Patient Department)

Dentist
Harry A. Goldberg, D.D.S.

Associate Dentists
Ralph H. Brodsky, D.M.D.   Joseph Schroff, M.D., D.D.S.
Leo Stern, D.D.S.

Adjunct Dentists
Charles H. Cohen, D.D.S.   Denis D. Glucksman, D.D.S.
Nathaniel Freeman, D.D.S.   Arthur A. Kulick, D.D.S.

Senior Clinical Assistants
Robert E. Arlt, D.D.S.   Joseph Grubman, D.D.S.
Miles Chelimer, D.D.S.   Daniel M. Kollen, D.D.S.
Samuel Colish, D.D.S.   Sydney Pollak, D.D.S.
Oscar C. Fink, D.D.S.   Elias Reiner, D.D.S.
Marvin G. Freid, D.D.S.   Louis Sabloff, D.D.S.
Maxwell Gershweir, D.D.S.   Milton Schwartz, D.D.S.
Herbert L. Goodfleish, D.M.D.   Bernard A. Sussman, D.D.S.
Max Greenspan, D.D.S.   Daniel L. Traub, D.D.S.
I. Edwin Zimmerman, D.D.S.

Clinical Assistants
Louis Arnowitz, D.D.S.   Louis Kroll, D.M.D.
Joseph, Bisaha, D.D.S.   Lee R. Kulick, D.D.S.
Edgar B. Biscow, D.D.S.   Morris L. Liebson, D.D.S.
Alex N. Cohen, D.D.S.   Nathan Marcus, D.D.S.
Henry I. Cohen, D.D.S.   Lloyd Markson, D.D.S.
Nathaniel Diner, D.D.S.   Ben Pine, D.D.S.
Samuel Donson, D.D.S.   Jacob C. Rachunow, D.D.S.
George Dubin, D.D.S.   Herman Reich, D.D.S.
Lester L. Eisner, D.D.S.   William Roth, D.D.S.
Robert R. Fagin, D.D.S.   David Rosenwasser, D.D.S.
Arthur M. Feltzin, D.D.S.   David Rubin, D.D.S.
Samuel Gervirtz, D.D.S.   Morris Schwartz, D.D.S.
Robert S. Gilbert, D.M.D.   Benjamin Seidner, D.D.S.
Samuel S. Gordon, D.D.S.   Jerome B. Singer, D.D.S.
Manuel Gottlieb, D.D.S.   Robert W. Slutzky, D.D.S.
Julius Helfand, D.D.S.   Arthur L. Smith, D.D.S.
Robert S. Hess, D.D.S.   Harry Spodak, D.D.S.
Jacob Hurwitz, D.D.S.   Abner T. Starr, D.D.S.
Herman Knobel, D.D.S.   Samuel Stolzberg, D.D.S.
Paul C. Kopf, D.D.S.   Sidney Sulzberg, D.D.S.
Ralph Korelitz, D.D.S.   George Trattner, D.D.S.
Abram J. Krasny, D.D.S.   Seymour Weinstein, D.D.S.
Henry H. Weishof, D.D.S.

HOUSE STAFF
(As of March 1st, 1939)

MEDICAL DEPARTMENT

Milton Landowne, M.D.
Irving Solomon, M.D.
Sidney Cohen, M.D.
Herbert M. Katzin, M.D.
Arthur W. Seligmann, Jr., M.D.
Alvin J. Gordon, M.D.
Selvan Davison, M.D.

Irving A. Beck, M.D.
Herman Anfanger, M.D.
Emanuel B. Schoenbach, M.D.
Clifford L. Spingarn, M.D.
Mary C. Tyson, M.D.
Samuel S. Dorrance, M.D.
George L. Engel, M.D.

Frank L. Engel, M.D.

SURGICAL DEPARTMENT

Nathan Adelman, M.D.
Emanuel Wachtel, M.D.
Alexander Thomas, M.D.
Elliott S. Hurwitt, M.D.
Gerson J. Lesnick, M.D.
Rudolph E. Drosd, M.D.
Leon M. Arnold, M.D.
Daniel Luger, M.D.

Joseph M. Szilagyi, M.D.
Samuel Diener, M.D.
Bernard S. Wolf, M.D.
Bernard E. Simon, M.D.
Daniel Stats, M.D.
William I. Glass, M.D.
David Miller, M.D.
Norman Rosenberg, M.D.

PATHOLOGICAL DEPARTMENT

Roy N. Barnett, M.D.

Merrill P. Haas, M.D.

DEPARTMENT OF RADIOLOGY

Roentgenology
Jack H. Levy, M.D.
Nathan Rudner, M.D.

Radiotherapy
Lester Freedman, M.D.

DENTAL DEPARTMENT

Manuel Burness, D.D.S.

Alfred R. Shepard, D.D.S.

RESIDENTS, WARD

Neurological
Eugene P. Mindlin, M.D.
Hyman E. Yaskin, M.D.
Bertram Schaffner, M.D.

Pediatric
Victor L. Szanton, M.D.
Jacob Danciger, M.D.

Gynecological
Nathan Mintz, M.D.
Jack Squire, M.D.

Ear, Nose and Throat
Samuel M. Bloom, M.D.
Michael S. Zeman, M.D.

Ophthalmological
Louis C. Ravin, M.D.

Orthopedic
Otto Lehmann, M.D.

RESIDENTS, PRIVATE PAVILION

Vernon A. Weinstein, M.D.
Leon N. Greene, M.D.

Sylvan Bloomfield, M.D.
Jerome S. Coles, M.D.

Milton H. Adelman, M.D.

RESIDENTS, SEMI-PRIVATE PAVILION

Arthur Gladstone, M.D.
Robert W. Mann, M. D.

Morris H. Kreeger, M.D.
Bernard Friedman, M.D.

DEPARTMENT OF GRADUATE MEDICAL INSTRUCTION

Conducted in Affiliation with

COLUMBIA UNIVERSITY

(University Extension and School of Medicine)

OFFICERS OF INSTRUCTION

HAROLD A. ABRAMSON, M.D..ASSISTANT IN MEDICINE TO
THE MOUNT SINAI HOSPITAL;
ASSISTANT PROFESSOR OF PHYSIOLOGY IN COLUMBIA UNIVERSITY
DAVID ADLERSBERG, M.D...........RESEARCH ASSISTANT IN CHEMISTRY AND CLINICAL
ASSISANT, MEDICAL DIVISION, OUT-PATIENT DEPARTMENT,
THE MOUNT SINAI HOSPITAL
SAMUEL H. AVERBUCK, M.D., ADJUNCT PHYSICIAN TO THE MOUNT SINAI HOSPITAL
GEORGE BAEHR, M.D...............................PHYSICIAN TO THE MOUNT SINAI HOSPITAL;
CLINICAL PROFESSOR OF MEDICINE IN COLUMBIA UNIVERSITY
MURRAY H. BASS, M.D.........ASSOCIATE PEDIATRICIAN TO THE MOUNT SINAI HOSPITAL;
ASSISTANT CLINICAL PROFESSOR OF DISEASES OF CHILDREN
IN COLUMBIA UNIVERSITY
DAVID BECK, M.D.........................ASSOCIATE PHYSICIAN TO THE MOUNT SINAI HOSPITAL;
ASSISTANT CLINICAL PROFESSOR OF MEDICINE IN COLUMBIA UNIVERSITY
MORRIS B. BENDER, M.D.......ADJUNCT NEUROLOGIST TO THE MOUNT SINAI HOSPITAL
PHINEAS BERNSTEIN, M.D., ADJUNCT GYNECOLOGIST TO THE MOUNT SINAI HOSPITAL
SOLON S. BERNSTEIN, M.D.......ADJUNCT PHYSICIAN TO THE MOUNT SINAI HOSPITAL
EDGAR M. BICK, M.D...............ADJUNCT ORTHOPEDIST TO THE MOUNT SINAI HOSPITAL
WILLIAM BIERMAN, M.D.........PHYSICAL THERAPIST TO THE MOUNT SINAI HOSPITAL;
ASSOCIATE IN MEDICINE IN COLUMBIA UNIVERSITY; ASSISTANT CLINICAL
PROFESSOR OF THERAPEUTICS AT NEW YORK UNIVERSITY COLLEGE OF MEDICINE
ERNST P. BOAS, M.D.................ASSOCIATE PHYSICIAN TO THE MOUNT SINAI HOSPITAL;
ASSISTANT CLINICAL PROFESSOR OF MEDICINE IN COLUMBIA UNIVERSITY
RICHARD M. BRICKNER,M.D...ASSOCIATE NEUROLOGIST TO
THE MOUNT SINAI HOSPITAL;
ASSISTANT PROFESSOR OF CLINICAL NEUROLOGY IN COLUMBIA UNIVERSITY
LOUIS CHARGIN, M.D.......ASSOCIATE DERMATOLOGIST TO THE MOUNT SINAI HOSPITAL
ASSOCIATE CLINICAL PROFESSOR OF DERMATOLOGY AND SYPHILOLOGY,
NEW YORK POST-GRADUATE MEDICAL SCHOOL, COLUMBIA UNIVERSITY
IRA COHEN, M.D....................................NEURO-SURGEON TO THE MOUNT SINAI HOSPITAL
RALPH COLP, M.D...SURGEON TO THE MOUNT SINAI HOSPITAL;
CLINICAL PROFESSOR OF SURGERY IN COLUMBIA UNIVERSITY
BURRILL B. CROHN, M.D.....ASSOCIATE IN MEDICINE TO THE MOUNT SINAI HOSPITAL;
ASSOCIATE IN MEDICINE IN COLUMBIA UNIVERSITY
SIMON DACK, M.D.........................RESEARCH ASSISTANT, CARDIOGRAPHIC LABORATORY AND
CLINICAL ASSISTANT, MEDICAL DIVISION, OUT-PATIENT DEPARTMENT,
THE MOUNT SINAI HOSPITAL
BERNARD S. DENZER, M.D., ADJUNCT PEDIATRICIAN TO THE MOUNT SINAI HOSPITAL
HENRY DOUBILET, M.D...............................CLINICAL ASSISTANT, SURGICAL DIVISION,
OUT-PATIENT DEPARTMENT, THE MOUNT SINAI HOSPITAL
JOSEPH G. DRUSS, M.D.............ASSOCIATE OTOLOGIST TO THE MOUNT SINAI HOSPITAL
GERTRUDE FELSHIN, M.D........RESEARCH ASSISTANT IN ENDOCRINOLOGY AND SENIOR
CLINICAL ASSISTANT, PEDIATRIC AND GYNECOLOGICAL DIVISIONS,
OUT-PATIENT DEPARTMENT, THE MOUNT SINAI HOSPITAL
ALFRED E. FISCHER, M.D.....ADJUNCT PEDIATRICIAN TO THE MOUNT SINAI HOSPITAL
ARTHUR M. FISHBERG, M.D., ASSOCIATE IN MEDICINE TO THE MOUNT SINAI HOSPITAL;
ASSOCIATE IN MEDICINE IN COLUMBIA UNIVERSITY
ROBERT T. FRANK, M.D...CONSULTING GYNECOLOGIST TO THE MOUNT SINAI HOSPITAL;
CLINICAL PROFESSOR OF GYNECOLOGY IN COLUMBIA UNIVERSITY
CHARLES K. FRIEDBERG, M.D., ADJUNCT PHYSICIAN TO THE MOUNT SINAI HOSPITAL
JOSEPH A. GAINES, M.D.......ADJUNCT GYNECOLOGIST TO THE MOUNT SINAI HOSPITAL
JOHN H. GARLOCK, M.D...............................SURGEON TO THE MOUNT SINAI HOSPITAL

DEPARTMENT OF GRADUATE MEDICAL INSTRUCTION

(Continued)

SAMUEL H. GEIST, M.D...................GYNECOLOGIST TO THE MOUNT SINAI HOSPITAL;
CLINICAL PROFESSOR OF GYNECOLOGY IN COLUMBIA UNIVERSITY

GEORGE J. GINANDES, M.D....ADJUNCT PEDIATRICIAN TO THE MOUNT SINAI HOSPITAL

JOSEPH H. GLOBUS, M.D.................ASSOCIATE NEUROLOGIST AND NEUROPATHOLOGIST
TO THE MOUNT SINAI HOSPITAL; ASSISTANT CLINICAL PROFESSOR
OF NEUROLGY IN COLUMBIA UNIVERSITY

MYER E. GOLAN, M.D.....ASSISTANT RADIOTHERAPIST TO THE MOUNT SINAI HOSPITAL

MORRIS A. GOLDBERGER, M.D......................................ASSOCIATE GYNECOLOGIST TO
THE MOUNT SINAI HOSPITAL

SAMUEL J. GOLDFARB, M.D., ASSOCIATE RADIOLOGIST TO THE MOUNT SINAI HOSPITAL;
ASSOCIATE IN RADIOLOGY IN COLUMBIA UNIVERSITY

ARON GOLDSCHMIDT, M.D............SENIOR CLINICAL ASSISTANT, SURGICAL DIVISION,
OUT-PATIENT DEPARTMENT, THE MOUNT SINAI HOSPITAL

EMIL GRANET, M.D..............................SENIOR CLINICAL ASSISTANT, MEDICAL DIVISION,
OUT-PATIENT DEPARTMENT, THE MOUNT SINAI HOSPITAL

EDWARD B. GREENSPAN, M.D.......................................ADJUNCT PHYSICIAN TO
THE MOUNT SINAI HOSPITAL

JOSEPH HARKAVY, M.D.....ASSOCIATE IN MEDICINE TO THE MOUNT SINAI HOSPITAL;
ASSOCIATE IN MEDICINE IN COLUMBIA UNIVERSITY

WILLIAM HARRIS, M.D.....................RADIOTHERAPIST TO THE MOUNT SINAI HOSPITAL;
ASSOCIATE IN RADIOLOGY IN COLUMBIA UNIVERSITY

HERMAN HENNELL, M.D........................ADJUNCT PHYSICIAN FOR CHEST DISEASES TO
THE MOUNT SINAI HOSPITAL

CECELE HERSCHBERGER, B.S.............................ASSISTANT BACTERIOLOGIST TO
THE MOUNT SINAI HOSPITAL

WILLIAM M. HITZIG, M.D......ADJUNCT PHYSICIAN TO THE MOUNT SINAI HOSPITAL

FRANKLIN HOLLANDER, PH.D...............................FELLOW IN GASTROENTEROLOGY TO
THE MOUNT SINAI HOSPITAL

HENRY HORN, M.D............ASSISTANT IN MORBID ANATOMY AND CLINICAL ASSISTANT,
MEDICAL DIVISION, OUT-PATIENT DEPARTMENT, THE MOUNT SINAI HOSPITAL

HAROLD T. HYMAN, M.D........ASSOCIATE PHYSICIAN TO THE MOUNT SINAI HOSPITAL;
ASSOCIATE PROFESSOR OF PHARMACOLOGY IN COLUMBIA UNIVERSITY

HARRY L. JAFFE, M.D............RESEARCH ASSISTANT, CARDIOGRAPHIC LABORATORY, AND
CLINICAL ASSISTANT, MEDICAL DIVISION, OUT-PATIENT DEPARTMENT,
THE MOUNT SINAI HOSPITAL

SAMUEL KARELITZ, M.D.......ADJUNCT PEDIATRICIAN TO THE MOUNT SINAI HOSPITAL

ALBERT KEAN, M.D........ASSOCIATE RADIOTHERAPIST TO THE MOUNT SINAI HOSPITAL;
ASSOCIATE IN RADIOLOGY IN COLUMBIA UNIVERSITY

PAUL KLEMPERER, M.D......................PATHOLOGIST TO THE MOUNT SINAI HOSPITAL;
CLINICAL PROFESSOR OF PATHOLOGY IN COLUMBIA UNIVERSITY

EMANUEL KLEMPNER, M.D.....FELLOW IN PATHOLOGY AND ASSISTANT GYNECOLOGIST,
OUT-PATIENT DEPARTMENT, THE MOUNT SINAI HOSPITAL

ALEXANDER KOLIN, PH.D........................PHYSICIST TO THE MOUNT SINAI HOSPITAL

JEROME L. KOHN, M.D............ADJUNCT PEDIATRICIAN TO THE MOUNT SINAI HOSPITAL

ABRAHAM L. KORNZWEIG, M.D....................VOLUNTARY ASSISTANT IN OPHTHALMO-
PATHOLOGY AND CLINICAL ASSISTANT, OPHTHALMOLOGICAL DIVISION,
OUT-PATIENT DEPARTMENT, THE MOUNT SINAI HOSPITAL

RUDOLPH KRAMER, M.D..................LARYNGOLOGIST TO THE MOUNT SINAI HOSPITAL

ROBERT K. LAMBERT, M.D.............................ASSOCIATE OPHTHALMIC SURGEON TO
THE MOUNT SINAI HOSPITAL

HERMAN LANDE, M.D...........ASSOCIATE IN MEDICINE TO THE MOUNT SINAI HOSPITAL;
ASSOCIATE IN MEDICINE IN COLUMBIA UNIVERSITY

MURRAY A. LAST, M.D.........VOLUNTARY ASSISTANT IN OPHTHALMO-PATHOLOGY AND
ASSISTANT OPHTHALMIC SURGEON, OUT-PATIENT DEPARTMENT,
THE MOUNT SINAI HOSPITAL

JOSEPH LAVAL, M.D...ADJUNCT OPHTHALMIC SURGEON TO THE MOUNT SINAI HOSPITAL

DEPARTMENT OF GRADUATE MEDICAL INSTRUCTION

(Continued)

SIDNEY D. LEADER, M.D..............Senior Clinical Assistant, Pediatric Division, Out-Patient Department, The Mount Sinai Hospital

OSCAR L. LEVIN, M.D.........Associate Dermatologist to The Mount Sinai Hospital; Associate in Dermatology in Columbia University

HYMAN LEVY, M.D.....................Clinical Assistant, Medical Division, Out-Patient Department, The Mount Sinai Hospital

SIDNEY LICHT, M.D.....Adjunct Physical Therapist to The Mount Sinai Hospital

S. S. LICHTMAN, M.D..................Adjunct Physician to The Mount Sinai Hospital

ROBERT K. LIPPMANN, M.D..................Orthopedist to the Mount Sinai Hospital

SYLVAN D. MANHEIM, M.D..........Assistant Surgeon in Charge of Rectal Clinic, Out-Patient Department, The Mount Sinai Hospital

HUBERT MANN, M.D.................Assistant in Medicine to The Mount Sinai Hospital

ARTHUR M. MASTER, M.D.....Associate in Medicine to The Mount Sinai Hospital; Associate in Medicine in Columbia University

JACOB L. MAYBAUM, M.D.........................Otologist to The Mount Sinai Hospital

MAX D. MAYER, M.D..........Associate Gynecologist to The Mount Sinai Hospital

SAUL MILLER, M.D..........Senior Clinical Assistant, Ophthalmological Division, Out-Patient Department, The Mount Sinai Hospital

HENRY MINSKY, M.D...Associate Ophthalmic Surgeon to The Mount Sinai Hospital

MAURICE E. MINTZ, M.D........Assistant Gynecologist, Out-Patient Department, The Mount Sinai Hospital

SYLVAN E. MOOLTEN, M.D......Adjunct Physician to The Mount Sinai Hospital

ELI MOSCHCOWITZ, M.D.........Associate Physician to The Mount Sinai Hospital; Assistant Clinical Professor of Medicine in Columbia University

HAROLD NEUHOF, M.D.............................Surgeon to The Mount Sinai Hospital; Clinical Professor of Surgery in Columbia University

ALBERT B. NEWMAN, M.D.............Senior Clinical Assistant, Pediatric Division, Out-Patient Department, The Mount Sinai Hospital

BERNARD S. OPPENHEIMER, M.D........Physician to The Mount Sinai Hospital; Clinical Professor of Medicine in Columbia University

SADAO OTANI, M.D..................Associate Pathologist to The Mount Sinai Hospital

REUBEN OTTENBERG, M.D.....Associate Physician to The Mount Sinai Hospital; Associate Clinical Professor of Medicine in Columbia University

SAMUEL M. PECK, M.D......Adjunct Dermatologist to The Mount Sinai Hospital

M. MURRAY PESHKIN, M.D....Assistant Pediatrician, Out-Patient Department, The Mount Sinai Hospital

HENRY PESKIN, M.D..Clinical Assistant, Surgical Division, Out-Patient Department, The Mount Sinai Hospital

DANIEL POLL, M.D...................Associate Physician to The Mount Sinai Hospital; Assistant Clinical Professor of Medicine in Columbia University

HERBERT POLLACK, M.D., Ph.D............................Assistant in Medicine to The Mount Sinai Hospital

COLEMAN B. RABIN, M.D..........Associate in Medicine and Assistant Radiologist to The Mount Sinai Hospital; Associate in Medicine in Columbia University

MIRIAM REINER, M.S....................Assistant Chemist to The Mount Sinai Hospital

SAMUEL RICHMAN, M.D...Assistant Radiotherapist to The Mount Sinai Hospital

ALFRED ROMANOFF, M.D............Assistant Physician, Out-Patient Department, The Mount Sinai Hospital

ISADORE ROSEN, M.D.......Dermatologist to The Mount Sinai Hospital; Professor of Clinical Dermatology and Syphilology, New York Post-Graduate Medical School, Columbia University

SAMUEL ROSEN, M.D...................Associate Otologist to The Mount Sinai Hospital

NATHAN ROSENTHAL, M.D..................Associate in Medicine and Hematologist to The Mount Sinai Hospital; Assistant Clinical Professor of Medicine in Columbia University

DEPARTMENT OF GRADUATE MEDICAL INSTRUCTION

(Continued)

HARRY ROSENWASSER, M.D.....Adjunct Otologist to The Mount Sinai Hospital
IRVING R. ROTH, M.D.........Associate in Medicine and Assistant Pediatrician to
    The Mount Sinai Hospital; Associate in Medicine in Columbia University
ISIDOR C. RUBIN, M.D.........................Gynecologist to The Mount Sinai Hospital;
    Clinical Professor of Gynecology in Columbia University
U. J. SALMON, M.D.....................Adjunct Gynecologist to The Mount Sinai Hospital
NATHAN SAVITSKY, M.D.........Adjunct Neurologist to The Mount Sinai Hospital
I. SCOTTY SCHAPIRO, M.D...Clinical Assistant, Medical and Surgical Divisions,
    Out-Patient Department, The Mount Sinai Hospital
MAX SCHEER, M.D...........Adjunct Dermatologist to The Mount Sinai Hospital;
    Associate Professor of Clinical Dermatology,
    New York Post-Graduate Medical School, Columbia University
ALBERT J. SCHEIN, M.D........Adjunct Orthopedist to The Mount Sinai Hospital
BELA SCHICK, M.D.....................................Pediatrician to The Mount Sinai Hospital;
    Clinical Professor of Diseases of Children in Columbia University
KAUFMAN SCHLIVEK, M.D....Ophthalmic Surgeon to The Mount Sinai Hospital
    Clinical Professor of Ophthalmology in Columbia University
HERMAN SCHWARZ, M.D.....Associate Pediatrician to The Mount Sinai Hospital;
    Assistant Clinical Professor of Diseases of Children,
    in Columbia University
SETH SELIG, M.D.....................................Orthopedist to The Mount Sinai Hospital
GREGORY SHWARTZMAN, M.D........Bacteriologist to The Mount Sinai Hospital
SAMUEL SILBERT, M.D....................Adjunct Surgeon to The Mount Sinai Hospital
SOLOMON SILVER, M.D.....Adjunct Physician to The Mount Sinai Hospital
EUGENE R. SNYDER, M.D.........Adjunct Otologist to The Mount Sinai Hospital
HARRY H. SOBOTKA, Ph.D.......................... Chemist to The Mount Sinai Hospital
LOUIS J. SOFFER, M.D...............Adjunct Physician to The Mount Sinai Hospital
MAX L. SOM, M.D...........Adjunct Laryngologist to The Mount Sinai Hospital
MARCY L. SUSSMAN, M.D......................Radiologist to The Mount Sinai Hospital;
    Associate in Radiology in Columbia University
ARTHUR S. W. TOUROFF, M.D...Associate Surgeon to The Mount Sinai Hospital
KAUFMAN WALLACH, M.D.........Adjunct Physician to The Mount Sinai Hospital
ROBERT I. WALTER, M.D.....................Fellow in Pathology; Clinical Assistant,
    Gynecological Division, Out-Patient Department, The Mount Sinai Hospital
ISRAEL S. WECHSLER, M.D............Neurologist to The Mount Sinai Hospital;
    Professor of Clinical Neurology in Columbia University
HARRY WEISS, M.D.....................Adjunct Physician to The Mount Sinai Hospital
DAVID WEXLER, M.D..Adjunct Ophthalmic Surgeon to The Mount Sinai Hospital
IRA S. WILE, M.D...................Associate in Pediatrics to The Mount Sinai Hospital
SEYMOUR WIMPFHEIMER, M.D....................Adjunct Gynecologist and Assistant
    Radiotherapist to The Mount Sinai Hospital
ASHER WINKELSTEIN, M.D...Associate in Medicine to The Mount Sinai Hospital;
    Associate in Medicine in Columbia University
HARRY YARNIS, M.D.................Clinical Assistant, Medical Division, Out-Patient
    Department, The Mount Sinai Hospital

EXECUTIVE OFFICERS AND HEADS OF DEPARTMENTS

HOSPITAL

JOSEPH TURNER, M.D. ....*Director*
JULIUS A. KATZIVE, M.D..............................*Assistant Director*
JANDON SCHWARZ, M.D..............................*Assistant Director*
MAXWELL S. FRANK, M.D............................*Assistant Director*
GEORGE T. COOK ....*Chief Clerk and Auditor*
JOHN B. CUBBERLEY ....*Supervising Engineer*
ISADORE ROGIN, PH.G. ....*Chief Apothecary*
MAY M. SLATOR, R.N................................*Supervisor, Out-Patient Dept.*
MARY R. ERWIN, R.N................................*Supervisor, Private Pavilion*
EDITH G. RYAN, R.N................................*Supervisor Semi-Private Pavilion*
FANNY LISSAUER MENDELSOHN, B.S.,R.N...*Director of Social Service*
HELEN SOMERS ....*Acting Supervising Dietitian*

SCHOOL OF NURSING

GRACE A. WARMAN, B.S., M.A., R.N.*Principal, School of Nursing, and Superintendent of Nurses*
MINNIE STRUTHERS, B.S., R.N........*Assistant Principal, School of Nursing*
LOTTIE M. PHILLIPS, R.N...............*Assistant Superintendent of Nurses*
PATIENCE EARNEST, R.N....................*Night Superintendent, School of Nursing*
LILLIAN LEESON, A.B., R.N.............*Supervisor of Nursing Education*
CLARE SKALING, R.N.........................*Instructor of Nursing Arts*
MARION CROZIER, M.A.....................*Instructor of Physical Education*
MAY M. SLATOR, R.N.......................*Supervisor of Nurses, Out-Patient Dept.*
MARY R. ERWIN, R.N.......................*Supervisor of Nurses, Private Pavilion*
EDITH G. RYAN, R.N.......................*Supervisor of Nurses, Semi-Private Pavilion*
RUTH GOEBEL, R.N............................*Supervisor of Nurses, Operating Room*
MITHYLDE REICH, R.N.....................*Supervisor of Nurses, Medical Pavilion*
BESSIE WOLFSON, B.A., R.N............*Supervisor of Nurses, Surgical Pavilion*
CORA BALL, R.N...............................*Supervisor of Nurses, Children's Pavilion*
LILLIE DIXON ....*Matron, Nurses' Residence*

REPORT OF THE MEDICAL STAFF

The President of the Medical Board takes pleasure in presenting the following report of the activities of the Medical Staff of the Hospital:

THE LABORATORIES: There has been a steady increase in the routine work in the past five years. This is a natural process, since scientific progress in the Hospital entails an increasing amount of contact with the various Laboratories.

A complete revision and standardization of classification of intestinal gram-negative bacilli has been made. For this purpose, the introduction of standard antigens, obtained from the International Committee on Bacteriology of the League of Nations, has proven especially advantageous. These antigens have been used for the preparation of an extensive series of standard agglutinating and precipitating sera. The method of Flossdorf and Mudd of rapid freezing in vacuo, already in operation for some years in bacteriology research, has been applied to preserve the new standard routine sera for future comparisons and identifications of new strains.

Suitable arrangements have been made with the Blood Transfusion Betterment Association, Inc., for an adequate supply of standard, high-titer blood-grouping sera. This arrangement has greatly relieved the Department of Bacteriology and placed the blood grouping on a standard basis.

The call for sterile 50 per cent glucose solution for intravenous use, prepared by the Department of Chemistry, has again increased, the increase being 38 per cent over the previous year. The amount of this solution dispensed during 1938 was 2,298,000 c.c. (45,960 vials) as compared with 1,663,350 c.c. (33,367 vials) in the preceding year.

The following new routine chemical tests have been introduced:

1. Volumetric Method for Amylase, Replacing Stalagometric Method.

2. Quantitative Determination of Sulfapyridine in Blood and Cerebrospinal Fluid.

3. Benzoic-Acid Test for Liver Function.

4. Vitamin C Excretion Test.

61

The services of a physicist have been secured for the Hospital. He is devoting his time to a number of routine procedures aiding the Departments of Physical Therapy, Radiotherapy and X-ray Diagnosis. The physicist has also been engaged in a research problem in association with members of these departments.

Work on the physico-chemical aspects of allergic skin reactions has been continued. A method has been devised which permits of obtaining permanent records of the rate of wheal growth, by measurements of the height and the area of wheal elevations. Studies are also being continued on demyelinization of the central nervous system in monkeys, with an attempt to duplicate the histological manifestations of multiple sclerosis. This is an elaboration of studies of Rivers, but under somewhat different conditions. Satisfactory progress in neurophysiology is being continued; work is being done on the relation between the sympathetic and parasympathetic hormones after devising a new operation of double denervation in monkeys; the effect of insulin hyperglycemia on the denervated pupil is also being studied. Investigations have been conducted regarding the pathogenesis of certain lesions of the cerebrospinal system which for years have been the center of much discussion among neuropathologists, such as tuberculous meningitis and its relation to tuberculous foci in the brain and massive cerebral hemorrhage. Studies on synthesis of triazines and other heterocyclic compounds are being continued; this work concerns protein structure with possible pharmacological applications. Work on male sex hormones and on estrogens is under way. The vaccination with pneumococcus Type III for prevention of intracranial complications following mastoiditis is being continued successfully. Morphological-histological studies have been carried out on the endometrium of patients who have been treated with testosterone. Interesting correlations have been established, which are of practical value in the diagnosis and treatment of various disorders of menstruation. These studies are being continued.

Investigative work in cardiopathology is being carried on. In close collaboration with the Pediatric Department, the collection of specimens obtained by means of the laryngoscope from children ill with pneumonia, is being supervised; diagnostic skin tests with pure carbohydrates in children at various stages of the disease are also being carried out. Histological studies of the phenomenon of local reactivity in lymph nodes are being conducted; the observations seem to indicate an interesting mechanism of dissemination of toxic disease by means of lymphatic channels. Research has been continued on the effect of concentrated spleen extract upon mouse tumors; these studies have now been extended to spontaneous mouse tumors which have a greater similarity to malignant neoplasms of man. Interesting observations were made during the year and the results obtained are encouraging. The growth of these otherwise very resistent tumors could be arrested, and in some instances the neoplasms have disappeared. The work on heavy oxygen exchange and protein structure carried out under a grant from the Rockefeller Foundation was completed, and has led to interesting conclusions regarding protein structure. Interesting studies have been completed on the effect of prontosil upon toxins of the phenomenon of local skin reactivity; these observations have added interesting information on a thus far unexplained mechanism of the therapeutic activity of this drug, and have also brought out the use of the phenomenon for purposes of determining the antitoxic properties not only of sera but also of therapeutic drugs. Studies were begun on the physiological aspects of infection and resistance, with special reference to neurotropic viruses and malignant transplantable neoplasms. A new toxin has been obtained from streptococcus viridans by means of the phenomenon of local tissue reactivity; the toxin is being used for immunization of horses in order to determine its ability of antitoxin production.

The extensive research on blood electrolytes has continued to yield promising results, especially by the unexpected observation of profound and regular changes in magnesium distribution in thyroid cases. A new laboratory, primarily designed for electrical neuro-diagnosis, has been constructed for the Department of Neurology.

The following papers were published from the Laboratories:

1. Argentaffine (Carcinoid) Tumors of the Small Intestine.

2. Thrombocytopenic Purpura; Failure of X-ray Therapy.

3. Sensitized Pupillary Dilator and Facial Muscles as Indicators of Sympathetic and Parasympathetic Substances in Blood.

4. The Fright Reaction after Section of the Facial, Trigeminal and Cervical Sympathetic Nerves.

5. Tuberculous Meningitis and its Relation to Tuberculous Foci in the Brain.

6. Pubertas Praecox: A Survey of the Reported Cases and Verified Anatomical Findings, with particular reference to Tumors of the Pineal Body.

7. Studies on Triazines. II. Lactim-Lactam Isomerism in Substituted Tetrahydrotriazines.

8. Urinary Cholesterol in Cancer.

9. Gradual Occlusion of a Coronary Artery—An Experimental Study.

10. Ulcer Recurrences Attributed to Upper Respiratory Infection: A Possible Illustration of the Shwartzman Phenomenon.

11. The Total Bile Acid-Cholesterol Ratio in Human and Canine Bile.

12. On the Absorption of Cholecystokinin and Secretion from the Colon and Rectum.

13. The Response of the Smooth Muscle of the Gall-bladder at Various Intravesical Pressures to Cholecystokinin.

14. A Characteristic Vacuolar Phenomenon in Monocytes.

15. Supravital Studies of Gaucher Cells.

16. The Comb of the Baby Chick as a Test for the Male Sex Hormone.

17. Pressor Substance in the Cortex of the Kidney.

18. Toxic Encephalopathy, Coal Tar Derivatives as a Probable Etiological Factor.

19. Morphologic Study of the Reactivity of Mouse Sarcoma 180 to Bacterial Filtrates.

20. Glioneuroma and Spongioneuroblastoma, Forms of Primary Neuro-ectodermal Tumors of the Brain.

21. Massive Cerebral Hemorrhage.

22. Clinical Neuropathological Conference.

23. Meningo-Encephalo-Myeloradiculitis (Clinico-pathological Study).

24. Hemodynamic Studies in Experimental Coronary Occlusion. V. Changes in Arterial Blood Pressure.

25. Pathologic Differentiation between Radiosensitive and Non-radiosensitive Malignant Neoplasms of the Larynx.

26. Pathology of Dirofilaria Infestation. Report of a Case with Chronic Pulmonary Arteritis.

27. Factors which Reduce Gastric Acidity. A Survey of the Problem.

28. Studies in Gastric Secretion. VI. A Statistical Analysis of the Neutral Chloride-Hydrochloric Acid Relation in Gastric Juice.

29. Preparation of Stomach Pouch without Interruption of Vagal Supply.

30. Gastric Vagi in the Dog. Erroneous Assumption of Uninterrupted Vagal Innervation in the Pavlow Pouch.

31. Origin of Carcinoma in Chronic Gastric Ulcer.

32. The Spalteholz Clearing Method applied to the Determination of Carcinomatous Metastases in Regional Lymph Nodes.

33. Cardiovascular Lesions in Avitaminoses.

34. Studies of Adenomatous Polyps and Carcinoma of the Colon.

35. A Case of Carcinoma of the Thyroid Gland with Metastases in the Lungs in a Gray Wolf (Canis Nebulus).

36. The Spleen, Chapter in Downey: Handbooks of Hematology.

37. Coronary Disease in Diabetes Mellitus.

38. Effect of Subcutaneous Injections of Concentrated Spleen Extract of Mouse Sarcoma 180.

39. The Use of Estrogenic Hormone in Experimental Peripheral Gangrene.

40. Cataphoretic Separation of Toxic Components of Moccasin Venom.

41. Colorimetric Determination of Equilenin and Dihydroequilenin.

42. The Oxygen Exchange Reaction of Glycine Hydrochloride and Water.

43. Chemical Investigations on the Active Principles of the Phenomenon of Local Skin Reactivity to Bacterial Filtrates. III. Application of Dialysis to the Production of the Active Principles of Fluid Media.

44. The Effects of Hydrogen Ion Concentration, Fatty Acids and Vitamin C on the Growth of Fungi.

45. The Gastric Absorption of Phenol Red in Humans.

46. Hypoglycemic Response of Patients using Protamine Zinc Insulin to Induced Hyperglycemia.

47. Protein as a Source of Carbohydrate for Patients using Protamine Zinc Insulin.

48. Effect of Fat on Rate of Availability of Orally Ingested Carbohydrate.

49. The Nasogenital Relationship.

50. Chapters on "Agranulocytosis", "Aplastic Anemia", "Blood-Platelets", and "Diseases of Blood-Platelets", for a book on "Blood Morphology".

51. A Slide Rule for Determining Lengths of Menstrual Cycles.

52. Naso-Genital Relationship, Endocrinology.

53. The Phenomenon of Tissue Reactivity in the Kidneys of Rabbits.

54. Chemical Investigations on the Active Principles of the Phenomenon of Local Skin Reactivity to Bacterial Filtrates. II. Physico-Chemical Properties.

55. Chemistry of Sterids.

56. Mono- and Polymolecular Films of Physiologically Active Substances, Chapter of Symposium on Surface Chemistry and Biology.

57. Built-up Films of Steroid Compounds.

58. Saccharosuria.

59. Role of the Uterus in the Production of Manometric Fluctuations During Uterotubal Insufflation (Rubin Test).

MEDICAL SERVICES: The Medical Services have continued their progress in clinical and scientific work and in the improvement of their organization. They have participated actively in the post-graduate teaching of outside physicians, both by means of the formal courses given under the auspices of Columbia University and by the clinical pathological and various clinical conferences. The Hospital is rapidly taking its place as a teaching institution. Over one hundred members of the staff are either actively teaching or offering courses. There has been a gratifying response to these efforts in the constantly increasing number of post-graduate students. It was gratifying to note that the Hospital Staff cooperated in the Eleventh Graduate Fortnight of the New York Academy of Medicine by many important contributions to its symposium.

There has been a continued co-ordination of the special medical services with the general medical staff by means of consultations, joint conferences and special group conferences. Reports of progress of the special groups and discussions of administrative problems at the monthly clinical meeting included the following subjects:

1. Clinical management and therapy of patients with pneumonia.
2. Activities of the Physical Therapy Department.
3. Administrative problems in obtaining necropsy examinations.
4. Report of activities of the metabolism group and dietitian.
5. Sulfanilamide therapy.
6. Proposals for residency in medicine and surgery.
7. Mechanisms in allergy and their clinical applications.
8. Medico-surgical aspects of ulcerative colitis.
9. Age, sex and hypertension in coronary occlusion.
10. Graves' Disease simulating muscular dystrophy.
11. Criteria in the diagnosis of Graves' Disease.

Inasmuch as many recent advances in medicine have been largely in the fields of physiology and chemistry, it seems unfortunate that we have a lack of facilities for physiological work in connection with the medical services. This need cannot be too strongly emphasized. There is comparatively little laboratory space for experimental work along these lines. Not only would efforts in this direction help elucidate many of the complicated medical problems, but they would also afford an opportunity for the best of the younger men who have recently been graduated from the Hospital, to continue their medical training. A partial solution of this problem might be achieved if there were more fellowships for younger men, to enable them to continue their work in physiology and chemistry.

The Out-Patient Department has maintained its high degree of excellence both as to personnel and clinical and scientific work. A number of emigré physicians have been given an opportunity to work in the medical clinics. The clinics have not only served a humanitarian purpose in aiding these men but have also performed a service to the community by training these physicians to maintain our own high standard of medical practice. The emigré physicians serve a period of apprenticeship under our own men before they are permitted to accept responsibility for the treatment of clinic patients. In the temporary contacts with patients in the clinics, the high standard of the work that is done in the wards cannot be maintained; however, through the constant presence in the clinics of associates and adjuncts from the Hospital service, the standard of medical care in these clinics is fast approaching the level of that in our wards. It is important to note that arrangements have been made, in the way of opportunity to assistants in the clinics, to rotate for four-month periods in various specialty clinics in the Out-Patient Department. The educational value of such training is obvious.

A number of scientific contributions has been made in the past year. Of special interest is the emphasis on the treatment of common but serious diseases. A special study was conducted of the relative merits of serum, Sulfanilamide and Sulfapyridine, in pneumonia therapy. Encouraging results have been obtained in the treatment of a few cases of subacute bacterial endocarditis. The investigation of a rapid treatment of syphilis by massive dosage of arsenicals has been continued, with important results. The inauguration of a blood bank has greatly facilitated the use of transfusion as a therapeutic measure.

The following papers were published during the past year:

1. Electrokinetic Phenomena XIII. Comparison of the Isoelectric points of dissolved and Crystalline Amino Acids.
2. Production of Wheals in the Human Skin.
3. Skin Reactions II. The Effect of Allergic and Histamine Wheals in the Rate of Absorption of Dyes and Blood from the Human Cutis.

4. Electrokinetic Aspects of Surface Chemistry V. Electric Mobility and Titration Curves of Proteins and their Relationship to the Calculation of Radius and Molecular Weight.

5. Reversed Iontophoresis of Histamine from Human Skin, Its Bearing on Histamine Theory of Allergic Wheal.

6. Skin Reactions III. The Elementary Theory of Electrophoresis of Drugs through the Skin.

7. Carbohydrate Diets in Relation to Uric Acid Excretion.

8. Nature of Glomerulonephritis.

9. Friedlaender Bacillus Infections of the Urinary Tract.

10. How Restricted is the Life of a Patient with Heart Disease?

11. Clinical Studies of Gitalin and Digitalis in the Treatment of Auricular Fibrillation.

12. The New York Heart Association.

13. Plague of Chronic Sickness.

14. Coronary Artery Thrombosis as a Delayed Postoperative Complication.

15. The Phenomenon of Tissue Reactivity in the Kidneys of Rabbits.

16. Tobacco Sensitization in Rats.

17. Hypersensitiveness and Biopsy Studies in Vascular Disease.

18. Cardiac Arrhythmias with Special Reference to Paroxysmal Tachycardia, Auricular Fibrillation, and Premature Beats in Constitutional Allergic Individuals.

19. Diffuse Dilatation of the Pulmonary Artery.

20. Relationship of Orthopedic Surgery to Internal Medicine.

21. The Creatine Tolerance Test in the Differential Diagnosis of Graves' Disease and Allied Conditions.

22. Oxygen Saturation of Arterial Blood in the Cyanosis from Sulphanilamide.

23. The Influence of Experimental Biliary Obstruction and Liver Injury upon the Total Bile Acid Content and Partition in Blood and Urine.

24. Mitral Stenosis: A Correlation of Electrocardiographic and Pathologic Observations.
25. Postoperative Coronary Artery Occlusion.
26. Optimism in Heart Disease.
27. Bundle Branch and Intraventricular Block in Acute Coronary Artery Occlusion.
28. Partial and Complete Heart Block in Acute Coronary Artery Occlusion.
29. Further Considerations of Radiology of the Chest.
30. Chemical Treatment of Spontaneous Pneumothorax.
31. Pleural Effusions.
32. The Effect of Testicular Extracts (Reynal's Spreading Factor) in Human Skin.
33. Value of the Sternal Puncture in the Diagnosis of Multiple Myeloma.
34. Course of Polycythemia.
35. Blood Platelets and Megakaryocytes.
36. Hemorrhagic Diatheses.
37. Aplastic Anemia and Osteosclerosis.
38. Agranulocytosis.
39. Observations on the Effects of Liver Extracts in Pernicious Anemia with Special Reference to the Paraplegic Form of Subacute Combined Sclerosis.
40. The Use of Intravenously Injected Sodium d-Lactate as a Test for Liver Function.
41. Acetylcholine Esterase in Serum in Jaundice and Biliary Disease.
42. Abdominal Manifestations of Hyperactive Carotid Sinus Reflex.
43. Pre-renal Azotemia and Pathology of Renal Blood Flow.
44. Unilateral Hemoglobinuria: Its Occurrence in Infarction of the Kidney.
45. Bile Salt Therapy in Gall Bladder Disease.
46. Transmission of Syphilis by Transfusion.
47. Angina Pectoris and Cardiac Infarction Induced by Trauma of Unusual Bodily Effort.

48. The Incidence, Mortality Figures, and Treatment of Gastric Hemorrhage due to Ulcer.
49. Primary Ileocecal Tuberculosis.
50. Chronic Gastritis.
51. Cardiac Sequellae of Pulmonary Embolism.
52. Nonrheumatic Calcific Aortic Stenosis.
53. Acute Myocardial Infarction not due to Coronary Artery Occlusion.
54. B. Influenza Endocarditis.
55. Recent Advances in 'Therapeutics.
56. Massive Dose Arsenotherapy of Syphilis by Intravenous Drip Method.
57. The Relative Value of the Basal Metabolic Rate, Velocity of Blood Flow, and Creatine Tolerance Test in the Differential Diagnosis of Graves' Disease and Allied Conditions.
58. The Influence of Intravenous Glucose upon Abnormal Sedimentation Rate in Relation to Activity of Infection.
59. Age, Sex, and Hypertension in Coronary Occlusion.
60. Pleural Effusions Following Pulmonary Infarcts.
61. Acute Mediastinitis.
62. The Pathogenesis of Lung Abscess.
63. Oblique Views in the Roentgen Ray Diagnosis of Lung Abscess.
64. The Course and Treatment of Thrombocytopenic Purpura.
65. Diabetic Gangrene and Infection.
66. Insulin Allergy.
67. Effects of Tissue Extracts on Diabetic Gangrene.
68. Nondiabetic Glycosurias.
69. Relationship of Carbohydrate Availability to Protamine Zinc Insulin.
70. The Treatment of Postarsphenamine Jaundice.
71. Perforations into the Free Peritoneal Cavity Occurring in the Hospital Wards.
72. Glycogen Storage Disease—Cardiac Form.
73. Clinical and Pathologic Findings in Scleroderma.

74. Recession of Renal Amyloidosis due to Multiple Skin Gangrene Associated with Arteritis of the Skin.

75. Acute Pancreatitis.

76. Hepatic Complications in Polycythemia Vera, with Particular Reference to Thrombosis of the Hepatic and Portal Veins and Hepatic Cirrhosis.

77. Arteriosclerosis.

78. Nosological Status of Periarteritis Nodosa.

79. The Treatment of Hemolytic Streptococcus Infections and the Newer Applications of Sulfanilamide.

80. Explanation for the Cyanosis of Sulfanilamide Therapy.

81. The Rate of Removal of Hemoglobin from the Circulation and Its Renal Threshold in Human Beings.

82. Sulfanilamide Therapy for Suppurative Pylephlebitis and Liver Abscesses.

83. The Diagnosis of Venous-Arterial Shunt by the Ether Circulation Time Method.

84. A Case of Primary Broncho-Pulmonary Aspergillosis.

85. Decreased Choline—Esterase Activity of Serum in Jaundice and Biliary Disease.

PEDIATRIC SERVICE: During the past year a number of clinical papers have appeared from this Service. Studies on the insensible perspiration in children, particularly with regard to the influence of the nervous system, the effect of salt, drugs and insulin have been continued. Studies of basal metabolism and tuberculosis in childhood have been made and reported. A second edition of the Diabetic Primer for children, larger and more complete than the earlier edition, has appeared. A simple patch test for tuberculosis has been developed and is now in general use. The subject of tetany of the newborn has been under investigation, and calcium studies in the newborn have been conducted in conjunction with the Chemistry Laboratory. A detailed study of the treatment of pneumonia in childhood has been undertaken, and the various newer methods of treatment are being evaluated.

Among the clinical articles that have appeared during the past year are the following:

1. A Study of the Behavior of 250 Children with Mental Age over Ten Years.

2. Personality Development and Social Control in Terms of Constitution and Culture.

3. Acute Phosphorous Poisoning.

4. Contusion Pneumonia.

5. Netting Restraint over Hospital Cribs.

6. Problems Arising during the Course of Sulfanilamide Therapy in Children.

7. Diffuse Dilation of the Pulmonary Artery.

NEUROLOGICAL SERVICE: The clinical activity of the Neurological Service has been continued at a high level. Investigative work is also in progress and many new problems are being studied. The Medical Board has approved the suggestion that an internist be assigned to both Neurological and Neuro-surgical Services, to the end that many borderland problems may be carefully studied on the wards. The Neurological and Neuro-surgical Services have, in cooperation, offered a course in advanced neurology.

DERMATOLOGICAL SERVICE: There has been a great deal of activity on this Service. Research is being carried out on a more intensive method of treating early syphilis. The results of this procedure have been very encouraging. Investigation from both the laboratory and clinical point of view is being conducted in the treatment of fungus infections. Fortunately, a number of volunteer physicians with a fairly good scientific training have applied for positions in the laboratory. Because of this, the scope of the work has widened materially. The acquisition of a pH meter has also enabled the laboratory staff to control the research on the treatment of fungus infections much more carefully. Investigation is also proceeding on the biology and immunology of the trichophytin reaction. Studies of the effect of snake venom on capillary fragility and various other dermatologic conditions are continuing.

Publications have appeared on a wide range of clinical and laboratory studies. Among these are included chemical studies of the analysis of sweat; the effect of fatty acids on the growth of fungi; chemical studies of snake venoms; as well as many other clinical reports.

SURGICAL SERVICES: During the past year, progress has been made in the problem of the surgical treatment of ulcerative colitis. A considerable number of patients are being subjected to graded procedures consisting of subtotal colectomy. There has been a decided decrease in the mortality rate and post-operative complications. In the field of surgical jaundice, studies are being continued in cholangiography, with the purpose of determining physiologic changes in the excretory system of the liver in disease processes of this organ. In the gastro-enterology laboratory, experimental work is being carried on in the production of acute and chronic cholecystitis, with and without stones, by a method heretofore not utilized. Interesting results are being obtained in this study and will be the subject of a future publication. In addition, considerable advance in the prevention of post-operative peritonitis and wound infections following small and large bowel surgery, has been made. As a result of careful bacteriological studies, the streptococcus hemolyticus was found to be the most important organism as the cause of post-operative peritonitis following colon operations. This organism was cultured in the majority of instances in association with B. Coli and the usual intestinal saphrophytes. As a result of this study, the routine pre-operative administration of sulfanilamide was started in all cases to be subjected to surgical operations on the small and large bowels. The change in the bacteriologic finding following the adoption of this treatment has indicated the elimination in practically every instance of the streptococcus hemolyticus. It is believed that this study will have far-reaching significance in the future development of intestinal surgery. There has been a noticeable absence of post-operative peritonitis as well as a marked diminution in wound complications since this plan was adopted. Studies are being continued, both clinically and pathologically, of the problem of regional and segmental ileitis.

During the past year, there was complete absence of mortality after operations for acute abscess of the lung. Progress has been made in the surgery of chronic abscess of the lung. Studies have been carried out on special varieties of empyema, non-putrid infections of the lung, non-cancerous tumors of lung and pleura, and on the respirator in conditions other than paralysis of respiration. A survey has been made of the problem of pulmonary embolism. An intestinal clamp for certain intestinal operations has been developed. The technique for the removal of all of the lung and of the lobes of the lung has been improved.

The following publications have appeared from these Services:

1. Failures Following Gastro-enterostomy for Gastro-duo-denal Ulcer.

2. Heminephrectomy in the Disease of the Double Kidney.

3. Operative X-ray Control in the Treatment of Renal Calculi.

4. The So-called Hemato-renal Syndrome.

5. Surgical Treatment of Carcinoma of the Esophagus.

6. Differential Diagnosis of Hyperparathyroidism.

7. An Unusual Type of Congenital Hernia.

8. Recurrent Epithelioma of the Arm. Method of Covering Defect after Radical Excision; Illustrating Two Useful Types of Skin Transplantation.

9. Surgical Treatment of Carcinoma of the Esophagus; Additional Experience; Late end-Results.

10. Parathyroidectomy in Treatment of Raynaud's Disease and Scleroderma.

11. Incisional Hernia Following Operation for Acute Appendicitis.

12. A New Colostomy Spur-crushing Clamp.

13. The Use of Sulfanilamide in Surgery of the Colon and Rectum.

14. Malignant Disease of the Thyroid Gland.

15. Diseases of the Double Kidney.

16. The Involvement of the Vena Cava in Renal Tumors.

17. Thrombophlebitis of the Prostatic Plexus.

18. Prostatic Hemorrhages.

19. Progressive Ileitis.

20. Operative X-ray Control of Renal Calculi.

21. Caliceal Pathology.

22. Anaerobic Infections following Operations on the Urinary Tract.

23. Late Wound Infections in Renal Tuberculosis.
24. The Influence of Vagotomy and Subtotal Gastrectomy on Acid Secretion and the Gastric Motility.
25. The Effect of Palliative Subtotal Gastrectomy on Cardiac Ulcers of the Stomach.
26. A Comparative Study of the Clinical and X-ray Evidences of Gastric Retention.
27. A Further Study of the Effect of Excision of the Sub-maxilliary Salivary Gland for Infections of the Floor of the Mouth.
28. A Study of the Bacteriology of a Diseased Gall Bladder.
29. A Study of the Bacteriology of Gastro-duodenal Ulceration of Carcinoma of the Stomach.
30. The Results of a Three Year Study of Multiple Stage Operations in Carcinoma of the Colon and Rectum.
31. The Value of Sodium Benzoate Test in the Jaundiced State.

NEURO-SURGICAL SERVICE: Probably the most important event on the Neuro-surgical Service during the past year was the rounding out of the Service by the appointment of an Associate and an Adjunct. The work on the Service has continued at about the same level as in previous years. Papers on subdural spinal infections and on papillomas of the choroid plexus of the fourth ventricle were published.

GYNECOLOGICAL SERVICES: These Services have been occupied with the endocrinological aspects of various gynecological diseases, particularly the treatment of menopause and functional derangements of gynecological physiology. Investigations have been carried out on the physiological and biological activity of estrogenic and androgenic hormones. The work in the field of gynecological pathology, both in relation to the histogenesis and the clinical aspects of pelvic neoplasms, has been extended. A method of diagnosing intrauterine tumors by hippuran (100%) and $C^{o}2$ has been worked out.

In the sterility clinic of the Out-Patient Department several problems are under investigation. In conjunction with the endocrine laboratory, ovulation studies are being made. The physiology of the fallopian tubes has been the subject of further investigation.

In addition, various clinical problems have been dealt with. These can best be illustrated by the following publications from the Services during 1938:

1. Theca Cell Tumors of the Ovaries.
2. Treatment of Carcinoma of the Ovaries.
3. Treatment of the Menopause Syndrome.
4. Treatment of Dysmenorrhea with Testosterone Propionate.
5. Treatment of Trichomonas Vaginitis.
6. Hematometra.
7. Method of Demonstration of Glycogen in the Human Vaginal Smear.
8. Production of Progestinal Changes in the Human Endometrium following Oral Administration of Pregneniolone.
9. Effect of Testosterone Propionate upon the Genital Tract.
10. Effect of Testosterone Propionate upon the Endometrial Cycle of the Human.
11. Treatment of Functional Bleeding with Testosterone Propionate.
12. Effect of Oestrogenic Hormone upon the Contractility of the Fallopian Tubes.
13. Effect of Progesterone upon the Contractility of the Fallopian Tubes.
14. Gonadatropic Effect of Androgen on the Immature Rat Ovary.
15. The Effect of Testosterone Propionate on Gonadatropic Hormone Excretion and Vaginal Smears of the Human Female Castrate.
16. The Skin Absorption of Dihydroxyesterin in Human.
17. Evaluation of the Human Vaginal Smear in Relation to the Histology of the Vaginal Mucosa.
18. The Role of the Uterus in the Production of Manometric Fluctuations as Determined by the Rubin Test.
19. The Patency of the Uterotubal Junction of the Rabbit as determined by the Rubin Test.
20. The Effect of Castration on the Tubal Contractility of the Rabbit Test.

21. Visualization of Tubal Peristalsis under Various Conditions by Means of the Formation of Abdominal Window.

22. Use of Opaque Media for Determining the Contour of the Endometrial Cavity and Tubes.

23. The Treatment of Oligospermia and Investigation of Azoospermia.

The following problems are under investigation:

1. The Study of Endocrine Products in Relation to the Tubes, Endometrium and Vagina.

2. Experiments in a New Method of Staining Vaginal Smears.

3. Studies in Treatment of Trichomonas Vaginalis.

4. Studies in Urinary Incontinence.

LARYNGOLOGICAL SERVICE: The Service made an extensive report on the results of treatment of laryngeal carcinoma and cylindroma of the respiratory tract and has continued the investigation of the bacteriology of sinusitis and its complications. Gastroscopy has been extensively used in both Hospital and Out-Patient Department. Through the cooperation of the College of Physicians and Surgeons, more thorough training in the basic sciences has been afforded the residents on the Service.

OTOLOGICAL SERVICE: This Service has made important clinical investigations as to the place of sulfanilamide in acute infections of the ear. The laboratory is continuing the very important correlation of studies with clinical material. In addition, special studies in otosclerosis are being made.

OPHTHALMOLOGICAL SERVICE: During the past year, there has been added interest in the departmental conferences, at which more important cases have been presented, and where more discussions by the younger men were stimulated by the head of the service. These discussions have great value in that the entire staff participates. In similar spirit, the post-graduate instruction, in collaboration with Columbia University, has more students. New courses have been given. The embryology collection has been increased, and new courses in histo-pathology and neuro-ophthalmology have been well received. The staff has been inspired by the realization of the importance of post-graduate teaching in the plans of Columbia University. A material step forward has been achieved in placing the residency on a three-year plan, in conformity with the American Board of Ophthalmic Examinations —the first year in basic sciences, the second as a junior residency followed by the final year as resident.

The following papers were published by the staff of this Service:

1. A Microscopic Study of the Coloboma of the Optic Nerve and Macula.
2. Hypersensitivity to Larocaine.
3. A Congenital Type of Endothelial Dystrophy.
4. Avertin Anesthesia in Ophthalmic Surgery.
5. Myopia and Vitamin D.
6. Necrosis of Lacrimal Gland and Frontal Bone.
7. Congenital Bilateral Ectopia Lentis with Arachnodactyly.

ORTHOPEDIC SERVICE: During the past year the increasing activity on this Service necessitated using more beds for patients than those assigned to the Service.

The following papers were published during the year:

1. The Relationship of Dental Infection to Arthritis.
2. Peroneal Nerve Palsy following Adhesive Traction.
3. Paraplegia after Manipulation for Sciatica.
4. The Effect of Large Doses of Lipiodol Injected in the Spinal Subarachnoid Space.
5. Tarsal Wedge Arthrodesis.
6. Meningococcus Arthritis.
7. Bone Changes in Hodgkin's Disease.
8. The Mechanism of Shoulder Derangements.
9. Surgical Tuberculosis.
10. Objections to the Use of Kirschner Wire in Femoral Neck Fractures.
11. The Management of Pathological Fractures.

The following studies are being carried out:

1. The Use of the Corkscrew Bolt in Hip Fractures.
2. Epiphysiodesis by Thermal Measures.
3. The Problems of Scoliosis following Empyema.

4. Adrenal Involvement in Bone Tuberculosis.

5. Buttonhole Dislocations of the Phalanges.

6. End Results in the Operative Treatment of Hallux Valgus.

DEPARTMENT OF ROENTGENOLOGY: In 1938, 16,751 patients were examined, compared with 16,520 in 1937, and 20,848 patients' visits were made, compared with 21,446 in 1937. The entire equipment in the Cystoscopic Department has been made electrically shockproof. The X-ray tube shields also provide protection from primary radiation. A three-phase generator has been installed and should be functioning at full capacity in the near future. Studies presented from this Department have included the following:

1. Influenzal Pneumonitis.

2. Contusion Pneumonia.

3. Non-putrid Pulmonary Suppuration.

4. Dilatation of the Left Auricle in Auricular Fibrillation.

5. Revised Contributions on the Roentgenology of Chest and Urinary Diseases.

6. The Oblique Views in Localization of Pulmonary Processes.

7. Roentgen Examination of the Aorta and Pulmonary Artery (Part of a Symposium on Cardiac Roentgenology).

DEPARTMENT OF RADIOTHERAPY: During the year 1938, there were 675 new patients admitted to this Department, representing an increase of 12% over the previous year and 596 patients were carried over from previous years, making the total 1,271 patients for the year.

Certain technical advancements in the treatment by radiotherapy called for an increase in the number of installations per patient, and with the increased number of new patients, there was a total of 14,890 in the previous year.

Due to the increasing amount of work necessitated by these technical changes, the need for additional apparatus became quite evident. An additional deep-therapy machine was purchased, which will be placed in the room where superficial skin therapy was formerly given. Plans have also been made for the installation of an X-ray machine for the treatment of skin diseases, in the Out-Patient Department. The conversion of the radium element into a more workable and modern form has been approved. This will make it possible to treat a greater variety of lesions and will eliminate the prolonged handling of radium applicators by the members of the Department who make up the forms.

Close co-operation was carried on with the Surgical Services in the treatment of breast cancer; with the Laryngological Department in the treatment of neoplasm of the upper air passages; and with the Gynecological Services in the treatment of neoplasm of the reproductive organs. More widespread use of radiation therapy in infections was also studied during the year. Studies were made with the Pathology Department on the role of tumor grading as an index to the prognosis of laryngeal tumors treated by radiotherapy. A paper, based on this study, was read before a National Society and published subsequently. The value of radiation therapy in the treatment of ovarian tumors was also studied and will be reported before the American Medical Association in May, 1939.

PHYSICAL THERAPY DEPARTMENT: During the past year, this Department experienced a major change. The small space allotted for the treatment of in-patients was greatly expanded. The entire fourth floor of the Administration Building, with the exception of a small section for the Physics Laboratory, was renovated to provide a new in-patient division of physical therapy. To it out-patients are also referred for special treatments not available in the out-patient section of the department. These special procedures consist of hydro-therapy, corrective exercise, cabinet bath, and fever therapy. A new physical therapy technician was attached to the in-patient staff, particularly for the care of patients receiving hydrotherapy and gymnastic exercise. The department has taken over the corrective exercise group. Because of these extra facilities, the department has ben able to care for an increased number of patients.

The presence of a physicist and a physics laboratory has permitted the inauguration of studies bearing on the relationship of physics to the diagnosis and treatment of disease.

The following papers were published by members of this Department:

1. Difference in Temperature of Skin and Muscle of the Lower Extremities, Following Various Procedures.
2. Medical Applications of the Short-Wave Current.

Post-graduate teaching is being continued. The trend of the work during the year indicated quite clearly that the Department is coming to play a more important part in the general activities of the Hospital.

In closing this, the last of my reports after twelve years as President of the Medical Board, I wish to express my sincere thanks to my colleagues for their interest and hearty co-operation. These have done much to lighten the burdens of my position. May I also extend to my successor my very best wishes.

ISIDORE FRIESNER, M.D.,

President, Medical Board.

BEQUESTS AND DONATIONS FOR SPECIAL PURPOSES DURING YEAR 1938

Estate of Amelia Meyers—For the alteration and dedication of the Laboratory Annex to be known as "The Abraham and Amelia Meyers Memorial" and for the support of research carried on therein $233,026.35

Estate of Charles Klingenstein—To be added to the Mr. and Mrs. Charles Klingenstein Fund—For non-budgetary purposes ... 50,000.00

Estate of William N. Cohen—For the William N. Cohen Research Fund; income to be used for research............................ 25,000.00

Estate of William N. Cohen—To be added to the Etta C. Lorsch Memorial Fund; income to be disbursed by the Social Service Auxiliary for the special country care of children ... 10,000.00

Committee on Neighborhood Health Development—For Intravenous Drip Therapy Project.. 8,625.33

David A. Schulte—For the Out-Patient Department Dental Clinic 8,000.00

Estate of Henry Esberg—For cardio-vascular research............... 5,000.00

Mr. and Mrs. George Blumenthal—For non-budgetary purposes ... 5,000.00

Blanche and Frank Wolf Foundation, Inc.—For Dr. Shwartzman's work in cancer research..................................... 3,000.00

Mrs. Paul Gottheil—In memory of daughter, Elsie Gottheil Jaretzki—For research fund... 3,000.00

Mr. and Mrs. Steven J. Hirsch—In memory of his brother, Walter A. Hirsch—To be added to the Morris J. and Carrie Hirsch Fund 2,500.00

Mrs. Arthur Lehman—For support of cancer research of Dr. Richard Lewisohn 2,500.00

The Friedsam Foundation, Inc.—Toward Fellowship for gastro-enterology research 2,500.00

Dr. I. C. Rubin—For Dr. Hiram N. Vineberg Fund for gynecology research 2,400.00

New York Foundation—For support of cancer research of Dr. Richard Lewisohn 2,250.00

Mrs. Paul Gottheil—In memory of daughter, Elsie Gottheil Jaretzki—For support of cancer research of Dr. Richard Lewisohn 2,000.00

The Friedsam Foundation, Inc.—For ear, nose and throat research 1,800.00

Mrs. Addie H. Homan—For the Isidor Hernsheim Fellowship in Chemistry 1,500.00

Mrs. Charles Klingenstein—To be added to the Charles Klingenstein Fellowship Fund 1,500.00

Ittleson Foundation—For support of cancer research of Dr. Richard Lewisohn 1,500.00

Frances and John L. Loeb Foundation—For support of cancer research of Dr. Richard Lewisohn............................ 1,500.00

"A Friend"—For a Fellowship in Gynecology to commemorate the 75th Birthday of Dr. Joseph Brettauer......................... 1,200.00

Carried Forward $373,801.68

BEQUESTS AND DONATIONS FOR SPECIAL PURPOSES DURING YEAR 1938

(Continued)

Brought Forward	$373,801.68
Eli Lilly & Company—For Eli Lilly Fellowship..........................	1,200.00
Josiah Macy, Jr. Foundation—For studies on the secretion of a para-sympathetic substance under emotional stress.................	1,000.00
Sam A. Lewisohn—For support of cancer research of Dr. Richard Lewisohn	1,000.00
Mrs. Levy Mayer—In memory of son-in-law, Walter A. Hirsch—For research fund	1,000.00
Mr. and Mrs. Frank Altschul—For cardio-vascular research......	996.26
Mount Sinai Hospital Research Foundation, Inc.—For venom research	900.00
Dr. Ralph Colp—For Fellowship in Bacteriology..........................	800.00
The Friedsam Foundation, Inc.—For special pediatric research on drug reactions	750.00
Josiah Macy, Jr. Foundation—For research on psychological and physiological aspects of angina pectoris............................	750.00
United Fruit Company—For studies on carbohydrate absorption	500.00
John Wyeth and Brother, Inc.—For the study of the continuous drip method in treatment of peptic ulcer....................................	500.00
Mrs. Benjamin J. Buttenwieser—For support of cancer research of Dr. Richard Lewisohn..	500.00
Mrs. Louis J. Grumbach—For support of cancer research of Dr. Richard Lewisohn	500.00
Frank Lewisohn—For support of cancer research of Dr. Richard Lewisohn.	500.00
Miss Adelaide Reckford—For support of cancer research of Dr. Richard Lewisohn	500.00
Mrs. Charles Altschul—For cardio-vascular research....................	500.00
Anonymous—For cardio-vascular research	500.00
Estate of S. Morgan Barber—For Research Fund........................	500.00
Dr. Ralph Colp—Toward Fellowship for gastro-enterology research	500.00
Mrs. Clara Klingenstein—Toward Fellowship for gastro-enterology research	500.00
Dr. Percy Klingenstein—Toward Fellowship for gastro-enterology research	500.00
Estate of Louise King Reckford—Toward Fellowship for gastro-enterology research	500.00
Steven J. Hirsch—For cost of air-conditioning unit....................	407.15
Dr. I. C. Rubin—For an insufflation apparatus and other new equipment	316.04
Anonymous—For Pediatric Lantern Slide Fund...........................	300.00
Mrs. D. Alan Dillenberg—For Research Fund..............................	250.00
Anonymous—For Lectures by Dr. George White Pickering........	200.00
Carried Forward	$390,171.13

BEQUESTS AND DONATIONS FOR SPECIAL
PURPOSES DURING YEAR 1938

(Continued)

Brought Forward	$390,171.13
Dr. Robert K. Lambert—For research in eye pathology	200.00
Philip J. Goodhart—For cardio-vascular research	200.00
Mr. and Mrs. Carl H. Pforzheimer—For Research Fund	200.00
Dr. Samuel M. Peck—For equipment	195.00
Dr. Samuel M. Peck—For venom research	176.57
American Medical Association—For the study of monomolecular layers of physiologically active substances	150.00
Mr. S. Klein—For thrombo-angiitis obliterans research	100.00
E. J. Block—In memory of Walter A. Hirsch—For Research Fund	100.00
Dr. Florence E. Sammis—For Research Fund	100.00
Howard M. Ernst—For non-budgetary purposes	100.00
Associated Alumni of The Mount Sinai Hospital—For Library Fund	100.00
Mrs. Charles Klingenstein—In memory of February 28th—For Library Fund	100.00
Dr. Joseph Laval—For Library Fund	100.00
Morton L. Adler—In memory of Frederica M. Adler—For Staff Loan and Relief Fund	100.00
Mrs. Max J. Breitenbach—In memory of Charles Klingenstein—For Staff Loan and Relief Fund	100.00
Mr. and Mrs. Isaac Friedenheit—"In memory of our dear son, Mr. Myron Goldsmith Friedenheit's birthday, September 7, 1898"	50.00
Bertha Brant—In memory of husband, Saul Brant—For Research Fund	50.00
Herbert L. Gardner, Walter L. Kahn, Milton Ferber, George Taylor, Howard Sinenberg, Irma Shlan—In memory of Alfred Lowenthal—For non-budgetary purposes of photography department	50.00
Dr. Kaufman Schlivek—For Research Fund	30.00
Miss N. Welt—For cancer research	25.00
Mrs. Samuel Stiefel—In memory of Mr. Ernst Rosenfeld—For Research Fund	25.00
Arthur M. Lamport—For Library Fund	25.00
Mr. and Mrs. Richard Hirsch—In memory of Charles Klingenstein—For Staff Loan and Relief Fund	25.00
Miss Grace M. Mayer—In memory of Dr. Leo Kessel—For Research Fund	10.00
Joseph H. Abraham—In memory of Alfred Lowenthal—For non-budgetary purposes of photography department	10.00
Smith Periodical Fund—For Library Fund	5.00
Total	$392,497.70

DONATIONS DURING YEAR 1938

The Workmen's Circle	$200.00
Mr. S. L. Buschman—Through Federation	150.00
Morris W. Haft	50.00
Third Panel Sheriff's Jury	50.00
Leila Saks Ranger—In memory of Mother, Jennie R. Saks—for Mother's Day	25.00
Paul C. DeBry	25.00
Walter J. Wolff—In memory of Mr. Walter A. Hirsch	25.00
Mrs. Paul Gottheil—In memory of Mr. Joseph F. Cullman	20.00
Mrs. Karl Kern	15.00
Leila Saks Ranger—In memory of her Mother's birthday	15.00
The Misses Albert	10.00
H. Seymour Eisman—In memory of Mrs. Bella R. Mirabeau	10.00
Mrs. Robert Barnett—In memory of Mrs. Samuel Edelman	10.00
Larry Barnett—In memory of Mrs. Samuel Edelman	10.00
Mr. and Mrs. Clarence M. Guggenheimer—In memory of Mrs. Annie Edelman	10.00
Mrs. John Welz—In memory of Mrs. Annie Edelman	10.00
Max Goldman	10.00
Jacques Passavant	10.00
Andrew R. McLaren—In memory of A. S. Rosenthal	10.00
Harold D. Wimpfheimer—In memory of Mr. Paul Adler	10.00
Harold P. Kurzman	10.00
Mrs. Otto V. Kohnstamm	10.00
Nathan Kaufman	10.00
Mr. and Mrs. Jesse Lilienthal—In memory of Dr. Edwin Beer	10.00
John Raiss—In memory of Mr. Walter A. Hirsch	10.00
Mr. and Mrs. Ralph Wolf—In memory of Mrs. M. B. Bernstein	10.00
Mrs. George L. Beer—In memory of Dr. Edwin Beer	10.00
Mr. and Mrs. Frank E. Karelsen, Jr.—In memory of Mr. Emanuel Van Raalte	10.00
Andrew R. McLaren—In memory of Dr. M. J. Sittenfield	10.00
Mrs. Josephine Price	10.00
Harold D. Wimpfheimer—In memory of Dr. Henry W. Berg	10.00
Miscellaneous donations	99.00
Total	$884.00

ENDOWMENTS FOR SPECIAL PURPOSES

Mr. and Mrs. Charles Klingenstein Fund..................................$105,000.00
> Established by Mr. and Mrs. Charles Klingenstein; income to be used for non-budgetary purposes as determined annually by the Board of Trustees.

Benjamin Altman Fund.. 100,000.00
> Established by provision in the will of Benjamin Altman; one-half of the income to be utilized to defray expenses of the Neurological Department, the remainder for the general purposes of the institution.

Marjorie Walter Goodhart and Florence Henrietta Walter Children's Clinic Endowment.. 100,000.00
> Founded by their parents, Florence B. and William I. Walter; income to be used for the purposes of Children's Clinic.

Marjorie Walter Goodhart and Florence Henrietta Walter Memorial Fund 25,000.00
> Established by provision in the will of Miss Rosie Bernheimer; income to be applied towards the running expenses of the Children's Clinic.

Babette Lehman Fund 100,000.00
> Founded by Mrs. Babette Lehman; income to be utilized for the advancement of preventive medicine.

Louis W. Neustadter Fund.. 100,000.00
> Founded by provision in the will of Mrs. Henry Neustadter; distribution of income to be made annually on the 16th day of March, a portion to needy and indigent patients in the Hospital on that date, the remainder for the general purposes of the Hospital.

Mount Sinai Hospital Fund for Medical Education............... 50,000.00
> Joseph F. and Zillah Cullman contributed $25,000.00 as a nucleus of said fund, and $25,000.00 contributed by the estate of Henry P. Goldschmidt; the income to be used to defray expenses arising out of clinical lectures, demonstrations and conferences, and for cognate purposes.

Alfred A. and Ruth M. Cook Fund....................................... 50,000.00
> Founded by Alfred A. and Ruth M. Cook; income to be applied to special experimental work in the Social Service Department.

Florette and Ernst Rosenfeld Foundation.............................. 50,000.00
> Founded by Florette and Ernst Rosenfeld; for the establishment and special support of a Department of Radium and Radiotherapy.

Dr. Isador Abrahamson Neurological Fund............................ 50,000.00
> Established by provision in the will of Stella Heidelberg Abrahamson; the income from this fund to be used for Fellowships for research work and study in the field of neurology and psychiatry.

George Blumenthal, Jr. Fellowship Fund............................... 45,000.00
> Founded by Mrs. Florence Blumenthal; income to be applied to the maintenance of two Fellowships in Pathology.

Helen B. Millhauser Fund.. 38,000.00

Etta C. Lorsch Memorial Fund.. $34,000.00
Established by provision in the will of Etta C. Lorsch
($10,000); by members of the Board of the Social Ser-
vice Auxiliary ($10,000.00); and by many of her friends
($4,370.00); the sum of $10,000.00 was added by provision
in the will of William N. Cohen; income to be disbursed
by the Social Service Auxiliary for the special country care
of children.

Jacob Mayer Fund.. 30,000.00
Founded in memory of Jacob Mayer for equipping and
maintaining a pneumonia room.

Harriet Meyer Memorial Fund.. 25,000.00
Founded by Eugene Meyer; income to be used for experi-
mental work in the Social Service Department.

Alice Goldschmidt Sachs Endowment Fund.............................. 25,000.00
Established by provision in the will of Alice Goldschmidt
Sachs; income to be used for medical education.

Moritz Rosenthal Fellowship Fund.. 25,000.00
Established by provision in the will of Moritz Rosenthal;
income to be used for medical, surgical, clinical or
laboratory Fellowships as granted to men selected by the
Board of Trustees.

Ambulance Fund 20,000.00
Established by Murry Guggenheim; income to be applied
toward the maintenance of the ambulance.

Murry Guggenheim Scholarship Fund...................................... 20,000.00
Founded by Murry Guggenheim; income to provide medals
and twelve scholarships of $100 each annually to nurses of
The Mount Sinai Hospital School of Nursing.

Moritz Warburg Social Service Fund.. 20,000.00
Founded by Felix M. and Paul M. Warburg; income to be
applied to the work of the Social Service Department.

Emanuel Van Raalte Endowment Fund for Medical
Education 20,000.00
Legacy; income to be used for medical education.

Minnie Kastor Memorial Fund.. 19,775.00
Founded by Alfred B. Kastor as a tribute to the memory
of his mother; income to be used for psychiatric work
through the service of a resident psychiatrist.

Charles Klingenstein Fellowship Fund...................................... 16,500.00
Established by Mrs. Charles Klingenstein; income to be
used for Fellowship in any clinical or laboratory department
of the Hospital as determined by the Board of Trustees.

Robert and John Kaufmann Vacation Fund.............................. 11,000.00
Founded by Max Kaufmann; income to be used for
providing vacations, preferably for crippled children.

Theodor Escherich Fellowship Fund.. 10,000.00
Founded by an anonymous donation; income to be applied
to the maintenance of a Fellowship in Pathology.

Moses Heineman Fellowship Fund.. 10,000.00
Founded by Moses Heineman; income to be applied to the
maintenance of a Fellowship in Pathology.

ENDOWMENTS FOR SPECIAL PURPOSES

(Continued)

Dr. Henry Koplik Fund... $10,000.00
  Established by provision in the will of Dr. Henry Koplik;
  income to be disbursed by the Social Service Department
  and devoted solely to the care of infants and children,
  whose parents are unable to pay ward fees.

Eugene Meyer, Jr. Fellowship Fund.............. .... 10,000.00
  Founded by Eugene Meyer, Jr.; income to be applied to
  the maintenance of a Fellowship in Pathology.

William Henry Welch Lecture Fund.............................. 10,000.00
  Established by Dr. Emanuel Libman; income to be used to
  provide lectures to be named after Dr. William Henry Welch
  of Johns Hopkins University.

Emil Wolff Social Service Fund.............................. 10,000.00
  Established by Emil Wolff; income to be applied to the
  work of the Social Service Department.

Library Funds 7,200.00
  Dr. Abraham Jacobi Library Fund of $5,000.00 established
  by the Board of Trustees to commemorate the eightieth
  birthday of Dr. Abraham Jacobi; income to be applied to
  the purchase of books for the Hospital Library.

  Dr. Fred S. Mandlebaum Memorial Fund of $2,200.00 con-
  tributed by many of his friends; income to be applied to the
  purchase of books for the Hospital Library.

Charles and Camilla Altschul Fund for Nursing in Wards.... 5,000.00
  Founded by Charles and Camilla Altschul; to defray the
  expense of special nursing in the wards.

Isaac C. Bishop Fund... 5,000.00
  Established by provision in the will of Morris Bishop;
  income to be used for the relief, care and benefit of poor
  patients suffering from cancer.

Edward Gamaliel Janeway Lecture Fund.............................. 5,000.00
  Founded by an anonymous donation; income to be utilized
  to bring important investigators to Mount Sinai Hospital,
  to present the result of their work.

Fannie C. Korn Fund... 5,000.00
  Founded by Mrs. Fannie C. Korn—In Memory of Henry
  Korn; for the establishing and maintaining of a splint and
  apparatus room for the Orthopedic Service.

Mount Sinai Hospital Alumni Fund.............................. 4,200.00
  Donation of Dr. H. F. L. Ziegel; income, and if necessary,
  capital, to be expended in defraying part or all of the cost
  of caring in private rooms of the Hospital for members of
  the Associated Alumni of Mount Sinai Hospital, the expenditures for any one case not to exceed $200.

Morris Littman Social Service Fund.............................. 3,000.00
  Established by provision in the will of Morris Littman;
  income to be applied to the work of the Social Service
  Department.

MEDICAL RESEARCH FUNDS

The Abraham and Amelia Meyers Memorial Fund......................$225,000.00
> Established by provision in the will of Amelia Meyers; income to be used in the furtherance of medical and scientific research.

S. S. Prince Research Fund.. 100,000.00
> Established by provision in the will of S. S. Prince; income to be used for research work.

Henry and Emma Rosenwald Foundation............................... 100,000.00
> Established by provision in the will of Mrs. Emma Rosenwald; income to be used for research work. If such work becomes impracticable or inadvisable, the income is to be used for any other purpose designated by the Trustees.

Kops Foundation for Pathological Research............................ 70,000.00
> Income to be used from time to time for special work in the Pathological Department, under the direction of the Board of Trustees, preference to be given to research.

The Lorsch-Sachs Endowment Fund for the Promotion of Medical Research 60,000.00
> Created by Josephine Lorsch, Nellie and Harry Sachs in memory of Albert Lorsch, Jenny and Sigmund Lorsch; income to be used for the study of some promising scientific problems especially for research work bearing upon the origin and cure of cancer.

Max Nathan Laboratory Fund... 30,000.00
> Established by his wife and daughters; income to be used primarily towards the payment of salaries in the Laboratory Research Department.

Eugene Littauer Research Fund... 25,000.00
> Founded by Eugene Littauer in memory of Nathan Littauer; income to be used for medical research work.

William N. Cohen Research Fund... 25,000.00
> Established by provision in the will of William N. Cohen; income to be used for research work.

Elias Asiel Research Fund... 21,000.00
> Founded by Irma A. Bloomingdale and Nelson I. Asiel; income of which is to be applied to the payment of salaries or fellowships in the research work of the Pathological Department.

Eugene Strauss Endowment Fund for Medical Research...... 20,000.00
> Established by provision in the will of Charles Strauss; income to be used for medical research.

Carried Forward $676,000.00

MEDICAL RESEARCH FUNDS

(Continued)

Brought Forward $676,000.00

Morris J. and Carrie Hirsch Fund.. 12,500.00
Established by Walter A. and Steven J. Hirsch in memory
of their parents ($10,000.00) ; and donation ($2,500.00) from
Mr. and Mrs. Steven J. Hirsch in memory of Walter A.
Hirsch; income to be devoted to work in connection with
the study of cancer.

Rosie Bernheimer Memorial Fund.. 10,000.00
Established by provision in the will of Miss Rosie Bern-
heimer; income to be used for clinical research work.

Morris Fatman Medical Research Fund.................................... 10,000.00
Founded by Morris Fatman in memory of Solomon A.
Fatman.

Etta C. and Arthur Lorsch Fund.. 10,000.00
Founded by Etta C. and Arthur Lorsch; income to be devoted
to Laboratory research work.

Elsie and Walter W. Naumburg Fund...................................... 10,000.00
Established by Mr. and Mrs. Walter W. Naumburg; income
to be used exclusively for Chemical Research at Mount Sinai
Hospital.

Virginia I. Stern Fund.. 10,000.00
Legacy; income to be used for medical research work.

**Herman Younker Fund for Clinical and Pathological
Research** 10,000.00
Established by Mrs. Herman Younker; income to be used
exclusively for clinical and pathological research.

Joel E. Hyams Fund.. 10,000.00
Established by provision in the will of Rosalie Hyams;
income to be devoted to research work in cancer.

Leo L. Doblin Endowment Fund for Research Work............ 9,250.00
Legacy; income to be used solely for research work in the
pathological laboratory (On account of $10,000.00 legacy).

Arthur E. Frank Medical Research Fund................................ 7,500.00
Established by provision in the will and in memory of
Arthur E. Frank; the income from this fund is to be
devoted to Laboratory research work, preferably in connection with the study and cure of cancer.

Total $775,250.00

ENDOWMENT FUNDS

THE CARRIE M. AND GUSTAV BLUMENTHAL FUND....	$35,000.00
THE GEORGE AND FLORENCE BLUMENTHAL FUND......	30,000.00
THE PHILIP J. AND HATTIE L. GOODHART FUND........	30,000.00
THE ELLIN P. AND JAMES SPEYER FUND.......................	30,000.00
THE ANNIE C. AND CHARLES A. WIMPFHEIMER FUND	30,000.00
THE MURRY AND LEONIE GUGGENHEIM FUND.............	25,000.00
THE TILLIE S. AND ALFRED JARETZKI FUND................	25,000.00
THE ADOLPH AND EMMA LEWISOHN FUND..................	20,000.00
THE EDWARD OPPENHEIMER FUND...............................	20,000.00
THE ESTELLE AND HUGO BLUMENTHAL FUND............	15,000.00
THE ELIAS AND LINA MEYER ASIEL FUND..................	10,000.00
THE JOHN A. AND HENRIETTA COOK FUND.................	10,000.00
THE DAVID L. AND CARRIE F. EINSTEIN FUND............	10,000.00
THE PAUL AND MIRIAM H. GOTTHEIL FUND..............	10,000.00
THE ALBERT N. HALLGARTEN FUND.............................	10,000.00
THE HENRY AND ROSA LEHMAN FUND........................	10,000.00
THE ALBERT A. LEVI FUND..	10,000.00
THE EUGENE AND HARRIET MEYER FUND...................	10,000.00
THE HENRY AND JOSEPHINE MORGENTHAU FUND......	10,000.00
THE ROSALIE AND MAX NATHAN FUND........................	10,000.00
THE MR. AND MRS. SAM S. STEINER FUND..................	10,000.00
THE ISAAC AND VIRGINIA STERN FUND........................	10,000.00
THE ALEXANDRE AND JULIE WEILL FUND....................	10,000.00

$390,000.00

TREASURER'S REPORT

STATEMENT OF CURRENT ACCOUNT RECEIPTS
FOR THE YEAR ENDED DECEMBER 31st, 1938

Payments of Patients:

Private Pavilion Patients	$534,755.64	
Semi-Private Pavilion Patients	298,863.65	
Ward Patients	74,331.30	
Out-Patient Department Patients	48,183.20	
Patients treated under Workmen's Compensation Act	8,650.88	
Total		$964,784.67

Payments by:

City of New York for Part Maintenance of Free Ward Patients and for Custodians....	197,558.39

Contributions:

Federation for the Support of Jewish Philanthropic Societies	185,178.11	
Greater New York Fund (through Federation)	55,742.93	
United Hospital Fund	69,313.09	
Donations	734.00	
Total		310,968.13

Permanent and Endowment Fund Income:

Permanent Fund	20,354.37	
Endowment Fund	16,806.48	
Total		37,160.85

Appropriations from Principal and Income of Special

Funds	131,238.08
Total Current Receipts (Hospital)	1,641,710.12

School of Nursing:

From Federation for the Support of Jewish Philanthropic Societies	242,984.00	
From Other Sources	9,425.30	
		252,409.30
Carried Forward		$1,894,119.42

Brought Forward		$1,894,119.42
Social Service Auxiliary:		
From Federation for the Support of Jewish Philanthropic Societies	$95,391.24	
From United Hospital Fund	19,500.00	
From Other Sources	4,176.45	
		119,067.69
Ladies' Auxiliary:		
From Federation for the Support of Jewish Philanthropic Societies		21,945.00
From Funds to Cover Cost of Operation in 1938:		
From Permanent Fund, for Hospital Deficit....	200,216.80	
From Permanent Fund, for School of Nursing Deficit	71,384.86	
From Permanent Fund, for Ladies' Auxiliary Deficit	4,257.53	
Total from Permanent Fund, for Deficits............	275,859.19	
From Social Service Auxiliary Special Account, for Deficit	18,682.87	
Total Deficit		*294,542.06*
Total Receipts		$2,329,674.17

STATEMENT OF CURRENT ACCOUNT
DISBURSEMENTS

FOR THE YEAR ENDED DECEMBER 31st, 1938

Administration:

Salaries and Wages of Officers and Clerks	$91,363.18	
Telephone Wages	11,132.64	
Salaries of Custodians	8,314.84	
Pensions	4,190.00	
Telephone Service	22,072.22	
Stationery and Printing	5,162.58	
Miscellaneous	2,009.38	
Total Administration		$144,244.84

Professional Care of Patients:
Salaries and Wages:

Physicians	44,721.27	
Nurses	28,644.50	
Druggists	13,459.73	
Orderlies	48,100.36	
Follow-up and Clinical Secretaries	23,616.60	
Medical and Surgical Supplies	162,665.49	
Total Professional Care of Patients		321,207.95

*Out-Patient Department:

Salaries and Wages	41,959.58	
Stationery and Printing	2,624.71	
Instruments	2,069.20	
Sundries	1,913.74	
Total Out-Patient Department		48,567.23

Radiograph Department:

Salaries and Wages	26,664.97	
Supplies	37,473.81	
Total Radiograph Department		64,138.78

Radiotherapy Department:

Salaries and Wages	8,805.46	
Supplies	3,650.13	
Radium	72.50	
Total Radiotherapy Department		12,528.09
Carried Forward		$590,686.89

* The items included under this heading are those which are chargeable directly and exclusively to the Out-Patient Department. The actual cost of conducting the Out-Patient Department, including the proportion of other expenses properly chargeable to it, is $366,754.90.

Brought Forward		$590,686.89
Electro-cardiograph Department:		
Salaries and Wages	$2,388.87	
Supplies	1,360.32	
Total Electro-cardiograph Department........		3,749.19
Department of Laboratories:		
Salaries and Wages	84,319.47	
Supplies	22,220.72	
Total Department of Laboratories:...............		106,540.19
Provisions		375,933.31
Dietary Department:		
Salaries and Wages	96,506.51	
Supplies	7,269.43	
Total Dietary Department		103,775.94
Housekeeping Department:		
Salaries and Wages	82,026.92	
Furniture and Housefurnishings	23,945.64	
Crockery and Silverware	6,711.42	
Dry Goods	8,583.93	
Beds and Bedding	5,039.14	
Total Housekeeping Department		126,307.05
Laundry Department:		
Salaries and Wages	44,251.95	
Supplies	10,470.65	
Total Laundry Department		54,722.60
General House and Property Expenses:		
Salaries and Wages	111,128.17	
Renewals and Repairs	108,288.13	
Light, Heat and Power	75,191.61	
Total General House and Property Expenses		294,607.91
Insurance		18,613.04
Carried Forward		$1,674,936.12

Brought Forward		$1,674,936.12

Auditing and Accounting:

Salaries and Wages	$37,417.28	
Sundries	7,432.92	
Stationery and Printing	2,114.80	
Postage	4,477.24	
Lettering of Tablets	970.17	
Awards to House Staff	650.00	
Annual Report	1,087.11	

Total Auditing and Accounting		54,149.52
Total General Current Account Disbursements		1,729,085.64
Current Disbursements from Principal and Income of Special Funds for Stated Purposes		112,841.28

Total Current Disbursements, Hospital........		1,841,926.92
Disbursements, School of Nursing	323,794.16	
Disbursements, Social Service Auxiliary	137,750.56	
Disbursements, Ladies' Auxiliary	26,202.53	

		487,747.25
Total Disbursements		$2,329,674.17

PERMANENT FUND

Received for Endowment of Wards, Rooms and Beds................$2,865,447.07
Cash and Securities on Hand	703,164.88

Deficit in Permanent Fund, December 31, 1938.......................$2,162.282.19

*This amount has been borrowed from the Permanent Fund mostly to provide for deficits in current expenses and in part for payment of real estate acquired for Hospital purposes. It is hoped that unrestricted donations and legacies, to enable repayment of this loan, will be received within a reasonable period of time.

COMPARATIVE STATEMENT OF STATISTICS

For the Year Ended December 31st, 1938
and the Year Ended December 31st, 1937

HOSPITAL PATIENTS
GENERAL WARDS AND PRIVATE ROOMS

	1938	1937
Patients in hospital at beginning of year #	583	603
Patients admitted during year (a)	16,074	15,745
Total number of patients treated in hospital during year (Emergency Ward not included)	16,657	16,348
Remaining in hospital at end of year #	634	583
Patients treated in Emergency Ward (not admitted) *	17,601	14,046
Total number of patients admitted since the Hospital was founded (b)	434,246	418,457

Patients discharged during year:		
Well or Improved	12,918	12,967
Unimproved	2,297	1,932
Died	808	866
Total (a)	16,023	15,765

	1938	1937
Maximum number of patients on any one day #	700	726
Minimum number of patients on any one day #	507	498
Average number of patients per day	634	627
Average hospital days per patient	14	14
Mortality rate for the year (all deaths including those which occurred on day of admission)	4.85	5.30

Distribution of days of hospital care for the year:	No. of Days	%	No. of Days	%
General Wards—free to patients	131,281	56.77	125,158	54.72
General Wards—part free to patients	24,719	10.69	28,382	12.40
Semi-Private Pavilion patients	42,487	18.37	42,013	18.37
Private Pavilion patients	32,756	14.17	33,191	14.51
Total	231,243		228,744	
Maintenance days (patients and employees included)	674,905		667,809	

(a) Not adjusted for approximately 285 internal transfers (1938) between private and ward services.

(b) Adjusted in 1938 to exclude all previously counted internal transfers between private and ward services.

* Includes Emergency Dental Treatments reported also in Hospital Dental Statistics for first time in 1938.

Midnight Census.

COMPARATIVE STATEMENT OF STATISTICS
(Continued)

	1938		1937	
	Patients		Patients	
Percentage of total number of patients	Treated	%	Treated	%
treated in various divisions:				
General Wards	11,547	69.32	11,398	69.72
Semi-Private Rooms	2,497	14.99	2,549	15.59
Private Rooms	2,613	15.69	2,401	14.69
Total	16,657		16,348	

	1938	1937
Dispositions of applications received during the year:		
Admitted to General Wards as free to patients	9,192	8,862
Admitted to General Wards as part free to patients	1,963	2,111
Admitted to Semi-Private Rooms at rates below cost	2,389	2,456
Admitted to Private Rooms	2,530	2,316
*Not admitted for various reasons (ward applications)	5,289	5,448
Total Applications	21,363	21,193

	1938	1937
*Reason for non-admission to Wards:		
Offered admission but refused by applicant	94	101
Referred to District Staff for care	342	343
Lack of room—referred elsewhere	495	551
Out of Borough—no room	104	113
Able to pay for private care	69	75
Minor ailments	2,664	2,737
Chronic incurable diseases (a)	921	941
Alcoholism (a)	58	36
Contagious diseases (a)	118	136
Infectious diseases (a)	124	115
Pregnancy (a)	76	81
Disturbing mental disorders (a)	224	219
Total	5,289	5,448

(a) Referred to appropriate hospital.

DISTRICT MEDICAL SERVICE

	1938	1937
**Applicants for admission visited at home	215	299
Patients cared for at home	64	44
Total number of patients visited	342	343
Total number of visits made by physicians	389	401
**Disposition of applicants for admission visited at home:		
Admission to hospital recommended	82	65
Admitted (included in general hospital statistics)	81	51
Admission refused by patient	1	14
Referred to other institutions	19	8
Not at home when doctor called	17	10
Minor ailments—treated at home	—	77
Unsuitable for hospital admission	48	124
Referred to Out-Patient Department	47	15
Patients ceased before arrival	2	—

COMPARATIVE STATEMENT OF STATISTICS

(Continued)

OUT-PATIENT DEPARTMENT STATISTICS

	1938	1937
Total consultations	343,862	327,068
Total prescriptions	141,513	137,163
Patients new in year	11,934	12,145
Patients from past years	21,349	17,924
Total Individuals	33,283	30,069
Out-Patient Department Days	303	304
Daily average prescriptions	467	452
Daily average consultations	1,135	1,076
Average daily attendance of physicians	181	163
Average daily attendance of nurses	24	23
Average daily attendance of volunteer aids	40	40
Maximum consultations on any one day	1,589	1,389
Maximum prescriptions on any one day	791	802

ANALYSIS OF CONSULTATIONS

Name of Clinic	Morning Session	Afternoon Session	1938 Total	1937 Total
Internal Medicine	9,387	27,937	37,324	36,370
Minor Medical	44	675	719	875
Basal Metabolism	1,713	—	1,713	1,668
Gastro-Enterology	9,006	—	9,006	7,779
Diabetic	8,274	2,938	11,212	11,311
Adult Cardiac	4,487	2,442	6,929	5,642
Adult Asthma	11,837	—	11,837	10,914
Chest	1,409	—	1,409	1,327
Hematology	—	7,214	7,214	7,636
Neurology and Mental Health	4,890	5,908	10,798	10,898
Dermatology	9,304	18,278	27,582	26,590
Arseno-Therapy	—	2,588	2,588	2,184
Surgical	13,440	11,937	25,377	26,010
Genito-Urinary	4,984	1,991	6,975	7,016
Rectal	4,762	—	4,762	4,535
Gynecological	8,603	12,408	21,011	14,854
Ear, Nose and Throat	2,074	17,816	19,890	20,205
Eye	3,805	10,410	14,215	14,227
Thrombo-Angiitis Obliterans	10,171	802	10,973	8,452
Orthopedic	873	14,333	15,206	13,658
Children's Medical	8,057	11,137	19,194	21,731
Children's Asthma	—	10,336	10,336	9,703
Children's Cardiac	1,596	—	1,596	1,443
Children's Health	—	1,877	1,877	1,970
Dental	10,511	5,566	16,077	15,860
Physical Therapy	13,928	10,408	24,336	23,289
Radiotherapy	7,526	7,453	14,979	13,464
Roentgenology	5,160	—	5,160	4,973
Electrocardiograph	1,278	—	1,278	1,258
Occupational Therapy	1,218	—	1,218	1,040
Breast	—	199	199	186
Nutrition	91	781	872	—
Total Consultations	158,428	185,434	343,862	327,068

COMPARATIVE STATEMENT OF STATISTICS
(Continued)

DEPARTMENT OF LABORATORIES
Examinations in Central Laboratory

	1938	1937
Laboratory for Bacteriology:		
Blood Groupings	8,095	7,385
Urine, Spinal Fluids, etc.	—	1
Nose and Throat Cultures	174	197
Blood Cultures	1,239	1,116
Pus Cultures, etc.	6,478	5,043
Post Mortem Cultures	97	117
Special Anaerobic Cultures	162	96
Bacteriophage Cultures	42	75
Loewenstein Cultures	14	6
Staphylococcus Pathogenicity	2,579	1,559
Streptococcus Pathogenicity	471	371
Pneumococcus Typings	426	233
Neufeld Tests	312	114
Vaccines	92	100
Bacteriophage Tests	10	17
Guinea Pig Inoculations	403	391
Miscellaneous Animal Inoculations	51	26
Widal Reactions	224	213
Wassermann Tests	11,083	10,450
Kahn Tests	4,345	3,268
Agglutination Reactions	475	407
Complement Fixation Tests	91	99
Precipitation Tests	145	128
Colloidal Gold Tests	787	705
Globulin Determinations	759	682
Heterophile Reactions	148	88
Cell Counts	8	9
Miscellaneous Tests	209	205
Total	38,919	33,101

Laboratory for Surgical Pathology:		
Examinations of Operative Specimens	5,577	5,047

Laboratory for Morbid Anatomy:		
Post-mortem Examinations	400	451

financial p

The cost of operating the Hospital was $2,216,833

> These operating costs were exclusive of costs of research, post-graduate medical education and other activities not directly connected with maintenance of the Hospital.
>
> More than $1,200,000 was used for salaries and wages.

To meet part of these costs patients paid to the Hospital only . . $ 975,576

The difference is the total philanthropic expense for the year, or $1,241,257

Grants from Federation, the United Hospital Fund, the Greater New York Fund and the City, supplied the Hospital with a total of $ 887,37○

Income from endowment funds, donations, etc., amounted to . $ 59,34

Leaving the Hospital with a final net shortage or deficit of . . $ 294,54

re for 1938

his deficit added to other deficits
since the depression years beginning with 1930, has now reached
a total of $1,544,505

he large deficits of the past nine years could
have been avoided only by curtailing in
quantity or quality, or both, the services
rendered by the Hospital to the sick poor
of the City. Because these services are urgently
needed, it has been the policy of the Board of
Trustees to maintain them as long as possible,
and the deficits have been met out of the
limited capital funds of the Hospital.

uch capital funds were expected to provide
income for maintenance purposes and the
depletion of these funds to keep the Hospital
going has correspondingly reduced such
income. There is obviously a limit to this
constant drain on the Hospital's reserves.

ue to this serious depletion of income, the
Hospital urgently appeals for increased capital
donations so that it may continue to serve
adequately and efficiently all who need its care.

COMPARATIVE STATEMENT OF STATISTICS
(Continued)

Laboratory for Chemistry:	1938		1937	
Complete Blood Chemistry	837		1,007	
Partial Blood Chemistry	10,382	(a)	8,821	(b)
Urine Chemistry	253		110	
Gastro Intestinal Contents	144		160	
Examinations for Heavy Metals	115		84	
Functional Tests	1,803		1,293	
Examinations for Spinal Fluid	979		860	
Miscellaneous Tests	222		303	
Total	14,735		12,638	

(a) Includes 33 emergency night and holiday examinations.
(b) Includes 26 emergency night and holiday examinations.

Laboratory for Hematology:		
Blood Counts	1,318	1,122
Blood Volumes	20	12
Fragility of Red Cells	48	43
Congo Red Tests	21	28
Sedimentation Tests	207	152
Hematocrit Determinations	110	49
Heterophile Reactions	5	35
Bone Marrow Examinations	214	125
Formalin Tests	25	—
Reticulocyte Counts	122	—
Miscellaneous Tests	43	61
Total	2,133	1,627

Laboratory for Routine Clinical Microscopy in Private Pavilion, Semi-Private Pavilion and Out-Patient Department

	———1938———			———1937———		
	PRIV. PAV.	SEMI-PRIV. PAV.	O.P.D.	PRIV. PAV.	SEMI-PRIV. PAV.	O.P.D.
Routine Urines	10,773	12,087	5,675	9,937	10,638	6,727
Phenolsulphonphthalein Tests	34	69	5	35	122	7
Blood Counts	2,969	3,399	2,774	2,576	3,197	2,408
Feces	557	523	558	299	543	548
Sputa	57	180	363	23	151	311
Smears	23	52	1,255	10	39	1,281
Gastric Contents	77	102	—	46	64	—
Spinal Fluids	63	26	—	20	29	—
Blood Sugars	—	—	735	—	—	1,221
Quantitative Urines	34	53	302	47	40	247
Galactose Tests	—	3	—	—	2	1
Sedimentation Tests	—	—	568	—	—	437
Concentration Tests	14	23	48	—	15	—
Janney Tests	3	3	145	—	1	30
Miscellaneous Tests	18	34	72	55	31	5
Total	14,622	16,554	12,500	13,048	14,872	13,223

COMPARATIVE STATEMENT OF STATISTICS

(Continued)

Clinic Laboratories in Out-Patient Department

	1938		1937	
Urinalysis:				
Genito-Urinary	3,056		2,333	
Gynecological	451		542	
Medical	3,514		3,124	
Diabetic	8,479		8,455	
Children's	1,509		1,312	
		17,009		15,766
Von Pirquets—Children's		856		831
Dark Field Examinations		77		11
Smears:				
Genito-Urinary	2,312		1,833	
Gynecological	3,691		559	
Miscellaneous	1		—	
		6,004		2,392
Gastric Analysis		1,153		823
Pneumo Thorax		433		243
Mantoux: Pediatric		—		8
Patch Tests—Pediatric		30		19
Total		25,562		20,093

Laboratory for Endocrinology

	1938	1937
Aschheim-Zondek Test	306	297
Frank-Goldberger Tests—Blood	174	127
Frank-Goldberger Tests—Urine	741	971
Pituitary Blood Tests	14	43
Pituitary Urine Tests	534	1,219
Pituitary Blood Serum	65	—
Estrogenic Substance and Gonadotropic Hormone Tests	652	573
Total	2,486	3,230

LABORATORY FOR BASAL METABOLISM

(Hospital Laboratory)*

	1938	1937
Private Patients	75	69
Semi-Private Patients	102	127
Ward Patients	1,050	1,095
Nurses	30	51
Total	1,257	1,342
Maximum number of examinations on any one day	10	10

* O. P. D. examinations reported in O. P. D. Statistics.

COMPARATIVE STATEMENT OF STATISTICS
(Continued)
DEPARTMENT OF RADIOLOGY

	1938	1937
Radiography:		
Number of Patients Examined	16,751	16,530
Number of Examinations	22,334	22,703
Number of Plates Taken	68,241	66,421
Number of Fluoroscopic Examinations	8,623	8,694
Radiotherapy:		
Number of New Patients	675	638
Number of Visits (old and new patients)	*16,582	**14,835
Number of Treatments (old and new patients)	11,117	10,218

Radiotherapy Treatments:		P.P.	SEMI-P.P.	WARD	O.P.D. AND FOLLOW-UP	TOTAL
High Frequency	1938	0	0	0	32	32
	1937	0	0	0	42	42
Radium	1938	0	0	32	28	60
	1937	0	0	38	24	62
Superficial Therapy	1938	1	0	94	2,583	2,678
	1937	23	5	128	2,336	2,492
Deep Therapy	1938	177	150	1,414	6,606	8,347
	1937	156	211	1,174	6,081	7,622
Total	1938	178	150	1,540	9,249	11,117
Total	1937	179	216	1,340	8,483	10,218

* Includes 14,979 Visits which were reported in O. P. D. Consultations.
** Includes 13,464 Visits which were reported in O. P. D. Consultations.

DEPARTMENT OF PHYSIOTHERAPY
(Hospital)

	1938	1937
Massage	1,114	1,077
Exercise	1,885	822
Electric Reaction	262	285
Infra Red	—	315
Hydrotherapy	1,814	—
Diathermia	225	321
Hyperthermy	562	390
Short Wave	1,573	809
Ultra Violet	1,923	1,940
Phototherapy	7,341	3,606
Carbon Arc	20	12
Thermostatic Cradle	1,659	275
Total number of treatments for year	18,378	9,852
Maximum number on any one day	69	37

COMPARATIVE STATEMENT OF STATISTICS

(Continued)

DENTAL DEPARTMENT

(Hospital)

	1938	1937
Extractions	789	1,130
Fillings	362	769
Oral Surgery	20	57
Mechanical Work	49	6
Root Canal Therapy	16	1
Pyorrhea Treatments	183	216
X-Ray Examinations	936	1,286
Cultures	43	45
Vaccines	13	2
Fractures	5	—
Other Treatments	1,706	1,612
	4,122	5,124
Examinations only	4,941	4,582
Emergency Ward Treatments, Miscellaneous	1,299	—
Total number for year	10,362	9,706
Maximum number on any one day	56	37

DENTAL DEPARTMENT

(Out-Patient)

	1938	1937
Extractions	1,713	1,676
Fillings	1,655	1,682
Orthodontia	711	684
Oral Surgery	84	122
Mechanical Work	3,727	3,087
Root Canal Therapy	61	100
Pyorrhea Treatments	265	240
X-Ray Examinations	1,322	1,237
Cultures	237	462
Fractures	11	—
Other Treatments	3,939	3,662
	13,725	12,952
Examinations only	2,601	3,084
Total number of services for year	16,326	16,036
Total number of visits	*16,077	*15,860
Maximum number of visits on any one day	92	99

* Included in O. P. D. Consultations.

COMPARATIVE STATEMENT OF STATISTICS
(Continued)
ELECTRO-CARDIOGRAPH DEPARTMENT

	1938	1937
Private Patients Examinations	156	137
Semi-Private Patients Examinations	152	120
Ward Patients Examinations	4,515	4,029
Out-Patient Examinations	*1,278	*1,258
Total number of examinations	6,101	5,544
Maximum number on any one day	39	30

* Included in O. P. D. Consultations—Morning Session.

FOLLOW-UP CLINICS
REPORT FOR 1938

	No. of Clinic Sessions	No. of Appointments Given	Kept	Cases Closed	Referred for Further Treatment	Referred for Readmission
Medical	85	2,233	1,725	181	387	32
Surgical	130	6,631	4,993	500	756	234
Gynecological	48	2,543	1,886	197	314	59
Orthopedic	23	1,109	873	73	169	62
Pediatric	47	1,110	801	65	95	14
Neurological	23	676	435	42	15	9
Ear, Nose and Throat	24	1,568	1,081	254	50	82
Eye	12	509	324	31	20	24
Radiotherapy	85	2,035	1,681	5	175	34
Physiotherapy	11	95	63	6	13	——
Hematology	12	111	84	14	8	——
Total	500	18,620	*13,946	1,368	2,002	550

* Included in O. P. D. Consultations.

CONSULTATION SERVICE

	1938	1937
Patients admitted	2,786	2,658
Referring Doctors	632	*625

* Estimated.

REPORT OF COMMITTEE ON
OUT-PATIENT DEPARTMENT

The importance of the service rendered to the community by the Out-Patient Department was reflected in the demands for ambulatory medical care which totaled almost 344,000 patient visits in 1938. This represented an increase of 17,000 clinic visits above the previous year. Not since the organization of the Out-Patient Department in 1872 have so many consultations been made in one year. The total number of individuals treated during 1938 was 33,283, showing an average of ten visits per patient per clinic. This represents a high average of consultations and inter-clinic refers, indicative of the high standard of medical care given to those for whom we have accepted responsibility. In order to maintain this standard, and to prevent the replacement of quality by quantity of care, it was necessary to maintain restrictive rules for admission, and to limit for temporary periods the acceptance of new admissions to some clinics. Another factor which increased the clinic load was the policy of the Out-Patient Department of co-operation with the various agencies assisting refugees from foreign countries. Regulations governing admission were often waived in order to offer succor to these oppressed individuals whose burdens were weighted with illness and disability.

An average of 1,135 consultations were made during each out-patient day throughout the year. The patients were attended daily by an average of 181 physicians and 24 nurses. That this service met a vital community need was evident from the high rate of return visits of more than 21,000 patients, and by a total of 12,000 new patients who were accepted for admission. In fulfilling its community obligations, the Out-Patient Department utilized fully and made available to the indigent sick the principles of modern preventive medicine. In this way the earning capacity of many patients was maintained during illness and many were saved from becoming public charges. In addition, disabilities were prevented, and incipient illnesses diagnosed early when most could be accomplished to effect a favorable outcome.

Despite the large number of consultations, every patient was considered as an individual, each with his special need. The intimate association of the Out-Patient Department with the work of the Hospital made available a complete service to the sick, with thorough study of each patient before, during and after

Hospital admission. Essentially the aim of the Out-Patient Department is to offer to its patients a type of service approximating that of private care in its medical quality. Wherever practicable, patients are attended by the same physician at each clinic visit. Strict adherence to an appointment system and careful case control has made this possible in most cases. The availability of modern facilities for diagnosis and treatment has stimulated thorough and accurate study and therapy of the patients. Ambulatory care was regarded as much of a community responsibility of the Hospital as its in-patient care.

The co-operation of the Social Service Department with the activities of the Out-Patient Department made possible the realization of a broad concept of medical care. Social and economic maladjustments, which in many cases retarded or nullified the beneficial effects of medical therapy, were studied jointly by the clinic physicians and the social workers. Frequently the solution of these problems spelled the difference between success and failure of the therapeutic outcome. Domiciliary care was provided whenever necessary at the request of the clinic physicians. The services of volunteer aids, whose daily attendance averaged 40, were invaluable in making it possible to lighten still further the clerical and other non-professional work required of physicians and nurses, thus allowing more time for professional care.

Political and racial persecution abroad has driven to America for refuge many capable foreign physicians. During 1938 the Out-Patient Department was able to accommodate 137 German, Austrian, Italian and other displaced physicians on its staff, thereby being instrumental in assisting these physicians in their adjustment during a difficult transitional period. Emigre physicians were represented on the staffs of almost every clinic, both general and specialty, and worked side by side with the regular staff in caring for the patients.

There has been a steady annual increase in the use of the clinical facilities for advanced educational activities. In many of the clinics formal post-graduate instruction was conducted during the courses of instruction given in affiliation with the College of Physicians and Surgeons of Columbia University. The abundance and variety of cases available for teaching purposes attracted 299 physicians from five states for post-graduate study, the largest enrollment since these courses were established. Although the clinic rooms were not planned for extensive medical teaching, they were also widely used for extra-curricular informal teaching at staff meetings held regularly in the Out-Patient Department. In addition, administrators, physicians, educators, nurses and social workers visited many of the clinics to study their organization and activities.

Interclinic co-operation has been encouraged and the studies of the specialty clinics have been closely integrated with those of the general clinics, thus offering to the patients a unified diagnostic approach and continuity of treatment. During the year 3,150 patients were referred to the Hospital for further study and treatment.

An important by-product of the activities of a large number of clinics has been research activities and the publication of many scientific papers. The clinical observations on which these publications were based were made almost entirely in the Out-Patient clinics. The increased emphasis placed on the improvements of the clinical records has made them more valuable from a scientific point of view as well as conducive to better patient care. The Thrombo-Angiitis Obliterans Clinic has pursued studies of the physiology and circulation in the legs. The Allergy Clinics have followed the clinical course of many of their patients for almost twenty years and have gathered data which is invaluable in the determination of the course and prognosis of these patients. The lines of research of the Endocrine Clinics were carried out in affiliation with the Endocrine Research Laboratory. In the Cardiac Clinics studies were made on the mechanism of heart failure and on the effect of hypertonic salt solution on coronary artery disease. It is impossible to do more than mention some of these activities. The report of the Medical Staff contains a review of the results of the investigative clinical research carried out in the Out-Patient Department.

The voluntary co-operation of the clinic physicians in the humanitarian work of the Out-Patient Department deserves particular mention, for without their devoted and unselfish efforts in furthering the activities of the Out-Patient Department its work could not be carried out.

Respectfully submitted,

LEONARD A. HOCKSTADER,

Chairman.

111

OFFICERS AND DIRECTORS OF THE MOUNT SINAI HOSPITAL SCHOOL OF NURSING

Hugo Blumenthal ....*President*
Alfred L. Rose ....*Vice-President*
W. D. Scholle ....*Treasurer*
Edwin M. Berolzheimer ....*Secretary*

Directors

Edwin M. Berolzheimer   Carl H. Pforzheimer, Jr.
George Blumenthal   Alfred L. Rose
Hugo Blumenthal   Paul M. Rosenthal
Waldemar Kops   W. D. Scholle
                Harold D. Wimpfheimer

For the Term Expiring April, 1941

Waldemar Kops   W. D. Scholle
                *Joseph F. Cullman, Jr.

For the Term Expiring April, 1943

Hugo Blumenthal   Paul M. Rosenthal
                Harold D. Wimpfheimer

For the Term Expiring April, 1945

Edwin M. Berolzheimer   Carl H. Pforzheimer, Jr.
George Blumenthal   Alfred L. Rose

Honorary Director

Philip J. Goodhart

---

* Elected 1939.

REPORT OF THE MOUNT SINAI HOSPITAL
SCHOOL OF NURSING

To the Board of Trustees of The Mount Sinai Hospital:

Gentlemen:

The Fifty-eighth year of the history of our School has been one of further progress. An examination of the work during the year discloses advancements which are important to the educational standing of the School and to the nursing service.

In a modern school of nursing the curriculum must be reviewed and revised frequently in order to keep in line with the advancement in medical science and to prepare students to function efficiently in present-day society. During the past year, particular thought has been given to the courses in medical and surgical nursing: a revision has been made in order to effect a closer relationship between the two subjects. Students entering into this period of classwork receive ward experience in medical and surgical nursing. Their experience is divided into two ten-week periods, one in medical nursing and the other in surgical nursing.

Faculty members have carried on special studies of the types of examinations that have been in current use, so that we might discover and measure the success of our teaching. One of the results of this study has been the attempt to plan and soon introduce the integrated comprehensive examination. This type of test, which is very new, encourages more effective learning and is more likely to measure the adjustment of the student to actual nursing situations. The faculty have recently completed and presented graphically a year's study of the number and variety of disease conditions available for student experience. Although we know that our Hospital is rich in clinical material, which is also evidenced in our students' case records, we feel that the study has been profitable and will prove of great value in our teaching.

We are happy to report a further reduction of student hours on duty, which gives the student a weekly schedule of forty-eight hours, including classes. The new arrangement provides for a straight eight-hour night duty, with one night off each week, and provides two free afternoons for students assigned to evening duty. At the time the change was made in students' hours we added to our personnel twenty-three additional graduates for general staff nursing. This brought about two other important accomplishments; the provision for a better-balanced clinical program for our students, and an improvement in the quality of our nursing service through the addition of these experienced graduates.

There has been only one resignation from the executive faculty personnel. In September we regretfully accepted the resignation of Miss Claire Favreau, who had been assistant principal for over three years. Miss Favreau left us to accept a position with the State Department in Albany. At the time this vacancy occurred we were fortunate to have well-qualified faculty members who were available for this important position. Miss Minnie Struthers, Assistant Superintendent of Nurses, was appointed Assistant Principal, while Miss Lottie M. Phillips, Surgical Supervisor, was selected to fill the vacancy of Assistant Superintendent of Nurses. Other faculty re-alignments included Miss Bessie Wolfson, Assistant Nursing Arts Instructor, who was appointed Surgical Supervisor, and Miss Blanche Gubersky, who transferred from a head nurse position to succeed Miss Wolfson in the Nursing Arts Department. Miss Cecile Lattimer was appointed to fill the new position of Pediatric Ward Instructor.

The School of Nursing granted a leave of absence to Miss Clare Skaling to attend the spring and summer semesters at Columbia University. The following members of the faculty completed the requirements for the Bachelor of Science degree: Miss Minnie Struthers, Miss Elizabeth Clanton, and Miss Cecile Lattimer. Miss Lattimer also completed a post-graduate course in pediatric nursing.

Miss Minnie Struthers, Assistant Principal, has been appointed by the Board of Regents of New York State as a member of the State Board of Nurse Examiners. As a member of this Board, Miss Struthers has charge of one of the stations where groups of nurses take their practical licensing examination.

Social activities increased during 1938 under the direction of the Student Association and the Faculty Advisory Committee. Extra-curricular interests were fostered by frequent dramatic and sports programs. An outstanding cultural event, which was greatly enjoyed, occurred on November 14 when Mischa Elman gave a private recital in our residence in appreciation of the hospital service and care given to his father. The personnel of the dietary department have co-operated, as usual, in all of the functions in our social program, and we thank them for their splendid assistance.

The health service in the past year has carried on its usual systematic program. As time lost through illness is costly both to the hospital and to the nurses, we make every effort to safeguard the well-being of our staff. The illness report for the year presents many interesting statistics, and indicates that the average number of days illness per student was 5.7. This is the best record we have had for several years.

On behalf of the staff and the students of the School I wish to express the gratitude of the Board to the School physicians and consultants who have contributed their time and skillful efforts in the professional care of our nurses.

One of the most important educational projects of the past year in the nursing profession has been the development of a plan by the National League of Nursing Education for accrediting schools of nursing. The League, after a long period of study and consideration, has accepted the responsibility of accrediting nursing schools on a national basis. At present, an extensive study is being made of various types of nursing schools throughout the country so that accurate criteria may be outlined for evaluating schools desiring accreditation. This program will give public recognition to schools that voluntarily seek and are considered worthy of accreditation, and will undoubtedly raise the standards of nursing education throughout the country.

During 1938 ninety-four new students were admitted. Our records show that of this number sixty-nine have remained in the School. It is interesting to note that in last year's enrollment alone fourteen states were represented.

As of January 1, 1939, the School had a total of 227 students divided as follows:

Preliminary students 41
First year students 28
Second year students 81
Third year students 77

We also had 97 graduates on the staff engaged in administration, teaching and supervision, as well as 124 graduates engaged in general staff nursing.

The commencement exercises were held February 8, 1939 in the Blumenthal Auditorium. Seventy-seven students were graduated, and will soon complete their nursing course. These young graduates are going into various fields of nursing, and their interests show that the curriculum of the School allows for a wide choice of professional opportunities.

The Alumnæ Association, of which Miss Nan T. Cuming is President, has a membership of 775. The Association has had a very active year, and continues to carry on its progressive welfare program whereby comfort and security are assured to members requiring assistance. Through the co-operation of the Medical Staff, interesting lectures stressing newer developments in medicine, have been presented at the monthly meetings.

The Registry records show an enrollment of over 450 nurses for private duty, with a daily average of 67 on the call list. During the year 7,846 calls for nurses were received, almost all of which were filled by nurses on our list.

The Board expresses its warm appreciation to the Director of the Hospital, Dr. Joseph Turner, for the support and counsel that he has given toward the solution of the problems of the School.

Finally, it gives me great pleasure to express to the faculty and staff the grateful thanks of the Board for their faithful efforts and excellent work. To the Principal of the School and Superintendent of Nurses, Miss Grace A. Warman, we extend our deep appreciation for her splendid work which has made this such a successful year.

Respectfully submitted,

HUGO BLUMENTHAL,

*President of The Mount Sinai Hospital
School of Nursing.*

SPECIAL FUNDS OF THE MOUNT SINAI HOSPITAL SCHOOL OF NURSING

Albert W. Scholle Memorial Fund... $40,000.00
  . Founded by William and Frederic Scholle as a tribute to
  the memory of their father, to provide a vacation and
  recreation fund for Mount Sinai Hospital student nurses.

Estelle and Hugo Blumenthal Scholarship and Graduation
  Fund 35,000.00
  Founded by Estelle and Hugo Blumenthal to provide an
  annual scholarship to the student of the graduating class
  chosen for special fitness to advance in the profession of
  nursing by taking a Post Graduate course at Columbia
  University. This fund also provides a prize of $15.00
  to each graduating student.

Emil Berolzheimer Memorial Fund... 20,000.00
  Founded by Mrs. Emil Berolzheimer in memory of her
  husband, Emil Berolzheimer; the income to be used for
  higher education of nurses.

Murry Guggenheim Scholarship Fund.. 20,000.00
  Established in 1905 by Murry Guggenheim; income to
  provide annually twelve scholarship awards of $100.00
  each to students who have shown exceptional ability
  during the year.

Jacques D. Wimpfheimer Memorial Fund.. 10,000.00
  Founded by Charles A. Wimpfheimer in memory of his son,
  Jacques D. Wimpfheimer. Any student requiring financial
  assistance during training may call upon this fund.

Charles A. Wimpfheimer Emergency Relief Fund.................................. 2,500.00
  Established by Charles A. Wimpfheimer; income and, if
  necessary, principal not to exceed $100.00 in any one year
  to be used for the relief of members of the Alumnae
  Association.

Lillie Stern Scholle Pleasure Fund.. 9,000.00
  Founded by Albert W. Scholle; the income to be used
  largely to defray the expenses of parties, dances and social
  gatherings of the students.

Mr. and Mrs. Sam S. Steiner Fund... 5,000.00
  Founded by Mr. and Mrs. Sam S. Steiner in memory of
  their beloved son, William J. H. Steiner; the income to be
  used for the relief of needy graduate nurses of the School.

Carrie M. and Gustav Blumenthal Graduating Class Prize
  Fund 5,000.00
  Established by provision in the will of Gustav Blumenthal;
  income to be distributed annually as a prize or prizes among
  the graduating class in such manner as the Directors may
  from time to time deem advisable.

SPECIAL FUNDS OF THE MOUNT SINAI HOSPITAL SCHOOL OF NURSING

(Continued)

Kalman and Harriet F. Haas Fund $3,000.00
Founded by Kalman Haas; the income to be used for the general purposes of the School.

Carrie Untermeyer Fund 2,600.00
Founded by Mrs. Carrie Untermeyer; to establish an award of $100.00 annually to the student graduating who has the best record for kindness and proficiency in actual bedside nursing.

Solomon and Betty Loeb Fund 2,500.00
Founded by Solomon Loeb; income to provide annual prizes to students.

Educational Fund 2,500.00
Founded by Mrs. Berthold Levi in memory of Berthold Levi; the income to be used for higher education of students.

Mr. and Mrs. Morris Fatman Relief Fund for Graduate Nurses 2,500.00
Founded by Mr. and Mrs. Morris Fatman; income to be used for the relief of graduate nurses.

Eugene Meyer, Jr. Library Fund 2,000.00
Founded by Eugene Meyer, Jr.; the income to be used to supply books and magazines for the school library.

Amy C. and Fred H. Greenebaum Fund 2,000.00
Established by Mr. and Mrs. Fred H. Greenebaum; income to be used for an annual award to the most deserving student nurse in any class.

Isabella Freedman Fund 1,500.00
Established by Mrs. Isabella Freedman; the income to be used for one or two awards to students in the graduating class who have shown marked ability, proficiency and interest in their work.

Daniel Kops Prize Fund 1,000.00
Founded by Employees of the House of Kops in memory of Daniel Kops; the income to be applied to the awarding of a prize to the nurse who holds the best record for bedside nursing and kindness to patients.

Pension Fund Mount Sinai Alumnae Association. Approx. 180,000.00
Established to provide pensions to nurses after many years of service.

REPORT OF THE MOUNT SINAI HOSPITAL SCHOOL OF NURSING

TREASURER'S REPORT

Statement of Receipts and Disbursements for Year Ended
December 31st, 1938

Receipts from:

Federation	$242,984.00
Matriculation Fees	4,490.00
Registry Fees	4,158.50
Sundry Fees	46.80
Permanent Fund Income	615.00
Haas Fund Income	115.00
Mount Sinai Hospital for 1938—*Deficit*	*71,384.86*
Total Receipts	$323,794.16

Disbursements:

Payroll:

Student Nurses	$15,720.96
Graduate Nurses	205,918.43
Office Assistants	8,738.24
Housekeeping	33,630.17
Attendants	24,596.53
Tuition	16,977.09
Postage	229.31
Sundries	696.65
Stationery and Printing	1,864.20
Household Supplies	3,776.67
Telephone	1,730.78
Advertising	1,890.00
Books	1,842.35
Uniforms	4,540.86
Graduation Exercises	1,641.92
Total Disbursements	$323,794.16

SOCIAL SERVICE AUXILIARY OF THE MOUNT SINAI HOSPITAL

COMMITTEE

Mrs. Alfred A. Cook ....*President*
Mrs. Myron I. Borg ....*Vice-President*
Mrs. Henry S. Glazier ....*Treasurer*
Mrs. Siegfried F. Hartman ....*Assistant Treasurer*
Miss Angie Jacobson ....*Secretary*

Mrs. George Backer
Mrs. Paul Baerwald
Mrs. Robert M. Benjamin
Mrs. Robert E. Binger
Mrs. Robert G. Blumenthal
Mrs. Arthur J. Cohen
Mrs. Leonard A. Cohn
Mrs. Frederick M. Heimerdinger
Mrs. Walter A. Hirsch
Mrs. William de Young Kay
Mrs. Alan H. Kempner
Mrs. Herbert H. Lehman

*Mrs. Richard Percy Limburg
Mrs. Louis M. Loeb
Mrs. George W. Naumburg
Mrs. Carl H. Pforzheimer, Jr.
Mrs. Moritz Rosenthal
Mrs. Philip A. Roth
Miss Edith Sachs
Mrs. William D. Scholle
Mrs. Henry Siegbert
Mrs. E. L. Smith
Mrs. Albert Stern
Mrs. Roger W. Straus

Mrs. Frank L. Weil

* Resigned.

STANDING COMMITTEES

Mrs. Frederick M. Heimerdinger..........*Cardiac Clinics*
Mrs. Philip A. Roth................................*Children's Health*
Mrs. Arthur J. Cohen, *Chairman* }
Mrs. Robert M. Benjamin } ....*Children's Social Service*
Mrs. Paul Baerwald, *Chairman* }
Mrs. William D. Scholle, } ....*Clothing*
  Associate Chairman }
Mrs. Walter A. Hirsch }
Mrs. Carl H. Pforzheimer, Jr. } ....*Gynecological Service*
Mrs. William de Young Kay................*Library*
Mrs. Louis M. Loeb................................*Medical Clinics*
Mrs. Frank L. Weil................................*Medical Wards*
*Mrs. Richard Percy Limburg................*Mental Health*
Mrs. Henry Siegbert, *Chairman* ⎤
Mrs. Robert M. Benjamin |
Mrs. Henry S. Glazier   ⎬.......*Nominating*
Mrs. Walter A. Hirsch |
Mrs. Moritz Rosenthal   ⎦
Mrs. Leonard A. Cohn..........................*Occupational Therapy—In-Patient*
Mrs. Frank L. Weil................................*Volunteers*
Miss Edith Sachs, *Chairman* ⎤
Mrs. Robert E. Binger   ⎬.........*Workshop*
Mrs. Siegfried F. Hartman ⎦

* Resigned.

120

CONFERENCE COMMITTEE

MRS. ALFRED A. COOK ....*Chairman*

DR. SAMUEL H. AVERBUCK
DR. MURRAY H. BASS
DR. IRA COHEN
DR. SOL W. GINSBURG
DR. HAROLD T. HYMAN
DR. WILLIAM H. MENCHER

MRS. ARTHUR J. COHEN
MRS. LEONARD A. COHN
MRS. FREDERICK M. HEIMERDINGER
MRS. WALTER A. HIRSCH
MRS. LOUIS M. LOEB
MRS. FRANK L. WEIL

DR. JOSEPH TURNER *(ex-officio)*
MRS. FANNY L. MENDELSOHN *(ex-officio)*

VOLUNTEERS

MRS. FRANK L. WEIL..*Chairman*

MISS KATHRYN ALEXANDER
MISS MARJORIE ALSBERG
MRS. VIRGINIA ANDERSON
MRS. HARRY ANGELO
MISS FLORENCE BAERWALD
MISS DORIS BAIZLEY
MRS. HAROLD BARNETT
MRS. JOSEPH BAUMANN
MRS. HARRY BENJAMIN
MISS LEAH BENNETT
MISS EILEEN BERMAN
MISS ADRIENNE BERNSTEIN
MISS JOY BERNSTEIN
MRS. THEODORE BERNSTEIN
MRS. THEODORE M. BERNSTEIN
MRS. DAVID BLOCK
MRS. LOUIS BLOOMBERG
MRS. HARRY BORDEN
MISS BARBARA J. CASSEL
MISS GERTRUDE COHEN
MRS. PETER A. COHN
MISS ETHEL LYNN DeHAAN
MRS. CHARLES DEITSCH
MRS. BERNARD DENZER
MRS. D. ALAN DILLENBERG
MRS. GILBERT DREIFUS
MRS. WALTER DREYFOUS
MRS. CHARLES DREYFUS
MRS. GEORGE C. ENGEL
MISS DOROTHY EPSTEIN
MRS. WILLIAM ERDMANN
MISS JEAN ETTMAN
MISS HELEN FALK

MISS LILLIAN FIDLER
MISS SARA FISHMAN
MISS REGINA FRANKENBERG
MRS. BURT FRANKLIN
MRS. SARA FRENKEL
MRS. MARCUS FRIEDLANDER
MRS. PERCY FROWENFELD
MRS. JOHN H. GARLOCK
MRS. VICTOR GETTNER
MISS BERNICE GLASER
MRS. SOLON GLASS
MRS. SAMUEL GOLDBERG
MISS KATE GOLDSMITH
MRS. SAM GOLDSMITH
MISS SHIRLEY GRABER
MISS MARION GREENBERG
MRS. HENRY GROSSMAN
MRS. IRVING HARRIS
MISS JEANNE HAYFLICH
MISS SYBILLA K. HECHT
MRS. J. HEIDEN
MISS JEANNE D. HUBSHMAN
MRS. STEPHEN JACOBY
MISS GRACE JEROME
MISS RUTH KAHN
MRS. JOHN KARGER
MRS. JEROME KATZ
MRS. BRANDON KEIBEL
MISS RUTH KIRSCHNER
MISS CORINNE KLAFTER
MRS. CHARLES KLINGENSTEIN
MRS. HENRY KLINGENSTEIN
MISS MURIEL KLUBOCK

VOLUNTEERS (CONTINUED)

Mrs. Florence F. Korkus
Mrs. Abraham Landesman
Mrs. Edwin Lane
Mrs. Percy W. Lansburgh
Miss Jane Ann Layman
Mrs. Phillip Leavitt
Mrs. William Lehman
Mrs. Edward Levy
Miss Miriam Levy
Mrs. Irving Lowenstein
Mrs. Henry T. Luria
Mrs. Arthur Marcus
Miss Elise Marcus
Miss Ann Meuer
Mrs. Herbert Meyer
Mrs. Jerome Meyer
Miss Rita Michaels
Mrs. Gustave Minton
Mrs. Irving Moskowitz
Mrs. Louis Napoleon
Miss Matilda Osmansky
Miss Madeline Edith Pearl
Mrs. Fred Perlberg
Miss Ruth H. Pinsky
Miss Jamie Porter
Miss Jane Posner
Mrs. William Rabkin
Mrs. A. Lee Reade
Miss Caroline Reicher
Miss Rachel Roitman
Miss Jean Rosenthal
Mrs. Moses L. Roth
Miss Esther Rothenberg
Miss Minna Rothenberg
Mrs. Leon Rothschild

Mrs. Abraham Austin Salmon
Miss Corinne Samek
Mrs. Oscar Schafer
Mrs. Arthur Schlichter
Mrs. Sigmond Schwartz
Miss Barbara Scofield
Mrs. Marian Seiniger
Mrs. Emanuel Shapiro
Mrs. Gregory Shwartzman
Miss Sadie Siegel
Miss Anita Siegman
Mrs. Solomon Silver
Miss Katherine Sloss
Miss Fanny Sokal
Mrs. Oscar J. Sokoloff
Mrs. Laurence Stein
Mrs. Max Steinberg
Miss Peggy Steinhardt
Mrs. Joseph Stenbuck
Mrs. Leo Stern
Miss Anne Stone
Miss Marjorie Stone
Mrs. Irving Taylor
Mrs. Ralph W. Watsky
Mrs. Beatrice F. Weil
Mrs. Max Weintraub
Miss Estelle Weisen
Mrs. Robert M. Werblow
Mrs. Leroy Whitelaw
Miss Leah Wiener
Miss Helen Isabel Wile
Mrs. Eli Winkler
Miss Janet Wise
Mrs. Fredric U. Witty
Miss Miriam Yellin

Miss Muriel Zinoroy

REPORT OF THE SOCIAL SERVICE DEPARTMENT

There have been no events particularly significant to us since we published our review last year for the years 1928 to 1937. Reports of world conditions with accounts of widespread appalling human suffering are apt at times to divert attention from our own daily experiences with human drama. We are, nevertheless, confronted with world problems in miniature, and our clientele numbers many from the oppressed minority groups of Europe. The painful process of adjustment to a new and often lower standard of living by those who have recently come to the United States concerns us deeply and taxes our case work skills to the utmost. Our own neighborhood (one of the worst slum areas in the city) furnishes many problems of inter-racial adjustments. The prolonged depression has made it necessary for our workers to devote much time in helping our patients obtain the bare necessities of life. More effective co-operation established with the various public relief agencies during the past years has enabled our staff to cope more expeditiously with the situation.

We have continued to improve our case work techniques, emphasizing the necessity of reaching a better understanding of the emotional and social implications which have so direct a bearing on our patients' diagnosis and treatment. One of our problems is to determine where the medical social worker's function begins and where it should end. The two case supervisors have been helpful in trying to clarify this problem by regular conferences with each worker. The task, however, is not easy since the supervisors must attempt this in addition to many other duties and many emergency consultations arise to interrupt the schedules. While it would be desirable to review each case with the worker before it is closed, we find that this is not possible at present.

In June, an additional social worker was placed in the Genito-Urinary Clinic where the need for one had long been expressed by the clinic physicians. The social worker is now present at all clinic sessions and it is now possible to interview all patients. The new worker is also able to give some time to one or two of the special Gynecological Clinics which are held on the same floor. An additional clerical worker has been added to give part time to the central file and part to answering numerous inquiries from public and private agencies. The installation of dictating machines has also facilitated our correspondence and case recording.

While there has been very little turn-over on the staff, a number of interdepartmental changes was made, often at the request of workers who wished to gain a more varied experience.

The death of Miss Rena Grossman was a great loss to the department. Miss Grossman had been associated with the Hospital since 1916 and had been on the Social Service staff as office manager for the past ten years. Her devotion to the Hospital, her cheerfulness, patience and kindness will be sadly missed.

The Corrective Exercise Class, which was conducted for many years as part of the Orthopedic Clinic, was transferred to the Physical Therapy Department. Although no longer supervising this activity, we keep in close personal touch with the enrolled children.

The American Association of Medical Social Workers has continued its study of statistics in order to devise a more uniform method of case accounting. In deference to its recommendations, we changed our statistical form at the beginning of the year, and at the request of the United Hospital Fund we made some changes again in September. It is, therefore, difficult to compare our figures with those of last year. We opened 9,359 new cases, reopened 1,778 cases, and closed 11,080 cases. 23,008 minor services were given to patients of the Hospital and Out-Patient Department and 13,467 visits were made outside the Hospital.

Thirty students from the School of Nursing spent eight weeks each in the department, and three students from Teachers' College spent three half days a week for a period of two months to gain supervised field work experience.

Several of our social workers, as well as the Occupational Therapist and our Kindergartner lectured to groups of student nurses to acquaint them with their particular activities and functions. The students in the School of Nursing attended a course of lectures given by speakers who presented subjects of important social movements and activities in the community. We are greatly indebted to these lecturers who include Mr. Milton E. Goldsmith, Assistant Consultant of the Housing Unit, Department of Welfare; Miss Eleanor Clifton, the Secretary of the Riverside District, Institute of Family Service; Mrs. Rachel M. Israel, the Superintendent of the Solomon and Betty Loeb Memorial Home; Mrs. Elsa Butler Grove, the Staff Educator of the Mount Sinai Social Service Department, and Instructor at Teachers' College; Miss Ruth Hill, the Associate Director of Public Assistance, Department of Welfare; Mr. Joel Earnest, the Director of the Home Relief Division, Department of Welfare; Mrs. Helen Harris Perlman, Supervisor of the Riverside District of the Jewish Social Service Association; and Mrs. Lillian L. Posses, Regional Attorney of the Social Security Board.

Requests for social service in the Adult Out-Patient Department clinics where we have no social workers at present, are increasing. With the advent in 1937 of a second worker in the Children's Allergy Clinic, more intensive treatment of many problems on a case-work level was established in this clinic, and it was possible to extend these services in relation to the problems of school and vocational adjustments, convalescence, and lessening of parental over-solicitude toward the patient. Prophylactic aspects of prenatal care for mothers of allergic children and treatment of minor allergic conditions of siblings were also stressed. There is a growing recognition by our physicians that long-term convalescence is the only method of treating recalcitrant cases where environmental adjustments and clinic treatment have been unsuccessful. Unfortunately, no facilities are available in this community for the care of the child suffering from severe asthma and we were obliged, therefore, to continue to use a few homes which had been found satisfactory in the past, and in which a number of these children could remain for long periods, until greatly improved or cured.

We sent 1,915 patients away for convalescent care. I take pleasure in reporting that the Neustadter Home for Convalescents, by changing its admitting policies, has enlarged its scope of work and it is now admitting patients requiring special diets as well as dressings, patients suffering from mild heart disease, and others for whom we did not have convalescent facilities in the past. This same care is still badly needed for male patients, and plans are now under consideration so that men can be admitted to the Neustadter Home during the coming year. No convalescent facilities are available anywhere for an increasing number of patients with colostomies and ileostomies, lung abscess, and severe asthma, nor can we find convalescent homes for negro patients. Whenever conditions permitted, home convalescence had to be provided for these patients. There is also no provision for non-ambulant orthopedic cases with casts which necessitate prolonged bed care, so that these cases often remain on the wards and occupy beds needed for other patients.

Our summer therapeutic program was very successful as an integrated part of our entire convalescent program. 351 children were sent away during the summer months as part of this activity. The Max J. Breitenbach Fund enabled us again to send 67 mothers and their children to the United Vacation Home in Long Branch, New Jersey.

As the clothing allowances by the Home Relief Division of the Department of Welfare continued to be inadequate, we were obliged to use our own limited resources to a great extent to help patients for whom clothing was necessary not only for their health but also to fill urgent minimum requirements for bare protection.

The Occupational Therapy Department cared for 1,760 ward patients of whom 130 patients were able to come to the ward workshop. Requests from the physicians for more functional work are increasing. There are likewise increasing demands to extend occupational therapy into the homes of those patients who will be homebound for long periods of time.

In November, Mrs. Leonard A. Cohn and five volunteers undertook to recondition many toys donated to us. As a result, 750 toys were made available for distribution during the holiday season. This work, which was undertaken as an experiment, has proved so successful that it is now organized as an all-year-round project.

The Social Service Library has given continuous service to the patients in the wards, the personnel and those of the medical staff who wished to avail themselves of the privileges of the Library. We have given out on the average of 550 books per month, exclusive of the summer months. Many new and interesting books have been placed on its shelves, almost all of which were contributed by friends of the Hospital. We have found it necessary, however, from time to time to purchase a few foreign-language books and current novels.

The Social Service Workroom reports another successful year and has taken care of as many patients as its limited space permits.

Much valuable service has again been given by our many loyal volunteers. 106 women gave on an average of six hours a week; many gave even more. A sitting room for volunteers, where they may go between appointments or between clinics, will be a great comfort and convenience when it can be provided.

The Federation for the Support of Jewish Philanthropic Societies and the United Hospital Fund deserve our most appreciative thanks for the financial support which we received from them. In recognition of the important communal needs which both serve, the women of our Social Service Board have made every effort to aid them in the arduous work of their campaigns.

We accepted with regret the resignation of Mrs. Richard P. Limburg, a member of our Board for many years. We are glad to count Mrs. Alan H. Kempner, Mrs. George W. Naumburg and Mrs. Carl H. Pforzheimer, Jr. as new members.

I wish to express my gratitude to the members of the Board who have continued to take a keen interest in the various activities of the Department and have not only devoted much of their time to the work but have contributed generously to its support.

The co-operation of the Medical Staff, the constant interest of the Director of the Hospital, Dr. Joseph Turner, the sympathetic understanding of the Board of Trustees of the Hospital, and the effective work of Mrs. Mendelsohn, Director of the Social Service Department, and her staff, have all contributed to successful accomplishment during the past year, and to all who have given their effort and aid I wish to express my most appreciative thanks.

Respectfully submitted,

RUTH M. COOK,

President of the Social Service Auxiliary.

THE MOUNT SINAI SOCIAL SERVICE AUXILIARY

REPORT OF THE TREASURER
For Year Ended December 31st, 1938

REGULAR ACCOUNT

RECEIPTS

Federation	$95,391.24	
United Hospital Fund	19,500.00	
Income from Investments	2,080.88	
Refunds from Patients, etc.	2,095.57	
Transferred from Special Account for Deficit	18,682.87	
Total Receipts		$137,750.56

DISBURSEMENTS

Appliances	11,472.69	
Extra Nourishment, Special Diets, etc.	2,838.11	
Boarding	33.00	
Convalescent Care	14,743.67	
Relief	2,571.41	
Shoes, Clothing, etc.	3,446.36	
Transportation	3,057.80	
Medication	154.16	
Education and Recreation Supplies	1,046.03	
Salaries	93,332.51	
Workers' Expenses	543.70	
Office Supplies (Including Stationery, Printing and Postage)	4,336.66	
Affiliation Dues	90.00	
Magazines and Newspapers	69.33	
Sundries	15.13	
Total Disbursements		$137,750.56

SPECIAL ACCOUNT

Balance, January 1st, 1938	$25,435.57	

RECEIPTS

Donations 1938	18,461.88	
Appropriation from Principal and Income of Special Funds	4,729.87	
Interest on Bank Acceptances	121.49	
Total Credits		$48,748.81

DISBURSEMENTS

Special Account	5,930.27	
Summer Work	5,254.70	
Transferred to Regular Account for 1938 Deficit	18,682.87	
Total Disbursements		29,867.84
Balance, December 31st, 1938		$18,880.97

DONATIONS FOR SPECIAL ACCOUNTS

Abramowitz, Mr. Irving	$25.00
Adler, Mr. Morton L.	100.00
Anonymous	500.00
Anonymous (In memory of Bella R. Mirabeau)	20.00
Bach, Mrs. Julian S. (In Memory of Mr. Marcus Stine)	5.00
Bach, Mrs. Julian S. (In Memory of Mr. Edward Kline)	10.00
Bach, Mrs. Julian S. (In Memory of Mr. Walter A. Hirsch)	5.00
Backer, Mrs. George	1,000.00
Baerwald, Mrs. Paul	650.00
Benjamin, Mrs. Robert M.	25.00
Binger, Mrs. Robert E.	50.00
Block, Mr. and Mrs. Philip D., Jr. (In Memory of Mr. Walter A. Hirsch)	10.00
Blumenthal, Mr. George	500.00
Blumenthal, Mrs. Robert G.	275.00
Borg, Mrs. Myron I.	25.00
Breitenbach, Mrs. Max J.—For Summer Work (1938)	1,000.00
Breitenbach, Mrs. Max J.—For Summer Work (1939)	600.00
Cohen, Mrs. Arthur J.	500.00
Cohen, Mr. and Mrs. Arthur J. (In Memory of Judge William N. Cohen)	1,000.00
Cohn, Mrs. Leonard A.	525.00
Cohn, Mr. and Mrs. Leonard A. (In Memory of Mr. Walter A. Hirsch)	10.00
Cook, Mrs. Alfred A.	1,050.00
Dammann, Mr. and Mrs. Richard (In Memory of Mr. Walter A. Hirsch)	10.00
Davis, Miss Hannah (In Memory of Miss Martha Nanke)	5.00
Davis, Miss Hannah (In Memory of Mrs. Henry Nanke)	3.00
Davis, Miss Hannah (In Memory of Edward and Elisa Davis)	15.00
Eisman, Mrs. Max (In Memory of Bella R. Mirabeau)	25.00
Elsinger, Mrs. W. H. (In Memory of Mr. Harry Kraus)	5.00
Epstein, Philip	2.00
Friedenheit, Mr. and Mrs. Isaac (In Memory of Myron Goldsmith Friedenheit)	50.00
Glazier, Mr. and Mrs. Henry S.	1,075.00
Guggenheim, The Harry Frank and Caroline Morton Foundation	40.00
Guggenheim, Mr. Simon	50.00
Hartman, Mrs. Siegfried F.	335.00
Heimerdinger, Mrs. Frederick M.	225.00
Heimerdinger, Miss Barbara and Master John	25.00
Hilb, Mrs. Hannah	30.00
Hirsch, Mrs. Richard	25.00
Hirsch, Mr. Steven J.	100.00
Hirsch, Mrs. Walter A.	685.00
Carried Forward	$10,590.00

DONATIONS FOR SPECIAL ACCOUNTS

(Continued)

Brought Forward $10,590.00

Israel, Mr. and Mrs. Charles (In Memory of Frederica Adler)	10.00
Israel, Mrs. Charles (In Memory of Mr. Charles Klingenstein)	10.00
Jacobson, Miss Angie (In Memory of Dr. Edwin Beer)	10.00
Jacobson, Miss Angie (In Memory of Mr. Walter A. Hirsch)	10.00
Jacobson, Miss Angie (In Memory of Mr. Maurice N. Sternberger)	5.00
Kaskel, Mrs. Max (In Memory of Mrs. Samuel Hammerslough)	10.00
Kaufman, Mrs. Gustave (In Memory of Bella R. Mirabeau)	5.00
Kay, Mrs. William de Young	60.00
Kaye, Mrs. E. D. (In Memory of Mr. Walter A. Hirsch)	10.00
Kempner, Mrs. Alan H.	10.00
Klingenstein, Mrs. Charles (In Memory of Dr. Edwin Beer)	15.00
Kohn, Mr. Walter W. (In Memory of Mr. Charles Klingenstein —February 10th)	25.00
Kops, Mr. and Mrs. Waldemar (In Memory of Mr. Moritz Mayer)	10.00
Kops, Mr. and Mrs. Waldemar (In Memory of Mr. Irving L. Ernst)	10.00
Kops, Mr. and Mrs. Waldemar (In Memory of Bertha Erenthal)	10.00
Lane, Mrs. Edwin (In Memory of Mr. Alexander Marcuse)	5.00
Lane, Mrs. Edwin (In Memory of Mr. Jerome Hanauer)	5.00
Lehman, Mrs. Herbert H.	1,020.00
Limburg, Mrs. Richard P.	15.00
Lissauer, Mrs. J. M. (In Memory of Bella R. Mirabeau)	5.00
Loeb, Mrs. Louis M.	175.00
Lorch, Mrs. John T. (In Memory of Mr. Walter A. Hirsch)	25.00
Martin, Mrs. Herbert S. (In Memory of Mr. Walter A. Hirsch)	25.00
Mayer, Mr. and Mrs. Isaac H. (In Memory of Mr. Walter A. Hirsch)	100.00
Mayer, Mr. and Mrs. Richard (In Memory of Mr. Walter A. Hirsch)	10.00
Mayer, Mr. Robert (In Memory of Mr. Walter A. Hirsch)	10.00
Mendelsohn, Mr. Louis (In Memory of Mr. Arthur C. Mendelsohn)	10.39
Meyer, Mr. M. A. and Mr. and Mr. Mrs. M. K. Schrager (In Memory of Mr. Walter A. Hirsch)	25.00
Miller, Louis Jr. (In Memory of Mr. Charles Klingenstein)	5.00
Moskowitz, Mrs. Lillian	100.00
Pforzheimer, Mrs. Carl H. Jr.	10.00
Pritz, Mr. Sidney E. (In Memory of Mr. Walter A. Hirsch)	20.00
Rice, Mrs. Jacques B. (In Memory of Bella R. Mirabeau)	10.00
Rosenfeld, Mrs. Maurice and Miss Grace (In Memory of Mr. Walter A. Hirsch)	15.00

Carried Forward $12,390.39

DONATIONS FOR SPECIAL ACCOUNTS

(Continued)

Brought Forward	$12,390.39
Rosenthal, Mrs. Moritz	530.00
Roth, Mrs. Philip A.—For Max J. Breitenbach Fund	4,000.00
Roth, Mrs. Philip A.	25.00
Roth, Mrs. Philip A. (In Memory of Mr. Charles Klingenstein's Birthday)	25.00
Sachs, Miss Edith	280.00
Scholle, Mrs. William D.	80.00
Schreiber, Dr. Martin	10.00
Schwarz, Mrs. Max	10.00
Seeley, Miss Helen	5.00
Selz, Mr. and Mrs. A. K. (In Memory of Mr. Walter A. Hirsch)	10.00
Siegbert, Mrs. Henry	160.00
Som, Dr. Max L.	20.21
Stern, Mrs. Albert	125.00
Strasburger, Mrs. Edgar L. (In Honor of Wedding Anniversary of Mr. and Mrs. Arthur J. Cohen)	3.00
Straus, Mr. Nathan	20.00
Straus, Mrs. Roger W.	100.00
Walter, Mrs. John I. (In Memory of Dr. Edwin Beer)	50.00
Weil, Mrs. Frank L.	65.00
Werblow, Mrs. Robert M.	25.00
Woolner, Mrs. Miriam S. (In Memory of Bella R. Mirabeau)	5.00
Wolff, Mrs. J. R. (In Memory of Mr. Joseph F. Cullman)	10.00
Miscellaneous: Refunds from patients, etc.	513.28
Total	$18,461.88

DONORS OF CLOTHING

Adler, Mr. Morton L.
Ansbacher, Mrs. David
Arnstein, Mrs. William E.
Atlas, Mrs. David
Bach, Mrs. Milton J.
Baerwald, Mrs. Paul
Bass, Dr. Murray H.
Becker, Mrs. Esther
Benjamin, Mrs. Robert M.
Berner, Mr. T. Roland
Bernheim, Mrs. I. J.
Berolzheimer, Mrs. Alfred C.
Berolzheimer, Mrs. Edwin M.
Binger, Mrs. Robert E.
Blum, Mr. Henry L.
Blumberg, Mrs. Louis
Blumenthal, Mr. George
Blun, Mrs. Edwin
Bullowa, Mrs. Arthur M.
Byk, Mrs. Paul M.
Cahn, Mrs. William M., Jr.
Carlebach, Mrs. Emil
Children's Relief
Cohen, Mrs. Arthur J.
Cohen, Miss Florence
Cohen, Mrs. George W.
Cohen, Mrs. Ira
Cohen, Mrs. Irving E.
Cohen, Miss Myra
Cohen, Mrs. Samuel
Cohen, Estate of Judge
  William N.
Cohn, Mrs. Leonard A.
Coleman, Mrs. Aaron
Conried, Mrs. Richard G.
Cook, Mrs. Alfred A.
Cook, Mr. and Mrs. John Alfred
Daniel, Miss Elaine
David, Mrs. Ferdinand
Delson, Mr. Harry
De Veglio, Miss Helen
Dillenberg, Mrs. D. Alan
Dixon, Mrs. Mary M.
Dwyer, Mrs.
Ehrich, Mrs. Jules S.
Eisner, Mrs. George S.

Engel, Miss Jean
Falk, Miss Mildred
Falk, Mrs. Myron S., Jr.
Farmer, Dr. Elsa
Fisher, Dr. Alfred A.
Flackston, Miss (In memory of
  Miss Elizabeth Lee)
Forsch, Mrs. Sidney
Frankel, Mr. Louis
Frankenheimer, Miss Ida
Frankenheimer, Miss Rose
Friedenheit, Mrs. Isaac
Friedland, Miss Mable
Friedlander, Misses Lottie and
  Marian
Friedlander, Dr. Mae L.
Friend, Mrs. Howard L.
Garlock, Mrs. John H.
Glass, Mrs. Ruth
Glazier, Mrs. Henry S.
Glazier, Mrs. William S.
Goldman, Mrs. Henry
Goldsmith, Miss Bessie J.
Goldstone, Mrs. M.
Gottheil, Mrs. Paul
Green, Mrs. Albert
Hamershlag, Mrs. Joseph
Harris, Mr. S. A.
Hartman, Mrs. Siegfried F.
Hecht, Mr. J.
Heming, Mrs. Charles E.
Herzog, Mr. Oscar M.
Hessberg, Mrs. Felix
Hessberg, Mrs. Lena
Hirsch, Mrs. Walter A.
Hitzig, Dr. William M.
Hochheimer. Miss Rita
Hochschild, Mrs. Walter
Holzman, Mrs. E.
Hyman, Mrs. M. S.
Indian Walk Footwear
Jacobs, Miss E.
Jacobson, Miss Angie
Janowitz, Mrs. J.
Jaretzski, Miss Josie
Kempner, Mrs. Alan H.

132

DONORS OF CLOTHING—(Continued)

Klauber, Mrs. Murray
Klieger, Dr. and Mrs. Israel S.
Klingenstein. Mrs. Charles
Kohn, Dr. Jerome L.
Kohn, Mrs. Leon A.
Kohnstamm, Mrs. Lothair S.
Kornzweig, Mrs. A. L.
Kratz, Miss Kathryn (In memory of
  Mrs. Emelia Hammerslough)
Kurzman, Mrs. George F.
Landsman, Miss Gertrude
Leventritt, Mrs. Edgar M.
Levi, Mrs. Harry
Liebman, Mrs. Charles J.
Liebman, Mrs. Thomas
Liebmann, Mrs. Alfred
Liebmann, Mrs. Samuel
Lippmann, Mr. David
Livingston, Mr. Samuel
Loeb, Mrs. Carl M.
Loeb, Mrs. Louis M.
Mack, Mrs. J. J.
Mailman Mr. Joseph (In memory of
  · Mr. Samuel Mailman)
Mantell, Mrs. B.
Mantell, Miss Charlotte
Marks, Miss Gertrude
Mayer, Dr. Max D.
Mayer, Mrs. Theresa
Meyer, Dr. and Mrs. Alfred
Meyer, Mrs. Jonas (Ladies' Thurs-
  day Sewing Circle)
Michael, Mrs. H.
Michaels, Mrs. Harold
Minton, Mr. Gustave M., Jr.
Moolten, Dr. Sylvan E.
Nahamkin, Mrs. Bluma
Napoleon, Mrs. Louis
Needlework Guild of America
Neuhof, Miss Rose
Oppenheimer, Dr. Gordon D.
Oppenheimer, Mrs. Stanton
Pforzheimer, Master Carl H., III
Pforzheimer, Mrs. Carl H., Jr.
Pforzheimer, Miss Nancy Carol
Pick, Mrs. Ruth (In memory of
  Mr. Felix Low)

Powell, Mrs. E.
Prince, Mrs. Leo M.
Rains, Mrs. S. E.
Reichenbach, Mrs. Max
Rheinstein, Mrs. Alfred
Rolshack, Mrs. L.
Rossbach, Mrs. Laurence B.
Sachs, Mrs. Howard J.
Sachs, Mrs. Julius
Scharff, Mrs. Maurice R.
Schlessinger, Mrs.
Scholle, Mrs. William D.
Schwabacher, Mrs. Herman S.
Schwabacher, Master Robert
Schwartz, Mrs. Anna
Seiniger, Mrs. Marian
Sicher, Mrs. Samuel A.
Siegel, Miss Sadie
Silesko, Mr. Abraham
Silver, Dr. Solomon
Sinai, Miss Mollie
Smith, Mrs. E. L.
Spelke, Miss Edith
Speyer, Mrs. Daniel
Spingarn, Mrs. Arthur B.
Stachelberg, Mrs. Charles G.
Stark, Mrs. Julian
Stein, Mrs. E. W.
Stein, Mrs. Rita W.
Straus, Mrs. Roger W.
Strauss, Mrs. Jacob
Stroock, Mrs. Samuel
Sweed, Mrs. Sophie
Tanenbaum, Mrs. I. Edwin
Tiedeman, Mrs. Adelaide
Turner, Dr. and Mrs. Joseph
Vondrak, Miss Vlasta
Werblow, Mrs. Robert M.
Weil, Mrs. Frank L.
Weintraub, Dr. Anna
Wile, Miss Birdie
Wimpfheimer, Mrs. Charles
Wolf, Mrs. Dorothy
Wyle, Mr. Milton
Zaft, Mrs. Henry

GIFTS OF ARTICLES

TOYS AND GAMES

Abrahams, Mrs. A. I.
Ackerland, Misses Nina and Jane
Alsberg, Miss Marjorie
American Legion (Through Colonel
  Henry Wolfson)
Baerwald, Mrs. Herman
Baerwald, Mrs. Paul
Berolzheimer, Mrs. Alfred C.
Berolzheimer, Master Kenneth
Blum, Mrs. Samuel
Blumenthal, Mr. George
Byk, Mrs. Paul M.
Cohen, Mrs. Anne E.
Cohen, Mrs. Arthur J.
Cohn, Mr. Bernard
Cohn, Mrs. Leonard A.
Cook, Mrs. Alfred A.
Dalton School
Dreyfus, Mrs. Charles
Flatauer, Mrs. George
Freedman, Miss Ida
Goldin, Masters Stanley and Victor
Greenwald, Mr. Bert L.
Hauff, Mrs. Hugo
Hebrew Orphan Asylum
Heineman, Mr. Joseph H.
Hilson, Mrs. Edwin
Hirsch, Mrs. Charles
Hirsch, Mrs. Steven J.
Hirsch, Mrs. Walter A.
Hochschild, Mrs. Walter
Holstein, Master Philip
Home for Aged and Infirm Hebrews,
  Occupational Therapy Committee
Karelitz, Dr. Samuel
Kay, Mrs. William de Young
Keschner, Dr. Harold W.
Kohnstamm, Mrs. Lothair S.

Krindler, Mrs. Maxwell A.
Leiter, Mrs. H. Evans
Levy, Mrs. Robert
Liberman, Master Horace
Liebman, Mrs. Charles J.
Loeb, Mrs. Louis M.
Lukas, Mrs. Edwin J.
Mayer-Hermann, Dr. William F.
Michael, Mrs. H.
Napoleon, Mrs. Louis
Oppenheimer, Mrs. Jerome H.
Pforzheimer, Mr. and Mrs. Carl H., Jr.
Pollack, Miss Lillian
Rains, Mrs. S. E.
Rosenstein, Miss Irma
Rosenthal, Miss Florence
Rosenthal, Mrs. Paul
Rosenwald, Mrs. James B.
Rubin, Mrs. I. C.
Schlivek, Dr. Kaufman
Schmee, Mrs. Mary B.
Schneierson, Master Dickie
Schuebel, Mrs. Regina
Schulte, Mrs. Arthur
Schwabacher, Master Robert
Seligman, Mr. Albert
Seligman, Mr. Louis (In memory of
  Mrs. Gertrude Hausman Seligman)
Siegman, Miss Anita
Stachelberg, Mrs. Charles G.
Stern, Mr. Carl J.
Strauss, Mr. Joseph
Stroock, Mr. and Mrs. Samuel
Tanenbaum, Mrs. I. Edwin
Touroff, Dr. Arthur S. W.
Vogel, Mr. Jerry
Weil, Mrs. Frank L.

BOOKS AND MAGAZINES

Aaron, Mr. M.
Abelson, L. & Son
Abrahams, Mrs. A. I.
Abrams, Mr. Morris
Agandy, Mr. A.
Alix, Masters Gerard, Guy, Lionel
and Norman
Alsofrom, Mr.
Altschul, Mrs. Charles
American Red Cross
Amsterdam, Mrs. Jack
Anna's Hats
Arnoff, Mrs. Ellis
Arrow, Mrs. H. I.
Asiel, Mrs. Elias
Atlas, Mrs. David
Auerbach, Dr. Julius
Auerbach, Mrs. Mortimer
Averbuck, Dr. Samuel H.
Bach, Mrs. Milton J.
Backer, Mrs. George
Baer, Mr. Arthur "Bugs"
Baerwald, Mrs. Herman F.
Baerwald, Mrs. Paul
Barnett, Mrs. S.
Bastian, Dr. Carlisle C.
Baumann, Mrs. Joseph
Baumann, Miss Rose
Becker, Miss Audry
Becker, Mr. Herman
Behrman, Master Ned
Benjamin, Mrs. John
Benjamin, Mrs. Robert M.
Bennett, Miss Sadie
Berman, Miss Rose L.
Bernard, Mrs. L.
Bernheim, Mrs. Isaac J.
Bernstein, Mrs. J. Sidney
Berolzheimer, Mrs. Alfred C.
Berolzheimer, Master Kenneth
Binger, Mrs. Gustav
Binger, Mrs. Robert E.
Black, Mrs. Albert
Bloomingdale, Mr. Donald
Blum, Mrs. Richard
Blumenthal, Mr. George

Blumenthal, Mrs. Maurice B.
Blun, Mrs. Edwin
Bodenheimer, Mrs. Irving H.
Borg, Mrs. Myron I.
Breitenbach, Mrs. Max J.
Bresnick, Mr. Samuel
Browne, Mr. Morton
Browning, Miss Dorothy
Browning, Mrs. S. Pearce, Jr.
Brownstein, Mr.
Bullowa, Mrs. Arthur M.
Bulowa, Miss Julia
Bunim, Mrs. David
Burnham, Mrs. Claude G.
Cahn, Mrs. William, Jr.
Carol, Mrs. Evelyn
Chinlund, Mrs. Edwin F.
Cohen, Estate of Judge
William N.
Cohn, Mrs. H.
Cohn, Mrs. Leonard A.
Coleman, Mrs. Aaron
Coleman, Miss Constance
Colp, Mrs. Ralph
Cone, Mrs. Paul
Cook, Mrs. Alfred A.
Cook, Phil (Columbia Broadcasting
System)
Cullman, Mrs. Joseph F., Jr.
Cuming, Mrs. Alice T.
Dannenbaum, Mrs. Max
Dantes, Dr. David
Danziger, Mrs. Max
Darling, Miss
Davies, Mrs. Josephine
Davis, Mrs. B. B.
Davis, Mrs. G. L.
Davis, Miss Hannah
Dickson, Mrs. Leonard
Diorio, Mrs.
Doctor, Mrs. Arthur
Eisman, Mrs. Max
Eliasoph, Dr. Benjamin
Elsinger, Mrs. W. H.
Engel, Mrs. Adolph
Engel, Mrs. George C.

BOOKS AND MAGAZINES—(Continued)

Engel, Mrs. Irving M.
Engel, Miss Jean
Epstein, Dr. Emanuel Z.
Erdman, Mr. Albert
Erdmann, Mrs. William
Falk, Mrs. David
Falk, Mrs. Myron S., Jr.
Farmer, Mrs. Alfred S.
Feiner, Miss Judy May
Feingold, Mrs. M. W.
Finkenberg, Mrs. I.
Flatauer, Mrs. George
Forsch, Mrs. Sidney
Frank, Mrs. Henry
Frank, Dr. Robert T.
Frankenthaler, Mrs. George
Freeman, Mrs. Milton W.
Freund, Mr. Joseph
Friedenheit, Mrs. Isaac
Friedlander, Mrs. Marcus S.
Friedman, Mrs. Stanleigh P.
Furchgott, Mrs. Leo
Galinger, Mrs. George W.
Games Digest
Garlock, Dr. John H.
Gates, Mrs. Samuel
Genn, Mrs. G. H.
Getz, Mrs. William
Glazier, Mrs. Henry S.
Goldberg, Dr. Harry A.
Goldman, Mrs. Henry
Goldman, Mrs. Henry, Jr.
Goldman, Dr. Irving B.
Goldman, Mrs. Julian
Goldman, Mrs. William
Goldsmith, Mrs. E. B.
Goldsmith, Mr. James A.
Goldsmith, Mr. Richard
Goldstone, Mrs. Lafayette A.
Gottheil, Mrs. Paul
Halle, Mrs. H. J.
Hanson, Mrs. Edward C.
Hartman, Mrs. Siegfried F.
Hartzberg, Mr. John M.
Hazeltine, Miss
Hearst Magazines, Inc.

Heimerdinger, Mrs. Frederick M.
Heimerdinger, Mrs. Joseph E.
Hellman, Mrs. Edgar A.
Hellman, Mrs. Marco Francis
Heming, Mrs. Charles E.
Henry, Miss F.
Henshel, Mr. and Mrs. H. D.
Herald Tribune
Herman, Mrs. Harry
Herrman, Mrs. A.
Heyman, Mrs. David M.
Hilson, Mrs. Edwin
Hirsch, Mrs. Steven J.
Hirsch, Mrs. Walter A.
Hirschfeld, Dr. Walter
Hochschild, Mrs. Walter
Hochstadter, Mrs. Albert F.
Hofheimer, Mrs. Lester
Holstein, Master Philip
Hotaling, Mr.
Hyman, Dr. Abraham
Hyman, Mrs. Mark
Hyman, Mr. Richard N.
Jablow, Mr. David
Jablow, I. & Co.
Jacobs, Mr. M.
Jacoby, Mrs. Arnold
Jaquet, Miss F.
Jarroff, Mrs. Clara
Kahn, Mrs. Gilbert W.
Kantor, Mrs. Ruth
Karelitz, Dr. Samuel
Karger, Mrs. John S.
Kaskel, Mrs. M.
Kastor, Mr. Adolph
Katzenstein, Mr. Milton
Katzive, Dr. Julius A.
Kaufmann, Mr. Ernst B.
Kay, Mrs. William de Young
Kelley, Mr. Joseph E.
Keschner, Dr. Harold W.
Klebman, Mrs. M. H.
Klein, Mr. Herman M.
Klingenstein, Mrs. Charles
Klingenstein, Mrs. Joseph
Kohn, Mrs. Harry R.

MAGAZINES—(Continued)

Lukas, Mrs. Edwin J.
Lurie, Rabbi B.
Mack, Mrs. Clarence E.
Mack, Mr. Walter S.
Marcus, Dr. Joseph H.
Marks, Mrs. Ferdinand
Marks, Mr. M. J.
Marx, Mr. Arthur
Mayer, Dr. Max D.
Meehan, Mrs. Alfred L.
Meinhard, Mrs. Leo I.
Mensch, Mr. Bernard L.
Meyer, Dr. and Mrs. Alfred
Meyer, Mrs. Arthur A.
Miller, Miss Belle
Mintz, Dr. M. Emanuel
Mintz, Dr. Maxwell
ing   Mitchell, Mrs. Harold M.
Moreland, Mr. and Mrs. Andrew
Morgenthau, Mrs. Henry
Morris, Miss Annie
Morris, Mr. Joseph
Morrison, Mrs. Joshua
Moschcowitz, Mrs. A. V.
Mullaney, Mr. P. J.
Naumburg, Mr. and Mrs. Walter W.
Neumeyer, Mrs. G. H.
Newell Emmett Company
Oppenheimer, Dr. and Mrs. B. S.
Osborne, Mrs. Martha W.
Parres, Mrs. David
Philco Radio and Television
    Corporation
Picker, Mrs. E.
Prelick, Mrs. Gussie
Prior, Mr. Howard
Proskauer, Mrs. Joseph M.
Pythian Sisters
Rains, Mrs. S. E.
Reichenbach, Mrs. Max
Reiss, Dr. Joseph
Rheinstein, Mrs. F.
Rittenberg, Mr. William C.
Rosenberg, Mrs. Alexander
Rosenfeld, Mrs. Ernst
Rosenstein, Mrs. Henry

BOOKS AND MAGAZINES—(Continued)

Rosenthal, Mrs. Moritz
Rosenwald, Mrs. Benno
Rosenwald, Mrs. James B.
Rossbach, Mrs. Max J.
Rothenberg, Mr. Philip
Rouse, Mrs. Arthur G.
Rubin, Mrs. I. C.
Ryan, Miss Edith
Sachs, Mrs. Arthur
Sachs, Miss Edith
Sachs, Mrs. Samuel
Schafer, Miss Natalie
Schlessinger, Mrs.
Schloss, Mrs. Hannah
Schoenberg, Master Robert
Scholle, Mrs. William D.
Schulte, Mrs. Joseph M.
Scofield, Mrs. Jerome B.
Seligman, Mr. Arthur
Shapiro, Mrs. B. J.
Shaw, Mrs. H.
Silver, Mrs. Solomon
Sobel, Mrs. Joseph
Solomon, Reverend Elias L.
Spencer, Mrs. Girard L.
Speyer, Mr. James
Stein, Mrs. E. W.
Stein, Mrs. Samuel
Stern, Mr. Carl J.
Stern, Mrs. Jennie R.
Stern, Mrs. June

Stern, Mrs. William
Steuer, Mr. and Mrs. Max D.
Stoloff, Dr. Gordon E.
Straus, Mrs. Hugh Grant
Stroock, Mrs. Stephen J.
Sulzberger, Mrs. Arthur Hays
Sulzberger, Mrs. David M.
Tanenbaum, Mrs. I. Edwin
Tanzer, Mrs. Laurence Arnold
Tiefenthal, Mrs. Ernst R.
Turner, Dr. Joseph
Van Raalte, Mr. T.
Van Schumis, Mr.
Vogel, Mrs. Arthur
Warburg, Mr. Edward M. M.
Warburg, Mrs. Felix M.
Ware, Mr. Robert R.
Weil, Mrs. Leon
Weiner, Mrs. Lucille
Weiner, Mr. Sheldon
Weis, Mrs. Walter M.
Werblow, Mrs. Robert M.
Western Electric Company
Wile, Mrs. Walter D.
Wiley, Mrs. B.
Wilheim, Mrs. William
Wimpfheimer, Mrs. Charles
Wolf, Mrs. Philip
Woolf, Mrs. Louis J.
Young, Miss Edith
Zuckerman, Mrs. Paul S.

FLOWERS AND PLANTS

Abeles, Mrs. Rose
Adler, Mr. Morton L.
Adler, Mrs. Paul
Asch, Mr. Sholom
Ansbacher, Mrs. David
Bass, Mr. William
Beer, Mrs. Edwin (In memory of Dr. Edwin Beer)
Behar, Mrs. Victor
Bernheimer, Miss Cora A.
Blue, Mr. Sidney

Brentano, Mrs. F.
Central Synagogue
Congregation Emanu-El Temple (In honor of Judge Irving Lehman)
Congregation Emanu-El Temple (In honor of Mr. Lewis L. Strauss)
Congregation Rodeph Sholom
Constant, Mr. George
Cook, Mrs. Alfred A.
Cullman, Mr. Howard S. (In memory of Mr. Joseph F. Cullman)

138

FLOWERS AND PLANTS—(Continued)

Cummings, Mr. Richard (In memory of Jane Cummings)
Danziger, Mrs. Max
Dubinsky, Mr. David
Elias, Mrs. Carrie (In memory of Mr. Herman Elias)
Flinn, Mr. John
Friedell and Bonollo, Inc.
Ginzburg, Mr. Nathan
Goldsmith, Mrs. Milton M.
Gruntal, Mrs. Herman
Guggenheim, Mrs. Murry
Haft, Mrs. Morris W.
Hart, Mr. Lorenz
Heineman, Mr. Bernard
Hertz, Mrs. Harry
Herz, Mrs. Louis
Hirsh, Dr. A. B.
Hirsh (In memory of Mrs. Flora)
Horn, Mrs. Walter
Jaches, Mrs. Leopold
Jaroff, Mrs. David
Kalter, Mr. Max
Kaye, Mrs. Alyce B.
Klein, Leo (Florist)
Klingenstein, Mrs. Charles (In memory of Mr. Charles Klingenstein)
Kogut, Dr. B.
Lamport, Mrs. Arthur M.
Lande, Mrs. Celia
Layman, Mrs. Joseph (In memory of Mr. Joseph Layman)
Lee, Mrs. Katherine
Levison, Mrs. L. C.
Levy, Mr. Leo
Levy, Mrs. Samuel D.
Lewisohn, Mrs. Samuel A.

Lichtenstein, Rabbi Morris
Liebmann, Mr. and Mrs. Alfred
Loeb, Mrs. Louis M.
Lowenstein, Mrs. Albert
Lubetkin, Mrs. Hannah
Luria, Mrs. Phillip
Marcuse, Mrs. Alexander J. (In memory of Mr. Alexander J. Marcuse)
Morgenthau, Mrs. Henry
Morrisey, Miss Grace
Moses, Mrs. N. A.
Necarsulmer, Mr. and Mrs. Edward, Jr.
Ohsie, Mr. Isidore
Osborne, Mrs. Martha W.
Price (In memory of Mr. Cyrus)
Randell, Mr. J. F.
Ring, Mrs. Morris
Robbins, Mrs. Eva
Rodeph Sholom Sisterhood
Rothschild, Mr. E. L.
Salmon, Dr. Udall J.
Schwarz, Mr. and Mrs. Herbert
Slazenger, Mrs. Frank L.
Solomon and Betty Loeb Memorial Home
Spiegelberg, Mrs. Flora
Stern, Mr. Abraham
Stern, Miss Constance
Straus, Mrs. Hugh Grant
Temple Emanu-El Sunday School
Till, Mrs. Joseph
Tremont Temple
Wallach, Mr. Harry
Weil, Mrs. Leon
Wein, Mr. Alfred
Wertheim, Mr. Albert

ICE CREAM, CAKE AND CANDY

Bass, Mr. William
Birk, Mrs. Minnie
Borg, Mrs. Myron I.
Brooks, Mrs. Ida
Cohn, Mrs. Leonard A.
Cook, Mrs. Alfred A.
Crystal, Mrs. Clement
Hartman, Mrs. Siegfried F.
Hirsch, Mrs. Walter A.
Hirschman, Mrs. Sue
Holstein, Master Philip
Israel, Mrs. Charles
Kaiser, Mrs. Hennie
Lee, Mrs. Clarence L.
Levinson, Master Jay
Lowenthal, Mr. Alfred

Mendelsohn, Mrs. Florence and Misses Paula and Annette (In memory of Mr. Joseph Layman)
Mendelsohn, Mr. and Mrs. Louis (In memory of Mr. Arthur C. Mendelsohn)
Mendelsohn, Mrs. Louis (In memory of Mr. Charles Klingenstein)
Sachs, Miss Edith
Schulte, Mr. Joseph M.
Siegman, Mrs. Arthur
Smolian, Miss Helene (In honor of her sister's birthday)
Stern, Mr. Gustave E.
Stern, Mr. Hubert B.
Sweig, Miss Carol
Vogel, Mr. Jerry

MISCELLANEOUS DONATIONS

Abrahams, Mrs. A. I.
Adler, Mr. Morton L.
Altmeyer, Miss M.
Back, Mrs. Bertha (In memory of Dr. Moses Back)
Baumgarten, Miss B.
Belias, Mr. Henry
Benjamin, Mrs. John
Bernheim, Miss C.
Bernheim, Mrs. I. J.
Blumenthal, Mrs. Maurice B.
Borg, Mrs. Myron I.
Bresnick, Mrs. Carl S.
Bulowa, Miss Julia
Carlebach, Mrs. Emil
Cohen, Mrs. Arthur J.
Cohen, Mrs. M. B.
Cohen, Estate of Judge William N.
Cohn, Mrs. Leonard A.
Coleman, Mrs. Aaron
Cullman, Mr. Howard S. (In memory of Mr. Joseph Cullman)
Davis, Mr. Severin

DeSola, Mr. Frederick
Dillenberg, Mrs. D. Alan
Director, Mrs. Helen
Elsinger, Mrs. W. H.
Feingold, Mr. M. William (In memory of mother, Mrs. Jessie Feingold)
Fishberg, Mrs. G.
Fisher, Miss Emma
Ford, Mrs. Edna
Franc, Mrs. James J.
Frankenheimer, Miss Ida
Frankenheimer, Miss Rose
Freeman, Mrs. Milton W.
Friedenheit, Mrs. Isaac
Friedlander, Mrs. Edwin M.
Furchgott, Mrs. Leo
Gimbel, Mr. Adam L.
Golding, Mr. Julius
Gottheil, Mrs. Paul
Greenberg, Mrs. Gussie
Greenebaum, Mrs. Fred, Jr.
Greenhut, Mrs. Benedict J.
Hampel, Miss Margaret

MISCELLANEOUS DONATIONS—(Continued)

Hartman, Mrs. Siegfried F.
Heimerdinger, Miss Barbara and
.Master John
Hendricks, Mrs. Henry S.
Herzfeld, Mrs. Emil G.
Hessberg, Mrs. Lena
Hirsch, Mrs. Walter A.
Hydeman, Mr. Edwin M.
Jaretzki. Mrs. Alfred
Johnston, Mrs. McEwen
Joyce, Mrs. J. A.
Kaufmann, Mrs. M. J.
Kessel, Mrs. Leo
Klingenstein, Mrs. Charles
Kornzweig, Mrs. A. L.
Ladies Fuel and Aid Society
Lehman, Mr. Philip
Lewy, Mrs. Theresa
Liebman, Mrs. Charles J.
Lippmann, Mrs. David
Lippman, Dr. Robert K.
Lissberger, Mrs. Benjamin
Loeb, Mrs. Louis M.
Lusher, Mrs. Dorothy
Manges, Dr. Morris
Manischewitz, B. Company
Marks, Mrs. Eric H.
Meyer, Dr. and Mrs. Alfred
Moschcowitz, Mrs. A. V.
Napoleon, Mrs. Louis
Nessler, Miss J.
Newman, Mrs. A. L.

Novogrod, Mr. Leonard
Oppelt, Mrs. C.
Picker, Mr. James
Pincus, Miss Leah
Pincus, Mrs. Robert M.
Rauh, Mrs. Milton A.
Reichenbach, Mrs. B.
Rheinstein, Mrs. Alfred
Rosenfeld, Mrs. Ernst
Rosenstein, Mrs. Henry
Rosenwald, Mrs. Benno
Schifrin, Dr. Arthur
Schoenfeld, Mr. Jacob
Scholle, Mrs. William D.
Schreidman, Mr. Benjamin
Schubart, Mrs. William Howard
Shonniger, Mr. Charles
Smith, Mrs. E. L.
Speyer, Mrs. Daniel
Stein, Mrs. E. W.
Steinberg, Mrs. Lillian
Straus, Mrs. Roger W.
Temple Emanu-El Religious School
Tillis, Mrs. Benny
Turner, Dr. Joseph
Wallach, Mr. Harry
Weinstein, Miss Ruth
Weis, Mrs. Walter M.
Weissman, Mr. Nathan
Werblow, Mrs. Robert M.
Whitelaw, Mrs. Leroy

CONTRIBUTIONS TO ABRAHAM JACOBI LIBRARY

BOOKS, PERIODICALS AND PICTURES

Associated Alumni of Mount Sinai Hospital

Bernstein, Mrs. Bertha

Beck, Dr. Irving A.

Bick, Dr. Edgar M.

Bierman, Dr. William

Bishop, Dr. Louis F., Jr.

Blumenthal, Mr. George

Block, Dr. Cecil

Boas, Dr. Ernst P.

Curtis Publishing Company

Dental Staff

Falk, Mr. Myron S.

Fischer, Dr. Alfred E.

Fox, Dr. Howard

Frank, Dr. Maxwell S.

Frank, Dr. Robert T.

Friesner, Dr. Isidore

Globus, Dr. Joseph H.

Goldberger, Dr. Morris A.

*Goldstein, Dr. Isidor (From Collection of)

*Jaches, Dr. Leopold

Karolinska Institutets Bibliotek

Klemperer, Dr. Paul

Klingenstein, Mrs. Charles (In memory of Mr. Charles Klingenstein)

Levy, Mrs. I. H.

Licht, Dr. Sidney

Lilienthal, Dr. Howard

Manges, Dr. Morris

Master, Dr. Arthur M.

Mayo Clinic

Meyer, Dr. Alfred

Moschcowitz, Dr. Eli

Neurological Institute of New York

New York Academy of Medicine

New York Medical Week

Pollack, Dr. Abou

Pollack, Dr. Herbert

Rosen, Dr. Samuel

Schlivek, Dr. Kaufman

Schwarz, Dr. Herman

Sea View Hospital

Sobotka, Dr. Harry

Sussman, Dr. Marcy L.

Szilagyi, Dr. Joseph

Turner, Dr. Joseph

Wolbach, Dr. S. B.

Yaskin, Dr. H. E.

* Deceased.

THE MOUNT SINAI HOSPITAL
LADIES' AUXILIARY SOCIETY

OFFICERS

MRS. LEOPOLD BERNHEIMER ....President
MRS. OSCAR ROSE ....Treasurer
MRS. JOSEPH A. ARNOLD ....Secretary

To the Board of Trustees of The Mount Sinai Hospital:
Gentlemen:

The hopes that I expressed in my former report for the year 1938 were fulfilled in good measure.

The past year has witnessed the continued devotion of our Ladies to the work at hand as evidenced by the many thousands of surgical dressings produced by them. My one regret is that I was unable to be with them at their many meetings. However, I have kept in constant touch with their activities and I know all that they have accomplished for which our thanks and whole-hearted approval are due them.

We look forward to even greater accomplishments for the year 1939.

Respectfully submitted,

Mrs. Leopold Bernheimer,

President.

TREASURER'S REPORT

Statement of Receipts and Disbursements for the Year Ended
December 31st, 1938

RECEIPTS

From Federation for the Support of Jewish Philanthropic Societies	$21,945.00	
Mount Sinai Hospital for 1938 *Deficit*	*4,257.53*	
Total Receipts		$26,202.53

DISBURSEMENTS

Linens and Bedding	$19,141.27	
Wearing Apparel	7,061.26	
Total Disbursements		$26,202.53
Cash Balance, December 31st, 1938		None

Dedicated Buildings

CHILDREN'S PAVILION

ERECTED IN LOVING REMEMBRANCE OF

LEWIS EINSTEIN

AND

MILLY EINSTEIN FALK

BY

HENRY L. EINSTEIN

1921

PRIVATE PAVILION

DEDICATED TO THE MEMORY OF

MEYER AND BARBARA GUGGENHEIM

BY THEIR CHILDREN

1920

Dedicated Buildings

OUT-PATIENT BUILDING

DEDICATED TO THE MEMORY OF

MAYER LEHMAN

BY HIS CHILDREN

1904

ADOLPH LEWISOHN
PATHOLOGICAL AND
LABORATORY BUILDING

DONATED BY

ADOLPH LEWISOHN

1904 - 1922

Dedicated Buildings

AUDITORIUM

DEDICATED TO THE
MEMORY OF

GEORGE BLUMENTHAL, JR.

BY

FLORENCE AND GEORGE BLUMENTHAL

1920

LABORATORY BUILDING

DEDICATED TO THE MEMORY OF

ABRAHAM AND AMELIA MEYERS

1938

Dedicated Buildings

CHILDREN'S CLINIC

DEDICATED TO THE MEMORY OF

FLORENCE HENRIETTA WALTER

AND

MARJORIE WALTER GOODHART

BY THEIR PARENTS

FLORENCE B. AND WILLIAM I. WALTER

1916 - 1923

Endowment of Wards

THE
CHARLES A. WIMPFHEIMER WARDS
FOR
SURGICAL TREATMENT
OF
DISEASES OF STOMACH AND INTESTINES
FOUNDED BY
CHARLES A. WIMPFHEIMER
1916

THE ADOLPH BERNHEIMER MEMORIAL WARD

———

FOUNDED BY HIS DAUGHTER ROSIE
FEBRUARY 16TH, 1897

THE MRS. ADOLPH BERNHEIMER MEMORIAL WARD

———

FOUNDED BY HER DAUGHTERS
ROSIE BERNHEIMER AND FLORENCE B. WALTER
FEBRUARY 16TH, 1916

Endowment of Wards

MAIN OPERATING ROOM

DEDICATED TO THE MEMORY OF

ISAAC AND BABETTE BLUMENTHAL

BY

ALFRED, GUSTAV, HUGO, BENJAMIN
AND GEORGE BLUMENTHAL

1904

GENITO-URINARY WARD

DEDICATED TO THE MEMORY OF

JOEL GOLDENBERG

BY PROVISION IN HIS WILL

1904

THE SIMON ROTHSCHILD WARD

IN PERPETUITY

1905

Endowment of Wards

THE EMANUEL LEHMAN MEMORIAL WARD

DEDICATED FEBRUARY 15TH, 1911

FOUNDED BY

MRS. SIGMUND LEHMAN, MRS. EVELYN L. EHRICH,
MR. PHILIP LEHMAN

THE
JOSEPH AND SOPHIA SACHS MEMORIAL WARDS

DEDICATED TO THE MEMORY OF THEIR PARENTS BY

SAMUEL AND HARRY SACHS

1913

THE ELIAS WARD

IN THIS WARD BEDS WERE ENDOWED:

THREE BEDS IN MEMORY OF RAPHAEL ELIAS
THREE BEDS IN MEMORY OF SARAH ELIAS
THREE BEDS IN MEMORY OF ROBERT F. ELIAS
THREE BEDS IN MEMORY OF HENRY F. ELIAS

ALL FOUNDED BY THE PROVISION OF THE WILL OF
HENRY F. ELIAS

1928

Endowment of Wards

THE ALFRED AND HANNAH BLUMENTHAL WARD

FOUNDED 1922

THE LOUIS N. KRAMER MEMORIAL

FOUNDED BY PROVISION
OF HIS WILL

1930

Endowment of Rooms

DEDICATED TO THE
MEMORY OF
LINA MEYER ASIEL
BY
ELIAS ASIEL
1904

THE EDWARD LAUTERBACH ROOM
DEDICATED IN PERPETUITY
BY THE
BOARD OF TRUSTEES
OF
THE MOUNT SINAI HOSPITAL
IN GRATEFUL RECOGNITION OF HIS
EMINENT SERVICES
1904

DEDICATED BY
DISTRICT GRAND LODGE No. 1
INDEPENDENT ORDER
FREE SONS OF ISRAEL
M. SAMUEL STERN, GRAND MASTER
1901
FOUR BEDS

DEDICATED FOR THE BENEFIT OF
THE ALUMNAE
OF THE
MOUNT SINAI HOSPITAL SCHOOL OF NURSING
BY
MRS. MAX NATHAN
1904

Endowment of Rooms

DEDICATED TO THE ALUMNAE OF

THE MOUNT SINAI HOSPITAL SCHOOL OF NURSING

BY

MR. AND MRS. CHARLES KLINGENSTEIN

1931

IN MEMORY OF

ISAAC STRAUSS

1825-1876

ENDOWED BY HIS SON

CHARLES STRAUSS

1934

IN MEMORY OF

HENRIETTA STRAUSS

1819-1893

ENDOWED BY HER SON

CHARLES STRAUSS

1934

THE JACOB AND HENRIETTA SNEUDAIRA ROOM

FOUNDED BY PROVISION IN THE WILL OF

MOSES J. SNEUDAIRA

1935

Tablets

ERECTED IN X-RAY MUSEUM

IN MEMORY OF

BERTHA WEHLE NAUMBURG

FOUNDED BY HER SON

WALTER W. NAUMBURG

MARCH 3RD, 1922

ERECTED IN RADIO-THERAPY
DEPARTMENT

DEPARTMENT OF
RADIUM AND RADIO-THERAPY

FLORETTE AND ERNST ROSENFELD FOUNDATION

1923

ERECTED IN X-RAY DEPARTMENT

EQUIPPED BY

LOUISA AND SAMUEL SACHS

IN MEMORY OF THEIR DAUGHTER

ELLA SACHS PLOTZ

1923

𝕮𝖆𝖇𝖑𝖊𝖙𝖘

ERECTED IN OUT-PATIENT DEPARTMENT

OUT-PATIENT DEPARTMENT DENTAL CLINIC
EQUIPPED AND SUPPORTED BY

DAVID A. SCHULTE

1925

ERECTED IN PATHOLOGICAL LECTURE HALL

DEDICATED TO THE MEMORY OF

ISAAC AND SARAH ERDMANN

1925

ERECTED IN LABORATORY NORTH BUILDING

ERECTED BY

CHARLES A. WIMPFHEIMER

A MOST GENEROUS FRIEND OF THE HOSPITAL

1926

ERECTED IN SOCIAL SERVICE DEPARTMENT

IN LOVING MEMORY OF

ETTA COHEN LORSCH

1928

Perpetual Beds

In Memory of
Louis W. Neustadter
Dedicated by his wife
1873

In Memory of
Daniel Joseph Jaffe
Dedicated by the family
1874

In Memory of
Isaac Dittenhoefer
Dedicated by
Abram J. Dittenhoefer
1874

In Memory of
Lewis Einstein
1875

In Memory of
Katy White
Wife of J. L. Englehart
Niece of Jonas and Yette Heller
1875

In Memory of
Mary Rosenbaum
By her husband,
Sigmund D. Rosenbaum
1876

Endowed in Memory of
Lazarus Hallgarten
1876

In Memory of
Martin and Joseph Bachrach
Beloved sons of
Samuel and Babette Bachrach
1877

In Memory of our beloved mother
Mina Schafer
Wife of Mayer Schafer
1878

In Memory of
Benjamin Nathan
Dedicated by will of his wife
1879

Dedicated by
Sarah Heinemann
1879

In Memory of
Abraham Scholle
1880

In Memory of
Leonora Wormser
Vice-President of the Ladies' Auxiliary
Society
Wife of Simon Wormser
1880

In Memory of
Nathan Blun
Endowed by his children
1880

In Memory of
Mary S. Sahlein
Wife of William Sahlein
1881

In Memory of
William Sahlein
1881

In Memory of
David Wallerstein
1881

In Memory of
Harris Aronson
1881

In Memory of
Arnold Uhlman
Dedicated by the family
1883

In Memory of
Joseph Reckendorfer
Dedicated by his wife
1883

In Memory of
Isaac and Ida Meyer
Dedicated by their children
1883

157

Perpetual Beds

In Memory of
Herman Friedlander
Dedicated by his family
1883

In Memory of
Nathan Asiel
Dedicated by his family
1883

In Memory of our beloved brother
Siegmund Spingarn
1884

In Memory of
Emanuel Hoffman
Dedicated by the family
1884

In Memory of
Adolph Hallgarten
1885

In Memory of
Siphra Stern
Dedicated by her children
1887

In Memory of
Benjamin F. Meyer
Dedicated by his brother
1887

In Memory of
Jonas Heller
Dedicated by the family
1887

In Memory of
Henry Herrman
Endowed by Esther Herrman
1889

In Memory of
Henryette Mortimer
and Edward Rosenfeld
Dedicated by the husband and father
1889

In Memory of
Maurie E. Ansbacher
Dedicated by
Adolph B. and Frances E. Ansbacher
1889

In Memory of
Sidney Speyer
Dedicated by his brother
James Speyer
1890

In Memory of
Nathan Littauer
1891

Dedicated to the Memory of
Hirsch Wallach and
Bienchen Wallach
By their son, Isaac Wallach
1891

Endowed in Memory of
Louise Littauer
Daughter of Nathan and Harriet Littauer
1891

In Memory of
Rosa Veit
1892

To the Memory of
Sophia Roth
Dedicated by her husband
Ludwig Roth
1892

In Memory of
Bernard L. and Fanny Tim
Endowed by Louis and Solomon Tim
1892

In Memory of
Sigmund Robertson
Dedicated by the family
1892

Perpetual Beds

In Memory of
Grace A. L. Cullman
Dedicated by her husband
1892

In Memory of
Esther Asiel
Dedicated by her son
1892

Dedicated to the Memory of
Moses Wasserman
1893

In Memory of
Dr. Joseph Mainzer
Dedicated by his brother
1893

In Memory of
Johanna Fatman
Dedicated by S. A. Fatman
1893

In Memory of
**Sylvester Brush
and Sarah, His Wife**
Dedicated by their children
1893

In Memory of
Jesse Seligman
Dedicated by the family
1894

In Memory of our beloved mother
Babette Scholle
1894

Dedicated to the Memory of
Albert S. Rosenbaum
1894

In Memory of
Israel D. and Henrietta Walter
Dedicated by their son
William I. Walter
1894

In Memory of
Isaac Bernheimer
1894

In Memory of
Moritz Josephthal
Dedicated by his widow
1895

To the Memory of
Leopold Boscowitz
Dedicated by his brothers and sisters
1837—1895

In Memory of her beloved son
Joseph Louis Myers
Dedicated by Louisa Myers
1895

In Memory of
Adolph T. Scholle
Dedicated by his father
1895

In Memory of
Adolph Bernheimer
Dedicated by his daughter
Miss Rosie Bernheimer
1895

In Memory of
Bertha Morris
Dedicated by her relatives
1896

Founded by and in Memory of
David Wallach
Chicago, Ill.
1896

In Memory of
Mayer Goldsmith
Dedicated by his widow
1896

159

Perpetual Beds

In Memory of
Mathilda Oppenheimer
Dedicated by her husband
1897

In Memory of
Bernard Mainzer
Dedicated by the family
1897

Dedicated by Antoinette Mayer
In Memory of her son
Carl Theodor Mayer
1897

In Memory of
Adelaide Ballin King
Dedicated by her husband
1897

In Memory of
Mariane Ickelheimer
Dedicated by Mrs. Julie Heidelbach
1897

In Memory of
Julius L. Goldenberg
Dedicated by his mother
1897

In Memory of
Bernard Cohen
1897

In Memory of
S. J. Spiegelberg
A former Director of this Institution
1898

In Memory of
Elias Jacobs
Dedicated by his wife
1898

Dedicated by
Mr. and Mrs. George Blumenthal
1898

**The Rosalie Nathan
Perpetual Bed**
Dedicated to the Cause of Humanity
1899

In Memory of
Martin H. Lehmaier
1899

Dedicated to the Memory of
Lydia Wolff
Wife of Abraham Wolff
1900

Dedicated to the Memory of
Abraham Wolff
1900

In Memory of
David Marks
Dedicated by his wife
1900

In Memory of
Louise Hoffman
Dedicated by her children
1900

Housman Memorial Beds
Dedicated by Arthur A. Housman
(Two Beds)
1900

In Memory of
Robert Graham Dun
1900

In Memory of
**His Wife, Bertha,
and Daughter, Sophie**
Dedicated by David Kohn
1900

160

Perpetual Beds

In Memory of My Beloved Parents
Simon and Rosetta S. Bernheimer
Dedicated by Jacob S. Bernheimer
1900

In Memory of
Henrietta Rubens
Dedicated by her husband
Charles Rubens, Paris
1901

In Memory of
Lazarus and Babette Morgenthau
Dedicated by Henry Morgenthau
1901

In Memory of
Edward B. Simon
Dedicated by his wife
1901

In Memory of
Josiah L. Webster
Dedicated by C. B. Webster
1901

In Memory of
Joseph Kaufman
Founded by provision in his will
1901

In Memory of
Emanuel Lauer
Dedicated by his daughters
Carrie Lehman and Sophie Goodhart
1901

In Memory of
Bernard and Henrietta Heineman
Dedicated by their son
Moses Heineman
1901

In Memory of
Marx and Sophie Hornthal
Dedicated by their children
1901

In Memory of
Moses Bruhl
Dedicated by his wife and daughters
1901

In Memory of
Moritz and Ernestine Cohn
Dedicated by their children
1901

In Memory of
Betty Loeb
Dedicated by her husband
Solomon Loeb
1902

In Memory of
Elizabeth Jeffries Garvey
Dedicated by Andrew Jeffries Garvey
(Two Beds)
1902

In Memory of
Louis and Yetta Stix
1902

In Memory of
Theodore G. Weil
1902

Two Beds
The Jacob Rubino Beds
1902

In Memory of
Fanny Myers
Dedicated by David E. Sicher
1902

In Memory of
Jacob S. Bernheimer
Dedicated by his wife and children
1902

In Memory of
Bernard Baruch
Endowed by his grandson
1902

Dedicated by
**The Hebrew Mutual Benefit
Society**
To Commemorate Its Seventy-fifth
Anniversary
1902

In Memory of
**Rachel V. and Charles
Sternbach**
Dedicated by their son
Sidney M. Sternbach
1903

In Memory of
Florentine Weinberg
Dedicated by Philip Weinberg
1903

In Memory of
Clara Wertheim
Dedicated by Henry P. Wertheim
1903

Dedicated to the Memory of
Jacob Bookman
1903

In Memory of
Edward J. King
Dedicated by his wife
Rosalie King
1904

In Memory of
Marcus L. Stieglitz
Dedicated by his wife
Sarah Stieglitz
1904

In Memory of
Joseph Freedman
Dedicated by his son
Andrew Freedman
1904

In Memory of
Simon Borg
Dedicated by his wife
Cecelia Borg
1905

In Memory of
Ruth M. Gross
By her parents
Morris and Carrie L. Gross
1905

In Memory of
Hannah Vogel
Dedicated by her husband
William Vogel
1905

In Memory of
M. S. Mork
Dedicated by his wife
Minnie Mork
1905

Dedicated by
Mr. and Mrs. Eugene Meyer
1905

In Memory of
Joseph B. Bloomingdale
1905

In Memory of
Adolph Herrmann
Founded by provision in his will
1906

Endowed by Emma B. Hendricks
In memory of her sons
**Edgar Hendricks
Henry H. Hendricks
and Clifford B. Hendricks**
1906

Endowed by Emma B. Hendricks
In Memory of her Husband
Joshua Hendricks
1906

Perpetual Beds

In Memory of
Bennett and Sarah B. King
1906

In Memory of
Samuel E. and Mary Halle
Endowed by Jacques S. Halle
1906

In Memory of
Cecelia Borg
Dedicated by her children
1906

The Lyman C. and Hattie Bloomingdale Perpetual Bed
1906

In Memory of
Walter A. Schiffer
Dedicated by his wife
1907

In Memory of
Isaac Wallach
Founded by provision in his will
1907.

In Memory of
Louis Josephthal
Founded by provision in his will
1907

In Memory of
Isabella Arnold Bernheimer
Dedicated by her children
1907

In Memory of
Hedwig Rosenbaum
By her husband
Sigmund D. Rosenbaum
1908

The Leopold Laderer Caroline Laderer and Samuel L. Laderer Perpetual Bed
1908

In Memory of
Emily Lazarus
Founded by provision in the will of
Amelia B. Lazarus
1908

In Memory of
Simon W. Glazier
Dedicated by his wife and children
1908

In Memory of
Isaac S. and Sarah Erdmann
1909

The Ernest Ehrmann Bed
Founded by provision in his will
1909

In Memory of
Solomon Herzog
Founded by Edward N. Herzog
1909

In Memory of
Arthur A. Housman
Founded by provision in his will
(Two Beds)
1909

In Memory of
Abraham B. Frank
Dedicated by his wife
1909

In Memory of
Leopold Gusthal
Dedicated by his sisters
1909

In Memory of
Gustav Bernheim
Dedicated by his wife and children
1909

163

Perpetual Beds

In Memory of
Mary Mayer
Founded by David Mayer
1910

In Memory of
Therese Josephthal
Founded by provision in her will
1910

In Memory of
Edward A. and Bertha R. Price
Founded by Julie Price Erdman
1910

In Memory of
Dr. Joseph Schnetter
Founded by provision in his will
(Three Beds)
1910

In Memory of
Bertha Horn
Founded by provision in the will of
Michael Horn
1910

In Memory of
Rev. Dr. Gustave Gottheil
Rabbi, Temple Emanu-El
1873-1899
Founded by Paul Gottheil
1910

In Memory of
Dr. Herman Baerwald
Founded by Paul Baerwald
1910

In Memory of
Valentine and Fanny Loewi
Dedicated by the family
1911

In Memory of
Edna Saks Levy
Dedicated by Mr. and Mrs. Andrew Saks
1911

The Emma Rosenwald Bed
Founded by provision in her will
1911

In Memory of
Henry Rosenwald
Founded by Mrs. Henry Rosenwald
1911

In Memory of
**Allen L. Mordecai
and Kate Mordecai**
Dedicated by their children
1911

In Memory of
Alexander L. Kaufmann
Founded by provision in his will
1911

In Memory of
Julius Ehrmann
Founded by provision in the will of
Mathilda Ehrmann
1912

In Memory of
James and Amelia Strauss
Founded by provision in the will
of their son, Nathan F. Strauss
1912

In Memory of
Dr. Max Herzog
Founded by
Mr. and Mrs. Abram N. Stein
1912

In Memory of
Dr. Wolfgang Mack
1808-1883
Founded by provision in the will of
Jacob W. Mack
1912

164

Perpetual Beds

In Memory of
Jacob Wolfgang Mack
1845-1912
Dedicated by Jennie and Ella Heyman
1912

In Memory of
Luise Mack
1808-1887
Founded by provision in the will of
Jacob W. Mack
1912

In Memory of
Mathilda Ehrmann
Founded by provision in her will
1912

In Memory of
Florence Henrietta Walter
Dedicated by her aunt
Rosie Bernheimer
1913

In Memory of
Marcus and Bertha Goldman
1913

In Memory of
Lewis S. Levy
Founded by provision in his will
1914

In Memory of
Mary Levy
Founded by provision in the will of
Lewis S. Levy
1914

In Memory of
Julius and Fanny Robertson
Founded by provision in his will
1915

In Memory of
Maurice and Mathilde Seligmann
Dedicated by
George and Arthur Seligmann
1915

In Memory of
Erwin Beit Von Speyer
Founded by his uncle
James Speyer
1915

In Memory of
Max and Nina Herzog
Dedicated by their daughter
Bella H. Kaufmann
1915

In Memory of
Samuel and Helene Prince
Dedicated by their children
1915

In Memory of
Leonard S. Prince
Dedicated by his father and mother
December 23, 1915

In Memory of
Madge N. Haas
1915

In Memory of
David, Gustave B. and Charles Calman
Founded by provision in the will of
Emma Calman
1915

In Memory of
Tillie Hochschild
1916

In Memory of
Mrs. Samuel H. Spingarn
Endowed by provision in the will of
Samuel H. Spingarn
1916

In Memory of
Samuel H. Spingarn
Endowed by provision in his will
1916

In Memory of
Henrietta Bondy
Founded by her son
Emil C. Bondy
1916

In Memory of
Jacob and Rosina Erdmann
Founded by Albert J. Erdmann
1916

In Memory of
Charles. Bondy
Founded by his son
Emil C. Bondy
1916

In Memory of
Karl Schwabach
Founded by his uncle
James Speyer
1917

In Memory of
**Henry and Rosalie
Klingenstein**
Dedicated by their son
Charles Klingenstein
1917

In Memory of his Parents
Josephine and David Salzer
Dedicated by Leopold Salzer
1917

In Memory of
Mrs. Isaac Wallach
Founded by provision in her will
1917

In Memory of
Johanna and Rosalie Moses
Dedicated by their sister
Julia R. Ballerstein
1917

In Memory of
Bernhard Stern
Dedicated by his brother
Benjamin Stern
1917

In Memory of
Amelia Heidelberg
Dedicated by Isaac N. Heidelberg
1917

In Memory of
Rachel H. Pfeiffer
Founded by provision in her will
1917

In Memory of
Belle Glazier Bernheimer
Founded by provision in her will
1917

In Memory of
Charles E. Schafer
Endowed by his wife
1917

Endowed by
Mr. and Mrs. Philip J. Goodhart
1918

In Memory of
Theresa and Joseph Fox
1918

In Memory of their Parents
Louise and Leopold Salzer
Dedicated by their children
(Two Beds)
1918

166

Perpetual Beds

In Memory of
Joshua Rothblatt
Dedicated by his parents
Bernard and Ida Rothblatt
1919

In Celebration of the
Ninetieth Birthday of
Max Nathan
April 15, 1919
Presented by his daughter
Irma N. Straus

In Memory of
Meyer H. Lehman
Dedicated by his sisters
Mrs. Harriet Weil
and Mrs. Bertha Rosenheim
1919

In Memory of
Julius Lewisohn
London, England
Dedicated by his son
1919

In Memory of
William Klingenstein
of London, England
Dedicated by his nephew
Charles Klingenstein
1919

In Memory of
Emma and Albert Kaskel
Founded by provision in the will of
Emma H. Kaskel
1919

In Memory of
**Mayer Lehman and
Babette Lehman**
Dedicated
(Two Beds)
1919

Dedicated to
The Clara de Hirsch Home
By Dr. Josephine Walter
1919

The Louis M. Sonnenberg Bed
Founded by provision in his will
1919

In Memory of
Alan Harry Simon
Dedicated by
Mr. and Mrs. Harry G. Simon
1919

In Memory of
Ferdinand A. Straus
Dedicated by his son
Lionel F. Straus
1919

In Memory of
Henry Bendheim
Dedicated by his brother
Adolph D. Bendheim
1919

In Memory of
Levi Bamberger
Founded by Albert and Clara Blum
1919

The Three
J. D. Wendel Beds
Endowed in Memory of the Former
Tenants of John D. Wendel
1919

In Memory of
Sara Sonnenberg Beck
Dedicated by Martin Beck
1919

In Memory of
Aron Weil
Dedicated by his wife
Dora Weil
1919

167

Perpetual Beds

In Memory of his Parents
Vitus and Fanny Lambert
Dedicated by their son
August V. Lambert
1920

In Memory of
Oscar M. Leiser
Founded by provision in his will
1920

In Memory of
Edith Stine Schiffer
Founded by her husband
Jack W. Schiffer
1920

In Memory of
Mayer and Babette Lehman
Dedicated by
Mr. and Mrs. Morris Fatman
1920

In Memory of
Alphons Lewis
Founded by provision in his will
1920

In Memory of
David Lehman
Dedicated by his sisters
Mrs. Harriet Weil and
Mrs. Bertha Rosenheim
1920

In Memory of
Matilda Ollendorff
Dedicated by her husband
1920

In Memory of
Marjorie Walter Goodhart
Founded by her aunt
Rosie Bernheimer
October 19, 1920

In Celebration of the
Seventy-fifth birthday of
Frances M. Fechheimer
September 4, 1920
Dedicated by her son
Sam M. Fechheimer

Dedicated by
Mr. and Mrs. Henry Budge
1920

In Memory of
Max J. Breitenbach
Dedicated by his wife and children
1920

In Memory of
Aaron and Johanna Fatman
Dedicated by
Mr. and Mrs. Morris Fatman
1920

In Memory of
Aline Bernheim
Founded by her sons
George B. and Alfred L. Bernheim
1921

In Memory of
Ellin Prince Speyer
Founded by her husband
James Speyer
1921

In Memory of
Arnold and Fannie Falk
Dedicated by Myron S. Falk
and K. George Falk
1921

In Memory of
Rosalie, Fannie, Charles, Simon and Joseph Lederer
Founded by provision in the will of
Charlotte Lederer
1921

Perpetual Beds

In memory of her parents
Samuel and Bella Haas
Founded by Mrs. Dudley D. Sicher

In Memory of
Henry and Hanna Herrmann
Dedicated by their son
Frederick Herrmann
1921

In Memory of
Jacob L. and Sophie Kops
Dedicated by their children
1921

In Memory of
Esther Wyman
Founded by provision in her will
1921

In Memory of
Sydney Michael Hyman
Dedicated by his parents
Michael and Rose Hyman
1921

In Memory of
Clara Glazier
Founded by provision in her will
1922

In Memory of
Carrie Rapp and Samuel Rapp
Founded by provision in the will of
Samuel Rapp
1922

In Memory of
**David James King and
Adelaide Ballin King**
Dedicated by their daughter
Louise King Reckford
1922

In Memory of
Caroline Bookman
Founded by provision in her will
1922

In Memory of
Dorothea Haas Weiler
Founded by provision in the will of
her son
Charles H. Weiler
1923

In Memory of
Jacob H. Semel
Founded by provision in his will
1923

In Memory of
Marks Weiler
Founded by provision in the will of
his son
Charles H. Weiler
1923

In Memory of
**Morris S. Barnet
and
Alvina Barnet**
Dedicated by Morris S. Barnet
(Two Beds)

Dedicated by
Addie W. Kahn
1923

In Memory of
Walter J. Rose
Dedicated by his mother
1924

In Memory of
**Gabriel Mayer
Antoinette Mayer
Otto L. Mayer**
Founded by provision in the will of
Otto L. Mayer
1924

Endowed by
Abraham Erlanger
1924

Perpetual Beds

Founded by
Charles Hendricks
1924

The Ella Hellman Bed
Founded by provision in her will
1924

In Memory of
Solomon C. Guggenheimer
March 24th, 1924

In Memory of
Jacob Wertheim
Dedicated by his wife
Emma Stern Wertheim
1925

In Memory of
Louis S. Frankenheimer
Dedicated by
Ida and Rose Frankenheimer
1925

In Memory of
Pauline Mayers
Endowed by her husband.
Morris Mayers
1925

In Memory of
Elkan and Bertha Naumburg
Dedicated by their son
Walter W. Naumburg
1926

In Memory of
Siegfried W. Mayer
Founded by provision in his will
1926

In Memory of
Samuel Baumann
Dedicated by his wife
Henrietta Baumann
1926

In Memory of
Henrietta Rawitser
Dedicated by her daughter
Theresa V. Rawitser
1926

In Memory of
Morris Rossin
Dedicated by his wife
Martha S. Rossin
1927

In Memory of
Lewis Schoolhouse
Endowed by
Joseph Runsheim
1927

Dedicated to their friends
George and Florence Blumenthal
By
Edmond and Suzanne King Bruwaert
1927

In Memory of
Samuel J. and Esther Gans
Dedicated by their son
Simeon C. Gans
1927

Endowed by
Mr. and Mrs. Albert E. Goodhart
1927

In Memory of
Arthur E. Frank
1927

In Memory of
Solomon Friedman and Amelia G. Friedman
1928

In Memory of
Samuel Bachrach and Babette Bachrach
1928

In Memory of
Richard M. Homberg
Founded by provision in the will
of his mother
Florence N. Homberger
1928

In Memory of
Isaac N. Heidelberg
Dedicated by his daughters
1928

In Memory of
William Vogel
Dedicated by his sons
Harry Wm. and Bernard Wm. Vogel
1928

In Memory of
Herman Rawitser
Dedicated by his wife
Theresa V. Rawitser
1929

In Memory of
Al and Minnie Hayman
Founded by provision in the will of
Minnie Hayman
(Two Beds)
1929

In Memory of
Ada Heidelberg Strauss
Dedicated by her husband
Seymour A. Strauss
1929

The Rebecca Friedlander Bed
Founded by provision in her will
1929

In Memory of
**Heinemann and Rosa
Vogelstein**
Dedicated by their children
1929

In Memory of
Mayer Mayer and Fanny Mayer
Beloved Father and Mother of
Bernhard Mayer
1929

In Memory of
Mary Small Einstein
Dedicated by her husband
I. D. Einstein
1930

In Memory of
Henry Stern and Mathilda Stern
Dedicated by their son
Meyer Stern
1930

The Selina E. Summerfield Bed
Founded by provision in her will
1931

In Memory of
Lucy Herzfeld
Dedicated by
Felix and Ida Herzfeld
1932

In Memory of
Richard and Matilda Sidenberg
1932

In Memory of
Henry Block
Bequest of
Alice A. Kohler
1932

The Fred H. Greenebaum Bed
Founded by provision in his will
1933

171

Perpetual Beds

In Memory of
Jacob Hirsh
Dedicated by his wife
Julia Hirsh
1927
and
In Memory of
Julia Hirsh
Dedicated by her children
(Two Beds)
1933

In Memory of
Heyman and Martha Pincus
Founded by provision in the will of
Martha Pincus
1933

In Memory of
Adolph
Charlotte and Mary Arber
Founded by provision in the will of
Adolph Arbor
1933

In Memory of
Ludwig and Rebecca Dreyfuss
Founded by provision in the will of
Ludwig Dreyfuss
(Two Beds)
1934

Dedicated in memory of
William Hyams
and Emma Hyams
1935

In Memory of
Sarah King
1935

In Memory of
Myron Goldsmith Friedenheit
Born, September 7, 1898
Died, January 15, 1936
Dedicated by his parents

In Memory of
Elizabeth P. Hewes
Founded by provision in her will
1936

The Straus Memorial Beds
In Memory of
Lionel F. Straus
Dedicated by his wife, May H. Straus
(Two Beds)
1937

In Memory of
Nathan and Ella Necarsulmer
Bequeathed by their daughter
Helena Necarsulmer
1937

In Memory of
Ralph J. Jacobs
Founded by provision in his will
1937

In Memory of
Virginia Guinzburg Kleinert
1937

Perpetual Beds

Children's Pavilion

In Memory of
Henry L. Einstein
Founded by Cecilia Einstein
1922

In Memory of
Sol H. Kohn
Dedicated by Lillie V. Kohn
1922

Founded by
Benjamin Mordecai
1922

In Memory of
Nellie M. Rice
(Two Beds)
1922

In Memory of
Robert Reis
Dedicated by Sarah Reis
1922

In Memory of
Carrie Wormser
Founded by provision·in the will of
her daughter, Julia Seligman
(Four Beds)
1922

In Memory of
Constance Davis Mordecai
Founded by Benjamin Mordecai
(Two Beds)
1923

Dedicated by
Dr. A. V. Moschcowitz
To commemorate the marriage of his
daughter, Frances Ethel Frowenfeld
1923

In Memory of
Joseph and Babet Semel
Founded by provision in the will of
Mrs. George Heyman
1924

In Memory of
George and Hannah Heyman
Founded by provision in the will of
Hannah Heyman
1924

Endowed by
Cecilia Einstein
1924

In Memory of
William Frankenheimer
Dedicated by
Ida and Rose Frankenheimer
1925

In Memory of
Abraham Leipzig
Founded by provision in his will
1925

In Memory of
Adolph Frank Hochstadter
Endowed by Rosa Hayman Hochstadter
1926

In Memory of
Rosa Hayman Hochstadter
Founded by provision in her will
1926

In Memory of
Solomon and Amalia Bondy
Founded by provision in the will of
Maurice S. Bondy
1926

In Memory of
Babette Rothschild
Dedicated by her daughter
Ida R. Cullman
1926

Marx Rothschild
Dedicated by his daughter
Ida R. Cullman
1926

173

Perpetual Beds

Children's Pavilion

In Memory of
Charles and Mary Weisberger
1926

The Aaron Bachrach and Jennie Bachrach Bed
1927

In Memory of
Marcus Loew
Dedicated by Caroline Loew
1928

The Peter F. Meyer Beds
Founded by provision in his will
(Five Beds)
1929

In Memory of
Samuel and Hattie Binswanger
1929

The Adelaide F. Pfeiffer Bed
Founded by provision in her will
1929

Ludwig Ulmann
In memory of his brother
Bernard Ulmann
1930

In Memory of
Agnes C. Rice
Founded by provision in her will
1930

In Memory of
Laura Rossman
Dedicated by will of Selma Rossman
1932

In Memory of
Robert Rossman
Dedicated by will of Selma Rossman
1932

In Memory of
Simon and Lucy Drukker
Dedicated by the will of their daughter
Jeannette D. Beaumont
1933

In Memory of
Elias Kempner
Founded by provision in his will
1933

In Memory of
Louis B. G. Garland
Dedicated by his parents
Edward S. Garland and
Lillian B. Garland
1933

The Samuel and Isabella Kritzman Beds
Founded by provision in the will of
Isabella Kritzman
(Five Beds)
1935

In Memory of
Herman Loevy
Dedicated by
Edwin F. Young
(Two Beds)
1936

In Loving Memory of
Frances Clayton Moses
Dedicated by her aunt
Catherine Sampson
1936

In Memory of
Lena Kemp
Founded by provision in her will
1937

In Memory of
Celia and Solomon Oppenheimer
Founded by provision in the will of
Solomon Oppenheimer
1938

174

Memorial Beds

In Memory of
Emanuel de Castro
Dedicated by Margaret D. Plant
1902

In Memory of
Joseph E. Heimerdinger
Dedicated by his brother and sisters
1904

In Memory of
Samuel R. and Jane Jacobs
Dedicated by their children
1904

In Memory of
Babetta Adelsberger
Dedicated by her daughter
Mrs. Emanuel M. Gattle
1905

In Memory of
Samuel Adelsberger
Dedicated by his daughter
Mrs. Emanuel M. Gattle
1905 .

In Memory of
Isaac A. and Sarah J. Singer
Dedicated by a son
1906

In Memory of Our Beloved Son
Max Reutlinger
Dedicated by
Mr. and Mrs. Emanuel Reutlinger
1908

The Charles Mayer Bed
Founded by Max W. Mayer
January 18, 1909

In Memory of
Sigmund Neustadt
Dedicated by Mrs. Agnes Neustadt
1909

Dedicated by Max Loewenstein
In Memory of
Edward I. Loewenstein
Died July 20, 1912

In Memory of
Seligman and Therese Oppenheimer
Dedicated by their children
1913

In Memory of
Michaelis H. Ziegel
Founded by his son
H. F. L. Ziegel
1913

In Memory of My Beloved Mother
Fannie Mandelbaum
and My Beloved Brother
Max Mandelbaum
Bella Del Monte
1914

In Memory of
Henry Liebmann
Dedicated by his wife
Emma Liebmann
1915

The Pauline, Jacob and Edward S. Bamberger Bed
1915

In Memory of
Edward C. Heymann
Dedicated by his parents
Chas. E. and Helen R. Heymann
1915

In Memory of
Richard Limburg
Dedicated by Mrs. Clara L. Limburg
1916

Frederick Jacobi Memorial Bed.
Endowed by Flora and Frederick Jacobi
1916

175

Memorial Beds

In Memory of
Mayer and Yette Katzenberg
Dedicated by their children
1916

In Memory of
Rachel Kaufmann
Dedicated by her husband
Gustav Kaufmann
1918

In Memory of
Mr. and Mrs. Emanuel S. Kuh
Dedicated by their daughter
Nellie Kuh
1918

In Memory of
Nathan Cohen
Founded by his parents
Mr. and Mrs. Isaac Cohen
1921

In Memory of
Alfred Frank
Dedicated by his brothers and sisters
1923

In Memory of
George and Rose Epstein
and Their Son David
1927

In Memory of
Morris Woititz
and Frances S. Woititz
1937

In Memory of
Levi and Sarah Goldenberg
Founded by their daughter
Helen B. Chaim
1938

Life Beds

Founded by
Mrs. DeWitt J. Seligman
1882

Founded by
Ethel F. Seligman
Daughter of
Mr. and Mrs. DeWitt J. Seligman
1897

Dedicated to
Elsie Nathan
1902

The May S. Harlow nee Stern Life Bed
Founded by her April 28, 1904

The Lucile M. S. van Heukelom Life Bed
Founded November 24, 1904

The Helen Fox Life Bed
Founded by Henry Morgenthau
April 7, 1906

Founded by
A Friend
1907

In Memory of
Joseph Dannenberg
of Macon, Georgia

The Dr. Manges Life Bed
Founded by a Friend of The Hospital
1912

In Memory of
Fannie Behrens Wolfe
and Solomon Baird Wolfe, M.D.

In Memory of
Max Weil
Dedicated by his wife
1914

In Memory of
Joseph Honig
Founded by Louise H. Mandelbaum
1916

In Memory of
Isidore Jackson
Dedicated by his wife and son
September 14, 1920

In Memory of
Leonard M.
Dedicated by his parents
Alexander and Rose M. Joseph
1920

In Memory of
Morris Goldstein and Pauline Goldstein
Endowed by their children
1921

Endowed by
Francois Kleinberger
1921

In Honor of
Minnie Kastor
Endowed by her husband,
Adolph Kastor
1922

In Memory of
Benjamin Ehrlich
Endowed by his wife
Fannie Ehrlich
1929

In Memory of
Julius Kaufmann
Endowed by his wife
Emma H. Kaufmann
1930

Founded by
Pauline F. Baerwald
March 26, 1931

Dedicated to Humanity by
Solomon and Dora Shapiro
(Nee Monness)
1932

In Memory of
Clara L. Limburg
Dedicated by her children
1935

LEGACIES AND BEQUESTS

Previous to 1867			
	Judah Touro	$20,000	00
1867	Jacob Abrahams	5,000	00
1869	Benjamin Nathan	10,000	00
	Joseph Fatman	10,000	00
1872	Dr. S. Abrahams (1872-1873)	14,020	00
1876	Lewis Philips	11,711	51
1879	Michael Reese	25,000	00
1882	Simeon Abrahams	10,980	00
1883	Mrs. Judith Einstein	5,000	00
1885	Julius Hallgarten	10,000	00
1886	Miss Sarah Burr (1886-1893)	54,900	00
1888	Isaac Hoechster	5,000	00
1889	Henry Herrman	5,000	00
	William Meyer (1889-1891)	12,252	34
1891	Daniel B. Fayerweather (1891-1897)	9,933	03
1893	Joseph Rosenberg (1893-1926)	9,995	54
	Abraham Kuhn	5,000	00
1895	Adolph Bernheimer	5,000	00
1897	Mayer Lehman	17,958	00
1902	Andrew J. Garvey (1902-1937)	15,205	28
	Jacob F. Cullman	10,000	00
1903	Julius Beer	10,000	00
	Adolph Openhym	5,000	00
1904	Solomon Loeb	10,000	00
1905	Simon Rothschild	50,000	00
	Salomon Rothfeld	5,000	00
	Meyer Guggenheim	20,000	00
1906	Frederick Uhlmann	5,000	00
	Mathilde C. Weil (1906-1907)	12,144	99
1907	Emanuel Walter	7,500	00
	Marx W. Mendel	16,044	10
1908	Amelia B. Lazarus (1908-1909)	29,995	76
1910	Adolph Kerbs	5,000	00
	Emanuel Einstein	9,525	00
	Chas. Rubens	5,695	00
	Ludwig Stettheimer (1910-1913)	24,748	39
	Rosa Schreiber	6,267	74
	Margaret J. P. Graves	10,000	00

1911	John Stemme	$5,000 00
	Charles E. Tilford (1911-1938)	151,783 38
	Martin Herman	5,000 00
1912	Jacob Small (1912-1929)	14,864 30
	Andrew Saks	5,000 00
	Moses Weinman	5,000 00
	Samuel Lilienthal	14,762 08
1913	John J. Clancy (1913-1914)	25,000 00
	Ernst Thalmann	10,000 00
	Benjamin Guggenheim	10,000 00
	William Scholle	10,000 00
	Nathan Herrmann	5,000 00
1914	Lewis S. Levy (1914-1916)	16,343 74
1915	Constant Mayer	13,948 09
	David E. Sicher	10,000 00
	Jacob Langeloth	5,000 00
	Moses Lowenstein	5,000 00
1916	Andrew Freedman	5,000 00
	Solomon Wolf (1916-1917)	11,860 18
	Amelia Lavanburg (1916-1917)	10,175 84
	Emil Bondy	10,000 00
	Herman N. Walter	5,000 00
1917	J. S. Halle	5,000 00
	Rachel H. Pfeiffer	15,000 00
	Esther Schlesinger	22,002 42
1918	Meyer H. Lehman	25,000 00
1919	Kalman Haas	10,000 00
	Benjamin Blumenthal	15,000 00
	Henry J. Duveen	5,000 00
	Margaret Olivia Sage (1919-1921)	100,000 00
1920	Joseph Frank	447,374 70
	Pearl Weinman	7,065 85
	Isaac N. Seligman	5,000 00
	Babette Lehman	5,000 00
	Julius Kayser	10,000 00
	Baruch Kaufman	14,250 00
1921	William Salomon	10,000 00

179

1922	Adolph D. Bendheim	$5,000 00
	Mary Helen Finch	5,000 00
	Julia Seligman (1922-1936)	12,682 29
1923	Morris S. Barnet	35,000 00
	Eleanor von Koppenfels	25,000 00
1924	Jacob Rossbach	5,000 00
1925	Eugene Meyer	10,000 00
	Emily A. Watson	24,998 20
	Emanuel Spiegelberg	5,000 00
	Michael Dreicer	10,000 00
1926	Emil Wolff	29,794 12
	Adolph Boskowitz	20,000 00
	Solomon A. Fatman	20,000 00
	Louis S. Stroock	5,000 00
	Albert Lorsch	5,000 00
	Harriet Weil	5,000 00
	Morris J. Hirsch	5,000 00
	Lewis Schoolhouse	5,000 00
	Jonathan Nathan (1926-1933)	5,130 89
1927	Alexander Herman (1927-1928)	100,000 00
	Lottie Estelle Mayer (1927-1928)	33,461 87
	Sophie W. Low	8,457 47
	Charles Altschul	7,500 00
	Mortimer H. Heyman	5,000 00
	Morris Weinstein	5,000 00
	Harry Mayer	5,000 00
1928	Al Hayman	25,000 00
	Aline Myers	15,027 87
	Morris Rossin	10,000 00
	Isaac J. Bernheim	5,000 00
	Marmaduke Richardson	5,000 00
1929	Simon R. Weil (1929-1934)	156,468 28
	Michael P. Rich	20,000 00
	Emma Blumenberg—In memory of her brothers, Marc A. and Louis Blumenberg (1929-1930)	12,473 66
	Harriet F. Haas	10,000 00
	Harmon W. Hendricks	10,000 00
1930	Harry H. Meyer (1930-1937)	206,260 10
	Betsy S. Korminsky	5,000 00
	Pauline Myers	5,000 00
	Louis C. Raegner	5,000 00

1931	Julius Marcus	$19,185 83
	Louis Marshall (1931-1937)	11,581 27
	William Hartfield (1931-1936)	10,061 59
	Alfred M. Heinsheimer	5,000 00
	Frieda Wimpfheimer	5,000 00
1933	Isaac Marx	7,500 00
	Sophie Reiser	4,520 37
1934	Rudolph J. Schaefer (1934-1937)	64,845 88
	Ludwig Dreyfuss	25,000 00
	Benjamin Stern (1934-1937)	25,000 00
	Josephine Jacobs	2,500 00
	Alexis V. Moschcowitz	2,500 00
1935	Bertha Weinman—In memory of her brother, Moses Weinman (1935-1936)	1,514,554 82
	Joseph Runsheim (1935-1937)	17,872 25
	Lawrence Pike (1935-1937)	4,102 89
1936	Edward J. King—For the Edward J. King and Jennie I. King Memorial Fund (1936-1938)	1,630,899 52
	Isa Nordlinger (1936-1937)	9,199 21
	Augustus W. Openhym (1936-1938)	37,372 52
	Louise C. Colten	2,800 29
	Abraham Cohn	2,622 65
	Henry F. Wolff	2,503 47
1937	Marco Fleishman—For the Rosetta and Marco Fleishman Memorial Fund (1937-1938)	743,810 79
	Carrie L. Lehman	10,000 00
	Henry Ollesheimer (1937-1938)	9,770 98
	Ephraim B. Levy	5,000 00
	Leah Simpson	5,000 00
	Jacob W. Gutman	2,500 00
	Henry Jacoby (1937-1938)	2,703 99
	Emil Kiss—In Memory of Laura Kiss	1,445 00
1938	Henry W. Putnam	50,000 00
	Bettie Meierhoff	36,543 07
	Harry J. D. Plaut	5,107 50
	Charles S. Erlanger	5,000 00
	Emanuel Felsenheld	1,250 00
	Morris Drey	1,000 00
	David J. Frankel	1,000 00
	Sara T. Lowman	1,000 00
	Fannie Metzger	465 31
	Louis Lauer	250 00
	Emanuel Tunis	200 00
	William Brill	166 67
	Jacob Richman	166 66
	Joseph N. Frank (1937-1938)	128 73
	Israel Wien	100 00

181

LIFE MEMBERS

HARRY CONTENT ....111 Broadway

ABRAM I. ELKUS...40 Wall Street

MRS. E. B. HART...2111 Madison Avenue

MRS. ELSIE WALLACH KRIDEL............................1075 Park Avenue

SAMUEL A. LEWIS...7 Warren Street

MRS. J. S. MENKEN...104 East 79th Street

ARTHUR MEYER.....................71 Fitzjohn Avenue, London, N. W.

WALTER W. NAUMBURG................................121 East 64th Street

MRS. FLORENCE S. ROBERTS.....................Hotel Villa Del Arroyo,
Pasadena, Cal.

JAMES SPEYER...24 Pine Street

MRS. ALBERT D. STEIN

ISADOR M. STETTENHEIM...17 Cedar Street

OFFICERS AND TRUSTEES

of

THE MOUNT SINAI HOSPITAL

SINCE ITS FOUNDATION

*SAMPSON SIMSON	1852-1855	President, 1852-1855.
*JOHN I. HART	1852-1856	Vice-President, 1852-1855; President, 1855-1856.
*HENRY HENDRICKS	1852-1861	Treasurer, 1852-1861.
*BENJAMIN NATHAN	1852-1870	Secretary, 1852-1853; Vice-President, 1855-1856; President, 1856-1870.
*REV. SAMUEL M. ISAACS	1852-1857	Vice-President, 1856-1857.
*JOHN M. DAVIES	1852-1857	
*THEO. I. SEIXAS	1852-1856	Secretary, 1853-1856.
*ISAAC PHILLIPS	1852-1856	
*J. D. PHILLIPS	1852-1858	Vice-President, 1857-1858.
*JOSEPH FATMAN	1855-1869	Treasurer, 1861-1869.
*LEWIS MAY	1855-1876	Treasurer, 1869-1876.
*JOSEPH SELIGMAN	1855-1862	
*SAMUEL A. LEWIS	1856-1874	Secretary, 1858-1870; Vice-President, 1870-1874.
*N. K. ROSENFELD	1857-1867	Vice-President, 1858-1866.
*EMANUEL B. HART	1857-1876	Vice-President, 1866-1870; President, 1870-1876.
*L. M. MORRISON	1857-1862	
*L. HOLLANDER	1857-1858	
*WILLIAM HELLER	1857-1861	
*H. J. HART	1858-1863	
*HARRIS ARONSON	1858-1879	Vice-President, 1875-1879; President, 1879.
*S. L. COHEN	1861-1869	Re-elected, 1871-1876.
*ANSEL LEO	1861-1867	
*WILLIAM SELIGMAN	1862-1867	
*S. J. SPIEGELBERG	1862-1866	
*JOHN M. LAWRENCE	1863-1872	Secretary, 1871-1872.
*HENRY GITTERMAN	1866-1916	
*JONAS HELLER	1866-1870	
*SOLOMON SOMMERICH	1867-1889	
*ISAAC HERRMANN	1867-1869	
*J. S. ABECASIS	1869-1872	
*LEWIS FATMAN	1869-1878	Vice-President, 1874-1875. Re-elected, 1880-1884.
*A. S. ROSENBAUM	1870-1875	Secretary, 1872-1875.
*MAX STADLER	1870-1876	
*ISAAC S. SOLOMON	1871-1878	
*JOS. RECKENDORFER	1871-1872	

*Deceased

*ADOLPH HALLGARTEN	1871-1883	President, 1876-1879.
*J. B. GUTTENBERG	1871-1872	
*V. HENRY ROTHSCHILD	1871-1887	
*ABRAHAM SIMM	1871-1874	
*ISAAC PHILLIPS	1872-1874	
*FERDINAND KURZMAN	1872-1878	
*A. B. ANSBACHER	1872-1876	Re-elected, 1877-1887.
*DAVID SALOMON	1872-1876	
*M. S. FECHHEIMER	1873-1875	Re-elected, 1883-1888.
*JULIUS J. LYONS	1874-1875	
*SAMUEL ZEIMER	1874-1877	
*NATHAN LITTAUER	1875-1879	Secretary, 1875-1877.
*J. M. STINE	1875-1878	
*EDW. OPPENHEIMER	1875-1876	Re-elected, 1892-1894. Re-elected, 1897-1910. Honorary Trustee, 1910-1919.
*SAMUEL M. SCHAFER	1875-1891	Treasurer, 1875-1891.
*EDW. EINSTEIN	1875-1880	
*LEVI SAMUELS	1875-1878	
*HARMON H. NATHAN	1875-1896	Secretary, 1877-1880.
*HYMAN BLUM	1875-1896	Vice-President, 1879; President, 1879-1896.
*LOUIS STIX	1875-1901	Honorary Trustee, 1901-1902.
*ISAAC BLUMENTHAL	1875-1901	Honorary Trustee, 1901-1902.
*ISAAC WALLACH	1877-1907	Vice-President, 1879-1896; President, 1896-1907.
*SOLOMON SULZBERGER	1877-1896	
*NATHAN BARNETT	1878-1879	
*MAYER LEHMAN	1878-1897	
*LEONARD LEWISOHN	1879-1880	
*JACOB H. SCHIFF	1879-1882	Re-elected, 1883-1885.
*HENRY ROSENWALD	1879-1885	
*LOUIS GANS	1879-1889	
*MOSES G. HANAUER	1879-1882	Secretary, 1879-1882.
*L. M. HORNTHAL	1880-1897	Secretary, 1882-1885.
*MICHAEL DINKELSPIEL	1881-1883	
*DEWITT J. SELIGMAN	1881-1888	Secretary, 1885-1888.
*SIMON ROTHSCHILD	1884-1905	
*S. L. FATMAN	1885-1898	
*ALBERT HENDRICKS	1885-1886	
*SOLOMON LOEB	1885-1897	
*ELIAS ASIEL	1886-1920	Treasurer, 1892-1915.
*WILLIAM VOGEL	1887-1893	
*ANTHONY WALLACH	1887-1888	
*ADOLPH HERRMANN	1887-1901	Honorary Trustee, 1901-1906.
*HENRY GOLDMAN	1888-1891	Secretary, 1888-1891.
*LEON MANDEL	1888-1891	

184

*Deceased

*HENRY L. CALMAN	1906-1930	Second Vice-President, 1917-1919.
PHILIP J. GOODHART	1907-1933	Vice-President, 1910-1917. Honorary Trustee, 1933. In office.
MILTON C. HERRMANN	1907-1909	
SAMUEL E. JACOBS	1907-1918	Honorary Trustee, 1918. In office.
SIEGFRIED H. KAHN	1908-1909	
*ABRAM N. STEIN	1909-1912	
EDWARD N. HERZOG	1909-1915	
EDGAR A. HELLMAN	1910-1912	Secretary, 1910-1911.
*PAUL GOTTHEIL	1910-1915	
*EMANUEL VAN RAALTE	1910-1930	
WILLIAM I. WALTER	1910-1927	
*ALBERT W. SCHOLLE	1910-1916	
EUGENE MEYER, JR.	1911-1920	
*S. HERBERT WOLFE	1911-1921	Secretary, 1911-1918; Second Vice-President, 1919-1921.
LOUIS J. HOROWITZ	1912-1919	
NORMAN S. GOLDBERGER	1912-1919	
BERNARD F. GIMBEL	1912-1920	
*DANIEL KOPS	1913-1923	
E. J. WILE	1915-1922	
G. F. SULZBERGER	1915-1917	
WALTER E. SACHS	1915-1933	Secretary, 1918-1921.
*SIDNEY S. PRINCE	1915-1929	Treasurer, 1915-1925.
*MAURICE FRANKFORT	1916-1928	Second Vice-President, 1921-1928; Honorary Trustee, 1928-1936.
MYRON S. FALK	1916	In office.
WALTER W. NAUMBURG	1916	In office.
MRS. ARTHUR L. CARNS	1917-1920	
MRS. ALFRED A. COOK	1917	In office.
ALBERT FORSCH	1919	Secretary, 1921-1923; Third Vice-President, 1924-1928; Second Vice-President, 1928-1937. In office.
BENJAMIN MORDECAI	1919	In office.
HERBERT H. LEHMAN	1919-1920	
JACK W. SCHIFFER	1920-1928	
BENEDICT ERSTEIN	1920-1931	
*CHARLES KLINGENSTEIN	1920-1936	
MRS. ROGER W. STRAUS	1920	In office.
NELSON I. ASIEL	1920	Treasurer, 1926. In office.
MRS. H. H. LEHMAN	1920	In office.
*ERNST ROSENFELD	1921-1937	
ARTHUR H. HARLOW	1922	Secretary, 1928-1938. In office.
MARTIN BECK	1922-1929	
DAVID A. SCHULTE	1922	In office.

187

SUPERINTENDENTS AND DIRECTORS SINCE 1855

Superintendents—Directors#

*1855-1866   JULIUS RAYMOND
*1867-1875   G. SCHWARZBAUM
*1876-1878   LEOPOLD B. SIMON
*1879-1892   THEODORE HADEL
*1892-1899   LEOPOLD MINZESHEIMER
*1899-1904   S. L. FATMAN
 1904-1928   S. S. GOLDWATER, M.D.
 1928-   JOSEPH TURNER, M.D.

Associate Director

1927-1928   JOSEPH TURNER, M.D.

Assistant Superintendents—Assistant Directors#

*1892-1892   LEOPOLD MINZESHEIMER
*1896-1902   GUSTAVE ABRAMS
*1903-1904   SOLON J. RIESER
 1903-1904   S. S. GOLDWATER, M.D.
 1906-1908   SIDNEY E. GOLDSTEIN
*1908-1909   D. M. BLOOM, M.D.
 1910-1915   H. J. MOSS, M.D.
 1914-1916   A. J. BELLER, M.D.
 1917-1920   HERMAN SMITH, M.D.
*1918-1919   SIMON TANNENBAUM, M.D.
 1920-1921   LEOPOLD BRAHDY, M.D.
 1920-1925   E. M. BLUESTONE, M.D.
 1922-1927   JOSEPH TURNER, M.D.
 1925-1927   J. J. GOLUB, M.D.
 1927-1937   STEPHEN MANHEIMER, M.D.
 1927-1934   LOUIS MILLER, JR.
 1934-   J. A. KATZIVE, M.D.
 1935-   JANDON SCHWARZ, M.D.
 1937-1938   M. A. GREEN, M.D.
 1938-   MAXWELL S. FRANK, M.D.

Title changed to Director and Assistant Director in 1917.
* Deceased

188

GRADUATES OF THE HOUSE STAFF
PRIOR TO 1884

*Deceased

*Mark Blumenthal
*F. Tilden Brown
*R. M. Cramer
*R. B. Coleman
D. H. Davison
Wm. L. Estes
*Benson M. Feldman
*Albert Fridenberg
*O. Froelich

Alfred Meyer
*J. R. Nilsen
R. Offenbach
*S. Rapp
J. M. Rice
*J. Rudisch
*John Van Der Poel
Julius Weiss

SURGEONS	PHYSICIANS
1884 *James L. Shiland	1884 Edward Burns
*Walter Hitchcock	Charles H. May
1885 *J. Clark Steward	1885 Arthur B. Coffin
*Herman J. Schiff	*Josephine Walter
	*Charles F. Mason
1886 *F. C. Husson	1886 *E. L. H. Swift
*Alfred N. Strouse	*Edward J. Ware
1887 *William H. Wilmer	1887 Charles G. Giddings
*H. S. Stark	*Abraham Korn
1888 Guy C. Rich	1888 *E. H. Walsh
Howard Lilienthal	*H. E. Sanderson
1889 L. J. Ladin	1889 *Simon D. Elsner
Geo. B. Cowell	G. L. Nicholas
1890 Samuel L. Weber	1890 R. H. Cunningham
A. D. Mewborn	*Max Jackson
1891 *Southgate Leigh	1891 *Fred S. Mandlebaum
David B. Lovell	H. P. Palmer
1892 *Edwin C. Sternberger	1892 *E. C. Levy
	Percy H. Fridenberg
1893 Geo. L. Broadhead	1893 Henry A. Cone
*S. M. Brickner	
1894 Martin W. Ware	1894 *W. Jarvis Barlow
Thomas T. Tuttle	
1895 Charles A. Elsberg	1895 *Sidney Yankauer
*Nathan Breiter	*J. Ralston Lattimore
1896 Albert A. Berg	1896 Emanuel Libman
*William H. Luckett	William P. Loth
1897 Charles Goodman	1897 Herman B. Baruch
J. B. Morrison	Sidney V. Haas
1898 *Harry Rodman	1898 Louis Hauswirth
*Walter M. Brickner	
1899 Sidney Ulfelder	1899 William G. Eckstein
L. W. Allen	A. F. Foord
1900 Leo B. Meyer	1900 Israel Strauss
Eugene H. Eising	

189

GRADUATES OF THE HOUSE STAFF

(Continued)

SURGEONS		PHYSICIANS	
1901	M. Thorner Truman Abbe	1901	*I. W. Becker Herman Schwarz
1902	*Edwin Beer Major G. Seelig	1902	*Edward A. Aronson Milton Gerschel
1903	*Meyer M. Stark Robert T. Frank Eli Moschcowitz	1903	*Herbert L. Celler *Alfred Fabian Hess David Kramer
1904	D. Lee Hischler Albert G. Swift Fred H. MacCarthy C. F. Jellinghaus	1904	Bernard S. Oppenheimer Arthur Bookman *H. F. L. Ziegel Louis Bauman
1905	Sol. Hyman Isadore Seff William J. Haber Horace Leiter	1905	Geo. W. T. Mills *Samuel Feldstein *Gustav A. Fried *Leo Kessel
1906	C. Morris Hathaway Milton Bodenheimer Ernest Sachs Solomon Wiener	1906	Julius J. Hertz Jesse G. M. Bullowa Julian J. Meyer Max Taschman
1907	Orville H. Schell Eben Alexander, Jr. Aims R. Chamberlain Harold Neuhof	1907	Alfred E. Cohn *Louis Jacobs *Louis G. Kaempfer *Walter J. Highman
1908	John C. A. Gerster Abraham Hyman Isidor C. Rubin	1908	*Jacob Wisansky Abraham E. Jaffin Albert A. Epstein Max Scheer
1909	Howard E. Lindeman Herbert D. Mandelbaum *Charles Ryttenberg Fred. G. Oppenheimer	1909	Abraham Sophian Joseph Rosenthal *Maurice T. Munker Murray H. Bass
1910	Abraham O. Wilensky Benjamin F. May George Baehr Samuel H. Geist	1910	Bernard H. Eliasberg Burrill B. Crohn *Milton Hahn Richard H. Hoffmann
1911	Louis Greenberg Philip Liebling Irving Simons Leo Mayer	1911	Harry Wessler Nathaniel Barnett H. W. Emsheimer Hiram Olsan
1912	Herman Jaffe Sidney Cohn Isidor Kross Julius Blum	1912	Salo N. Weber *Morris H. Kahn *Abraham Zingher Meyer Rosensohn
1913	Abraham J. Beller Oscar Baumann Jesse D. Schwartz Ira Cohen	1913	*Alexander Hofheimer Jacob Sachs Edward Mahler Daniel Poll

GRADUATES OF THE HOUSE STAFF

(Continued)

SURGEONS	PHYSICIANS
1914 Hyman R. Miller C. Koenigsberger Edward Bleier Abraham Strauss	1914 Arthur S. Rosenfeld Maurice F. Lautman John L. Kantor Louis H. Levy
1915 Ralph M. Bruckheimer Sol. Shlimbaum Paul W. Aschner *John F. Grattan	1915 A. I. Loewenthal David Beck Louis G. Shapiro Jacob Piller
1916 Joseph A. Landy Nathan Rosenthal Adolf A. Weiss Waldemar R. Metz	1916 Willard D. Mayer Lester J. Unger Ernst P. Boas Joseph Harkavy
1917 Harry C. Saltzstein David M. Natanson Max D. Mayer Leo Edelman	1917 Harry Plotz Charles G. Giddings, Jr. Louis Berman William Rosenson
1918 *Eugene Klein Louis Carp Samuel Kahn Julius Gottesman Leopold Brahdy Lewis T. Mann	1918 Joseph Felsen William Friedman Max Harrison Reuben Steinholz Harold T. Hyman Louis Hausman
1919 Herman Sharlit Morris Brooks Morris A. Goldberger Emanuel Salwen Joseph A. Lazarus Barney M. Kully Henry S. Fischer Jerome M. Ziegler	1919 Jerome L. Kohn Asher Winkelstein Edward Hollander Irving R. Roth Abraham Kardiner Kaufman Wallach
1920 Leo J. Hahn Charles Green Rudolph Kramer Samuel Hirshfeld Max Schneider *Harold L. Meierhof	1920 Ira M. Olsan Leo Loewe Philip Finkle Edward Lehman Harry D. Pasachoff Nathan Sobel
1921 Laurence Jones William Harris Martin A. Furman Leonard M. Lyons Sylvan D. Manheim Joseph B. Stenbuck	1921 Morris J. Lavine Saul A. Ritter Benj. B. Eichner Philip Astrowe Frederic D. Zeman Alton M. Amsterdam
1922 Joseph M. Marcus Samuel Silbert Percy Klingenstein Joseph S. Somberg Henry Milch Samuel Gaines	1922 Nathan Muskin Sydney C. Feinberg Samuel Z. Levine David Gaberman David Soletsky Leon Ginzburg

SURGEONS	PHYSICIANS
1923 Benj. N. Berg	1923 Samuel Rosen
Julian B. Herrmann	Samuel Rosenfeld
Arthur H. Aufses	Arthur M. Master
Louis Kleinfeld	Louis Hodes
Saul S. Samuels	Philip Cohen
Edwin A. Seidman	William S. Collens
1924 Seth Selig	1924 Roland I. Grausman
David Warshaw	Alfred M. Goltman
Seymour Wimpfheimer	Coleman B. Rabin
Sidney Friedman	Ephraim Shorr
Elias L. Stern	Robert K. Lambert
Gordon D. Oppenheimer	David Ball
1925 Robert K. Lippmann	1925 Leon Goldsmith
Edward A. Horowitz	Benj. Eliasoph
Robert H. Feldman	Richard M. Brickner
Martin Schreiber	Harold A. Abramson
Leon Ginzburg	Alfred E. Fischer
Irving A. Frisch	Harry I. Weinstock
1926 *A. Philip Zemansky, Jr.	1926 Harry Schwartz
Edward O. Finestone	J. Lester Kobacker
Mayer E. Ross	Nathan Cherwin
Edward J. Bassen	Harry S. Mackler
Samuel Mufson	Joseph Laval
Clarence K. Weil	David Wexler
1927 Ernest E. Arnheim	1927 Abraham L. Goldwyn
Walter F. Welton	William J. Bearman
Hyman Rosenfeld	Ameil Glass
Arthur S. W. Touroff	Milton J. Matzner
1928 Moses Swick	1928 Jacob E. Holzman
Abraham Firestone	Elmer S. Gais
Sidney Grossman	Abraham L. Kornzweig
William H. Mencher	*John Cohen
1929 William Leifer	1929 Samuel H. Averbuck
Sidney Hirsch	Joseph Uttal
Monroe A. Rosenbloom	Herman Zazeela
Robert L. Craig	Alfred Romanoff
1930 Lester R. Tuchman	1930 Solomon Silver
Ameil Glass	Samuel Melamed
Isidore Schapiro	William J. Hochbaum
William L. Ferber	Shirley H. Baron
1931 Maurice M. Berck	1931 Sylvan E. Moolten
Lyon Steine	Arthur Schifrin
Borris A. Kornblith	*Herbert M. Klein
Herbert S. Talbot	Rose Spiegel
1932 Samuel H. Klein	1932 Arthur R. Sohval
Erwin K. Gutmann	Robert V. Sager
Joseph A. Gaines	Albert B. Newman
William Sheinfeld	William M. Hitzig

GRADUATES OF THE HOUSE STAFF

(Continued)

SURGEONS		PHYSICIANS	
1933	Perry S. Horenstein	1933	Herman S. Roth
	H. Evans Leiter		Frederick Bridge
	Abraham J. Gitlitz		Jacob E. Stern
	Alexander H. Rosenthal		Saul W. Jarcho
1934	Meyer Abrahams	1934	Hyman Levy
	Sidney Rosenburg		Harry L. Jaffe
	Jacob S. Goltman		Abraham Penner
	Leonard J. Druckerman		Frederick H. Theodore
1935	Albert Schein	1935	David A. Dantes
	Emanuel Klempner		Israel Schiller
	Edward E. Jemerin		Sheppard Siegal
	Herman J. Meisel		Benjamin Rubin
1936	Irving A. Sarot	1936	Milton Mendlowitz
	Paul Kaufman		Henry Dolger
	Sidney M. Silverstone		Morton W. Willis
	Alan N. Leslie		Morris F. Steinberg
1937	Gabriel P. Seley	1937	Samuel Nisnewitz
	Leon G. Berman		Edward R. Schlesinger
	Herman R. Nayer		Sidney L. Penner
	Ralph W. Flax		Eugene Somkin
	Robert C. Elitzik		Edgar A. Baron
	Nathan Mintz		Morton Yohalem
1938	Julius L. Weissberg	1938	Samuel C. Bukantz
	Vernon A. Weinstein		Max Ellenberg
	Abner Kurtin		S. Zelig Sorkin
	Sylvan Bloomfield		Robert A. Newburger
	Leonard S. Bases		Ralph E. Moloshok
	Leon N. Greene		Sydney G. Margolin

ONE-YEAR INTERNS AND EXTERNS

1898 L. A. S. Bodine
      W. M. Lazard
1899 E. A. Rosenberg
      E. D. Lederman
      *A. W. Roff
1900 Edward J. Miller
      *Chas. E. Rosenwasser
      J. Howard Staub
1901 Leon Bandler
      *Eugene P. Bernstein
1902 S. S. Goldwater
1906 Kaufman Schlivek
      *Isadore Goldstein
      William Branower
      Isadore Kaufman
1907 B. Rein
      Edgar D. Oppenheimer
      P. Fiaschi
      Jerome S. Leopold
1908 *Wm. I. Wallach
      M. Reuben
      M. C. Pease, Jr.
      Michael Barsky
1909 H. C. Fleming
      E. W. Abramowitz
      Wm. Lapatnikoff
      E. M. Carson
      I. Shapiro
      Jerome Roemer
1910 Charles Gluck
      Mark Cohen
      Jerome Zuckerman
      Charles Gottlieb
      Ralph H. Goss
1911 D. Tannenbaum
      Arthur J. Bendick
      *J. J. Fabian
      *Hugo Blum
      William Thalhimer
      Clarence Brown
1912 Harry G. Goldman
      Saul Levy
      Harold A. Cohen
      Samuel Wetchler
      *Samuel Silverman
      Abraham J. Newman
      Carl C. Franken

1913 S. Aronowitz
      Oscar L. Levin
      A. Levy
      *Marcus A. Rothschild
      M. Lobsenz
      H. L. Sherman
      S. Genovese
1914 C. G. Ratner
      *J. S. Meltzer
      W. Rosen
      A. Unger
      T. Halpern
      D. H. Bluestone
      A. Mendelson
1915 J. Sinkowitz
      D. Kronman
      I. Pelzman
      J. Haimann
      I. W. Jacobs
      A. Brody
1916 *J. L. Furst
      M. A. Sager
      *J. A. Rosenberg
      Joseph Reiss
      I. Rosen
      L. L. Roth
1917 M. Varzahbedian
      *H. Martinson
      A. Jerskey
      J. Rosenfeld
      Louis Nahum
      J. J. Wiener
      B. E. Strode
1918 A. Altschul
      Samuel K. Levy
      Leon Antell
      W. Sellinger
      M. J. Radin
      Max Dobrin
      Jacob Branower
1920 Harold Rypins
      S. S. Dann
1923 Sol. S. Lichtman
1924 M. Biederman
      M. L. Guttmacher
      Max Brahdy
      Isabel Beck

* Deceased.

194

1925 Wm. B. Rose
Julius Kavee
Gertrude Felshin

1926 Emanuel W. Benjamin
Eli Y. Shorr

1927 Harry Weiss
Sidney D. Leader
Paul S. Rosenberg
Walter Bromberg
Ben. Z. Steine
Hudythe M. Levin
Moses R. Buchman
S. I. Kooperstein
Herman Slass

1928 Murray A. Last
P. Goolker
William Chester
J. Fuhrman Heinrich
Isabel Globus
S. P. Carp
Sidney D. Leader
Harry Rosenwasser
Harry Feld

1929 George Frumkes
Michael C. Kemelhor
Louis Schneider
Saul Miller
Bernard S. Brody
Marcy L. Sussman
David Beres

1930 Harold A. Abel
Charles K. Friedberg
Harry Keil
Clement H. Golden
Henry A. Baron
Sidney Housman
Charles Sutro
Herbert Lampert
Nathan H. Sachs

1931 Hyman Lieber
Edward B. Greenspan
Harry Yarnis

1931 Henry Peskin
Robert H. Abrahamson
Ralph T. Levin
Max L. Som
Bernard Amsterdam

1932 David R. Levine
Bernard Amsterdam
Samuel A. Feldman
Sidney E. Lenke
Irving Kowaloff
Alice I. Bernheim
Charles J. Sage
Carl Zelson
F. J. de Frume

1933 Benjamin Allen
Bension Calef
Simon Dack
Edward Greenberger
Harold W. Keschuer
Arnold Treitman
Fred R. Schechter
Robert Ullman
I. Oscar Weisman

1934 Meyer Emanuel
Ralph W. Flax
Sidney L. Gottlieb
David Littauer
M. Edward Hipsh
Charles W. Rieber
Louis M. Rosati
Jandon Schwarz

1935 Albert D. Kistin
Vernon A. Weinstein
Morris M. Kessler
William Finkelstein
Herman I. Kantor
Jean Pakter
William Epstein
M. Edward Hipsh
Samuel B. Weiner

1936 Simon H. Nagler
Samuel M. Bloom
Max Ellenberg
Jean Pakter

INTERNS IN PATHOLOGY

1913 Paul W. Aschner
1914 Harry Plotz
1915 William Rosenson
1916 Julius Gottesman
1917 Lewis T. Mann
1918 Martin Vorhaus
1919 Maurice Rashbaum
1920 Percy Klingenstein
1921 Saul S. Samuels
1922 Sol. S. Lichtman
1923 Martin Schreiber
1924 Lionel S. Auster
    Clarence K. Weil
1925 Abraham Firestone
1926 William Leifer
    Alfred Romanoff
1927 Irving Nachamie
    S. David Glusker
1928 Henry H. Lichtenberg
    Arthur Schifrin

1929 Reuben Cares
    Harry Moskowitz
1930 Harold A. Aaron
    Victor H. Kugell
1931 Sidney E. Lenke
    Jacob S. Goltman
1932 Sidney Licht
1933 Milton Mendlowitz
    Irving A. Sarot
1934 Leon G. Berman
    *Milton Steiner
1935 Samuel C. Bukantz
    Nathan Mintz
1936 Nathan S. Hiatt
    Joseph M. Szilagyi
1937 Alexander Thomas
    Bernard S. Wolf
1938 Tibor J. Greenwalt
    Daniel Luger

INTERNS, EXTERNS AND RESIDENTS IN RADIOLOGY

1921 Sidney H. Levy
1922 Rubin Lavine
    Barnett P. Freedman
1923 Harry S. Olin
    Harry Gross
1924 Irving Schwartz
    Max Newer
1925 Jacob R. Freid
    Nathaniel H. Robin
    Emanuel J. Wexler
1926 William Snow
    Sol. Taubin
1927 Albert Kean
    Samuel Poplack
    Samuel Sinberg
1928 Carye-Belle Henle
    Benjamin J. Sax
    Emanuel W. Benjamin

1929 Myer E. Golan
    Charles Lipsky
    Samuel Richman
1930 Isidore Klein
    Saul J. Tomarkin
1931 Harry Herscher
1932 Simon Shulman
    Louis E. Zaretski
    Gerald J. Bernath
1933 Mitchell Burdick
    Gayland L. Hagelshaw
1934 Israel Kirsh
    Edward D. Sherman
1936 Irving I. Cowan
    Joseph Jellen
    Benjamin Copleman
1937 Max Schenck
    Marston T. Woodruff
1938 Arnold Bachman
    Robert J. Ruby

RESIDENT STAFF

PRIVATE AND SEMI-PRIVATE PAVILIONS

SURGEONS		PHYSICIANS	
1905	Albert G. Swift		
1906	Edwin A. Riesenfeld		
1907	Milton Bodenheimer		
1908	Wm. Branower	1908	Julius Kaunitz
1909	Eben Alexander, Jr.	1909	J. Russell Verbrycke
	Harold Neuhof		
1910	Abraham E. Jaffin	1910	*Jacob Wisansky
1911	J. C. Wooldridge	1911	Joseph Rosenthal
1912	J. Irving Fort	1912	Oris S. Warr
	A. O. Wilensky		
1913	J. W. Brennan	1913	A. B. James
	J. E. King		
1914	A. J. Beller	1914	B. M. Dear
	H. E. Schorr		*Morris H. Kahn
1915	Jesse D. Schwartz	1915	Edward Mahler
1916	*H. S. Marcley	1916	Joseph D. Kelley
	Edward Bleier		
1917	Sol Shlimbaum	1917	Joseph Reiss
	J. Ramsay Crawford		
	Joseph A. Landy		
1918	Adolf A. Weiss	1918	Joseph Rosenfeld
	David M. Natanson		
1919	Max D. Mayer	1919	Hubert Mann
	G. D. Von Deylen		
	Milton S. Fine		
1920	Wm. A. Flick	1920	Louis Sacks
	Thomas J. Sullivan		
	Joseph Lazarus		
1921	Arnold Messing	1921	Selian Hebald
	Paul S. Lowenstein		
1922	Joseph Heyman	1922	A. Isaacman
	L. W. Fritchett		
1923	Benjamin Kogut	1923	Stanley S. Myers
	Edward Lorentzen		
	Samuel Gaines		
1924	Seymour F. Wilhelm	1924	Bernard Appel
	Ernst Springer		
	Abram A. Weiss		
	A. J. Sparks		
	Elias Rubin (10 months)		

* Deceased.

197

RESIDENT STAFF

PRIVATE AND SEMI-PRIVATE PAVILIONS
(Continued)

SURGEONS		PHYSICIANS	
1925	Franklin I. Harris	1925	Samuel Schindelhelm
	George S. Lachman		
	Elias L. Stern		
	Nathaniel H. Blumenkranz		
1926	Norman F. Laskey		
	Samuel Hochman		
	Edward O. Finestone		
1927	Joseph M. Frehling	1927	Abraham M. Schaefer
	M. Lester Levy		
	C. D. Moore		
1928	Harold W. Goldberg	1928	Henry Z. Goldstein
	Edward Jacobs		
	Myron A. Sallick		
	David Sloane		
1929	Jacob J. Enkelis	1929	Max E. Panitch
	Samuel S. Hanflig		
	Robert I. Hiller		
	Bernard D. Kulick		
1930	Samuel Imboden	1930	Bernard S. Brody
	Samuel P. Suffin		
	Eske H. Windsberg		
1931	Sidney Rosenburg	1931	Harold A. Abel
	Henry A. Baron		
	Lyon Steine		
1932	David A. Susnow	1932	Harry Yarnis
	Joseph Tomarkin		
	Erwin K. Gutmann		
	Meyer Corff		
1933	Joseph Tartakoff	1933	Frank A. Bassen
	Robert Turell		
	Perry S. Horenstein		
1934	H. Evans Leiter		
	Robert H. Abrahamson		
	Arthur J. Harris		
1935	Meyer Abrahams	1935	Abraham Penner
	Zachary R. Cottler		
	Albert M. Schwartz		
	Jerome Gross		
	Anthony Kohn		
	Leonard J. Druckerman		
1936	Leo H. Pollock		
	Seebert J. Goldowsky		
	Edward E. Jemerin	1936	Samuel Baer
	Irwin P. Train		

RESIDENT STAFF

PRIVATE AND SEMI-PRIVATE PAVILIONS
(Continued)

SURGEONS

1937 Ernest D. Bloomenthal
   Aaron Prigot
   Meyer L. Goldman
   Louis Scheman
   Leon M. Caplan
   Sigmund A. Siegel
   Gabriel P. Seley

1938 Julian A. Jarman
   Philip Cooper
   Ralph W. Flax
   Lawrence Essenson
   Benjamin Gitlitz
   H. Earle Tucker

PHYSICIANS

1937 David E. Scheinberg
   William Finkelstein
   Albert Cornell

1938 Herman G. Helpern
   Philip M. Gottlieb

199

WARD SERVICES

Neurology

1924	William Malamud
	David Rothschild
1925	M. Weinstock Bergman
	David I. Arbuse
1926	Herman G. Selinsky
1927	Sol W. Ginsburg
	Jacob J. Kasanin
1928	Lewis J. Doshay
	Walter Bromberg
1929	William Berman
	Isabel Globus
1930	P. Goolker
	Lewis H. Loeser
1931	Paul Sloane
	Bernard S. Brody
1932	William Schick
	Samuel A. Sandler
	Louis Levenstim
1933	Daniel E. Schneider
	Jacob H. Friedman
1934	Abraham Blau
	Morris B. Bender
1935	Norman Reider
1936	Sidney Tarachow
	Norman A. Levy
1937	Morris M. Kessler
	Laurence M. Weinberger
	Jerome E. Alderman
1938	Mark G. Kanzer
	Edwin A. Weinstein

Pediatrics

1924	Philip Cohen
	Alfred Nathans
1925	E. Gordon Stoloff
	Isabel Beck
1926	Samuel Karelitz
	Samuel J. Levin
1927	Alfred E. Fischer
	Gustave F. Weinfeld
1928	Abbot L. Winograd
	Harry S. Mackler
1929	Moses R. Buchman
	Sidney D. Leader
1930	David Beres
	Peter Vogel
1931	Jacob L. Rothstein
	A. E. Cohen
1932	George J. Ginandes.
	Albert A. Rosenberg
1933	Martin L. Stein
	Carl Zelson
1934	Louise Rauh
1935	Jacob Brem
	Samuel Ehre
1936	Howard C. Leopold
	Sidney Blumenthal
1937	Arthur Lesser
	Samuel B. Weiner
	Jean Pakter
1938	Howard G. Rapaport
	David B. Davis

Oto-Laryngology

1924	Louis Kleinfeld
1925	Samuel Rosen
1927	Joseph G. Druss
1928	Irving B. Goldman
1929	Ben Z. Steine
1930	Harry Rosenwasser
1931	Joseph L. Goldman
1932	William J. Hochbaum
1933	Max L. Som

Gynecology

1924	Arthur Katzenstein
	Karl Polifka
1925	Morris R. Matus
	Seymour Wimpfheimer
1926	Howard A. Power
	Edward A. Horowitz
1927	Frank Spielman
1928	Jacques D. Soifer
	Alan F. Guttmacher
1929	Oscar Glassman
1930	Benj. E. Urdan
	Maurice Feresten
1931	Irving Nachamie
	Mervin A. Henschel
1932	Phineas Bernstein
	Henry A. Baron
1933	Joseph A. Gaines

RESIDENT STAFF

WARD SERVICES
(Continued)

Oto-Laryngology		Gynecology	
1934	Eugene R. Snyder	1934	Sidney N. Mendelsohn
			U. J. Salmon
1935	Benj. I. Allen	1935	Robert Turell
			H. Melvin Radman
		1936	Emanuel Klempner
1937	A. H. Neffson	1937	Robert I. Walter
			Norman Margolius
			Herbert F. Newman
1938	Lester L. Coleman	1938	Arthur M. Davids
			Phoenix M. Sales

Ophthalmology

1928	David Wexler	1934	Abraham L. Kornzweig
1929	Robert K. Lambert	1935	Nathan S. Rubin
1930	Murray A. Last	1936	Frederick H. Theodore
1931	Saul Miller	1937	Jacob Goldsmith
1932	Herman I. Weiss	1938	Morris Greenberg
1933	Samuel L. Saltzman		

Orthopedics

1938　Samuel R. Rubert

INTERNS IN DENTISTRY

1933	Marvin G. Freid	1936	Robert S. Gilbert
	Herbert L. Goodfleish		Manuel Gottlieb
1934	Henry I. Cohen	1937	Ben Pine
	Harry A. Suslow		Robert W. Slutzky
1935	Louis Kroll	1938	Robert S. Hess
			Lee R. Kulick

ADMITTING PHYSICIANS

1908-1911	Max Rosenberg	1928	Sidney Grossman
1912-1913	Herbert W. Emsheimer	1928	Elmer S. Gais
1914-1915	Daniel Poll	1929	Samuel H. Averbuck
1916	David Beck	1930	Herman Zazeela
1917-1918	Joseph Harkavy	1931	Isidore Schapiro
1919	Asher Winkelstein	1931-1933	Rose Spiegel
1920-1921	Philip Finkle	1934	Herman S. Roth
1922	Leon Ginzburg	1935	Hyman Levy
1923	Arthur M. Master	1936	Alfred Dantes
1924	Coleman B. Rabin	1937	Alan N. Leslie
1925-1927	Lewis E. Persoff	1938	Herman I. Kantor

EIGHTY-SEVENTH

ANNUAL REPORT

OF

THE MOUNT SINAI HOSPITAL

OF THE

CITY OF NEW YORK

For the Year 1939

Act of Incorporation Filed February, 1852

CONTENTS

2

Extracts from the Constitution on Endowed Beds and Other Endowment Funds

A contribution of $2,500 to the general funds of the corporation, if accepted by the Board of Trustees, shall endow a Life Bed. Such contribution shall entitle the donor thereof, during his or her lifetime, to name a patient from time to time to occupy one bed in the wards of the Hospital, free of charge.

A contribution of $3,500 to the general funds of the corporation, if accepted by the Board of Trustees, shall endow a Memorial Bed. Such a contribution shall entitle the donor thereof, during his or her lifetime, to name a patient from time to time to occupy one bed in the wards of the Hospital, free of charge. Such donor may bequeath that right to a successor appointed by the said donor in his or her last will and testament, or by any other instrument under seal. In the event of such successor being appointed, the rights hereinbefore mentioned shall continue for a period of not over fifty years from the date of such contribution, provided, however, that such period shall be extended so that it shall in no event end until ten years after the death of the donor.

A contribution of $5,000 to the general funds of the corporation, if accepted by the Board of Trustees, shall endow a Perpetual Bed in the Children's Pavilion. Such contribution shall entitle the donor thereof, during his or her lifetime, to name a patient from time to time to occupy one bed in the wards of the Children's Pavilion free of charge. Such donor may bequeath that right to a successor appointed by said donor in his or her last will and testament or by any other instrument under seal. When a corporation is the donor, the privilege shall expire at the end of twenty-five years from the date of such contribution.

A contribution of $7,500 to the general funds of the corporation, if accepted by the Board of Trustees, shall endow a Perpetual Bed, but where, under the provision of any will executed prior to March 20, 1921, the sum of $5,000 or more is bequeathed to the corporation in payment of any Perpetual Bed, the Board of Trustees may, at their option, accept such sum in payment of such Perpetual Bed. Such contribution shall entitle the donor thereof, during his or her lifetime, to name a patient from time to time to occupy one bed in a ward of the Hospital, free of charge. Such donor may bequeath that right to a successor appointed by said donor in his or her last will and testament, or by any other instrument under seal. When a corporation is the donor, the privilege shall expire at the end of twenty-five years from the date of such contribution.

Tablets to commemorate the endowment of Life, Memorial and Perpetual Beds shall be placed in a ward or in such other place as may be set aside for the purpose. Tablets for Life Beds shall be maintained during the life of the donor. Tablets for Memorial Beds shall be maintained for a period not beyond fifty years from the date of their endowment, provided, however, that such period shall be extended so that it shall in no event end until ten years after the death of the donor. Tablets for Perpetual Beds shall be maintained in perpetuity.

A donor may change a Life Bed endowed by him or her to a Memorial Bed by making an additional contribution of $1,000 or to a Perpetual Bed by making an additional contribution of $5,000, or may change a Memorial Bed to a Perpetual Bed by making an additional contribution of $4,000.

No patient shall be admitted to the privileges pertaining to a Life, Memorial or Perpetual Bed unless he shall comply with the current rules of the corporation and be a proper subject for treatment under its regulations.

An endowment for the establishment of any special fund may be accepted by a resolution of the Board of Trustees. Such fund may be created for special or general purposes under the name of one or more persons or otherwise. If created for a special purpose the fund shall be used only for that purpose. Additions to any fund may be made at any time and in any amount, but no fund shall be created with an initial endowment of less than Ten Thousand Dollars.

Gifts of any sums whatsoever may be made to one or more special funds for non-budgetary purposes, the principal and income of which may be appropriated by the Board of Trustees as the needs may arise for purposes not covered by the regular budget of the corporation.

In the case of a bequest which does not in all respects conform to the conditions herein set forth, the Board of Trustees may, in its discretion, accept the same in accordance with the provisions of such bequest.

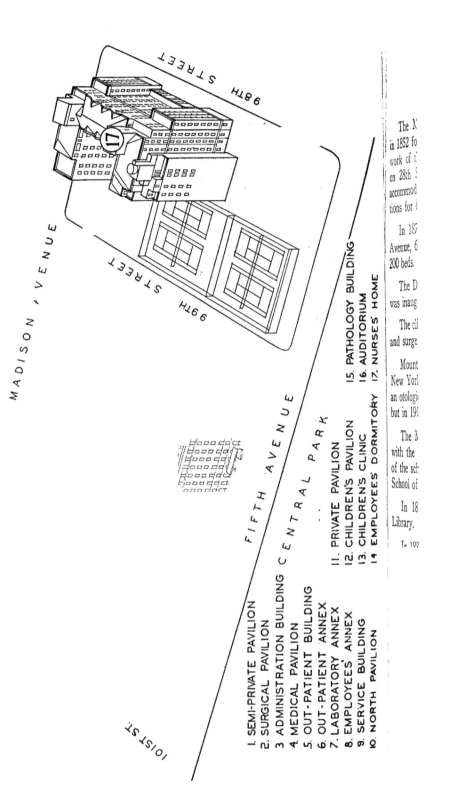

MADISON AVENUE

98TH STREET

99TH STREET

FIFTH AVENUE

CENTRAL PARK

101ST ST.

1. SEMI-PRIVATE PAVILION
2. SURGICAL PAVILION
3. ADMINISTRATION BUILDING
4. MEDICAL PAVILION
5. OUT-PATIENT BUILDING
6. OUT-PATIENT ANNEX
7. LABORATORY ANNEX
8. EMPLOYEES' ANNEX
9. SERVICE BUILDING
10. NORTH PAVILION
11. PRIVATE PAVILION
12. CHILDREN'S PAVILION
13. CHILDREN'S CLINIC
14. EMPLOYEES' DORMITORY
15. PATHOLOGY BUILDING
16. AUDITORIUM
17. NURSES' HOME

The M
in 1852 fo
work of t
on 28th S
accommod
tions for 8

In 187
Avenue, 6
200 beds.

The D
was inaug

The cli
and surge

Mount
New York
an otologi
but in 191

The M
with the
of the sch
School of

In 18
Library,

In 193

HISTORICAL NOTE

The Mount Sinai Hospital was organized and incorporated in 1852 for "benevolent, charitable and scientific purposes." The work of the Hospital was begun in a small four-story building on 28th Street, between Seventh and Eighth Avenues, which accommodated 28 patients. The Hospital now has accommodations for 856 patients, including 18 beds in the receiving ward.

In 1872 the Hospital completed and occupied, at Lexington Avenue, 66th and 67th Streets, a building having a capacity of 200 beds.

The Dispensary, now known as the Out-Patient Department, was inaugurated in 1873.

The clinical departments first organized were those of medicine and surgery; a gynecologist was appointed in 1877.

Mount Sinai created precedents among the hospitals of New York by setting up a distinct pediatric service in 1878 and an otologic service in 1879; the latter was at first combined with, but in 1910 was separated from, ophthalmology and laryngology.

The Mount Sinai Training School for Nurses, in affiliation with the Hospital, was incorporated in March, 1881; the name of the school was changed in 1923 to The Mount Sinai Hospital School of Nursing.

In 1883 a committee was formed to develop a Medical Library.

In 1886 a district medical service was inaugurated.

Formal provision for the care of private patients was made in 1886; an intermediate or "semi-private" ward was opened in 1904.

In 1893 a Pathological Department was established, and consultants in dermatology and neurology were appointed.

The corner stone of the group of ten hospital buildings occupying the block bounded by Fifth and Madison Avenues, 100th and 101st Streets, was laid May 22nd, 1901; the buildings were completed and occupied March 15th, 1904, when 500 beds became available for the care of the sick.

A Department of Dietetics was established in 1905.

A Social Service Department was inaugurated in 1906.

A Tuberculosis Clinic was organized in 1908.

The first of a series of "Fellowship" funds was created in 1908 to assist investigators engaged in scientific medical work.

The Hospital's first X-ray machine was installed in 1900. In 1910 a full-fledged Department of Radiology was formed and in 1924 the department was subdivided into separate branches for (a) radiography and (b) X-ray and radium therapy.

In 1910 the three-story Out-Patient Building, which had been completed in 1904 was altered to a five-story building, and the Nurses' Home was enlarged from a six-story to an eight-story building. At the same time new isolation wards were erected on the roof of the Medical Building.

A Dental Department was established for the benefit of in-patients in 1910; this work was extended to the Out-Patient Department in 1925.

An orthopedic surgeon and a physio-therapist were named in 1911.

Roof wards for outdoor treatment were erected on the Medical and Surgical Pavilions in 1912.

The Hospital in 1912 accepted a fund "for the advancement of preventive medicine." A "health class" for children was promptly established.

In 1913 the erection of seven additional buildings south of 100th Street was begun; four of these buildings were occupied in 1915, and three, namely, the Private Pavilion, the Children's Pavilion and the Auditorium, were completed in the spring of 1922. With these additions, the Hospital was able to care for 654 patients.

The first of a series of lectureship funds was established in 1913. These funds provide honoraria for distinguished visiting lecturers.

Electro-cardiography was instituted in 1915.

In 1917, Mount Sinai Hospital became a constituent member of the Federation for the Support of Jewish Philanthropic Societies, which was organized in that year.

6

Until 1917, tonsillectomies were performed in the Dispensary, often without anesthesia; in the year mentioned, a "tonsil and adenoid" ward, with a fully equipped operating room, was opened.

A Mount Sinai Hospital Unit, organized as a section of the Medical Department of the United States Army, was sent to France in 1918.

Post-Graduate medical instruction was formally organized in 1923, in affiliation with the College of Physicians and Surgeons of Columbia University.

A permanent fund for the support of medical research was inaugurated in 1925, prior to which research was precariously supported by occasional donations.

The construction of a new school and residence building for the School of Nursing, fronting on 98th Street, between Fifth and Madison Avenues, was begun in 1925 and completed in 1927; the residence accommodates 490 nurses.

The new Semi-Private Pavilion for the care of patients of moderate means was completed and opened to the public in 1931.

Group or cooperative special nursing was introduced for the first time in 1931.

A Consultation Service for ambulant out-patients of moderate means was organized in 1931.

Neuro-surgery was included in General Surgery until 1932, when a separate service was created.

The modernization of the Out-Patient Department Building was completed in 1933.

New facilities for cystoscopy were built and occupied in 1933.

In 1934, the vacant former laboratory on 101st Street, was renovated and restored to use, providing space for a number of exiled German scientists and others.

Renovation and modernization of the Medical and Surgical Pavilions, part of the group of 10 buildings built in 1901, was begun in 1935 and completed in 1936.

The Isolation Ward was rebuilt in 1936 and, with the approval of the Department of Health, became the first Isolation Unit in New York City to be made available for use of private patients.

The Clinical Photographic Department, on a volunteer basis for more than a score of years, was established on a full time basis in 1936.

The Research Foundation of The Mount Sinai Hospital was incorporated in 1936 "to conduct, promote, encourage, and assist investigation in the services and arts of hygiene, medicine, and surgery and allied subjects."

Renovation of the Administration Building—after more than 30 years of use—was undertaken in 1937 and completed in 1938, providing enlarged facilities for Physiotherapy, Hydrotherapy, Occupational Therapy, Dentistry and other diagnostic and therapeutic services. Improved classroom and amphitheatre facilities for postgraduate medical instruction were also provided.

In 1939 a close affiliation was arranged with The Neustadter Foundation making it the Convalescent Branch of the Mount Sinai Hospital.

STATISTICAL SUMMARY

Year	Patients Treated in Hospital	Hospital Days	Consultations in Out-Patient Department	Total Disbursements for all Maintenance and Non-Budgetary Purposes (Non-Capital)
1857	216	6,048*	None	$9,000.00
1860	297	8,316*	None	14,000.00
1870	663	18,564*	None	20,000.00
1880	1,474	43,164	9,922	44,376.10
1890	2,862	65,255	43,560	100,000.00
1900	3,145	75,113	86,431	135,272.00
1910	7,613	149,198	115,726	410,000.00
1920	9,548	146,841	173,682	899,704.97
1930	12,179	193,482	222,489	1,785,244.23
1938	16,657	231,243	343,862	2,329,674.17
1939	17,360	232,292	343,041	2,374,088.01

* Estimated.

8

REPORT OF THE PRESIDENT

The close of 1939 marked ten years, beginning in 1930, of a period of disturbing and mixed experiences for the Hospital. There were highlights and low shadows. There were heartwarming advances and heartbreaking retreats. On the side of new medical procedures, I might mention sulfanilamide, sulfapyridine, fever therapy, the Shwartzman Phenomenon and the intravenous drip therapy for the rapid treatment of syphilis. On the economic side, discouragements were many—temporary payroll cuts, heavy budgetary losses, unemployment and the impact of refugee physicians and patients. All in all it was an exciting decade, one which I hope to review in greater detail, as it affected Mount Sinai Hospital, in a later report.

Among the casualties of the decade was our general purpose fund, euphemistically called the "Permanent Fund." It was our fond hope before 1930 that this fund, which had been growing slowly but steadily over the years, would in time, with the help of the Hospital's many friends, become an endowment sufficient in amount to assure in a fair measure the future financial security of the charitable work of the Hospital. It had never been the expectation or even the hope that this fund would become large enough in itself to make the Hospital independent of current gifts, but it was, in a sense, a substantial fund and on its way to its second million when 1930 came upon us. The story in the past ten years can be epitomized in the statement that through these years the accumulated deficits have amounted to more than $1,700,000., and this fund has been used to meet such deficits. At this writing there are remaining in the fund quick assets of less than $400,000.

During these years, we have tried to maintain the standards which have made for Mount Sinai's reputation. 1939 was no exception to this rule. Our principal aim had been to maintain this same quality of service rather than to increase quantity for statistical aggrandizement. There was no expansion into newer and larger fields, but there was progress into better methods with the adoption of practices required by the most recent advances in scientific knowledge and medical practice.

Of physical changes there were few, the most important one being the installation of two Diesel-driven generators to take the place of the old power plant, which, after nearly 40 years of service, was worn out and was unable to carry the normal load and to

9

provide enough reserve to function in case of emergency. Much study was devoted to this problem by the Committee on Building under the able leadership of Mr. Benjamin Mordecai. The new plant has been functioning for several months and the anticipated saving in operating costs is being realized.

Several changes in staff organization were necessitated by modern medical advances and the need to improve departmental efficiency. Under this head I might mention the separation of the Radiotherapy from the Roentgenology Department, which heretofore had been organized as a single division. Part of the old high-voltage X-ray equipment of the Radiotherapy Department was replaced with a new and up-to-date modern unit, the cost being met by a special gift. Some of the 20-year old machines in the laundry were replaced by modern equipment in order to meet the ordinary laundering needs.

The total number of patients treated in the entire hospital in 1939 was 17,360, an increase of about 5% over 1938, and the total number of days' care to in-patients was 232,292, establishing a new high record. The largest number of bed patients in the Hospital in any one given day was 733, likewise the greatest number since the Hospital was founded.

In the Out-Patient Department there was an average daily attendance of 198 physicians, who gave a total of 343,041 consultations and treatments in 1939 as against 343,862 in 1938. In addition, 19,713 emergency treatments were given in the accident ward.

It is of interest to note that the Mount Sinai Hospital received from the United Hospital Fund the largest amount allotted for free work.

The Consultation Service which has continued to function most successfully in the interest of ambulant patients of moderate means admitted 2,829 individuals as against 2,786 in 1938.

The Private Pavilion, although not operating to capacity at all times, has met a real community need, and I am glad to say that the standard of service rendered has met with the approval of practically all of its patients. The Semi-private Pavilion has had a waiting list almost constantly, and here also we have been receiving many encouraging letters praising the care given its patients.

These few statistics may be dry reading but are none the less presented to show that without increase in the number of beds or size of the Hospital, the public is being served in increasing measure, and I think I may safely say, with improving results. Fuller statistical summaries will be found in other pages of this report.

The reconditioned amphitheatre, completed late in 1938 and first used in January 1939, has been steadily growing as a factor in the educational work of the institution. Surgical demonstrations and medical clinics are held there several times a week, often with every seat filled by physicians and medical students.

The clinical pathological conferences have again been held every week in the Blumenthal Auditorium and their value to the community seems to be appreciated increasingly each year. The average attendance was upwards of 450.

Another educational feature which has prospered during the year is the Journal of the Mount Sinai Hospital, which in its sixth year has increased in circulation by 8% over 1938. An indication of its increasing acceptance in medical circles is the listing of its articles in the Journal of the American Medical Association.

These opportunities and services as well as others to which I shall refer would not have been possible of accomplishment if we did not have the continuing loyal support of many friends who through legacies and donations have put the Hospital and the community under deep obligations by the following benefactions:

DEDICATION OF BEDS

Estate of Jacob Newman (on Account)—For the endowment of beds—In memory of Jacob Newman...$257,250.75

Perpetual Bed:

Ellen Ida Cardozo—Provided in the Will of Benjamin N. Cardozo 7,500.00

Children's Perpetual Bed:

In memory of Louise Renskorf—Provided in the Will of her mother, Millie H. Renskorf............ 5,000.00

Estate of Alfred Blumenthal—For the Alfred and Hannah Blumenthal Ward—(Received to 12/31/39 $69,132.63) 6,294.80

BEQUESTS

Estate of John Frankel ....

Estate of Flora Hirsh ....

Estate of Jerome Rice ....

Estate of Carl W. Stern—In memory of his mother,
Louise Marie Stern..

LEGACIES AND DONATIONS OF $500 AND MORE F
SPECIAL PURPOSES DURING YEAR 1939

Committee on Neighborhood Health Development, Inc.
—For Intravenous Drip Therapy Project....................

David A. Schulte—For Dental Clinic................................

Philip Lehman—To be used in the interest of the
Physical Therapy Department ....

Mount Sinai Hospital Research Foundation—To provide equipment for Dr. Shwartzman's research........

Estate of Amelia A. Meyers—For support of research
in Abraham and Amelia Meyers Memorial Labora-
tory (additional) ....

Josiah Macy, Jr. Foundation—To continue support of
studies on the secretion of a para-sympathetic substance under emotional stress.......................................

Mrs. Charles Klingenstein—For the Charles Klingenstein Fellowship Fund (additional)..............................

Dr. Ralph Colp—Toward Fellowship for gastro-
enterology research ....

The Friedsam Foundation, Inc.—For ear, nose and
throat research ....

The Friedsam Foundation, Inc.—For special hormone
research ....

"A Friend"—For a Fellowship in gynecology to commemorate the 76th birthday of Dr. Joseph Brettauer

Mrs. Walter A. Hirsch—In memory of Walter A.
Hirsch—For leukemia research ....

12

Mrs. Levy Mayer—In memory of Walter A. Hirsch—
For leukemia research 1,000.00

Mr. Joseph Klingenstein—For non-budgetary purposes 1,000.00

The Mount Sinai Hospital Research Foundation—For
venom research 900.00

Josiah Macy, Jr. Foundation—For research on psycho-
logical and physiological aspects of angina pectoris 750.00

John Wyeth & Brother, Inc.—For the study of the
continuous drip method in treatment of peptic ulcer 750.00

Dazian Foundation for Medical Research—To continue
support of neurophysiology research.............................. 500.00

Dazian Foundation for Medical Research—For gastric
physiology research 500.00

Dr. Percy Klingenstein—Toward Fellowship for gastro-
enterology research 500.00

Mr. and Mrs. Walter W. Naumburg—For Research
Fund 500.00

Max J. Shapiro—For support of neurology research... 500.00

DONATIONS OF $500 AND MORE FOR SUPPORT OF CANCER RESEARCH WORK OF DR. RICHARD LEWISOHN

New York Foundation.. $3,000.00

Frances and John Loeb Foundation............................ 2,500.00

Mrs. Arthur Lehman 2,500.00

Miss Adelaide Reckford 1,500.00

Ittleson Foundation 1,500.00

Adeline and Carl M. Loeb Foundation—In memory
of Lee J. Moses 1,000.00

Adelaide and Carl M. Loeb Foundation........................... 900.00

Mrs. Louis J. Grumbach 500.00

Total... $13,400.00

DONATIONS OF $500 AND MORE FOR CARDIO-VASCULAR RESEARCH

Mr. and Mrs. Frank Altschul	$1,000.00
Mrs. Charles Altschul	500.00
Anonymous	500.00
Frances and John Loeb Foundation	500.00
Mrs. Arthur M. Master	500.00
Total	$3,000.00

Mr. William Rosenwald presented to the Hospital a 3-ton air-conditioning unit, which was greatly needed to cool the telephone exchange room which is situated directly under the hot copper roof.

In a previous report there was reference to the establishment of a closer relationship with the Neustadter Home. During the past year this affiliation has become more definite, and as you will see from the report of its President, Mrs. Walter A. Hirsch, published in this volume, great progress has been made in making needed types of convalescent care available to patients of the Hospital. We are greatly indebted to the Officers and Board of Directors of the Home for their successful handling of a difficult subject.

We are particularly proud of the work done in our laboratories, both as to the dependability of its routine service and the worth of its research. Those interested in the scientific work of the Hospital will find detailed statements in the separate reports of the Medical Board and of the Laboratories. I wish merely in this place to acknowledge gratefully the fine work done by Drs. Klemperer, Shwartzman, Sobotka, Globus and their staffs, under the supervision of the Laboratory Administrative Committee to whose accomplishment Drs. Isidore Friesner and Robert T. Frank contributed generously of their time and effort.

In my last year's report I referred to the experiment in the intravenous drip method for rapid treatment of syphilis which was being carried on at that time. This work continued throughout 1939 with constantly improving results. It is expected that the experiment will be completed in 1940 at which time the results will be at the disposal of the United States Public Health Service and of the medical profession in general. We are indebted to the New York Foundation and the Friedsam Foundation for the continued support of this work which has been administered through the Committee on Neighborhood Health Development under the direction of Dr. Walter Clarke, Consultant to the Department of Health.

In an organization of the size of Mount Sinai Hospital, with its daily census of 600 to 700 in-patients, with its daily service to more than 1,100 out-patients, and with its volunteer medical staff of more than 800, with its full-time professional, nursing, technical, executive, administrative, maintenance and service staffs of more than 1,400, there are of necessity many changes in policy and in organization in the course of each year. Of these, I should like to refer to only a few.

A more comprehensive plan for giving financial assistance to members of the House Staff was put into effect in 1939, and it is believed that under the guidance of an understanding committee of the Board of Trustees, this plan will prove to be of definite help to these young men and women.

· The maximum ward rate for ward patients was established at $4.00 per day, in keeping with practices in leading and comparable metropolitan hospitals. The rate is, of course, reduced in suitable cases and is in fact remitted entirely in most cases, for, unfortunately, the majority of those who apply to us for medical service are unable to pay anything toward the cost of their care.

Salaries and wages paid in 1939 were nearly $57,000 more than in 1938, of which sum, $22,000 represents increases in rates of pay, most of which went to employees in the lower wage brackets, this being the sixth consecutive year of wage increases. The balance represents wages paid to new employees required by a program of shortening hours of service. As the shorter work-week was extended during the year to an additional number of employee categories, this of course necessitated additional employees to take care of the loss in hours of service. The same policy of reduction in hours was carried out in connection with nurses who are on duty in the wards of the Hospital.

To permit members on the House Staff to qualify for certificates and diplomas issued by the various American Boards for Specialties, a plan for residencies on a much broader scale than heretofore in vogue has been outlined with the hope of putting it into effect in the Fall of 1941.

As will be referred to at greater length in the report of the Social Service Department, the old building, formerly used as an employees' dormitory annex, is now used in part by the Social Service Workshop, a sheltered workshop attended by selected patients from the Out-Patient Department. This workshop is ably directed by Miss Edith Sachs and Mrs. Robert E. Binger.

At the annual meeting of the Medical Board, held in January, Dr. George Baehr was elected President of the Medical Board to succeed Dr. Isidore Friesner, who had for so many years as President sedulously guarded the interests of the institution. During the balance of the year, our Medical Staff under Dr. Baehr's able leadership has again devoted itself selflessly to the welfare of the Hospital and its patients. I find it difficult to give adequate expression for the fine work done by this group of men and women which, year in and year out, render such great service to the community.

A number of changes have, as usual, taken place on the staff. Dr. Bernard S. Oppenheimer, who, as Physician to the Hospital, was at the head of one of the medical services, resigned his position in December 1939 for reasons of health. Dr. Oppenheimer, who has won an enviable name as internist and cardiologist in the community, served this Hospital for over thirty-five years with the greatest devotion. We are truly sorry that he has found it necessary to sever his active connection with the Hospital but are pleased that he was willing to continue as consulting physician to which office he was appointed. Other changes on the staff are as follows:

New Appointments on the Medical Staff

Dr. Robert K. Lippmann.............................Orthopedist to Hospital

Dr. Seth Selig...Orthopedist to Hospital

Dr. Marcy L. Sussman.................................Radiologist to Hospital

Dr. Joseph G. Druss.....................................Associate Otologist

Dr. Lawrence S. Kubie ....Associate Psychiatrist

Dr. Ernst P. Pick ....Associate Pharmacologist

Dr. M. Murray Peshkin ....Associate in Pediatrics

Dr. Ben Friedman ....Adjunct Physician

Dr. Benjamin I. Allen...................................Adjunct Otologist

RESIGNATIONS FROM THE MEDICAL STAFF

Dr. Otto Marburg................................Associate Neuro-Pathologist

Dr. Sandor Lorand................................Associate Psychiatrist

Dr. Clarence P. Oberndorf ....Associate Psychiatrist

Dr. Albert Slutsky ....Adjunct Psychiatrist

We are pleased to record the fact that Dr. Richard Lewisohn, Consulting Surgeon, was elected President of the New York Surgical Society, the fourth Mount Sinai surgeon to occupy that distinguished position.

Changes in personnel included the resignation of Miss M. May Slator, who had been supervisor of the Out-Patient Department since 1913 and who could no longer continue her duties because of ill health. Her connection with the Hospital dates back to 1903 when she entered the School of Nursing as a pupil nurse, and from that time until last September, with the exception of two years, she was connected with the Hospital in various capacities, in all of which she showed great ability and she was always most conscientious in the performance of her duties. To fill the vacancy caused by Miss Slator's resignation, Miss May Shamp was appointed Supervisor of the Out-Patient Department.

We have continued to co-operate with the Associated Hospital Service of New York, the three-cents-a-day plan for voluntary group hospitalization insurance. During 1939, various problems with which the Associated Hospital Service was faced resulted in the reduction or deferment of payments by the Associated Hospital Service to the hospitals, but we are confident that its problems will be satisfactorily solved. We still believe wholeheartedly in the philosophy underlying this plan and that it is entitled to the continued support and cooperation of the hospitals.

The expenditure for current purposes of the Hospital including the School of Nursing, the Social Service Department, and the Ladies' Auxiliary in 1939 amounted to..........................$2,374,088.01

Receipts applicable to current expenditures were......... 2,204,601.61

Leaving a net deficit of.. $169,486.40

Included in the receipts are the following:

Received from Federation $664,531.21

Received from The Greater New York Fund (through
    Federation) 46,139.00

From the United Hospital Fund—For the Hospital
    and the Social Service Auxiliary.................................... 75,998.16

From the City of New York:
    For custodians and payment of part of the cost
    of cases approved by the City... 192,010.67

I have referred above to the reduction in our so-called Permanent Fund during the past decade. The situation arising from this decrease due to insufficient income to carry on the work of the Hospital at its accustomed high standard of service has given your officers and Board of Trustees great concern. With the continuance of large operating deficits and with the reduced funds available to meet these deficits, we shall be confronted with a real emergency in the near future. Federation has again during the past year carried on a vigorous and successful campaign for funds, under the able leadership of the Honorable George Z. Medalie. This campaign was very successful, taking into consideration the handicaps under which it operated. The objectives set up by Federation was the amount appropriated for the constituent societies plus the deficits which had been incurred by the societies in 1938. The first of these objectives was approximately achieved, but the second one relative to the deficits failed of accomplishment. The operating deficit experience of Mount Sinai Hospital is not unique, for all of the Federation hospitals in varying degrees have found it impossible to operate under the appropriations made available to them. Such total hospital deficits for 1938 for Manhattan and Bronx hospitals amounted to a little less than $600,000. The experience of Federation during the past year would appear to indicate that the community does not at the moment give the amount of money which will take care of the full requirements of its societies. Federation, recognizing that some change had to be made in its budget procedure, appointed a committee to study this subject, and Mount Sinai's representative on that committee is urging certain fundamental changes in the budget-making procedure. We are of the opinion that in the light of insufficient support from the community, the underlying principles upon which the budget procedure is now based must be modified if we are to maintain our present high standards. We are of the firm conviction that the Mount Sinai Hospital stands for so much in the medical world and in the community generally, that any retrogression with respect to standards would be of lasting injury.

We have again been honored by having distinguished visitors deliver a number of lectures in the Blumenthal Aditorium, as follows:

Dr. Otto Marburg, formerly Director of the Neurological Institute in Vienna: "Hydrocephalus: Clinical Manifestations, Pathogenesis and Therapy."

Sir Alfred Webb-Johnson, C.B.E., D.S.O., M.B., F.R.C.S., (England) Hon. F.A.C.S.: "The History of Surgery in England."

Dr. Max Bergmann, Member of The Rockefeller Institute for Medical Research, New York, delivered the Edward Gamaliel Janeway Lecture on: "Some Biological Aspects of Protein Chemistry."

Dr. Herbert M. Evans of the Institute of Experimental Biology, University of California, Berkley, California, delivered the William Henry Welch Lectures on: "New Light on the Biological Role of the Anti-Sterility Vitamin E" and "Some Unsolved Problems in Anterior Pituitary Physiology."

The Twelfth Annual Graduate Fortnight was held at the New York Academy of Medicine, and as usual, the members of our Medical Staff contributed clinics, delivered lectures and presented scientific exhibits, this time on the subject of "The Endocrine Glands and their Disorders."

In January of this year, we were saddened by the death of Dr. Leopold Jaches, who had served the Hospital in the capacity of Radiologist for more than thirty years. He occupied a high position in his profession and had the respect and the affection of the entire community. From the estate of Dr. Jaches, the Hospital received a fine X-ray library which is now housed in the X-ray Department. The resolution adopted by the Board of Trustees at the time of his death appeared in last year's Annual Report.

We also record with regret the passing of Mr. Murry Guggenheim, who served as Trustee of the Hospital from 1901 to 1907 and whose benefactions to this institution and to the School of Nursing were most generous.

Mr. Benjamin H. Jacobs, who had served the Hospital as Assistant Chief Clerk in the Auditing and Accounting Department, passed away and we are glad to offer this testimonial to his faithful service.

It is with sorrow that we likewise make mention of the death of Mr. Samuel Sicher, who was a Director of the Neustadter Home since its inception and at all times offered the Hospital generous cooperation.

Dr. Jandon Schwarz resigned as Assistant Director and Dr. Milton L. Dryfus as Administrative Assistant; the latter was succeeded by Dr. Morris H. Kreeger as of the first of January, 1940.

Mr. Joseph F. Cullman, Jr. was elected a Trustee, and we were particularly happy to welcome him as a member of the Board on which his father had served with distinction for a period of over forty years.

I wish to extend sincere thanks to Mayor LaGuardia, Comptroller McGoldrick and the Board of Estimate as well as Commissioners Goldwater, Rice and Hodson for the unremitting cooperation which we have received from them.

Whenever I speak of the Hospital, I include in the picture the auxiliary services without which its operation would be impossible. The School of Nursing under the liberal leadership of Mr. Hugo Blumenthal and the direction of Miss Grace A. Warman, the Social Service Department with its untiring leader, Mrs. Alfred A. Cook and its Director, Mrs. Fanny L. Mendelsohn, as well as the Ladies' Auxiliary Society, headed by Mrs. Leopold Bernheimer, are all entitled to our sincerest thanks for their splendid cooperation and fine accomplishment. The Mount Sinai Social Service Department has for three years in succession been awarded the $1,000 prize by the United Hospital Fund for securing the largest number of individual contributions in its drive.

A group of over 134 volunteers, men and women, who have been devoting their time to assisting in the Social Service Department, Out-Patient Department and Consultation Service for many hours a week, have earned our warm thanks for this service which would not be available in any other way.

The Board of Trustees joins me in expressing thanks to the administrative staff, ably led by Dr. Joseph Turner and seconded

20

by his Assistants and Department Heads, and to all workers in the Hospital and its auxiliaries for their devoted service to the Hospital and the community.

The United Hospital Fund and the Greater New York Fund through their efficient campaigns and their generous distribution of the funds collected have been of incalculable aid to the Hospital in its work.

Needless to say, we are deeply indebted to Federation for the large amount of support that we have received from that organization which carried on its work under the influence and inspiration of its President, Mr. Benjamin Buttenwieser.

I wish to thank our many friends for their continued interest in the work of the Hospital, and we shall leave no stone unturned to have the Hospital serve the community as proficiently as possible.

LEO ARNSTEIN,

President.

TRUSTEES

23

24

25

OFFICERS AND STANDING COMMITTEES OF THE MEDICAL BOARD FOR 1940

GEORGE BAEHR, M.D...*President*
HAROLD NEUHOF, M.D...*Vice-President*
IRA COHEN, M.D...*Secretary*

Executive (Conference) Committee

HAROLD NEUHOF, M.D...*Chairman*

GEORGE BAEHR, M.D.
RALPH COLP. M.D.
RUDOLPH KRAMER, M.D.

ISIDOR C. RUBIN, M.D.
KAUFMAN SCHLIVEK, M.D.
GREGORY SHWARTZMAN, M.D.

Committee on Medical Instruction

REUBEN OTTENBERG, M.D...(Acting) Chairman*

*BURRILL B. CROHN, M.D.
*JOSEPH H. GLOBUS, M.D.
*CHARLES K. FRIEDBERG, M.D.

PAUL KLEMPERER, M.D.
*ARTHUR M. MASTER, M.D.
*ELI MOSCHCOWITZ, M.D.

Committee on Intern Examinations

RALPH COLP, M.D...*Chairman*

*ARTHUR M. FISHBERG, M.D.

ISRAEL S. WECHSLER, M.D.

Surgical Committee

HAROLD NEUHOF, M.D...*Chairman*

IRA COHEN, M.D.
RALPH COLP, M.D.
JOHN H. GARLOCK, M.D.
SAMUEL H. GEIST, M.D.
ROBERT K. LIPPMANN, M.D.

ABRAHAM HYMAN, M.D.
RUDOLPH KRAMER, M.D.
JACOB L. MAYBAUM, M.D.
ISIDOR C. RUBIN, M.D.
SETH SELIG, M.D.

KAUFMAN SCHLIVEK, M.D.

Committee on Fellowships

SAMUEL H. GEIST, M.D...*Chairman*

JOHN H. GARLOCK, M.D.
*ERNST P. BOAS, M.D.
PAUL KLEMPERER, M.D.

RUDOLPH KRAMER, M.D.
GREGORY SHWARTZMAN, M.D.
HARRY H. SOBOTKA, Ph.D.

Committee on Laboratories

RALPH COLP, M.D...*Chairman*

PAUL KLEMPERER, M.D.

HARRY H. SOBOTKA, Ph.D.

GREGORY SHWARTZMAN, M.D.

---

* Not a member of the Medical Board.

OFFICERS AND STANDING COMMITTEES OF THE MEDICAL BOARD FOR 1940

(Continued)

Committee on Radiology

ABRAHAM HYMAN, M.D...*Chairman*
WILLIAM BIERMAN, M.D.   WILLIAM HARRIS, M.D.
*HARRY A. GOLDBERG, D.D.S.   *COLEMAN B. RABIN, M.D.
MARCY L. SUSSMAN, M.D.

Committee on Out-Patient Department

JOHN H. GARLOCK, M.D...*Chairman*
*LEONARD J. DRUCKERMAN, M.D.   JACOB L. MAYBAUM, M.D.
WILLIAM HARRIS, M.D.   ISADORE ROSEN, M.D.
RUDOLPH KRAMER, M.D.   SETH SELIG, M.D.
KAUFMAN SCHLIVEK, M.D.

Committee on Nurses

BELA SCHICK, M.D...*Chairman*
*DAVID BECK, M.D.   ISIDOR C. RUBIN, M.D.

Committee on Records

RUDOLPH KRAMER, M.D...*Chairman*
*MURRAY BASS, M.D.   *SIGMUND MAGE, M.D.
*FREDERICK H. KING, M.D.   SETH SELIG, M.D.
*PERCY KLINGENSTEIN, M.D.   *SOLOMON SILVER, M.D.

Committee on Cardiography

*ERNST P. BOAS, M.D...*Chairman*
*ARTHUR M. FISHBERG, M.D.   *WILLIAM M. HITZIG, M.D.
*ARTHUR M. MASTER, M.D.   *IRVING R. ROTH, M.D.

Committee on Social Service

ISRAEL S. WECHSLER, M.D...*Chairman*
*BERNARD S. DENZER, M.D.   *LAWRENCE S. KUBIE, M.D.
*EDWARD B. GREENSPAN, M.D.   *WILLIAM H. MENCHER, M.D.
*HERMAN ZAZEELA, M.D.

Dental Committee

RALPH COLP, M.D. ....*Chairman*
*CHARLES K. FRIEDBERG, M.D.   *JOSEPH SCHROFF, M.D., D.D.S.
*HARRY A. GOLDBERG, D.D.S.   *ARTHUR R. SOHVAL, M.D.
*LEO STERN, D.D.S.

---

* Not a member of the Medical Board.

OFFICERS AND STANDING COMMITTEES OF THE MEDICAL BOARD FOR 1940

(Continued)

Committee on Economy

HAROLD NEUHOF, M.D...*Chairman*
*ALFRED E. FISCHER, M.D. MARCY L. SUSSMAN, M.D.
SAMUEL H. GEIST, M.D. *ARTHUR S. W. TOUROFF, M.D.
*GORDON D. OPPENHEIMER, M.D. *FREDERIC D. ZEMAN, M.D.

Committee on Pharmacy

*HAROLD T. HYMAN, M.D...*Chairman*
*MORRIS A. GOLDBERGER, M.D. *ROBERT K. LAMBERT, M.D.
*SAMUEL KARELITZ, M.D. *DANIEL POLL, M.D.
*FREDERICK H. KING, M.D. .. *LESTER R. TUCHMAN, M.D.

Committee on Dietetics

BELA SCHICK, M.D...*Chairman*
*BURRILL B. CROHN, M.D. *HERBERT POLLACK, M.D.
*HERMAN LANDE, M.D. *ASHER WINKELSTEIN, M.D.

Committee on Library

*ELI MOSCHCOWITZ, M.D...*Chairman*
WILLIAM BIERMAN, M.D. *LEON GINZBURG, M.D.
*LEO EDELMAN, M.D. *SYLVAN E. MOOLTEN, M.D.
KAUFMAN SCHLIVEK, M.D.

Committee on Medical Publications

IRA COHEN, M.D. ....*Chairman*
RALPH COLP, M.D. RUDOLPH KRAMER, M.D.
*JOSEPH H. GLOBUS, M.D. *LOUIS J. SOFFER, M.D.

OFFICERS OF THE ASSOCIATION OF THE JUNIOR MEDICAL STAFF

FREDERIC D. ZEMAN, M.D...*Chairman*
MORRIS A. GOLDBERGER, M.D..............................*Vice-Chairman*
SOLOMON SILVER, M.D...*Secretary*
DAVID BECK, M.D.
PERCY KLINGENSTEIN, M.D. } *.Delegates to the Medical Board*

---

* Not a member of the Medical Board.

30

MEDICAL AND SURGICAL STAFF

(With changes up to April 30, 1940)

CONSULTING STAFF

Physicians

Emanuel Libman, M.D.

Morris Manges, M.D.

Alfred Meyer, M.D.

Bernard S. Oppenheimer, M.D.

Pediatrician

Henry Heiman, M.D.

Neurologists

Bernard Sachs, M.D.

Israel Strauss, M.D.

Surgeons

Albert A. Berg, M.D.

Charles A. Elsberg, M.D.

Richard Lewisohn, M.D.

Howard Lilienthal, M.D.

Gynecologists

Joseph Brettauer, M.D.

Robert T. Frank, M.D.

Hiram N. Vineberg, M.D.

Otologists

Isidore Friesner, M.D.

Fred Whiting, M.D.

Ophthalmic Surgeons

Carl Koller, M.D.

Charles H. May, M.D.

Julius Wolff, M.D.

Orthopedist

Philip D. Wilson, M.D.

Physical Therapist

Heinrich F. Wolf, M.D.

Chemist

Samuel Bookman, Ph.D.

31

MEDICAL AND SURGICAL STAFF

MEDICAL SERVICE
Physicians

George Baehr, M.D.   ***Bernard S. Oppenheimer, M.D.

Associate Physicians

David Beck, M.D.   Eli Moschcowitz, M.D.
Ernst P. Boas, M.D.   Reuben Ottenberg, M.D.
Harold T. Hyman, M.D.   Daniel Poll, M.D.

Associates in Medicine

Burrill B. Crohn, M.D.   Arthur M. Master, M.D.
Arthur M. Fishberg, M.D.   Coleman B. Rabin, M.D.
Joseph Harkavy, M.D.   Nathan Rosenthal, M.D.
Herman Lande, M.D.   Irving R. Roth, M.D.
                   Asher Winkelstein, M.D.

Adjunct Physicians

#Samuel H. Averbuck, M.D.   Frederick H. King, M.D.
#Solon S. Bernstein, M.D.   **S. S. Lichtman, M.D.
**Emanuel Z. Epstein, M.D.   #Sylvan E. Moolten, M.D.
#Philip Finkle, M.D.   (a)Abraham Penner, M.D.
 Charles K. Friedberg, M.D.   Arthur Schifrin, M.D.
 Ben Friedman, M.D.   Solomon Silver, M.D.
 Edward B. Greenspan, M.D.   Louis J. Soffer, M.D.
 Herman Hennell, M.D.   Arthur R. Sohval, M.D.
   (For Chest Diseases)   #Lester R. Tuchman, M.D.
 William M. Hitzig, M.D.   **Kaufman Wallach, M.D.
(a)Saul W. Jarcho, M.D.   #Harry Weiss, M.D.
                  Frederic D. Zeman, M.D.

Assistant Physicians

(In charge of Out-Patient Department Clinics)

Morris Blum, M.D.   Alfred Romanoff, M.D.

Assistants in Medicine

(Hospital or Out-Patient Department)

Harold A. Abel, M.D.   Hubert Mann, M.D.
Harold A. Abramson, M.D.   Herbert Pollack, M.D.

\# For Special Service.
** Off Service.
*** Resigned.
(a) Appointed 1940.

32

MEDICAL AND SURGICAL STAFF

MEDICAL SERVICE—(Continued)

Senior Clinical Assistants

(Out-Patient Department)

Salvatore Amato, M.D.
Frank A. Bassen, M.D.
Kurt Berliner, M.D.
Herbert Blau, M.D.
N. W. Chaikin, M.D.
Morris Chamurich, M.D.
Simon Dack, M.D.
Henry Feibes, M.D.
Sydney C. Feinberg, M.D.
Samuel A. Feldman, M.D.
Walter Fischbein, M.D.
Emil Granet, M.D.
Selian Hebald, M.D.
Joseph Herzstein, M.D.
Harry L. Jaffe, M.D.
Abraham Jezer, M.D.
Abraham Jerskey, M.D.
Herbert Lampert, M.D.
Sidney Levinson, M.D.
Aaron Levinsky, M.D.
Frederick J. Lewy, M.D.
Jacob Liff, M.D.
Adolph A. Lilien, M.D.

Fred E. Maisel, M.D.
Charles R. Messeloff, M.D.
P. N. Ortiz, M.D.
David Paley, M.D.
Frank Pierson, M.D.
Philip Reichert, M.D.
Joseph Reiss, M.D.
Alfred Romanoff, M.D.
Herman S. Roth, M.D.
Robert V. Sager, M.D.
Isidore Schapiro, M.D.
Siegfried S. Schatten, M.D.
S. Stanley Schneierson, M.D.
Sheppard Siegal, M.D.
Morris T. Siegel, M.D.
David I. Singer, M.D.
Joseph Singer, M.D.
Rose Spiegel, M.D.
J. Edward Stern, M.D.
Abraham Sternbach, M.D.
Peter Vogel, M.D.
Harry Yarnis, M.D.
Bernard M. Zussman, M.D.

Clinical Assistants

(Out-Patient Department)

Frederic S. Adler, M.D.
David Adlersberg, M..D.
Bernard H. Alberg, M.D.
John Amoruso, M.D.
Ludwig Anfanger, M.D.
Victor Apt, M.D.
Joseph Bandes, M.D.
Aaron Barcham, M.D.
Perry Blumberg, M.D.
Jack Brandes, M.D.
William H. Branch, M.D.
David M. Bressler, M.D.
Joseph Bronstein, M.D.
Paul N. Bulova, M.D.
Anne F. Casper, M.D.
Ralph Cohen, M.D.

Felix Cohn, M.D.
George C. Cole, M.D.
Salvatore Contento, M.D.
Albert Cornell, M.D.
D. Alfred Dantes, M.D.
Max David, M.D.
Henry Dolger, M.D.
Henry L. Dorfmann, M.D.
Morris L. Drazin, M.D.
Rudolph R. Ebert, M.D.
Milton Eisen, M.D.
Max Ellenberg, M.D.
Alan Emanuel, M.D.
Kurt Esser, M.D.
Paul Fagin, M.D.
A. Stuart Ferguson, M.D.

MEDICAL SERVICE—(Continued)
Clinical Assistants (Continued)
(Out-Patient Department)

I. E. Gerber, M.D.
Sidney L. Gottlieb, M.D.
I. M. Greenberger, M.D.
Richard Gubner, M.D.
Edward B. Grossman, M.D.
Herbert L. Gutstein, M.D.
Ernst Hammerschlag, M.D.
Samuel A. Handelsman, M.D.
Herman G. Helpern, M.D.
Leo Hennell, M.D.
Henry Horn, M.D.
Morris Hyman, M.D.
Friedrich Kach, M.D.
Edward Kahn, M.D.
Henry H. Kalter, M.D.
David Kastoff, M.D.
Harold W. Keschner, M.D.
Goodell G. Klevan, M.D.
J. John Kristal, M.D.
Victor H. Kugel, M.D.
Nicholas Langer, M.D.
Alan N. Leslie, M.D.
Carl L. Levenson, M.D.
William Levison, M.D.
Hyman Levy, M.D.
Richard Levy, M.D.
Walter Loewenberg, M.D.
Walter Loewenstein, M.D.
Harold L. Margulies, M.D.
Rafael A. Marin, M.D.
Milton Mendlowitz, M.D.
Martin Meyer, M.D.
Nathan Meyer, M.D.
Herman R. Nayer, M.D.
Harvey Nussbaum, M.D.

Louis Part, M.D.
Samuel J. Penchansky, M.D.
Arthur Post, M.D.
Irving Rapfogel, M.D.
Jerome Ritter, M.D.
Randolph Rosenthal, M.D.
Harry N. Rothman, M.D.
Hyman J. Rubenstein, M.D.
Benjamin Rubin, M.D.
Norman A. Samuels, M.D. .
Irving A. Sarot, M.D.
Maxwell Sayet, M.D.
Gerhard Schauer, M.D.
Siegfried Schoenfeld, M.D.
Alfred Selinger, M.D.
Isadore M. Siegel, M.D.
David E. Silberman, M.D.
Alexander G. Silberstein, M.D.
Irving Somach, M.D.
Eugene Somkin, M.D.
Arthur Sonnenfeld, M.D.
Morris F. Steinberg, M.D.
Milton H. Stillerman, M.D.
Oscar Tannenbaum, M.D.
Sidney Tarachow, M.D.
Meyer Texon, M.D.
Alexander Thomas, M.D.
John V. Waller, M.D.
Louis R. Wasserman, M.D.
Charles Weisberg, M.D.
Marcus Widmann, M.D.
Victor Willner, M.D.
E. Gunther Wolff, M.D.
Morton Yohalem, M.D.
Albert M. Yunich, M.D.

Volunteers

(b) Henry Dolger, M.D.
(b) Edward B. Grossman, M.D.
(b) Eugene Somkin, M.D.
(b) Rose Spiegel, M.D.
Jenny Stricker, M.D.

(b) Until April 30, 1940.

MEDICAL AND SURGICAL STAFF

PEDIATRIC SERVICE
Pediatrician
Bela Schick, M.D.

Associate Pediatricians
Murray H. Bass, M.D.   Herman Schwarz, M.D.

Associates in Pediatrics
M. Murray Peshkin, M.D.   Ira S. Wile, M.D.

Adjunct Pediatricians
Bernard S. Denzer, M.D.   Samuel Karelitz, M.D.
Alfred E. Fischer, M.D.   Jerome L. Kohn, M.D.
#George J. Ginandes, M.D.   **Sara Welt, M.D.

Assistant Pediatricians
(In charge of Out-Patient Department Clinics)
U. Himmelstein, M.D.   Irving R. Roth, M.D.
William Rosenson, M.D.   Henry M. Weisman, M.D.
                    Harry O. Zamkin, M.D.

Assistants in Pediatrics
(Hospital or Out-Patient Department)
Margit Freund, M.D.   Anne Topper, M.D.

Senior Clinical Assistants
(Out-Patient Department)
John Bauer, M.D.   Raphael Isaacs, M.D.
Henry H. Blum, M.D.   M. J. Karsh, M.D.
Max Chidekel, M.D.   Sidney D. Leader, M.D.
Harry J. Cohen, M.D.   Edward Lehman, M.D.
Samuel Ehre, M.D.   Harry S. Mackler, M.D.
Jacob Elitzak, M.D.   Joseph Mayeroff, M.D.
Else Farmer, M.D.   William Messer, M.D.
Gertrude Felshin, M.D.   Bessie Metrick, M.D.
A. H. Fineman, M.D.   Hanna Mulier, M.D.
Maurice Gelb, M.D.   Arthur Nathan, M.D.
Fred Glucksman, M.D.   Albert B. Newman, M.D.
Henry L. Greene, M.D.   Harry D. Pasachoff, M.D.
Gertrude Greenstein, M.D.   Abraham I. Rosenstein, M.D.
Ferenc Grossman, M.D.   Gustave Salomon, M.D.
Maurice Grozin, M.D.   Joseph Schapiro, M.D.
Harold Herman, M.D.   William A. Schonfeld, M.D.
Jacob Hirsh, M.D.

For Special Service.
** Off Service.

35

MEDICAL AND SURGICAL STAFF

PEDIATRIC SERVICE—(Continued)
Senior Clinical Assistants (Continued)
(Out-Patient Department)

J. Schwarsbram, M.D.
Adele Sicular, M.D.
Morris Sonberg, M.D.
Rose G. Spiegel, M.D.
Jacob Sugarman, M.D.
Anna Weintraub, M.D.
Carl Zelson, M.D.

Clinical Assistants
(Out-Patient Department)

George Bair, M.D.
Arthur J. Berger, M.D.
Eugene Bernstein, M.D.
Victor Blass, M.D.
Sidney Blumenthal, M.D.
Harvey Brandon, M.D.
Joseph Bronstein, M.D.
Paul N. Bulova, M.D.
Ralph Cohen, M.D.
Samuel H. Dender, M.D.
Albert Dingmann, M.D.
Ralph Feig, M.D.
Irving Feuer, M.D.
Franz H. Hanan, M.D.
Charles R. Hayman, M.D.
Lotte Heinemann, M.D.
Walter Hirschfeld, M.D.
Wilfred C. Hulse, M.D.
Herman Hochstaedt, M.D.
Godel I. Hunter, M. D.
Mark Imberman, M.D.
Dora Joelson, M.D.
Eva C. Kivelson, M.D.
Israel S. Klieger, M.D.
Walter H. Levy, M.D.
Saul Lieb, M.D.
Morton R. Milsner, M.D.
Lydia Shapiro-Mindlin
Stephan Mussliner, M.D.
George Neuhaus, M.D.
William Neuland, M.D.
Antoine Noti, M.D.
Harry L. Orlov, M.D.
Jean Pakter, M.D.
Carl Pototzky, M.D.
Howard G. Rapaport, M.D.
Jerome Ritter, M.D.
Elwood Roodner, M.D.
Jacob L. Rothstein, M.D.
B. M. Schegloff, M.D.
Eugene E. Schwarz, M.D.
Bertha Spiegel, M.D.
Ernst Steinitz, M.D.
Fannie Stoll, M.D.
Rudolf Strauss, M.D.
Herman Vollmer, M.D.
Fritz Weil, M.D.
Hans Weil, M.D.
Samuel B. Weiner, M.D.
Morton W. Willis, M.D.
Alexander Winter, M.D.

Volunteers

(b) Sidney D. Leader, M.D.
(b) Arthur Lesser, M.D.
(b) Sidney Blumenthal, M.D.
(b) Sidney H. Miller, M.D.
Howard G. Rapaport, M.D.
Freda Rath, M.D.
Rose G. Spiegel, M.D.
Samuel B. Weiner, M.D.
Herman Vollmer, M.D.

(b) Until April 30, 1940.

MEDICAL AND SURGICAL STAFF

NEUROLOGICAL SERVICE

Neurologist
Israel S. Wechsler, M.D.

Associate Neurologists
Joseph H. Globus, M.D. Richard M. Brickner, M.D.

Associate Psychiatrists
Lawrence S. Kubie, M.D. **Sandor Lorand, M.D.
**Clarence P. Oberndorf, M.D.

Adjunct Neurologists
***Benjamin H. Balser, M.D. Judah Marmor, M.D.
Morris B. Bender, M.D. William Needles, M.D.
Irving Bieber, M.D. **Nathan Savitsky, M.D.

Adjunct Psychiatrists
Arnold Eisendorfer, M.D. (a)Rene A. Spitz, M.D.
Sol W. Ginsburg, M.D. Leo Stone, M.D.
***Albert Slutsky, M.D. (a)Johan H. W. van Ophuijsen, M.D.
(a)Bettina Warburg, M.D.

Assistants in Neurology
(Hospital or Out-Patient Department)
Joseph Salan, M.D. John Scharf, M.D.

Assistant in Psychiatry
(Hospital or Out-Patient Department)
Arpad Pauncz, M.D.

Senior Clinical Assistant
(Out-Patient Department)
(Neurology)
Sidney Elpern, M.D.

Senior Clinical Assistants
(Out-Patient Department)
(Psychiatry)
P. Goolker, M.D. Herman G. Selinsky, M.D.
Harry I. Weinstock, M.D.

Clinical Assistants
(Out-Patient Department)
(Neurology)
David Beres, M.D. Alexis Gottlieb, M.D.
Alfred Dannhauser, M.D. Jakob Leffkowitz, M.D.
Felix O. Durham, M.D. Viva Schatia, M.D.
Frank P. Eves, M.D. George Trefousse, M.D.
David Gersten, M.D. Herman Vollmer, M.D.

** Off Service.
*** Resigned.
(a) Appointed 1940.

NEUROLOGICAL SERVICE—(Continued)

Clinical Assistants
(Out-Patient Department)
(Psychiatry)

Abraham Apter, M.D.
George G. Arato, M.D.
Emil A. Gutheil, M.D.
Samuel Kahn, M.D.
Edith Laszlo, M.D.

David M. Lipshutz, M.D.
Max Loeb, M.D.
Meyer Maskin, M.D.
Ernest Rothe, M.D.
Edgar C. Trautmann, M.D.

Volunteer
(b) Daniel E. Schneider, M.D.

Research Assistant
Hans Strauss, M.D.

Clinical Psychologist
Silas Cohen, M.A.

DERMATOLOGICAL SERVICE

Dermatologist
Isadore Rosen, M.D.

Associate Dermatologists
Louis Chargin, M.D.   Oscar L. Levin, M.D.

Adjunct Dermatologists
Samuel M. Peck, M.D.   Max Scheer, M.D.

Assistant Dermatologists
(In charge of Out-Patient Department Clinics)
Lewis A. Goldberger, M.D.
Arthur Sayer, M.D.

Henry Silver M.D.
Charles Wolf, M.D.

Assistant in Dermatology
(Hospital or Out-Patient Department)
Herbert Rosenfeld, M.D.

Senior Clinical Assistants
(Out-Patient Department)
D. B. Ballin, M.D.
Max Berkovsky, M.D.
Eugene T. Bernstein, M.D.
Raphael Breakstone, M.D.
Frank E. Cross, M.D.
Julius Davis, M.D.
Philip S. Greenbaum, M.D.
H. C. Herrman, M.D.

H. J. Kohnstam, M.D.
William Leifer, M.D.
Sidney B. Rooff, M.D.
G. Rubin, M.D.
Joel Schweig, M.D.
Harry Sherwood, M.D.
Harry E. Slatkin, M.D.
Samuel Strumwasser, M.D.

Maurice Umansky, M.D.

(b) Until April 30, 1940.

MEDICAL AND SURGICAL STAFF

DERMATOLOGICAL SERVICE—(Continued)
Clinical Assistants
(Out-Patient Department)

Ernest Bass, M.D.
Howard T. Behrman, M.D.
Erich Buechler, M.D.
Willy Flegenheimer, M.D.
Hirsch L. Gordon, M.D.
Arthur W. Glick, M.D.
Alfred Hess, M.D.
Moses H. Holland, M.D.
S. Lawrence Kaman, M.D.
David Kane, M.D.
Adolf Krakauer, M.D.
Abner Kurtin, M.D.

Moritz Lewinski, M.D.
Adrian Neumann, M.D.
Kermit E. Osserman, M.D.
Samuel J. Rabinowitz, M.D.
Ferd. Rosenberger, M.D.
Irving H. Silverstein, M.D.
Julius Simon, M.D.
Kona Simon, M.D.
Abraham M. Skern, M.D.
Adolf Sternberg, M.D.
E. N. Winograd, M.D.
Morton Yohalem, M.D.

Arseno-Therapy Clinic
(Out-Patient Department)
Associate Dermatologist
Louis Chargin, M.D.

Senior Clinical Assistants
Harry Sherwood, M.D.   Maurice Umansky, M.D.

SURGICAL SERVICE
Surgeons
Ralph Colp, M.D.   Abraham Hyman, M.D.
John H. Garlock, M.D.   Harold Neuhof, M.D.

Associate Surgeons
Leo Edelman, M.D.   Percy Klingenstein, M.D.
Leon Ginzburg, M.D.   Arthur S. W. Touroff, M.D.

Adjunct Surgeons
Ernest E. Arnheim, M.D.   H. Evans Leiter, M.D.
Arthur H. Aufses, M.D.   Sigmund Mage, M.D.
Maurice M. Berck, M.D.   William H. Mencher, M.D.
Leonard J. Druckerman, M.D.   Gordon D. Oppenheimer, M.D.
Ameil Glass, M.D.   Myron A. Sallick, M.D.
Samuel H. Klein, M.D.   #Samuel Silbert, M.D.
Moses Swick, M.D.

Assistant Surgeon
(In charge of Out-Patient Department Clinic)
Sylvan D. Manheim, M.D.

For Special Service.

39

SURGICAL SERVICE—(Continued)

Senior Clinical Assistants
(Out-Patient Department)

Moses Benmosche, M.D.
Daniel Casten, M.D.
Benjamin Damsky, M.D.
Milton M. Eckert, M.D.
Norman L. Goldberg, M.D.
Aron Goldschmidt, M.D.
Milton H. Goolde, M.D.

Sidney Grossman, M.D.
Sidney Hirsch, M.D.
Borris A. Kornblith, M.D.
Norman F. Laskey, M.D.
H. G. Rose, M.D.
Isidore Schapiro, M.D.
Ralph W. Watsky, M.D.

Herman Zazeela, M.D.

Clinical Assistants
(Out-Patient Department)

Robert H. Abrahamson, M.D.
Aaron Berger, M.D.
Harry Bergman, M.D.
Harry Bettauer, M.D.
William Braunstein, M.D.
Sydney Bressler, M.D.
Jerome S. Coles, M.D.
Kurt Cronheim, M.D.
Henry Doubilet, M.D.
Walter Edkins, M.D.
Celia Ekelson, M.D.
Robert C. Elitzik, M.D.
Fritz Falk, M.D.
Benjamin Glick, M.D.
Meyer L. Goldman, M.D.
William Hayn, M.D.
Nathan B. Hirschfeld, M.D.
Max Jacoby, M.D.
Harry Kassop, M.D.
Abner Kurtin, M.D.
Mark J. Markham, M.D.
Helmuth Nathan, M.D.
Hellmuth Oppenheimer, M.D.
Henry Peskin, M.D.
Willy Perez, M.D.
Erich Plocki, M.D.

Aaron Prigot, M.D.
Irving R. Rachlin, M.D.
Benjamin Ritter, M.D.
Gustav Rosenburg, M.D.
Gerhard Sachs, M.D.
M. Salzberg, M.D.
Emil Schnebel, M.D.
David Schwartz, M.D.
Emil Schwarzmann, M.D.
Gabriel P. Seley, M.D.
Sigmund A. Siegel, M.D.
Richard Silberstein, M.D.
Arthur Simon, M.D.
Meyer M. Stone, M.D.
David J. Surrey, M.D.
Joseph A. Tamerin, M.D.
Alexander Thomas, M.D.
Irwin P. Train, M.D.
Leonard J. Trilling, M.D.
Robert Turell, M.D.
Herbert G. Weichsel, M.D.
Leonard Weinroth, M.D.
Vernon A. Weinstein, M.D.
Julius L. Weissberg, M.D.
Eric Wohlauer, M.D.
Saul Zager, M.D.

Thomas S. Zimmer, M.D.

Volunteers

Sidney Blumenthal, M.D.
Henry Doubilet, M.D.
Edward E. Jemerin, M.D.
Irving A. Sarot, M.D.
Gabriel P. Seley, M.D.

Alfred R. Shepard, D.D.S.
Alexander Thomas, M.D.
Irwin P. Train, M.D.
Harry I. Weinstock, M.D.
Vernon A. Weinstein, M.D.

Julius L. Weissberg, M.D.

MEDICAL AND SURGICAL STAFF

NEURO-SURGICAL SERVICE

Neuro-Surgeon
Ira Cohen, M.D.

Associate Neuro-Surgeon
Abraham Kaplan, M.D.

Adjunct Neuro-Surgeon
Sidney W. Gross, M.D.

GENITO-URINARY DIVISION OF OUT-PATIENT DEPARTMENT OF SURGICAL SERVICE

Assistant Surgeons
(In charge of Out-Patient Department Clinics)

William Bisher, M.D.   Lewis T. Mann, M.D.
Jerome M. Ziegler, M.D.

Senior Clinical Assistants
(Out-Patient Department)

N. D. Benezra, M.D.   Abraham Firestone, M.D.
Jacob Birnbaum, M.D.   Joseph Haas, M.D.
George F. Dayton, M.D.   Edward Jacobs, M.D.
Henry Feibes, M.D.   Leo Jacoby, M.D.
William L. Ferber, M.D.   Bernard D. Kulick, M.D.
Edward O. Finestone, M.D.   Norman F. Laskey, M.D.

Clinical Assistants
(Out-Patient Department)

Maurice Alden, M.D.   Edward E. Jemerin, M.D.
Lawrence Essenson, M.D.   Herman I. Kantor, M.D.
Frank E. Fink, M.D.   Bruno Mark, M.D.
Joseph Graham, M.D.   Pasquale Montilli, M.D.
Paul E. Gutman, M.D.   George E. Raskin, M.D.
Kurt A. Heinrich, M.D.   Natale A. Sabatino, M.D.
Harry D. Italiener, M.D.   David Schreiber, M.D.

GYNECOLOGICAL SERVICE

Gynecologists

Samuel H. Geist, M.D.   Isidor C. Rubin, M.D.

Associate Gynecologists

Morris A. Goldberger, M.D.   Max D. Mayer, M.D.

Adjunct Gynecologists

Phineas Bernstein, M.D.   U. J. Salmon, M.D.
Joseph A. Gaines, M.D.   Seymour Wimpfheimer, M.D.

MEDICAL AND SURGICAL STAFF

GYNECOLOGICAL SERVICE—(Continued)

Assistant Gynecologists
(In charge of Out-Patient Department Clinics)

Morris Feresten, M.D.   Maurice E. Mintz, M.D.
Emanuel Klempner, M.D.   Frank Spielman, M.D.

Senior Clinical Assistants
(Out-Patient Department)

Isabel Beck, M.D.   H. C. Herrman, M.D.
Samuel G. Berkow, M.D.   Samuel Hochman, M.D.
Gertrude Felshin, M.D.   Monroe A. Rosenbloom, M.D.
Oscar Glassman, M.D.   Paul Steinweg, M.D.
Leonard Zweibel, M.D.

Clinical Assistants
(Out-Patient Department)

Hans Auerbach, M.D.   Walter B. Neubauer, M.D.
Bernard Berglas, M.D.   Herbert F. Newman, M.D.
Johanna N. Bulova, M.D.   Josef Novak, M.D.
Arthur M. Davids, M.D.   John O. Porges, M.D.
Richard Fleischer, M.D.   Louis Portnoy, M.D.
Eleanor B. Gutman, M.D.   James A. Rosen, M. D.
Sello Leopold, M.D.   Raymond W. Sass, M.D.
Maximilian Lewitter, M.D.   Abbey D. Seley, M.D.
H. Richard Mayer, M.D.   Robert I. Walter, M.D.
Nathan Mintz, M.D.   Elvira L. Wasserman, M.D.

OTOLOGICAL AND LARYNGOLOGICAL SERVICES

Otologist
Jacob L. Maybaum, M.D.

Associate Otologists
Joseph G. Druss, M.D.   Samuel Rosen, M.D.

Adjunct Otologists
Benjamin I. Allen, M.D.   Harry Rosenwasser, M.D.
Eugene R. Snyder, M.D.

Laryngologist
Rudolph Kramer, M.D.

Associate Laryngologists
Morris S. Bender, M.D.   Irving B. Goldman, M.D.

Adjunct Laryngologists
Joseph L. Goldman, M.D.   Louis Kleinfeld, M.D.
Max L. Som, M.D.

Assistant Oto-Laryngologist
(In charge of Out-Patient Department Clinic)
Harry D. Cohen, M.D.

42

MEDICAL AND SURGICAL STAFF

OTOLOGICAL AND LARYNGOLOGICAL SERVICES
(Continued)

Senior Clinical Assistants
(Out-Patient Department)

Adolph N. Abraham, M.D.   William J. Hochbaum, M.D.
Julius Golembe, M.D.   S. Mencher, M.D.

Clinical Assistants
(Out-Patient Department)

Samuel M. Bloom, M.D.   Karl O. Lowy, M.D.
Lester L. Coleman, M.D.   Wm. F. Mayer-Hermann, M.D.
Maurice R. Goodwin, M.D.   Hans Meinrath, M.D.
Bruno Griessmann, M.D.   A. Harry Neffson, M.D.

OPHTHALMOLOGICAL SERVICE

Ophthalmic Surgeon
Kaufman Schlivek, M.D.

Associate Ophthalmic Surgeons
Robert K. Lambert, M.D.   Henry Minsky, M.D.

Adjunct Ophthalmic Surgeons
Joseph Laval, M.D.   David Wexler, M.D.

Assistant Ophthalmic Surgeons
(In charge of Out-Patient Department Clinics)
Murray A. Last, M.D.   Herman Ostrow, M.D.

Senior Clinical Assistants
(Out-Patient Department)

Edward J. Bassen, M.D.   Saul Miller, M.D.
Bertha Gladstern, M.D.   Meta Mueller, M.D.
Abraham L. Kornzweig, M.D.   M. Rosenbaum, M.D.

Clinical Assistants
(Out-Patient Department)

Philip L. Adalman, M.D.   Alfred Kestenbaum, M.D.
Richard Baruch, M.D.   Franz J. Langendorff, M.D.
Eva C. Dienst, M.D.   Norbert Lewin, M.D.
Benjamin Esterman, M.D.   Max Mannheimer, M.D.
Joseph Fried, M.D.   Philip L. Masor, M.D.
Jacob Goldsmith, M.D.   Ernst L. Metzger, M.D.
Frank M. Green, M.D.   David I. Mirow, M.D.
Frederick H. Theodore, M.D.

Refractionists
(Out-Patient Department)
Bertha Gladstern, M.D.   M. Rosenbaum, M.D.

MEDICAL AND SURGICAL STAFF

ORTHOPEDIC SERVICE
Orthopedists
Robert K. Lippmann, M.D.   Seth Selig, M.D.

Associate Orthopedist
(a) Edgar M. Bick, M.D.

Adjunct Orthopedist
Albert J. Schein, M.D.

Senior Clinical Assistants
(Out-Patient Department)
Herman S. Lieberman, M.D.   Jacob Mandel, M.D.

Clinical Assistants
(Out-Patient Department)
Ernst Bettmann, M.D.   Lydia Shapiro-Mindlin, M.D.
Max Kliger, M.D.   Rudolf Selig, M.D.
H. R. Landmann, M.D.   Stephan Wahl, M.D.

ISOLATION SERVICE
Associate Physician
Benjamin Eliasoph, M.D.

PHYSICAL THERAPY DEPARTMENT
Physical Therapist
William Bierman, M.D.

Adjunct Physical Therapist
Sidney Licht, M.D.

Assistant Physical Therapists
Erich Levy, M.D.   A. W. Schenker, M.D.

Clinical Assistants
(Out-Patient Department)
Victor Feith, M.D.   Alexander Hersh, M.D.
Eugene Neuwirth, M.D.

CARDIOGRAPHIC LABORATORY
Associate in Medicine
Arthur M. Master, M.D.

Assistant in Medicine
Hubert Mann, M.D.

Research Assistants
Simon Dack, M.D.   Harry L. Jaffe, M.D.
Abraham Jezer, M.D.

Volunteers
Rudolph Friedmann, M.D.   Arthur Grishman, M.D.
Richard Gubner, M.D.

(a) Appointed 1940.

MEDICAL AND SURGICAL STAFF

THE LABORATORIES

Pathologist
Paul Klemperer, M.D.

Bacteriologist
Gregory Shwartzman, M.D.

Chemist
Harry H. Sobotka, Ph.D.

Neuro-pathologist
Joseph H. Globus, M.D.

Hematologist
Nathan Rosenthal, M.D.

Associate Pathologist
Sadao Otani, M.D.

Associate Pharmacologist
Ernst P. Pick, M.D.

Assistant Pathologist
Abou D. Pollack, M.D.

Assistant Bacteriologist
Cecele Herschberger, B.S.

Assistant Chemist
Miriam Reiner, M.S.

Assistant in Morbid Anatomy
Henry Horn, M.D.

Assistants in Bacteriology
Lewis H. Koplik, M.D.   S. Stanley Schneierson, M.D.

SPECIAL LABORATORY APPOINTMENTS
Fellows
1939-1940

Arthur C. Allen, M.D.......George Blumenthal, Jr. Fellowship
Ben Friedman, M.D...........Lionel Sutro Fellowship
Franklin Hollander, Ph.D. Fellowship in Gastro-enterology
Mark G. Kanzer, M.D.......Minnie Kastor Fellowship in Psychiatry
Nathan Mintz, M.D.............Dr. Joseph Brettauer Fellowship
Leo Moschkowitz, M.D...George Blumenthal, Jr. Fellowship
Joseph Pick, M.D...............Theodor Escherich Fellowship
Martin Rubin, Ph.D...........Hernsheim Fellowship in Chemistry
Eugene Somkin, M.D........Charles Klingenstein Fellowship
H. E. Yaskin, M.D.............Dr. Isadore Abrahamson Memorial Fellowship
Joseph M. Zucker, M.D.....Moritz Rosenthal Fellowship

MEDICAL AND SURGICAL STAFF

MEDICAL AND SURGICAL STAFF

SPECIAL LABORATORY APPOINTMENTS—(Continued)
Voluntary Assistants (Continued)
MORBID ANATOMY .

George C. Escher, M.D.
J. Gudemann, M.D.
Vitali Kogan, M.D.
Morris F. Steinberg, M.D.

Emanuel Wachtel, M.D.
M. Wachstein, M.D.
Tobias Weinberg, M.D.
Bernard S. Wolf, M.D.

NEURO-PATHOLOGY

Samuel M. Bloom, M.D.
(b) Jacob H. Friedman, M.D.
(b) Mark Gerstle, Jr. M.D.

H. Kuhlenbeck, M.D.
Theodore Meltzer, M.D.
James F. McDonald, M.D.

OPHTHALMO-PATHOLOGY

Murray A. Last, M.D.

Abraham L. Kornzweig, M.D.

SURGICAL PATHOLOGY

Max Ellenberg, M.D.
Julian A. Jarman, M.D.
Borris A. Kornblith, M.D.

(b) Abner Kurtin, M.D.
A. Harry Neffson, M.D.
(b) Max Schenk, M.D.

Julius Winer, M.D.

PHARMACOLOGY
Consultant
Charles L. Lieb, M.D.

DEPARTMENT OF ROENTGENOLOGY
Radiologist
Marcy L. Sussman, M.D.

Associate Radiologists
Arthur J. Bendick, M.D.

Samuel J. Goldfarb, M.D.

Assistant Radiologists
John Beck, M.D.

Benjamin Copleman, M.D.

Coleman B. Rabin, M.D.

Volunteers
(b) Henry L. Dorfmann, M.D.

Morris F. Steinberg, M.D.

DEPARTMENT OF RADIOTHERAPY
Radiotherapist
William Harris, M.D.

Associate Radiotherapist
Albert Kean, M.D.

(b) Until April 30, 1940.

MEDICAL AND SURGICAL STAFF

DEPARTMENT OF RADIOTHERAPY—(Continued)

Assistant Radiotherapists

Myer E. Golan, M.D.
Samuel Richman, M.D.
Sidney M. Silverstone, M.D.

Seymour Wimpfheimer, M.D.
Charles Wolf, M.D.
Louis E. Zaretski, M.D.

Volunteers

Arnold Bachman, M.D.

Moses H. Holland, M.D.

Physicists

Carl B. Braestrup, B.Sc.

Alexander Kolin, Ph.D.

DEPARTMENT OF ANESTHESIA

Visiting Anesthetists

William Branower, M.D.

Bernard H. Eliasberg, M.D.

Harry G. Goldman, M.D.

Anesthetists in Out-Patient Department

Sidney Grossman, M.D.

Barney Isaacson, M.D.

Resident Anesthetists

Helen E. Almour, R.N.
Fanny Bergmann, M.D.
Ryta M. Canty, R.N.

Florence Califano, R.N.
Evelyn T. Clerico, M.D.
Dorothy Newland, R.N.

DISTRICT SERVICE

Physicians

Abraham Jerskey, M.D.

Morris F. Steinberg, M.D.

ADMITTING SERVICE

Irving Solomon, M.D.

ASSISTANT PHYSICIAN TO EMPLOYEES

D. Alfred Dantes, M.D.

MEDICAL AND SURGICAL STAFF

DENTAL DEPARTMENT

(Hospital and Out-Patient Department)

Dentist

Harry A. Goldberg, D.D.S.

Associate Dentists

Ralph H. Brodsky, D.M.D.   Joseph Schroff, M.D., D.D.S.

Leo Stern, D.D.S.

Adjunct Dentists

Charles H. Cohen, D.D.S.   Denis D. Glucksman, D.D.S.
Nathaniel Freeman, D.D.S.   Arthur A. Kulick, D.D.S.

Senior Clinical Assistants

Robert E. Arlt, D.D.S.   Paul C. Kopf, D.D.S.
Miles Chelimer, D.D.S.   Abram J. Krasny, D.D.S.
Henry I. Cohen, D.D.S.   Sydney Pollak, D.D.S.
Lester L. Eisner, D.D.S.   Elias Reiner, D.D.S.
Oscar C. Fink, D.D.S.   Louis Sabloff, D.D.S.
Marvin G. Freid, D.D.S.   Milton Schwartz, D.D.S.
Herbert L. Goodfleish, D.M.D.   Arthur L. Smith, D.D.S.
Max Greenspan, D.D.S.   Bernard A. Sussman, D.D.S.
Daniel M. Kollen, D.D.S.   Daniel L. Traub, D.D.S.

I. Edwin Zimmerman, D.D.S.

Clinical Assistants

Louis Arnowitz, D.D.S.   Benjamin A. Klein, D.D.S.
Joseph Bisaha, D.D.S.   Louis Kroll, D.M.D.
Edgar B. Biscow, D.D.S.   Lee R. Kulick, D.D.S.
Alex N. Cohen, D.D.S.   Jacob C. Rachunow, D.D.S.
Abraham Dinim, D.D.S.   Herman Reich, D.D.S.
Samuel Donson, D.D.S.   Sidney Retzker, D.D.S.
Frederick T. Doob, D.D.S.   William Roth, D.D.S.
George Dubin, D.D.S.   David Rubin, D.D.S.
Robert S. Gilbert, D.M.D.   Eric D. Sachs, D.D.S.
Samuel Gordon, D.D.S.   Morris Schwartz, D.D.S.
Edward Gottesman, D.D.S.   Leonard B. Shapiro, D.D.S.
Jack Hausberg, D.D.S.   I. Arnold Simon, D.D.S.
Robert S. Hess, D.D.S.   Daniel H. Spector, D.D.S.
Jacob Hurwitz, D.D.S.   Harry Spodak, D.D.S.
Jack Kantor, D.D.S.   George Trattner, D.D.S.
Harry W. Katz, D.D.S.   Seymour Weinstein, D.D.S.

Henry H. Weishof, D.D.S.

HOUSE STAFF
(As of March 1st, 1940)

MEDICAL DEPARTMENT

Daniel Stats, M.D.
Arthur W. Seligmann, Jr., M.D.
Alvin J. Gordon, M.D.
Selvan Davison, M.D.
Merrill P. Haas, M.D.
Bernard M. Schwartz, M.D.
Harry D. Janowitz, M.D.
Jonas E. Salk, M.D.

Clifford L. Spingarn, M.D.
Mary C. Tyson, M.D.
Samuel S. Dorrance, M.D.
George L. Engel, M.D.
Frank L. Engel, M.D.
Maurice Franks, M.D.
John B. DeHoff, M.D.
Herman L. Jacobius, M.D.

SURGICAL DEPARTMENT

Elliott S. Hurwitt, M.D.
Gerson J. Lesnick, M.D.
Rudolph E. Drosd, M.D.
Leon M. Arnold, M.D.
Daniel Luger, M.D.
Ernst L. Sarason, M.D.
Alvin I. Goldfarb, M.D.
Lester Narins, M.D.

Bernard E. Simon, M.D.
Herbert M. Katzin, M.D.
William I. Glass, M.D.
David Miller, M.D.
Norman Rosenberg M.D.
Roy Barnett, M.D.
George J. Sabrin, M.D.
Norman Simon, M.D.

PATHOLOGICAL DEPARTMENT

Irving G. Kroop, M.D.

Robert Landesman, M.D.

DEPARTMENT OF RADIOLOGY

Roentgenology
Harold G. Jacobson, M.D.
Abraham Melamed, M.D.

Radiotherapy
Jack Levy, M.D.
Nathan Rudner, M.D.

DENTAL DEPARTMENT

Lester H. Sablow, D.M.D.

Henry Ellison, D.D.S.

RESIDENTS, WARD

Neurological
Bertram Schaffner, M.D.
Sydney G. Margolin, M.D.
Milton Sapirstein, M.D.

Pediatric
Herschel J. Kaufman, M.D.
Arnold Widerman, M.D.

Gynecological
Norbert B. Reicher, M.D.
Irving L. Frank, M.D.

Ear, Nose and Throat
Michael S. Zeman, M.D.
Leonard S. Bases, M.D.

Ophthalmological
Herman K. Goldberg, M.D.
Milton G. Rosoff, M.D.

Orthopedic
Alvin M. Arkin, M.D.

RESIDENTS, PRIVATE PAVILION

Leon J. Taubenhaus. M.D.
Albert S. Lyons, M.D.

Nathaniel C. Schlossman, M.D.
Earl M. Edison, M.D.

William Kaufman, M.D.

RESIDENTS, SEMI-PRIVATE PAVILION

Bernard Friedman, M.D.
David Brezin, M.D.

Marvin P. Rhodes, M.D.
Martin A. Zionts, M.D.

DEPARTMENT OF GRADUATE MEDICAL INSTRUCTION

Conducted in Affiliation with
COLUMBIA UNIVERSITY
(University Extension and School of Medicine)

OFFICERS OF INSTRUCTION

HAROLD A. ABRAMSON, M.D._____ASSISTANT IN MEDICINE TO
THE MOUNT SINAI HOSPITAL;
ASSISTANT PROFESSOR OF PHYSIOLOGY IN COLUMBIA UNIVERSITY

DAVID ADLERSBERG, M.D._____RESEARCH ASSISTANT IN CHEMISTRY AND CLINICAL
ASSISANT, MEDICAL DIVISION, OUT-PATIENT DEPARTMENT,
THE MOUNT SINAI HOSPITAL

SAMUEL H. AVERBUCK, M.D., ADJUNCT PHYSICIAN TO THE MOUNT SINAI HOSPITAL

GEORGE BAEHR, M.D._____PHYSICIAN TO THE MOUNT SINAI HOSPITAL;
CLINICAL PROFESSOR OF MEDICINE IN COLUMBIA UNIVERSITY

MURRAY H. BASS, M.D._____ASSOCIATE PEDIATRICIAN TO THE MOUNT SINAI HOSPITAL;
ASSISTANT CLINICAL PROFESSOR OF PEDIATRICS IN COLUMBIA UNIVERSITY

DAVID BECK, M.D._____ASSOCIATE PHYSICIAN TO THE MOUNT SINAI HOSPITAL;
ASSISTANT CLINICAL PROFESSOR OF MEDICINE IN COLUMBIA UNIVERSITY

MORRIS B. BENDER, M.D._____ADJUNCT NEUROLOGIST TO THE MOUNT SINAI HOSPITAL

PHINEAS BERNSTEIN, M.D., ADJUNCT GYNECOLOGIST TO THE MOUNT SINAI HOSPITAL

SOLON S. BERNSTEIN, M.D.____ADJUNCT PHYSICIAN TO THE MOUNT SINAI HOSPITAL

EDGAR M. BICK, M.D._____ASSOCIATE ORTHOPEDIST TO THE MOUNT SINAI HOSPITAL

WILLIAM BIERMAN, M.D._____PHYSICAL THERAPIST TO THE MOUNT SINAI HOSPITAL;
ASSOCIATE IN MEDICINE IN COLUMBIA UNIVERSITY

ERNST P. BOAS, M.D._____ASSOCIATE PHYSICIAN TO THE MOUNT SINAI HOSPITAL;
ASSISTANT CLINICAL PROFESSOR OF MEDICINE IN COLUMBIA UNIVERSITY

WILLIAM BRANOWER, M.D._____SUPERVISING ANESTHETIST TO
THE MOUNT SINAI HOSPITAL

RICHARD M. BRICKNER,M.D._____ASSOCIATE NEUROLOGIST TO
THE MOUNT SINAI HOSPITAL;
ASSISTANT PROFESSOR OF CLINICAL NEUROLOGY IN COLUMBIA UNIVERSITY

LOUIS CHARGIN, M.D._____ASSOCIATE DERMATOLOGIST TO THE MOUNT SINAI HOSPITAL
ASSOCIATE CLINICAL PROFESSOR OF DERMATOLOGY AND SYPHILOLOGY,
NEW YORK POST-GRADUATE MEDICAL SCHOOL, COLUMBIA UNIVERSITY

IRA COHEN, M.D._____NEURO-SURGEON TO THE MOUNT SINAI HOSPITAL

RALPH COLP, M.D._____SURGEON TO THE MOUNT SINAI HOSPITAL;
CLINICAL PROFESSOR OF SURGERY IN COLUMBIA UNIVERSITY

BURRILL B. CROHN, M.D._____ASSOCIATE IN MEDICINE TO THE MOUNT SINAI HOSPITAL;
ASSOCIATE IN MEDICINE IN COLUMBIA UNIVERSITY

SIMON DACK, M.D._____RESEARCH ASSISTANT, CARDIOGRAPHIC LABORATORY AND
SENIOR CLINICAL ASSISTANT, MEDICAL DIVISION, OUT-PATIENT DEPARTMENT,
THE MOUNT SINAI HOSPITAL

BERNARD S. DENZER, M.D., ADJUNCT PEDIATRICIAN TO THE MOUNT SINAI HOSPITAL

HENRY DOLGER, M.D._____VOLUNTARY ASSISTANT IN CHEMISTRY,
AND CLINICAL ASSISTANT, MEDICAL DIVISION, OUT-PATIENT DEPARTMENT,
THE MOUNT SINAI HOSPITAL

HENRY DOUBILET, M.D._____CLINICAL ASSISTANT, SURGICAL DIVISION,
OUT-PATIENT DEPARTMENT, THE MOUNT SINAI HOSPITAL

JOSEPH G. DRUSS, M.D._____ASSOCIATE OTOLOGIST TO THE MOUNT SINAI HOSPITAL

MAX ELLENBERG, M.D._____VOLUNTARY ASSISTANT IN SURGICAL PATHOLOGY
AND CLINICAL ASSISTANT, MEDICAL DIVISION, OUT-PATIENT DEPARTMENT,
THE MOUNT SINAI HOSPITAL

E. Z. EPSTEIN, M.D._____ADJUNCT PHYSICIAN TO THE MOUNT SINAI HOSPITAL

SERGEI FEITELBERG, M.D._____RESEARCH ASSISTANT IN PHARMACOLOGY TO
THE MOUNT SINAI HOSPITAL

GERTRUDE FELSHIN, M.D._____RESEARCH ASSISTANT IN CHEMISTRY AND SENIOR
CLINICAL ASSISTANT, PEDIATRIC AND GYNECOLOGICAL DIVISIONS,
OUT-PATIENT DEPARTMENT, THE MOUNT SINAI HOSPITAL

ALFRED E. FISCHER, M.D._____ADJUNCT PEDIATRICIAN TO THE MOUNT SINAI HOSPITAL

ARTHUR M. FISHBERG, M.D., ASSOCIATE IN MEDICINE TO THE MOUNT SINAI HOSPITAL;
ASSOCIATE IN MEDICINE IN COLUMBIA UNIVERSITY

DEPARTMENT OF GRADUATE MEDICAL INSTRUCTION

(Continued)

ROBERT T. FRANK, M.D...CONSULTING GYNECOLOGIST TO THE MOUNT SINAI HOSPITAL;
CLINICAL PROFESSOR OF GYNECOLOGY IN COLUMBIA UNIVERSITY
CHARLES K. FRIEDBERG, M.D., ADJUNCT PHYSICIAN TO THE MOUNT SINAI HOSPITAL
BEN FRIEDMAN, M.D.................ADJUNCT PHYSICIAN TO THE MOUNT SINAI HOSPITAL
JOSEPH A. GAINES, M.D......ADJUNCT GYNECOLOGIST TO THE MOUNT SINAI HOSPITAL
JOHN H. GARLOCK, M.D................................SURGEON TO THE MOUNT SINAI HOSPITAL
SAMUEL H. GEIST, M.D.........................GYNECOLOGIST TO THE MOUNT SINAI HOSPITAL
CLINICAL PROFESSOR OF GYNECOLOGY IN COLUMBIA UNIVERSITY
I. E. GERBER, M.D...RESEARCH ASSISTANT IN MORBID ANATOMY
AND CLINICAL ASSISTANT, MEDICAL DIVISION, OUT-PATIENT DEPARTMENT,
THE MOUNT SINAI HOSPITAL
GEORGE J. GINANDES, M.D....ADJUNCT PEDIATRICIAN TO THE MOUNT SINAI HOSPITAL
JOSEPH H. GLOBUS, M.D.................ASSOCIATE NEUROLOGIST AND NEUROPATHOLOGIST
TO THE MOUNT SINAI HOSPITAL; ASSISTANT CLINICAL PROFESSOR
OF NEUROLGY IN COLUMBIA UNIVERSITY
MYER E. GOLAN, M.D.....ASSISTANT RADIOTHERAPIST TO THE MOUNT SINAI HOSPITAL;
INSTRUCTOR IN RADIOLOGY IN COLUMBIA UNIVERSITY
MORRIS A. GOLDBERGER, M.D.......................................ASSOCIATE GYNECOLOGIST TO
THE MOUNT SINAI HOSPITAL; ASSOCIATE IN GYNECOLOGY IN COLUMBIA UNIVERSITY
SAMUEL J. GOLDFARB, M.D., ASSOCIATE RADIOLOGIST TO THE MOUNT SINAI HOSPITAL;
ASSOCIATE IN RADIOLOGY IN COLUMBIA UNIVERSITY
JOSEPH L. GOLDMAN, M.D...ADJUNCT LARYNGOLOGIST TO THE MOUNT SINAI HOSPITAL
ARON GOLDSCHMIDT, M.D.............SENIOR CLINICAL ASSISTANT, SURGICAL DIVISION,
OUT-PATIENT DEPARTMENT, THE MOUNT SINAI HOSPITAL
EMIL GRANET, M.D.............................SENIOR CLINICAL ASSISTANT, MEDICAL DIVISION,
OUT-PATIENT DEPARTMENT, THE MOUNT SINAI HOSPITAL
EDWARD B. GREENSPAN, M.D...ADJUNCT PHYSICIAN TO
THE MOUNT SINAI HOSPITAL
JOSEPH HARKAVY, M.D.....ASSOCIATE IN MEDICINE TO THE MOUNT SINAI HOSPITAL;
ASSOCIATE IN MEDICINE IN COLUMBIA UNIVERSITY
WILLIAM HARRIS, M.D.....................RADIOTHERAPIST TO THE MOUNT SINAI HOSPITAL;
ASSOCIATE IN RADIOLOGY IN COLUMBIA UNIVERSITY
HERMAN HENNELL, M.D.........................ADJUNCT PHYSICIAN FOR CHEST DISEASES TO
THE MOUNT SINAI HOSPITAL
CECELE HERSCHBERGER, B.S.............................ASSISTANT BACTERIOLOGIST TO
THE MOUNT SINAI HOSPITAL
ALEXANDER HERSH, M.D.............CLINICAL ASSISTANT, PHYSICAL THERAPY DIVISION,
OUT-PATIENT DEPARTMENT, THE MOUNT SINAI HOSPITAL
WILLIAM M. HITZIG, M.D.......ADJUNCT PHYSICIAN TO THE MOUNT SINAI HOSPITAL
FRANKLIN HOLLANDER, PH.D.......................FELLOW IN GASTROENTEROLOGY TO
THE MOUNT SINAI HOSPITAL
HENRY HORN, M.D............ASSISTANT IN MORBID ANATOMY AND CLINICAL ASSISTANT,
MEDICAL DIVISION, OUT-PATIENT DEPARTMENT, THE MOUNT SINAI HOSPITAL
HAROLD T. HYMAN, M.D........ASSOCIATE PHYSICIAN TO THE MOUNT SINAI HOSPITAL;
ASSOCIATE PROFESSOR OF PHARMACOLOGY IN COLUMBIA UNIVERSITY
HARRY L. JAFFE, M.D...........RESEARCH ASSISTANT, CARDIOGRAPHIC LABORATORY, AND
SENIOR CLINICAL ASSISTANT, MEDICAL DIVISION, OUT-PATIENT DEPARTMENT,
THE MOUNT SINAI HOSPITAL
SAMUEL KARELITZ, M.D.......ADJUNCT PEDIATRICIAN TO THE MOUNT SINAI HOSPITAL
ALBERT KEAN, M.D.........ASSOCIATE RADIOTHERAPIST TO THE MOUNT SINAI HOSPITAL;
ASSOCIATE IN RADIOLOGY IN COLUMBIA UNIVERSITY
PAUL KLEMPERER, M.D........................PATHOLOGIST TO THE MOUNT SINAI HOSPITAL;
CLINICAL PROFESSOR OF PATHOLOGY IN COLUMBIA UNIVERSITY
EMANUEL KLEMPNER, M.D.......RESEARCH ASSISTANT IN CHEMISTRY AND ASSISTANT
GYNECOLOGIST, OUT-PATIENT DEPARTMENT, THE MOUNT SINAI HOSPITAL
ALEXANDER KOLIN, PH.D.....................PHYSICIST TO THE MOUNT SINAI HOSPITAL
JEROME L. KOHN, M.D.............ADJUNCT PEDIATRICIAN TO THE MOUNT SINAI HOSPITAL
LEWIS H. KOPLIK, M.D..ASSISTANT IN BACTERIOLOGY TO THE MOUNT SINAI HOSPITAL
ABRAHAM L. KORNZWEIG, M.D...............VOLUNTARY ASSISTANT IN OPHTHALMO-
PATHOLOGY AND CLINICAL ASSISTANT, OPHTHALMOLOGICAL DIVISION,
OUT-PATIENT DEPARTMENT, THE MOUNT SINAI HOSPITAL

DEPARTMENT OF GRADUATE MEDICAL INSTRUCTION

(Continued)

RUDOLPH KRAMER, M.D.............LARYNGOLOGIST TO THE MOUNT SINAI HOSPITAL
ROBERT K. LAMBERT. M.D.................ASSOCIATE OPHTHALMIC SURGEON TO
THE MOUNT SINAI HOSPITAL
HERMAN LANDE, M.D.........ASSOCIATE IN MEDICINE TO THE MOUNT SINAI HOSPITAL;
ASSOCIATE IN MEDICINE IN COLUMBIA UNIVERSITY
MURRAY A. LAST, M.D......VOLUNTARY ASSISTANT IN OPHTHALMO-PATHOLOGY AND
ASSISTANT OPHTHALMIC SURGEON, OUT-PATIENT DEPARTMENT,
THE MOUNT SINAI HOSPITAL
JOSEPH LAVAL. M.D...ADJUNCT OPHTHALMIC SURGEON TO THE MOUNT SINAI HOSPITAL
SIDNEY D. LEADER, M.D.................SENIOR CLINICAL ASSISTANT, PEDIATRIC DIVISION,
OUT-PATIENT DEPARTMENT, THE MOUNT SINAI HOSPITAL
OSCAR L. LEVIN, M.D........ASSOCIATE DERMATOLOGIST TO THE MOUNT SINAI HOSPITAL;
ASSOCIATE IN DERMATOLOGY IN COLUMBIA UNIVERSITY
HYMAN LEVY, M.D.................CLINICAL ASSISTANT, MEDICAL DIVISION, OUT-PATIENT
DEPARTMENT, THE MOUNT SINAI HOSPITAL
SIDNEY LICHT, M.D.....ADJUNCT PHYSICAL THERAPIST TO THE MOUNT SINAI HOSPITAL
S. S. LICHTMAN, M.D.................ADJUNCT PHYSICIAN TO THE MOUNT SINAI HOSPITAL
ROBERT K. LIPPMANN, M.D.................ORTHOPEDIST TO THE MOUNT SINAI HOSPITAL
SYLVAN D. MANHEIM, M.D..........ASSISTANT SURGEON IN CHARGE OF RECTAL CLINIC,
OUT-PATIENT DEPARTMENT, THE MOUNT SINAI HOSPITAL
HUBERT MANN, M.D.................ASSISTANT IN MEDICINE TO THE MOUNT SINAI HOSPITAL
ARTHUR M. MASTER, M.D.....ASSOCIATE IN MEDICINE TO THE MOUNT SINAI HOSPITAL;
ASSOCIATE IN MEDICINE IN COLUMBIA UNIVERSITY
JACOB L. MAYBAUM, M.D.................OTOLOGIST TO THE MOUNT SINAI HOSPITAL
MAX D. MAYER, M.D.............ASSOCIATE GYNECOLOGIST TO THE MOUNT SINAI HOSPITAL;
ASSOCIATE IN GYNECOLOGY IN COLUMBIA UNIVERSITY
SAUL MILLER, M.D.........SENIOR CLINICAL ASSISTANT, OPHTHALMOLOGICAL DIVISION,
OUT-PATIENT DEPARTMENT, THE MOUNT SINAI HOSPITAL
HENRY MINSKY, M.D.................ASSOCIATE OPHTHALMIC SURGEON TO
THE MOUNT SINAI HOSPITAL
MAURICE E. MINTZ, M.D.........ASSISTANT GYNECOLOGIST, OUT-PATIENT DEPARTMENT,
THE MOUNT SINAI HOSPITAL
NATHAN MINTZ, M.D.................FELLOW IN GYNECOLOGY AND CLINICAL ASSISTANT,
GYNECOLOGICAL DIVISION, OUT-PATIENT DEPARTMENT, THE MOUNT SINAI HOSPITAL
SYLVAN E. MOOLTEN. M.D.......ADJUNCT PHYSICIAN TO THE MOUNT SINAI HOSPITAL
ELI MOSCHCOWITZ, M.D.........ASSOCIATE PHYSICIAN TO THE MOUNT SINAI HOSPITAL;
ASSISTANT CLINICAL PROFESSOR OF MEDICINE IN COLUMBIA UNIVERSITY
HAROLD NEUHOF, M.D.................SURGEON TO THE MOUNT SINAI HOSPITAL;
CLINICAL PROFESSOR OF SURGERY IN COLUMBIA UNIVERSITY
ALBERT B. NEWMAN, M.D.............SENIOR CLINICAL ASSISTANT, PEDIATRIC DIVISION,
OUT-PATIENT DEPARTMENT, THE MOUNT SINAI HOSPITAL
PEDRO ORTIZ, M.D.....VOLUNTEER ASSISTANT IN HEMATOLOGY AND CLINICAL ASSISTANT,
MEDICAL DIVISION, OUT-PATIENT DEPARTMENT, THE MOUNT SINAI HOSPITAL
REUBEN OTTENBERG, M.D.....ASSOCIATE PHYSICIAN TO THE MOUNT SINAI HOSPITAL;
ASSISTANT CLINICAL PROFESSOR OF MEDICINE IN COLUMBIA UNIVERSITY
SADAO OTANI, M.D.................ASSOCIATE PATHOLOGIST TO THE MOUNT SINAI HOSPITAL
SAMUEL M. PECK. M.D......ADJUNCT DERMATOLOGIST TO THE MOUNT SINAI HOSPITAL
M. MURRAY PESHKIN, M.D...ASSOCIATE IN PEDIATRICS TO THE MOUNT SINAI HOSPITAL
HENRY PESKIN, M.D.................CLINICAL ASSISTANT, SURGICAL DIVISION,
OUT-PATIENT DEPARTMENT, THE MOUNT SINAI HOSPITAL
ERNST P. PICK, M.D.......ASSOCIATE PHARMACOLOGIST TO THE MOUNT SINAI HOSPITAL;
CLINICAL PROFESSOR OF PHARMACOLOGY IN COLUMBIA UNIVERSITY
DANIEL POLL, M.D.................ASSOCIATE PHYSICIAN TO THE MOUNT SINAI HOSPITAL;
ASSISTANT CLINICAL PROFESSOR OF MEDICINE IN COLUMBIA UNIVERSITY
HERBERT POLLACK, M.D., PH.D.................ASSISTANT IN MEDICINE TO
THE MOUNT SINAI HOSPITAL
COLEMAN B. RABIN, M.D..........ASSOCIATE IN MEDICINE AND ASSISTANT RADIOLOGIST
TO THE MOUNT SINAI HOSPITAL; ASSOCIATE IN MEDICINE
IN COLUMBIA UNIVERSITY
MIRIAM REINER, M.S.................ASSISTANT CHEMIST TO THE MOUNT SINAI HOSPITAL
SAMUEL RICHMAN, M.D...ASSISTANT RADIOTHERAPIST TO THE MOUNT SINAI HOSPITAL

DEPARTMENT OF GRADUATE MEDICAL INSTRUCTION

(Continued)

ALFRED ROMANOFF, M.D..............Assistant Physician, Out-Patient Department, The Mount Sinai Hospital

ISADORE ROSEN, M.D..........................Dermatologist to The Mount Sinai Hospital; Clinical Professor of Dermatology and Syphilology, New York Post-Graduate Medical School, Columbia University

NATHAN ROSENTHAL, M.D....................Associate in Medicine and Hematologist to The Mount Sinai Hospital; Assistant Clinical Professor of Medicine in Columbia University

IRVING R. ROTH, M.D........Associate in Medicine and Assistant Pediatrician to The Mount Sinai Hospital; Associate in Medicine in Columbia University

ISIDOR C. RUBIN, M.D.......................Gynecologist to The Mount Sinai Hospital; Clinical Professor of Gynecology in Columbia University

U. J. SALMON, M.D.....................Adjunct Gynecologist to The Mount Sinai Hospital

NATHAN SAVITSKY, M.D.........Adjunct Neurologist to The Mount Sinai Hospital

I. SCOTTY SCHAPIRO, M.D.........Senior Clinical Assistant, Medical and Surgical Divisions, Out-Patient Department, The Mount Sinai Hospital

MAX SCHEER, M.D.............Adjunct Dermatologist to The Mount Sinai Hospital; Associate Clinical Professor of Dermatology and Syphilology, New York Post-Graduate Medical School, Columbia University

ALBERT J. SCHEIN, M.D........Adjunct Orthopedist to The Mount Sinai Hospital

BELA SCHICK, M.D.................................Pediatrician to The Mount Sinai Hospital; Clinical Professor of Pediatrics in Columbia University

KAUFMAN SCHLIVEK, M.D....Ophthalmic Surgeon to The Mount Sinai Hospital Clinical Professor of Ophthalmology in Columbia University

S. S. SCHNEIERSON, M.D..................Assistant in Bacteriology and Senior Clinical Assistant, Medical Division, Out-Patient Department, The Mount Sinai Hospital

HERMAN SCHWARZ, M.D.....Associate Pediatrician to The Mount Sinai Hospital; Assistant Clinical Professor of Pediatrics in Columbia University

G. P. SELEY, M.D.........................Research Assistant in Bacteriology; Volunteer on Dr. Colp's Service and Clinical Assistant, Surgical Division, Out-Patient Department, The Mount Sinai Hospital

SETH SELIG, M.D...................................Orthopedist to The Mount Sinai Hospital

GREGORY SHWARTZMAN, M.D........Bacteriologist to The Mount Sinai Hospital Clinical Professor of Bacteriology in Columbia University

SAMUEL SILBERT, M.D...................Adjunct Surgeon to The Mount Sinai Hospital

SOLOMON SILVER, M.D...............Adjunct Physician to The Mount Sinai Hospital

HARRY H. SOBOTKA, Ph.D........................... Chemist to The Mount Sinai Hospital

LOUIS J. SOFFER, M.D..........Adjunct Physician to The Mount Sinai Hospital

MAX L. SOM, M.D.................Adjunct Laryngologist to The Mount Sinai Hospital

MARCY L. SUSSMAN, M.D.....................Radiologist to The Mount Sinai Hospital; Associate in Radiology in Columbia University

ARTHUR S. W. TOUROFF, M.D...Associate Surgeon to The Mount Sinai Hospital

ROBERT I. WALTER, M.D...............Research Assistant in Chemistry and Clinical Assistant, Gynecological Division, Out-Patient Department, The Mount Sinai Hospital

LOUIS R. WASSERMAN, M.D.....Research Assistant in Hematology and Clinical Assistant, Medical Division, Out-Patient Department, The Mount Sinai Hospital

ISRAEL S. WECHSLER, M.D............Neurologist to The Mount Sinai Hospital; Professor of Clinical Neurology in Columbia University

HARRY WEISS, M.D....................Adjunct Physician to The Mount Sinai Hospital

DAVID WEXLER, M.D..Adjunct Ophthalmic Surgeon to The Mount Sinai Hospital

IRA S. WILE, M.D.....................Associate in Pediatrics to The Mount Sinai Hospital

SEYMOUR WIMPFHEIMER, M.D...................Adjunct Gynecologist and Assistant Radiotherapist to The Mount Sinai Hospital

ASHER WINKELSTEIN, M.D..Associate in Medicine to The Mount Sinai Hospital; Associate in Medicine in Columbia University

HARRY YARNIS, M.D.....Senior Clinical Assistant, Medical Division, Out-Patient Department, The Mount Sinai Hospital

EXECUTIVE OFFICERS AND HEADS OF DEPARTMENTS

HOSPITAL

JOSEPH TURNER, M.D. ....*Director*
JULIUS A. KATZIVE, M.D.............................*Assistant Director*
MAXWELL S. FRANK, M.D............................*Assistant Director*
MORRIS H. KREEGER, M.D............................*Assistant Director*
GEORGE T. COOK ....*Chief Clerk and Auditor*
JOHN B. CUBBERLEY ....*Supervising Engineer*
ISADORE ROGIN, PH.G. ....*Chief Apothecary*
MARY R. ERWIN, R.N................................*Supervisor, Private Pavilion*
EDITH G. RYAN, R.N................................*Supervisor Semi-Private Pavilion*
MAY E. SHAMP, R.N................................*Supervisor, Out-Patient Dept.*
FANNY LISSAUER MENDELSOHN, B.S.,R.N...*Director of Social Service*
HELEN SOMERS ....*Acting Supervising Dietitian*

SCHOOL OF NURSING

GRACE A. WARMAN, B.S., M.A., R.N.*Principal, School of Nursing, and Superintendent of Nurses*
MINNIE STRUTHERS, B.S., R.N........*Assistant Principal, School of Nursing*
LOTTIE M. PHILLIPS, R.N.............*Assistant Superintendent of Nurses*
MARION KIMBALL, R.N.................*Night Superintendent, School of Nursing*
LILLIAN LEESON, A.B., R.N...........*Supervisor of Nursing Education*
CLARE SKALING, B.S., R.N.............*Instructor of Nursing Arts*
MARION CROZIER, M.A.................*Instructor of Physical Education*
MARY R. ERWIN, R.N.................*Supervisor of Nurses, Private Pavilion*
EDITH G. RYAN, R.N.................*Supervisor of Nurses, Semi-Private Pavilion*
MAY E. SHAMP, R.N.................*Supervisor of Nurses, Out-Patient Dept.*
RUTH GOEBEL, R.N.................*Supervisor of Nurses, Operating Room*
MITHYLDE REICH, R.N.................*Supervisor of Nurses, Medical Pavilion*
BESSIE WOLFSON, B.A., R.N..........*Supervisor of Nurses, Surgical Pavilion*
CORA BALL, R.N.................*Supervisor of Nurses, Children's Pavilion*
LILLIE DIXON ....*Matron, Nurses' Residence*

REPORT OF THE MEDICAL STAFF

The medical staff of the Hospital is primarily concerned with the routine care of the sick. In reviewing its activities during the year of 1939, it may be of interest to report that the staff contributed its services without remuneration to 12,000 ward patients and more than 31,000 patients in the Out-Patient Department of the Hospital. During the year many administrative and technical improvements were introduced for the purpose of coordinating the activities of the various clinical services more effectively. More than ever before, the scientific work of the year was concerned with the application of new or improved methods of therapy. Postgraduate teaching under the auspices of Columbia University continued to form a significant feature of the staff's activities.

MEDICAL SERVICES: Aside from the formal postgraduate courses, the educational activities of the medical department have been extended to an increasing number of practicing physicians. More than 400 practitioners and specialists from all parts of the metropolitan area are attending the weekly clinical pathological conferences in the Blumenthal Auditorium, the number being limited only by the seating capacity and the standing room. Public clinics, previously called Grand Rounds, have been conducted every Friday afternoon in the renovated clinical amphitheater and have also attracted a capacity audience of 150 to 160 physicians. The conferences on electrocardiography, clinical roentgenology, thoracic diseases, and other specialties of internal medicine have also been exceedingly popular. In this manner the Hospital has steadily expanded its influence upon the practice of medicine outside its walls.

The increasing complexity of modern medicine has been reflected in a rapidly growing need for a variety of highly trained experts and specialized services. The introduction of new techniques for diagnosis and for therapy has transformed the medical service into a highly complicated organization which bears little resemblance to the medical service of 25 or 30 years ago.

Aside from the general medical work on the wards and ambulatory clinics, the rapid growth of medical knowledge and the refinement of medical techniques has necessitated the organization of six groups of medical specialists for gastro-enterology, hematology, allergy, thoracic diseases, cardio-vascular diseases and diseases of metabolism and nutrition. Each of these groups of specialists is headed by a physician holding the rank of Associate

56

in Medicine. They collaborate with the general medical staff in the diagnostic and therapeutic problems related to their specialties, and function not only on the medical wards but on all clinical services of the Hospital, wherever patients may present clinical problems in the solution of which their assistance is required. In addition each of these six groups of specialists conducts the Out-Patient Clinic related to its specialty and each is concerned with one of the laboratories. For example, the hematology group has its own clinical laboratory, the cardio-vascular conducts the cardiological laboratory for the study of the physiological abnormalities found in cardio-vascular diseases, the group of specialists for thoracic diseases is responsible for the interpretation of all x-ray work on the chest, whereas the other three special groups work in the laboratory of pathology, bacteriology or chemistry.

Few laymen can appreciate the complexities of a modern medical department of a large general hospital. The administrative responsibilities grow from year to year. In order that the medical service may be manned in all its essential branches with a variety of highly trained experts, the staff must be replenished periodically by the addition of new men, the younger physician must be stimulated and assisted to acquire training in fields of work for which the other members of the staff are not adequately qualified by education and experience, promising recent graduates must be directed into basic science work which will form the groundwork for their future career in clinical medicine or in one of its branches. All this must be accomplished in addition to efficient medical care of the patients in the wards and clinics. Scientific research must be stimulated if the Hospital is to fulfill its complete function and a large staff of interns and residents must constantly be trained and encouraged.

It is astonishing that so much has been accomplished by an unpaid staff in the time which they can spare from the private practice of medicine. The medical service has need for a large number of clinical fellowships for the younger members of the staff so that they can continue to devote all or most of their time to Hospital work.

From an administrative standpoint it may be of interest to report that the monthly staff conferences of the medical service have been largely devoted during the past year to the discussion of interdepartmental problems. They have been organized into a series of monthly round table conferences with other departments of the Hospital concerned with administrative as well as clinical matters. Various surgical and other special services have participated as well as the Social Service Department, the Out-Patient Department staff, the new psychiatric staff, the several laboratory departments. By this means numerous improvements in interdepartmental relationships have been established and substantial economies have been initiated. Some of these departmental meetings have been attended by Trustees and by representatives of the administrative staff.

The staff conferences have resulted in the curtailment of unnecessary laboratory and x-ray work, in the reduction in the number of special diets and in improvement in the methods of diagnosis and therapy. The field of oxygen therapy may be mentioned as one example of substantial monetary saving by the substitution of masks in suitable cases for oxygen tents, by the use of large in place of small oxygen tanks for anesthesia and by eliminating the loss involved in returning incompletely emptied tanks.

Due to improvement in recent years in physical facilities of the Out-Patient Department, in the character of supervision and in the relationship to the indoor services of the Hospital, the quality of the work of the medical clinics is now comparable in every way with that of the wards. The number of applications from capable physicians for clinic positions has resulted in the selection of a staff which is comparable to the indoor division. In addition to these two large afternoon clinics there are two equally efficient morning clinics for general medicine and a large number of morning and afternoon clinics for each of the various specialties of medicine.

Mention should also be made of the work which has been carried on in the various clinics of the Out-Patient Department in the retraining of a group of refugee physicians, in order that they may have an opportunity to familiarize themselves with American methods of medical practice.

Clinical research in the past year has emphasized the treatment of disease by new bacteriostatic chemicals, vitamines and new endocrine products. There has been some increase in physiologic and chemical research corresponding to the general trend in scientific medicine throughout the country, but the facilities in the Hospital for physiologic work are still inadequate.

Observations have been made of the effects of sulfanilamide and sulfapyridine and more recently of sulfathiazol in a variety of infectious processes, notably in lobar pneumonia, meningitis and subacute bacterial endocarditis. Investigations are under way on vitamine B 1 and its excretion in normal individuals and in various diseases. The therapeutic effect of various other fractions of the vitamin B complex is being studied intensively. Interesting observations have been made on the treatment of Addison's disease by the subcutaneous implantation of pellets of desoxy-corticosterone acetate, a synthetically created hormone of the adrenal gland. A variety of other investigations has been carried on by members of the medical service in connection with the various divisions of the laboratory, which are presented in more detail in the report of the laboratories.

The group interested in gastro-enterology has been elaborating our knowledge of the disease known as regional ileitis which was first described in this Hospital. The Hospital has become a center to which patients from neighboring states as well as the vicinity of the city have been attracted for medical and surgical care. The gastro-enterologic group of physicians has also been studying the treatment of ulcerative colitis and encouraging results have been obtained in this disease with an antitoxic B. coli serum prepared in collaboration with our bacteriological laboratories. The treatment of peptic ulcer by means of a continuous drip containing milk or aluminum salts is still under investigation. Further investigations have been made in the practice and interpretation of test meals for gastric acidity.

The thoracic group has developed a spot method for the more exact localization of pulmonary abscess. It has also studied the clinical picture and pathology of suppurative broncho-pneumonia, the clinical and roentgenographic appearance of acute mediastinitis, the pathogenic interrelationships of acute inflammatory diseases of the lung and the treatment of chronic spontaneous pneumothorax by the induction of a chemical pleuritis.

The chief contribution of the year by the division of hematology has been the successful operation of the blood bank. In addition, valuable observations have been made on the value of material obtained by the puncture of the lymph nodes or spleen for the differentiation of the leukemias and purpuras. The allergy division has continued the study of tobacco sensitiveness and of the immunologic properties of the several chemical fractions of ragweed pollen. Various allergic cutaneous manifestations have been studied by the application of physio-chemical principles, particularly as applied to the wheal. The possibility of the administration of drugs and other chemicals by iontophoresis has been demonstrated in an ingenious research. Extensive studies on angina pectoris and coronary artery occlusion previously reported have now been further elaborated, especially with regard to the use of fluoroscopy and roentgenkymography for the diagnosis of coronary artery occlusion. The study of the electrocardiogram after exercise has been developed as a test of coronary artery disease. Diffuse sclero-derma has been relieved by means of dihydrotachysterol and the relationship of this disease to lupus erythematosis and to dermato-myositis is about to be reported.

Two important pieces of original clinical investigation published during 1939 from the medical service concerned the relationship of the element magnesium to hyperthyroidism and myxoedema and the cure of syphilis within five days by means of a new technique. Although the total magnesium in the blood is quite constant, it has been discovered that in hyperthyroidism the element is largely bound to some protein, possibly thyroglobulin, whereas in myxo-edema all the magnesium in the blood is free and can be dialyzed through a permeable membrane. Experimentally, hyperthyroidism (exophthalmic goitre) has been produced in guinea pigs by means of the thyrotropic hormone of the pituitary gland and the chemical observations made in human sufferers have been confirmed.

The five day treatment of syphilis by means of a slow intra-venous drip for 10 to 12 hours a day can now be stated to result in a complete cure in more than 85 percent of all cases treated within the first four months after acquiring the infection. The remaining 15 percent will require a second five-day course of treatment after an interval of 3 months in order to establish a cure. The group of investigators who have been carrying on this important investigation have now an experience with more than 350 cases. Their work has been supervised by a distinguished committee composed of representatives of the U. S. Public Health Service, the Department of Health of the City of New York, the American Social Hygiene Association, the heads of the depart-ments of medicine at Columbia and Cornell University and the head of the department of pharmacology at Columbia. The follow up and interpretation of the results has been the responsibility of the departments of syphilis at the New York and Bellevue Hospitals, so that the conclusions may be regarded as truly objective. Since changing the arsenical to arsenoxide (mapharsen) practically all toxic effects have been eliminated. These results open up new possibilities in public health. This new form of treatment takes the infected person out of circulation and discharges him a week later free of the ability to transmit his infection to others. Although the method is not yet to be recommended for general practitioners, it is immediately applicable for use in hospital therapy.

PEDIATRIC SERVICE: Investigations on the pediatric service have been concerned with a variety of clinical problems. Many of these were in the field of vitamines, including a study of the distribution of vitamine D in the body after the administration of massive doses, the treatment of rickets and tetany with a single dose of vitamine D, the effect of hyperthermia on vitamine C in the blood plasma, the determination of vitamine C in children by intradermal injection, biophotometric studies in cases of ulcerative colitis, the relationship of vitamine A deficiency to eczema, the relation of vitamines C and K to capillary fragility and the influence of vitamines C and E on asthma.

· The work on insensible perspiration and basal metabolism has been continued and has resulted in a number of publications. A comprehensive review of the use of sulfapyridine in the cases of pneumonia on the service was presented before the American Academy of Pediatrics. The management of cases of whooping cough has been reviewed in order to achieve better control of the communicability and mortality of this disease which is now responsible for more deaths in children under five years of age than all other communicable diseases of childhood combined.

A special Out-Patient Department section was devoted to the study of the growth and development of children. The allergy clinic has ‹been conducting scientific studies upon the problems of immunization against tetanus and scarlet fever. The cardiac clinic is studying bacteremias following dental extractions and tonsillectomies with a view to using bacteriastatic substances such as surfanilamide to prevent a complicating subacute bacterial endocarditis in children with valvular disease. Other studies from the pediatric service included an investigation designed to improve the tuberculin patch test, and researches upon the mechanism of serum sickness. There has been an increase in the postgraduate teaching and in the attendance at the weekly pediatric conferences.

61

NEUROLOGIC SERVICE: The new work with electroencephalography has been concerned with a number of problems, which it is hoped, will soon provide material worthy of report. An exhibit on clinical electroencephalography was presented at the American Congress of Physiotherapy. Postgraduate courses have been organized.

The psychiatric division has been entirely reorganized during the past year. More expert psychiatric service is now available on the medical and some of the surgical wards and in medical clinics of the Out-Patient Department. The psychiatrists are now working shoulder to shoulder with the internists and surgeons and giving immeasurable assistance in the understanding and relief of many psychosomatic factors in disease. The reorganization of the psychiatric service constitutes an important change in the clinical services of the Hospital.

DERMATOLOGICAL SERVICE: This service is participating in the important work on the treatment of syphilis by massive doses of arsenicals. Chemical studies of snake venom have been continued. There have been several investigations of fungi and a special mycologic group has been formed to study fungus infection. The radiotherapy department has arranged its staff during the past year so as to provide closer collaboration with the dermatological service in the treatment of skin diseases.

SURGICAL SERVICES: A number of important surgical problems have been the subject of special studies. Unsolved problems of peptic ulcer have continued to constitute one of the major investigations. The methods of surgical resection have been restudied as have problems concerned with bacteriology, chemistry and the rôle of psychogenic factors. A member of the psychiatric department has been associated with the surgical service in an effort to correlate the psyche to gastroduodenal ulceration. Studies in regional ileitis have been continued, particularly in regard to the value and methods of performing intestinal resections and anastomosis in this disease. Advances have been made in the surgical treatment of intractable ulcerative colitis. The mortality rate for the operation of ileostomy has been reduced to approximately 14 per cent, a remarkably low figure for this serious disease. Many patients with ulcerative colitis who were formerly lifetime chronic invalids, are now being restored to social and economic self-sufficiency.

Studies in the normal and abnormal physiological activity of the excretory apparatus of the liver have been continued. The value of vitamine K in the treatment of patients with jaundice and determinations of the prothrombin time in the prognosis of jaundiced patients is under investigation. Operations were performed on a large number of patients with carcinoma of the colon. In order to be able in the future to evaluate the permanent results obtained, the operative procedure for this condition has been standardized. Further experiences in the resection of carcinoma of the esophagus continue to yield encouraging results. Studies have been initiated on post-operative hiccough and serious disturbances of water balance which sometimes follow extensive surgical procedures.

The surgical service interested in thoracic diseases has continued to obtain favorable results in the surgical treatment of acute putrid pulmonary abscess of which there are now 104 operated cases. Progress has been made in the study of constrictive pericarditis, empyema, pulmonary neoplasms, suppurative bronchial pneumonia, cervico-mediastinal infections, pulmonary embolism, acute intestinal obstruction, acute peritonitis, subpectoral abscess and phlebitis of the axillary vein, the viability of fat grafts in the pulmonary cavities, and the viability of the testicle after severance of the cord. The technique of pneumonectomy has been improved and an operative procedure for the cure of direct hernia has been developed.

On the neurosurgical service experimental and clinical work has been conducted on the visualization of the cerebral vessels. Publications were also made on epidural spinal infections, phrenic nerve interruption in para-esophageal hernia, surgical therapy of certain convulsive disorders, and sunray hemangioma of the skull.

GYNECOLOGIC SERVICE: This service has continued its studies on the endocrinological aspects of various gynecological disturbances and particularly on the treatment of the menopause and other functional derangements of female physiology. New investigations have dealt with the physiological and biological activity of estrogenic and androgenic hormones and the application of these hormones to the treatment of gynecologic diseases.

The subcutaneous implantation of synthetic ovarian hormones represents an important practical contribution to the problem of the therapy of the menopause. Over 100 patients have now been treated. This method has proved effective in various types of ovarian deficiency. It has also been employed prophylactically at the time of surgical removal of the ovaries in order to prevent the development of symptoms of the artificial menopause. Synthetic male hormone (testosterone propionate) has also been found efficacious in the treatment of certain forms of menorrhagia, metrorrhagia, dysmenorrhea, premenstrual tension and in refractory types of menopausal symptoms. Presentations, conferences and exhibits on these important subjects have been held at a number of scientific meetings including the New York State Medical Society, the American Medical Association, the Third International Cancer Congress and the Twelfth Postgraduate Fortnight of the New York Academy of Medicine.

The work in gynecological pathology has been extended, especially on the histogenesis and pathology of ovarian neoplasms. Studies in experimental pathology were conducted in order to determine the effect of sex hormones upon the endometrium. Attempts are being made to improve various tests used in gynecology and endocrinology. The endocrine division of the gynecologic service has also been collaborating with other services and departments in the study of problems of joint interest.

Hormonal studies on sterility have been pursued in selected cases. An investigation of stress incontinence has been continued in order to reveal its cause and develop methods for improving the operative results. Anatomical studies have provided the basis for the development of improved operative techniques. The contractions of the uterine tubes were correlated with the hormonal status of women, and the effects have been noted of estrogenic, androgenic, and gonadotropic substances on the tubal muscle. A new visualization technique has also been devised which will demonstrate the presence of submucous myomata.

LARYNGOLOGICAL SERVICE: New operative procedures on the sinuses for infection and malignancy were developed. The operative treatment of sinusitis has provided new opportunities to study the influence of focal infections upon asthma. These investigations have included bacteriological and immunological studies. The pathological basis for cerebro-spinal rhinorrhea was elucidated. Observations have also been made on laryngeal lesions which result from endocrine therapy. A report was made on the pathology and treatment of juvenile nasal fibroma.

OTOLOGICAL SERVICE: Clinical investigations were conducted on the hazards and value of sulfanilamide in otogenous infections, particularly on the effect of this drug in masking the clinical picture. This has resulted in extending our knowledge of the indications and contraindications to the use of sulfanilamide in mastoiditis. Observations on the clinical course of otogenous infections due to the type III pneumococcus have provided a more comprehensive concept of the varied clinical pictures encountered. The installation in the clinic of an audiometer has provided increased interest in the diagnosis and treatment of impaired hearing. A number of men on the staff have been organized into a group in order to conduct studies on hearing disturbances, especially those due to otosclerosis. Neuro-otologic studies have been undertaken to stimulate the interest of members of the staff in this subject and one of the members of the service has been pursuing investigations in the neuropathological laboratory.

OPHTHALMOLOGICAL SERVICE: No great change in the routine work of this service has occurred during the year. Postgraduate instruction has grown considerably, and two new courses on functional testing and physiological optics have been added. Almost every branch of ophthalmology is now covered in the courses. The enlarged residency plan is now in operation and is proving very satisfactory to the Hospital and to the residents. Scientific work is in progress on fundus photography, the etiology of iritis, the structure of the ocular circulation, sarcoid of the lacrymal gland, the anatomic structure of myopic eyes and ocular complications in various types of meningitis.

ORTHOPEDIC SERVICE: During 1939 there was increased interest in the monthly conferences and the attendance was much greater than previously. This was due chiefly to the new policy of having a prominent guest speaker at each meeting. The activity of the service has continued essentially as in the previous year. There has been a special interest in the clinical aspects of low back pain and this subject has been investigated by the entire staff.

DEPARTMENT OF ROENTGENOLOGY: In 1939, 21,581 patient visits were made as compared with 20,848 in 1938. In spite of this increase, the number of films used decreased from 68,241 to 66,451. The efficiency of the department has been improved by the reorganization of the filing system and reclassification of the museum.

Considerable experimental work was performed to evaluate the results obtainable by body section radiography and by photography of the fluoroscopic screen. Other studies in progress include air and opaque myelography, biliary dyskinesia, the pattern of the small bowel with various media, and the use of an ionization chamber as an aid in roentgenologic diagnostic technique. By invitation, a symposium on the small bowel was given. This included presentations on the roentgenologic diagnosis of regional ileitis, the small bowel in states of deficient nutrition and the pattern of the small bowel with varying bowel content and under the influence of drugs. The postgraduate courses given in radiology in connection with Columbia University have been continued. There has been a progressive increase in the size of the classes and a decided improvement in the qualifications of the students who have come from various parts of the country.

DEPARTMENT OF RADIOTHERAPY: Radiotherapy was administered to 562 new patients and to 696 patients who had been treated previously. There was a slight diminution in the number of new patients because of an interruption in the treatment of skin cases for several months while a new machine was installed for this purpose and another was modernized. Dermatological cases previously treated in the Radiotherapy Department are now being treated in the Out-Patient Department to which a roentgen-ray machine for superficial therapy was transferred. This new arrangement has reduced overcrowding in the Radiotherapy Department and has afforded more opportunities in radiation therapy to the members of the dermatological staff.

Part of the Hospital's radium supply was converted into more flexible units during the year. This has made possible the elimination of the use of radon in certain cases and has resulted in more effective treatment.

Throughout the Hospital, greater use of roentgen-ray was made in the treatment of benign inflammatory disease; studies on more precise methods for the administration of radiation therapy were carried out with the cooperation of our physicists.

Close cooperation is being maintained with the laryngological service in the treatment and follow-up of neoplasms of the upper respiratory passages. Similar cooperation is being maintained with the hematological department in the management of patients with diseases of the blood-forming organs. Weekly departmental conferences were inaugurated in 1939, all new cases being discussed by the entire staff. Bimonthly conferences are also held in collaboration with the Department of Roentgenology.

DEPARTMENT OF PHYSICAL THERAPY: A variety of original investigations in physical therapy was initiated during the past year and are being continued. These include the observations on physically induced fever, changes following local application of cold, intra-muscular temperature of the human calf, chronaxie, and the clinical evaluation of the short wave current. Studies were made on the effect of fever therapy upon bile flow, on gastric secretion, on the contraction of the sphincter of Oddi and of the cardiac sphincters. Physiologic investigations have also been made to determine the effect of local applications of cold on the temperature of various body tissues, on blood flow in the extremities, on neurologic alterations and on modification of local tissue immunity. The clinical application of cold has been employed successfully in cases of peripheral vascular disease, cardiac disease, localized malignancy, acute inflammatory states and in a variety of other conditions. The possibility of undertaking the study of systemic refrigeration is under consideration by a special committee.

A number of scientific exhibits were presented at the annual meeting of the American Congress of Physical Therapy, at which a silver medal was awarded for one of the exhibits on temperature studies in the human calf.

· DENTAL DEPARTMENT: The dental department has continued to provide a great variety of dental services. There were 1,162 new patients treated in the Out-Patient Department and a total of 15,808 patient visits. The lectures on dental medicine given in collaboration with other services and departments in the Hospital were continued. Clinical demonstrations were also given at a number of dental society meetings.

In this outline it has only been possible to mention the major scientific activities of the various clinical divisons of the Hospital. Many other research activities, which were carried on in collaboration with the laboratories, are listed in the annual report of the Department of Laboratories. The volume and variety of the clinical and laboratory investigations are an indication of that spirit of scientific inquiry which must animate the staff of a truly modern hospital. The knowledge and the technical skills of the staff must be maintained constantly at a high level in order that there may be no lag between scientific progress and its prompt application to the care of the sick. If our medical staff is to continue to represent the best standards of medical practice, additional support for scientific research must be secured.

GEORGE BAEHR, M.D.

President of the Medical Board.

BEQUESTS AND DONATIONS FOR SPECIAL
PURPOSES DURING YEAR 1939

Committee on Neighborhood Health Development, Inc.—For Intravenous Drip Therapy Project	$9,483.39
David A. Schulte—For Dental Clinic	8,000.00
New York Foundation—For support of cancer research of Dr. Richard Lewisohn	3,000.00
Mount Sinai Hospital Research Foundation—For equipment of Dr. Shwartzman's research	2,878.49
✔ Estate of Amelia A. Meyers—For support of research in Abraham and Amelia Meyers Memorial Laboratory—Additional	2,504.29 ✔
Mrs. Arthur Lehman—For support of cancer research of Dr. Richard Lewisohn	2,500.00
Frances and John Loeb Foundation—For support of cancer research of Dr. Richard Lewisohn	2,500.00
Josiah Macy, Jr. Foundation—To continue support of studies on the secretion of a para-sympathetic substance under emotional stress.	1,750.00
Ittleson Foundation—For support of cancer research of Dr. Richard Lewisohn	1,500.00
Miss Adelaide Reckford—For support of cancer research of Dr. Richard Lewisohn	1,500.00
Mrs. Charles Klingenstein—For the Charles Klingenstein Fellowship Fund	1,500.00
Dr. Ralph Colp—Toward Fellowship for gastro-enterology research	1,250.00
The Friedsam Foundation, Inc.—For ear, nose and throat research	1,200.00
The Friedsam Foundation, Inc.—For special hormone research	1,200.00
"A Friend"—For a Fellowship in Gynecology to commemorate the 76th Birthday of Dr. Joseph Brettauer	1,200.00
Mr. and Mrs. Frank Altschul—For cardio-vascular research	1,000.00
Mrs. Walter A. Hirsch—In memory of Walter A. Hirsch—For leukemia research	1,000.00
Mrs. Levy Mayer—In memory of Walter A. Hirsch—For leukemia research	1,000.00
Mr. Joseph Klingenstein—For non-budgetary purposes	1,000.00
Adeline and Carl M. Loeb Foundation—In memory of Lee J. Moses—For support of cancer research of Dr. Richard Lewisohn	1,000.00
Adeline and Carl M. Loeb Foundation—For support of cancer research of Dr. Richard Lewisohn	900.00
The Mount Sinai Hospital Research Foundation—For venom research	900.00
Josiah Macy, Jr. Foundation—For research on psychological and physiological aspects of angina pectoris	750.00
John Wyeth & Brother, Inc.—For the study of the continuous drip method in treatment of peptic ulcer	750.00
Mrs. Charles Altschul—For cardio-vascular research	500.00
Carried Forward	$50,766.17

68

BEQUESTS AND DONATIONS FOR SPECIAL PURPOSES DURING YEAR 1939

(Continued)

Brought Forward	$50,766.17
Anonymous—For cardio-vascular research	500.00
Dazian Foundation for Medical Research—To continue support of neurophysiology research	500.00
Dazian Foundation for Medical Research—For gastric physiology research	500.00
Mrs. Louis J. Grumbach—For support of cancer research of Dr. Richard Lewisohn	500.00
Frances and John Loeb Foundation—For cardio-vascular research	500.00
Dr. Percy Klingenstein—Toward Fellowship for gastro-enterology research	500.00
Mrs. Arthur M. Master—For cardio-vascular research	500.00
Mr. and Mrs. Walter W. Naumburg—For Research Fund	500.00
Max J. Shapiro—For support of neurology research	500.00
Greater New York Chapter of the National Foundation for Infantile Paralysis, Inc.—For the care and after-treatment of Infantile Paralysis	439.21
Dr. Samuel H. Geist—For centrifuge	330.30
Dr. Ralph Colp—For Fellowship in Bacteriology	300.00
Louis S. Weiss—For Vitamin A research	300.00
Dr. Clarence Buttenwieser—Toward Fellowship for gastro-enterology research	250.00
Philip J. Goodhart—For cardio-vascular research	200.00
Mrs. Edward S. Kaufman—In memory of Rosalie Nathan—For Research Fund	200.00
Dr. Samuel M. Peck—For venom research	168.15
Mrs. Charles Klingenstein—In celebration of Mr. Charles Klingenstein's birthday—For Staff Loan and Relief Fund	150.00
Sidney J. Eisman—For Staff Loan and Relief Fund	150.00
M. L. Seidman—Toward Fellowship for gastro-enterology research	150.00
John Wyeth & Brother, Inc.—For gastro-intestinal research	150.00
Associated Alumni of The Mount Sinai Hospital—For Library Fund	100.00
Morton L. Adler—For the "Anniversary of a birthday"—For the Staff Loan and Relief Fund	100.00
Anonymous—For non-budgetary purposes	100.00
Louis Flaster—For special non-budgetary needs of the Physical Therapy Department	100.00
"A Friend"—For Research Fund	100.00
Hon. Amy Guest—For Research Fund	100.00
Lawrence M. and Miss Carol M. Hirsch—In memory of Walter A. Hirsch—For Research Fund	100.00
Carried Forward	$58,753.83

BEQUESTS AND DONATIONS FOR SPECIAL PURPOSES DURING YEAR 1939

(Continued)

Brought Forward	$58,753.83
Mrs. Charles Klingenstein—To commemorate an anniversary—For Staff Loan and Relief Fund	100.00
Mrs. Charles Klingenstein—For Staff Loan and Relief Fund	100.00
Samuel Marcus—For Research Fund	100.00
Mrs. Roger W. Straus—For support of cancer research of Dr. Richard Lewisohn	100.00
Lou Schneider—Toward the support of neurology research	100.00
Joseph Stroock—Toward Fellowship for gastro-enterology research	100.00
Edwin Trent—Toward Fellowship for gastro-enterology research	100.00
Dr. Robert K. Lambert—For research in eye pathology	67.19
Anonymous—(Through Dr. Herbert Pollack)—For research on Vitamin B-1	50.00
Mrs. Bertha Brant—In memory of Saul Brant—For Research Fund	50.00
Mrs. Isaac Friedenheit—In memory of her son, Myron Friedenheit's birthday—For Research Fund	50.00
Mrs. M. L. Seidman—Toward Fellowship for gastro-enterology research	50.00
Mrs. Lewis M. Bloomingdale—For non-budgetary purposes	25.00
Sidney Blumenthal—In memory of Murry Guggenheim—For the Murry Guggenheim Scholarship Fund	25.00
Mr. and Mrs. Richard Hirsch—In memory of Charles Klingenstein—For Staff Loan and Relief Fund	25.00
Mrs. Settie Hirsch—In memory of Charles Klingenstein's birthday—For Staff Loan and Relief Fund	25.00
Mr. Walter W. Kohn—In celebration of Charles Klingenstein's birthday—For Staff Loan and Relief Fund	25.00
Mrs. Milly Frank Mayer—For non-budgetary purposes	25.00
First New Sandez Society, Inc.—For Research Fund	25.00
Mr. and Mrs. Sam Levine—For Research Fund	21.00
Mrs. Harry G. Hockstadter—In celebration of Billy's birthday, April 26th—For a treat in the Children's Wards	10.00
Robert J. Misch—For Library Fund	10.00
Miss Grace M. Mayer—In memory of Dr. Leo Kessel—For Research Fund	10.00
Mrs. Charles A. Wimpfheimer—In memory of Murry Guggenheim—For the Murry Guggenheim Scholarship Fund	10.00
Dr. Maurice B. Hexter—For Staff Loan and Relief Fund	5.00
Smith Periodical Fund—For Library Fund	5.00
Hendrick Van Loon—In memory of Charles J. Mendelsohn—For Research Fund	5.00
Total	$59,972.02

70

DONATIONS DURING YEAR 1939

Bing Fund, Inc.—In memory of Cora G. Edelmuth.......................... $25.00
Ralph M. Freydberg 10.92
The Misses Albert 10.00
Mrs. Samuel L. Dinkelspiel—In memory of Mr. Henry S. Glazier 10.00
Bernard Feigen 10.00
William Guthman—In memory of Cora G. Edelmuth.................... 10.00
Mr. and Mrs. Frank E. Karelsen, Jr.—In memory of Emanuel
    Van Raalte 10.00
Nathan Kaufman 10.00
John Raiss—In memory of Mr. Henry S. Glazier......................... 10.00
Miss Evelyn Rosenfeld—In memory of Joseph Moschcowitz........ 10.00
Mrs. K. Ulan.. 10.00
Miss N. Welt 10.00
Miscellaneous donations 57.50

    Total... $193.42

𝔍𝔫 𝔐𝔢𝔪𝔬𝔯𝔦𝔞𝔪

BENJAMIN HARRISON JACOBS
Employed 14 Years
ACCOUNTING DEPARTMENT
Died Aug. 31, 1939

ENDOWMENTS FOR SPECIAL PURPOSES

Mr. and Mrs. Charles Klingenstein Fund................................$109,000.00
Established by Mr. and Mrs. Charles Klingenstein; income
to be used for non-budgetary purposes as determined
annually by the Board of Trustees.

Benjamin Altman Fund.. 100,000.00
Established by provision in the will of Benjamin Altman;
one-half of the income to be utilized to defray expenses of
the Neurological Department, the remainder for the general
purposes of the institution.

**Marjorie Walter Goodhart and Florence Henrietta Walter
Children's Clinic Endowment**.. 100,000.00
Founded by their parents, Florence B. and William I.
Walter; income to be used for the purposes of Children's
Clinic.

**Marjorie Walter Goodhart and Florence Henrietta Walter
Memorial Fund** 25,000.00
Established by provision in the will of Miss Rosie Bern-
heimer; income to be applied towards the running expenses
of the Children's Clinic.

Babette Lehman Fund 100,000.00
Founded by Mrs. Babette Lehman; income to be utilized
for the advancement of preventive medicine.

Louis W. Neustadter Fund.. 100,000.00
Founded by provision in the will of Mrs. Henry Neustadter;
distribution of income to be made annually on the 16th day
of March, a portion to needy and indigent patients in the
Hospital on that date, the remainder for the general purposes
of the Hospital.

Mount Sinai Hospital Fund for Medical Education................. 50,000.00
Joseph F. and Zillah Cullman contributed $25,000.00 as a
nucleus of said fund, and $25,000.00 contributed by the
estate of Henry P. Goldschmidt; the income to be used to
defray expenses arising out of clinical lectures, demonstrations and conferences, and for cognate purposes.

Alfred A. and Ruth M. Cook Fund.. 50,000.00
Founded by Alfred A. and Ruth M. Cook; income to be
applied to special experimental work in the Social Service
Department.

Florette and Ernst Rosenfeld Foundation............................... 50,000.00
Founded by Florette and Ernst Rosenfeld; for the estab-
lishment and special support of a Department of Radium
and Radiotherapy.

Dr. Isador Abrahamson Neurological Fund............................. 50,000.00
Established by provision in the will of Stella Heidelberg
Abrahamson; the income from this fund to be used for
Fellowships for research work and study in the field of
neurology and psychiatry.

George Blumenthal, Jr. Fellowship Fund................................ 45,000.00
Founded by Mrs. Florence Blumenthal; income to be applied
to the maintenance of two Fellowships in Pathology.

Helen B. Millhauser Fund... 38,000.00

ENDOWMENTS FOR SPECIAL PURPOSES
(Continued)

Etta C. Lorsch Memorial Fund $34,000.00
 Established by provision in the will of Etta C. Lorsch
 ($10,000); by members of the Board of the Social Ser-
 vice Auxiliary ($10,000.00); and by many of her friends
 ($4,370.00); the sum of $10,000.00 was added by provision
 in the will of William N. Cohen; income to be disbursed
 by the Social Service Auxiliary for the special country care
 of children.
Jacob Mayer Fund 30,000.00
 Founded in memory of Jacob Mayer for equipping and
 maintaining a pneumonia room.
Harriet Meyer Memorial Fund 25,000.00
 Founded by Eugene Meyer; income to be used for experi-
 mental work in the Social Service Department.
Alice Goldschmidt Sachs Endowment Fund 25,000.00
 Established by provision in the will of Alice Goldschmidt
 Sachs; income to be used for medical education.
Moritz Rosenthal Fellowship Fund 25,000.00
 Established by provision in the will of Moritz Rosenthal;
 income to be used for medical, surgical, clinical or
 laboratory Fellowships as granted to men selected by the
 Board of Trustees.
Ambulance Fund 20,000.00
 Established by Murry Guggenheim; income to be applied
 toward the maintenance of the ambulance service.
Murry Guggenheim Scholarship Fund 20,000.00
 Founded by Murry Guggenheim; income to provide medals
 and twelve scholarships of $100 each annually to nurses of
 The Mount Sinai Hospital School of Nursing.
Moritz Warburg Social Service Fund 20,000.00
 Founded by Felix M. and Paul M. Warburg; income to be
 applied to the work of the Social Service Department.
Emanuel Van Raalte Endowment Fund for Medical
 Education 20,000.00
 Legacy; income to be used for medical education.
Minnie Kastor Memorial Fund 19,775.00
 Founded by Alfred B. Kastor as a tribute to the memory
 of his mother; income to be used for psychiatric work
 through the service of a Fellow in psychiatry.
Charles Klingenstein Fellowship Fund 18,000.00
 Established by Mrs. Charles Klingenstein; income to be
 used for Fellowship in any clinical or laboratory department
 of the Hospital as determined by the Board of Trustees.
Robert and John Kaufmann Vacation Fund 11,000.00
 Founded by Max Kaufmann; income to be used for
 providing vacations, preferably for crippled children.
Theodor Escherich Fellowship Fund 10,000.00
 Founded by Edward S. Steinam; income to be applied
 to the maintenance of a Fellowship in Pathology.
Moses Heineman Fellowship Fund 10,000.00
 Founded by Moses Heineman; income to be applied to the
 maintenance of a Fellowship in Pathology.

ENDOWMENTS FOR SPECIAL PURPOSES

(Continued)

Dr. Henry Koplik Fund... $10,000.00
Established by provision in the will of Dr. Henry Koplik;
income to be disbursed by the Social Service Department
and devoted solely to the care of infants and children,
whose parents are unable to pay ward fees.

Eugene Meyer, Jr. Fellowship Fund............... .... 10,000.00
Founded by Eugene Meyer, Jr.; income to be applied to
the maintenance of a Fellowship in Pathology.

William Henry Welch Lecture Fund...................... 10,000.00
Established by Dr. Emanuel Libman; income to be used to
provide lectures to be named after Dr. William Henry Welch
of Johns Hopkins University.

Emil Wolff Social Service Fund.................... 10,000.00
Established by Emil Wolff; income to be applied to the
work of the Social Service Department.

Library Funds 7,200.00
Dr. Abraham Jacobi Library Fund of $5,000.00 established
by the Board of Trustees to commemorate the eightieth
birthday of Dr. Abraham Jacobi; income to be applied to
the purchase of books for the Hospital Library.

Dr. Fred S. Mandlebaum Memorial Fund of $2,200.00 con-
tributed by many of his friends; income to be applied to the
purchase of books for the Hospital Library.

Charles and Camilla Altschul Fund for Nursing in Wards.... 5,000.00
Founded by Charles and Camilla Altschul; to defray the
expense of special nursing in the wards.

Isaac C. Bishop Fund... 5,000.00
Established by provision in the will of Morris Bishop;
income to be used for the relief, care and benefit of poor
patients suffering from cancer.

Edward Gamaliel Janeway Lecture Fund.................................. 5,000.00
Founded by Edward S. Steinam; income to be utilized
to bring important investigators to Mount Sinai Hospital,
to present the result of their work.

Fannie C. Korn Fund... 5,000.00
Founded by Mrs. Fannie C. Korn—In Memory of Henry
Korn; for the establishing and maintaining of a splint and
apparatus room for the Orthopedic Service.

Mount Sinai Hospital Alumni Fund.. 4,400.00
Donation of Dr. H. F. L. Ziegel; income, and if necessary,
capital, to be expended in defraying part or all of the cost
of caring in private rooms of the Hospital for members of
the Associated Alumni of Mount Sinai Hospital, the expenditures for any one case not to exceed $200.

Morris Littman Social Service Fund....................................... 3,000.00
Established by provision in the will of Morris Littman;
income to be applied to the work of the Social Service
Department.

MEDICAL RESEARCH FUNDS

The Abraham and Amelia Meyers Memorial Fund...................$227,000.00
> Established by provision in the will of Amelia Meyers; income to be used in the furtherance of medical and scientific research.

S. S. Prince Research Fund... 100,000.00
> Established by provision in the will of S. S. Prince; income to be used for research work.

Henry and Emma Rosenwald Foundation................................ 100,000.00
> Established by provision in the will of Mrs. Emma Rosenwald; income to be used for research work. If such work becomes impracticable or inadvisable, the income is to be used for any other purpose designated by the Trustees.

Kops Foundation for Pathological Research............................ 70,000.00
> Income to be used from time to time for special work in the Pathological Department, under the direction of the Board of Trustees, preference to be given to research.

The Lorsch-Sachs Endowment Fund for the Promotion of Medical Research 60,000.00
> Created by Josephine Lorsch, Nellie and Harry Sachs in memory of Albert Lorsch, Jenny and Sigmund Lorsch; income to be used for the study of some promising scientific problems especially for research work bearing upon the origin and cure of cancer.

Max Nathan Laboratory Fund... 30,000.00
> Established by his wife and daughters; income to be used primarily towards the payment of salaries in the Laboratory Research Department.

Eugene Littauer Research Fund... 25,000.00
> Founded by Eugene Littauer in memory of Nathan Littauer; income to be used for medical research work.

William N. Cohen Research Fund... 25,000.00
> Established by provision in the will of William N. Cohen; income to be used for research work.

Elias Asiel Research Fund... 21,000.00
> Founded by Irma A. Bloomingdale and Nelson I. Asiel; income of which is to be applied to the payment of salaries or fellowships in the research work of the Pathological Department.

Eugene Strauss Endowment Fund for Medical Research...... 20,000.00
> Established by provision in the will of Charles Strauss; income to be used for medical research.

Carried Forward $678,000.00

MEDICAL RESEARCH FUNDS

(Continued)

Brought Forward $678,000.00

Morris J. and Carrie Hirsch Fund... 12,500.00
Established by Walter A. and Steven J. Hirsch in memory
of their parents ($10,000.00); and donation ($2,500.00) from
Mr. and Mrs. Steven J. Hirsch in memory of Walter A.
Hirsch; income to be devoted to work in connection with
the study of cancer.

Rosie Bernheimer Memorial Fund.. 10,000.00
Established by provision in the will of Miss Rosie Bern-
heimer; income to be used for clinical research work.

Morris Fatman Medical Research Fund................................... 10,000.00
Founded by Morris Fatman in memory of Solomon A.
Fatman.

Etta C. and Arthur Lorsch Fund... 10,000.00
Founded by Etta C. and Arthur Lorsch; income to be devoted
to Laboratory research work.

Elsie and Walter W. Naumburg Fund..................................... 10,000.00
Established by Mr. and Mrs. Walter W. Naumburg; income
to be used exclusively for Chemical Research at Mount Sinai
Hospital.

Virginia I. Stern Fund.. 10,000.00
Legacy; income to be used for medical research work.

**Herman Younker Fund for Clinical and Pathological
Research** 10,000.00
Established by Mrs. Herman Younker; income to be used
exclusively for clinical and pathological research.

Joel E. Hyams Fund... 10,000.00
Established by provision in the will of Rosalie Hyams;
income to be devoted to research work in cancer.

Leo L. Doblin Endowment Fund for Research Work............ 9,250.00
Legacy; income to be used solely for research work in the
pathological laboratory (On account of $10,000.00 legacy).

Arthur E. Frank Medical Research Fund................................ 7,500.00
Established by provision in the will and in memory of
Arthur E. Frank; the income from this fund is to be
devoted to Laboratory research work, preferably in connection with the study and cure of cancer.

Total $777,250.00

ENDOWMENT FUNDS

The Jacob Newman Fund...$257,000.00

The Carrie M. and Gustav Blumenthal Fund.... 35,000.00

The George and Florence Blumenthal Fund...... 30,000.00

The Philip J. and Hattie L. Goodhart Fund........ 30,000.00

The Ellin P. and James Speyer Fund...................... 30,000.00

The Annie C. and Charles A. Wimpfheimer Fund 30,000.00

The Murry and Leonie Guggenheim Fund............ 25,000.00

The Tillie S. and Alfred Jaretzki Fund................ 25,000.00

The Adolph and Emma Lewisohn Fund.................. 20,000.00

The Edward Oppenheimer Fund.............................. 20,000.00

The Estelle and Hugo Blumenthal Fund............ 15,000.00

The Elias and Lina Meyer Asiel Fund.................. 10,000.00

The John A. and Henrietta Cook Fund.................. 10,000.00

The David L. and Carrie F. Einstein Fund............ 10,000.00

The Paul and Miriam H. Gottheil Fund.............. 10,000.00

The Albert N. Hallgarten Fund.............................. 10,000.00

The Henry and Rosa Lehman Fund........................ 10,000.00

The Albert A. Levi Fund.. 10,000.00

The Eugene and Harriet Meyer Fund.................... 10,000.00

The Henry and Josephine Morgenthau Fund...... 10,000.00

The Rosalie and Max Nathan Fund........................ 10,000.00

The Mr. and Mrs. Sam S. Steiner Fund.................. 10,000.00

The Isaac and Virginia Stern Fund........................ 10,000.00

The Alexandre and Julie Weill Fund.................... 10,000.00

$647,000.00

TREASURER'S REPORT

STATEMENT OF CURRENT RECEIPTS

FOR THE YEAR ENDED DECEMBER 31st, 1939

HOSPITAL:

Payments of Patients:

Private Pavilion Patients	$587,833.62	
Semi-Private Pavilion Patients	286,428.67	
Ward Patients	102,495.74	
Ward Patients treated under Workmen's Compensation Act	8,995.52	
Out-Patient Department Patients	49,263.18	
Total		$1,035,016.73

Payments by:

City of New York for Part Maintenance of Free Ward Patients and for Custodians....	192,010.67

Contributions:

Federation for the Support of Jewish Philanthropic Societies	264,757.98	
Greater New York Fund (through Federation)	46,139.00	
United Hospital Fund	56,498.16	
Donations	193.42	
Total		367,588.56

Income from Investments:

Permanent Fund	17,420.57	
Endowment Fund	15,325.94	
Other Special Funds for Budgetary Purposes....	17,490.80	
Total		50,237.31
Total Budgetary Receipts (Hospital)		1,644,853.27

SCHOOL OF NURSING:

From Federation for the Support of Jewish Philanthropic Societies	275,956.47	
From Other Sources for Budgetary Purposes	9,104.66	
Total Budgetary Receipts (School of Nursing)		285,061.13

SOCIAL SERVICE AUXILIARY:

From Federation for the Support of Jewish Philanthropic Societies	98,502.44	
From United Hospital Fund	19,500.00	
From Other Sources for Budgetary Purposes....	4,548.55	
Total Budgetary Receipts (Social Service Auxiliary)		122,550.99
Carried Forward		2,052,465.39

Brought Forward	$2,052,465.39

LADIES' AUXILIARY:

From Federation for the Support of Jewish Philanthropic Societies	25,492.00
Total Receipts for Budgetary Purposes (Four Societies)	2,077,957.39
Appropriations from Principal and/or Income of Special Funds for Stated Non-Budgetary Purposes (per contra)	126,644.22
Total Receipts (Budgetary and Non-Budgetary) (Four Societies)...................	$2,204,601.61

Taken from Permanent Fund to meet 1939 Deficits from Budgetary Operations:

Hospital	*$82,727.44*
School of Nursing..	*73,217.95*
Ladies' Auxiliary	*1,089.69*
Total from Permanent Fund for 1939 Deficits	*157,035.08*
Taken from Social Service Auxiliary Special Account for 1939 Deficit..	*12,451.32*
Total taken from Capital to meet the 1939 Deficits from Operations	**$169,486.40**

STATEMENT OF CURRENT DISBURSEMENTS
FOR THE YEAR ENDED DECEMBER 31st, 1939

HOSPITAL:

Administration:

Salaries and Wages of Officers and Clerks	$99,715.41	
Telephone Wages	11,452.94	
Salaries of Custodians	8,763.84	
Pensions	3,960.00	
Telephone Service	22,394.08	
Stationery and Printing	5,349.86	
Miscellaneous	1,483.29	
Total Administration		$153,119.42

Professional Care of Patients:

Salaries and Wages:

Physicians	46,638.99	
Nurses	27,791.00	
Druggists	13,812.86	
Orderlies	52,734.27	
Follow-up and Clinical Secretaries	22,986.50	
Medical and Surgical Supplies	164,197.03	
Total Professional Care of Patients		328,160.65

*Out-Patient Department:

Salaries and Wages	39,985.87	
Stationery and Printing	2,471.81	
Supplies	3,860.36	
Total Out-Patient Department		46,318.04

Radiograph Department:

Salaries and Wages	25,070.41	
Supplies	29,074.95	
Total Radiograph Department		54,145.36

Radiotherapy Department:

Salaries and Wages	9,105.57	
Supplies	4,078.48	
Radium	140.01	
Total Radiotherapy Department		13,324.06
Carried Forward		$595,067.53

*The items included under this heading are those which are chargeable directly and exclusively to the Out-Patient Department. The actual cost of conducting the Out-Patient Department, including the proportion of other expenses properly chargeable to it, is $361,531.72.

Brought Forward $595,067.53

Electro-cardiograph Department:
Salaries and Wages $2,217.61
Supplies 1,721.46

Total Electro-cardiograph Department 3,939.07

Department of Laboratories:
Salaries and Wages 86,569.66
Supplies 22,723.03

Total Department of Laboratories 109,292.69
Provisions 350,573.20

Dietary Department:
Salaries and Wages 98,853.99
Supplies 11,104.47

Total Dietary Department 109,958.46

Housekeeping Department:
Salaries and Wages 81,451.03
Furniture and Housefurnishings 23,353.03
Crockery and Silverware 6,730.48
Dry Goods 9,031.02
Beds and Bedding 5,850.09

Total Housekeeping Department 126,415.65

Laundry Department:
Salaries and Wages 44,710.91
Supplies 10,122.27

Total Laundry Department 54,833.18

General House and Property Expenses:
Salaries and Wages 111,558.34
Renewals and Repairs 124,997.29
Light, Heat and Power 63,153.28

Total General House and Property Expenses 299,708.91
Insurance 24,243.68

Carried Forward $1,674,032.37

Brought Forward		$1,674.032.37
Auditing and Accounting:		
Salaries and Wages	$38,859.87	
Sundries	6,273.09	
Stationery and Printing	2,219.19	
Postage	4,185.12	
Lettering of Tablets	132.08	
Awards to House Staff	650.00	
Annual Report	1,228.99	
Total Auditing and Accounting		53,548.34
Total Budgetary Disbursements (Hospital)		1,727,580.71
SCHOOL OF NURSING—Total Budgetary Disbursements		358,279.08
SOCIAL SERVICE—Total Budgetary Disbursements....		135,002.31
LADIES' AUXILIARY—Total Budgetary Disbursements		26,581.69
Total Disbursements for Budgetary Purposes (Four Societies)		2,247,443.79
Disbursements from Principal and/or Income of Special Funds for Stated Non-Budgetary Purposes (per contra)		126,644.22
Total Disbursements (Budgetary and Non-Budgetary) (Four Societies)		$2,374,088.01

PERMANENT FUND

Received for Endowment of Wards, Rooms and Beds	$2,884,241.87
Cash and Securities on Hand	586,864.42
*Deficit in Permanent Fund, December 31, 1939	$2,297,377.45

---

*This amount has been borrowed from the Permanent Fund mostly to provide for deficits in current expenses and in part for payment of real estate acquired for Hospital purposes. It is hoped that unrestricted donations and legacies, to enable repayment of this loan, will be received within a reasonable period of time.

COMPARATIVE STATEMENT OF STATISTICS

For the Year Ended December 31st, 1939
And the Year Ended December 31st, 1938

HOSPITAL PATIENTS
GENERAL WARDS AND PRIVATE ROOMS

	1939	1938
Patients in hospital at beginning of year [1]	634	583
Patients admitted during year [2]	16,726	16,074
Total number of patients treated in hospital during year (Emergency Ward not included)	17,360	16,657
Remaining in hospital at end of year [1]	607	634
Patients treated in Emergency Room (not admitted) [3]	19,713	17,601
Total number of patients admitted since the Hospital was founded [4]	450,600	434,246

Patients discharged during year:		
Well or Improved	13,678	12,918
Unimproved	2,276	2,297
Died	799	808
Total [2]	16,753	16,023

Maximum number of patients on any one day [1]	733	700
Minimum number of patients on any one day [1]	402	507
Average number of patients per day	636	634
Average hospital days per patient	13	14
Mortality rate for the year (all deaths including those which occurred on day of admission)	4.6	4.85

Distribution of days of hospital care for the year:	No. of Days	%	No. of Days	%
General Wards—free to patients	127,206	54.76	131,281	56.77
General Wards—part free to patients	27,251	11.73	24,719	10.69
Semi-Private Pavilion patients	42,170	18.16	42,487	18.37
Private Pavilion patients	35,665	15.35	32,756	14.17
Total	232,292		231,243	
Maintenance days (patients and employees included)	684,143		674,905	

[1] Midnight Census.

[2] Not adjusted for approximately 372 internal transfers (1939) between private and ward services.

[3] Includes Emergency Dental Treatments reported also in Hospital Dental Statistics. These must be added to O.P.D. Statistics to give complete record of out-patient services.

[4] Excludes internal transfers between private and ward services.

83

The cost of operating the Hospital was $

These operating costs were exclusive of costs of research, post-graduate medical education and other activities not directly connected with maintenance of the Hospital.

More than $1,200,000 was used for salaries and wages. This sum, of course, does not include the value of the services given gratis to the sick poor by our unpaid professional staff.

To meet part of these costs patients paid to the Hospital only . $

The difference is the total philanthropic expense for the year, or $

Grants from Federation, the United Hospital Fund, the Greater New York Fund and the City, supplied the Hospital with a total of $

Income from endowment funds, donations, etc., amounted to   .$

...leaving the Hospital with a final
  net shortage or deficit of . .$ 169,486
This deficit added to other deficits
  since the depression years beginning with 1930, has now reached
  a total of . . . .$ 1,706,924
The large deficits of the past ten years could
  have been avoided only by curtailing in
  quantity or quality, or both, the services
  rendered by the Hospital to the sick poor
  of the City. Because these services are urgently
  needed, it has been the policy of the Board of
  Trustees to maintain them as long as possible,
  and the deficits have been met out of the
  limited capital funds of the Hospital.

Such capital funds were expected to provide
  income for maintenance purposes and the
  depletion of these funds to keep the Hospital
  going has correspondingly reduced such
  income. There is obviously a limit to this
  constant drain on the Hospital's reserves.

Due to this serious depletion of income, the
  Hospital urgently appeals for increased capital
  donations so that it may continue to serve
  adequately and efficiently all who need its care.

COMPARATIVE STATEMENT OF STATISTICS

(Continued)

	1939		1938	
Percentage of total number of patients treated in various divisions:	Patients Treated	%	Patients Treated	%
General Wards	11,893	68.51	11,547	69.32
Semi-Private Rooms	2,662	15.33	2,497	14.99
Private Rooms	2,805	16.16	2,613	15.69
Total	17,360		16,657	

	1939	1938
Disposition of applications received during the year:		
Admitted to General Wards as free to patients	9,252	9,192
Admitted to General Wards as part free to patients	2,207	1,963
Admitted to Semi-Private Rooms at rates below cost	2,540	2,389
Admitted to Private Rooms	2,727	2,530
[5] Not admitted for various reasons (ward applications)	4,770	5,289
Total Applications	21,496	21,363

[5] Reason for non-admission to Wards:	1939	1938
Offered admission but refused by applicant	82	94
Referred to District Staff for care	346	342
Lack of room—referred elsewhere	291	495
Out of Borough—no room	146	104
Able to pay for private care	53	69
Minor ailments	2,439	2,664
Chronic incurable diseases [6]	757	921
Alcoholism [6]	51	58
Contagious diseases [6]	102	118
Infectious diseases [6]	131	124
Pregnancy [6]	54	76
Disturbing mental disorders [6]	318	224
Total	4,770	5,289

[6] Referred to appropriate hospital.

DISTRICT MEDICAL SERVICE

	1939	1938
Applicants for admission visited at home	259	215
Patients cared for at home	130	64
Total number of patients visited	346	342
[7] Total number of visits made by physicians	387	389

[7] Analysis of total visits made by physicians:	1939	1938
Admission to hospital recommended	102	82
Admitted (included in general hospital statistics)	102	81
Admission refused by patient	—	1
Referred to other institutions	26	19
Not at home when doctor called	14	10
Minor ailments—treated at home	35	—
Unsuitable for hospital admission	162	222
Referred to Out-Patient Department	38	47
Patients ceased before arrival	2	2
Not found at given address	8	7

COMPARATIVE STATEMENT OF STATISTICS
(Continued)
OUT-PATIENT DEPARTMENT STATISTICS

	1939	1938
Total visits	343,041 [8]	343,862
Total prescriptions	146,397	141,513
Patients new in year	10,157	11,934
Patients from past years	21,292	21,349
Total individuals	31,449	33,283
Out-Patient Department days	302	303
Daily average prescriptions	485	467
Daily average consultations	1,136	1,135
Average daily attendance of physicians	198	181
Average daily attendance of nurses	24	24
Average daily attendance of volunteer aids	33	40
Maximum consultations on any one day	1,456	1,589
Maximum prescriptions on any one day	899	791

8 This figure does not inculde 19,713 emergency visits to out-patients in accident and emergency room outside of regular clinic hours. Inclusive total is 362,754.

ANALYSIS OF CONSULTATIONS

Name of Clinic	Morning Session	Afternoon Session	1939 Total	1938 Total
Internal Medicine	11,039	27,882	38,921	37,324
Minor Medical	199	381	580	719
Basal Metabolism	1,377	——	1,377	1,713
Gastro-Enterology	8,374	——	8,374	9,006
Diabetic	8,920	——	8,920	11,212
Adult Cardiac	4,662	2,353	7,015	6,929
Adult Asthma	12,569	——	12,569	11,837
Chest	1,421	——	1,421	1,409
Hematology	——	7,902	7,902	7,214
Neurology and Psychiatry	4,758	6,482	11,240	10,798
Dermatology	9,408	15,960	25,368	27,582
Arseno-Therapy	——	1,907	1,907	2,588
Surgical	14,311	11,202	25,513	25,377
Genito-Urinary	4,943	1,548	6,491	6,975
Rectal	4,206	——	4,206	4,762
Gynecological	10,287	11,841	22,128	21,011
Ear, Nose and Throat	2,466	16,938	19,404	19,890
Eye	3,862	11,469	15,331	14,215
Thrombo-Angiitis Obliterans	10,867	496	11,363	10,973
Orthopedic	946	13,296	14,242	15,206
Children's Medical	8,746	11,681	20,427	19,194
Children's Asthma	——	9,869	9,869	10,336
Children's Cardiac	1,476	——	1,476	1,596
Children's Health	——	2,200	2,200	1,877
Dental	9,610	5,953	15,563	16,077
Physical Therapy	14,007	11,371	25,378	24,336
Radiotherapy	5,455	6,533	11,988	14,979
Roentgenology	4,857	——	4,857	5,160
Electrocardiography	1,493	——	1,493	1,278
Occupational Therapy	1,233	——	1,233	1,218
Breast	——	226	226	199
Nutrition	43	4,016	4,059	872
Total Consultations	161,535	181,506	343,041	343,862

COMPARATIVE STATEMENT OF STATISTICS

(Continued)

DEPARTMENT OF LABORATORIES
Examinations in Central Laboratory

	1939	1938
Bacteriology:		
Blood Groupings	6,648	8,095
Nose and Throat Cultures	99	174
Blood Cultures	1,558	1,239
Pus Cultures, etc.	6,527	6,478
Post Mortem Cultures	123	97
Special Anaerobic Cultures	185	162
Bacteriophage Cultures	7	42
Loewenstein Cultures	4	14
Staphylococcus Pathogenicity	2,642	2,579
Streptococcus Pathogenicity	461	471
Pneumococcus Typings	678	426
Neufeld Tests	547	312
Vaccines	84	92
Bacteriophage Tests	7	10
Guinea Pig Inoculations	338	403
Miscellaneous Animal Inoculations	51	51
Widal Reactions	241	224
Wassermann Tests	10,866	11,083
Kahn Tests	3,265	4,345
Agglutination Reactions	506	475
Complement Fixation Tests	102	91
Precipitation Tests	420	145
Colloidal Gold Tests	854	787
Globulin Determinations	802	759
Heterophile Reactions	281	148
Cell Counts	4	8
Miscellaneous Tests	207	209
Total	37,507	38,919

	1939	1938
Surgical Pathology and Morbid Anatomy:		
Examinations of Operative Specimens	6,031	5,577
Post-Mortem Examinations	344	400

	1939	1938
Chemistry:		
Complete Blood Chemistry	818	837
Partial Blood Chemistry	10,921	10,382
Urine Chemistry	173	253
Gastro Intestinal Contents	68	144
Examinations for Heavy Metals	81	115
Functional Tests	2,534	1,803
Examinations for Spinal Fluid	1,080	979
Miscellaneous Tests	182	222
Total	15,857	14,735

COMPARATIVE STATEMENT OF STATISTICS
(Continued)
DEPARTMENT OF LABORATORIES—(Continued)
Examinations in Central Laboratory—(Continued)

	1939	1938
Hematology:		
Blood Counts	566	1,318
Blood Volumes	22	20
Fragility of Red Cells	38	48
Congo Red Tests	21	21
Sedimentation Tests	259	207
Hematocrit Determinations	78	110
Heterophile Reactions	2	5
Bone Marrow Examinations	168	214
Formalin Tests	8	25
Reticulocyte Counts	180	122
Miscellaneous Tests	164	43
Total	1,506	2,133
Endocrinology:		
Aschheim-Zondek Tests	287	306
Frank-Goldberger Tests—Blood	258	174
Frank-Goldberger Tests—Urine	569	741
Pituitary Blood Tests	9	14
Pituitary Urine Tests	437	534
Pituitary Blood Serum	177	65
Estrogenic Substance and Gonadotropic Hormone Tests	609	652
Total	2,346	2,486
Blood Bank:		
Volunteer Donors Used	2,052	
Transfusions Given with Stored Blood	1,910	

Laboratory for Routine Clinical Microscopy in Private Pavilion, Semi-Private Pavilion and Out-Patient Department

	1939			1938		
	PRIV. PAV.	SEMI-PRIV. PAV.	O.P.D.	PRIV. PAV.	SEMI-PRIV. PAV.	O.P.D.
Routine Urines	10,537	12,401	6,138	10,773	12,087	5,675
Phenolsulphonphthalein Tests	26	27	4	34	69	5
Blood Counts	3,707	3,617	3,142	2,969	3,399	2,774
Feces	343	422	541	557	523	558
Sputa	47	136	420	57	180	363
Smears	33	15	1,174	23	52	1,255
Gastric Contents	53	96	——	77	102	——
Spinal Fluids	60	44	——	63	26	——
Blood Sugars	——	——	687	——	——	735
Quantitative Urines	31	53	415	34	53	302
Galactose Tests	4	——	2	——	3	——
Sedimentation Tests	——	——	659	——	——	568
Concentration Tests	17	20	88	14	23	48
Janney Tests	3	5	171	3	3	145
Miscellaneous Tests	15	37	68	18	34	72
Total	14,876	16,873	13,509	14,622	16,554	12,500

COMPARATIVE STATEMENT OF STATISTICS
(Continued)
Clinic Laboratories in Out-Patient Department

	1939	1938
Urinalysis:		
Genito-Urinary	2,729	3,056
Gynecological	619	451
Medical	3,539	3,514
Diabetic	9,026	8,479
Children's	1,527	1,509
	17,440	17,009
Tuberculin Tests	3,240	886
Dark Field Examinations	39	77
Smears:		
Genito-Urinary	2,729	2,312
Gynecological	4,016	3,691
Miscellaneous	—	1
	6,745	6,004
Gastric Analysis	985	1,153
Total	28,449	25,129

LABORATORY FOR BASAL METABOLISM
(Hospital Laboratory)[9]

	1939	1938
Private Patients	70	75
Semi-Private Patients	175	102
Ward Patients	1,154	1,050
Nurses	32	30
Total	1,431	1,257
Maximum number of examinations on any one day	11	10

[9] O. P. D. examinations reported in O. P. D. Statistics.

DEPARTMENT OF RADIOLOGY

	1939	1938
Radiography:		
Number of Examinations	23,152	22,334
Number of Plates Taken	66,451	68,241
Number of Fluoroscopic Examinations	7,576	8,623
Radiotherapy:		
Number of New Patients	562	675
Number of Visits (old and new patients)	13,516[10]	16,582[11]
Number of Treatments (old and new patients)	8,618	11,117

Radiotherapy Treatments:		P.P.	SEMI-P.P.	WARD	O.P,D.	TOTAL
High Frequency	1939	1	0	1	17	19
	1938	0	0	0	32	32
Radium	1939	0	1	35	8	44
	1938	0	0	32	28	60
Superficial Therapy	1939	2	6	24	1,327	1,359
	1938	1	0	94	2,583	2,678
Deep Therapy	1939	185	277	1,424	5,284	7,170
	1938	177	150	1,414	6,606	8,347
Total	1939	188	284	1,484	6,636	8,592
	1938	178	150	1,540	9,249	11,117

[10] Includes 11,988 visits which were reported in O. P. D. Consultations.
[11] Includes 14,979 visits which were reported in O. P. D. Consultations.

COMPARATIVE STATEMENT OF STATISTICS

(Continued)

DEPARMENT OF PHYSIOTHERAPY

(Hospital)

	1939	1938
Massage	988	1,114
Exercise	705	1,885
Gymnasium Treatments	2,204	——
Low Tension Currents	406	262
Hydrotherapy	2,990	1,814
Diathermia	64	225
Hyperthermia	525	562
Short Wave	1,446	1,573
Ultra Violet	1,712	1,923
Photothermia (Infra-Red Lamp)	2,710	7,341
Carbon Arc	——	20
Thermo Hood	1,047	1,659
Total number of treatments for year	14,797	18,378
Maximum number on any one day	40	69

DENTAL DEPARTMENT

(Hospital)

	1939	1938
Extractions	332	789
Fillings	188	362
Oral Surgery	34	20
Mechanical Work	6	49
Root Canal Therapy	5	16
Pyorrhea Treatments	51	183
X-Ray Examinations	831	936
Cultures	25	43
Vaccines	10	13
Fractures	6	5
Other Treatments	952	1,706
	2,440	4,122
Examinations only	1,397	4,941
Emergency Ward Treatments, Miscellaneous	2,261	1,299
Total number for year	6,098	10,362
Maximum number on any one day	23	56

COMPARATIVE STATEMENT OF STATIST.

(Continued)

DENTAL DEPARTMENT

(Out-Patient Department)

	1939
Extractions	1,615
Fillings	1,357
Orthodontia	601
Oral Surgery	229
Mechanical Work	3,574
Root Canal Therapy	99
Pyorrhea Treatments	267
X-Ray Examinations	1,224
Cultures	35
Fractures	77
Other Treatments	3,305
	12,383
Examinations only	3,425
Total number of services for year	15,808
Total number of visits [12]	15,563
Maximum number of visits on any one day	95

[12] Included in O. P. D. Consultations.

ELECTRO-CARDIOGRAPH DEPARTMENT

	1939
Private Patients Examinations	184
Semi-Private Patients Examinations	163
Ward Patients Examinations	4,591
Out-Patient Examinations [13]	1,493
Total number of examinations	6,431
Maximum number on any one day	38

[13] Included in O. P. D. Consultations—Morning Session.

CONSULTATION SERVICE

	1939
Patients admitted	2,829
Referring doctors	635

COMPARATIVE STATEMENT OF STATISTICS

(Continued)

FOLLOW-UP CLINICS

REPORT FOR 1939

	No. of Clinic Sessions	No. of Appointments Given	Kept 14	Cases Closed	Referred for Further Treatment	Referred for Readmission
Medical	84	2,670	2,026	266	459	66
Surgical	126	6,727	5,053	435	746	258
Gynecological	48	2,846	2,045	208	288	53
Orthopedic	23	1,245	946	125	163	46
Pediatric	45	984	729	65	65	8
Neurological	24	802	510	53	32	15
Ear, Nose and Throat	24	1,613	1,064	215	80	104
Eye	11	489	363	37	70	45
Radiotherapy	84	1,945	1,622	4	143	32
Physiotherapy	11	84	50	3	6	——
Hematology	10	91	72	6	9	——
Total	490	19,496	14,480	1,417	2,061	627

14 Included in O. P. D. Consultations.

REPORT OF THE COMMITTEE ON
OUT-PATIENT DEPARTMENT

In 1939, in the sixty-seventh year since its beginning, the Out-Patient Department has again fulfilled to a generous degree its important community responsibilities. Striking commentary on current economic conditions was afforded by the fact that more than 31,000 individuals applied for the medical philanthropy of the Hospital and of its staff. Careful investigation of the financial and social background of every applicant for admission made it clear than none of these patients was able to purchase medical service. The experience of the Out-Patient Department is further support of the findings of various surveys, which have demonstrated the existence of a close relationship between poverty and illness among the unemployed. The demands on the Out-Patient Department for medical services, in excess of its capacity, were so pressing that it was necessary to apply district limitations for admission somewhat more strictly than in previous years, for it would obviously be unfair to accept for clinic care patients living at a distance, and to refuse admission to the Hospital's nearby neighbors.

On the other hand, district limitations were waived where possible in order to assist helpless refugees from foreign lands. These individuals are very limited in their choice of medical care, and a large proportion of those residing in New York City found their way into the Hospital's Out-Patient Department. In the latter half of 1939, several surveys of new patients revealed an intake of refugees amounting to 25% of the total number of new admissions. Special considerations frequently entered into the care of these individuals, requiring time-consuming adjustments, correspondence and follow-up procedures. On the whole, they constituted a grateful group, extremely appreciative of the help which was given to them without question of charges or fees.

The expansion of clinic activities has been so great that this department of the Hospital is now reported to be carrying a larger free clinic load than any other voluntary hospital in the United States. More than two-thirds of the patients paid no fees whatever for their treatment and medication. By careful supervision of administrative procedures, admission policies, employment of an appointment system, and rejection of those individuals financially able to secure private professional services at modest rates, it was possible to maintain the traditionally high quality of service.

Expeditious handling of these large numbers of patients in an efficient manner was found to be consistent with individualization of treatment. High standards of privacy and courtesy, and sympathetic consideration of the problems of the physically and mentally ailing members of the community who sought care at our hands, were maintained. In practically all cases, patients received continuous treatment by the same physicians at successive clinic visits.

The magnitude and scope of the work performed in the clinics of the Out-Patient Department may be indicated by a short statistical summary. In 1939 the average daily number of 1,136 consultations was higher than in any previous year. Visits to the more than fifty separate clinical divisions totalled 343,041, to which might be added 19,713 emergency visits to the accident ward. 31,449 individuals received treatment during the year, the average patient making 10.9 clinic visits. This figure indicates a high average of consultations and inter-clinic refers, typical of high standards of medical care. 10,157 new patients were admitted to the Out-Patient Department during the year to receive treatment from an average of 198 physicians and 24 nurses in daily attendance. Unselfish and loyal assistance was given to the professional staff by 64 lay volunteers, whose efforts made it possible for the medical personnel to devote their time solely to patient care. Each volunteer lady spent 6 hours every week in the clinics, unobtrusively and efficiently advancing the quality of the service given to the patient. The number of prescriptions dispensed during the year totalled 146,397, almost 5,000 more than during the previous year, an average of 485 prescriptions daily.

But a mere recital of cold statistics, although suggestive of the magnitude of the community service rendered, cannot reflect the personality of the Out-Patient Department. Institutions, like individuals, possess distinct personalities, and it was heartwarming to observe the gratitude of the "ill-housed, ill-clothed, and ill-fed" portion of the community for whom the Hospital has voluntarily accepted responsibility.

The professional staff of the Out-Patient Department, without whose freely-donated efforts and devotion this humanitarian undertaking could not be carried on, deserves commendation for their cooperation. The staff now numbers 628 physicains, well-trained, conscious of their social obligations, and untiring in the discharge of their duties. Opportunities to become truly American have been afforded to more than 200 displaced foreign physicians, whose loss to their native countries was our gain. They have proven to be an eager and industrious group, whose association with the Hospital constitutes a valuable asset to the community which it serves. In addition to these physicians on the clinic staff, a group of 20 emigre physicians were attached to the various clinics in rotation for a period of one year, during which, under supervision of the chiefs of clinics, they were introduced to American medical techniques, ideals and standards of work.

The services of trained medical social workers were available to every clinic in the Out-Patient Department. Their liaison efforts between physician and patient, and their translation into reality of the physicians' recommendations, contributed greatly to the medical and social effectiveness of the Hospital's efforts. Too great emphasis cannot be placed upon the fact that without the services of the social workers an appreciable proportion of our work might have fallen upon barren soil.

In order to enhance the value of the Out-Patient Department to the general practitioner, rotational assignments to the various specialty clinics were encouraged. Interest was stimulated thereby, and the development of better-trained practitioners, familiar with new and specialized techniques and clinical approaches, was encouraged. Highly specialized work was pursued in many of the specialty clinics, e.g., endocrine studies, allergy research, investigation of cardiac abnormalities, treatment of peripheral vascular diseases, the complications of diabetes and other metabolic diseases, the ravages of arthritis—the list is well-nigh endless. These clinics functioned in close cooperation with other departments, utilizing, when necessary, the facilities of special laboratories, in-patient accommodations for more intensive study and treatment of the patients, and medical social service. The clinic physicians attended ward rounds, pathological conferences, special lectures and the many other educational activities of the Hospital. Staff meetings were held at frequent intervals in the clinics for the discussion and presentation of interesting problems of diagnosis and therapy. The staff also formed journal clubs, met at evening seminars and participated in demonstrations and lectures at the meetings of the local and national professional societies.

Many of the clinic physicians enrolled for the post-graduate courses given at the Hospital in affiliation with the College of

Physicians and Surgeons of Columbia University. This formal type of post-graduate instruction, conducted to a considerable extent in the Out-Patient Department, had a total enrollment of 310 physicians from 10 states and 3 foreign countries, a substantial increase over the previous recorded enrollment of 1938. The Out-Patient Department also accepted as volunteer clerks during the summer months senior medical students, who were given an opportunity to act as observers and, under the tutelage and guidance of experienced physicians, to learn the fundamental principles of practical clinical medicine.

Many of the resident and assistant resident physicians regularly attended the various specialty clinics associated with their hospital services, e.g., ophthalmology, orthopedic surgery, psychiatry, pediatrics, gynecology, etc. Under the supervision of their attending physicians, they observed the patients prior to admission to the Hospital and followed their courses after discharge from the wards. It can readily be seen that with all of these activities being pursued concurrently with patient care, the physical facilities of the eight floors housing the Out-Patient Department were utilized to their fullest extent.

The extension of the admitting-examining-physician schedule to include the morning as well as afternoon clinics assured every new patient of adequate preliminary examination and routing to the proper clinic. A new clinic was established and equipped as a sub-division of the otolaryngological service, for the purpose of audiometric testing of individuals who are hard of hearing. The arthritis clinic was given enlarged quarters and its staff expanded so that the increasing number of patients suffering from this disabling disease might be restored to gainful participation in the life of the community and prevented from becoming public charges. The nutrition clinic was also expanded and the service of its physicians and full-time staff dietitian made available at all times to all the clinics. The diabetic, gastro-intestinal, thyroid, medical and many other departments, availed themselves constantly of the services of the nutrition clinic for consultation and dietary prescription. Research activities were pursued in all the clinics in order to widen the horizon of medical knowledge and extend the usefulness of clinical therapeutics. Many scientific papers, based upon studies conducted in the Out-Patient Department, were published and accepted for publication. A more complete survey of the results of the investigative clinical research carried out in the Out-Patient Department may be found in the reports of the President of the Medical Board and the Chairman of the Committee on Laboratories. Clinic restrictions were lifted in some instances in order to make available to worthy patients the facilities of the Out-Patient Department for the study of obscure and unusual diseases and conditions.

The activities of the Out-Patient Department were closely correlated with those of the Hospital Follow-up Department. The treatment of the patients thus became a continuous, coordinated process with the transition from Out-Patient Department to Hospital to Follow-up Clinic accomplished with a minimum of psychic trauma to the patient or disruption of his usual mode of life.

It was found possible to decrease the number of working hours of the non-professional clerical personnel to 7 hours daily. For the comfort of the personnel and convenience of the patients, a revolving door was installed in the main entrance to the Out-Patient Department. All of the stairs used by patients were fitted with carborundum safety treads to reduce to a minimum the possibility of accidents. Maintenance of the buildings and equipment was kept at a high level throughout the year.

After more than a quarter of a century of loyal service, Miss M. May Slator, Supervisor of the Out-Patient Department, retired because of illness. An Assistant Director was assigned to the direct supervision of the Out-Patient Department, assisted by a Nursing Supervisor, who, in addition to her administrative duties, is also an instructor in the School of Nursing, and responsible for the instruction of the pupil nurses during the scheduled assignment to the Out-Patient Department. It is believed that this direct administrative supervision of the Out-Patient Department will bring about a still greater usefulness of this department of the Hospital to its patients and to its professional staff.

Respectfully submitted,

LEONARD A. HOCKSTADER,

Chairman.

REPORT OF COMMITTEE ON LABORATORIES

The following reports of the major laboratory departments for 1939 include statistical data and a general survey of routine activities and research projects, many of which were stimulated by current clinical interest and made possible by the cooperation of the clinical services.

A total of sixty-nine papers were published from the laboratories of the Hospital in 1939. Another fifty-four papers have been completed and are in press. The Laboratory Administrative Committee approved research on thirty-six new problems and extended the time limit on twenty-one problems. Forty-three problems were terminated during the year; twelve of these were recorded as ending without results and thirty-one investigations terminated with results deemed worthy of publication. Fifty-three problems are presently under investigation.

LABORATORY OF BACTERIOLOGY

TRENDS AND SUBJECTS OF RESEARCH: A series of publications deals with the application of physico-chemical principles and mathematical analyses to allergic skin manifestations in humans. This appears to be a new method of approach to the problems of allergy. Some encouraging results have followed the substitution in allergy desensitization of the injection method by the method of iontophoresis, namely, the transport of the substances into the skin layers by means of electric current.

Satisfactory progress has been shown in the studies on the humoral transmitters of nervous stimuli. Recent investigations have brought this work into the sphere of interest and supervision of this department because of the immunological aspects of the humoral transmitters recovered in erythrocytes.

Observations have been made concerning the possible rôle of the Forssman antigen in allergic disease which may be of further clinical significance.

The work on pre- and post-operative bacteriology of the colon and gastric surgical cases has resulted in contributions which seem to improve the immediate prognosis following gastric carcinoma resections. The findings of the streptococcus hemolyticus pre-operatively in colon cases prompted the introduction of prophylactic sulfanilamide therapy with encouraging results.

During the summer of 1939 an outbreak of bacillary dysentery in the Nurses' Home necessitated a complete mobilization of the facilities of the department. The investigations made enabled the isolation of the causative agent in all the cases. Since many of the nurses who were affected are likely to be employed in the institution for many years, a rather unique opportunity has presented itself for well controlled long-time follow-up observations.

The use of methods of preservation of labile antigens and sera and the acquirement of standard strains from the Standard Laboratories, Oxford, England, as developed by the Health Organization of the League of Nations has resulted in a complete revision and accurate serological identification of the important group of gram-negative bacilli responsible for many diseases in the intestinal tract. This has proven already of considerable value in the early diagnosis of this group of diseases and has shown possibilities for valuable epidemiological observations on obscure entities in families.

Because of additional training received by a member of the staff in anaerobic bacteriology at the Pasteur Institute in Paris and in parasitology at the London School of Tropical Medicine it was possible to undertake investigations of routine materials with the view in mind of accumulating additional clinical facts for evaluation of the rôle of anaerobic bacteria which is obscure and frequently overlooked, and of diseases of semi-tropical origin which are believed to be more prevalent than shown by present statistics.

The Department of Pediatrics has collaborated in efforts to develop methods for better utilization of materials difficult to secure in children and towards development of a blood culture technique using amounts of blood considerably smaller than in adults.

The immunization of cases of pneumococcus Type III mastoiditis has continued with apparent success. In cases of pneumococcus type III mastoiditis intracranial complications (meningitis, brain abscesses, etc.) are likely to occur not earlier than a few weeks after the onset of the infection of the mastoid. In view of this fact, it seemed advisable to use this interval of time for active immunization with an autogenous vaccine. In a preliminary publication in 1934 a report had been made on the apparent lowering of the incidence of intracranial complications in vaccinated patients. The work has been continued up-to-date and has confirmed earlier findings on lowering of death rate in a large series of cases and has also brought out the fact that the operative infected wounds of the patients heal better through the effect of vaccinaion.

The use of an anti-coli serum prepared by a commercial laboratory and based on the phenomenon of local tissue reactivity continued successfully on a large group of cases. Presentation of a complete clinical report on the cases treated in this Hospital is under way.

The department aims now to use its facilities for wider studies on physiological aspects of immunology. Some of the present investigations deal with the physiological evaluation of bacterial intoxication, the experiments allowing close analysis of the mechanism of the production of toxemia with special reference to the rôle of the autonomic nervous system.

The Massachusetts General Hospital of Boston has undertaken the treatment of rather extensive series of cases with the filtrates active in the elicitation of the phenomenon of local tissue reactivity for treatment of skin tumors and warts. The materials of ascertained potency will be prepared and supplied to the investigators by our laboratory.

LABORATORY OF CHEMISTRY

I. ROUTINE ACTIVITIES: The totals for the routine analyses carried out in the Central Laboratory in 1939, also in Endocrinology and in Clinical Microscopy will be reported elsewhere. They show an increasing trend, not only for the total number of analyses performed but also for the number per patient, indicating the steadily augmenting significance, which the clinicians attribute to chemical laboratory findings.

The out-put of 50% sterile glucose solution for transfusion and other intravenous uses has increased 10% over 1938. Over 50,000 ampoules are now prepared annually.

II. EDUCATIONAL ACTIVITIES: In addition to the postgraduate courses and to those general purposes of instruction outlined further below, a short course was conducted in our routine methods for the rehabilitation of a number of emigré laboratory technicians. The monthly Physiological Chemistry Seminar, because of its mounting attendance, was transferred this fall from the homes of the staff to the Hospital with increasing participation of the Attending and House Staff and guests from the various universities.

101

III. Trend and Subjects of Research : A number of problems are an outgrowth of routine observations of chemical compo-
sition of the blood, urine, etc. and could only be carried out in
an Institution like ours with its wealth of clinical material.

a. Investigations Resulting from Clinical Problems—A very
important contribution of clinical significance was the discovery
of changes in the magnesium partition in thyroid disease, this
discovery, based on observations of clinical material, is the basis
of investigations under way on various physiological and pathological aspects, these include the study of magnesium and other
blood electrolytes in sleep and in hibernation, which in turn seems
of special interest in view of the recent exploits of cold temperature treatment in cancer.

The groups working on clinical and physiological problems in
the field of endocrinology have carried on numerous investigations
linking the blood and urine content of the various female and male
sex hormones with pathological and physiological conditions met
with by the gynecologist. These studies comprise the bio-assay of
androgen based on the three day chick comb test, and in combination with this, simultaneous study of the estrogens and gonadotropic excretion in both sexes in health and disease, and the
influence of medication on these excretions. This laboratory work
is of course, at the same time, ancillary to hormonal therapy.

The research group interested in gastro-enterology has continued their progress and were able to establish valuable new
principles in the practice and interpretation of test meals for
gastric acidity. In conjunction with the corresponding medical
and surgical services other practical problems such as the effect
of vagotomy and the use of neutralizing drips are under way.

The occurrence of increased amounts of cholesterol in urine of
cancer patients observed by us previously in 3,000 liters of pooled
urine was investigated in 100 individual cases from our own wards
and our explanation of this phenomenon was confirmed by our-
selves and elsewhere.

In close conjunction with the chemical routine, variations of
calcium in infants and the nature of jaundice in the new born were
studied. Other clinical problems under investigation comprise
study of vitamins in multiple sclerosis and in diabetes, the determination of uric acid in the blood of the gouty.

b. Contributions to Diagnosis and Therapy: New Methods—
Several services have become interested in the study of new
chemicals containing iodine for certain visualization problems.
Fundamental laboratory research, carried out under the Hernsheim Fellowship, on the nature of enzymes and their behavior in
monomolecular films indicates among other findings a hitherto
unsuspected chemical relation to the group of hormones.

Experiments have been instigated with a view to synthesize
highly water soluble sulfanyl derivative for chemo-therapy. A
chemical check up on the blood chemistry of chemo-therapy with
arsenicals is being conducted in connection with the intravenous
drip therapy experiment in the wards.

Important routine methods for cholesterol and blood proteins,
sulfapyridine and sulfathiazol have been improved. The time
saving photoelectric colorimeter has been adapted to additional
routine procedures, also for the quantitative determination of traces
of arsenic of one part in the million and of Vitamin A and carotene.
Parallel to the trend of the research in physiological chemistry,
there has been an increasing number of requests for routine
determinations of blood electrolytes (magnesium, sodium and
potàssium). The purchase of a calculating machine with the aid
of the Helen B. Millhauser Fund has been of great benefit and
value for the correct statistical interpretation of experimental
results in gastro-enterology, endocrinology and biochemistry.

LABORATORY OF MORBID ANATOMY AND SURGICAL PATHOLOGY

Statistics on the routine work of the laboratory appear elsewhere in this book. The performance of postmortem examinations
continues to have, apart from the determination of the precise
causes of death, a very distinct educational value for the assistants
in the laboratory as well as for the house and attending staffs of
the Hospital. A good number of the cases have aided in the many
scientific investigations under way.

I. *The more formal educational activity consists of:*

A. THE WEEKLY CLINICAL PATHOLOGICAL CONFERENCES
which have been conducted as heretofore before an average audience of more than 300 physicians not only affiliated with the Hospital, but also many physicians from the metropolitan area. These
conferences are conducted like postgraduate courses correlating
the clinical observations with the findings at autopsy. The cases

presented are selected according to their teaching value. The interest in these conferences has been stimulated by the participation of the attending physicians and surgeons in the discussion of the cases.

B. POSTGRADUATE COURSES have been given by members of the department under the auspices of Columbia University in general pathology as well as in selected subjects, such as diseases of the circulatory and nervous system, the gastro-intestinal tract and the liver and biliary ducts. Several courses were given in ophthalmo- and oto-pathology. A series of lectures on pathology were delivered last spring under the auspices of the Hudson County Medical Society in Jersey City. A series of courses in neuroanatomy and neurophysiology were given under the auspices of the Graduate School of New York University. Lectures on tuberculosis were given by invitation for the undergraduate students of the College of Physicians and Surgeons.

C. WEEKLY MICROSCOPIC SEMINARS were held for the staff of the department at which the current autopsy specimens were demonstrated, discussed, and the final diagnosis and conclusion made in each case.

D. MONTHLY JOURNAL CLUB meetings were held at which articles in the current medical journals were reviewed and discussed by all the members of the department.

E. The material of the *department of neuropathology* was demonstrated and discussed at *weekly seminars* and routinely presented before the neurologic conference. Cases of general medical interest were presented at the clinical pathological conferences.

II. *The result of the research activities of the department* is revealed by the list of publications which appeared during the past year in medical journals, several of which might warrant additional comment.

Reports on visceral lesions in shock were the result of analytical studies of clinical cases and post mortem material as well as of well planned animal experiments. The broader aspect of this investigation is the recognition and evaluation of the importance of transient and prolonged vascular spasm in the genesis of human disease.

An analysis of a large number of cardiac deaths established that in a relatively high percentage of these cases myocardial infarction was the result of insufficiency of coronary perfusion and not of actual occlusion of the vessels. These studies are of special interest for the proper interpretation of pathologic electrocardiograms.

It was shown that Renin, the hypothetical blood pressure raising substance obtained from ischemic kidneys, is inactive in adrenalectomized animals.

By renewed investigation of a large amount of material, the concept that massive cerebral hemorrhage is a terminal phase in a series of events which antecede it was strengthened.

The common theme of these reports and others in preparation is the relation of vascular disease and disturbed function of blood vessels to hypertension and its sequelæ. This subject is one of the main lines of investigation in the department.

Of further interest is the report at the Third International Cancer Congress in Atlantic City of the ability to cause a permanent disappearance of spontaneous breast carcinoma in mice in about twenty-five per cent of animals by the repeated injection of concentrated spleen extract.

III. *Problems which were the immediate result of cooperation between clinical departments and the laboratory.*

Close cooperation has existed between the laboratories of morbid anatomy and electrocardiography and the material from autopsies is studied at weekly joint conferences. There were several joint publications.

The necessity of coordination of the departments of surgical pathology and radiotherapy is evident. Joint publications on the treatment of ovarian carcinoma and a joint presentation on solid teratoma of the ovary were given before the New York Roentgen Society.

The special interest of the Laryngology Service in the pathology of the nose and paranasal sinuses necessitates the regular affiliation of a person familiar with the clinical problems and trained in pathology. This has resulted in a paper on Cylindroma of the upper air passages and the completion of a long and well illustrated article on Intracranial pathways of infection from the spheno-ethmoid sinuses.

In ophthalmopathology, there was completed a detailed anatomic-histologic study of the vascularization of the eye which will

105

be among the scientific exhibits at the annual meeting of the American Medical Association.

The close cooperation of the neuropathology department with clinical neurology need hardly be stressed and its research has been guided as usual by considerations of clinical significance. The result was articles on the topography of the sleep regulating center, on massive cerebral hemorrhage, on the midline tumors, on the effect of thorotrast on the brain, on tuberous sclerosis, metastatic brain tumors and on trauma in relation to brain tumors.

IV. *Problems originating in observations of routine material.*

The finding of unusual vascular lesions of the internal organs in diffuse scleroderma was reported before the New York Pathological Society. These observations indicate that this disease can be linked with other apparently heterogenous maladies such as diffuse lupus erythematosus and dermatomyositis. An exhaustive survey is in preparation.

The association with the department of an emigré who is an anatomist has stimulated the interest in malformations and two observations of unusual anomalies of the heart have been placed on record.

The material available from the association with the New York Zoological Park has led to several case reports on unusual diseases in animals. The increasing information in comparative pathology resulted, during the past year, in a paper on mammary tumors in dogs which dealt mainly with the structural differences in human and animal tumors of this organ.

Studies on solitary bone granuloma simulating malignant neoplasms were completed. The material for this study as well as for the report on argentaffine tumors of the small intestine and on sarcoma of the trachea, was supplied by routine observations in the past years.

Publications also dealt with studies on the myocytes in the heart, on adenoma of the Brunner's glands, an accidental, but unusual, observation at autopsy.

V. *Problems in experimental pathology.*

A number of investigations have been completed and the articles published can be found in the list of publications or are in press.

These investigations were concerned with the effect in the viscera of vaso constriction due to adrenalin and its relation to shock; with questions of hypertension; the production of ovarian neoplasms by irradiation. Experimental work under progress is not specifically mentioned in this report.

VI. *Routine:*

Some of the research work carried out in the past has led to an improvement in the routine activity of the department. Last year, there was published a short report on the search for lymph node metastases in colon carcinomas which were made transparent with oil of wintergreen. The relatively high incidence of cases in which metastases were found by this method while careful routine examination had failed to disclose them, suggested the routine use of the same method in cancer of the stomach and of the breast. This improved method of examination gives more information upon which the surgeon will be able to base his prognosis of the case.

GENERAL SUMMARY: In summing up, the nature of the activities and the apparent trend of development of the laboratories in the near future may be broadly indicated. The facts point to a definite progress in research as well as to the rôle assumed in the life of the Hospital by its Laboratories.

The researches above described bear testimony to a steady growth and accomplishments in widely diverse fields of medical sciences. Some of the investigations have already definitely brought credit to the Hospital and others unquestionably will justify the efforts in the future. A certain proportion of the investigative work is in the nature of pure science accomplished by the use of special technical modern methods equal to those employed by Institutions devoted exclusively to research. It is of interest worthy of special emphasis, that these researches do not bring about a detachment from the clinical services and do not lack coordination with the purposes of the Institution as a whole. On the contrary, the work is closely interwoven with the clinical problems since the ultimate object of pure scientific investigations is invariably directed to help to diagnose and treat disease. In addition to the investigative value, research makes possible constant improvement of the routine, the application of modern methods to clinical sciences and the lifting of the scientific standards of those who come for postgraduate training to the Hospital. The educational value of the laboratories is not only, of course, rendered possible by the research activities but is carried out also in informal discussions with the Visiting Staffs and House Staff, interpretations and correlation of the laboratory reports, formal postgraduate courses, weekly presentations at conferences, and finally, in the training of assistants in laboratory medicine. A limited number of the younger men active in the laboratory intend to embark upon a laboratory career. A far greater percentage has constantly utilized the laboratory facilities in order to obtain training in the fundamental sciences preparatory to their further clinical activities.

The efforts of the laboratory in these directions are based upon the feeling that modern medicine demands more than the knowledge of facts and methods. Above all and most essential is the application of scientific logic and scientific attitude to problems of human diseases.

Respectfully submitted,

GEORGE B. BERNHEIM,

Chairman, Committee on Laboratories.

OFFICERS AND DIRECTORS OF THE MOUNT SINAI HOSPITAL SCHOOL OF NURSING

Hugo Blumenthal ....*President*
Alfred L. Rose ....*Vice-President*
W. D. Scholle ....*Treasurer*
Edwin M. Berolzheimer ....*Secretary*

Directors

Leo Arnstein

Edwin M. Berolzheimer

George Blumenthal

Hugo Blumenthal

Joseph F. Cullman, Jr.

Waldemar Kops

Carl H. Pforzheimer, Jr.

Alfred L. Rose

Paul M. Rosenthal

W. D. Scholle

Harold D. Wimpfheimer

For the Term Expiring April, 1941

Leo Arnstein

Joseph F. Cullman, Jr.

Waldemar Kops

W. D. Scholle

For the Term Expiring April, 1943

Hugo Blumenthal

Paul M. Rosenthal

Harold D. Wimpfheimer

For the Term Expiring April, 1945

Edwin M. Berolzheimer

George Blumenthal

Carl H. Pforzheimer, Jr.

Alfred L. Rose

Honorary Director

Philip J. Goodhart

REPORT OF THE MOUNT SINAI HOSPITAL SCHOOL OF NURSING

To the Board of Trustees of The Mount Sinai Hospital :

Gentlemen:

During the past year, two groups of preliminary students were admitted to the School; the February division of 35, and the September division of 54; a total of 89. Of this group, 69 remain in the School. Although the best possible techniques of selection are used in choosing our applicants it is still difficult to predict the percentage of students who will complete the course. The general average of resignations in most schools of nursing is approximately 30%. The record of our graduating class this year was particularly noteworthy because 83% of the original group admitted completed their course.

On January 1, 1940 the School had a total of 217 students, divided as follows:

Preliminary students 49
First year students 27
Second year students 63
Third year students 78

We also had 92 graduates on our staff engaged in administration, teaching, and supervision, as well as 136 graduates engaged in general staff nursing.

Nursing education and nursing service, although in themselves different, are so closely interwoven that to change and improve one means to directly affect the other. A sound educational program, therefore, ultimately results in better nursing service to patients. Since our school seeks to offer a well-rounded preparation, and since prevention of disease is inherent in the whole concept of nursing, we have made further changes in the curriculum, which we feel have strengthened and developed the student's understanding of the social and preventive aspects of nursing. In order to get a clearer focus on the social components in sickness and more continuity in the discussion of social adjustment, a separate course was introduced on Social Problems in Nursing Service. This course is given concurrently with the practical experience in the Social Service Department, which is now available to all students entering the School.

On behalf of the Board and faculty of the School I wish to .express warm appreciation to Mrs. A. A. Cook, Chairman of the Social Service Committee, and Mrs. Mendelsohn, Director of the Department, for their helpful assistance in making Social Service experience available to all our students.

Another change has been to introduce the student, early in her course, to family health work through observations in the Out-Patient Department. This is followed by a lecture course which aims to prepare her for the practical experience in this department. While she is assigned to this service further instruction is given in the prevention of disease, the use of community health and social resources for disease prevention, and the purpose of public health in the community. A course in Modern Social Problems and their special implications to the nurse completes the separate courses dealing with the social and preventive aspects of nursing.

The affiliation for psychiatric nursing with the New York Hospital, Westchester Division, has been increased. It is now possible for twenty-four students to receive this elective annually.

The curriculum of the School now includes 1,075 hours of formal class-room instruction, and 200 hours of clinical teaching on the wards. The hours devoted to nursing practice on the wards, in special departments and in affiliated services, total approximately 5,571. Student nurses are now initiated more gradually into nursing responsibilities, thus making their practical work more productive educationally, and giving better nursing care to patients.

Twenty graduate nurses were added to the staff during the year, so that a reduction could be made in the hours on duty of the head nurses and general staff nurses. The increase in graduate staff nurses also enabled us to assign permanent senior nurses to the wards in the medical and surgical pavilions, thus stabilizing still further the nursing service of the Hospital and increasing its efficiency.

There have been three resignations and one retirement from the faculty. Miss Suzanne Charles and Miss Harley Savage, ward instructors, and Miss Nell Ballenger, assistant science instructor, resigned in August. Miss Alice Herzig, B.A., and Miss Anna Hoffman, B.A., graduates of the class of 1938, were promoted to the positions of ward instructor, while Miss Myrtle Larsen, B.S., a graduate of the Norwegian Lutheran Hospital, was appointed to

111

fill the vacancy of science instructor. Miss M. May Slator retired after giving twenty-eight years of faithful service as supervisor of the Out-Patient Department. Miss May Shamp, a graduate of the class of 1933, was appointed to this position. Miss Shamp's experience in the public health field has made her an invaluable asset to the faculty of the School.

Faculty members have represented the School at state and national professional conventions, and on occasions have participated in the programs presented at these meetings. An educational exhibit from the School was included in those displayed at the National League of Nursing Education convention at New Orleans last April.

For the past few years there has been a steady growth in the extra-curricular activities in the School. Planned social and recreational activities contribute to broaden and enrich the personal development of the student and make for happier living in the future. Activities on the year's program were planned by committees of the Student Association, and guided by faculty advisors. A noteworthy example of the work of the students was the senior class play, an original comic production "All This and Sinai Too."

The commencement exercises of the Class of 1940 were held on February 14, in the Blumenthal Auditorium. Eighty nurses received their diplomas. The address to the graduating class was delivered by Dr. George Baehr, the President of the Medical Board of the Hospital. Special recognition was accorded at the commencement exercises to Miss Cora L. Ball, Supervisor of the Pediatric Pavilion, who has given twenty-five years of commendable service to the School and Hospital.

Once again, on behalf of the Board, I wish to thank Doctors Bernstein, Silver and Klingenstein and the consultants who have so wholeheartedly aided in maintaining high health standards for our nursing department personnel. Only those closely connected with the School realize how many hours of devoted and valuable service are given during each year by the members of our medical staff.

The Alumnae Association, with a membership of 770, has had a very busy year. The desire of the Association to help members professionally is evidenced by the stimulating programs presented at the monthly meetings. Their genuine interest in welfare work has been demonstrated by the enthusiasm and willingness with which activities were undertaken to provide benefit for others.

The report of our Nurses' Registry for the year affords many interesting figures:

Total enrollment 461
Daily average on call 63
Total calls received 8,387
Nurses supplied from our own registry......................8,273
Cases for which outside registry nurses were called 114

The total calls for this year exceeded last year's figure by 541.

We are grateful to Dr. Joseph Turner, the Director of the Hospital, for his valuable cooperation and unfailing attention to our problems at all times.

It gives me great pleasure to express on behalf of the Board to the faculty and staff our deep appreciation for the work well done and to Miss Grace Warman, the Principal of the School and the Superintendent of Nurses for her efficient services which have brought the School and the Nursing Service of the Hospital to their present high level.

HUGO BLUMENTHAL,

*President of The Mount Sinai Hospital
School of Nursing.*

SPECIAL FUNDS OF THE MOUNT SINAI HOSPITAL SCHOOL OF NURSING

Albert W. Scholle Memorial Fund.. **$40,000.00**
Founded by William and Frederic Scholle as a tribute to
the memory of their father; income to be used to provide vacations and recreation for nurses and students of
the School of Nursing.

**Estelle and Hugo Blumenthal Scholarship and Graduation
Fund** 35,000.00
Founded by Estelle and Hugo Blumenthal to provide an
annual scholarship to the student of the graduating class
chosen for special fitness to advance in the profession of
nursing by taking a Post Graduate course at Columbia
University. This fund also provides a prize of $15.00
to each graduating student.

Emil Berolzheimer Memorial Fund.................................... 20,000.00
Founded by Mrs. Emil Berolzheimer in memory of her
husband, Emil Berolzheimer; the income to be used for
higher education of nurses.

Murry Guggenheim Scholarship Fund.............................. 20,000.00
Established in 1905 by Murry Guggenheim; income to
provide annually twelve scholarship awards of $100.00
each to students who have shown exceptional ability
during the year.

Jacques D. Wimpfheimer Memorial Fund......................... 10,000.00
Founded by Charles A. Wimpfheimer in memory of his son,
Jacques D. Wimpfheimer. Any student requiring financial
assistance during training may call upon this fund.

Charles A. Wimpfheimer Emergency Relief Fund................ 2,500.00
Established by Charles A. Wimpfheimer; income and, if
necessary, principal not to exceed $100.00 in any one year
to be used for the relief of members of the Alumnae
Association.

Lillie Stern Scholle Pleasure Fund................................... 9,000.00
Founded by Albert W. Scholle; the income to be used
largely to defray the expenses of parties, dances and social
gatherings of the students.

Mr. and Mrs. Sam S. Steiner Fund.................................. 5,000.00
Founded by Mr. and Mrs. Sam S. Steiner in memory of
their beloved son, William J. H. Steiner; the income to be
used for the relief of needy graduate nurses of the School.

**Carrie M. and Gustav Blumenthal Graduating Class Prize
Fund** 5,000.00
Established by provision in the will of Gustav Blumenthal;
income to be distributed annually as a prize or prizes among
the graduating class in such manner as the Directors may
from time to time deem advisable.

114

SPECIAL FUNDS OF THE MOUNT SINAI HOSPITAL SCHOOL OF NURSING

(Continued)

Kalman and Harriet F. Haas Fund... $3,000.00
    Founded by Kalman Haas; the income to be used for
    the general purposes of the School.

Carrie Untermeyer Fund... 2,600.00
    Founded by Mrs. Carrie Untermeyer; to establish an
    award of $100.00 annually to the student graduating who
    has the best record for kindness and proficiency in actual
    bedside nursing.

Solomon and Betty Loeb Fund.. 2,500.00
    Founded by Solomon Loeb; income to provide annual
    prizes to students.

Educational Fund 2,500.00
    Founded by Mrs. Berthold Levi in memory of Berthold Levi;
    the income to be used for higher education of students.

Mr. and Mrs. Morris Fatman Relief Fund for Graduate Nurses   2,500.00
    Founded by Mr. and Mrs. Morris Fatman; income to be
    used for the relief of graduate nurses.

Eugene Meyer, Jr. Library Fund....................................... 2,000.00
    Founded by Eugene Meyer, Jr.; the income to be used to
    supply books and magazines for the school library.

Amy C. and Fred H. Greenebaum Fund............................. 2,000.00
    Established by Mr. and Mrs. Fred H. Greenebaum; income
    to be used for an annual award to the most deserving
    student nurse in any class.

Isabella Freedman Fund.. 1,500.00
    Established by Mrs. Isabella Freedman; the income to be
    used for one or two awards to students in the graduating
    class who have shown marked ability, proficiency and
    interest in their work.

Daniel Kops Prize Fund... 1,000.00
    Founded by Employees of the House of Kops in memory
    of Daniel Kops; the income to be applied to the awarding
    of a prize to the nurse who holds the best record for bedside
    nursing and kindness to patients.

Pension Fund Mount Sinai Alumnae Association. Approx. 180,000.00
    Established to provide pensions to nurses after many years
    of service.

REPORT OF THE MOUNT SINAI HOSPITAL SCHOOL OF NURSING

TREASURER'S REPORT

Statement of Disbursements and Receipts for the Year Ended
December 31st, 1939

Disbursements:

Payroll:

Student Nurses	$15,134.01
Graduate Nurses	238,281.73
Office Assistants	9,077.60
Housekeeping	34,490.25
Attendants	26,829.45
Tuition	16,827.44
Postage	235.00
Sundries	698.59
Stationery and Printing	1,850.42
Household Supplies	3,825.17
Telephone	1,735.08
Advertising	1,890.00
Books	1,923.79
Uniforms	4,103.86
Graduation Exercises	1,376.69

Total Disbursements $358,279.08

Receipts from:

Federation	$275,956.47
Matriculation Fees	4,290.00
Registry Fees	4,053.50
Sundry Receipts	61,16
Permanent Fund Income	585.00
Haas Fund Income	115.00

Total Receipts 285,061.13

*Deficit** *$73,217.95*

* *Taken from Permanent Fund of Hospital.*

116

SOCIAL SERVICE AUXILIARY OF THE MOUNT SINAI HOSPITAL

COMMITTEE

Mrs. Alfred A. Cook ....*President*
Mrs. Myron I. Borg ....*Vice-President*
Mrs. Henry S. Glazier ....*Treasurer*
Mrs. Siegfried F. Hartman ....*Assistant Treasurer*
Mrs. Robert M. Benjamin ....*Secretary*

Mrs. George Backer	Mrs. Herbert H. Lehman
Mrs. Paul Baerwald	Mrs. Louis M. Loeb
Mrs. Robert E. Binger	Mrs. George W. Naumburg
Mrs. Robert G. Blumenthal	Mrs. Carl H. Pforzheimer, Jr.
Mrs. Arthur J. Cohen	Mrs. Moritz Rosenthal
Mrs. Leonard A. Cohn	Mrs. Philip A. Roth
Mrs. Frederick L. Ehrman	Miss Edith Sachs
Mrs. Frederick M. Heimerdinger	Mrs. William D. Scholle
Mrs. Marco F. Hellman	Mrs. Henry Siegbert
Mrs. Walter A. Hirsch	Mrs. E. L. Smith
Miss Angie Jacobson	Mrs. Albert Stern
Mrs. William de Young Kay	Mrs. Roger W. Straus
Mrs. Alan H. Kempner	Mrs. Irwin Untermyer

Mrs. Frank L. Weil

STANDING COMMITTEES

Mrs. Frederick M. Heimerdinger...........*Cardiac Clinics*
Mrs. Philip A. Roth.............................*Children's Health*
Mrs. Arthur J. Cohen, *Chairman* ⎫
Mrs. Robert M. Benjamin   ⎬ ......*Children's Social Service*
Mrs. Frederick L. Ehrman   ⎭
Mrs. Paul Baerwald, *Chairman*   ⎫
Mrs. William D. Scholle   ⎬ ......*Clothing*
   Associate Chairman   ⎭
Mrs. William de Young Kay.................*Library*
Mrs. Louis M. Loeb.........................*Medical Clinics*
Mrs. Frank L. Weil.........................*Medical Wards*
Mrs. Walter A. Hirsch......................*Neustadter Home*
Mrs. Henry Siegbert, *Chairman* ⎫
Mrs. Robert M. Benjamin   ⎪
Mrs. Henry S. Glazier   ⎬.....*Nominating*
Mrs. Walter A. Hirsch   ⎪
Mrs. Moritz Rosenthal   ⎭
Mrs. Leonard A. Cohn ....*Occupational Therapy—In-Patient*
Mrs. Irwin Untermyer ....*Orthopedic Clinics*
Mrs. Frank L. Weil ....*Volunteers*
Miss Edith Sachs, *Chairman*   ⎫
Mrs. Robert E. Binger   ⎬ ....*Workshop*
Mrs. Siegfried F. Hartman   ⎭

117

CONFERENCE COMMITTEE

MRS. ALFRED A. COOK ....*Chairman*

DR. ISRAEL WECHSLER
DR. SAMUEL H. AVERBUCK
DR. DAVID BECK
DR. WILLIAM H. MENCHER
DR. HERMAN SCHWARZ

MRS. ARTHUR J. COHEN
MRS. LEONARD A. COHN
MRS. WALTER A. HIRSCH
MRS. LOUIS M. LOEB
MRS. FRANK L. WEIL

DR. JOSEPH TURNER *(ex-officio)*
MRS. FANNY L. MENDELSOHN *(ex-officio)*

VOLUNTEERS

MRS. FRANK L. WEIL..*Chairman*

MISS VIOLA ALBERT
MISS MARJORIE ALSBERG
MRS. HARRY ANGELO
MISS DORIS BAIZLEY
MRS. HAROLD BARNETT
MRS. IRVING BARON
MRS. JOSEPH BAUMANN
MISS EILEEN BERMAN
MRS. PHILIP BERNHEIM
MRS. THEODORE BERNSTEIN
MRS. THEODORE M. BERNSTEIN
MRS. GEORGE S. BICKWIT
MRS. TOBY BIEBER
MRS. DAVID BLOCK
MR. ELLAN BORENFREUND
MISS SELMA CHUCK
MISS GERTRUDE COHEN
MISS LUCILLE COHEN
MR. SANFORD F. COHEN
MRS. PETER A. COHN
MISS FLORENCE DALY
MISS ANN DAVID
MRS. DAVID S. DAVIDSON
MRS. CHARLES DEITSCH
MRS. BERNARD DENZER
MRS. HENRY DOUBILET
MISS HELEN DOYLE
MRS. GILBERT DREIFUS
MRS. WALTER A. DREYFOUS
MRS. GEORGE C. ENGEL
MRS. JACK EPSTEIN
MRS. WILLIAM ERDMANN
MISS JEAN ETTMAN
MRS. MILDRED FALK
MRS. IRVING FEIG

MISS DORIS FELDMAN
MISS EDITH FELDBRAU
MISS LILLIAN FIDLER
MRS. GUS FIELD
MISS PEGGY FILER
MRS. ALFRED FISCHER
MISS IRENE ELISE FISCHER
MRS. ARTHUR FLASH
MISS REGINA B. FRANKENBERG
MRS. SARA FRENKEL
MISS LISBETH FRIED
MR. JOSEPH LEWIS FRIEDMAN
MRS. HENRY J. FRIENDLY
MRS. GUS FULD
MISS RITA GALEWSKI
MRS. VICTOR GETTNER
MISS BERNICE GLASER
MRS. SAM GOLDSMITH
. MISS BEULAH GRANT
MRS. JACOB GRAY
MISS MARION GREENBERG
MISS MARY GREENHUT
MISS HELEN HAAS
MISS IRMA J. HENRY
MISS THERESA HERRMAN
MRS. ROBERT HERZOG
MISS MURIEL C. HESS
MRS. MARTIN HIRSCHFELD
MISS JANET HOCHSTADTER
MISS ELAINE HOLZMAN
MISS JULIETTE INGAUF
MR. HANS JELINEK
MISS GRACE JEROME
MISS BABETTE JUDSON

118

VOLUNTEERS—(Continued)

Miss Ruth Kahn
Mrs. Frank Kalisch
Miss Shirley Kaplan
Mrs. John Karger
Mrs. Jerome Katz
Mrs. Brandon Keibel
Mrs. Roger King
Miss Hortense Lee Kinsman
Miss Sylvia Klein
Miss Doris Jane Kleinman
Mrs. Charles Klingenstein
Mrs. Henry Klingenstein
Miss Muriel Klubock
Miss Ruth Kreis
Mrs. Abraham Landesman
Miss Debra Landsberg
Mrs. Edwin Lane
Mrs. Percy W. Lansburgh
Mrs. Joseph Laval
Mrs. Sidney.D. Leader
Mrs. Phillip Leavitt
Mrs. William Lehman
Miss Beatrice Levinson
Mrs. Monroe Levoy
Mrs. Edward Levy
Miss Jayne Levy
Mrs. Saul Lewis
Mrs. Irving Lowenstein
Miss Sylvia C. Lowenstein
Miss Sydelle Lubev
Mrs. Henry T. Luria
Mr. Boris Magasanik
Mrs. Arthur Marcus
Mrs. Mortimer Marcus
Miss Dorothy Maybaum
Mrs. Irving Meister
Mrs. Herbert Meyer
Mrs. Jerome Meyer
Miss Rita Michaels
Miss Helga Michelson
Mrs. Gustave Minton

Miss Rhoda Lucille Mintz
Mrs. Harold Moneysmith
Mrs. Louis Napoleon
Mrs. Cyrus H. Nathan
Mrs. Julius Palleri
Mrs. Fred Perlberg
Miss Shirley Robinson
Miss Suzanne Rosener
Mrs. Leon Rothschild
Miss Bobbie Sable
Mr. Abraham Austin Salmon
Miss Janet Samuels
Miss Peggy Samuels
Miss Evelyn Saphir
Miss Barbara Scofield
Miss Muriel Seligman
Miss Gladys Selverne
Mrs. Nelson Sharfman
Mrs. Gregory Shwartzman
Miss Sadie Siegel
Mrs. Solomon Silver
Mrs. Norman Silverstein
Miss Audrey Simons
Miss Edna Stein
Mrs. Laurence B. Stein
Mrs. Edward Sulzberger
Miss May Taif
Mrs. Irving Taylor
Mrs. Abraham Topkis
Miss Edith Tuchman
Miss Gertrude Urquhart
Mrs. Beatrice F. Weil
Mrs. Jacob Weinstein
Mrs. Max Weintraub
Mrs. Robert M. Werblow
Mrs. Leroy Whitelaw
*Miss Leah Wiener
Mrs. Eli Winkler
Mrs. Arthur M. Wolfson
Miss Muriel Wurtzel
Miss Muriel Zinoroy

--- —

* Ceased.

REPORT OF THE SOCIAL SERVICE DEPARTMENT

During the past year, the continued economic depression and the worldwide unrest were again important factors in dealing with the many patients who came to our attention. We had hoped that changes in public assistance would lessen our responsibilities, but on the contrary, we found that in many ways they have increased. The influx of refugees into New York has continued to bring us increasingly complex problems, and the subsequent demands made upon us for various forms of assistance have multiplied during the year. The varied types of our clientele are evidence that our city is truly a "melting pot." That our patients are representative of all classes is well illustrated by the following story:

On one of the wards were a gypsy baby and the child of a former wealthy Viennese refugee. The family of each child came to see the social worker at the same time, and the scene was significant to anyone sensitive to human drama. The gypsy mother, a tall, commanding figure, was clad in full regalia with long, swinging petticoats, colorful but not too clean. The non-resident gypsy family, applying for relief, not welcome as tenants because of their habit of moving without notice, seemed to have little sense of security, although they were citizens and had a claim on State, even if not on municipal funds. The refugee family appeared to have all that the gypsy lacked. The mother, an aunt, and an older child were dressed in furs, which, incidentally, the gypsy eyed intently. A feeling of security was lacking in both women. With rich furs but no money, in a strange land, with memories but no knowledge of how to manage without resources, the refugee mother, a recent widow, was coping with the problem of caring for her children unassisted by servants. Though worlds apart, these two women shared common problems—insecurity, poverty, and illness.

THE STAFF: Owing to the fact that some agencies enlarged their personnel and that new positions were created in public welfare work, there was a greater turnover on our staff than during the previous year. Considerable time was lost in replacing staff members, as we found it difficult to secure social workers with the particular experience and ability necessary to carry on our work. In addition to this, absence on account of illness was greater than in 1938.

STATISTICS: It is to the credit of the staff that, in spite of the many changes and illnesses, the case load showed very little variation. We had 9,341 new cases, only 18 less than in 1938; 821 more cases were reopened and 613 more were closed. There is a tendency in the field of medical social service to close cases as soon as the immediate problem is solved, and to reopen them later, if necessary, rather than to carry a large inactive case load. We are not in complete agreement with this practice, particularly when the patient continues to be under active medical care. Although the interviews and consultations in the Hospital have shown a large increase, visits outside of the Hospital have decreased. This is accounted for by the fact that the demands made upon the workers' time in the Hospital make it necessary to limit home visits.

DEPARTMENTAL ACTIVITIES: We are cognizant of the newer trends in medical social work but we have made comparatively few changes in our own techniques. Change is not always improvement, and before we abandon a tried and familiar method, we wish to be assured that we are substituting a better and a sounder one, which ultimately will afford the greatest benefit to the patient, to the Hospital and to the community.

Owing to the large number of patients attending the Psychiatric Clinic, it was not possible to accept new admissions during a large part of the year. Since February, one of the psychiatric social workers has given part of her time to the Neurological Ward and Clinic cases. This, however, can be only a temporary arrangement, and eventually it will be necessary to add another psychiatric social worker to the department.

During the past year, a psychiatrist was assigned to each medical service, with whom the social workers have weekly conferences, resulting in better and more understanding service.

An effort was made to effect more efficient planning in the discharge of our patients. The social worker continues to take a great share of the responsibility, and it is felt that progress is being made and more thought is being given to the individual patient's needs.

The plan for full coverage of the Genito-Urinary Clinic was working out with increasing satisfaction until October 1, when the worker, who had started the service, resigned. It is regrettable that the slow, steady building up of social service participation in the clinic was disturbed and that considerable momentum was lost.

For many years, some physicians have placed emphasis on the importance of climatic change for certain types of diseases. During the year, we placed two bronchiectasis cases with a private family in Arizona, the families of the patients being able to assume a large part of the expenses.

CONFERENCE COMMITTEE ON SOCIAL SERVICE: The Conference Committee on Social Service held one meeting during the year. A report on the large increase in the number of appliances provided by us was presented. The problem of replying to the numerous inquiries from social agencies, particularly the Home Relief Bureau, regarding the employability of patients, was considered. The question of who should impart diagnoses, such as cancer and tuberculosis, to patients and patients' families was also discussed. The physicians on the Committee showed keen interest, and their suggestions proved most helpful.

STUDENT NURSES: In September, the education assignment of student nurses to the Social Service Department was shortened from eight weeks to four weeks, thus making it possible for every student, instead of only a limited few, to have some experience in Social Service. This has resulted in a complete change in our program, requiring the social workers and supervisors to give much more attention to the students; but the students' ability to render assistance to us has thereby been greatly diminished. We are, however, gratified to be able to make our contribution to the training of the student nurses, since we believe that every nurse should have an understanding of the social and emotional problems of a patient and familiarize herself with the resources in the community.

CONVALESCENCE: The closer affiliation of The Neustadter Home for Convalescents with the Hospital has been one of the bright spots of the year. In February, male patients were admitted to the Home for the first time, thus helping to meet one of our most urgent convalescent needs. It has been particularly helpful to have a continuity of service between the Hospital and the Home, and the marked improvement found in the condition of patients upon their return has been heart-warming. To have participated with the Hospital in making an existing Home more adequately meet the needs of the patients in a large hospital has been an interesting and stimulating experience. The admitting procedure underwent a radical change. All patients now assemble at the Hospital and are seen by the admitting physician. They are sent directly to the Home in a large, well heated taxi, thus causing the patients as little exertion as possible. We have continued to use other convalescent facilities. and in all have provided convalescent care for 2,170 patients, an increase of 255 over last year.

CONVALESCENT DAY CAMP: The Convalescent Day Camp on Welfare Island, which was opened last summer, provided another convalescence resource. We sent 64 patients to the camp and anticipate sending a larger number during the coming year. We hope that the Department of Hospitals may find it possible to arrange for transportation so that patients from distant parts of the city can avail themselves of the Camp's beneficial facilities.

SUMMER THERAPEUTIC PROGRAM: The summer therapeutic program was carried out very satisfactorily; 412 children and 16 working boys and girls were sent to the country, an increase of 156 over last year. Through the Max J. Breitenbach Fund, we were able to send 89 mothers and their children to the United Vacation Home. Although we secured more vacancies for colored children, there was still an insufficient number to meet the needs of this group. Facilities for caring for adolescent boys and girls, asthmatics, cardiacs, and diabetic children were also lacking.

WORKROOM: Near the end of the year, the Social Service Workroom was moved to more spacious quarters, making it possible for an increased number of patients to participate in its activities. It continued to play an important part in their rehabilitation. The total attendance during the year was 39, averaging 15 women and 9 men daily. Four young girls, recent trade-school graduates, who were under treatment in our clinics, attended the Workroom until they were well enough to look for regular employment. The habit of work which they acquired, as well as the money which they earned, encouraged them to seek employment elsewhere, which they did successfully as soon as their physical conditions permitted.

VOLUNTEERS: 134 volunteers gave conscientious assistance to the Hospital, the largest number ever registered. The high quality of their work is evidenced by the number of physicians who requested that volunteers be assigned to them. We have been exceedingly fortunate to have so large a group of women whose sustained enthusiasm keeps them with us year after year. Each volunteer has contributed a share toward the achievement of smooth and efficient functioning of the Hospital, for which, we know, the Trustees are most grateful.

OCCUPATIONAL THERAPY: The demands for Occupational Therapy, as a part of medical treatment, are increasing to such an extent that they can no longer be met by the present staff, and the need for another therapist is apparent. A group of volunteers, who assist the occupational therapists, also reconditioned and distributed to the ward and clinic children 1,600 toys which had been donated to the Hospital.

LIBRARY: The Patient's Library continued to function as in the past, and many of our friends again remembered us with generous donations of books and magazines.

CHANGES IN COMMUNITY ACTIVITIES WHICH AFFECT OUR WORK: The many changes of policy which were made in the Works Progress Administration and by the various categorical divisions of the Department of Welfare are bound to bring reactions from our patients, and naturally they turn to the medical social workers for assistance in these crises. We were particularly affected by the drastic cut in the housekeeping services; although we foresaw that this would eventually happen, it proved none the less difficult when it came. The emotional response of many families to the sudden withdrawal of housekeepers made us more than ever conscious of the need for a more permanent service of this type. One of our greatest problems continues to be the reporting on physical condition and degree of disability of those of working age, requested by the Home Relief Bureau of the Department of Welfare. This is a complicated and difficult question, and one which confronts all metropolitan hospitals accepting recipients of relief.

The workers recognize the advantages gained through the sharing of information and joint planning with other agencies, and many helpful conferences were held during the year. We appreciate greatly the cooperation accorded us by the numerous organizations throughout the city.

SOCIAL SERVICE COMMITTEE: We welcomed Mrs. Irwin Untermyer, Mrs. Marco Hellman and Mrs. Frederick L. Ehrman as members of the Social Service Committee. Mrs. Robert M. Benjamin was appointed secretary to replace Miss Angie Jacobson, who resigned after many years of faithful service. Miss Jacobson's resignation was accepted with regret, but we are pleased that she will continue to serve as a member of our Board.

CONTRIBUTIONS: As in past years, we wish to express our sincere thanks for the financial assistance given us by the Federation of Jewish Philanthropic Societies, the United Hospital Fund and by many generous friends, thus enabling us to meet the expenses of the Department.

To Dr. Joseph Turner, Director of the Hospital, and his assistants, to Mrs. Louis Mendelsohn, our director, and her loyal staff, as well as to the Board of Trustees of the Hospital, we extend our deep appreciation for their cooperation on all occasions. As in previous years, the members of the Social Service Board have taken a very active part in the work of the department, and I am most grateful for all their accomplishments in furthering medical social service in the Hospital.

Respectfully submitted,

RUTH M. COOK,

President of the Social Service Auxiliary.

THE MOUNT SINAI SOCIAL SERVICE AUXILIARY

REPORT OF THE TREASURER
For Year Ended December 31st, 1939

REGULAR ACCOUNT
DISBURSEMENTS

Appliances	$12,993.39
Extra Nourishment, Special Diets, etc.	2,118.44
Boarding	19.50
Convalescent Care	14,139.66
Relief	2,388.76
Shoes, Clothing, etc.	3,244.12
Transportation	2,652.73
Medication	245.40
Education and Recreation Supplies	985.68
Salaries	94,015.31
Workers' Expenses	525.17
Office Supplies (Including Stationery, Printing and Postage)	1,491.66
Affiliation Dues	88.50
Magazines and Newspapers	87.74
Sundries	6.25

Total Disbursements	$135,002.31

RECEIPTS

Federation	98,502.44
United Hospital Fund	19,500.00
Income from Investments	1,883.56
Refunds from Patients, etc.	2,664.99

Total Receipts	122,550.99

*Deficit**	*$12,451.32*

* Taken from Non-budgetary Special Accounts of Social Service Auxiliary (See below under Special Account).

SPECIAL ACCOUNT

Balance, January 1st, 1939	$18,880.97

RECEIPTS

Donations, etc. 1939	17,516.70
Appropriation from Principal and Income of Special Funds	5,002.71
Interest on Bank Acceptances	99.94

Total Credits	$41,500.32

DISBURSEMENTS

Special Account	5,715.81
Summer Work	5,851.00
Transferred to Regular Account for 1939 Deficit	*12,451.32*

Total Disbursements	24,018.13

Balance, December 31st, 1939	$17,482.19

126

DONATIONS FOR SPECIAL ACCOUNTS

Anonymous	$550.00
Anonymous (In Memory of Mr. David S. Hays)	50.00
Anonymous (In Memory of Mr. Walter A. Hirsch)	25.00
Anonymous	2.00
Bach, Mrs. Julian S. (In Memory of Mr. Joseph Saks)	10.00
Bach, Mrs. Julian S. (In Memory of Mr. Lloyd Wimpfheimer)	5.00
Backer, Mrs. George	250.00
Baerwald, Mrs. Paul	550.00
Benjamin, Mrs. Robert M.	120.00
Blumenthal, Mr. George	508.27
Blumenthal, Mrs. Gustav M. (In Memory of Mrs. Harry Sachs)	10.00
Blumenthal, Mrs. Robert G.	275.00
Bookman, Miss Nellie (In Memory of Mrs. Harry Sachs)	5.00
Borg, Mrs. Myron I.	25.00
Breitenbach, Mrs. Max J. (In Memory of Mr. Max J. Breitenbach)	1,000.00
Breitenbach, Mrs. Max J. (In Memory of the birthday of the late Mr. Charles Klingenstein)	100.00
Breitenbach, Mrs. Max J. (In Memory of Mrs. Morton L. Adler)	50.00
Buchman, Miss Helen (In Memory of Mrs. Lottie R. Norman)	5.00
Cohen, Mrs. Arthur J.	550.00
Cohn, Mrs. Leonard A.	525.00
Cohn, Mr. and Mrs. Leonard A. (In Memory of Mrs. Lottie R. Norman)	5.00
Cook, Mrs. Alfred A.	1,050.00
Davis, Miss Hannah (In Memory of parents Edward and Elisa Davis)	15.00
Ehrman, Mrs. Frederick L.	100.00
Elsinger, Mrs. W. H. (In Memory of Mrs. Lottie R. Norman)	5.00
Feingold, Miss Jessica (In Memory of Mr. Joseph Moschcowitz)	5.00
Fleming, Miss Winifred (In Memory of Mr. Charles Klingenstein)	25.00
Frank, Mr. and Mrs. Clifton (In Memory of Mrs. Harry Sachs)	2.00
Friedenheit, Mr. and Mrs. Isaac (In Memory of Myron Goldsmith Friedenheit)	50.00
Glazier, Mr. and Mrs. Henry S.	1,075.00
Hartman, Mr. and Mrs. Siegfried F.	325.00
Heimerdinger, Mrs. Frederick M.	225.00
Heimerdinger, Miss Barbara and Master John	25.00
Hellman, Mrs. Marco F.	110.00
Hilb, Mrs. Hannah	20.00
Hirsch, Mr. Steven J. (In Memory of Mr. Walter A. Hirsch)	100.00
Hirsch, Mrs. Walter A.	785.00
Hirsch, Mrs. Walter A. (In Memory of Miss Mildred Klein)	10.00
Carried Forward	$8,547.27

DONATIONS FOR SPECIAL ACCOUNTS

(Continued)

Brought Forward	$8,547.27
Hurt, Mrs. Edna M. (In Memory of Mrs. Herman Goldenberg)	5.00
Hyman, Dr. and Mrs. Harold T. (In Memory of Miss Mildred Klein)	10.00
Jacobson, Miss Angie (In Memory of Mr. Harry R. Kohn)	5.00
Jacobson, Miss Angie (In Memory of Mr. Maurice Goodman)	5.00
Jacobson, Miss Angie (In Memory of Mr. Lloyd Wimpfheimer)	10.00
Jacobson, Miss Angie (In Memory of Mr. Henry S. Glazier)	10.00
Kaufman, Mrs. H. M. (In Memory of Mrs. Fannie C. Korn)	15.00
Kay, Mrs. William de Young	60.00
Kempner, Mrs. Alan H.	225.00
Klingenstein, Mrs. Charles (In Memory of Mrs. Morton L. Adler)	50.00
Kops, Mrs. Max and Family (In Memory of Mr. Joseph Gitterman)	15.00
Kops, Mr. and Mrs. Waldemar (In Memory of Mrs. Robert Lambert)	10.00
Kops, Mr. and Mrs. Waldemar (In Memory of Mrs. H. Kaiser)	5.00
Kops, Mr. and Mrs. Waldemar (In Memory of Hetty Lambert)	5.00
Lehman, Mrs. Herbert H.	1,020.00
Loeb, Mrs. Louis M.	150.00
Lorch, Master Thomas	10.00
Lorsch, Mrs. Josie M. (In Memory of Mrs. Harry Sachs)	30.00
Meyer, The Brothers (In Memory of Mr. Moses J. Hess)	10.00
Naumburg, Mrs. George W.	530.00
Oppenheimer, Mrs. F. J. (for Lucille J. Oppenheimer Fund for special designated purposes)	2,000.00
Pforzheimer, Mrs. Carl H. Jr.	110.00
Rosenthal, Mrs. Moritz	530.00
Roth, Mrs. Philip A. (For Max J. Breitenbach Fund)	4,000.00
Roth, Mrs. Philip A. (In Memory of Mrs. Morton L. Adler)	100.00
Roth, Mrs. Philip A. (In Memory of Mr. Charles Klingenstein)	100.00
Sachs, Miss Edith	280.00
Schamberg, Mrs. Lucile (In Memory of Mrs. Harry Sachs)	5.00
Scholle, Mrs. William D.	200.00
Siegbert, Mrs. Henry	210.00
Solomon, Mrs. P.	10.00
Som, Dr. Max L.	20.20
Stern, Mrs. Albert	125.00
Straus, Mrs. Roger W.	250.00
Strauss, Mrs. Jacob (In Memory of Mrs. Harry Sachs)	15.00
Strauss, Mr. Maurice J. (In Memory of Mrs. Harry Sachs)	10.00
Strauss, Mr. Walter C. (In Memory of Mrs. Harry Sachs)	5.00
Carried Forward	$18,697.47

DONATIONS FOR SPECIAL ACCOUNTS

(Continued)

Brought Forward $18,697.47
Untermyer, Mrs. Irwin 125.00
Von Phul, Mrs. William (In Honor of the silver wedding anni-
    versary of Mr. and Mrs. Arthur J. Cohen................................. 3.00
Weil, Mrs. Frank L. 125.00
Weil, Mrs. Leopold 20.00
Wimpfheimer, Mrs. Charles A. (In Memory of Mrs. Harry Sachs) 10.00
Miscellaneous: Refunds from patients, etc..................................... 536.23

Total.. $19,516.70

DONORS OF CLOTHING

Abel, Dr. Harold A.
Adoff, Mrs. Frederick
Asiel, Mrs. Nelson I.
Baar, Miss Elinor A.
Bach, Mrs. Milton J.
Bache, Mrs. Leopold S.
Baehr, Dr. George
Baerwald, Mrs. Paul
Barnett, Mrs. Harold
Barnett, Miss Rosalind L.
Bass, Dr. Murray H.
Becker, Mrs. Herman
Bendheim, Mr. John
Benjamin, Mrs. Robert M.
Bernheim, Mrs. Isaac J.
Berolzheimer, Mrs. Alfred C.
Berolzheimer, Master Kenneth
Bethill, Miss Ruth
Binger, Mrs. Gustav
Binger, Mrs. Robert E.
Bixer, Mrs. Herman
Blun, Mrs. Edwin
Boggess, Mrs. Albert S.
Byk, Mrs. Paul M.
Cardozo, Mr. Michael H., Jr.
Carlebach, Mrs. Emil
Chargin, Dr. Louis
Cohen, Mrs. Arthur J.
Cohen, Miss Florence
Cohen, Dr. and Mrs. Ira
Cohen, Dr. Jerome L.
Cohen, Mrs. Norman H.
Cohen, Mrs. Samuel
Cohn, Mrs. Leonard A.
Cohn, Mrs. Peter A.
Cole, Mrs. Robert
Cone, Mrs. Arthur L.
Cook, Mrs. Alfred A.
Cook, Miss Madeleine R.
Cuming, Miss Nan
Deitsch, Mrs. Charles
DeMenasce, Mrs. Elinor
DeVeglio, Miss Helen
Dillenberg, Mrs. D. Alan
Dorsey, Miss Julia P.
Dreicer, Mrs. Mary
Dreyfus, Mrs. Charles, Jr.
Ehrich, Mrs. Jules S.
Ehrman, Mrs. Frederick L .
Einstein, Mrs. L.

Elsinger, Mrs. W. H.
Engel, Miss Jean
Erdmann, Mrs. William
Falk, Miss Mildred
Falk, Mr. Myron S.
Farmer, Dr. Elsie
Fischer, Dr. Alfred E.
Frank, Dr. and Mrs. Maxwell S.
Frank, Dr. Robert T.
Frankenheimer, Miss Ida
Frankenheimer, Miss Rose
Friedlander, Mrs. Marcus S.
Friend, Miss Alice J.
Friestner, Mr. William
Garfinkel, Mrs. Harry P.
Glass, Mrs. Ruth
Glassman, Mr. Julius (In memory
   of Mr. Mayer Glassman)
Glazier, Mrs. Henry S.
Glazier, Mrs. William S.
Globus, Dr. and Mrs. Joseph H.
Goldsmith, Mrs. B. J.
Goldsmith, Mrs. Samuel
Gottheil, Mrs. Paul
Haas, Mrs. Robert K.
Hamerschlag, Mrs. Joseph
Handelman, Miss Beatrice
Hartman, Mrs. Siegfried F.
Heming, Mrs. Charles E.
Henry, Mrs. H. Maud
Herrman, Mrs. A.
Hersch, Mrs. Albert M.
Herzog, Mr. Oscar
Hessberg, Mrs. Felix
Hessberg, Mrs. Lena
Heyman, Mrs. David M.
Hirsch, Mrs. Elizabeth S.
Hirsch, Mrs. Walter A.
Hyman, Mrs. Harold Thomas
Hyman, Mrs. M. S.
Jonas, Mrs. A. (Through Mrs.
   Charles Israel)
Jonas, Mrs. Edouard
Kanzer, Dr. Mark
Katzive, Dr. Julius A.
Kay, Mrs. William de Young
Kempner, Mrs. Alan H.
Keschner, Dr. Harold W.
Kiebel, Mrs. Brandon
Klauber, Mrs. Murray

DONORS OF CLOTHING—(Continued)

Klieger, Dr. and Mrs. I. S.
Klingenstein, Mrs. Charles
Klotsky, Mrs. Mack G.
Kohnstamm, Mrs. Lothair S.
Korn, Mrs. F. C.
Krindler, Mrs. Maxwell A.
Lampert, Mrs. Harry (In memory of Master Solomon Lampert)
Landesman, Mrs. Abraham
Leader, Dr. and Mrs. Sidney D.
Lenzner, Mrs. Joseph B.
Leventritt, Mrs. Edgar M.
Levy, Miss Edith L.
Lewisohn, Mrs. Sam A.
Liberman, Mrs. Isaac
Liebman, Mrs. Charles J.
Liebman, Miss Margaret
Liebman, Mrs. Thomas
Liebmann, Mrs. Samuel
Lifschey, Miss Ella
Lippmann, Mr. and Mrs. David
Loeb, Mrs. Carl M.
Loeb, Miss Dorothy
Loeb, Mrs. Louis M.
Loewe, Miss Jewel (In memory of Mrs. Selma Loewe)
Lowenstein, Mrs. Irving
Mendelsohn, Mr. and Mrs. Sigmund
Meyerhoff, Mr. and Mrs. William
Michaels, Mrs. Harold
Michaels, Mrs. Herbert L.
Millhauser, Mrs. DeWitt
Minton, Mr. G. M., Jr.
Moolten, Dr. Sylvan E.
Napoleon, Mrs. Louis
Neaman, Mrs. Pearson E.
Neary, Miss Lucy M.
Needlework Guild of America
Paymer, Miss Adell
Perper, Mr. D. (In memory of Mr. Israel Perper)
Pforzheimer, Mr. and Mrs. Carl H., Jr.
Pofcher, Mrs. Jacob F.
Prince, Mrs. Leo M.
Reichstein, Mrs. Albert H.
Reiss, Dr. Joseph
Rosenstock, Mrs. David G.
Rosenthal, Mrs. Nathan

Rossbach, Mrs. Lawrence B.
Rossbach, Mrs. Leopold
Rubel, Mrs. Tillie
Sabloff, Dr. Louis
Sachs, Mrs. Julius
Sachs, Mr. Walter E.
Salomon, Mr. Percy F.
Schafer, Mrs. Myron
Scharff, Mrs. Maurice R.
Schatia, Dr. Viva
Schick, Dr. Bela
Schlivek, Mrs. Kaufman
Scholle, Mrs. William D.
Schwartz, Miss Esther (In memory of Mrs. Tony Schwartz
Seligman, Mr. Milton
Sicher, Mrs. Frank E.
Siegel, Miss Sadie
Silberstein, Mrs. Abraham
Silver, Mrs. Solomon
Sperber, Mrs. Jacob
Speyer, Mrs. Daniel
Spingarn, Mrs. Arthur B.
Spingarn, Mr. Sigmund
Springer, Miss Bessie
Stachelberg, Mrs. Charles G.
Stein, Mrs. Emanuel W.
Stein, Mrs. Lawrence B.
Stein, Mrs. William H.
Stern, Mr. Carl J.
Stettenheim, Mr. and Mrs. I. M.
Straus, Mrs. Roger W.
Strauss, Mrs. Israel
Strauss, Mrs. Jacob
Tiedemann, Mrs. Carl
Turner, Dr. Joseph
Weil, Mrs. Frank L.
Weil, Mr. George L.
Weil, Mrs. Leon
Weinberg, Mrs. Akiba
Werblow, Mrs. Robert M.
Wile, Miss Birdie
Williams, Mrs. Jesse
Wimpfheimer, Mrs. Charles A.
Wimpfheimer, Mr. Harold D.
Wimpfheimer, Miss Susan
Zamkin, Dr. Harry O.
Zelson, Dr. Carl

GIFTS OF ARTICLES

TOYS AND GAMES

Abraham, Mrs. Otto
Barnett, Miss Marjorie
Benjamin, Mrs. Robert M.
Berolzheimer, Mrs. Alfred C.
Blackstone, Miss Barbara
Blum, Mrs. Samuel
Blumenthal, Mr. George
Cahn, Mrs. William M., Jr.
Cohen, Mrs. Arthur J.
Cohn, Mrs. Leonard A.
Cohn, Mrs. Peter A.
Cole, Mrs. Robert
Collier, Master Gilman
Cook, Mrs. Alfred A.
Dalton School
Dammann, Mrs. Richard W.
Davis, Mrs. Richard
Dreyfus, Mrs. Charles, Jr.
Ehrman, Mrs. Frederick L.
Elias, Mrs. Henry H.
Erdmann, Mrs. William
Frankenheimer, Miss Ida
Frankenheimer, Miss Rose
Glazier, Mrs. William S.
Goldsmith, Mrs. James A., Jr.
Good Cheer Doll Group (Through
  Mrs. A. Millhauser)
Gottlieb, Mrs. Leo
Greenspan, Dr. Edward B.
Grossman, Master Ronald
Hartig, Mrs. Morris
Heimerdinger, Mrs. Frederick M.
Heming, Mrs. Charles E.
Hilson, Mrs. Edwin
Hirsch, Mrs. Steven J.
Horowitz, Mrs. Herman
Hyman, Mrs. Abraham
Hyman, Mrs. M. S.
Ittleson, Mrs. Henry, Jr.
Klingenstein, Mrs. Joseph
Krindler, Mrs. Maxwell A.

Leiter, Dr. H. Evans
Leventritt, Mrs. Leo L.
Levinsohn, Mrs. I. (Through Dr.
  Sol W. Ginsburg)
Liebman, Mrs. Thomas
Liebmann, Mrs. Samuel
Loeb, Mrs. Carl M., Jr.
Loeb, Mrs. John L.
Loeb, Mrs. Louis M.
Luber, Mr. Solomon
Luber, Miss Sydelle
March, Mrs. Henry
Meyer, Mrs. Robert T.
Neaman, Mrs. Pearson E.
Newman, Master Daniel
Oppenheimer, Mr. and Mrs.
  Jerome H.
Picker, Mrs. Eugene
Rashbaum, Dr. Maurice
Riesner, Master Gordon
Rifkind, Mrs. Albert J.
Rosenthal, Mrs. John
Roth, Master Sanford
Sadowsky, Mrs. Jack P.
Schlossberg, Mr. Alfred
Scholle, Mrs. William D.
Schwartz, Mr. William
Spindler, Mrs. Jack
Steefel, Mrs. Robert D.
Stern, Miss Elizabeth
Stern, Master Hubert
Stroock, Mrs. Samuel
Touroff, Dr. Arthur S. W.
Warburg, Mrs. Jean S.
Weiser, Master Sammy
Wiener, Mr. Harry
Willis, Mrs. G. F.
Works Progress Administration
  (Toy Mending Project)
Zuckerman, Mrs. Henry

BOOKS AND MAGAZINES

Abrams, Miss Hessie
Abrams, Miss Sadie
Adler, Mr. Morton L.
Alix, Master Andrew
Alix, Master Guy
Alkus, Mrs. I. Jack
Altschul, Mrs. Frank
American Red Cross
Amsterdam, Mr. Isador
Amsterdam, Mrs. Jack
Arnheim, Dr. Ernest E.
Arthur Kudner Company
Atlas, Mrs. David
Baar, Miss Elinor A.
Bach, Mrs. Milton J.
Backer, Mrs. George
Baerwald, Mrs. Herman F.
Baerwald, Mrs. Paul
Bandler, Mrs. Evon F.
Barnard, Miss Selina
Bastian, Dr. Carlisle C.
Becker, Mrs. Herman
Bendheim, Mr. John
Benjamin, Mrs. Robert M.
Bennett, Miss Leah
Berger, Mrs. Sidney A.
Berman, Miss Rose L.
Bernheim, Mrs. Isaac J.
Bernheim, Mrs. Sidney
Bernstein, Dr. Phineas
Berolzheimer, Mrs. Alfred C.
Berolzheimer, Master Kenneth
Bick, Dr. Edgar M.
Binger, Mrs. Robert E.
Block, Mrs. J. Horace
Blumenthal, Mr. and Mrs. George
Blumenthal, Mrs. Irving
Blun, Mrs. Edwin
Borg, Mrs. Myron I.
Breitenbach, Mrs. Max J.
Bresnick, Mr. Samuel H.
Brickner, Dr. Richard M.
Browning, Mrs. S. Pearce, Jr.
Brumer, Dr. Nathan
Bullowa, Mrs. Arthur M.
Bulowa, Miss Julia
Burr, Miss Jane

Byk, Mrs. Paul M.
Cardozo, Mrs. Michael H., Jr.
Chester, Mr. Jacob
Clear, Mrs. Virginia
Cohen, Mrs. Arthur J.
Cole, Mrs. Ralph M.
Cole, Mrs. Robert
Collier, Master Gilman
Colp, Mrs. Ralph A.
Cone, Mrs. Paul
Cook, Mrs. Alfred A.
Cook, Phil (Columbia Broadcasting System)
Cullman, Mrs. Joseph F., Jr.
Cuming,, Miss Nan
Dalton School
Dammann, Mrs. Richard W.
Danowsky, Dr. Rabbi Joseph
Danziger, Mrs. Max
Davidson, Master Edward
Davies, Mrs. Josephine
Deutsch, Mr. Armand S.
Dickson, Mrs. Leonard
Dillenberg, Mrs. D. Alan
Doctor, Mrs. Arthur
Dorman, Mrs. Stanley J.
Dushkind, Mrs. Davis S.
Ehrich, Mrs. Jules S.
Eliasoph, Dr. Benjamin
Elkin, Mr. Paul
Epstein, Dr. Emanuel Z.
Erdmann, Mrs. William
Erlanger, Mrs. Sydney B.
Fadiman, Master Edwin
Farmer, Mrs. Alfred
Feiner, Miss Judy
Feist, Mrs. Leonard
Finkenberg, Mrs. Israel
Finkle, Mr. Jacob
Finkle, Dr. Philip
Frank, Mrs. Henry
Frank, Dr. Robert T.
Friedlander, Mrs. Charles
Friedlander, Mrs. Marcus S.
Friedlander, Miss Mary Ellen
Friedman, Mr. Elisha M.
Furchgott, Mrs. Leo

BOOKS AND MAGAZINES—(Continued)

Fuerst, Mrs. William F.
Galinger, Mrs. George W.
Garlock, Dr. John H.
Gates, Mrs. Samuel
Gelb, Mrs. Lena K.
Gelfer, Master Lloyd
Genn, Mrs. G. H.
Genn, Miss Lillian G.
Geyer, Cornell & Newell Inc.
Gilbert, Mrs. Seymour
Gold, Mr. Morris
Goldman, Mrs. William
Goldsmith, Mrs. Harry B.
Goldsmith, Mr. Richard
Goodman, Mr. B.
Goodman, Mrs. Edwin
Gottheil, Mrs. Paul
Gottlieb, Mrs. Arnold
Greenberg, Mrs. Max
Guinzburg, Mrs. Harold A.
Halle, Mr. H. J.
Hanson, Mrs. Edward C.
Hart, Mrs. Henry
Hartig, Mrs. Morris
Hartman, Mrs. Siegfried F.
Heiman, Mr. Arthur S.
Heimerdinger, Mrs. Frederick M.
Heimerdinger, Mrs. Joseph E.
Heming, Mrs. Charles E.
Henry, Mrs. H. Maud
Henshel, Mr. and Mrs. Harry D.
Herald Tribune
Herman, Mr. Arthur
Herrmann, Mrs. John A.
Hersch, Mrs. Albert
Heyman, Mrs. David M.
Heyman, Mr. Jacob
Hilson, Mrs. Edwin
Hirsch, Mrs. Steven J.
Hirsch, Mrs. Walter A.
Hirschfeld, Dr. Walter
Hober, Miss Beal
Hochstadter, Mrs. Albert F.
Hospital Service Plan of Technical
  Publicity Assn., Inc.
Hyman, Mrs. M. S.
Hyman, Mrs. Mark

Hyman, Mr. N. Richard
Isaacs, Mrs. Jerome L.
James, Mrs. Lee Warren
Jonas, Mrs. Edouard
Kahn, Mrs. Ely Jacques
Kaiser, Mr. Charles
Kaplan, Miss Adele
Kaplan, Miss Ailene
Karelitz, Dr. Samuel
Karger, Mrs. John S.
Karnel, Master Harold
Kastor, Mr. Adolph
Kaufmann, Mr. Ernest B.
Kaufmann, Mr. Herbert M.
Kempner, Mrs. Alan H.
Kempner, Mrs. Marshall S.
Keschner, Dr. Harold W.
Kirsch, Mrs. I.
Klein, Mrs. F.
Klein, Dr. Samuel H.
Klingenstein, Mrs. Charles
Klingenstein, Mrs. Joseph
Klingenstein, Mrs. William
Kops, Mrs. Adolph
Kops, Mr. Waldemar
Koretsky, Mrs. Yetta
Korn, Mr. Albert R.
Korn, Mrs. Ff C.
Krampner, Mr. William
Krauss, Mr. Max
Kreisler, Miss Mona and Club
Krellberg, Mr. Alfred S.
Kridel, Mrs. Robert H.
Kroll, Mrs. Pearl
Kulick, Dr. Bernard D.
Kurzman, Mrs. George F.
Lampert, Mr. Harry (In memory
  of Master Solomon Lampert)
Landesman, Mrs. Abraham
Lane, Mrs. Edwin
Larus, Mr. Dudley J.
Lawson, Master Irvil
Lazarus, Mrs. Louis
Lehman, Mrs. Irving
Leidesdorf, Mr. Arthur
Leventritt, Mrs. Edgar H.
Levy, Mrs. Benjamin J.

BOOKS AND MAGAZINES—(Continued)

Levy, Miss Edith L.
Levy, Mrs. I. H.
Levy, Mr. and Mrs. Joseph
Levy, Mrs. Joseph A.
Levy, Mrs. L. Napoleon
Levy, Mrs. Marvin L.
Lowengood, Mrs. Abraham
Liebman, Mrs. Charles J.
Liebmann, Mrs. Samuel
Lilienthal, Dr. Howard
List, Mrs. Edna
Loeb, Mrs. Louis M.
Loeb, Mrs. Morris
Loeb, Mrs. Otto S.
Long, Mrs. Louis
Lorsch, Mr. Henry
Lowenstein, Mrs. Oscar
Lowman, Miss Evelyn
Makenken, Miss Anne
Magazine, Dr. Joseph
March, Mrs. Henry
Marks, Miss Gertrude
Maurer, Mr. Harris W.
May, Dr. Charles H.
Mayer, Dr. Max D.
Meinhard, Mrs. Leo I.
Mensch, Mr. Bernard L.
Metwood Office Equip. Corp.
Meuer, Miss Ann
Meyer, Dr. and Mrs. Alfred
Michaels, Mrs. Joseph
Miller, Miss Belle
Millhauser, Mrs. DeWitt
Mintz, Dr. Maurice E.
Moch, Mrs. E. W.
Monk, Mr. Lawrence
Mordecai, Mr. Benjamin
Moreland, Mrs. Andrew
Morris, Mrs. S. Fred
Nachman, Mrs. M.
Napoleon, Mrs. Louis
Oppenheimer, Mrs. B. S.
Paris, Mrs. Harold
Pichel, Mrs. H.
Pimsleur, Master Paul
Posner, Mrs. Edwin
Preis, Mrs. Julius

Price, Mrs. Louis R.
Proskauer, Mrs. Joseph M.
Rains, Mr. and Mrs. S. E.
Ranger, Miss Edna A.
Reichenbach, Mrs. Max
Reiss, Mrs. Jac M.
Reiss, Dr. Joseph
Reubens, Mrs. Raymond
Rifkind, Mrs. Albert J.
Rimelbach, Mrs. Sigmund
Rittenberg, Mr. L.
Rosenfeld, Mrs. Ernst
Rosenstein, Mrs. Henry
Rosenthal, Mrs. John
Rosenthal, Mrs. Moritz
Rossbach, Mrs. Lawrence
Rossbach, Mrs. Max J.
Roth, Mr. Samuel
Sachs, Miss Edith
St. Vincent de Paul Society
Samuel, Mr. and Mrs. Morris
Sandler, Miss Rose
Sanger, Mr. Alan B.
Schafer, Mrs. Myron
Schlivek, Mrs. Max
Schneider. Mr. Hyman
Scholle, Mrs. William D.
Schulte, Mrs. Joseph M.
Schulte, Mrs. John S.
Schwabacher, Mrs. Herman S.
Schwartz, Mr. William
Selig, Dr. Seth
Seligman, Mrs. Arthur
Shapiro, Mrs. B. J.
Shapiro, Mrs. Benjamin
Siegbert, Mrs. Henry
Sobel, Mr. Joseph
Spencer, Mrs. Girard L.
Sperry, Mrs. Eugene E.
Springer, Miss Bessie
Stern, Miss Elizabeth
Stern, Mrs. Samuel
Stettenheim, Mr. and Mrs. I. M.
Straus, Mr. Hugh Grant, Jr.
Strauss, Miss Florence
Strauss, Mrs. Florence
Strauss, Mrs. Maurice J.

BOOKS AND MAGAZINES—(Continued)

Stroock, Mrs. Stephen J.
Sulzberger, Mrs. Arthur Hays
Towne, Mr. W. L.
Trachtenberg, Dr. Harold B.
Trent, Mrs. Edwin
Untermyer, Miss Louise
Wachtel, Mrs. P.
Wald, Master Edwin
Walter, Mrs. Edwin J.
Warburg, Mr. Edwin M. M.
Warburg, Mrs. Jean S.
Watters, Mrs. Leon Laizer
Weitz, Miss Francine
Werblow, Mrs. Robert M.
Werner, Mrs. Gerard B.
Wheeler, Mr. F. R.
Wildenstein, Mrs. Felix

Wile, Mrs. Walter D.
Wiley, Mrs. B.
Wimpfheimer, Mrs. Charles A.
Wimpfheimer, Mrs. Edward
Wimpfheimer, Mr. Harold D.
Wing, Mr. Willis Kingsley
Wise, Mrs. Edmond E.
Wood, Mrs. Roland
Woolf, Mrs. Louis J.
Wyle, Mrs. Milton
Young Israel
Zamkin, Dr. Harry O.
Zimmerman, Mrs. William
Zimmern, Mr. Lee D.
Zuckerman, Mrs. Henry
Zuckerman, Mrs. Paul S.
Zunz, Mrs. E.

FLOWERS AND PLANTS

Abram, Mrs. Sadie (In memory of Sidney Spier)
Adams, Mrs. Saul
Amsterdam, Mrs. Isador
Bernheim, Mrs. Alfred L.
Bernheim, Mrs. Henry J.
Blacher, Mr. Samuel
Blech, Mrs. Israel
Bloom, Mr. Jacob
Brentano, Mrs. Simon
Brodsky, Mrs. Miriam
Brooks, Mrs. Leo L.
Chasan, Mrs. Harry
Claster, Mr. Lester
Cohen, Mrs. Arthur J.
Cohen, Miss Ernestine
Collier, Master Gilman
Colp, Mrs. Ralph A.
Community Church (Through Dr. John Haines Holmes)
Congregation Emanu-El Temple
Congregation Rodeph Sholom
Cook, Mrs. Alfred A.
Danziger, Mrs. Max
Daum, Mrs. Charles
Dinson, Mr. Hyman
Drubin, Mrs. Arthur W.

Ehrman, Mrs. Frederick L.
Elias, Mr. Sam
Fine, Mrs. Anna
Frankenthaler, Hon. and Mrs. Alfred
Frankenthaler, Mrs. George
Frankfurter, Mr. Paul (In memory of Mrs. Paul Frankfurter)
Frohnknecht, Mr. O. C.
Gilbert, Mrs. Seymour (In memory of Mrs. Fritz Loeb)
Glazier, Mrs. Henry S.
Guinzburg, Mrs. George K.
Harris, Mr. Wolf
Heller, Mrs. Samuel
Herman, Mrs. David
Hirsch, Mrs. Richard
Horowitz, Mrs. I. S.
Kaiser, Master Bruce
Kasler, Mr. and Mrs. J.
Klein, Leo (Florist) (Through Dr. William M. Hitzig)
Klingenstein, Mrs. Charles
Lane, Mrs. Edwin
Leavitt, Mr. Ezra G.
Lederer, Mrs. E.
Leidesdorf, Mr. and Mrs. Samuel D.
Levy, Miss Anna

FLOWERS AND PLANTS—(Continued)

Liberman, Mr. and Mrs. Isaac
Loeb, Mrs. Milton B.
Margolin, Mr. William
Mayer, Mrs. Joseph L. B.
Mendel, Mrs. Esther A.
Meyer, Mrs. Harrison D.
Mizzi, Miss Eleanor
Morgenthau, Mrs. Henry
Nordlinger, Mrs. Louis
Norman, Mrs. Aaron E.
Ogden, Miss Peggy Ann
Oppenheimer, Dr. B. S.
Parodi, Mrs. Flaviano
Popper, Miss Louise
Popper, Miss Rebecca
Price, Mr. and Mrs. George
Rabin, Miss Bessie
Robinson, Mr. Louis H.
Robson, Mrs. Herman
Rodeph Sholom Sisterhood

Sadowsky, Mrs. Jack P.
Salmon, Mrs. David Leon (In memory of Mr. David Leon Salmon)
Schafer, Mrs. Oscar S. (In memory of Mr. Samuel M. Grier)
Silverstone, Miss Eleanor Barbara
Silverstone Miss Marilyn
Stein, Mrs. Alix J.
Stengel, Mr. Arthur W.
Stroock, Mr. Joseph
Surat, Miss Elaine
Tim, Mrs. Louis B.
Veit, Mrs. Arthur B. (In memory of Rose Hollander)
Weatherwax, Mrs. Clifford
Weil, Mrs. Leon
Weisgal, Mrs. Meyer W.
Wheeler, Miss Joan
Williams, Miss Anna Freid
Wormser, Mr. and Mrs. Morton

ICE CREAM, CAKE AND CANDY

Cohn, Mrs. Maurice
Colp, Dr. Ralph A.
Colp, Mrs. Ralph A. (In memory of Mrs. Alice Kaye) .
Collier, Master Gilman
Congregation Emanu-El Temple (Through Brightside Work)
Cook, Mrs. Alfred A.
Danziger, Mrs. Max
Fried, Miss Ruth
Grossman, Master Ronald
Handy Helpers Craft Club (Through Miss Hanna Fischbein)
Hartman, Mrs. Siegfried F.
Hochstader, Mrs. Harvey C.
Kay, Mrs. William de Young
Klauber, Master William
Leiter, Mrs. H. Evans
Levinsohn, Mrs. I. (Through Dr. Sol W. Ginsburg)
Lieberman, Dr. Elias
Mendelsohn, Mr. and Mrs. Louis (In memory of Mr. Julius Judell)

Mendelsohn, Mr. and Mrs. Louis (In memory of Mr. Arthur C. Mendelsohn)
Mendelsohn, Mrs. Louis (In memory of Miss Rena Grossman)
Mendelsohn, Mrs. Louis (In memory of Mrs. Robert Lambert)
Metropolitan Post Jewish War Veterans of United States (Through Dr. Arthur J. Berger)
Moss, Mrs. Charles B.
Phillips, Mrs. Daniel
Rains, Mrs. S. E.
Robert Louis Stevenson School (Sophomore Class)
Roth, Mr. Michael
Sachs, Miss Edith
Scholle, Mrs. Albert H.
Schulte, Mrs. Joseph M.
Siegman, Miss Anita
Siegman, Mrs. Arthur
Tim, Mrs. Louis B.
Vogel, Mr. Jerry

MISCELLANEOUS DONATIONS

American Red Cross
Arnstein, Mrs. C.
Atlas, Mrs. David
Averbuck, Dr. Samuel H.
Bach, Mr. Edmond
Baerwald, Mrs. Paul
Ballin, Dr. David B.
Bernheimer, Miss Cora A.
Bick, Dr. Edgar M.
Binger, Mrs. Robert E.
Bloom, Miss Doris
Blumenthal, Mrs. George
Blun, Mrs. Edwin
Borg, Mrs. Myron I.
Bresnick, Mrs. Carl S.
Brummel, Mrs. Emanuel
Cahen, Mrs. Celia G.
Cohen, Mrs. Arthur J.
Cohn, Mrs. Leonard A.
Cole, Mrs. Robert
Colp, Dr. Ralph A.
Cook, Mrs. Alfred A.
Coshland, Mrs. L. B.
Deitsch, Mrs. Charles
DeMenasce, Mrs. Elinor
Dillenberg, Mrs. D. Alan
Dreicer, Mrs. Mary
Dreyfus, Mrs. Charles, Jr.
Dunham, Miss Ella P.
Erdman, Mr. Bert
Falk, Mrs. William
Fidler, Miss Lillian
Field, Mrs. Neva Rooks (In memory of Mrs. Aaron E. Norman)
Frank, Dr. Maxwell S.
Frank, Dr. Robert T.
Frankenheimr, Miss Ida
Frankenheimer, Miss Rose
Friedman, Mrs. Henry Weisenfeld
Friend, Miss Alice J.
Glanz, Miss Grace
Goldstone, Mrs. Lafayette A. (Through Mrs. Walter A. Dreyfous)
Goodman, Mrs. Edwin
Gottheil, Mrs. Paul
Greenwald, Miss Marjorie
Grossman, Master Ronald
Haas, Mrs. Robert K.

Hartman, Mrs. Siegfried F.
Hays, Mrs. David S.
Helfstein, Mr. Max
Heming, Mrs. Charles E.
Henry, Mrs. Charles I.
Herrman, Mrs. A.
Herzog, Mr. Oscar
Hessberg, Mrs. Lena
Heyman, Mrs. David M.
Hirsch, Mrs. Walter A.
Horowitz, Mrs. Joseph
Hydeman, Mr. Edwin M.
Janowitz, Mrs. Jacob J.
Joyce, Mrs. Joseph A.
Klingenstein, Mrs. Charles
Kutchai, Mrs. David
Lane, Mrs. Edwin
Lederer, Mrs. E.
Lehman, Mrs. Irving
Leiter, Mrs. H. Evans
Lenzner, Mrs. Joseph B.
Levison, Mrs. Jesse W.
Lilienthal, Dr. Howard
Lippmann, Dr. Robert K.
Loeb, Mrs. Louis M.
Loewe, Miss Jewel (In memory of Mrs. Selma Loewe)
Mayer, Mrs. Louis
Mayer, Mrs. Max D.
Meyer, Dr. Alfred
Meyer, Mrs. Herbert
Moses, Mrs. Leila G.
Price, Mrs. Louis R.
Reiss, Mrs. Jack
Rodner, Mr. Harold
Rosenberg, Mr. Theodore
Rosenfeld, Miss Evelyn
Rosenstock, Mrs. David G.
Rosenthal, Mrs. Emanuel M.
Rossbach, Miss Laurie
Rubel, Mrs. Beno
Scholle, Mrs. Albert H.
Scholle, Mrs. William D.
Spier, Mrs. S.
Stein, Mrs. E. W.
Straus, Mrs. Roger W.
Weil, Mrs. Leon
Wolfson, Mrs. Max

CONTRIBUTIONS TO ABRAHAM JACOBI LIBRARY

BOOKS, PERIODICALS AND PICTURES

Associated Alumni of The Mount Sinai Hospital
Benmosche, Dr. Moses
Brazilian Pavilion, New York World's Fair
Bick, Dr. Edgar M.
Fishberg, Dr. Arthur M.
Frank, Dr. Maxwell S.
Friesner, Dr. Isidore
Garlock, Dr. John H.
Genner, Professor V.
Globus, Dr. Joseph H.
Greene, Dr. Leon N.
Haas, Dr. Merrill P.
Hess, Mrs. Alfred F.
*Jaches, Dr. Leopold (From Collection of)
Karolinska Institutets Bibliotek
Klemperer, Dr. Paul
Levy, Mrs. I. H.
Licht, Dr. Sidney
Lilienthal, Dr. Howard
London, Dr. Louis S.
Macmillan Company
Master, Dr. Arthur M.
Manges, Dr. Morris
May, Dr. Charles H.
Mayo Clinic
Mead, Johnson and Company
Meyer, Dr. Alfred
Moschcowitz, Dr. Eli
Neuhof, Dr. Harold
Neurological Institute of New York
New York Academy of Medicine
New York Medical Week
Orndorff, Dr. B. H.
Pollack, Dr. Herbert
Reiner, Miss Miriam
Rosen, Dr. Samuel
Schwarz, Dr. Herman
Sea View Hospital
Surgeon General's Office
Sussman, Dr. Marcy L.
Turner, Dr. Joseph
Volterra, Professor Mario
Webb-Johnson, Sir Alfred E.
Wechsler, Dr. Israel S.
Wile, Dr. Ira S.

* Deceased.

REPORT OF
THE MOUNT SINAI HOSPITAL
LADIES' AUXILIARY SOCIETY

OFFICERS

MRS. LEOPOLD BERNHEIMER ....President
MRS. OSCAR ROSE ....Treasurer
MRS. JOSEPH A. ARNOLD ....Secretary

To the Board of Trustees of The Mount Sinai Hospital:

Gentlemen:

Since addressing you last year it has been my great regret that I have been unable to give to the Ladies' Auxiliary Society the time and personal service that had always been of so much interest to me.

I know, however, that owing to the continued devotion of the ladies of our group, the splendid work of our Society goes steadily forward. Our thanks are due them for the work of their hands, and also for the spirit of service which pervades their weekly meetings.

Respectfully submitted,

Mrs. Leopold Bernheimer,

President.

TREASURER'S REPORT

Statement of Disbursements and Receipts for the Year Ended
December 31st, 1939

DISBURSEMENTS

Linens and Bedding	$17,606.69	
Wearing Apparel	8,975.00	
Total Disbursements		$26,581.69

RECEIPTS

From Federation for the Support of Jewish Philanthropic Societies	25,492.00
Deficit*	*$1,089.69*

* Taken from Permanent Fund of Hospital.

REPORT OF NEUSTADTER HOME

During 1939 we accepted 521 female patients and 276 male patients, making a total of 797 patients. Our capacity is 56 patients—36 women and 20 men. Of the 797 patients accepted, 731 were referred to us from the wards of Mount Sinai Hospital and 66 came from other sources. The average length of stay was 23 days. The gain in weight of our patients ranged from 1 to 24 lbs.

Our professional staff includes a physician, a member of the Medical Staff of Mount Sinai Hospital on call at all times, five graduate nurses, two female attendants, one dietitian, one full-time recreational worker, and one secretary. In addition, we have available the valuable advice as Medical Consultant of Dr. George Baehr, Physician to Mount Sinai Hospital.

During the past year, several important changes have been made:

(1) The Neustadter Home has become more closely affiliated with the Mount Sinai Hospital with a resultant closer relationship in medical and social service matters, giving the Home the benefit of the Hospital's experience in administration, medicine, social service, dietetics, therapeutics, and other institutional services.

Miss Mary J. Henderson of the Hospital's Dietary Department has given much time to the problem of readjusting the service schedules of our internal nursing and domestic staffs so that now we are able to arrange sufficient free time for every member of the staff.

(2) In February 1939, we discontinued accepting children and for the first time opened the Home to men, since we had learned that there was more need for convalescent care for men and that there were adequate convalescent facilities for children available elsewhere in the Metropolitan area.

(3) We have made many improvements in the physical set-up of the Home, including the following:

A Utility Room was installed and equipped.

The Children's larger playroom was redecorated and equipped for a women's sitting room.

The large room on the ground floor was furnished as a special recreation room for men by the Board in memory of Walter A. Hirsch.

An elevator is in process of installation.

(4)   In the field of Recreation, we have instituted many innovations making the atmosphere happier and more cheerful for our patients:

Miss Mina Davie, full-time occupational therapy and recreational worker, has been engaged. Her work is based on its therapeutic value and is aimed at keeping patients occupied at knitting, handsewing, modeling, weaving, etc. Patients participate on a voluntary basis. Miss Davie also supervises all forms of recreation.

A moving picture machine and a piano have been donated to the Home.

A permanent out-door fireplace has been built for picnics for patients.

Various forms of simple entertainment and recreation were made available for the enjoyment of the patients.

At the recent Conference on Convalescent Care, held at the Academy of Medicine, Dr. Herman Zazeela, the physician to the Neustadter Home, and Mrs. Fanny Mendelsohn, in charge of the Social Service Department of the Hospital, read papers on the work of the Home which were very favorably received. At the final session of the Conference, Neustadter Home was mentioned as having made an outstanding contribution to the principles and practices of convalescent care, especially in view of the fact that we have a building which was not built originally for the purpose for which it is now being used—thereby proving that under certain circumstances, properly planned physical equipment can be adjusted to meet new needs; that we are caring for sicker types of patients than other homes, and are accepting patients for care that would not be available in other convalescent homes. These include special diet cases, special treatment cases, cardiacs, etc.

On another occasion, the Lay Medical Social Service Committee of the United Hospital Fund held a morning conference at which Neustadter Home was again singled out as having made a real contribution to convalescent care practices. I mention these facts merely to show that we are meeting some of the urgent convalescent needs of the community.

There have been problems, of course, but with the cooperation of our able Board and Staff, we have been enabled to settle them so as not to interfere with the smooth running of the Home.

During the year, the sum of $53,219.55 was spent in maintaining the routine activities of the Home. For meeting these expenses, $37,311.72 was available from income of the Neustadter Fund, a grant from the Greater New York Fund, and small payments by some of the patients, leaving a net operating deficit of $15,907.83.

It is interesting to mention that for the first time some patients able to do so paid part of the cost of their care and transportation. This justifies our decision to maintain a sliding scale of charges for those patients who can pay a little.

Mr. Samuel Sicher, a Director and the Secretary of this Society since its early years passed away on January 1, 1940. Having been so closely in touch with its affairs for many years, he has left an ineradicable impress upon its history. To record its sense of loss, the Board has adopted fitting resolutions embodied in its minutes.

In closing, I want to express the gratitude of the Board, as well as my own, to those various members who have given unstintingly of their time and efforts to making the year 1939 the successful one that it has been. I wish also to thank the Mount Sinai Hospital Administration, particularly Dr. Joseph Turner, Mrs. Fanny Mendelsohn, Miss Mary Hallahan, Mr. John B. Cubberley and Miss Mary J. Henderson, the Staff of the Neustadter Home, so ably headed by Miss Helen Butler, Dr. Herman Zazeela, Mr. Sidney Goldstone, who has been ready at all times to assist, and all others who have joined in helping the Home serve so well the many in this community who are in need of convalescent care.

Respectfully submitted,

HORTENSE M. HIRSCH,

President.

Dedicated Buildings

CHILDREN'S PAVILION

ERECTED IN LOVING REMEMBRANCE OF

LEWIS EINSTEIN

AND

MILLY EINSTEIN FALK

BY

HENRY L. EINSTEIN

1921

PRIVATE PAVILION

DEDICATED TO THE MEMORY OF

MEYER AND BARBARA GUGGENHEIM

BY THEIR CHILDREN

1920

Dedicated Buildings

OUT-PATIENT BUILDING

DEDICATED TO THE MEMORY OF

MAYER LEHMAN

BY HIS CHILDREN

1904

ADOLPH LEWISOHN
PATHOLOGICAL AND
LABORATORY BUILDING

DONATED BY

ADOLPH LEWISOHN

1904 - 1922

Dedicated Buildings

AUDITORIUM

DEDICATED TO THE
MEMORY OF

GEORGE BLUMENTHAL, JR.

BY

FLORENCE AND GEORGE BLUMENTHAL

1920

LABORATORY BUILDING

DEDICATED TO THE MEMORY OF

ABRAHAM AND AMELIA MEYERS

1938

Dedicated Buildings.

CHILDREN'S CLINIC

DEDICATED TO THE MEMORY OF

FLORENCE HENRIETTA WALTER

AND

MARJORIE WALTER GOODHART

BY THEIR PARENTS

FLORENCE B. AND WILLIAM I. WALTER

1916 - 1923

Endowment of Wards

THE
CHARLES A. WIMPFHEIMER WARDS
FOR
SURGICAL TREATMENT
OF
DISEASES OF STOMACH AND INTESTINES
FOUNDED BY
CHARLES A. WIMPFHEIMER
1916

THE ADOLPH BERNHEIMER
MEMORIAL WARD

———

FOUNDED BY HIS DAUGHTER ROSIE
FEBRUARY 16TH, 1897

THE MRS. ADOLPH BERNHEIMER
MEMORIAL WARD

———

FOUNDED BY HER DAUGHTERS
ROSIE BERNHEIMER AND FLORENCE B. WALTER
FEBRUARY 16TH, 1916

Endowment of Wards

MAIN OPERATING ROOM

DEDICATED TO THE MEMORY OF

ISAAC AND BABETTE BLUMENTHAL

BY

ALFRED, GUSTAV, HUGO, BENJAMIN
AND GEORGE BLUMENTHAL

1904

GENITO-URINARY WARD

DEDICATED TO THE MEMORY OF

JOEL GOLDENBERG

BY PROVISION IN HIS WILL

1904

THE SIMON ROTHSCHILD WARD

IN PERPETUITY

1905

Endowment of Wards

THE EMANUEL LEHMAN MEMORIAL WARD

DEDICATED FEBRUARY 15TH, 1911

———

FOUNDED BY

MRS. SIGMUND LEHMAN, MRS. EVELYN L. EHRICH,
MR. PHILIP LEHMAN

THE

JOSEPH AND SOPHIA SACHS MEMORIAL WARDS

———

DEDICATED TO THE MEMORY OF THEIR PARENTS BY

SAMUEL AND HARRY SACHS

1913

THE ELIAS WARD

———

IN THIS WARD BEDS WERE ENDOWED:

THREE BEDS IN MEMORY OF RAPHAEL ELIAS
THREE BEDS IN MEMORY OF SARAH ELIAS
THREE BEDS IN MEMORY OF ROBERT F. ELIAS
THREE BEDS IN MEMORY OF HENRY F. ELIAS

ALL FOUNDED BY THE PROVISION OF THE WILL OF
HENRY F. ELIAS

1928

151

Endowment of Wards

THE ALFRED AND HANNAH BLUMENTHAL WARD

FOUNDED 1922

THE LOUIS N. KRAMER MEMORIAL

FOUNDED BY PROVISION
OF HIS WILL

1930

Endowment of Rooms

DEDICATED TO THE
MEMORY OF

LINA MEYER ASIEL

BY

ELIAS ASIEL

1904

THE EDWARD LAUTERBACH ROOM

DEDICATED IN PERPETUITY
BY THE
BOARD OF TRUSTEES
OF
THE MOUNT SINAI HOSPITAL
IN GRATEFUL RECOGNITION OF HIS
EMINENT SERVICES
1904

DEDICATED BY

DISTRICT GRAND LODGE No. 1

INDEPENDENT ORDER
FREE SONS OF ISRAEL
M. SAMUEL STERN, GRAND MASTER
1901
FOUR BEDS

DEDICATED FOR THE BENEFIT OF

THE ALUMNAE

OF THE

MOUNT SINAI HOSPITAL SCHOOL OF NURSING

BY

MRS. MAX NATHAN

1904

Endowment of Rooms

DEDICATED TO THE ALUMNAE OF
THE MOUNT SINAI HOSPITAL SCHOOL OF NURSING
BY
MR. AND MRS. CHARLES KLINGENSTEIN

1931

IN MEMORY OF
ISAAC STRAUSS
1825-1876

ENDOWED BY HIS SON
CHARLES STRAUSS

1934

IN MEMORY OF
HENRIETTA STRAUSS
1819-1893

ENDOWED BY HER SON
CHARLES STRAUSS

1934

THE JACOB AND HENRIETTA SNEUDAIRA ROOM

FOUNDED BY PROVISION IN THE WILL OF

MOSES J. SNEUDAIRA

1935

Tablets

ERECTED IN X-RAY MUSEUM

IN MEMORY OF

BERTHA WEHLE NAUMBURG

FOUNDED BY HER SON

WALTER W. NAUMBURG

MARCH 3RD, 1922

ERECTED IN RADIO-THERAPY DEPARTMENT

DEPARTMENT OF
RADIUM AND RADIO-THERAPY

FLORETTE AND ERNST ROSENFELD FOUNDATION

1923

ERECTED IN X-RAY DEPARTMENT

EQUIPPED BY

LOUISA AND SAMUEL SACHS

IN MEMORY OF THEIR DAUGHTER

ELLA SACHS PLOTZ

1923

Tablets

ERECTED IN OUT-PATIENT
DEPARTMENT

OUT-PATIENT DEPARTMENT DENTAL CLINIC
EQUIPPED AND SUPPORTED BY
DAVID A. SCHULTE
1925

ERECTED IN PATHOLOGICAL
LECTURE HALL

DEDICATED TO THE MEMORY OF
ISAAC AND SARAH ERDMANN
1925

ERECTED IN LABORATORY
NORTH BUILDING

ERECTED BY
CHARLES A. WIMPFHEIMER
A MOST GENEROUS FRIEND OF THE HOSPITAL
1926

ERECTED IN SOCIAL SERVICE
DEPARTMENT

IN LOVING MEMORY OF
ETTA COHEN LORSCH
1928

Perpetual Beds

In Memory of
Louis W. Neustadter
Dedicated by his wife
1873

In Memory of
Daniel Joseph Jaffe
Dedicated by the family
1874

In Memory of
Isaac Dittenhoefer
Dedicated by
Abram J. Dittenhoefer
1874

In Memory of
Lewis Einstein
1875

In Memory of
Katy White
Wife of J. L. Englehart
Niece of Jonas and Yette Heller
1875

In Memory of
Mary Rosenbaum
By her husband,
Sigmund D. Rosenbaum
1876

Endowed in Memory of
Lazarus Hallgarten
1876

In Memory of
Martin and Joseph Bachrach
Beloved sons of
Samuel and Babette Bachrach
1877

In Memory of our beloved mother
Mina Schafer
Wife of Mayer Schafer
1878

In Memory of
Benjamin Nathan
Dedicated by will of his wife
1879

Dedicated by
Sarah Heinemann
1879

In Memory of
Abraham Scholle
1880

In Memory of
Leonora Wormser
Vice-President of the Ladies' Auxiliary
Society
Wife of Simon Wormser
1880

In Memory of
Nathan Blun
Endowed by his children
1880

In Memory of
Mary S. Sahlein
Wife of William Sahlein
1881

In Memory of
William Sahlein
1881

In Memory of
David Wallerstein
1881

In Memory of
Harris Aronson
1881

In Memory of
Arnold Uhlman
Dedicated by the family
1883

In Memory of
Joseph Reckendorfer
Dedicated by his wife
1883

In Memory of
Isaac and Ida Meyer
Dedicated by their children
1883

157

Perpetual Beds

In Memory of
Herman Friedlander
Dedicated by his family
1883

In Memory of
Nathan Asiel
Dedicated by his family
1883

In Memory of our beloved brother
Siegmund Spingarn
1884

In Memory of
Emanuel Hoffman
Dedicated by the family
1884

In Memory of
Adolph Hallgarten
1885

In Memory of
Siphra Stern
Dedicated by her children
1887

In Memory of
Benjamin F. Meyer
Dedicated by his brother
1887

In Memory of
Jonas Heller
Dedicated by the family
1887

In Memory of
Henry Herrman
Endowed by Esther Herrman
1889

In Memory of
Henryette Mortimer
and Edward Rosenfeld
Dedicated by the husband and father
1889

In Memory of
Maurie E. Ansbacher
Dedicated by
Adolph B. and Frances E. Ansbacher
1889

In Memory of
Sidney Speyer
Dedicated by his brother
James Speyer
1890

In Memory of
Nathan Littauer
1891

Dedicated to the Memory of
Hirsch Wallach and
Bienchen Wallach
By their son, Isaac Wallach
1891

Endowed in Memory of
Louise Littauer
Daughter of Nathan and Harriet Littauer
1891

In Memory of
Rosa Veit
1892

To the Memory of
Sophia Roth
Dedicated by her husband
Ludwig Roth
1892

In Memory of
Bernard L. and Fanny Tim
Endowed by Louis and Solomon Tim
1892

In Memory of
Sigmund Robertson
Dedicated by the family
1892

Perpetual Beds

In Memory of
Grace A. L. Cullman
Dedicated by her husband
1892

In Memory of
Esther Asiel
Dedicated by her son
1892

Dedicated to the Memory of
Moses Wasserman
1893

In Memory of
Dr. Joseph Mainzer
Dedicated by his brother
1893

In Memory of
Johanna Fatman
Dedicated by S. A. Fatman
1893

In Memory of
Sylvester Brush
and Sarah, His Wife
Dedicated by their children
1893

In Memory of
Jesse Seligman
Dedicated by the family
1894

In Memory of our beloved mother
Babette Scholle
1894

Dedicated to the Memory of
Albert S. Rosenbaum
1894

In Memory of
Israel D. and Henrietta Walter
Dedicated by their son
William I. Walter
1894

In Memory of
Isaac Bernheimer
1894

In Memory of
Moritz Josephthal
Dedicated by his widow
1895

To the Memory of
Leopold Boscowitz
Dedicated by his brothers and sisters
1837—1895

In Memory of her beloved son
Joseph Louis Myers
Dedicated by Louisa Myers
1895

In Memory of
Adolph T. Scholle
Dedicated by his father
1895

In Memory of
Adolph Bernheimer
Dedicated by his daughter
Miss Rosie Bernheimer
1895

In Memory of
Bertha Morris
Dedicated by her relatives
1896

Founded by and in Memory of
David Wallach
Chicago, Ill.
1896

In Memory of
Mayer Goldsmith
Dedicated by his widow
1896

Perpetual Beds

In Memory of
Mathilda Oppenheimer
Dedicated by her husband
1897

In Memory of
Bernard Mainzer
Dedicated by the family
1897

Dedicated by Antoinette Mayer
In Memory of her son
Carl Theodor Mayer
1897

In Memory of
Adelaide Ballin King
Dedicated by her husband
1897

In Memory of
Mariane Ickelheimer
Dedicated by Mrs. Julie Heidelbach
1897

In Memory of
Julius L. Goldenberg
Dedicated by his mother
1897

In Memory of
Bernard Cohen
1897

In Memory of
S. J. Spiegelberg
A former Director of this Institution
1898

In Memory of
Elias Jacobs
Dedicated by his wife
1898

Dedicated by
Mr. and Mrs. George Blumenthal
1898

The Rosalie Nathan
Perpetual Bed
Dedicated to the Cause of Humanity
1899

In Memory of
Martin H. Lehmaier
1899

Dedicated to the Memory of
Lydia Wolff
Wife of Abraham Wolff
1900

Dedicated to the Memory of
Abraham Wolff
1900

In Memory of
David Marks
Dedicated by his wife
1900

In Memory of
Louise Hoffman
Dedicated by her children
1900

Housman Memorial Beds
Dedicated by Arthur A. Housman
(Two Beds)
1900

In Memory of
Robert Graham Dun
1900

In Memory of
His Wife, Bertha,
and Daughter, Sophie
Dedicated by David Kohn
1900

Perpetual Beds

In Memory of My Beloved Parents
Simon and Rosetta S. Bernheimer
Dedicated by Jacob S. Bernheimer
1900

In Memory of
Henrietta Rubens
Dedicated by her husband
Charles Rubens, Paris
1901

In Memory of
Lazarus and Babette Morgenthau
Dedicated by Henry Morgenthau
1901

In Memory of
Edward B. Simon
Dedicated by his wife
1901

In Memory of
Josiah L. Webster
Dedicated by C. B. Webster
1901

In Memory of
Joseph Kaufman
Founded by provision in his will
1901

In Memory of
Emanuel Lauer
Dedicated by his daughters
Carrie Lehman and Sophie Goodhart
1901

In Memory of
Bernard and Henrietta Heineman
Dedicated by their son
Moses Heineman
1901

In Memory of
Marx and Sophie Hornthal
Dedicated by their children
1901

In Memory of
Moses Bruhl
Dedicated by his wife and daughters
1901

In Memory of
Moritz and Ernestine Cohn
Dedicated by their children
1901

In Memory of
Betty Loeb
Dedicated by her husband
Solomon Loeb
1902

In Memory of
Elizabeth Jeffries Garvey
Dedicated by Andrew Jeffries Garvey
(Two Beds)
1902

In Memory of
Louis and Yetta Stix
1902

In Memory of
Theodore G. Weil
1902

Two Beds
The Jacob Rubino Beds
1902

In Memory of
Fanny Myers
Dedicated by David E. Sicher
1902

In Memory of
Jacob S. Bernheimer
Dedicated by his wife and children
1902

161

Perpetual Beds

In Memory of
Bernard Baruch
Endowed by his grandson
1902

Dedicated by
**The Hebrew Mutual Benefit
Society**
To Commemorate Its Seventy-fifth
Anniversary
1902

In Memory of
**Rachel V. and Charles
Sternbach**
Dedicated by their son
Sidney M. Sternbach
1903

In Memory of
Florentine Weinberg
Dedicated by Philip Weinberg
1903

In Memory of
Clara Wertheim
Dedicated by Henry P. Wertheim
1903

Dedicated to the Memory of
Jacob Bookman
1903

In Memory of
Edward J. King
Dedicated by his wife
Rosalie King
1904

In Memory of
Marcus L. Stieglitz
Dedicated by his wife
Sarah Stieglitz
1904

In Memory of
Joseph Freedman
Dedicated by his son
Andrew Freedman
1904

In Memory of
Simon Borg
Dedicated by his wife
Cecelia Borg
1905

In Memory of
Ruth M. Gross
By her parents
Morris and Carrie L. Gross
1905

In Memory of
Hannah Vogel
Dedicated by her husband
William Vogel
1905

In Memory of
M. S. Mork
Dedicated by his wife
Minnie Mork
1905

Dedicated by
Mr. and Mrs. Eugene Meyer
1905

In Memory of
Joseph B. Bloomingdale
1905

In Memory of
Adolph Herrmann
Founded by provision in his will
1906

Endowed by Emma B. Hendricks
In memory of her sons
**Edgar Hendricks
Henry H. Hendricks
and Clifford B. Hendricks**
1906

Endowed by Emma B. Hendricks
In Memory of her Husband
Joshua Hendricks
1906

Perpetual Beds

In Memory of
Bennett and Sarah B. King
1906

In Memory of
Samuel E. and Mary Halle
Endowed by Jacques S. Halle
1906

In Memory of
Cecelia Borg
Dedicated by her children
1906

**The Lyman C. and Hattie
Bloomingdale Perpetual Bed**
1906

In Memory of
Walter A. Schiffer
Dedicated by his wife
1907

In Memory of
Isaac Wallach
Founded by provision in his will
1907

In Memory of
Louis Josephthal
Founded by provision in his will
1907

In Memory of
Isabella Arnold Bernheimer
Dedicated by her children
1907

In Memory of
Hedwig Rosenbaum
By her husband
Sigmund D. Rosenbaum
1908

**The Leopold Laderer
Caroline Laderer and
Samuel L. Laderer
Perpetual Bed**
1908

In Memory of
Emily Lazarus
Founded by provision in the will of
Amelia B. Lazarus
1908

In Memory of
Simon W. Glazier
Dedicated by his wife and children
1908

In Memory of
Isaac S. and Sarah Erdmann
1909

The Ernest Ehrmann Bed
Founded by provision in his will
1909

In Memory of
Solomon Herzog
Founded by Edward N. Herzog
1909

In Memory of
Arthur A. Housman
Founded by provision in his will
(Two Beds)
1909

In Memory of
Abraham B. Frank
Dedicated by his wife
1909

In Memory of
Leopold Gusthal
Dedicated by his sisters
1909

In Memory of
Gustav Bernheim
Dedicated by his wife and children
1909

Perpetual Beds

In Memory of
Mary Mayer
Founded by David Mayer
1910

In Memory of
Therese Josephthal
Founded by provision in her will
1910

In Memory of
Edward A. and Bertha R. Price
Founded by Julie Price Erdman
1910

In Memory of
Dr. Joseph Schnetter
Founded by provision in his will
(Three Beds)
1910

In Memory of
Bertha Horn
Founded by provision in the will of
Michael Horn
1910

In Memory of
Rev. Dr. Gustave Gottheil
Rabbi, Temple Emanu-El
1873-1899
Founded by Paul Gottheil
1910

In Memory of
Dr. Herman Baerwald
Founded by Paul Baerwald
1910

In Memory of
Valentine and Fanny Loewi
Dedicated by the family
1911

In Memory of
Edna Saks Levy
Dedicated by Mr. and Mrs. Andrew Saks
1911

The Emma Rosenwald Bed
Founded by provision in her will
1911

In Memory of
Henry Rosenwald
Founded by Mrs. Henry Rosenwald
1911

In Memory of
Allen L. Mordecai
and Kate Mordecai
Dedicated by their children
1911

In Memory of
Alexander L. Kaufmann
Founded by provision in his will
1911

In Memory of
Julius Ehrmann
Founded by provision in the will of
Mathilda Ehrmann
1912

In Memory of
James and Amelia Strauss
Founded by provision in the will
of their son, Nathan F. Strauss
1912

In Memory of
Dr. Max Herzog
Founded by
Mr. and Mrs. Abram N. Stein
1912

In Memory of
Dr. Wolfgang Mack
1808-1883
Founded by provision in the will of
Jacob W. Mack
1912

164

Perpetual Beds

In Memory of
Jacob Wolfgang Mack
1845-1912
Dedicated by Jennie and Ella Heyman
1912

In Memory of
Luise Mack
1808-1887
Founded by provision in the will of
Jacob W. Mack
1912

In Memory of
Mathilda Ehrmann
Founded by provision in her will
1912

In Memory of
Florence Henrietta Walter
Dedicated by her aunt
Rosie Bernheimer
1913

In Memory of
Marcus and Bertha Goldman
1913

In Memory of
Lewis S. Levy
Founded by provision in his will
1914

In Memory of
Mary Levy
Founded by provision in the will of
Lewis S. Levy
1914

In Memory of
Julius and Fanny Robertson
Founded by provision in his will
1915

In Memory of
Maurice and Mathilde Seligmann
Dedicated by
George and Arthur Seligmann
1915

In Memory of
Erwin Beit Von Speyer
Founded by his uncle
James Speyer
1915

In Memory of
Max and Nina Herzog
Dedicated by their daughter
Bella H. Kaufmann
1915

In Memory of
Samuel and Helene Prince
Dedicated by their children
1915

In Memory of
Leonard S. Prince
Dedicated by his father and mother
December 23, 1915

In Memory of
Madge N. Haas
1915

In Memory of
David, Gustave B. and Charles Calman
Founded by provision in the will of
Emma Calman
1915

In Memory of
Tillie Hochschild
1916

Perpetual Beds

In Memory of
Mrs. Samuel H. Spingarn
Endowed by provision in the will of
Samuel H. Spingarn
1916

In Memory of
Samuel H. Spingarn
Endowed by provision in his will
1916

In Memory of
Henrietta Bondy
Founded by her son
Emil C. Bondy
1916

In Memory of
Jacob and Rosina Erdmann
Founded by Albert J. Erdmann
1916

In Memory of
Charles Bondy
Founded by his son
Emil C. Bondy
1916

In Memory of
Karl Schwabach
Founded by his uncle
James Speyer
1917

In Memory of
Henry and Rosalie Klingenstein
Dedicated by their son
Charles Klingenstein
1917

In Memory of his Parents
Josephine and David Salzer
Dedicated by Leopold Salzer
1917

In Memory of
Mrs. Isaac Wallach
Founded by provision in her will
1917

In Memory of
Johanna and Rosalie Moses
Dedicated by their sister
Julia R. Ballerstein
1917

In Memory of
Bernhard Stern
Dedicated by his brother
Benjamin Stern
1917

In Memory of
Amelia Heidelberg
Dedicated by Isaac N. Heidelberg
1917

In Memory of
Rachel H. Pfeiffer
Founded by provision in her will
1917

In Memory of
Belle Glazier Bernheimer
Founded by provision in her will
1917

In Memory of
Charles E. Schafer
Endowed by his wife
1917

Endowed by
Mr. and Mrs. Philip J. Goodhart
1918

In Memory of
Theresa and Joseph Fox
1918

In Memory of their Parents
Louise and Leopold Salzer
Dedicated by their children
(Two Beds)
1918

166

Perpetual Beds

In Memory of
Joshua Rothblatt
Dedicated by his parents
Bernard and Ida Rothblatt
1919

In Celebration of the
Ninetieth Birthday of
Max Nathan
April 15, 1919
Presented by his daughter
Irma N. Straus

In Memory of
Meyer H. Lehman
Dedicated by his sisters
Mrs. Harriet Weil
and Mrs. Bertha Rosenheim
1919

In Memory of
Julius Lewisohn
London, England
Dedicated by his son
1919

In Memory of
William Klingenstein
of London, England
Dedicated by his nephew
Charles Klingenstein
1919

In Memory of
Emma and Albert Kaskel
Founded by provision in the will of
Emma H. Kaskel
1919

In Memory of
Mayer Lehman and
Babette Lehman
Dedicated
(Two Beds)
1919

Dedicated to
The Clara de Hirsch Home
By Dr. Josephine Walter
1919

The Louis M. Sonnenberg Bed
Founded by provision in his will
1919

In Memory of
Alan Harry Simon
Dedicated by
Mr. and Mrs. Harry G. Simon
1919

In Memory of
Ferdinand A. Straus
Dedicated by his son
Lionel F. Straus
1919

In Memory of
Henry Bendheim
Dedicated by his brother
Adolph D. Bendheim
1919

In Memory of
Levi Bamberger
Founded by Albert and Clara Blum
1919

The Three
J. D. Wendel Beds
Endowed in Memory of the Former
Tenants of John D. Wendel
1919

In Memory of
Sara Sonnenberg Beck
Dedicated by Martin Beck
1919

In Memory of
Aron Weil
Dedicated by his wife
Dora Weil
1919

Perpetual Beds

In Memory of his Parents
Vitus and Fanny Lambert
Dedicated by their son
August V. Lambert
1920

In Memory of
Oscar M. Leiser
Founded by provision in his will
1920

In Memory of
Edith Stine Schiffer
Founded by her husband
Jack W. Schiffer
1920

In Memory of
Mayer and Babette Lehman
Dedicated by
Mr. and Mrs. Morris Fatman
1920

In Memory of
Alphons Lewis
Founded by provision in his will
1920

In Memory of
David Lehman
Dedicated by his sisters
Mrs. Harriet Weil and
Mrs. Bertha Rosenheim
1920

In Memory of
Matilda Ollendorff
Dedicated by her husband
1920

In Memory of
Marjorie Walter Goodhart
Founded by her aunt
Rosie Bernheimer
October 19, 1920

In Celebration of the
Seventy-fifth birthday of
Frances M. Fechheimer
September 4, 1920
Dedicated by her son
Sam M. Fechheimer

Dedicated by
Mr. and Mrs. Henry Budge
1920

In Memory of
Max J. Breitenbach
Dedicated by his wife and children
1920

In Memory of
Aaron and Johanna Fatman
Dedicated by
Mr. and Mrs. Morris Fatman
1920

In Memory of
Aline Bernheim
Founded by her sons
George B. and Alfred L. Bernheim
1921

In Memory of
Ellin Prince Speyer
Founded by her husband
James Speyer
1921

In Memory of
Arnold and Fannie Falk
Dedicated by Myron S. Falk
and K. George Falk
1921

In Memory of
**Rosalie, Fannie, Charles,
Simon and Joseph Lederer**
Founded by provision in the will of
Charlotte Lederer
1921

168

Perpetual Beds

In memory of her parents
Samuel and Bella Haas
Founded by Mrs. Dudley D. Sicher

In Memory of
Henry and Hanna Herrmann
Dedicated by their son
Frederick Herrmann
1921

In Memory of
Jacob L. and Sophie Kops
Dedicated by their children
1921

In Memory of
Esther Wyman
Founded by provision in her will
1921

In Memory of
Sydney Michael Hyman
Dedicated by his parents
Michael and Rose Hyman
1921

In Memory of
Clara Glazier
Founded by provision in her will
1922 .

In Memory of
Carrie Rapp and Samuel Rapp
Founded by provision in the will of
Samuel Rapp
1922

In Memory of
David James King and Adelaide Ballin King
Dedicated by their daughter
Louise King Reckford
1922

In Memory of
Caroline Bookman
Founded by provision in her will
1922

In Memory of
Dorothea Haas Weiler
Founded by provision in the will of
her son
Charles H. Weiler
1923

In Memory of
Jacob H. Semel
Founded by provision in his will
1923

In Memory of
Marks Weiler
Founded by provision in the will of
his son
Charles H. Weiler
1923

In Memory of
Morris S. Barnet
and
Alvina Barnet
Dedicated by Morris S. Barnet
(Two Beds)

Dedicated by
Addie W. Kahn
1923

In Memory of
Walter J. Rose
Dedicated by his mother
1924

In Memory of
Gabriel Mayer
Antoinette Mayer
Otto L. Mayer
Founded by provision in the will of
Otto L. Mayer
1924

Endowed by
Abraham Erlanger
1924

Perpetual Beds

Founded by
Charles Hendricks
1924

The Ella Hellman Bed
Founded by provision in her will
1924

In Memory of
Solomon C. Guggenheimer
March 24th, 1924

In Memory of
Jacob Wertheim
Dedicated by his wife
Emma Stern Wertheim
1925

In Memory of
Louis S. Frankenheimer
Dedicated by
Ida and Rose Frankenheimer
1925

In Memory of
Pauline Mayers
Endowed by her husband
Morris Mayers
1925

In Memory of
Elkan and Bertha Naumburg
Dedicated by their son
Walter W. Naumburg
1926

In Memory of
Siegfried W. Mayer
Founded by provision in his will
1926

In Memory of
Samuel Baumann
Dedicated by his wife
Henrietta Baumann
1926

In Memory of
Henrietta Rawitser
Dedicated by her daughter
Theresa V. Rawitser
1926

In Memory of
Morris Rossin
Dedicated by his wife
Martha S. Rossin
1927

In Memory of
Lewis Schoolhouse
Endowed by
Joseph Runsheim
1927

Dedicated to their friends
George and Florence Blumenthal
By
Edmond and Suzanne King Bruwaert
1927

In Memory of
Samuel J. and Esther Gans
Dedicated by their son
Simeon C. Gans
1927

Endowed by
Mr. and Mrs. Albert E. Goodhart
1927

In Memory of
Arthur E. Frank
1927

In Memory of
Solomon Friedman and Amelia G. Friedman
1928

In Memory of
Samuel Bachrach and Babette Bachrach
1928

170

Perpetual Beds

In Memory of
Richard M. Homberg
Founded by provision in the will
of his mother
Florence N. Homberger
1928

In Memory of
Isaac N. Heidelberg
Dedicated by his daughters
1928

In Memory of
William Vogel
Dedicated by his sons
Harry Wm. and Bernard Wm. Vogel
1928

In Memory of
Herman Rawitser
Dedicated by his wife
Theresa V. Rawitser
1929

In Memory of
Al and Minnie Hayman
Founded by provision in the will of
Minnie Hayman
(Two Beds)
1929

In Memory of
Ada Heidelberg Strauss
Dedicated by her husband
Seymour A. Strauss
1929

The Rebecca Friedlander Bed
Founded by provision in her will
1929

In Memory of
Heinemann and Rosa Vogelstein
Dedicated by their children
1929

In Memory of
Mayer Mayer and Fanny Mayer
Beloved Father and Mother of
Bernhard Mayer
1929

In Memory of
Mary Small Einstein
Dedicated by her husband
I. D. Einstein
1930

In Memory of
Henry Stern and Mathilda Stern
Dedicated by their son
Meyer Stern
1930

The Selina E. Summerfield Bed
Founded by provision in her will
1931

In Memory of
Lucy Herzfeld
Dedicated by
Felix and Ida Herzfeld
1932

In Memory of
Richard and Matilda Sidenberg
1932

In Memory of
Henry Block
Bequest of
Alice A. Kohler
1932

The Fred H. Greenebaum Bed
Founded by provision in his will
1933

Perpetual Beds

In Memory of
Jacob Hirsh
Dedicated by his wife
Julia Hirsh
1927
and
In Memory of
Julia Hirsh
Dedicated by her children
(Two Beds)
1933

In Memory of
Heyman and Martha Pincus
Founded by provision in the will of
Martha Pincus
1933

In Memory of
Adolph
Charlotte and Mary Arber
Founded by provision in the will of
Adolph Arber
1933

In Memory of
Ludwig and Rebecca Dreyfuss
Founded by provision in the will of
Ludwig Dreyfuss
(Two Beds)
1934

Dedicated in memory of
William Hyams
and Emma Hyams
1935

In Memory of
Sarah King
1935

In Memory of
Myron Goldsmith Friedenheit
Born, September 7, 1898
Died, January 15, 1936
Dedicated by his parents

In Memory of
Elizabeth P. Hewes
Founded by provision in her will
1936

The Straus Memorial Beds
In Memory of
Lionel F. Straus
Dedicated by his wife, May H. Straus
(Two Beds)
1937

In Memory of
Nathan and Ella Necarsulmer
Bequeathed by their daughter
Helena Necarsulmer
1937

In Memory of
Ralph J. Jacobs
Founded by provision in his will
1937

In Memory of
Virginia Guinzburg Kleinert
1937

In Memory of
Ellen Ida Cardozo
Provided in the will of
Benjamin N. Cardozo
1938

Perpetual Beds

Children's Pavilion

In Memory of
Henry L. Einstein
Founded by Cecilia Einstein
1922

In Memory of
Sol H. Kohn
Dedicated by Lillie V. Kohn
1922

Founded by
Benjamin Mordecai
1922

In Memory of
Nellie M. Rice
(Two Beds)
1922

In Memory of
Robert Reis
Dedicated by Sarah Reis
1922

In Memory of
Carrie Wormser
Founded by provision in the will of
her daughter, Julia Seligman
(Four Beds)
1922

In Memory of
Constance Davis Mordecai
Founded by Benjamin Mordecai
(Two Beds)
1923

Dedicated by
Dr. A. V. Moschcowitz
To commemorate the marriage of his
daughter, Frances Ethel Frowenfeld
1923

In Memory of
Joseph and Babet Semel
Founded by provision in the will of
Mrs. George Heyman
1924

In Memory of
George and Hannah Heyman
Founded by provision in the will of
Hannah Heyman
1924

Endowed by
Cecilia Einstein
1924

In Memory of
William Frankenheimer
Dedicated by
Ida and Rose Frankenheimer
1925

In Memory of
Abraham Leipzig
Founded by provision in his will
1925

In Memory of
Adolph Frank Hochstadter
Endowed by Rosa Hayman Hochstadter
1926

In Memory of
Rosa Hayman Hochstadter
Founded by provision in her will
1926

In Memory of
Solomon and Amalia Bondy
Founded by provision in the will of
Maurice S. Bondy
1926

In Memory of
Babette Rothschild
Dedicated by her daughter
Ida R. Cullman
1926

Marx Rothschild
Dedicated by his daughter
Ida R. Cullman
1926

In Memory of
Charles and Mary Weisberger
1926

173

Perpetual Beds

Children's Pavilion

The Aaron Bachrach
and Jennie Bachrach Bed
1927

In Memory of
Marcus Loew
Dedicated by Caroline Loew
1928

The Peter F. Meyer Beds
Founded by provision in his will
(Five Beds)
1929

In Memory of
Samuel and Hattie Binswanger
1929

The Adelaide F. Pfeiffer Bed
Founded by provision in her will
1929

Ludwig Ulmann
In memory of his brother
Bernard Ulmann
1930

In Memory of
Agnes C. Rice
Founded by provision in her will
1930

In Memory of
Laura Rossman
Dedicated by will of Selma Rossman
1932

In Memory of
Robert Rossman
Dedicated by will of Selma Rossman
1932

In Memory of
Simon and Lucy Drukker
Dedicated by the will of their daughter
Jeannette D. Beaumont
1933

In Memory of
Elias Kempner
Founded by provision in his will
1933

In Memory of
Louis B. G. Garland
Dedicated by his parents
Edward S. Garland and
Lillian B. Garland
1933

The Samuel and Isabella
Kritzman Beds
Founded by provision in the will of
Isabella Kritzman
(Five Beds)
1935

In Memory of
Herman Loevy
Dedicated by
Edwin F. Young
(Two Beds)
1936

In Loving Memory of
Frances Clayton Moses
Dedicated by her aunt
Catherine Sampson
1936

In Memory of
Lena Kemp
Founded by provision in her will
1937

In Memory of
**Celia and Solomon
Oppenheimer**
Founded by provision in the will of
Solomon Oppenheimer
1938

In Memory of
Louise Renskorf
Provided in the will of her mother
Millie H. Renskorf
1938

174

Memorial Beds

In Memory of
Emanuel de Castro
Dedicated by Margaret D. Plant
1902

In Memory of
Joseph E. Heimerdinger
Dedicated by his brother and sisters
1904

In Memory of
Samuel R. and Jane Jacobs
Dedicated by their children
1904

In Memory of
Babetta Adelsberger
Dedicated by her daughter
Mrs. Emanuel M. Gattle
1905

In Memory of
Samuel Adelsberger
Dedicated by his daughter
Mrs. Emanuel M. Gattle
1905

In Memory of
Isaac A. and Sarah J. Singer
Dedicated by a son
1906

In Memory of Our Beloved Son
Max Reutlinger
Dedicated by
Mr. and Mrs. Emanuel Reutlinger
1908

The Charles Mayer Bed
Founded by Max W. Mayer
January 18, 1909

In Memory of
Sigmund Neustadt
Dedicated by Mrs. Agnes Neustadt
1909

Dedicated by Max Loewenstein
In Memory of
Edward I. Loewenstein
Died July 20, 1912

In Memory of
Seligman and Therese Oppenheimer
Dedicated by their children
1913

In Memory of
Michaelis H. Ziegel
Founded by his son
H. F. L. Ziegel
1913

In Memory of My Beloved Mother
Fannie Mandelbaum
and My Beloved Brother
Max Mandelbaum
Bella Del Monte
1914

In Memory of
Henry Liebmann
Dedicated by his wife
Emma Liebmann
1915

The Pauline, Jacob and Edward S. Bamberger Bed
1915

In Memory of
Edward C. Heymann
Dedicated by his parents
Chas. E. and Helen R. Heymann
1915

In Memory of
Richard Limburg
Dedicated by Mrs. Clara L. Limburg
1916

Frederick Jacobi Memorial Bed
Endowed by Flora and Frederick Jacobi
1916

Memorial Beds

In Memory of
Mayer and Yette Katzenberg
Dedicated by their children
1916

In Memory of
Rachel Kaufmann
Dedicated by her husband
Gustav Kaufmann
1918

In Memory of
Mr. and Mrs. Emanuel S. Kuh
Dedicated by their daughter
Nellie Kuh
1918

In Memory of
Nathan Cohen
Founded by his parents
Mr. and Mrs. Isaac Cohen
1921

In Memory of
Alfred Frank
Dedicated by his brothers and sisters
1923

In Memory of
**George and Rose Epstein
and Their Son David**
1927

In Memory of
**Morris Woititz
and Frances S. Woititz**
1937

In Memory of
Levi and Sarah Goldenberg
Founded by their daughter
Helen B. Chaim
1938

Life Beds

Founded by
Mrs. DeWitt J. Seligman
1882

Founded by
Ethel F. Seligman
Daughter of
Mr. and Mrs. DeWitt J. Seligman
1897

Dedicated to
Elsie Nathan
1902

**The May S. Harlow nee Stern
Life Bed**
Founded by her April 28, 1904

**The Lucile M. S. van Heukelom
Life Bed**
Founded November 24, 1904

The Helen Fox Life Bed
Founded by Henry Morgenthau
April 7, 1906

Founded by
A Friend
1907

In Memory of
Joseph Dannenberg
of Macon, Georgia

The Dr. Manges Life Bed
Founded by a Friend of The Hospital
1912

In Memory of
**Fannie Behrens Wolfe
and Solomon Baird Wolfe, M.D.**

In Memory of
Max Weil
Dedicated by his wife
1914

In Memory of
Joseph Honig
Founded by Louise H. Mandelbaum
1916

In Memory of
Isidore Jackson
Dedicated by his wife and son
September 14, 1920

In Memory of
Leonard M.
Dedicated by his parents
Alexander and Rose M. Joseph
1920

In Memory of
**Morris Goldstein and
Pauline Goldstein**
Endowed by their children
1921

Endowed by
Francois Kleinberger
1921

In Honor of
Minnie Kastor
Endowed by her husband,
Adolph Kastor
1922

In Memory of
Benjamin Ehrlich
Endowed by his wife
Fannie Ehrlich
1929

In Memory of
Julius Kaufmann
Endowed by his wife
Emma H. Kaufmann
1930

Founded by
Pauline F. Baerwald
March 26, 1931

Dedicated to Humanity by
Solomon and Dora Shapiro
(Nee Monness)
1932 .

In Memory of
Clara L. Limburg
Dedicated by her children
1935

177

LEGACIES AND BEQUESTS

Previous to 1867		
	Judah Touro	$20,000 00
1867	Jacob Abrahams	5,000 00
1869	Benjamin Nathan	10,000 00
	Joseph Fatman	10,000 00
1872	Dr. S. Abrahams (1872-1873)	14,020 00
1876	Lewis Philips	11,711 51
1879	Michael Reese	25,000 00
1882	Simeon Abrahams	10,980 00
1883	Mrs. Judith Einstein	5,000 00
1885	Julius Hallgarten	10,000 00
1886	Miss Sarah Burr (1886-1893)	54,900 00
1888	Isaac Hoechster	5,000 00
1889	Henry Herrman	5,000 00
	William Meyer (1889-1891)	12,252 34
1891	Daniel B. Fayerweather (1891-1897)	9,933 03
1893	Joseph Rosenberg (1893-1926)	9,995 54
	Abraham Kuhn	5,000 00
1895	Adolph Bernheimer	5,000 00
1897	Mayer Lehman	17,958 00
1902	Andrew J. Garvey (1902-1939)	15,283 65
	Jacob F. Cullman	10,000 00
1903	Julius Beer	10,000 00
	Adolph Openhym	5,000 00
1904	Solomon Loeb	10,000 00
1905	Simon Rothschild	50,000 00
	Salomon Rothfeld	5,000 00
	Meyer Guggenheim	20,000 00
1906	Frederick Uhlmann	5,000 00
	Mathilde C. Weil (1906-1907)	12,144 99
1907	Emanuel Walter	7,500 00
	Marx W. Mendel	16,044 10
1908	Amelia B. Lazarus (1908-1909)	29,995 76
1910	Adolph Kerbs	5,000 00
	Emanuel Einstein	9,525 00
	Chas. Rubens	5,695 00
	Ludwig Stettheimer (1910-1913)	24,748 39
	Rosa Schreiber	6,267 74
	Margaret J. P. Graves	10,000 00
1911	John Stemme	5,000 00
	Charles E. Tilford (1911-1939)	151,883 38
	Martin Herman	5,000 00

1912	Jacob Small (1912-1929)	$14,864 30
	Andrew Saks	5,000 00
	Moses Weinman	5,000 00
	Samuel Lilienthal	14,762 08
1913	John J. Clancy (1913-1914)	25,000 00
	Ernst Thalmann	10,000 00
	Benjamin Guggenheim	10,000 00
	William Scholle	10,000 00
	Nathan Herrmann	5,000 00
1914	Lewis S. Levy (1914-1916)	16,343 74
1915	Constant Mayer	13,948 09
	David E. Sicher	10,000 00
	Jacob Langeloth	5,000 00
	Moses Lowenstein	5,000 00
1916	Andrew Freedman	5,000 00
	Solomon Wolf (1916-1917)	11,860 18
	Amelia Lavanburg (1916-1917)	10,175 84
	Emil Bondy	10,000 00
	Herman N. Walter	5,000 00
1917	J. S. Halle	5,000 00
	Rachel H. Pfeiffer	15,000 00
	Esther Schlesinger	22,002 42
1918	Meyer H. Lehman	25,000 00
1919	Kalman Haas	10,000 00
	Benjamin Blumenthal	15,000 00
	Henry J. Duveen	5,000 00
	Margaret Olivia Sage (1919-1921)	100,000 00
1920	Joseph Frank	447,374 70
	Pearl Weinman	7,065 85
	Isaac N. Seligman	5,000 00
	Babette Lehman	5,000 00
	Julius Kayser	10,000 00
	Baruch Kaufman	14,250 00
1921	William Salomon	10,000 00
1922	Adolph D. Bendheim	5,000 00
	Mary Helen Finch	5,000 00
	Julia Seligman (1922-1936)	12,682 29
1923	Morris S. Barnet	35,000 00
	Eleanor von Koppenfels	25,000 00
1924	Jacob Rossbach	5,000 00

LEGACIES AND BEQUESTS

1925	Eugene Meyer	$10,000 00
	Emily A. Watson	24,998 20
	Emanuel Spiegelberg	5,000 00
	Michael Dreicer	10,000 00
1926	Emil Wolff	29,794 12
	Adolph Boskowitz	20,000 00
	Solomon A. Fatman	20,000 00
	Louis S. Stroock	5,000 00
	Albert Lorsch	5,000 00
	Harriet Weil	5,000 00
	Morris J. Hirsch	5,000 00
	Lewis Schoolhouse	5,000 00
	Jonathan Nathan (1926-1933)	5,130 89
1927	Alexander Herman (1927-1928)	100,000 00
	Lottie Estelle Mayer (1927-1928)	33,461 87
	Sophie W. Low	8,457 47
	Charles Altschul	7,500 00
	Mortimer H. Heyman	5,000 00
	Morris Weinstein	5,000 00
	Harry Mayer	5,000 00
1928	Al Hayman	25,000 00
	Aline Myers	15,027 87
	Morris Rossin	10,000 00
	Isaac J. Bernheim	5,000 00
	Marmaduke Richardson	5,000 00
1929	Simon R. Weil (1929-1934)	156,468 28
	Michael P. Rich	20,000 00
	Emma Blumenberg—In memory of her brothers, Marc A. and Louis Blumenberg (1929-1930)	12,473 66
	Harriet F. Haas	10,000 00
	Harmon W. Hendricks	10,000 00
1930	Harry H. Meyer (1930-1939)	206,383 06
	Betsy S. Korminsky	5,000 00
	Pauline Myers	5,000 00
	Louis C. Raegner	5,000 00
1931	Julius Marcus	19,185 83
	Louis Marshall (1931-1937)	11,581 27
	William Hartfield (1931-1936)	10,061 59
	Alfred M. Heinsheimer	5,000 00
	Frieda Wimpfheimer	5,000 00
1933	Isaac Marx	7,500 00

1934	Rudolph J. Schaefer (1934-1937)	$64,845 88
	Ludwig Dreyfuss	25,000 00
	Benjamin Stern (1934-1937)	25,000 00
1935	Bertha Weinman—In memory of her brother, Moses Weinman (1935-1939)	1,514,554 82
	Joseph Runsheim (1935-1937)	17,872 25
	Lawrence Pike (1935-1939)	4,113 64
1936	Edward J. King—For the Edward J. King and Jennie I. King Memorial Fund (1936-1939)	1,631,319 44
	Isa Nordlinger (1936-1937)	9,199 21
	Augustus W. Openhym (1936-1939)	37,501 96
	Louise C. Colten	2,800 29
	Abraham Cohn	2,622 65
	Henry F. Wolff	2,503 47
1937	Marco Fleishman—For the Rosetta and Marco Fleishman Memorial Fund (1937-1939)	743,810 79
	Carrie L. Lehman	10,000 00
	Henry Ollesheimer (1937-1939)	10,020 98
	Ephraim B. Levy	5,000 00
	Leah Simpson	5,000 00
	Jacob W. Gutman	2,500 00
	Henry Jacoby (1937-1938)	2,732 30
	Emil Kiss—In Memory of Laura Kiss	1,445 00
	Joseph N. Frank (1937-1939)	404 63
1938	Henry W. Putnam	50,000 00
	Bettie Meierhoff	36,543 07
	Harry J. D. Plaut	5,107 50
	Charles S. Erlanger	5,000 00
	Fannie Metzger (1938-1939)	1,285 31
	Emanuel Felsenheld	1,250 00
	Morris Drey	1,000 00
	David J. Frankel	1,000 00
	Sara T. Lowman	1,000 00
1939	John Frankel	1,000 00
	Flora Hirsh	1,000 00
	Jerome Rice	1,000 00
	Carl W. Stern (In memory of mother, Louise Marie Stern)	1,000 00
	Henry Katzenberg	750 00
	Isaac Fry	620 05
	Isaac D. Einstein (through Federation)	500 00
	John E. Kaliski	200 00
	Isidor Wagner	100 00
	Isaac T. Carpenter	68 96
	Barnet Green	22 58

LIFE MEMBERS

HARRY CONTENT ....111 Broadway

ABRAM I. ELKUS...40 Wall Street

MRS. E. B. HART...2111 Madison Avenue

MRS. ELSIE WALLACH KRIDEL...........................1075 Park Avenue

SAMUEL A. LEWIS...7 Warren Street

MRS. J. S. MENKEN.......................................104 East 79th Street

ARTHUR MEYER....................71 Fitzjohn Avenue, London, N. W.

WALTER W. NAUMBURG................................121 East 64th Street

MRS. FLORENCE S. ROBERTS...................Hotel Villa Del Arroyo,
                                                        Pasadena, Cal.

JAMES SPEYER..24 Pine Street

MRS. ALBERT D. STEIN

ISADOR M. STETTENHEIM...17 Cedar Street

186

187

SUPERINTENDENTS AND DIRECTORS SINCE 1855

Superintendents—Directors#

*1855-1866   JULIUS RAYMOND
*1867-1875   G. SCHWARZBAUM
*1876-1878   LEOPOLD B. SIMON
*1879-1892   THEODORE HADEL
*1892-1899   LEOPOLD MINZESHEIMER
*1899-1904   S. L. FATMAN
 1904-1928   S. S. GOLDWATER, M.D.
 1928-   JOSEPH TURNER, M.D.

Associate Director

1927-1928   JOSEPH TURNER, M.D.

Assistant Superintendents—Assistant Directors#

*1892-1892   LEOPOLD MINZESHEIMER
*1896-1902   GUSTAVE ABRAMS
*1903-1904   SOLON J. RIESER
 1903-1904   S. S. GOLDWATER, M.D.
 1906-1908   SIDNEY E. GOLDSTEIN
*1908-1909   D. M. BLOOM, M.D.
 1910-1915   H. J. MOSS, M.D.
 1914-1915   A. J. BELLER, M.D.
 1915-1916   EMANUEL GIDDINGS, M.D.
 1916-1920   HERMAN SMITH, M.D.
*1918-1919   SIMON TANNENBAUM, M.D.
 1920-1922   LEOPOLD BRAHDY, M.D.
 1920-1926   E. M. BLUESTONE, M.D.
 1922-1927   JOSEPH TURNER, M.D.
 1925-1927   J. J. GOLUB, M.D.
 1927-1937   STEPHEN MANHEIMER, M.D.
 1927-1934   LOUIS MILLER, JR.
 1934-   J. A. KATZIVE, M.D.
 1935-1939   JANDON SCHWARZ, M.D.
 1937-1938   M. A. GREEN, M.D.
 1938-   MAXWELL S. FRANK, M.D.
 1940-   MORRIS H. KREEGER, M.D.

Title changed to Director and Assistant Director in 1917.
* Deceased

GRADUATES OF THE HOUSE STAFF

PRIOR TO 1884

*Mark Blumenthal
*F. Tilden Brown
*R. M. Cramer
*R. B. Coleman
D. H. Davison
Wm. L. Estes
*Benson M. Feldman
*Albert Fridenberg
*O. Froelich

Alfred Meyer
*J. R. Nilsen
R. Offenbach
*S. Rapp
J. M. Rice
*J. Rudisch
*John Van Der Poel
Julius Weiss

	SURGEONS		PHYSICIANS
1884	*James L. Shiland	1884	Edward Burns
	*Walter Hitchcock		Charles H. May
1885	*J. Clark Steward	1885	Arthur B. Coffin
	*Herman J. Schiff		*Josephine Walter
			*Charles F. Mason
1886	*F. C. Husson	1886	*E. L. H. Swift
	*Alfred N. Strouse		*Edward J. Ware
1887	*William H. Wilmer	1887	Charles G. Giddings
	*H. S. Stark		*Abraham Korn
1888	Guy C. Rich	1888	*E. H. Walsh
	Howard Lilienthal		*H. E. Sanderson
1889	L. J. Ladin	1889	*Simon D. Elsner
	Geo. B. Cowell		G. L. Nicholas
1890	Samuel L. Weber	1890	R. H. Cunningham
	A. D. Mewborn		*Max Jackson
1891	*Southgate Leigh	1891	*Fred S. Mandlebaum
	David B. Lovell		*H. P. Palmer
1892	*Edwin C. Sternberger	1892	*E. C. Levy
			Percy H. Fridenberg
1893	Geo. L. Brodhead	1893	Henry A. Cone
	*S. M. Brickner		
1894	Martin W. Ware	1894	*W. Jarvis Barlow
	Thomas T. Tuttle		
1895	Charles A. Elsberg	1895	*Sidney Yankauer
	*Nathan Breiter		
	*J. Ralston Lattimore		
1896	Albert A. Berg	1896	Emanuel Libman
	*William H. Luckett		William P. Loth
1897	Charles Goodman	1897	Herman B. Baruch
	J. B. Morrison		Sidney V. Haas
1898	*Harry Rodman	1898	Louis Hauswirth
	*Walter M. Brickner		
1899	Sidney Ulfelder	1899	William G. Eckstein
	*L. W. Allen		A. F. Foord
1900	Leo B. Meyer	1900	Israel Strauss
	Eugene H. Eising		

GRADUATES OF THE HOUSE STAFF

(Continued)

Surgeons	Physicians
1901 M. Thorner	1901 *I. W. Becker
Truman Abbe	Herman Schwarz
1902 *Edwin Beer	1902 *Edward A. Aronson
Major G. Seelig	Milton Gerschel
1903 *Meyer M. Stark	1903 *Herbert L. Celler
Robert T. Frank	*Alfred Fabian Hess
Eli Moschcowitz	David Kramer
1904 D. Lee Hischler	1904 Bernard S. Oppenheimer
Albert G. Swift	Arthur Bookman
Fred H. MacCarthy	*H. F. L. Ziegel
C. F. Jellinghaus	Louis Bauman
1905 Sol. Hyman	1905 Geo. W. T. Mills
Isadore Seff	*Samuel Feldstein
William J. Haber	*Gustav A. Fried
Horace Leiter	*Leo Kessel
1906 C. Morris Hathaway	1906 Julius J. Hertz
Milton Bodenheimer	Jesse G. M. Bullowa
Ernest Sachs	Julian J. Meyer
Solomon Wiener	Max Taschman
1907 Orville H. Schell	1907 Alfred E. Cohn
Eben Alexander, Jr.	*Louis Jacobs
Aims R. Chamberlain	*Louis G. Kaempfer
Harold Neuhof	*Walter J. Highman
1908 John C. A. Gerster	1908 *Jacob Wisansky
Abraham Hyman	Abraham E. Jaffin
Isidor C. Rubin	Albert A. Epstein
	Max Scheer
1909 Howard E. Lindeman	1909 Abraham Sophian
Herbert D. Manley	Joseph Rosenthal
*Charles Ryttenberg	*Maurice T. Munker
Fred. G. Oppenheimer	Murray H. Bass
1910 Abraham O. Wilensky	1910 Bernard H. Eliasberg
Benjamin F. May	Burrill B. Crohn
George Baehr	*Milton Hahn
Samuel H. Geist	Richard H. Hoffmann
1911 Louis Greenberg	1911 Harry Wessler
Philip Liebling	Nathaniel Barnett
Irving Simons	*H. W. Emsheimer
Leo Mayer	Hiram Olsan
1912 Herman Jaffe	1912 Salo N. Weber
Sidney Cohn	*Morris H. Kahn
Isidor Kross	*Abraham Zingher
Julius Blum	Meyer Rosensohn
1913 Abraham J. Beller	1913 *Alexander Hofheimer
Oscar Baumann	Jacob Sachs
Jesse D. Schwartz	Edward Mahler
Ira Cohen	Daniel Poll

GRADUATES OF THE HOUSE STAFF
(Continued)

	SURGEONS		PHYSICIANS
1914	Hyman R. Miller C. Koenigsberger Edward Bleier Abraham Strauss	1914	Arthur S. Rosenfeld Maurice F. Lautman John L. Kantor Louis H. Levy
1915	Ralph M. Bruckheimer Sol. Shlimbaum Paul W. Aschner *John F. Grattan	1915	A. I. Loewenthal David Beck Louis G. Shapiro Jacob Piller
1916	Joseph A. Landy Nathan Rosenthal Adolf A. Weiss Waldemar R. Metz	1916	Willard D. Mayer Lester J. Unger Ernst P. Boas Joseph Harkavy
1917	Harry C. Saltzstein David M. Natanson Max D. Mayer Leo Edelman	1917	Harry Plotz Charles G. Giddings, Jr. Louis Berman William Rosenson
1918	*Eugene Klein Louis Carp Samuel Kahn Julius Gottesman Leopold Brahdy Lewis T. Mann	1918	Joseph Felsen William Friedman Max Harrison Reuben Steinholz Harold T. Hyman Louis Hausman
1919	Herman Sharlit Morris Brooks Morris A. Goldberger Emanuel Salwen Joseph A. Lazarus Barney M. Kully Henry S. Fischer Jerome M. Ziegler	1919	Jerome L. Kohn Asher Winkelstein Edward Hollander Irving R. Roth Abraham Kardiner Kaufman Wallach
1920	Leo J. Hahn Rudolph Kramer Samuel Hirshfeld Max Schneider *Harold L. Meierhof Nathan Sobel	1920	Ira M. Olsan Charles Green Leo Loewe Philip Finkle Edward Lehman Harry D. Pasachoff
1921	Laurence Jones William Harris Martin A. Furman Leonard M. Lyons Sylvan D. Manheim Joseph B. Stenbuck	1921	Morris J. Lavine Saul A. Ritter *Benj. B. Eichner Philip Astrowe Frederic D. Zeman Alton M. Amsterdam
1922	Joseph M. Marcus Samuel Silbert Percy Klingenstein Joseph S. Somberg Henry Milch Samuel Gaines	1922	Nathan Muskin Sydney C. Feinberg Samuel Z. Levine David Gaberman David Soletsky Leon Ginzburg

SURGEONS	PHYSICIANS
1923 Benj. N. Berg	**1923** Samuel Rosen
Julian B. Herrmann	Samuel Rosenfeld
Arthur H. Aufses	Arthur M. Master
Louis Kleinfeld	Louis Hodes
Saul S. Samuels	Philip Cohen
Edwin A. Seidman	William S. Collens
1924 Seth Selig	**1924** Roland I. Grausman
David Warshaw	Alfred M. Goltman
Seymour Wimpfheimer	Coleman B. Rabin
Sidney Friedman	Ephraim Shorr
Elias L. Stern	Robert K. Lambert
Gordon D. Oppenheimer	David Ball
1925 Robert K. Lippmann	**1925** Leon Goldsmith
Edward A. Horowitz	Benj. Eliasoph
Robert H. Feldman	Richard M. Brickner
Martin Schreiber	Harold A. Abramson
Leon Ginzburg	Alfred E. Fischer
Irving A. Frisch	Harry I. Weinstock
1926 *A. Philip Zemansky, Jr.	**1926** Harry Schwartz
Edward O. Finestone	J. Lester Kobacker
Mayer E. Ross	Nathan Cherwin
Edward J. Bassen	Harry S. Mackler
Samuel Mufson	Joseph Laval
Clarence K. Weil	David Wexler
1927 Ernest E. Arnheim	**1927** Abraham L. Goldwyn
Walter F. Welton	William J. Bearman
Hyman Rosenfeld	Ameil Glass
Arthur S. W. Touroff	Milton J. Matzner
1928 Moses Swick	**1928** Jacob E. Holzman
Abraham Firestone	Elmer S. Gais
Sidney Grossman	Abraham L. Kornzweig
William H. Mencher	*John Cohen
1929 William Leifer	**1929** Samuel H. Averbuck
Sidney Hirsch	Joseph Uttal
Monroe A. Rosenbloom	Herman Zazeela
Robert L. Craig	Alfred Romanoff
1930 Lester R. Tuchman	**1930** Solomon Silver
Ameil Glass	Samuel Melamed
Isidore Schapiro	William J. Hochbaum
William L. Ferber	Shirley H. Baron
1931 Maurice M. Berck	**1931** Sylvan E. Moolten
Lyon Steine	Arthur Schifrin
Borris A. Kornblith	*Herbert M. Klein
Herbert S. Talbot	Rose Spiegel
1932 Samuel H. Klein	**1932** Arthur R. Sohval
Erwin K. Gutmann	Robert V. Sager
Joseph A. Gaines	Albert B. Newman
William Sheinfeld	William M. Hitzig

GRADUATES OF THE HOUSE STAFF

(Continued)

SURGEONS | PHYSICIANS

1933 Perry S. Horenstein
H. Evans Leiter
Abraham J. Gitlitz
Alexander H. Rosenthal

1934 Meyer Abrahams
Sidney Rosenburg
Jacob S. Goltman
Leonard J. Druckerman

1935 Albert Schein
Emanuel Klempner
Edward E. Jemerin
Herman J. Meisel

1936 Irving A. Sarot
Paul Kaufman
Sidney M. Silverstone
Ale.i N. Leslie

1937 Gabriel P. Seley
Leon G. Berman
Herman R. Nayer
Ralph W. Flax
Robert C. Elitzik
Nathan Mintz

1938 Julius L. Weissberg
Vernon A. Weinstein
Abner Kurtin
Sylvan Bloomfield
Leonard S. Bases
Leon N. Greene

1939 Nathan Adelman
Joseph M. Szilagyi
Emanuel Wachtel
Samuel Diener
Alexander Thomas
Bernard S. Wolf

1933 Herman S. Roth
Frederick Bridge
Jacob E. Stern
Saul W. Jarcho

1934 Hyman Levy
Harry L. Jaffe
Abraham Penner
Frederick H. Theodore

1935 David A. Dantes
Israel Schiller
Sheppard Siegal
Benjamin Rubin

1936 Milton Mendlowitz
Henry Dolger
Morton W. Willis
Morris F. Steinberg

1937 Samuel Nisnewitz
Edward R. Schlesinger
Sidney L. Penner
Eugene Somkin
Edgar A. Baron
Morton Yohalem

1938 Max Ellenberg
Samuel C. Bukantz
S. Zelig Sorkin
Robert A. Newburger
Ralph E. Moloshok
Sydney G. Margolin

1939 Milton Landowne
Irving A. Beck
Irving Solomon
Herman Anfanger
Sidney Cohen
Emanuel B. Schoenbach

ONE-YEAR INTERNS AND EXTERNS

1898 L. A. S. Bodine
     W. M. Lazard
1899 E. A. Rosenberg
     E. D. Lederman
     *A. W. Roff
1900 Edward J. Miller
     *Chas. E. Rosenwasser
     J. Howard Staub
1901 Leon Bandler
     *Eugene P. Bernstein
1902 S. S. Goldwater
1906 Kaufman Schlivek
     *Isadore Goldstein
     William Branower
     Isadore Kaufman
1907 B. Rein
     Edgar D. Oppenheimer
     P. Fiaschi
     Jerome S. Leopold
1908 *Wm. I. Wallach
     M. Reuben
     M. C. Pease, Jr.
     Michael Barsky
1909 H. C. Fleming
     E. W. Abramowitz
     Wm. Lapatnikoff
     E. M. Carson
     I. Shapiro
     Jacob Roemer
1910 Charles Gluck
     Mark Cohen
     Jerome Zuckerman
     Charles Gottlieb
     Ralph H. Goss
1911 D. Tannenbaum
     Arthur J. Bendick
     *J. J. Fabian
     *Hugo Blum
     William Thalhimer
     Clarence Brown
1912 Harry G. Goldman
     Saul Levy
     Harold A. Cohen
     Samuel Wetchler
     *Samuel Silverman
     Abraham J. Newman
     Carl C. Franken

1913 S. Aronowitz
     Oscar L. Levin
     A. Levy
     *Marcus A. Rothschild
     M. Lobsenz
     H. L. Sherman
     S. Genovese
1914 C. G. Ratner
     *J. S. Meltzer
     W. Rosen
     A. Unger
     T. Halpern
     D. H. Bluestone
     A. Mendelson
1915 J. Sinkowitz
     D. Kronman
     I. Pelzman
     J. Haimann
     I. W. Jacobs
     A. Brody
1916 *J. L. Furst
     M. A. Sager
     *J. A. Rosenberg
     Joseph Reiss
     I. Rosen
     L. L. Roth
1917 M. Varzahbedian
     *H. Martinson
     A. Jerskey
     J. Rosenfeld
     Louis Nahum
     J. J. Wiener
     B. E. Strode
1918 A. Altschul
     Samuel K. Levy
     Leon Antell
     W. Sellinger
     M. J. Radin
     Max Dobrin
     Jacob Branower
1920 *Harold Rypins
     D. S. Darm
1923 S. S. Lichtman
1924 M. Biederman
     M. L. Guttmacher
     Max Brahdy
     Isabel Beck

* Deceased.

194

ONE-YEAR INTERNS AND EXTERNS
(Continued)

1925 Wm. B. Rose
Julius Kavee
Gertrude Felshin

1926 Emanuel W. Benjamin
Eli Y. Shorr

1927 Harry Weiss
Sidney D. Leader
Paul S. Roland
Walter Bromberg
Ben. Z. Steine
Hudythe M. Levin
Moses R. Buchman
S. I. Kooperstein
Herman Slass

1928 Murray A. Last
P. Goolker
William Chester
J. Fuhrman Heinrich
Isabel Globus
S. P. Carp
Sidney D. Leader
Harry Rosenwasser
Harry Feld

1929 George Frumkes
Michael C. Kemelhor
Louis Schneider
Saul Miller
Bernard S. Brody
Marcy L. Sussman
David Beres

1930 Harold A. Abel
Charles K. Friedberg
Harry Keil
Clement H. Golden
Henry A. Baron
Sidney Housman
Charles Sutro
Herbert Lampert
Nathan H. Sachs

1931 Hyman Lieber
Edward B. Greenspan
Harry Yarnis

1931 Henry Peskin
Robert H. Abrahamson
Ralph T. Levin
Max L. Som
Bernard Amsterdam

1932 David R. Levine
Bernard Amsterdam
Samuel A. Feldman
Sidney E. Lenke
Irving Kowaloff
Alice I. Bernheim
Charles J. Sage
Carl Zelson
F. J. de Prume

1933 Benjamin Allen
Bension Calef
Simon Dack
Edward Greenberger
Harold W. Keschner
Arnold Treitman
Fred R. Schechter
Robert Ullman
I. Oscar Weisman

1934 Meyer Emanuel
Ralph W. Flax
Sidney L. Gottlieb
David Littauer
M. Edward Hipsh
Charles W. Rieber
Louis M. Rosati
Jandon Schwarz

1935 Albert D. Kistin
Vernon A. Weinstein
Morris M. Kessler
William Finkelstein
Herman I. Kantor
Jean Pakter
William Epstein
M. Edward Hipsh
Samuel B. Weiner

1936 Simon H. Nagler
Samuel M. Bloom
Max Ellenberg
Jean Pakter

INTERNS IN PATHOLOGY

1911 Daniel Poll
1912 Louis H. Levy
1913 Paul W. Aschner
1914 Harry Plotz
1915 William Rosenson
1916 Julius Gottesman
1917 Lewis T. Mann
1918 Martin Vorhaus
1919 Maurice Rashbaum
1920 Percy Klingenstein
1921 Saul S. Samuels
1922 Sol. S. Lichtman
1923 Martin Schreiber
1924 Lionel S. Auster
     Clarence K. Weil
1925 Abraham Firestone
1926 William Leifer
     Alfred Romanoff
1927 Irving Nachamie
     S. David Glusker
1928 Henry H. Lichtenberg
     Arthur Schifrin

1929 Reuben Cares
     Harry Moskowitz
1930 Harold A. Aaron
     Victor H. Kugell
1931 Sidney E. Lenke
     Jacob S. Goltman
1932 Sidney Licht
1933 Milton Mendlowitz
     Irving A. Sarot
1934 Leon G. Berman
     *Milton Steiner
1935 Samuel C. Bukantz
     Nathan Mintz
1936 Nathan S. Hiatt
     Joseph M. Szilagyi
1937 Alexander Thomas
     Bernard S. Wolf
1938 Tibor J. Greenwalt
     Daniel Luger
1939 Roy N. Barnett
     Merrill P. Haas

INTERNS, EXTERNS AND RESIDENTS IN RADIOLOGY

1921 Sidney H. Levy
1922 Rubin Lavine
     Barnett P. Freedman
1923 Harry S. Olin
     Harry Gross
1924 Irving Schwartz
     Max Newer
1925 Jacob R. Freid
     Nathaniel H. Robin
     Emanuel J. Wexler
1926 William Snow
     Sol. Taubin
1927 Albert Kean
     Samuel Poplack
     Samuel Sinberg
1928 Carye-Belle Henle
     Benjamin J. Sax
     Emanuel W. Benjamin

1929 Myer E. Golan
     Charles Lipsky
     Samuel Richman
1930 Isidore Klein
     Saul J. Tamarkin
1931 Harry Herscher
1932 Simon Shulman
     Louis E. Zaretski
     Gerald J. Bernath
1933 Mitchell Burdick
     Gayland L. Hagelshaw
1934 Israel Kirsh
     Edward D. Sherman
1936 Irving I. Cowan
     Joseph Jellen
     Benjamin Copleman
1937 Max Schenck
     Marston T. Woodruff
1938 Arnold Bachman
     Robert J. Ruby
1939 Lester Freedman

* Deceased.

RESIDENT STAFF

PRIVATE AND SEMI-PRIVATE PAVILIONS

	SURGEONS		PHYSICIANS
1905	Albert G. Swift		
1906	Edwin A. Riesenfeld		
1907	Milton Bodenheimer		
1908	Wm. Branower	1908	Julius Kaunitz
1909	Eben Alexander, Jr.	1909	J. Russell Verbrycke
	Harold Neuhof		
1910	Abraham E. Jaffin	1910	*Jacob Wisansky
1911	J. C. Wooldridge	1911	Joseph Rosenthal
1912	J. Irving Fort	1912	Oris S. Warr
	A. O. Wilensky		
1913	J. W. Brennan	1913	A. B. James
	J. E. King		
1914	A. J. Beller	1914	B. M. Dear
	H. E. Schorr		*Morris H. Kahn
1915	Jesse D. Schwartz	1915	Edward Mahler
1916	*H. S. Marcley	1916	Joseph D. Kelley
	Edward Bleier		
1917	Sol Shlimbaum	1917	Joseph Reiss
	J. Ramsay Crawford		
	Joseph A. Landy		
1918	Adolf A. Weiss	1918	Joseph Rosenfeld
	David M. Natanson		
1919	Max D. Mayer	1919	Hubert Mann
	G. D. Von Deylen		
	Milton S. Fine		
1920	Wm. A. Flick	1920	Louis Sacks
	Thomas J. Sullivan		
	Joseph Lazarus		
1921	Arnold Messing	1921	Selian Hebald
	Paul S. Lowenstein		
1922	Joseph Heyman	1922	A. Isaacman
	L. W. Pritchett		
1923	Benjamin Kogut	1923	Stanley S. Myers
	Edward Lorentzen		
	Samuel Gaines		
1924	Seymour F. Wilhelm	1924	Bernard Appel
	Ernst Springer		
	Abram A. Weiss		
	A. J. Sparks		
	Elias Rubin (10 months)		

* Deceased.

RESIDENT STAFF

PRIVATE AND SEMI-PRIVATE PAVILIONS
(Continued)

SURGEONS	PHYSICIANS
1925 Franklin I. Harris	1925 Samuel Schindelhelm
George S. Lachman	
Elias L. Stern	
Nathaniel H. Blumenkranz	
1926 Norman F. Laskey	
Samuel Hochman	
Edward O. Finestone	
1927 Joseph M. Frehling	1927 Abraham M. Schaefer
M. Lester Levy	
C. D. Moore	
1928 Harold W. Goldberg	1928 Henry Z. Goldstein
Edward Jacobs	
Myron A. Sallick	
David Sloane	
1929 Jacob J. Enkelis	1929 Max E. Panitch
Samuel S. Hanflig	
Robert I. Hiller	
Bernard D. Kulick	
1930 Samuel Imboden	1930 Bernard S. Brody
Samuel P. Suffin	
Eske H. Windsberg	
1931 Sidney Rosenburg	1931 Harold A. Abel
Henry A. Baron	
Lyon Steine	
1932 David A. Susnow	1932 Harry Yarnis
Joseph Tomarkin	
Erwin K. Gutmann	
Meyer Corff	
1933 Joseph Tartakoff	1933 Frank A. Bassen
Robert Turell	
Perry S. Horenstein	
1934 H. Evans Leiter	
Robert H. Abrahamson	
Arthur J. Harris	
1935 Meyer Abrahams	1935 Abraham Penner
Zachary R. Cottler	
Albert M. Schwartz	
Jerome Gross	
Anthony Kohn	
Leonard J. Druckerman	
1936 Leo H. Pollock	
Seebert J. Goldowsky	
Edward E. Jemerin	1936 Samuel Baer
Irwin P. Train	

RESIDENT STAFF

PRIVATE AND SEMI-PRIVATE PAVILIONS
(Continued)

SURGEONS	PHYSICIANS
1937 Ernest D. Bloomenthal	1937 David E. Scheinberg
Aaron Frigot	William Finkelstein
Meyer L. Goldman	Albert Cornell
Louis Scheman	
Leon M. Caplan	
Sigmund A. Siegel	
Gabriel P. Seley	
1938 Julian A. Jarman	1938 Herman G. Helpern
Philip Cooper	Philip M. Gottlieb
Ralph W. Flax	
Lawrence Essenson	
Benjamin Gitlitz	
H. Earle Tucker	
1939 Arthur Gladstone	1939 Milton H. Adelman
Sylvan Bloomfield	Morris H. Kreeger
Vernon A. Weinstein	
Leon N. Greene	
Robert W. Mann	
Jerome S. Coles	

RESIDENT STAFF

WARD SERVICES

Neurology

1924	William Malamud
	David Rothschild
1925	M. Weinstock Bergman
	David I. Arbuse
1926	Herman G. Selinsky
1927	Sol W. Ginsburg
	Jacob J. Kasanin
1928	Lewis J. Doshay
	Walter Bromberg
1929	William Berman
	Isabel Globus
1930	P. Goolker
	Lewis H. Loeser
1931	Paul Sloane
	Bernard S. Brody
1932	William Schick
	Samuel A. Sandler
	Louis Levenstim
1933	Daniel E. Schneider
	Jacob H. Friedman
1934	Abraham Blau
	Morris B. Bender
1935	Norman Reider
1936	Sidney Tarachow
	Norman A. Levy
1937	Morris M. Kessler
	Laurence M. Weinberger
	Jerome E. Alderman
1938	Mark G. Kanzer
	Edwin A. Weinstein
1939	Eugene P. Mindlin
	Hyman E. Yaskin

Pediatrics

1924	Philip Cohen
	Alfred Nathans
1925	E. Gordon Stoloff
	Isabel Beck
1926	Samuel Karelitz
	Samuel J. Levin
1927	Alfred E. Fischer
	Gustave F. Weinfeld
1928	Abbot L. Winograd
	Harry S. Mackler
1929	Moses R. Buchman
	Sidney D. Leader
1930	David Beres
	Peter Vogel
1931	Jacob L. Rothstein
	A. E. Cohen
1932	George J. Ginandes.
	Albert A. Rosenberg
1933	Martin L. Stein
	Carl Zelson
1934	Louise Rauh
1935	Jacob Brem
	Samuel Ehre
1936	Howard C. Leopold
	Sidney Blumenthal
1937	Arthur Lesser
	Samuel B. Weiner
	Jean Pakter
1938	Howard G. Rapaport
	David B. Davis
1939	Victor L. Szanton
	Jacob Danciger

Oto-Laryngology

1924	Louis Kleinfeld
1925	Samuel Rosen
1927	Joseph G. Druss
1928	Irving B. Goldman
1929	Ben Z. Steine
1930	Harry Rosenwasser
1931	Joseph L. Goldman
1932	William J. Hochbaum
1933	Max L. Som

Gynecology

1924	Arthur Katzenstein
	Karl Polifka
1925	Morris R. Matus
	Seymour Wimpfheimer
1926	Howard A. Power
	Edward A. Horowitz
1927	Frank Spielman
1928	Jacques D. Soifer
	Alan F. Guttmacher
1929	Oscar Glassman
1930	Benj. E. Urdan
	Maurice Feresten
1931	Irving Nachamie
	Mervin A. Henschel
1932	Phineas Bernstein
	Henry A. Baron
1933	Joseph A. Gaines

WARD SERVICES
(Continued)

Oto-Laryngology
1934 Eugene R. Snyder

1935 Benj. I. Allen

1937 A. H. Neffson

1938 Lester L. Coleman

1939 Samuel M. Bloom

Gynecology
1934 Sidney N. Mendelsohn
     U. J. Salmon
1935 Robert Turell
     H. Melvin Radman
1936 Emanuel Klempner
1937 Robert I. Walter
     Norman Margolius
     Herbert F. Newman
1938 Arthur M. Davids
     Phoenix M. Sales
1939 Nathan Mintz
     Jack Squire

Ophthalmology
1928 David Wexler
1929 Robert K. Lambert
1930 Murray A. Last
1931 Saul Miller
1932 Herman I. Weiss
1933 Samuel L. Saltzman

1934 Abraham L. Kornzweig
1935 Nathan S. Rubin
1936 Frederick H. Theodore
1937 Jacob Goldsmith
1938 Frank M. Green
1939 Louis C. Ravin

Orthopedics
1938 Samuel R. Rubert

1939 Otto Lehmann

INTERNS IN DENTISTRY
1933 Marvin G. Freid
     Herbert L. Goodfleish
1934 Henry I. Cohen
     Harry A. Suslow
1935 Louis Kroll
1936 Robert S. Gilbert
     Manuel Gottlieb

1937 Ben Pine
     Robert W. Slutzky
1938 Robert S. Hess
     Lee R. Kulick
1939 Manuel Burness
     Alfred R. Shepard

ADMITTING PHYSICIANS
1908-1911	Max Rosenberg	1928	Elmer S. Gais
1912-1913	Herbert W. Emsheimer	1929	Samuel H. Averbuck
1914-1915	Daniel Poll	1930	Herman Zazeela
1916	David Beck	1931	Isidore Schapiro
1917-1918	Joseph Harkavy	1931-1933	Rose Spiegel
1919	Asher Winkelstein	1934	Herman S. Roth
1920-1921	Philip Finkle	1935	Hyman Levy
1922	Leon Ginzburg	1936	D. Alfred Dantes
1923	Arthur M. Master	1937	Alan N. Leslie
1924	Coleman B. Rabin	1938	Herman I. Kantor
1925-1927	Lewis E. Persoff	1939	Julius L. Weissberg
1928	Sidney Grossman		

EIGHTY-EIGHTH

ANNUAL REPORT

OF

THE MOUNT SINAI HOSPITAL

OF THE

CITY OF NEW YORK

For the Year 1940

Act of Incorporation Filed February, 1852

CONTENTS

Extracts from the Constitution on Endowed Beds and Other Endowment Funds

A contribution of $2,500 to the general funds of the corporation, if accepted by the Board of Trustees, shall endow a Life Bed. Such contribution shall entitle the donor thereof, during his or her lifetime, to name a patient from time to time to occupy one bed in the wards of the Hospital, free of charge.

A contribution of $3,500 to the general funds of the corporation, if accepted by the Board of Trustees, shall endow a Memorial Bed. Such a contribution shall entitle the donor thereof, during his or her lifetime, to name a patient from time to time to occupy one bed in the wards of the Hospital, free of charge. Such donor may bequeath that right to a successor appointed by the said donor in his or her last will and testament, or by any other instrument under seal. In the event of such successor being appointed, the rights hereinbefore mentioned shall continue for a period of not over fifty years from the date of such contribution, provided, however, that such period shall be extended so that it shall in no event end until ten years after the death of the donor.

A contribution of $5,000 to the general funds of the corporation, if accepted by the Board of Trustees, shall endow a Perpetual Bed in the Children's Pavilion. Such contribution shall entitle the donor thereof, during his or her lifetime, to name a patient from time to time to occupy one bed in the wards of the Children's Pavilion free of charge. Such donor may bequeath that right to a successor appointed by said donor in his or her last will and testament or by any other instrument under seal. When a corporation is the donor, the privilege shall expire at the end of twenty-five years from the date of such contribution.

A contribution of $7,500 to the general funds of the corporation, if accepted by the Board of Trustees, shall endow a Perpetual Bed, but where, under the provision of any will executed prior to March 20, 1921, the sum of $5,000 or more is bequeathed to the corporation in payment of any Perpetual Bed, the Board of Trustees may, at their option, accept such sum in payment of such Perpetual Bed. Such contribution shall entitle the donor thereof, during his or her lifetime, to name a patient from time to time to occupy one bed in a ward of the Hospital, free of charge. Such donor may bequeath that right to a successor appointed by said donor in his or her last will and testament, or by any other instrument under seal. When a corporation is the donor, the privilege shall expire at the end of twenty-five years from the date of such contribution.

Tablets to commemorate the endowment of Life, Memorial and Perpetual Beds shall be placed in a ward or in such other place as may be set aside for the purpose. Tablets for Life Beds shall be maintained during the life of the donor. Tablets for Memorial Beds shall be maintained for a period not beyond fifty years from the date of their endowment, provided, however, that such period shall be extended so that it shall in no event end until ten years after the death of the donor. Tablets for Perpetual Beds shall be maintained in perpetuity.

A donor may change a Life Bed endowed by him or her to a Memorial Bed by making an additional contribution of $1,000 or to a Perpetual Bed by making an additional contribution of $5,000, or may change a Memorial Bed to a Perpetual Bed by making an additional contribution of $4,000.

No patient shall be admitted to the privileges pertaining to a Life, Memorial or Perpetual Bed unless he shall comply with the current rules of the corporation and be a proper subject for treatment under its regulations.

An endowment for the establishment of any special fund may be accepted by a resolution of the Board of Trustees. Such fund may be created for special or general purposes under the name of one or more persons or otherwise. If created for a special purpose the fund shall be used only for that purpose. Additions to any fund may be made at any time and in any amount, but no fund shall be created with an initial endowment of less than Ten Thousand Dollars.

Gifts of any sums whatsoever may be made to one or more special funds for non-budgetary purposes, the principal and income of which may be appropriated by the Board of Trustees as the needs may arise for purposes not covered by the regular budget of the corporation.

In the case of a bequest which does not in all respects conform to the conditions herein set forth, the Board of Trustees may, in its discretion, accept the same in accordance with the provisions of such bequest.

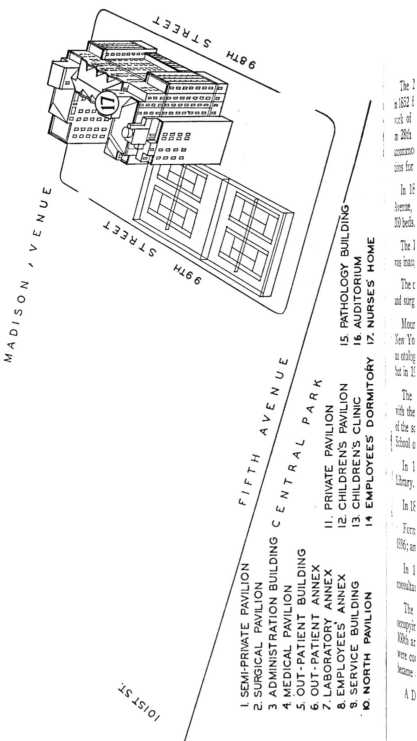

MADISON AVENUE

98TH STREET

99TH STREET

100TH ST.

FIFTH AVENUE

CENTRAL PARK

1. SEMI-PRIVATE PAVILION
2. SURGICAL PAVILION
3. ADMINISTRATION BUILDING
4. MEDICAL PAVILION
5. OUT-PATIENT BUILDING
6. OUT-PATIENT ANNEX
7. LABORATORY ANNEX
8. EMPLOYEES' ANNEX
9. SERVICE BUILDING
10. NORTH PAVILION
11. PRIVATE PAVILION
12. CHILDREN'S PAVILION
13. CHILDREN'S CLINIC
14. EMPLOYEES' DORMITORY
15. PATHOLOGY BUILDING
16. AUDITORIUM
17. NURSES' HOME

The M
in 1852 f
work of
on 28th
accommo
tions for

In 18
Avenue,
200 beds.

The L
was inau

The c
and surg

Mour
New Yo
an otolog
but in 19

The
with the
of the sc
School o

In 1
Library.

In 18

Form
1886; an

In 1
consultai

The
occupyir
100th an
were cor
became

A D

HISTORICAL NOTE

The Mount Sinai Hospital was organized and incorporated in 1852 for "benevolent, charitable and scientific purposes." The work of the Hospital was begun in a small four-story building on 28th Street, between Seventh and Eighth Avenues, which accommodated 28 patients. The Hospital now has accommodations for 856 patients, including 18 beds in the receiving ward.

In 1872 the Hospital completed and occupied, at Lexington Avenue, 66th and 67th Streets, a building having a capacity of 200 beds.

The Dispensary, now known as the Out-Patient Department, was inaugurated in 1873.

The clinical departments first organized were those of medicine and surgery; a gynecologist was appointed in 1877.

Mount Sinai created precedents among the hospitals of New York by setting up a distinct pediatric service in 1878 and an otologic service in 1879; the latter was at first combined with, but in 1910 was separated from, ophthalmology and laryngology.

The Mount Sinai Training School for Nurses, in affiliation with the Hospital, was incorporated in March, 1881; the name of the school was changed in 1923 to The Mount Sinai Hospital School of Nursing.

In 1883 a committee was formed to develop a Medical Library.

In 1886 a district medical service was inaugurated.

Formal provision for the care of private patients was made in 1886; an intermediate or "semi-private" ward was opened in 1904.

In 1893 a Department of Pathology was established, and consultants in dermatology and neurology were appointed.

The corner stone of the group of ten hospital buildings occupying the block bounded by Fifth and Madison Avenues, 100th and 101st Streets, was laid May 22nd, 1901; the buildings were completed and occupied March 15th, 1904, when 500 beds became available for the care of the sick.

A Department of Dietetics was established in 1905.

A Social Service Department was inaugurated in 1906.

A Tuberculosis Clinic was organized in 1908.

The first of a series of "Fellowship" funds was created in 1908 to assist investigators engaged in scientific medical work.

The Hospital's first X-ray machine was installed in 1900. In 1910 a full-fledged Department of Radiology was formed and in 1924 the department was subdivided into separate branches for (a) radiography and (b) X-ray and radium therapy.

In 1910 the three-story Out-Patient Building, which had been completed in 1904 was altered to a five-story building, and the Nurses' Home was enlarged from a six-story to an eight-story building. At the same time new isolation wards were erected on the roof of the Medical Building.

A Dental Department was established for the benefit of in-patients in 1910; this work was extended to the Out-Patient Department in 1925.

An orthopedic surgeon and a physio-therapist were named in 1911.

Roof wards for outdoor treatment were erected on the Medical and Surgical Pavilions in 1912.

The Hospital in 1912 accepted a fund "for the advancement of preventive medicine." A "health class" for children was promptly established.

In 1913 the erection of seven additional buildings south of 100th Street was begun; four of these buildings were occupied in 1915, and three, namely, the Private Pavilion, the Children's Pavilion and the Auditorium, were completed in the spring of 1922. With these additions, the Hospital was able to care for 654 patients.

The first of a series of lectureship funds was established in 1913. These funds provide honoraria for distinguished visiting lecturers.

Electro-cardiography was instituted in 1915.

In 1917, Mount Sinai Hospital became a constituent member of the Federation for the Support of Jewish Philanthropic Societies, which was organized in that year.

Until 1917, tonsillectomies were performed in the Dispensary, often without anesthesia; in the year mentioned, a "tonsil and adenoid" ward, with a fully equipped operating room, was opened.

A Mount Sinai Hospital Unit, organized as a section of the Medical Department of the United States Army, was sent to France in 1918.

Post-Graduate medical instruction was formally organized in 1923, in affiliation with the College of Physicians and Surgeons of Columbia University.

A permanent fund for the support of medical research was inaugurated in 1925, prior to which research was precariously supported by occasional donations.

The construction of a new school and residence building for the School of Nursing, fronting on 98th Street, between Fifth and Madison Avenues, was begun in 1925 and completed in 1927; the residence accommodates 490 nurses.

. The new Semi-Private Pavilion for the care of patients of moderate means was completed and opened to the public in 1931.

Group or cooperative special nursing was introduced for the first time in 1931.

A Consultation Service for ambulant out-patients of moderate means was organized in 1931.

Neuro-surgery was included in General Surgery until 1932, when a separate service was created.

The modernization of the Out-Patient Department Building was completed in 1933.

New facilities for cystoscopy were built and occupied in 1933.

The Journal of The Mount Sinai Hospital was established in 1934 for the publication of the scientific work of the Hospital's Medical Staff.

In 1934, the vacant former laboratory on 101st Street, was renovated and restored to use, providing space for a number of exiled German scientists and others.

Renovation and modernization of the Medical and Surgical Pavilions, part of the group of 10 buildings built in 1901, was begun in 1935 and completed in 1936.

The Isolation Ward was rebuilt in 1936 and, with the approval of the Department of Health, became the first Isolation Unit in New York City to be made available for use of private patients.

The Research Foundation of The Mount Sinai Hospital was incorporated in 1936 "to conduct, promote, encourage, and assist investigation in the services and arts of hygiene, medicine, and surgery and allied subjects."

Renovation of the Administration Building—after more than 30 years of use—was undertaken in 1937 and completed in 1938, providing enlarged facilities for Physiotherapy, Hydrotherapy, Occupational Therapy, Dentistry and other diagnostic and therapeutic services. Improved classroom and amphitheatre facilities for postgraduate medical instruction were also provided.

In 1939 a close affiliation was arranged with The Neustadter Foundation making it the Convalescent Branch of The Mount Sinai Hospital.

STATISTICAL SUMMARY

Year	Patients Treated in Hospital	Hospital Days	Consultations in Out-Patient Department	Total Disbursements for all Maintenance and Non-Budgetary Purposes (Non-Capital)
1857	216	6,048*	None	$9,000.00
1860	297	8,316*	None	14,000.00
1870	663	18,564*	None	20,000.00
1880	1,474	43,164	9,922	44,376.10
1890	2,862	65,255	43,560	100,000.00
1900	3,145	75,113	86,431	135,272.00
1910	7,613	149,198	115,726	410,000.00
1920	9,548	146,841	173,682	899,704.97
1930	12,179	193,482	222,489	1,785,244.23
1939	16,988	232,292	345,093	2,374,088.01
1940	17,275	236,851	357,567	2,398,595.02

* Estimated.

8

REPORT OF THE PRESIDENT

During the year 1940, international events have cast their shadow across the work of the Hospital and its activities have been affected in many ways by the approaching storm. In July, the Mount Sinai Hospital was invited by the Surgeon General to organize a military hospital to be known as General Hospital No. 3, just as in the last war it organized Base Hospital No. 3 which did splendid service with the American Expeditionary Force in France. Dr. George Baehr was appointed Unit Director of this new military hospital and it has been in the process of organization since authorized. Considerable headway has been made and a number of commissions have been received by members of the Medical Staff, but the process is not as yet completed. In addition to this, a number of men who held commissions in the Medical Reserve Corps of the Army and Navy have been called into service both from the attending staff and the resident staff and our medical organization will doubtless be subject to repeated and radical changes dependent upon the course of events.

Another angle of the war situation was reflected in the Blood-Plasma-for-England Project which was carried out by the Hospital in collaboration with the Blood Transfusion Association and the American Red Cross. In the middle of August six hospitals in the City offered their participation in furnishing blood plasma of which Mount Sinai was one. Later, three more hospitals joined the group. Mount Sinai's initial group consisted of six donors, and, from that small beginning, the organization quickly increased until at the end it was functioning during four sessions weekly, each one planned for sixty-five donors, or a weekly total of 260. The daily numbers, of course, varied; on one night there were as many as seventy-three donors. The total number of those who volunteered to contribute their blood at the Hospital was 2,938 of whom 2,862 proved to be acceptable donors whose blood was processed into plasma and shipped abroad as fast as space could be found on Britain-bound ships. It is with considerable satisfaction that I can state that, with the exception of about forty bottles which were part of a shipment lost when the S. S. "Western Prince" was torpedoed, the entire quantity is reported to have reached England.

To carry out this project required professional skill, organization and an enthusiastic group of willing volunteer workers. Dr. Nathan Rosenthal, who was in charge of the professional work, earned our gratitude as did the many other volunteers who served in various capacities. The total volunteer personnel numbered 450 and included the following: doctors—93; nurses—232; technicians and clerks—29; receptionists—31; porters and maids—60; volunteers for surgical supplies and dressings—5. There were employees from all departments. Many were private nurses who came after hours of duty, some were married nurses no longer practicing their profession, some were our own graduate and student nurses, social workers, technicians, clerks, waitresses, porters and maids. Five members from the Ladies' Auxiliary Committee came in regularly to prepare dressing bundles. Two volunteers were in attendance practically every day that the bank was in operation; others came on regularly scheduled week days and still others occasionally. To provide for continuity and uniformity of direction in processing the blood, four temporary persons were employed with special funds, the salary of one being met by private donation.

A letter of thanks and appreciation on the part of the Hospital to all blood donors was sent currently and, after the work was completed, a letter of appreciation went forward to the volunteers who donated their services.

In spite of these diversions from the regular work of the Hospital, I think I may safely say that the past year has not been without steady gains in a number of different directions. Gains in quantity of service are gains only if the quality of such service has been strictly maintained or improved. This can be stated without fear of contradiction, both as to quantity and quality. The number of admissions of in-patients, namely 16,668, as well as the total number of hospital days, 236,851, are new highs of service. Semi-Private admissions numbered 2,703, and Private patient admissions totaled 2,746. The total number of OPD visits exceeded 350,000 for the first time. Due to the change in the character of the neighborhood, there has been a great increase in the number of emergency treatments in the Accident Ward which have now reached a level of 21,807 as against a range of from 10,000 to 12,000 only a few years ago. The Consultation Service continues to grow as is indicated by the fact that the total for 1940 of 3,098 patients is two and one-half times as great as the number accepted in 1934.

These statistics have been quoted in a rather sketchy way to indicate the general trend of the service rendered; more are set forth in greater detail in other pages of this printed report.

Next year we shall celebrate the 90th anniversary of the formation of the Hospital and it is, after these many years, a constant source of satisfaction to the Board of Trustees that its efforts to maintain the Hospital as an outstanding institution, comparable with any in the land, appeared to be appreciated by a considerable number of friends who continue to make this work possible by generous support. During the past year, the following gifts were made either by way of legacies or donations:

DEDICATION OF BEDS

Estate of Jacob Newman (additional).................................$16,635.41
> For the endowment of beds in memory of Jacob Newman.

Perpetual Beds:

> To the memory of Adolf F. and Rosa H. Hochstadter
> (two beds) 15,000.00
> Endowed by their son, Edwin A. Hochstadter.

Memorial Beds:

> In memory of Aaron and Amy H. Coleman............... 3,500.00
> Endowed by their daughters Constance Coleman
> and Janet E. Dillenberg.
>
> In memory of Moses Tanenbaum.. 2,650.83
> Founded by provision in his will.

Estate of Bella Stiefel.. 50,000.00
> For the endowment of the Bella Stiefel Ward

11

BEQUESTS

Estate of James Ulmann	$50,000.00
Estate of Ida Meyer	14,813.35
Estate of Fanny H. Cox	9,377.34
Estate of Emanuel Felsenheld (additional)	1,250.00
Estate of Alfred A. Kohn	1,000.00
Estate of Bertha Y. Lambert	1,000.00

LEGACIES AND DONATIONS OF $500 AND MORE FOR SPECIAL PURPOSES

Estate of Joseph F. Cullman (Received January 7, 1941—for Medical Education Fund).	50,000.00
Estate of Amalia F. Morse (special purposes)	15,000.00
David A. Schulte—For Dental Clinic	8,000.00
Friedsam Foundation, Inc.—For gastro-enterology research	5,000.00
Friedsam Foundation, Inc.—for research on nasal nerve pathways	1,350.00
Friedsam Foundation, Inc.—for research on the hypothalamus	1,200.00
Committee on Neighborhood Health Development, Inc. for intravenous Drip Therapy Project	5,006.11
Estate of Florentine S. Sutro—for the Florentine S. Sutro Research Fund	5,000.00
Dazian Foundation for Medical Research—for research in physiology and pharmacology of brain	2,000.00
Dazian Foundation for Medical Research—for studies on secretions of para-sympathetic substance	500.00
Dazian Foundation for Medical Research—for study of the chemical and physiological characteristics of intestinal secretions	500.00
John and Mary R. Markle Foundation—for research on amyotrophic lateral sclerosis	2,500.00

12

Josiah Macy, Jr. Foundation—for study of mechanism
of skin reactivity 1,650.00

Josiah Macy, Jr. Foundation—for studies on secretion
of parasympathetic substance 1,250.00

Hiram C. Bloomingdale and Samuel J. Bloomingdale
—In memory of Corrine B. Popper—for research
on multiple sclerosis 1,500.00

Mrs. Addie H. Homan—for the Isidore Hernsheim
Fellowship in Chemistry 1,500.00

Hoffman-La Roche, Inc.—for research on vitamins 1,500.00

John Wyeth and Brothers, Inc.—for study of intestinal
secretions 700.00

John Wyeth and Brothers, Inc.—for study of the continuous drip treatment 600.00

Williams, Waterman Fund—for Vitamin B-1 Research 1,250.00

Dr. Ralph Colp—for gastro-enterology research 1,250.00

Lucius N. Littauer Foundation, Inc.—for research on
Vitamins 1,200.00

Dr. I. C. Rubin—for Dr. Hiram N. Vineberg Fund for
gynecology research 1,200.00

American Lecithin Co., Inc.—for multiple sclerosis
Vitamin A research 1,025.00

Mr. and Mrs. Walter W. Naumburg—for non-
budgetary needs of Laboratory 1,000.00

Mrs. Levy Mayer—In memory of Walter A. Hirsch—
for leukemia research 1,000.00

Mount Sinai Hospital Research Foundation, Inc.—for
venom research 850.00

Mark and William Bernstein—for bacteriology re-
search 800.00

Louis Chiron—for special needs of the surgical group
in urology 500.00

"A Friend"—For Dr. Joseph Brettauer Fellowship
Fund (part payment toward a $1,200 grant)............ 500.00

Emergency Committee in Aid of Displaced Foreign
Medical Scientists-Stipend for Dr. Erich Kuznitzky 500.00

Max J. Shapiro—for support of neurology research...... 500.00

American Medical Association—to investigate the influence of nutrition and drugs on the cardiac output
in coronary occlusion 500.00

DONATIONS OF $500 OR MORE FOR SUPPORT OF CANCER RESEARCH
WORK OF DR. RICHARD LEWISOHN

New York Foundation, Inc. $6,500.00

Mrs. Arthur Lehman 3,500.00

The International Cancer Research Foundation............ 3,233.32

Frances and John Loeb Foundation.................................... 2,500.00

Miss Adelaide Reckford 1,500.00

Mrs. Louis J. Grumbach 500.00

DONATIONS OF $500 AND MORE FOR CARDIO-VASCULAR RESEARCH

Frank Altschul (through Greater New York Fund)... $1,000.00

Mrs. Charles Altschul 500.00

Anonymous 500.00

The expenditure for current purposes of the Hospital, including the School of Nursing, the Social Service Department and
the Ladies' Auxiliary in 1940 amounted to $2,398,595.02. Receipts
applicable to current expenditures were $2,309,225.96, leaving a
net deficit of $89,369.06. Included in these receipts are the
following:

Received from Federation $682,235.90

Received from Greater New York Fund (through
Federation)
Hospital Group $41,626.00
Social Service as part of United
Hospital Fund allotment for 1940   6,925.00

Total from Greater New York Fund
(through Federation) $48,551.00

Although I regret to have to report that we have not as yet succeeded in balancing our budget, it is pleasing to note that the deficit is less by about $80,000.00 than in the previous year. In my last year's report I referred to investigations that were being made with a view to reducing the deficits of hospitals and that Mount Sinai's representative was urging that certain changes in budget procedure be adopted. This was done at least for the current year and the more favorable outcome so far as the deficit of the Hospital is concerned is due in large part to such change in procedure. Income from practically all sources was calculated on a non-adjustable basis and more freedom in administering their budgets was given to all institutions. As a result, the Hospital has increased its income from a number of sources and has also instituted economies with the understanding that it would receive continuing benefit from both of these policies, at least until such time as its budget is balanced. I might also mention that Federation changed its budget year so that it now runs from July 1st to June 30th instead of from January 1st to December 31st. I wish also to refer to the fact that a plan was developed by Federation during the past year with a view to reducing the operating deficits of its societies. According to this so-called "Goetz Plan," a special fund of upward of $200,000 was raised which is to be used to pay institutions which reduce their deficits for the year 1940-41 on the basis of a dollar for each dollar of such reduction. This offer has also been an incentive to reduce the deficit as much as possible even though in some cases it has resulted to postponing expenditures for items which good management would ordinarily have cared for but which could be postponed for a later period, without undue risk of deterioration.

The Federation campaign, under the dynamic and able leadership of Judge Proskauer, was very successful and particularly so in view of the handicaps that it had to overcome in the shape of a hectic political campaign and the drives being made on behalf of many appealing over-seas causes. Judge Proskauer and the Businessmen's Council, as well as its able staff, are to be congratulated upon their fine results.

We have lost by death since the issuance of our last report our beloved colleague, Arthur Lorsch, who served the Hospital with great fidelity and generosity since his election as Trustee in 1928.

15

The resolution which was adopted on the occasion of his death is printed in full in this Annual Report. We also record with sorrow the death of two former Trustees of the Hospital who passed away during the past year; Mr. Martin Beck who was Trustee from 1922-29, and Mr. Henry R. Ickelheimer who was a Trustee from 1897 to 1904. We record with regret the deaths of the following employees and I take this opportunity of expressing our appreciation of their faithful service: Albert Littmann, Almo Baker, Martina Glass, and Kate Fitzgerald, a very old employee who had been pensioned in 1932 after forty-two years of active service in the Hospital.

Miss Cora Ball, R.N., Supervisor of the Children's Pavilion, was awarded a gold medal for twenty-five years of devoted service to the Hospital. Starting as a pupil nurse in 1911, after graduation she became a head nurse and, in 1916, was appointed Supervisor of the Children's Pavilion which position she held from that time until the present with only an interruption for the time during which she served overseas with Base Hospital No. 3.

In my last year's report I referred to the experiment which was being carried on in the intravenous drip method for the rapid treatment of syphilis and which it was expected would be completed in 1940. This proved to be the case and on April 12th a meeting was held in the George Blumenthal Auditorium to make public the details of the work which had been carried on at the Hospital for over two years on Dr. George Baehr's service under the direction of Drs. Harold T. Hyman, Louis Chargin and William Leifer. A distinguished group of syphilologists from many parts of the country was present and the new therapy was acclaimed as an important advance in the treatment of syphilis.

At the annual meeting of the Medical Society of the City of New York, held on May 1st, a prize was awarded in the clinical group to Dr. Arthur M. Master, who, in collaboration with Dr. Arthur Grishman, Dr. Simon Dack and Dr. Harry Jaffe, had given a demonstration of the fluorscopic diagnosis of coronary occlusion.

Our former Director and Trustee, Dr. S. S. Goldwater, received the 1940 award of merit from the American Hospital Association. During the year Dr. Goldwater resigned his post as Commissioner.

of Hospitals in New York City to assume the position of President of the Associated Hospital Service of New York.

Dr. George Baehr was again elected President of the Medical Board and has devoted himself unstintingly to the advancement of the Hospital's interests during the past year. He has been loyally supported by all the members of the medical staff who have, as usual, given of their time and effort with a degree of devotion which mere words cannot measure. Changes in the attending staff during the past year have consisted of resignations and new appointments as follows:

NEW APPOINTMENTS ON THE MEDICAL STAFF

Dr. Edgar M. Bick ....Associate Orthopedist

Dr. Saul W. Jarcho ....Adjunct Physician

Dr. Abraham Penner ....Adjunct Physician

Dr. Rene A. Spitz ....Adjunct Psychiatrist

Dr. Johan H. W. van Ophuijsen ....Adjunct Psychiatrist

Dr. Bettina Warburg ....Adjunct Psychiatrist

Dr. Edwin A. Weinstein ....Adjunct Neurologist

Dr. Benjamin B. Greenberg ....Adjunct Orthopedist

Dr. Sidney Blumenthal ....Adjunct Pediatrician

RESIGNATIONS FROM MEDICAL STAFF

Dr. Bernard S. Denzer ....Adjunct Pediatrician

Dr. Nathan Savitsky ....Adjunct Neurologist

Dr. Benjamin H. Balser ....Adjunct Neurologist

Dr. Harold T. Hyman asked to be relieved of his active duties for a period, so that he might devote more time to writing and his name is being carried on the roster of the Hospital as "Associate Physician, off duty."

Our laboratories have continued to work at top speed under the direction of Drs. Klemperer, Shwartzman, Sobotka, Globus and their staffs. Full reports on the work accomplished during 1940 will appear elsewhere in this volume. The Laboratory Administrative Committee, to which Drs. Isidore Friesner and

Robert T. Frank have given much of their time and thought, has continued to guide the general policy of the laboratories. The need of laboratory space is giving the Administration more and more concern as the serious effects of this growing bottleneck are being felt on all of the clinical services. The continually growing demand for diagnostic laboratory tests of all kinds and especially on the chemical side has developed into an almost insoluble problem. Additions to the present laboratories by using space in other departments have been made wherever practicable, but these have been merely stop-gaps. If the high reputation of the clinical services of the Hospital is to be maintained, some major additions to the laboratory facilities will have to be forthcoming very soon. This subject has been studied quite carefully and the best solution appears to be a new laboratory building on an available site which would not only take care of this urgent demand but would also house a number of other facilities of which the Hospital is in urgent need.

The other great need of the Hospital which we constantly sense is a maternity service. While we have often spoken of this in the past, the need has become more urgent of late because of the requirements which the Specialty Boards are setting up for qualifying and certifying specialists in various branches. The Mount Sinai Hospital is practically the only large general hospital in the City of New York which does not have its own obstetrical service and, as a result, the interns and residents are unable to secure this experience. Energetic efforts have been made during the past year to secure an affiliation with some hospital having an obstetrical service, but so far without result. The property on which such a maternity pavilion could be erected is available on 99th Street but the funds for construction unfortunately are lacking. Such a service would be in large measure self-supporting and I earnestly hope that we may in the not too distant future, be in a position to proceed with this development.

During the past year four new trustees were elected as follows:

Mr. George Lee—for the term expiring 1942.

Mr. Herman F. Baerwald—for the term expiring 1943.

Mr. Phillip W. Haberman, Jr.—for the term expiring 1943.

Mr. Jacob C. Stone—for the term expiring 1943.

18

We are very happy to welcome these gentlemen to the Board, all of whom have shown their great interest in the work of the Hospital.

No alterations of a major nature were made during this year, although one might mention a number of necessary repairs and replacements which inevitably occur in a plant as large as this.

The medical instruction program has been continued and enlarged. The clinical pathological conferences continue to draw large interested professional audiences ranging upward from 350, and the surgical demonstrations and medical clinics, which are held throughout the year in the renovated amphitheatre are very well attended.

The post-graduate courses given in affiliation with Columbia University registered their largest attendance numbering 329 in 1940. The Hospital, as usual, participated in the annual Graduate Fortnight of the New York Academy of Medicine which dealt with "Medical and Surgical Aspects of Infections." Many members of our staff contributed clinics, lectures and scientific exhibits. The George Blumenthal Auditorium has again been the scene of many lectures by distinguished members of the medical profession.

A symposium was held on Sigmund Freud, in which Dr. Fritz Wittles, Dr. Israel S. Wechsler and Dr. Lawrence S. Kubie participated. There was also a series of eight lectures on Vitamins as follows:

"Vitamin A and Vision," by Dr. Selig Hecht ,Professor Biophysics, Columbia University.

"Clinical Aspects of Vitamin B Deficiencies," by Dr. Norman Jolliffe, Associate Professor of Medicine, New York University College of Medicine, Chief of the Medical Service, Psychiatric Division, Bellevue Hospital.

"Physiological and Clinical Significance of Vitamin K," by Dr. A. M. Snell, Mayo Clinic, Rochester, Minn.

"Vitamin C," by Dr. Gilbert Dalldorf, Chief of Laboratories, Grasslands Hospital, Valhalla, N. Y.

"Vitamin A," by Dr. Hans Popper, Cook County Graduate School of Medicine, Chicago, Ill.

"Lesions of the Nervous System and Skeletal Muscles in Diet Deficient in Vitamin E," by Dr. Alwin ` Pappenheimer, Professor of Pathology, Columbia University.

"Vitamin D—Formation, Clinical Pathology and Therapeutic Indication," by Dr. Benjamin Kramer, Chief of Pediatrics, Jewish Hospital, Brooklyn, N. Y.

"Riboflavin," by Dr. William H. Sebrell, United States Public Health Service, Washington, D. C.

The William Henry Welch Lecture was given by Dr. Peyton Rous, member of the Rockefeller Institute for Medical Research, on "Conditions Determining Cancer and the Known Causes of Cancer," and the Edward Gamaliel Janeway Lecture by Dr. Max Bergmann, also of the Rockefeller Institute, on "Some Biological Aspects of Protein Chemistry."

The Mount Sinai Journal is another educational factor which continues on the upgrade. Subscribers are increasing in number and the Journal continues to have a wider and more important number of outlets. One of the special features during the past year was the volume published in the honor of the eightieth birthday of Dr. Howard Lilienthal to whom a reception was given on this occasion.

Although the School of Nursing will publish its own report in this volume, I cannot refrain from referring to the fact that at the end of 1940, Mr. Hugo Blumenthal, its President for a period of almost twenty-five years, resigned from that office and was elected Honorary President. His devotion to the interests of the School and his sympathetic understanding of the needs of its pupils for this long period could not have been excelled. His decision to withdraw from the office was a source of universal regret which is somewhat tempered by the fact that he continues his active interest in the School. The School is fortunate in having as his successor Mr. Alfred L. Rose who, for a number of years, has acted as Vice-President. The Hospital, as always, is indebted to the School of Nursing for its valuable contribution to the success of the Hospital's work and this, of course, is due in large part to the able direction given by Miss Grace Warman, the Principal of the School.

One of the gratifying accomplishments of the year was the completion of the gradual process which has been going on for some time of reducing the hours of nurses on the wards to a maximum of forty-eight hours a week. In the Private Pavilion the optional method by which doctors, nurses and patients are able to choose whether they wish the eight hour or the twelve hour service was continued and there was little variation from previous experience in the number of those who elect either method.

A large number of patients admitted into the Private and Semi-Private Pavilions are subscribers to the Associated Hospital Service. The total number of days' care covered by these policies was about 16% less than in 1939.

Throughout the year, Mr. George Blumenthal, President Emeritus, has been most helpful on every occasion in being available for advice with respect to broad policy, and I feel deeply indebted to him for his help.

The Social Service Department, under the able leadership of Mrs. Alfred A. Cook and her associates, and under the direction of Mrs. Fanny H. Mendelsohn, maintained its high standard of work of the past. The Social Service Workroom, which is operating in the building formerly used as an isolation building, continued as an important factor in the therapeutic work of the Out-Patient Department and, under the direction of the Workroom Committee consisting of Miss Edith Sachs, Mrs. Robert E. Binger and Mrs. Siegfried F. Hartman, did a fine piece of work. The outlet for its products was increased by providing additional work for the patients through the generosity of Miss Edith Sachs who donated funds and her time for making articles for the Red Cross. Mrs. Leonard Cohn, in the field of occupational therapy, made an outstanding contribution to the welfare of our patients.

I wish there were some way of informing the public of the large amount of fine work done by the lay volunteers in the Hospital. There are not less than 135 volunteers who give unstintingly of their time without other compensation than the satisfaction of doing work of an essential character for those who need such help. It is a pleasure to pay this slight tribute to their unselfish devotion.

21

A separate report, covering the work of the Neustadter Home, will appear in this volume, but I wish to stress the great advance which has been made during the past year in the care of our convalescents. Mrs. Walter A. Hirsch as President and the other Officers and Directors of this affiliated institution have won recognition from experts in the field of convalescent care and this Home is now regarded as one of the most progressive institutions of its kind.

Mrs. Leopold Bernheimer, President of the Ladies' Auxiliary, and her associates have again placed the Hospital under lasting obligation by their continued interest and devotion to their important work.

We wish once more to express our sincere gratitude for the sympathetic cooperation received from Mayor LaGuardia, Comptroller McGoldrick and the other members of the Board of Estimate, as well as from the Commissioners of Hospitals, Health and Welfare, all of which we deeply appreciate.

To our able Director, Dr. Joseph Turner, and to his associates, Drs. Katzive, Frank and Kreeger, we wish to pay tribute for the excellent service rendered. Our many Department Heads and their staffs have all contributed to the success of the operation of the Hospital and we are deeply appreciative of their services.

The United Hospital Fund and the Greater New York Fund have once more performed a signal service to the social work of the community by raising funds from the public and distributing them to the constituent societies on the basis of work performed and urgent needs. To both these organizations we extend our heartfelt thanks.

To all the friends and supporters of the Hospital, I wish to extend sincere thanks for their unswerving loyalty without which the work of the Hospital could not be successfully carried on.

LEO ARNSTEIN,
President.

In Memoriam

ALBERT LITTMAN
Employed 13½ Years
X-RAY
Died March 2, 1940

KATE FITZGERALD
Employed 42 Years
HOUSEKEEPING
(Pensioned May 1, 1932)
Died May 15, 1940

ALMO BAKER
Employed 3 Years
OUT-PATIENT
Died August 12, 1940

MARTINA GLASS
Employed 8 Years
LAUNDRY
Died December 11, 1940

TRUSTEES

25

28

OFFICERS AND STANDING COMMITTEES OF THE
MEDICAL BOARD FOR 1941

GEORGE BAEHR, M.D...*President*
HAROLD NEUHOF, M.D..*Vice-President*
IRA COHEN, M.D...*Secretary*

Executive (Conference) Committee

HAROLD NEUHOF, M.D..*Chairman*

GEORGE BAEHR, M.D.   KAUFMAN SCHLIVEK, M.D.
RALPH COLP. M.D.   HARRY H. SOBOTKA, PH.D.
ISIDOR C. RUBIN, M.D.   ISRAEL S. WECHSLER, M.D.

Committee on Medical Instruction

REUBEN OTTENBERG, M.D.........................(Acting) Chairman*

*BURRILL B. CROHN, M.D.   PAUL KLEMPERER, M.D.
*JOSEPH GLOBUS, M.D.   ELI MOSCHCOWITZ, M.D.
*CHARLES K. FRIEDBERG, M.D.   *ARTHUR M. MASTER, M.D.
.**B. S. Oppenheimer, M.D.

Committee on Intern Examinations

RALPH COLP, M.D. ....*Chairman*
*ARTHUR M. FISHBERG, M.D.   ISRAEL S. WECHSLER, M.D.

Committee on Residencies

HAROLD NEUHOF, M.D. ....*Chairman*
PAUL KLEMPERER, M.D.   GREGORY SHWARTZMAN, M.D.
and the Head of the Clinical Service

Surgical Committee

HAROLD NEUHOF, M.D. ....*Chairman*

IRA COHEN, M.D.   RUDOLPH KRAMER, M.D.
RALPH COLP, M.D.   ROBERT K. LIPPMANN, M.D.
JOHN H. GARLOCK, M.D.   JACOB L. MAYBAUM, M.D.
SAMUEL H. GEIST, M.D.   ISIDOR C. RUBIN, M.D.
ABRAHAM HYMAN, M.D.   SETH SELIG, M.D.
KAUFMAN SCHLIVEK, M.D.

Committee on Fellowships

SAMUEL H. GEIST, M.D...*Chairman*

*ERNST P. BOAS, M.D.   RUDOLPH KRAMER, M.D.
JOHN H. GARLOCK, M.D.   GREGORY SHWARTZMAN, M.D.
PAUL KLEMPERER, M.D.   HARRY H. SOBOTKA, Ph.D.

---

* Not a member of the Medical Board.
** On Consulting Staff.

OFFICERS AND STANDING COMMITTEES OF THE MEDICAL BOARD FOR 1941

(Continued)

Committee on Laboratories

RALPH COLP, M.D..Chairman
PAUL KLEMPERER, M.D. HARRY H. SOBOTKA, Ph.D.
GREGORY SHWARTZMAN, M.D.

Committee on Radiology

ABRAHAM HYMAN, M.D...Chairman
WILLIAM BIERMAN, M.D. WILLIAM HARRIS, M.D.
*HARRY A. GOLDBERG, D.D.S. *COLEMAN B. RABIN, M.D.
MARCY L. SUSSMAN, M.D.

Committee on Out-Patient Department

JOHN H. GARLOCK, M.D..Chairman
*LEONARD J. DRUCKERMAN, M.D. JACOB L. MAYBAUM, M.D.
WILLIAM HARRIS, M.D. ISADORE ROSEN, M.D.
RUDOLPH KRAMER, M.D. SETH SELIG, M.D.
KAUFMAN SCHLIVEK, M.D.

Committee on Nurses

BELA SCHICK, M.D. ....Chairman
*DAVID BECK, M.D. RALPH COLP, M.D.
ISIDOR C. RUBIN, M.D.

Committee on Records

RUDOLPH KRAMER, M.D..Chairman
*MURRAY H. BASS, M.D. *SIGMUND MAGE, M.D.
*FREDERICK H. KING, M.D. SETH SELIG, M.D.
*PERCY KLINGENSTEIN, M.D. *SOLOMON SILVER, M.D.

Committee on Cardiography

*ERNST P. BOAS, M.D...Chairman
*ARTHUR M. FISHBERG, M.D. *ARTHUR M. MASTER, M.D.
*WILLIAM M. HITZIG, M.D. *IRVING R. ROTH, M.D.

Committee on Social Service

ISRAEL S. WECHSLER, M.D. ....Chairman
*SAMUEL H. AVERBUCK, M.D. *LAWRENCE S. KUBIE, M.D.
*SIDNEY BLUMENTHAL, M.D. *WILLIAM H. MENCHER, M.D.
*HERMAN ZAZEELA, M.D.

---

* Not a member of the Medical Board.

OFFICERS AND STANDING COMMITTEES OF THE MEDICAL BOARD FOR 1941

(Continued)

Dental Committee

JACOB L. MAYBAUM, M.D. ....*Chairman*
*CHARLES K. FRIEDBERG, M.D.   *JOSEPH SCHROFF, M.D., D.D.S.
*HARRY A. GOLDBERG, D.D.S.   *ARTHUR R. SOHVAL, M.D.
*LEO STERN, D.D.S.

Committee on Economy

HAROLD NEUHOF, M.D. ....*Chairman*
*ALFRED E. FISCHER, M.D.   MARCY L. SUSSMAN, M.D.
SAMUEL H. GEIST, M.D.   *ARTHUR S. W. TOUROFF, M.D.
*GORDON D. OPPENHEIMER, M.D.   *FREDERIC D. ZEMAN, M.D.

Committee on Pharmacy

*ARTHUR M. FISHBERG, M.D. ....*Chairman*
*MORRIS A. GOLDBERGER, M.D.   *ROBERT K. LAMBERT, M.D.
*SAMUEL KARELITZ, M.D.   *DANIEL POLL, M.D.
*FREDERICK H. KING, M.D. ..   *LESTER R. TUCHMAN, M.D.

Committee on Dietetics

BELA SCHICK, M.D. ....*Chairman*
*BURRILL B. CROHN, M.D.   *HERMAN LANDE, M.D.
*EDWARD B. GREENSPAN, M.D.   *HERBERT POLLACK, M.D.
*ASHER WINKELSTEIN, M.D.

Committee on Library

ELI MOSCHCOWITZ, M.D. ....*Chairman*
WILLIAM BIERMAN, M.D.   *LEON GINZBURG, M.D.
*LEO EDELMAN, M.D.   *SYLVAN E. MOOLTEN, M.D.
KAUFMAN SCHLIVEK, M.D.

Committee on Medical Publications

IRA COHEN, M.D. ....*Chairman*
RALPH COLP, M.D.   RUDOLPH KRAMER, M.D.
*JOSEPH H. GLOBUS, M.D.   *LOUIS J. SOFFER, M.D.

OFFICERS OF THE ASSOCIATION OF THE JUNIOR MEDICAL STAFF

ARTHUR S. W. TOUROFF, M.D. ....*Chairman*
MURRAY H. BASS, M.D. ....*Vice-Chairman*
SOLOMON SILVER, M.D. ....*Secretary*
PERCY KLINGENSTEIN, M.D. } *Delegates to the Medical Board*
FREDERIC D. ZEMAN, M.D. }

---

* Not a member of the Medical Board.

MEDICAL AND SURGICAL STAFF

(As of May 1, 1941)

CONSULTING STAFF

Physicians

Emanuel Libman, M.D. Alfred Meyer, M.D.
Morris Manges, M.D. Bernard S. Oppenheimer, M.D.

Pediatrician
Henry Heiman, M.D.

Neurologists

Bernard Sachs, M.D. Israel Strauss, M.D.

Surgeons

Albert A. Berg, M.D. Richard Lewisohn, M.D.
Charles A. Elsberg, M.D. Howard Lilienthal, M.D.

Gynecologists

Joseph Brettauer, M.D. Robert T. Frank, M.D.
Hiram N. Vineberg, M.D.

Otologists

Isidore Friesner, M.D. Fred Whiting, M.D.

Ophthalmic Surgeons

Carl Koller, M.D. Charles H. May, M.D.
Julius Wolff, M.D.

Orthopedist
Philip D. Wilson, M.D.

Physical Therapist
Heinrich F. Wolf, M.D.

Chemist
Samuel Bookman, Ph.D.

ASSOCIATE CONSULTING STAFF

Pediatrician
(c) Herman Schwarz, M.D.

Dermatologist
(c) Louis Chargin, M.D.

(c) Appointed 1941.

MEDICAL AND SURGICAL STAFF

MEDICAL SERVICE
Physicians

George Baehr, M.D.
(c) Eli Moschcowitz, M.D.

Associate Physicians

David Beck, M.D.
Ernst P. Boas, M.D.
(c) Arthur M. Fishberg, M.D.
**Harold T. Hyman, M.D.
Reuben Ottenberg, M.D.
Daniel Poll, M.D.
(c) Solomon Silver, M.D.

Associates in Medicine

Burrill B. Crohn, M.D.
Joseph Harkavy, M.D.
Herman Lande, M.D.
Arthur M. Master, M.D.
Coleman B. Rabin, M.D.
Nathan Rosenthal, M.D.
Irving R. Roth, M.D.
Asher Winkelstein, M.D.

Adjunct Physicians

#Samuel H. Averbuck, M.D.
#Solon S. Bernstein, M.D.
**Emanuel Z. Epstein, M.D.
#Philip Finkle, M.D.
**Charles K. Friedberg, M.D.
Ben Friedman, M.D.
#Edward B. Greenspan, M.D.
Herman Hennell, M.D.
(For Chest Diseases)
William M. Hitzig, M.D.
(c) Henry Horn, M.D.
Saul W. Jarcho, M.D.
Frederick H. King, M.D.
**S. S. Lichtman, M.D.
Sylvan E. Moolten, M.D.
Abraham Penner, M.D.
Arthur Schifrin, M.D.
Louis J. Soffer, M.D.
Arthur R. Sohval, M.D.
Lester R. Tuchman, M.D.
**Kaufman Wallach, M.D.
#Harry Weiss, M.D.
Frederic D. Zeman, M.D.

Assistant Physicians
(Out-Patient Department)

Morris Blum, M.D.
Alfred Romanoff, M.D.

Assistants in Medicine
(Hospital or Out-Patient Department)

Harold A. Abel, M.D.
Harold A. Abramson, M.D.
Hubert Mann, M.D.
Herbert Pollack, M.D.

** Off Service.
# For Special Service.
(c) Appointed 1941.

34

MEDICAL AND SURGICAL STAFF

MEDICAL SERVICE—(Continued)
Senior Clinical Assistants
(Out-Patient Department)

Salvatore Amato, M.D.
Frank A. Bassen, M.D.
Kurt Berliner, M.D.
Herbert Blau, M.D.
N. W. Chaikin, M.D.
Morris Chamurich, M.D.
Simon Dack, M.D.
Henry Dolger, M.D.
Joseph Echtman, M.D.
Henry Feibes, M.D.
Sydney C. Feinberg, M.D.
Samuel A. Feldman, M.D.
(a) Emil Granet, M.D.
Selian Hebald, M.D.
Joseph Herzstein, M.D.
Harry L. Jaffe, M.D.
Abraham Jezer, M.D.
Herbert Lampert, M.D.
Sidney Levinson, M.D.
Frederick J. Lewy, M.D.
Hyman Levy, M.D.
Adolph A. Lilien, M.D.

Fred E. Maisel, M.D.
Charles R. Messeloff, M.D.
Pedro N. Ortiz, M.D.
David Paley, M.D.
Frank Pierson, M.D.
Philip Reichert, M.D.
Joseph Reiss, M.D.
Alfred Romanoff, M.D.
Herman S. Roth, M.D.
Robert V. Sager, M.D.
I. Scotty Schapiro, M.D.
Siegfried S. Schatten, M.D.
(a) S. Stanley Schneierson, M.D.
Sheppard Siegal, M.D.
Morris T. Siegel, M.D.
David A. Singer, M.D.
Joseph I. Singer, M.D.
J. Edward Stern, M.D.
Abraham Sternbach, M.D.
Peter Vogel, M.D.
Harry Yarnis, M.D.
(a) Bernard M. Zussman, M.D.

Clinical Assistants
(Out-Patient Department)

Frederic S. Adler, M.D.
David Adlersberg, M..D.
John Amoruso, M.D.
Ludwig Anfanger, M.D.
Victor Apt, M.D.
(a) Joseph Bandes, M.D.
Hans W. Baum, M.D.
(a) Samuel H. Belgorod, M.D.
Bennett W. Billow, M.D.
Hyman B. Birnbaum, M.D.
Perry Blumberg, M.D.
William H. Branch, M.D.
Jack S. Brandes, M.D.
Frederick Bridge, M.D.
Paul N. Bulova, M.D.
Anne F. Casper, M.D.
Ralph Cohen, M.D.
Felix Cohn, M.D.
George C. Cole, M.D.
Hans R. Coler, M.D.
Salvatore J. Contento, M.D.

Albert Cornell, M.D.
D. Alfred Dantes, M.D.
Max David, M.D.
Henry L. Dorfmann, M.D.
Morris L. Drazin, M.D.
Morton H. Edelman, M.D.
Milton E. Eisen, M.D.
Max Ellenberg, M.D.
Alan Emanuel, M.D.
Kurt Esser, M.D.
Paul Fagin, M.D.
Josef Faltitschek, M.D.
Leon Figur, M.D.
(a) Leonard E. Field, M.D.
Rudolph Friedman, M.D.
Isadore E. Gerber, M.D.
Seymour Goldgraben, M.D.
Irving Goldmacher, M.D.
Sidney L. Gottlieb, M.D.
Isidore M. Greenberger, M.D.
Arthur Grishman, M.D.

(a) On Military Service.

35

MEDICAL AND SURGICAL STAFF

MEDICAL SERVICE—(Continued)

Clinical Assistants (Continued)

(Out-Patient Department)

Edward B. Grossman, M.D.
Farkas W. Gruber, M.D.
Herbert L. Gutstein, M.D.
Ernst Hammerschlag, M.D.
Samuel A. Handelsman, M.D.
Herman G. Helpern, M.D.
Leo Hennell, M.D.
Michael Iserman, M.D.
Louis A. Izenstein, M.D.
Friedrich Kach, M.D.
Edward Kahn, M.D.
Henry H. Kalter, M.D.
S. Lawrence Kaman, M.D.
David Kastoff, M.D.
Erich Kaufmann, M.D.
Goodell G. Klevan, M.D.
(a) J. John Kristal, M.D.
Victor H. Kugel, M.D.
Morton Kulick, M.D.
(a) H. Richard Landmann, M.D.
Nicholas Langer, M.D.
Daniel Laszlo, M.D.
Alan Leslie, M.D.
Carl L. Levenson, M.D.
William Levison, M.D.
Milton H. Levy, M.D.
Walter Loewenberg, M.D.
Walter Loewenstein, M.D.
Harold L. Margulies, M.D.
Rafael A. Marin, M.D.
Jacob D. Matis, M.D.
Milton Mendlowitz, M.D.
Martin M. Meyer, M.D.
Nathan Meyer, M.D.
Harvey Nussbaum, M.D.
Louis Part, M.D.
Samuel J. Penchansky, M.D.
Roman B. Perkul, M.D.

(a) Arthur Post, M.D.
Randolph Rosenthal, M.D.
Harry N. Rothman, M.D.
Fritz Riesenfeld, M.D.
(a) Norman A. Samuels, M.D.
Irving A. Sarot, M.D.
Maxwell Sayet, M.D.
Gerhard Schauer, M.D.
Siegfried Schoenfeld, M.D.
Arthur W. Seligmann, Jr., M.D.
Alfred Selinger, M.D.
Isadore M. Siegel, M.D.
David L. Silberman, M.D.
Alexander G. Silberstein, M.D.
Irving Solomon, M.D.
Irving Somach, M.D.
Eugene Somkin, M.D.
Arthur Sonnenfeld, M.D.
S. Zelig Sorkin, M.D.
Alfred Sorter, M.D.
Daniel Stats, M.D.
Morris F. Steinberg, M.D.
Milton H. Stillerman, M.D.
Jenny Stricker, M.D.
Oscar Tannenbaum, M.D.
Milton Tanzer, M.D.
Meyer Texon, M.D.
Alexander Thomas, M.D.
Mary C. Tyson, M.D.
(a) John V. Waller, M.D.
Louis R. Wasserman, M.D.
Charles Weisberg, M.D.
Marcus Widmann, M.D.
Victor Willner, M.D.
E. Gunther Wolff, M.D.
Morton Yohalem, M.D.
Mario Volterra, M.D.
Morris Zuckerbrod, M.D.

(a) On Military Service.

36

MEDICAL AND SURGICAL STAFF

PEDIATRIC SERVICE

Pediatrician
Bela Schick, M.D.

Associate Pediatricians
Murray H. Bass, M.D. (c)Jerome L. Kohn, M.D.
(b)Herman Schwarz, M.D.

Associates in Pediatrics
M. Murray Peshkin, M.D. Ira S. Wile, M.D.

Adjunct Pediatricians
Sidney Blumenthal, M.D. #George J. Ginandes, M.D.
***Bernard S. Denzer, M.D. Samuel Karelitz, M.D.
Alfred E. Fischer, M.D. (c)Samuel B. Weiner, M.D.
**Sara Welt, M.D.

Assistant Pediatricians
(Out-Patient Department)
U. Himmelstein, M.D. Irving R. Roth, M.D.
William Rosenson, M.D. Henry M. Weisman, M.D.
Harry O. Zamkin, M.D.

Assistants in Pediatrics
(Hospital or Out-Patient Department)
Margit Freund, M.D. Anne Topper, M.D.

Senior Clinical Assistants
(Out-Patient Department)

John Bauer, M.D.	Sidney D. Leader, M.D.
Eugene Bernstein, M.D.	Edward Lehman, M.D.
Henry H. Blum, M.D.	Harry S. Mackler, M.D.
Max Chidekel, M.D.	Joseph Mayeroff, M.D.
Harry J. Cohen, M.D.	William Messer, M.D.
Samuel Ehre, M.D.	Bessie Metrick, M.D.
Jacob Elitzak, M.D.	Morton R. Milsner, M.D.
Else Farmer, M.D.	Stephan Mussliner, M.D.
Gertrude Felshin, M.D.	Hanna Mulier, M.D.
Irving Feuer, M.D.	Arthur Nathan, M.D.
Maurice Gelb, M.D.	George Neuhaus, M.D.
Fred Glucksman, M.D.	William Neuland, M.D.
Henry L. Greene, M.D.	Albert B. Newman, M.D.
Ferenc Grossman, M.D.	Harry D. Pasachoff, M.D.
Maurice Grozin, M.D.	Abraham I. Rosenstein, M.D.
Harold Herman, M.D.	Gustav Salomon, M.D.
Wilfred C. Hulse, M.D.	J. Schwarsbram, M.D.
Godel I. Hunter, M.D.	William A. Schonfeld, M.D.
Raphael Isaacs, M.D.	Adele Sicular, M.D.
M. J. Karsh, M.D.	Morris Sonberg, M.D.
Eva C. Kivelson, M.D.	Rose G. Spiegel, M.D.
	Fannie Stoll, M.D.

** Off Service.
*** Resigned.
# For Special Service.
(b) Until April 30, 1941.
(c) Appointed 1941.

MEDICAL AND SURGICAL STAFF

PEDIATRIC SERVICE—(Continued)
Senior Clinical Assistants (Continued)
(Out-Patient Department)

Jacob Sugarman, M.D.
Fritz Weil, M.D.

Anna Weintraub, M.D.
Alexander Winter, M.D.

Carl Zelson, M.D.

Clinical Assistants
(Out-Patient Department)

George Bair, M.D.
Paul Barber, M.D.
(a) Arthur J. Berger, M.D.
Harvey Brandon, M.D.
Paul N. Bulova, M.D.
Ralph Cohen, M.D.
Samuel H. Dender, M.D.
Albert Dingmann, M.D.
Henry M. Eisenoff, M.D.
Ralph Feig, M.D.
Joseph A. Graham, M.D.
Franz H. Hanau, M.D.
(a) Charles R. Hayman, M.D.
Lotte Heinemann, M.D.
Mark Imberman, M.D.
Dora Joelson, M.D.
Else Kaufmann, M.D.
S. Lawrence Kaman, M.D.
Israel S. Klieger, M.D.
Walter H. Levy, M.D.

Saul Lieb, M.D.
Aron M. Martin, M.D.
Jacob D. Matis, M.D.
Lydia Shapiro-Mindlin, M.D.
Antoine Noti, M.D.
Rudolf Pollak, M.D.
Carl Pototzky, M.D.
Howard G. Rapaport, M.D.
Elwood Roodner, M.D.
Karl Rosenthal, M.D.
Frederick Redlich, M.D.
Jacob L. Rothstein, M.D.
Maury Sanger, M.D.
B. M. Schegloff, M.D.
Eugene E. Schwarz, M.D.
Victoria Soloway, M.D.
Ernst Steinitz, M.D.
Rudolf Strauss, M.D.
Philip Weissman, M.D.
Selma Wertheimer, M.D.

Morton W. Willis, M.D.

Volunteers

Howard G. Rapaport, M.D.
Frieda Rath, M.D.

Rose G. Spiegel, M.D.
(b) Herman Vollmer, M.D.

** Off Service.
(a) On Military Service.
(b) Until April 30, 1941.

MEDICAL AND SURGICAL STAFF

NEUROLOGICAL SERVICE

Neurologist
Israel S. Wechsler, M.D.

Associate Neurologists
Richard M. Brickner, M.D.   Joseph H. Globus, M.D.

Associate Psychiatrists
Lawrence S. Kubie, M.D.   **Sandor Lorand, M.D.
**Clarence P. Oberndorf, M.D.

Adjunct Neurologists
Morris B. Bender, M.D.   Judah Marmor, M.D.
Irving Bieber, M.D.   William Needles, M.D.
(a) Norman Q. Brill, M.D.   Edwin A. Weinstein, M.D.

Adjunct Psychiatrists
Arnold Eisendorfer, M.D.   Leo Stone, M.D.
Sol W. Ginsburg, M.D.   Johan H. W. van Ophuijsen, M.D.
Rene A. Spitz, M.D.   Bettina Warburg, M.D.

Assistant in Neurology
(Hospital or Out-Patient Department)
Joseph Salan, M.D.

Assistant in Psychiatry
(Hospital or Out-Patient Department)
Arpad Pauncz, M.D.

Senior Clinical Assistant
(Out-Patient Department)
(Neurology)
Alexis Gottlieb, M.D.   Jacob Leffkowitz, M.D.
George Trefousse, M.D.

Senior Clinical Assistants
(Out-Patient Department)
(Psychiatry)
Abraham H. Apter, M.D.   P. Goolker, M.D.
Herman G. Selinsky, M.D.

Clinical Assistants
(Out-Patient Department)
(Neurology)
Renato J. Almansi, M.D.   David Gersten, M.D.
David Beres, M.D.   Manfred L. Gorten, M.D.
Felix O. Durham, M.D.   Paul Loewy, M.D.
Frank P. Eves, M.D.   Kurt Spaeth, M.D.

(a) On Military Service.
** Off Service.

39

MEDICAL AND SURGICAL STAFF

NEUROLOGICAL SERVICE—(Continued)
Clinical Assistants—(Continued)
(Out-Patient Department)
(Psychiatry)

Harold Aaron, M.D.
George G. Arato, M.D.
Emil A. Gutheil, M.D.
Edward E. Harkavy, M.D.
Bela H. Heksh, M.D.
(a) Samuel Kahn, M.D.
Mark G. Kanzer, M.D.
Margaret Mahler-Schoenberger, M.D.
(a) Daniel M. Lipshutz, M.D.
Max L. Loeb, M.D.
Heinrich J. Lowenfeld, M.D.
Olga Lowenfeld, M.D.

Erich Mosse, M.D.
Annie Reich, M.D.
Nathaniel Ross, M.D.
Ernst Rothe, M.D.
Viva Schatia, M.D.
Judith Silberpfennig, M.D.
Melitta Sperling, M.D.
Otto Sperling, M.D.
Sidney Tarachow, M.D.
Edgar C. Trautmann, M.D.
Howard L. Werner, M.D.
Herbert Wiggers, M.D.

Research Assistants

Samuel Atkin, M.D.
George S. Goldman, M.D.
Hans Strauss, M.D.

DERMATOLOGICAL SERVICE
Dermatologist
Isadore Rosen, M.D.
Associate Dermatologists
(b) Louis Chargin, M.D.
Oscar L. Levin, M.D.
Adjunct Dermatologists
Samuel M. Peck, M.D.
Max Scheer, M.D.
Assistant Dermatologists
(Out-Patient Department)
Lewis A. Goldberger, M.D.
Arthur Sayer, M.D.
Henry Silver M.D.
Charles Wolf, M.D.

Senior Clinical Assistants
(Out-Patient Department)

D. B. Ballin, M.D.
Max Berkovsky, M.D.
Eugene T. Bernstein, M.D.
Raphael Breakstone, M.D.
Frank E. Cross, M.D.
Julius Davis, M.D.
H. C. Herrman, M.D.
David Kane, M.D.
H. J. Kohnstam, M.D.
William Leifer, M.D.

Adrian Neumann, M.D.
Kermit E. Osserman, M.D.
Sidney B. Rooff, M.D.
Herbert Rosenfeld, M.D.
G. Rubin, M.D.
Joel Schweig, M.D.
(d) Harry Sherwood, M.D.
Harry E. Slatkin, M.D.
Samuel Strumwasser, M.D.
(d) Maurice Umansky, M.D.

E. N. Winograd, M.D.

(a) On Military Service.
(b) Until April 30, 1941.
(d) Also in Arseno-Therapy Clinic.

MEDICAL AND SURGICAL STAFF

DERMATOLOGICAL SERVICE—(Continued)
Clinical Assistants
(Out-Patient Department)

Ernest Bass, M.D.
Howard T. Behrman, M.D.
Erich Buechler, M.D.
Friedrich J. Ebstein, M.D.
Arthur W. Glick, M.D.
Fritz W. Gutmann, M.D.
Alfred Hess, M.D.
Moses H. Holland, M.D.
Adolf Krakauer, M.D.
Abner Kurtin, M.D.
Frederick B. Laufer, M.D.
Ernest W. Nathan, M.D.
Alfred Petersen, M.D.

S. J. Rabinowitz, M.D.
Ellen Reiner, M.D.
Ferd. Rosenberger, M.D.
Moritz Salmonski-Rosen, M.D.
Irving H. Silverstein, M.D.
Julius Simon, M.D.
(a) Kona Simon, M.D.
Abraham M. Skern, M.D.
Adolf Sternberg, M.D.
Bruno Tyson, M.D.
Gustav Weissberg, M.D.
Karl Weissberger, M.D.
Morton Yohalem, M.D.

(a) Reuben Yontef, M.D.

Volunteer
Herbert Rosenfeld, M.D.

SURGICAL SERVICE
Surgeons
Ralph Colp, M.D.
John H. Garlock, M.D.

Abraham Hyman, M.D.
Harold Neuhof, M.D.

Associate Surgeons
Leo Edelman, M.D.
Leon Ginzburg, M.D.

Percy Klingenstein, M.D.
Arthur S. W. Touroff, M.D.

Adjunct Surgeons
Ernest E. Arnheim, M.D.
Arthur H. Aufses, M.D.
Maurice M. Berck, M.D.
Leonard J. Druckerman, M.D.
Ameil Glass, M.D.
Samuel H. Klein, M.D.

H. Evans Leiter, M.D.
Sigmund Mage, M.D.
William H. Mencher, M.D.
Gordon D. Oppenheimer, M.D.
Myron A. Sallick, M.D.
#Samuel Silbert, M.D.

Moses Swick, M.D.

Assistant Surgeon
(Out-Patient Department)
˙ Sylvan D. Manheim, M.D.

For Special Service.
(a) On Military Service.

MEDICAL AND SURGICAL STAFF

SURGICAL SERVICE—(Continued)
Senior Clinical Assistants
(Out-Patient Department)

Moses Benmosche, M.D.
Harry J. Bettauer, M.D.
(a) Sydney Bressler, M.D.
Daniel Casten, M.D.
George F. Dayton, M.D.
Milton M. Eckert, M.D.
Norman L. Goldberg, M.D.
Aron Goldschmidt, M.D.
Milton H. Goolde, M.D.
Sidney Grossman, M.D.

Borris A. Kornblith, M.D.
Norman F. Laskey, M.D.
Henry Peskin, M.D.
H. G. Rose, M.D.
Gustav Rosenburg, M.D.
Emil Schnebel, M.D.
Arthur Simon, M.D.
Rose Spiegel, M.D.
Irwin P. Train, M.D.
Ralph W. Watsky, M.D.

Herman Zazeela, M.D.

Clinical Assistants
(Out-Patient Department)

(a) Robert H. Abrahamson, M.D.
Maurice Alden, M.D.
Aaron Berger, M.D.
Harry Bergman, M.D.
Joseph Birnbaum, M.D.
William Braunstein, M.D.
Leon M. Caplan, M.D.
Jerome S. Coles, M.D.
Kurt Cronheim, M.D.
Arthur Dallos, M.D.
Henry Doubilet, M.D.
Walter Edkins, M.D.
Celia Ekelson, M.D.
Robert C. Elitzik, M.D.
Fritz Falk, M.D.
Bernard Friedman, M.D.
Benjamin Glick, M.D.
Meyer L. Goldman, M.D.
Hirsch L. Gordon, M.D.
William Hayn, M.D.
Nathan B. Hirschfeld, M.D.
Max Jacoby, M.D.
(a) Julian A. Jarman, M.D.
Herman I. Kantor, M.D.
Harry Kassop, M.D.
Mark J. Markham, M.D.

Helmuth Nathan, M.D.
Hellmuth Oppenheimer, M.D.
Jesse Patt, M.D.
Willy Perez, M.D.
Erich Plocki, M.D.
(a) Aaron Prigot, M.D.
(a) Irving R. Rachlin, M.D.
Benjamin Ritter, M.D.
Gerhart Sachs, M.D.
M. Salzberg, M.D.
David Schwartz, M.D.
Emil Schwarzmann, M.D.
Gabriel P. Seley, M.D.
Sigmund A. Siegel, M.D.
Richard Steen, M.D.
Meyer M. Stone, M.D.
David J. Surrey, M.D.
Joseph A. Tamerin, M.D.
Alexander Thomas, M.D.
Robert Turell, M.D.
Herbert G. Weichsel, M.D.
Leonard Weinroth, M.D.
Vernon A. Weinstein, M.D.
Julius L. Weissberg, M.D.
Eric Wohlauer, M.D.
Saul Zager, M.D.

Thomas S. Zimmer, M.D.

Volunteers

Henry Doubilet, M.D.
Edward E. Jemerin, M.D.
Irving A. Sarot, M.D.
Gabriel P. Seley, M.D.

Alfred R. Shepard, D.D.S.
Alexander Thomas, M.D.
(b) Irwin P. Train, M.D.
Vernon A. Weinstein, M.D.

Julius L. Weissberg, M.D.

(a) On Military Service.
(b) Until April 30, 1941.

42

MEDICAL AND SURGICAL STAFF

NEURO-SURGICAL SERVICE
Neuro-Surgeon
Ira Cohen, M.D.

Associate Neuro-Surgeon
Abraham Kaplan, M.D.

Adjunct Neuro-Surgeon
Sidney W. Gross, M.D.

GENITO-URINARY DIVISION OF OUT-PATIENT DEPARTMENT OF SURGICAL SERVICE
Assistant Surgeons
(Out-Patient Department)

William Bisher, M.D.   Lewis T. Mann, M.D.
Jerome M. Ziegler, M.D.

Senior Clinical Assistants
(Out-Patient Department)

N. D. Benezra, M.D.   Joseph Haas, M.D.
Jacob Birnbaum, M.D.   Edward Jacobs, M.D.
Henry Feibes, M.D.   Leo Jacoby, M.D.
William L. Ferber, M.D.   Edward E. Jemerin, M.D.
Edward O. Finestone, M.D.   Bernard D. Kulick, M.D.
Norman F. Laskey, M.D.

Clinical Assistants
(Out-Patient Department)

Max David, M.D.   Bruno Mark, M.D.
Lawrence Essenson, M.D.   David N. Marks, M.D.
Paul E. Gutman, M.D.   Pasquale Montilli, M.D.
Kurt A. Heinrich, M.D.   Natale A. Sabatino, M.D.
Harry D. Italiener, M.D.   David Schreiber, M.D.
Nathaniel C. Schlossmann, M.D.

GYNECOLOGICAL SERVICE
Gynecologists
Samuel H. Geist, M.D.   Isidor C. Rubin, M.D.

Associate Gynecologists
Morris A. Goldberger, M.D.   Max D. Mayer, M.D.

Adjunct Gynecologists
(a) Phineas Bernstein, M.D.   U. J. Salmon, M.D.
Joseph A. Gaines, M.D.   Seymour Wimpfheimer, M.D.

(a) On Military Service.

MEDICAL AND SURGICAL STAFF

GYNECOLOGICAL SERVICE—(Continued)
Assistant Gynecologists
(Out-Patient Department)
Morris Feresten, M.D.
Emanuel Klempner, M.D.
Maurice E. Mintz, M.D.
Frank Spielman, M.D.

Senior Clinical Assistants
(Out-Patient Department)
Isabel Beck, M.D.
Samuel G. Berkow, M.D.
Gertrude Felshin, M.D.
Eleanor B. Gutman, M.D.
H. C. Herrman, M.D.
Samuel Hochman, M.D.
(a) Monroe A. Rosenbloom, M..D
Paul Steinweg, M.D.
Leonard A. Zweibel, M.D.

Clinical Assistants
(Out-Patient Department)
Hans Auerbach, M.D.
Bernard Berglas, M.D.
Johanna N. Bulova, M.D.
Arthur M. Davids, M.D.
Hilliard Dubrow, M.D.
Irving C. Fischer, M.D.
Richard Fleischer, M.D.
Stephanie K. Haas, M.D.
Felix Jacobi, M.D.
Manes Klaften, M.D.
Bruno Kriss, M.D.
Maximilian Lewitter, M.D.
Harold S. Leopold, M.D.
H. Richard Mayer, M.D.
Nathan Mintz, M.D.
Walter B. Neubauer, M.D.
(a) Herbert F. Newman, M.D.
Josef Novak, M.D.
John O. Porges, M.D.
David N. Reiner, M.D.
James A. Rosen, M. D.
Raymond W. Sass, M.D.
Abbey D. Seley, M.D.
Robert Turell, M.D.
Robert I. Walter, M.D.
Louis Portnoy, M.D.
Elvira L. Wasserman, M.D.

OTOLOGICAL AND LARYNGOLOGICAL SERVICES
Otologist
Jacob L. Maybaum, M.D.

Associate Otologists
Joseph G. Druss, M.D.
Samuel Rosen, M.D.

Adjunct Otologists
Benjamin I. Allen, M.D.
Harry Rosenwasser, M.D.
Eugene R. Snyder, M.D.

Laryngologist
Rudolph Kramer, M.D.

Associate Laryngologists
Morris S. Bender, M.D.
Irving B. Goldman, M.D.

Adjunct Laryngologists
Joseph L. Goldman, M.D.
Louis Kleinfeld, M.D.
Max L. Som, M.D.

Assistant Oto-Laryngologist
(Out-Patient Department)
Harry D. Cohen, M.D.

(a) On Military Service.

44

MEDICAL AND SURGICAL STAFF

OTOLOGICAL AND LARYNGOLOGICAL SERVICES
(Continued)
Senior Clinical Assistants
(Out-Patient Department)

Adolph N. Abraham, M.D. William J. Hochbaum, M.L
Julius Golembe, M.D. S. Mencher, M.D.

Clinical Assistants
(Out-Patient Department)

Hans Brinitzer, M.D. Hans Meinrath, M.D.
Lester L. Coleman, M.D. A. Harry Neffson, M.D.
Wm. F. Mayer-Hermann, M.D. H. J. Rubenstein, M.D.
Fred L. Marx, M.D. Rudolf Singer, M.D.
(a) Michael S. Zeman, M.D.

OPHTHALMOLOGICAL SERVICE
Ophthalmic Surgeon
Kaufman Schlivek, M.D.

Associate Ophthalmic Surgeons
Robert K. Lambert, M.D. Henry Minsky, M.D.

Adjunct Ophthalmic Surgeons
Joseph Laval, M.D. David Wexler, M.D.

Assistant Ophthalmic Surgeons
(Out-Patient Department)
Murray A. Last, M.D. Herman Ostrow, M.D.

Senior Clinical Assistants
(Out-Patient Department)

Edward J. Bassen, M.D. Saul Miller, M.D.
Bertha Gladstern, M.D. Meta Mueller, M.D.
Abraham L. Kornzweig, M.D. M. Rosenbaum, M.D.

Clinical Assistants
(Out-Patient Department)

Philip L. Adalman, M.D. Alfred Kestenbaum, M.D.
Richard Baruch, M.D. Frank J. Langendorff, M.D.
Eva C. Dienst, M.D. Norbert Lewin, M.D.
Benjamin Esterman, M.D. Max Mannheimer, M.D.
Joseph Fried, M.D. Philip L. Masor, M.D.
Jacob Goldsmith, M.D. Ernst L. Metzger, M.D.
Frank M. Green, M.D. David I. Mirow, M.D.
Frederick H. Theodore, M.D.

Refractionists
(Out-Patient Department)
Bertha Gladstern, M.D. M. Rosenbaum, M.D.

(a) On Military Service.

45

MEDICAL AND SURGICAL STAFF

ORTHOPEDIC SERVICE
Orthopedists
Robert K. Lippmann, M.D.   Seth Selig, M.D.

Associate Orthopedists
(a) Edgar M. Bick, M.D.   **Edgar D. Oppenheimer, M.D.

Adjunct Orthopedists
Benjamin B. Greenberg, M.D.   Albert J. Schein, M.D.

Senior Clinical Assistant
(Out-Patient Department)
Jacob Mandel, M.D.

Clinical Assistants
(Out-Patient Department)
Alvin M. Arkin, M.D.   Lazarus Lippert, M.D.
Ernst Bettmann, M.D.   Frederick M. Marek, M.D.
Philip I. Burack, M.D.   Carlo Schapira, M.D.
David Goldberg, M.D.   Rudolf Selig, M.D.
Max Kliger, M.D.   Stephan Wahl, M.D.
Hans Wolff, M.D.

ISOLATION SERVICE

Associate Physician
Benjamin Eliasoph, M.D.

PHYSICAL THERAPY DEPARTMENT
Physical Therapist
William Bierman, M.D.

Adjunct Physical Therapist
Sidney Licht, M.D.

Assistant Physical Therapists
Eric Levy, M.D.   A. W. Schenker, M.D.

Clinical Assistants
(Out-Patient Department)
Victor Feith, M.D.   Alexander Hersh, M.D.
Eugene Neuwirth, M.D.

Research Assistant
Wladimir T. Liberson, M.D.

Volunteers
Joseph Moldaver, M.D.   Frank T. Woodbury, M.D.

** Off Service.
(a) On Military Service.

MEDICAL AND SURGICAL STAFF

CARDIOGRAPHIC LABORATORY
Associate in Medicine
Arthur M. Master, M.D.

Assistant in Medicine
(Hospital or Out-Patient Department)
Hubert Mann, M.D.

Research Assistants
Simon Dack, M.D.
Rudolph Friedman, M.D.
Arthur Grishman, M.D.
Harry L. Jaffe, M.D.
Abraham Jezer, M.D.
Milton Mendlowitz, M.D.
Jenny Stricker, M.D.

Volunteer
Nathan Silver, M.D.

THE LABORATORIES

Pathologist
Paul Klemperer, M.D.

Bacteriologist
Gregory Shwartzman, M.D.

Chemist
Harry H. Sobotka, Ph.D.

Neuro-pathologist
Joseph H. Globus, M.D.

Hematologist
Nathan Rosenthal, M.D.

Associate Pathologist
Sadao Otani, M.D.

Assistant Pathologist
Abou D. Pollack, M.D.

Assistant Bacteriologists
Cecele Herschberger, B.S.
Lewis H. Koplik, M.D.
(a) S. Stanley Schneierson, M.D

Assistant Chemist
Miriam Reiner, M.S.

SPECIAL LABORATORY APPOINTMENTS
Associates
Ernst P. Pick, M.D...Pharmacology
(c) Franklin Hollander, Ph.D...Gastric Physiology

(a) On Military Service.
(c) Appointed 1941.

THE LABORATORIES—(Continued)

SPECIAL LABORATORY APPOINTMENTS—(Continued)

Fellows

Corrado Ajo, M.D.......................Moritz Rosenthal Fellowship
Clarence Cohn, M.D.....................Eugene Meyer, Jr. Fellowship
Mark G. Kanzer, M.D................Minnie Kastor Fellowship in Psychiatry
Theodore Meltzer, M.D..............Charles Klingenstein Fellowship
Nathan Mintz, M.D.....................Dr. Joseph Brettauer Fellowship
Kurt Oster, M.D..........................George Blumenthal, Jr. Fellowship
Nathaniel C. Schlossmann, M.D..Theodore Escherich Fellowship
Saul Soloway, Ph.D....................Hernsheim Fellowship in Chemistry
H. E. Yaskin, M.D.......................Dr. Isadore Abrahamson Memorial
                                                        Fellowship

Research Assistants
BACTERIOLOGY

Frank M. Green, M.D.   Sheppard Siegal, M.D.
(b) Florence Sammis, M.D.   Gabriel P. Seley, M.D.
                 Emanuel Wachtel, M.D.

CHEMISTRY

David Adlersberg, M.D.   Edward E. Jemerin, M.D.
(a) Joseph Bandes, M.D.   Susan Kann, Ph.D.
Lester Blum, M.D.   Emanuel Klempner, M.D.
Albert Cornell, M.D.   Milton H. Levy, M.D.
(b) D. Alfred Dantes, M.D.   Gerda Gernsheim-Mayer, M.D.
Arthur M. Davids, M.D.   Charles S. Poole, M.D.
Max Ellenberg, M.D.   S. Zelig Sorkin, M.D.
Gertrude Felshin, M.D.   Robert I. Walter, M.D.
Edward B. Grossman, M.D.   Vernon A. Weinstein, M.D.
                 Morton Yohalem, M.D.

DERMATO-PATHOLOGY
Arthur W. Glick, M.D.

HEMATOLOGY

Peter Vogel, M.D.   Louis R. Wasserman, M.D.

MORBID ANATOMY

Alice I. Bernheim, M.D.   Daniel Laszlo, M.D.
Konrad Bloch, M.D.   Mrs. Cecele Leuchtenberger
I. E. Gerber, M.D.   Rudolf Leuchtenberger, M.D.
Abraham J. Gitlitz, M.D.   Manes Klaften, M.D.
                 Cesare Tedeschi, M.D.

PHARMACOLOGY
Sergei Feitelberg, M.D.

(a) On Military Service.
(b) Until April 30, 1941.
(c) Appointed 1941.

MEDICAL AND SURGICAL STAFF

THE LABORATORIES—(Continued)

SPECIAL LABORATORY APPOINTMENTS—(Continued)

Research Assistants—(Continued)

SURGICAL PATHOLOGY

Joseph C. Ehrlich, M.D.
(b)Leon Gerber, M.D.
(a)Julian A. Jarman, M.D.
Erich Kuznitzky, M.D.
Michael L. Lewin, M.D.
Josef Novak, M.D.
Eugene Somkin, M.D.
Rose Spiegel, M.D.
(b)Herbert G. Weichsel, M.D.

THROMBO-ANGIITIS OBLITERANS

Mae L. Friedlander, Ph.D.
(b)Norman F. Laskey, M.D.
(b)Herman Zazeela, M.D.

Voluntary Assistants

BACTERIOLOGY

Morton H. Edelman, M.D.

CHEMISTRY

Henry Dolger, M.D.
Louis A. Izenstein, M.D.

HEMATOLOGY

Frank A. Bassen, M.D.
Pedro N. Ortiz, M.D.
Mario Volterra, M.D.

MORBID ANATOMY

(b)Arthur C. Allen, M.D.
Jacob Churg, M.D.
George C. Escher, M.D.
Alvin J. Gordon, M.D.
Edith Grishman, M.D.
(b)J. Gudemann, M.D.
(a)Richard H. Marshak, M.D.
Leo Moschkowitz, M.D.
(a)Nathan Rudner, M.D.
Morris F. Steinberg, M.D.
M. Wachstein, M.D.
(b)Vitale Kogan, M.D.

NEURO-PATHOLOGY

Bernard R. Goldberg, M.D.
H. Kuhlenbeck, M.D.
James F. McDonald, M.D.
Joseph E. Rubenstein, M.D.

OPHTHALMO-PATHOLOGY

Abraham L. Kornzweig, M.D.
Murray A. Last, M.D.

OTO-PATHOLOGY

Lester L. Coleman, M.D.

SURGICAL PATHOLOGY

Jacob S. Aronoff, M.D.
Rudolph Drosd, M.D.
Elliott S. Hurwitt, M.D.
Borris A. Kornblith, M.D.
A. Harry Neffson, M.D.
Irving A. Sarot, M.D.

PHARMACOLOGY

Consultant

Charles L. Lieb, M.D.

(a) On Military Service.
(b) Until April 30, 1941.

MEDICAL AND SURGICAL STAFF

DEPARTMENT OF ROENTGENOLOGY

Radiologist
Marcy L. Sussman, M.D.

Associate Radiologists
Arthur J. Bendick, M.D.   Samuel J. Goldfarb, M.D.

Assistant Radiologists
Benjamin Copleman, M.D.   M. H. Poppel, M.D.
Jack H. Levy, M.D.   Coleman B. Rabin, M.D.

Volunteer
Morris F. Steinberg, M.D.

DEPARTMENT OF RADIOTHERAPY

Radiotherapist
William Harris, M.D.

Associate Radiotherapist
Albert Kean, M.D.

Assistant Radiotherapists
Arnold Bachman, M.D.   Seymour Wimpfheimer, M.D.
Samuel Richman, M.D.   Charles Wolf, M.D.
Sidney M. Silverstone, M.D.   Louis E. Zaretski, M.D.

Volunteers
Myer E. Golan, M.D.   Moses H. Holland, M.D.

Physicists
Carl B. Braestrup, B.Sc.   (b) Alexander Kolin, Ph.D.

DEPARTMENT OF ANESTHESIA

Visiting Anesthetists
William Branower, M.D.   Bernard H. Eliasberg, M.D.

Anesthetists in Out-Patient Department
Sidney Grossman, M.D.   ***Barney Isaacson, M.D.

Resident Anesthetists
Helen E. Almour, R.N.   Ryta M. Canty, R.N.
Fanny Bergmann, M.D.   Evelyn T. Clerico, M.D.
Florence Califano, R.N.   Dorothy Newland, R.N.
Marion J. Saks, R.N.

DISTRICT SERVICE

Physicians
Abraham Jerskey, M.D.   Morris F. Steinberg, M.D.

(b) Until April 30, 1941.
*** Resigned.

MEDICAL AND SURGICAL STAFF

ADMITTING SERVICE
Gerson J. Lesnick, M.D.

ASSISTANT PHYSICIAN TO EMPLOYEES
D. Alfred Dantes, M.D.

DENTAL DEPARTMENT

(Hospital and Out-Patient Department)

Dentist
Harry A. Goldberg, D.D.S.

Associate Dentists
Ralph H. Brodsky, D.M.D.   Joseph Schroff, M.D., D.D.S.
Leo Stern, D.D.S.

Adjunct Dentists
Charles H. Cohen, D.D.S.   Denis D. Glucksman, D.D.S.
Nathaniel Freeman, D.D.S.   Arthur A. Kulick, D.D.S.

Senior Clinical Assistants
Robert E. Arlt, D.D.S.   Paul C. Kopf, D.D.S.
Miles Chelimer, D.D.S.   Abram J. Krasny, D.D.S.
Henry I. Cohen, D.D.S.   Sydney Pollak, D.D.S.
Lester L. Eisner, D.D.S.   Elias Reiner, D.D.S.
Oscar C. Fink, D.D.S.   Louis Sabloff, D.D.S.
Marvin G. Freid, D.D.S.   Milton Schwartz, D.D.S.
Robert S. Gilbert, D.M.D.   Arthur L. Smith, D.D.S.
Herbert L. Goodfleish, D.M.D.   Bernard A. Sussman, D.D.S.
Samuel Gordon, D.D.S.   George Trattner, D.D.S.
Max Greenspan, D.D.S.   Seymour Weinstein, D.D.S.
Daniel M. Kollen, D.D.S.   I. Edwin Zimmerman, D.D.S.

Clinical Assistants
Louis Arnowitz, D.D.S.   Lee R. Kulick, D.D.S.
Sigmond Bergman, D.D.S.   David A. Langstein, D.D.S.
Alex N. Cohen, D.D.S.   Meyer Mehlman, D.D.S.
Lawrence Cohen, D.D.S.   Herman Reich, D.D.S.
Abraham Dinin, D.D.S.   Sidney Retzker, D.D.S.
Samuel Donson, D.D.S.   William Roth, D.D.S.
Frederick T. Doob, D.D.S.   David Rubin, D.D.S.
George Dubin, D.D.S.   Eric D. Sachs, D.D.S.
Edward Gottesman, D.D.S.   Morris Schwartz, D.D.S.
(a) Bernard L. Handel, D.D.S.   Julian Schroff, D.D.S.
Jack Hausberg, D.D.S.   Irwin Siegel, D.D.S.
Julius Helfand, D.D.S.   Ralph Siegel, D.D.S.
Robert S. Hess, D.D.S.   I. Arnold Simon, D.D.S.
Arthur E. Kahn, D.D.S   Maurice Stavin, D.D.S.
Jack Kantor, D.D.S.   Harry Spodak, D.D.S.
Harry W. Katz, D.D.S.   Milton Wechsler, D.D.S.
Henry H. Weishoff, D.D.S.

(a) On Military Service.

THE MOUNT SINAI HOSPITAL
HOUSE STAFF
(As of May 1st, 1941)

MEDICAL DEPARTMENT

Merrill P. Haas, M.D.
Bernard M. Schwartz, M.D.
Henry D. Yanowitz, M.D.
Jonas E. Salk, M.D.
Robert Landesman, M.D.
Robert H. Heavenrich, M.D.
Morley J. Kert, M.D.

Frank L. Engel, M.D.
Maurice Franks, M.D.
John B. DeHoff, M.D.
Herman L. Jacobius, M.D.
Irving G. Kroop, M.D.
Edward Meilman, M.D.
Mortimer B. Hermel, M.D.

SURGICAL DEPARTMENT

Daniel Luger, M.D.
Ernest L. Sarason, M.D.
Alvin I. Goldfarb, M.D.
Lester Narins, M.D.
Stanley J. Snitow, M.D.
Harvey K. Mechanik, M.D.
Jonas H. Sirota, M.D.

Norman Rosenberg, M.D.
Roy Barnett, M.D.
George J. Sabrin, M.D.
Norman Simon, M.D.
Irving L. Pavlo, M.D.
Maurice J. Keller, M.D.
Nathaniel B. Kurnick, M.D.

DEPARTMENT OF PATHOLOGY

Daniel Burdick, M.D.

Jacques L. Gabrilove, M.D.

DEPARTMENT OF RADIOLOGY

Roentgenology
Bernard S. Wolf, M.D.
(a) Eugene M. Holleb, M.D.

Radiotherapy
Harold G. Jacobson, M.D.
Abraham M. Melamed, M.D.

DENTAL DEPARTMENT

Leon Eisenbud, D.D.S.

Robin M. Rankow, D.D.S.

RESIDENTS, WARD

Neurological
Milton Sapirstein, M.D.
Aaron Stein, M.D.
Paul G. Myerson, M.D.

Pediatric
Ralph E. Moloshok, M.D.
Herman Anfanger, M.D.

Gynecological
Aaron L. Lichtman, M.D.
Louis S. Lapid, M.D.

Ear, Nose and Throat
Leonard S. Bases, M.D.
Nathan Adelman, M.D.

Ophthalmological
Milton G. Rosoff, M.D.
Alan H. Barnert, M.D.

Orthopedic
(a) Joel Hartley, M.D.

RESIDENTS, PRIVATE PAVILION

Seelig Freund, M.D.
Benjamin Greenspan, M.D.
Charles Ressler, M.D.

S. Ralph Friedlander, M.D.
(a) Sidney Katz, M.D.
Leon M. Arnold, M.D.

RESIDENTS, SEMI-PRIVATE PAVILION

(a) David Brezin, M.D.
(a) Theodore A. Fox, M.D.

Sidney S. Greenberg, M.D.
Heinz Lippmann, M.D.

(a) On Military Service

THE MOUNT SINAI HOSPITAL
DEPARTMENT OF GRADUATE MEDICAL
INSTRUCTION

(1941-1942)

Conducted in Affiliation with
COLUMBIA UNIVERSITY

(University Extension and School of Medicine)

OFFICERS OF INSTRUCTION

HAROLD A. ABEL, M.D..........ASSISTANT IN MEDICINE TO THE MOUNT SINAI HOSPITAL
HAROLD A. ABRAMSON, M.D...ASSISTANT IN MEDICINE TO
THE MOUNT SINAI HOSPITAL;
ASSISTANT PROFESSOR OF PHYSIOLOGY IN COLUMBIA UNIVERSITY
DAVID ADLERSBERG, M.D.....CLINICAL ASSISTANT, MEDICAL DIVISION, OUT-PATIENT
DEPARTMENT, THE MOUNT SINAI HOSPITAL
SAMUEL H. AVERBUCK, M.D., ADJUNCT PHYSICIAN TO THE MOUNT SINAI HOSPITAL
GEORGE BAEHR, M.D...........................PHYSICIAN TO THE MOUNT SINAI HOSPITAL;
CLINICAL PROFESSOR OF MEDICINE IN COLUMBIA UNIVERSITY
MURRAY H. BASS, M.D.........ASSOCIATE PEDIATRICIAN TO THE MOUNT SINAI HOSPITAL;
ASSISTANT CLINICAL PROFESSOR OF PEDIATRICS IN COLUMBIA UNIVERSITY
FRANK A. BASSEN, M.D.....................SENIOR CLINICAL ASSISTANT, MEDICAL DIVISION,
OUT-PATIENT DEPARTMENT, THE MOUNT SINAI HOSPITAL
DAVID BECK, M.D.....................ASSOCIATE PHYSICIAN TO THE MOUNT SINAI HOSPITAL
ASSISTANT CLINICAL PROFESSOR OF MEDICINE IN COLUMBIA UNIVERSITY
MORRIS B. BENDER, M.D. ....ADJUNCT NEUROLOGIST TO THE MOUNT SINAI HOSPITAL
PHINEAS BERNSTEIN, M.D., ADJUNCT GYNECOLOGIST TO THE MOUNT SINAI HOSPITAL
SOLON S. BERNSTEIN, M.D.......ADJUNCT PHYSICIAN TO THE MOUNT SINAI HOSPITAL
EDGAR M. BICK, M.D...........ASSOCIATE ORTHOPEDIST TO THE MOUNT SINAI HOSPITAL
WILLIAM BIERMAN, M.D.........PHYSICAL THERAPIST TO THE MOUNT SINAI HOSPITAL;
ASSOCIATE IN MEDICINE IN COLUMBIA UNIVERSITY
ERNST P. BOAS, M.D.................ASSOCIATE PHYSICIAN TO THE MOUNT SINAI HOSPITAL;
ASSISTANT CLINICAL PROFESSOR OF MEDICINE IN COLUMBIA UNIVERSITY
WILLIAM BRANOWER, M.D..SUPERVISING ANESTHETIST TO
THE MOUNT SINAI HOSPITAL
RICHARD M. BRICKNER,M.D...ASSOCIATE NEUROLOGIST TO
THE MOUNT SINAI HOSPITAL;
ASSISTANT PROFESSOR OF CLINICAL NEUROLOGY IN COLUMBIA UNIVERSITY
LOUIS CHARGIN, M.D., ASSOCIATE CONSULTING DERMATOLOGIST TO THE MOUNT SINAI
HOSPITAL; ASSOCIATE CLINICAL PROFESSOR OF DERMATOLOGY AND SYPHILOLOGY,
NEW YORK POST-GRADUATE MEDICAL SCHOOL, COLUMBIA UNIVERSITY
IRA COHEN, M.D...............................NEURO-SURGEON TO THE MOUNT SINAI HOSPITAL
RALPH COLP, M.D..SURGEON TO THE MOUNT SINAI HOSPITAL;
CLINICAL PROFESSOR OF SURGERY IN COLUMBIA UNIVERSITY
ALBERT CORNELL, M.D.............................CLINICAL ASSISTANT, MEDICAL DIVISION,
OUT-PATIENT DEPARTMENT, THE MOUNT SINAI HOSPITAL
BURRILL B. CROHN, M.D.....ASSOCIATE IN MEDICINE TO THE MOUNT SINAI HOSPITAL;
ASSOCIATE IN MEDICINE IN COLUMBIA UNIVERSITY
SIMON DACK, M.D................................SENIOR CLINICAL ASSISTANT, MEDICAL DIVISION,
OUT-PATIENT DEPARTMENT, THE MOUNT SINAI HOSPITAL
HENRY DOLGER, M.D..........................SENIOR CLINICAL ASSISTANT, MEDICAL DIVISION,
OUT-PATIENT DEPARTMENT, THE MOUNT SINAI HOSPITAL
HENRY DOUBILET, M.D..............................CLINICAL ASSISTANT, SURGICAL DIVISION,
OUT-PATIENT DEPARTMENT, THE MOUNT SINAI HOSPITAL
JOSEPH G. DRUSS, M.D..............ASSOCIATE OTOLOGIST TO THE MOUNT SINAI HOSPITAL
MAX ELLENBERG, M.D...................................CLINICAL ASSISTANT, MEDICAL DIVISION,
OUT-PATIENT DEPARTMENT, THE MOUNT SINAI HOSPITAL
EMANUEL Z. EPSTEIN, M.D.....ADJUNCT PHYSICIAN TO THE MOUNT SINAI HOSPITAL
SERGEI FEITELBERG, M.D.......................RESEARCH ASSISTANT IN PHARMACOLOGY TO
THE MOUNT SINAI HOSPITAL
ALFRED E. FISCHER, M.D.....ADJUNCT PEDIATRICIAN TO THE MOUNT SINAI HOSPITAL
ARTHUR M. FISHBERG, M.D., ASSOCIATE PHYSICIAN TO THE MOUNT SINAI HOSPITAL;
ASSOCIATE IN MEDICINE IN COLUMBIA UNIVERSITY

53

DEPARTMENT OF GRADUATE MEDICAL INSTRUCTION

(Continued)

CHARLES K. FRIEDBERG, M.D., Adjunct Physician to The Mount Sinai Hospital

BEN FRIEDMAN, M.D................Adjunct Physician to The Mount Sinai Hospital

JOSEPH A. GAINES, M.D.......Adjunct Gynecologist to The Mount Sinai Hospital

JOHN H. GARLOCK, M.D...............................Surgeon to The Mount Sinai Hospital; Clinical Professor of Surgery in Columbia University

SAMUEL H. GEIST, M.D.......................Gynecologist to The Mount Sinai Hospital Clinical Professor of Gynecology in Columbia University

I. E. GERBER, M.D...Clinical Assistant, Medical Division, Out-Patient Department, The Mount Sinai Hospital

GEORGE J. GINANDES, M.D....Adjunct Pediatrician to The Mount Sinai Hospital

JOSEPH H. GLOBUS, M.D................Associate Neurologist and Neuropathologist to The Mount Sinai Hospital; Assistant Clinical Professor of Neurolgy in Columbia University

MYER E. GOLAN, M.D...............................Volunteer in Radiotherapy Department, The Mount Sinai Hospital; Instructor in Radiology in Columbia University

MORRIS A. GOLDBERGER, M.D.......................Associate Gynecologist to The Mount Sinai Hospital; Associate in Gynecology in Columbia University

SAMUEL J. GOLDFARB, M.D., Associate Radiologist to The Mount Sinai Hospital; Associate in Radiology in Columbia University

JOSEPH L. GOLDMAN, M.D...Adjunct Laryngologist to The Mount Sinai Hospital

ARON GOLDSCHMIDT, M.D.............Senior Clinical Assistant, Surgical Division, Out-Patient Department, The Mount Sinai Hospital

EDWARD B. GREENSPAN, M.D..Adjunct Physician to The Mount Sinai Hospital

JOSEPH HARKAVY, M.D.....Associate in Medicine to The Mount Sinai Hospital; Associate in Medicine in Columbia University

WILLIAM HARRIS, M.D....................Radiotherapist to The Mount Sinai Hospital; Associate in Radiology in Columbia University

HERMAN HENNELL, M.D........................Adjunct Physician for Chest Diseases to The Mount Sinai Hospital

CECELE HERSCHBERGER, B.S.............................Assistant Bacteriologist to The Mount Sinai Hospital

ALEXANDER HERSH, M.D............Clinical Assistant, Physical Therapy Division, Out-patient Department, The Mount Sinai Hospital

WILLIAM M. HITZIG, M.D.......Adjunct Physician to The Mount Sinai Hospital

FRANKLIN HOLLANDER, Ph.D...........................Associate in Gastric Physiology to The Mount Sinai Hospital

HENRY HORN, M.D.......................Adjunct Physician to The Mount Sinai Hospital

HARRY L. JAFFE, M.D......................Senior Clinical Assistant, Medical Division, Out-Patient Department, The Mount Sinai Hospital

SAUL W. JARCHO, M.D............Adjunct Physician to The Mount Sinai Hospital

SAMUEL KARELITZ, M.D.......Adjunct Pediatrician to The Mount Sinai Hospital

ALBERT KEAN, M.D.........Associate Radiotherapist to The Mount Sinai Hospital; Associate in Radiology in Columbia University

PAUL KLEMPERER, M.D.......................Pathologist to The Mount Sinai Hospital; Clinical Professor of Pathology in Columbia University

EMANUEL KLEMPNER, M.D., Assistant Gynecologist, Out-Patient Department, The Mount Sinai Hospital

JEROME L. KOHN, M.D.........Associate Pediatrician to The Mount Sinai Hospital

LEWIS H. KOPLIK, M.D.....Assistant Bacteriologist to The Mount Sinai Hospital.

ABRAHAM L. KORNZWEIG, M.D., Senior Clinical Assistant, Ophthalmological Division, Out-Patient Department, The Mount Sinai Hospital

DEPARTMENT OF GRADUATE MEDICAL INSTRUCTION

(Continued)

ROBERT K. LAMBERT, M.D.................................ASSOCIATE OPHTHALMIC SURGEON TO
          THE MOUNT SINAI HOSPITAL
HERMAN LANDE, M.D.............ASSOCIATE IN MEDICINE TO THE MOUNT SINAI HOSPITAL;
        ASSOCIATE IN MEDICINE IN COLUMBIA UNIVERSITY
MURRAY A. LAST, M.D...........................ASSISTANT OPHTHALMIC SURGEON, OUT-PATIENT
        DEPARTMENT, THE MOUNT SINAI HOSPITAL
JOSEPH LAVAL, M.D., ADJUNCT OPHTHALMIC SURGEON TO THE MOUNT SINAI HOSPITAL
SIDNEY D. LEADER, M.D.................SENIOR CLINICAL ASSISTANT, PEDIATRIC DIVISION,
      OUT-PATIENT DEPARTMENT, THE MOUNT SINAI HOSPITAL
WILLIAM LEIFER, M.D........SENIOR CLINICAL ASSISTANT, DERMATOLOGICAL DIVISION,
      OUT-PATIENT DEPARTMENT, THE MOUNT SINAI HOSPITAL
OSCAR L. LEVIN, M.D.........ASSOCIATE DERMATOLOGIST TO THE MOUNT SINAI HOSPITAL;
      ASSOCIATE IN DERMATOLOGY IN COLUMBIA UNIVERSITY
ERIC LEVY, M.D.........ASSISTANT PHYSICAL THERAPIST TO THE MOUNT SINAI HOSPITAL
HYMAN LEVY, M.D.................................SENIOR CLINICAL ASSISTANT, MEDICAL DIVISION,
      OUT-PATIENT DEPARTMENT, THE MOUNT SINAI HOSPITAL
SIDNEY LICHT, M.D.....ADJUNCT PHYSICAL THERAPIST TO THE MOUNT SINAI HOSPITAL
S. S. LICHTMAN, M.D.................ADJUNCT PHYSICIAN TO THE MOUNT SINAI HOSPITAL
ROBERT K. LIPPMANN, M.D................ORTHOPEDIST TO THE MOUNT SINAI HOSPITAL
SYLVAN D. MANHEIM, M.D............ASSISTANT SURGEON, OUT-PATIENT DEPARTMENT,
      THE MOUNT SINAI HOSPITAL
HUBERT MANN, M.D.................ASSISTANT IN MEDICINE TO THE MOUNT SINAI HOSPITAL
ARTHUR M. MASTER, M.D.....ASSOCIATE IN MEDICINE TO THE MOUNT SINAI HOSPITAL;
      ASSISTANT CLINICAL PROFESSOR OF MEDICINE IN COLUMBIA UNIVERSITY
MAX D. MAYER, M.D.............ASSOCIATE GYNECOLOGIST TO THE MOUNT SINAI HOSPITAL;
      ASSOCIATE IN GYNECOLOGY IN COLUMBIA UNIVERSITY
SAUL MILLER, M.D.........SENIOR CLINICAL ASSISTANT, OPHTHALMOLOGICAL DIVISION,
      OUT-PATIENT DEPARTMENT, THE MOUNT SINAI HOSPITAL
HENRY MINSKY, M.D..ASSOCIATE OPHTHALMIC SURGEON TO
          THE MOUNT SINAI HOSPITAL
MAURICE E. MINTZ, M.D.........ASSISTANT GYNECOLOGIST, OUT-PATIENT DEPARTMENT,
      THE MOUNT SINAI HOSPITAL
NATHAN MINTZ, M.D............................CLINICAL ASSISTANT, GYNECOLOGICAL DIVISION,
      OUT-PATIENT DEPARTMENT, THE MOUNT SINAI HOSPITAL
SYLVAN E. MOOLTEN, M.D.......ADJUNCT PHYSICIAN TO THE MOUNT SINAI HOSPITAL
ELI MOSCHCOWITZ, M.D.................PHYSICIAN TO THE MOUNT SINAI HOSPITAL;
      ASSISTANT CLINICAL PROFESSOR OF MEDICINE IN COLUMBIA UNIVERSITY
HAROLD NEUHOF, M.D................SURGEON TO THE MOUNT SINAI HOSPITAL;
      CLINICAL PROFESSOR OF SURGERY IN COLUMBIA UNIVERSITY
ALBERT B. NEWMAN, M.D............SENIOR CLINICAL ASSISTANT, PEDIATRIC DIVISION,
      OUT-PATIENT DEPARTMENT, THE MOUNT SINAI HOSPITAL
JOSEF NOVAK, M.D................................CLINICAL ASSISTANT, GYNECOLOGICAL DIVISION,
      OUT-PATIENT DEPARTMENT, THE MOUNT SINAI HOSPITAL
PEDRO N. ORTIZ, M.D........................SENIOR CLINICAL ASSISTANT, MEDICAL DIVISION,
      OUT-PATIENT DEPARTMENT, THE MOUNT SINAI HOSPITAL
SADAO OTANI, M.D.................ASSOCIATE PATHOLOGIST TO THE MOUNT SINAI HOSPITAL
REUBEN OTTENBERG, M.D.....ASSOCIATE PHYSICIAN TO THE MOUNT SINAI HOSPITAL;
      ASSISTANT CLINICAL PROFESSOR OF MEDICINE IN COLUMBIA UNIVERSITY
SAMUEL M. PECK, M.D......ADJUNCT DERMATOLOGIST TO THE MOUNT SINAI HOSPITAL
M. MURRAY PESHKIN, M.D...ASSOCIATE IN PEDIATRICS TO THE MOUNT SINAI HOSPITAL
HENRY PESHKIN, M.D................SENIOR CLINICAL ASSISTANT, SURGICAL DIVISION,
      OUT-PATIENT DEPARTMENT, THE MOUNT SINAI HOSPITAL
ERNST P. PICK, M.D.....ASSOCIATE IN PHARMACOLOGY TO THE MOUNT SINAI HOSPITAL;
      CLINICAL PROFESSOR OF PHARMACOLOGY IN COLUMBIA UNIVERSITY
DANIEL POLL, M.D.....................ASSOCIATE PHYSICIAN TO THE MOUNT SINAI HOSPITAL;
      ASSISTANT CLINICAL PROFESSOR OF MEDICINE IN COLUMBIA UNIVERSITY
HERBERT POLLACK, M.D., PH.D.....................................ASSISTANT IN MEDICINE TO
         THE MOUNT SINAI HOSPITAL
COLEMAN B. RABIN, M.D.....ASSOCIATE IN MEDICINE TO THE MOUNT SINAI HOSPITAL;
      ASSOCIATE IN MEDICINE IN COLUMBIA UNIVERSITY
MIRIAM REINER, M.S....................ASSISTANT CHEMIST TO THE MOUNT SINAI HOSPITAL
SAMUEL RICHMAN, M.D...ASSISTANT RADIOTHERAPIST TO THE MOUNT SINAI HOSPITAL

DEPARTMENT OF GRADUATE MEDICAL INSTRUCTION

(Continued)

ALFRED ROMANOFF, M.D.............Assistant Physician, Out-Patient Department,
The Mount Sinai Hospital
ISADORE ROSEN, M.D.....................Dermatologist to The Mount Sinai Hospital;
Clinical Professor of Dermatology and Syphilology, New York
Post-Graduate Medical School, Columbia University
NATHAN ROSENTHAL, M.D................Associate in Medicine and Hematologist to
The Mount Sinai Hospital; Assistant Clinical Professor
of Medicine in Columbia University
IRVING R. ROTH, M.D.........Associate in Medicine and Assistant Pediatrician to
The Mount Sinai Hospital; Associate in Medicine in Columbia University
ISIDOR C. RUBIN, M.D.....................Gynecologist to The Mount Sinai Hospital;
Clinical Professor of Gynecology in Columbia University
U. J. SALMON, M.D.................Adjunct Gynecologist to The Mount Sinai Hospital .
I. SCOTTY SCHAPIRO, M.D.................Senior Clinical Assistant, Medical Division,
Out-Patient Department, The Mount Sinai Hospital
MAX SCHEER, M.D.............Adjunct Dermatologist to The Mount Sinai Hospital;
Associate Clinical Professor of Dermatology and Syphilology,
New York Post-Graduate Medical School, Columbia University
ALBERT J. SCHEIN, M.D.........Adjunct Orthopedist to The Mount Sinai Hospital
A. W. SCHENKER, M.D.....................................Assistant Physical Therpist to
The Mount Sinai Hospital
BELA SCHICK, M.D.....................Pediatrician to The Mount Sinai Hospital;
Clinical Professor of Pediatrics in Columbia University
KAUFMAN SCHLIVEK, M.D...Ophthalmic Surgeon to The Mount Sinai Hospital
Clinical Professor of Ophthalmology in Columbia University
HERMAN SCHWARZ, M.D.......................Associate Consulting Pediatrician to
The Mount Sinai Hospital; Assistant Clinical Professor of Pediatrics
in Columbia University
GABRIEL P. SELEY, M.D.....................Clinical Assistant, Surgical Division,
Out-Patient Department, The Mount Sinai Hospital
SETH SELIG, M.D.....................Orthopedist to The Mount Sinai Hospital
GREGORY SHWARTZMAN, M.D........Bacteriologist to The Mount Sinai Hospital
Clinical Professor of Bacteriology in Columbia University
SAMUEL SILBERT, M.D.................Adjunct Surgeon to The Mount Sinai Hospital
SOLOMON SILVER, M.D.........Associate Physician to The Mount Sinai Hospital
HARRY H. SOBOTKA, Ph.D.............. Chemist to The Mount Sinai Hospital
LOUIS J. SOFFER, M.D.............Adjunct Physician to The Mount Sinai Hospital
MAX L. SOM, M.D.................Adjunct Laryngologist to The Mount Sinai Hospital
HANS STRAUSS, M.D....................Research Assistant, Neurological Service,
The Mount Sinai Hospital
MARCY L. SUSSMAN, M.D.................Radiologist to The Mount Sinai Hospital;
Associate in Radiology in Columbia University
ARTHUR S. W. TOUROFF, M.D...Associate Surgeon to The Mount Sinai Hospital
LESTER R. TUCHMAN, M.D.....Adjunct Physician to The Mount Sinai Hospital
PETER VOGEL, M.D.....................Senior Clinical Assistant, Medical Division,
Out-Patient Department, The Mount Sinai Hospital
ROBERT I. WALTER, M.D................Clinical Assistant, Gynecological Division,
Out-Patient Department, The Mount Sinai Hospital
LOUIS R. WASSERMAN, M.D.....................Clinical Assistant, Medical Division,
Out-Patient Department, The Mount Sinai Hospital
ISRAEL S. WECHSLER, M.D............Neurologist to The Mount Sinai Hospital;
Professor of Clinical Neurology in Columbia University
DAVID WEXLER, M.D.................................Adjunct Ophthalmic Surgeon to
The Mount Sinai Hospital
IRA S. WILE, M.D.....................Associate in Pediatrics to The Mount Sinai Hospital
SEYMOUR WIMPFHEIMER, M.D..Adjunct Gynecologist to
The Mount Sinai Hospital
ASHER WINKELSTEIN, M.D...Associate in Medicine to The Mount Sinai Hospital;
Associate in Medicine in Columbia University
HARRY YARNIS, M.D....Senior Clinical Assistant, Medical Division, Out-Patient
Department, The Mount Sinai Hospital

56

EXECUTIVE OFFICERS AND HEADS OF DEPARTMENTS

HOSPITAL

JOSEPH TURNER, M.D.............*Director*
MAXWELL S. FRANK, M.D.............*Assistant Director*
MORRIS H. KREEGER, M.D.............*Assistant Director*
DAVID H. ROSS, M.D.............*Assistant Director*
GRACE A. WARMAN, B.S., M.A., R.N.,*Principal, School of Nursing and Superintendent of Nurses*
FANNY LISSAUER MENDELSOHN, B.S., R.N.............*Director of Social Service*
GEORGE T. COOK.............*Chief Clerk and Auditor*
JOHN B. CUBBERLEY.............*Supervising Engineer*
ISADORE ROGIN, PH.G.............*Chief Apothecary*
MARY R. ERWIN, R.N.............*Supervisor Private Pavilion*
EDITH G. RYAN, R.N.............*Supervisor, Semi-Private Pavilion*
MAY E. SHAMP, R.N.............*Supervisor, Out-Patient Department*
RUTH GOEBEL, R.N.............*Supervisor of Nurses, Operating Room*
HELEN SOMERS.............*Acting Supervising Dietitian*
ROBERT M. MORRISS.............*Laundry Manager*

SCHOOL OF NURSING

GRACE A. WARMAN, B.S., M.A., R.N.,*Principal, School of Nursing and Superintendent of Nurses*
MINNIE STRUTHERS, B.S., R.N.......*Assistant Principal, School of Nursing*
LOTTIE M. PHILLIPS, R.N.............*Assistant Superintendent of Nurses*
MARION KIMBALL, R.N.............*Night Superintendent of Nurses*
LILLIAN LEESON, A.B., R.N.............*Supervisor of Instructors*
BLANCHE GUBERSKY, R.N.............*Instructor of Nursing Arts*
MARION CROZIER, M.A.............*Instructor of Physical Education*
MARY R. ERWIN, R.N.............*Supervisor of Nurses, Private Pavilion*
EDITH G. RYAN, R.N.............*Supervisor of Nurses, Semi-Private Pav.*
MAY E. SHAMP, R.N.............*Supervisor of Nurses, Out-Patient Dept.*
RUTH GOEBEL, R.N.............*Supervisor of Nurses, Operating Room*
MATHILDE REICH, R.N.............*Supervisor of Nurses, Medical Pavilion*
BESSIE WOLFSON, B.S., R.N.............*Supervisor of Nurses, Surgical Pavilion*
CORA BALL, R.N.............*Supervisor of Nurses, Children's Pavilion*
LILLIE DIXON.............*Matron, Nurses Residence*

ON ACTIVE DUTY WITH THE DEFENSE FORCES
OF THE UNITED STATES

(As of July, 1941)

MEDICAL AND SURGICAL STAFF

Robert H. Abrahamson, M.D.
Joseph Bandes, M.D.
Samuel H. Belgorod, M.D.
Arthur J. Berger, M.D.
Phineas Bernstein, M.D.
Edgar M. Bick, M.D.
Sydney Bressler, M.D.
David Brezin, M.D.
Norman Q. Brill, M.D.
Leonard E. Field, M.D.
Theodore A. Fox, M.D.
Emil Granet, M.D.
Bernard Handel, D.D.S.
Joel Hartley, M.D.
Charles R. Hayman, M.D.
Eugene M. Holleb, M.D.
Julian A. Jarman, M.D.
Sidney Katz, M.D.

Samuel Kahn, M.D.
J. John Kristal, M.D.
H. Richard Landmann, M.D.
Daniel M. Lipshutz, M.D.
Richard Marshak, M.D.
Herbert F. Newman, M.D.
Arthur Post, M.D.
Aaron Prigot, M.D.
Monroe A. Rosenbloom, M.D.
Irving Rachlin, M.D.
Nathan Rudner, M.D.
Norman A. Samuels, M.D.
S. Stanley Schneierson, M.D.
Kona Simon, M.D.
John Waller, M.D.
Reuben Yontef, M.D.
Michael S. Zeman, M.D.
Bernard M. Zussman, M.D.

EMPLOYEES

Anthony Berezansky
Anthony Chepak
Frank Curry
Joseph Harasyn
John Harbove
Paul Hundley
Steven Juba
Harry Monahan
Santiago Padilla

John Rodriguez
Paul Ruppert
Leo Senuk
Rene Steiner
Igni Walles
Joseph Witzer
Anthony Yuskin
Bernard Zuckermandel

REPORT OF THE MEDICAL STAFF

During 1940, members of the medical staff of the Hospital contributed their services to 11,949 ward patients and attended more than 350,000 patient visits in the Out-Patient Department of the Hospital. The effective accomplishment of this duty was made possible by fine coordination of the numerous special divisions of the medical staff. Through these well trained, experienced, specialist groups, the patients received the benefits of the newest advances in diagnosis and therapeutics.

In addition to the direct application of medical knowledge to the care of the sick, the medical staff has continued to engage actively in research, both in the clinical and laboratory divisions of the Hospital, and has participated in numerous educational activities to improve the professional knowledge of our own physicians, our intern staff and physicians in the community. The clinical pathological conferences held in the George Blumenthal Auditorium continue to attract over 350 practitioners and specialists throughout the metropolitan area each week .This represents the attendance capacity of the auditorium. Similarly, capacity audiences of 150 or more physicians attend the Friday afternoon weekly public clinics (Grand Rounds) held in the clinical amphitheatre. There have also been regular weekly or bimonthly conferences on clinical roentgenology, electrocardiography, thoracic diseases and other specialties, as well as operative clinics which have been well attended by members of the Hospital staff and outside physicians.

The Committee on Medical Education has arranged lectures on subjects of current importance which were given by physicians of prominence in the respective fields. Special mention should be made of the valuable series of lectures on modern advances in our knowledge of the vitamins, and a lecture on aviation medicine. Postgraduate formal courses in the various branches of medicine and surgery under the auspices of Columbia University continued to form a significant feature of the educational activities of the medical staff. A special effort has been made to enhance the educational value of the internship by improving the opportunities of learning during the routine activities of the House Staff and by supplemental lectures and demonstrations.

MEDICAL SERVICES: The educational activities of the medical services have been continued by their participation in postgraduate courses, by the weekly Friday afternoon medical clinics and by weekly or irregular conferences in the various specialties such as electrocardiography, metabolic diseases, etc. In addition, members of the medical staff contributed to the annual Graduate Fortnight on Infections at the Academy of Medicine, and to the many programs of national, state and local medical societies.

A continued effort has been made to coordinate the activities of the various medical specialties with those of the general medical services and with other cognate branches of surgery and specialties. A consideration of these interdepartmental problems and of the scientific and clinical work of special groups have formed a major part of the monthly staff conferences.

Due to improvement both in physical facilities and in the caliber of physicians now engaged on the medical divisions of the Out-Patient department, the quality of work performed there is fully comparable with that in the wards. The Out-Patient department is also serving to retrain groups of refugee physicians so that they may become familiar with American methods of medical practice.

Clinical research has continued to emphasize the important newer developments in therapy, especially the use of the sulfonamide drugs, vitamins and endocrine products. While the administration of sulfanilamide and sulfapyridine has been continued when indicated, an evaluation has been made of the effectiveness of sulfathiazole, particularly in cases of lobar pneumonia and subacute bacterial endocarditis. A few cures have been obtained in that almost hopeless disease, subacute bacterial endocarditis, by the combined use of sulfapyridine or sulfanilamide and hyperthermia. A newer preparation, sulfanilylguanidine has been tested for the treatment of cases of ulcerative colitis. Continued observations have been conducted on the use of intramuscular injections and subcutaneous implantations of pellets of desoxycorticosterone acetate in the treatment of Addison's disease. Encouraging results have been obtained in the treatment of scleroderma by dihydrotachysterol.

Experimental and clinical studies as to the nature and cause of essential hypertension were continued, and attempts were made to determine the site of formation of the renal pressor substance. The relation of unilateral renal disease to certain cases of hypertension has also been studied and the knowledge obtained has been applied therapeutically.

Numerous reports upon these subjects have been published as well as others upon toxic and infectious jaundice, acute yellow atrophy following avertin narcosis, medical and surgical aspects of chronic constrictive pericarditis, gastrointestinal manifestations of shock, terminal ileitis, the Cushing syndrome, the nature of blood iodine, orthostatic circulatory insufficiency, painless gastrointestinal hemorrhage, serum magnesium partition studies in clinical and experimental hypothyroidism, aging of the cardiovascular system, cardiac hypertrophy in glycogen storage disease.

Massive arsenotherapy in early syphilis by the five day continuous intravenous drip method has attracted the attention of the entire country. The work, which has been in progress in our Hospital for more than seven years, was released for trial by other well organized treatment centers at a nationwide conference called by the Commissioner of Health of the City on April 12, 1940. The experience of the country is being tabulated by the U. S. Public Health Service and will be reported at the 1941 meeting of the American Medical Association.

The gastrointestinal group has continued its weekly rounds and conferences with the surgical services interested in gastrointestinal surgery. Studies in regional ileitis and jejunitis and in the treatment of peptic ulcer, ulcerative colitis and cardiospasm were continued. A more systematized and extensive use of gastroscopy was inaugurated. Papers were published on shock, gastric syphilis, the relationship of female sex hormones to peptic ulcer, the parenteral therapy of peptic ulcer, intestinal tuberculosis, true achlorhydria, antitoxic B. coli serum therapy of ulcerative colitis.

The thoracic group has published papers reporting the spot method it developed for the localization of pulmonary abscess. It has also published a report on acute mediastinitis and presented its study of suppurative broncho-pneumonia in children.

The cardiographic group has participated in the programs of many medical groups and presented its observations on various aspects of coronary occlusion and other cardiological subjects. Papers were published on the modes of onset of acute coronary occlusion, aneurysm of the aorta due to rheumatic fever, the roentgenkymogram in myocardial infarction, myocardial infarction due to acute hemorrhage, relation of effort and trauma to acute coronary artery occlusion, the relation of bundle branch block and cardiac enlargement, the diagnosis of coronary occlusion and myocardial infarction by fluoroscopic examination.

The metabolic clinics accounted for 9,129 patient visits including 180 new patients in the diabetic division and 4,865 patient visits with 555 new patients in the general nutrition division. An attempt has been made to evaluate the recent trends in dietary management of diabetes mellitus, including the use of low, moderate, high and unrestricted carbohydrate diets, respectively. The relationship of protamine zinc insulin to the absorption of food is under investigation.

The effects of hormonal pituitary inhibition on clinical diabetes is being studied in cooperation with the menopause clinic. Allergic reactions to insulin are being studied in cooperation with a member of the department of allergy. A clinical podiatrist has been appointed to the diabetic clinic; the importance of this association is obvious in view of the frequency of serious complications involving the feet, due to vascular disturbances and infections, in cases of diabetes.

The studies on Vitamin B excretion have been continued, and a test has been developed to determine early Vitamin B1 deficiency states. A study is also being made on the prevalence of Vitamin B2 deficiencies, in conjunction with the skin clinic and eye clinic. The metabolic group has shown that certain diseases of the gastrointestinal tract frequently result in vitamin deficiency states. Similarly a high incidence of acute pellagroid states was found in postoperative patients on the surgical wards. In conjunction with the neurological service, metabolic studies have been carried out on Vitamin E. These various studies indicate the importance of coordination of the problems of one specialty with those of various other specialty groups in the Hospital.

PEDIATRIC SERVICE: Studies on vitamins in childhood have been continued and articles have appeared or are in press on biophotometric studies in relation to Vitamin A, capillary fragility and ascorbic acid, the cutaneous manifestations of vitamin deficiencies. The possible role of vitamins in ichthyosis is being investigated.

The studies in insensible perspiration have been continued, particularly with regard to the effect of insulin and fever of unknown origin. Other studies are concerned with serum sickness and with numerous problems in allergy. The effects of estrogenic hormone on diabetic children are being investigated.

Reports have been published on cases of cryptorchidism and the effect of gonadotropic and male sex hormone, nephritis and nephrosis, diabetes mellitis in identical twins, the occurrence of the bullous Schick reaction in infectious diseases, the icteric index in hemolytic icterus, idiosyncrasy to ammoniated mercury, and on various subjects related to mental health.

NEUROLOGIC SERVICE: Research activities have been expanded, particularly in neurophysiology and experimental neuroanatomy. A coordinated study is being conducted on the relationship of Vitamin E (topocopherol) and of creatine metabolism to amyotrophic lateral sclerosis.

Studies in electroencephalography have been increased, the use of this procedure having been extended not only to neurological problems but also to those on other services. Electroencephalography has been utilized in the study of hypoglycemia, the carotid sinus syndrome, postural hypotension and hypertension and the convulsive state. The relation of vitamin deficiency to hypoglycemic manifestations has also been studied.

The neuropsychiatric service has been greatly enlarged during the past year. Four adjuncts in psychiatry are providing psychiatric consultations to all services in the Hospital and are also carrying on special studies. The psychiatric clinic has been greatly expanded so as to accommodate almost all applicants for treatment. There are now four instead of two morning psychiatric clinics. Psychiatrists have been placed in various clinics of the Out-Patient Department.

The publications in this branch of medicine during 1940 include the following subjects: vitamin therapy in diseases of the nervous system, recovery in amyotrophic lateral sclerosis treated with tocopherols, intravenous use of paraldehyde for the control of convulsions, topographic relations of the sleep regulating center, dissociated loss of deep sensibility at different levels of the central nervous system, effect of section of the medial lemniscus on weight discrimination, reactions of adrenaline and acetylcholine on the denervated iris of the cat and monkey, pupillodilator reactions in sciatic and diencephalic stimulation in cat and monkey, release of autonomic humoral substances in hypoglycemic cats and monkeys, paralysis of divergence, effects of adrenaline on tubal contractions of the rabbit in relation to sex hormones, relaxation effect of acetylcholine on the oviduct of the rabbit in relation to hormonal status, pneumoencephalographic and electroencephalographic localization of an epileptogenic focus, electroencephalography in cases of head injury, effect of metrazol injections on the electroencephalogram, applications of electroencephalography in the practice of medicine, Jacksonian seizures of reflex origin, transient organic mental reactions during shock therapy of the psychotic, a human cortical area producing repetitive phenomena when stimulated.

DERMATOLOGICAL SERVICE: This service continued to participate in the investigations on the treatment of syphilis by massive intravenous doses of arsenicals. Work on the perfection of a trychophytin is progressing. Evidence has been found of the probable role of Vitamin A deficiency in Darier's disease and patients with this disease have been improved by the correction of this deficiency. Other studies were concerned with pigment oxidases and nail growth. The incorporation of radiotherapy in the dermatological service has greatly enhanced the utilization of this form of treatment.

SURGICAL SERVICES: The surgical service interested in thoracic diseases has reported favorable results in the surgical treatment of acute putrid pulmonary abscess. Publications were also made on acute mediastinitis, acute suppurative bronchopneumonia with special reference to surgical aspects, constrictive pericarditis, surgery of pulmonary tuberculosis, treatment of pleural infections, interlobar perforated lung abscess (interlobar empyema), ligation of patent ductus arteriosus in subacute bacterial endocarditis and other subjects.

Studies on peptic ulcer and gastric carcinoma have been continued and work on the following has been completed or is in progress: The influence of jejunal feedings on gastric acidity, indications for jejunostomy for alimentation in gastroduodenal ulceration, insulin test meal in the evaluation of partial vagotomy, effect of vascular ligation in subtotal gastrectomy upon the histology of the mucosa of the stomach, the correlation of gastroscopic, x-ray, operative and histological findings in ulcer and carcinoma of the stomach, hemorrhage as a late sequel of subtotal gastrectomy, follow-up studies in cases of palliative gastrectomy for cardiac ulcers, surgical problems in the treatment of gastrojejunal ulcers, the bacteriology of gastroduodenal ulceration and carcinoma of the stomach, gastroduodenal ulceration in older age group, report of mortality and end results following use of partial gastrectomy in the treatment of gastric and duodenal ulcer.

Various other surgical problems are being studied or have been completed including: the effect of desoxycorticosterone on the postoperative course in major surgical procedures, endocholedochal sphincterotomy with a report of 4 cases, late sequelae in strangulated hernia, spasm as a cause of colonic obstruction, ileocolostomy with exclusion in regional ileitis, bleeding Meckel's diverticulum in infancy and childhood.

The service interested in abdominal surgery has occupied itself with a variety of problems, especially those concerned with regional ileitis, ulcerative colitis and carcinoma of the colon and the thoracic esophagus. In order to overcome the complication of wound evisceration, a new method of suturing the abdominal wall has been developed with excellent results thus far. The utilization of sulfonamide drugs preoperatively in the surgery of the small and large bowel has resulted in practical disappearance of the postoperative complication of peritonitis. The number of operative survivals following surgical treatment of carcinoma of the esophagus and cardiac end of the stomach is increasing. Encouraging results have been obtained in the attempt to reproduce the Banti syndrome experimentally.

Articles were published during the year or are in press on the following: fecal fistulae due to regional ileitis, enterocolostomy with exclusion in the treatment of regional ileitis, the conservative management of sigmoidoscopic perforation, extraperitoneal injuries simulating intraabdominal trauma, primary angiosarcoma of the spleen, surgical treatment of carcinoma of the esophagus, the surgical treatment of intractable ulcerative colitis, bleeding tendency in obstructive jaundice, management of the strangulatory type of intestinal obstruction, volvulus of the sigmoid with special reference to radiological diagnosis.

The surgical service interested particularly in genitourinary disease has published articles on the following subjects: reimplantation of the ureter into the bladder, ureteropelvic anastomosis following avulsion, evaluation of roentgenography of surgically exposed kidney in treatment of renal calculi, cases illustrating treatment of bilateral renal calculi including parathyroid exploration, hypernephroma of kidney with solitary metastases to cerebellum—successful removal of both. The following additional articles have been accepted for publication: diagnosis of bladder neoplasms in benign prostatic hypertrophy, xanthine calculi in the ureter, reimplantation of the ureter into the renal pelvis, surgery of the inferior vena cava in urological conditions, plastic procedures for hydronephrosis.

On the neurosurgical service, investigative work has been conducted with reference to the use of diodrast in the visualization of the cerebral vessels and a report on this subject has been completed.

GYNECOLOGIC SERVICE: The morphological and hormonological aspects of gynecoendocrinologic disorders have been investigated and correlated with practical clinical problems of diagnosis and therapy. Some of these problems have been studied in cooperation with other departments of the hospital including the diabetic, the gastrointestinal and roentgenological.

Studies have been conducted in the therapy of the menopause syndrome. These have included the relative advantages of different techniques and different estrogenic and androgenic substances in implantation therapy. The enteral and buccal administration of estrogenic substances has also been studied. Similar studies have been carried out with androgens utilized for the treatment of functional menorrhagia and dysmenorrhea and mastopathies. The therapeutic value of the gonadotropes has been investigated with respect to functional amenorrhea and sterility. The therapeutic value of prolactin and synthetic Vitamin E is also being studied. Other investigations are concerned with studies in vaginal cytology, therapy of kraurosis vulvae, hormonal control of peristalsis of the fallopian tubes and the excretion of sodium pregnandiol glucuronidate.

Articles were also published on the following: inhibitory effect of implanted crystals of estrogenic hormone upon the postmenopause and castration hypophysis of women, the biologic effect of androgens in women, effect of pregneninolene on the genital tract of immature female rats, local tissue reaction to the implantation of crystals and pellets of estrogenic hormone, absorption rate and biologic effects of pellets of estradiol and estradiol benzoate in women, inhibitory action of testosterone propionate on the human ovary, the appearance of gonadotropic hormone in the urine of women after ovariectomy, evaluation of stilboesterol as a therapeutic estrogen, biological properties of pregneninolene in women, buccal absorption of estradiol in propylene glycol.

The studies on the motility of the fallopian tubes have been continued. Reports have been published on: the biodynamic effects of the sex hormones on tubal motility contrasting testosterone propionate and estrogenic hormones, effects of adrenaline and related adrenergic substances on the motility of the fallopian tubes in relation to the sex hormones, effects of acetylcholine and related cholinergic substances on the motility of the fallopian tubes in relation to the sex hormones.

LARYNGOLOGICAL SERVICE: Investigations were made on the intracranial pathways of infection from the sphenoid and ethmoid sinuses, and the observations were published. Articles were also published on infections of the paranasal sinuses in relation to systemic disease with special reference to diagnostic lavage, cerebrospinal rhinorrhea, nasopharyngeal fibromas—juvenile and cellular types, prevention and correction of dorsal depressions by septal implants, and sphenoiditic hydrocephalus.

OTOLOGICAL SERVICE: Further investigation of the value of chemotherapy in otogenous infections has added considerably to our knowledge of the modification of the clinical course and the masking effect resulting from the use of these drugs. A clearer concept of the indications and contraindications for this important type of therapy has resulted from these studies.

As a result of the installation of an audiometer in the Out-Patient Department, increased interest in the diagnosis of various types of hearing impairment has been aroused. Investigation is being conducted regarding the etiological factors in each case, especially in children, and the proper corrective measures are being instituted so as to prevent, if possible, permanent hearing impairment in adult life. A new operative procedure for otosclerosis has been used recently and promises alleviation of this hitherto incurable condition.

In cooperation with the neurological service, neuro-otological clinical studies by means of vestibular examinations have served to stimulate the interest of members of the staff in this important subject. The value of the monthly staff conference conducted in the otological laboratory has been greatly enhanced by correlative investigation of clinical problems and histopathological studies.

Articles were published on the following: congenital fistula of the neck communicating with the middle ear, carcinoma of the nasopharynx with extension to the petrous pyramid, bacteremia of otitic origin, thrombophlebitis of the cavernous sinus of otitic origin, neoplasms involving the middle ear, lipoid granulomatosis, otitic hydrocephalus, meningitis and temporal lobe abscess secondary to suppurative petrositis.

OPHTHALMOLOGICAL SERVICE: Various embryological, anatomical, pathological and clinical studies were made. The anatomy of the lens, vitreous and ligamentum hyaloidea was investigated in relation to intracapsular cataract extraction. The anatomy of the limbus and anterior chamber angle was studied in relation to operations for glaucoma. An embryological study was completed on the development of the corneoscleral junction and the structures of the angle of the anterior chamber. Pathologic investigations were conducted on gastric carcinoma metastasizing to the ciliary body, anatomic variations in myopia and the intimate structure of the optic nerves in pituitary tumors. Clinical studies were made on the etiology and nature of iritis and on the etiology and treatment of vernal catarrh. Papers were published on vaccinia of the eyes, bilateral symmetrical cystoid detachment of the retina and anomalus retinal vein crossing the macula.

An exhibit was given at the American Medical Association convention on blood vessels of the eye which received an honorable mention. Another exhibit was given at the Annual Graduate Fortnight of the Academy of Medicine on ocular infections in meningitis.

ORTHOPEDIC SERVICE: The orthopedic service has been especially interested in improved therapeutic measures for the correction of orthopedic abnormalities and has published reports of new contributions to these problems. The publications include: Hammer toes (a new procedure for its correction), corkscrew bolt in intertrochanteric fracture, the Keller operation, emergency treatment and transportation of fractures, sulfonamide therapy in acute hematogenous osteomyelitis, irreducible buttonhole dislocations of fingers, bacillus pyocyaneus osteomyelitis of the spine.

DEPARTMENT OF ROENTGENOLOGY: Particular attention was paid to the development of a well-classified museum collection of roentgen films with explanatory clinical data. Experiments are still in progress to determine whether a photographic record of the films and clinical history might be adequate as well as more economical. Individual attention to requests for roentgen-ray examinations has resulted in decided economies in departmental operation.

There has been continued cooperation with other services of the Hospital. Weekly medical roentgen-ray conferences have continued. Cooperation of the department of pathology has been particularly gratifying.

The department has participated in symposia before the New York Roentgen Society and before the medical, neurological and pediatric services of the Hospital. Articles were published during 1940 on: the roentgen aspects of nonputrid pulmonary suppuration, interlobar perforated abscess of lung, roentgenkymogram in myocardial infarction.

DEPARTMENT OF RADIOTHERAPY: Although there was no marked increase in the number of new patients, there was an increase in the total number of treatments given, which exceeded 10,000 during 1940. This is explained by the new trend in radiation therapy according to which more treatments are given for malignant disease than formerly.

The addition of a resident to the department has facilitated the conduct of precise procedures and has made it possible for each member of the resident staff to attend various clinics and meetings and to participate more fully in the follow-up work of the department.

Clinical research is being carried out with new procedures in radiation therapy in cooperation with the various divisions of the Hospital. It is hoped that this cooperation will be even more successful when a tumor clinic is established.

Papers in press or published include: radiation therapy of carcinoma of the anus, roentgen therapy in carcinoma of the ovary, lymphosarcoma of the hard palate.

DEPARTMENT OF PHYSICAL THERAPY: Most of the investigations were concerned with the therapeutic applications of hyperthermia and cold. Articles were published on the following: effect of hyperpyrexia on tonus of human common bile duct and cardiac sphincters, the value of hyperthermia in the treatment of gonococcal infections in women, regulation of circulation in the skin and muscles of the lower extremeties, evaluation of some methods of treatment in peripheral vascular disease, the penetrative effect of cold, electrosurgery.

DENTAL DEPARTMENT: For the tenth year, an annual course of lectures on medical subjects relating to dentistry was given and attended by physicians and dentists throughout the city. Members of the staff have read papers, given clinics and presented cases before various dental societies. Research problems are being investigated in cooperation with the Physical Therapy department and the Ophthalmological service. Papers were published on Grenz ray therapy in periodontoclasia and oral tuberculous lesions, chemotherapy of dental infections, metastatic carcinoma of the mandible.

THIRD GENERAL HOSPITAL: Upon the invitation of the War Department, the organization of a military hospital drawn from the professional staff of the Hospital is rapidly nearing completion. It is a source of satisfaction to be able to report that almost the entire medical staff volunteered for service. In recognition of the services rendered during the last war by the Mount Sinai

70

Hospital Unit, Base Hospital No. 3, the new military hospital has been designated with the same number by The Surgeon General as The Third General Hospital. Its personnel will include 73 officers, 120 nurses and more than 500 enlisted men. It is designed for mobilization in the event of war, and will provide the organization for a hospital with a minimum capacity of 1,000 beds.

In order to alleviate the hardships of the families of those members of the medical staff who may be called for military duty either with the Third General Hospital or in any other capacity, the Medical Board and the Association of the Junior Medical Staff unanimously adopted a plan for the joint sharing of responsibilities. Under this plan members of the medical staff will contribute a designated percentage of their net income monthly for the purpose of creating a fund for the benefit of the dependents of those in military service. This Military Emergency Fund is to be administered by a committee of Trustees appointed by the President of the Hospital, on which the Presidents of the Medical Board and the Junior Medical Staff will serve in an advisory capacity.

THE LABORATORIES: References to the Laboratories have been omitted since these are covered by others in another section of this report.

GEORGE BAEHR, M.D.,

President, Medical Board.

BEQUESTS AND DONATIONS FOR SPECIAL PURPOSES DURING YEAR 1940

David A. Schulte—For Dental Clinic	$8,000.00
New York Foundation, Inc.—For support of cancer research of Dr. Richard Lewisohn	6,500.00
Committee on Neighborhood Health Development, Inc.—For Intravenous Drip Therapy Project	5,006.11
Philip Lehman—For special needs of Physical Therapy Department	5,000.00
The Friedsam Foundation, Inc.—For gastro-enterology research	5,000.00
Estate of Florentine S. Sutro—For the Florentine S. Sutro Research Fund	5,000.00
Mrs. Arthur Lehman—For support of cancer research of Dr. Rchard Lewisohn	3,500.00
The International Cancer Research Foundation—For support of cancer research of Dr. Richard Lewisohn	3,233.32
Frances and John Loeb Foundation—For support of cancer research of Dr. Richard Lewisohn	2,500.00
The John and Mary R. Markle Foundation—For support of research on amyotrophic lateral sclerosis	2,500.00
Dazian Foundation for Medical Research—For research in physiology and pharmacology of brain	2,000.00
Josiah Macy, Jr. Foundation—For study of mechanism of skin reactivity	1,650.00
Hiram C. Bloomingdale and Samuel J. Bloomingdale—In memory of Corrine B. Popper—For research on multiple sclerosis....	1,500.00
Mrs. Addie H. Homan—For the Isidore Hernsheim Fellowship in Chemistry	1,500.00
Miss Adelaide Reckford—For support of cancer research of Dr. Richard Lewisohn	1,500.00
Hoffman-La Roche, Inc.—For special research of Dr. Israel S. Wechsler	1,500.00
The Friedsam Foundation, Inc.—For special research of Dr Samuel Rosen	1,350.00
Blood Transfusion Betterment Association, Inc.—For Blood Plasma Project	1,273.84
Williams-Waterman Fund—For Vitamin B-1 Research	1,250.00
Josiah Macy, Jr. Foundation—For studies on secretion of parasympathetic substance	1,250.00
Dr. Ralph Colp—Toward Fellowship for gastro-enterology research	1,250.00
The Friedsam Foundation, Inc.—For research on the hypothalmus	1,200.00
The Lucius N. Littauer Foundation, Inc.—For research of Dr. Israel S. Wechsler	1,200.00
Dr. I. C. Rubin—For Dr. Hiram N. Vineberg Fund for gynecology research	1,200.00
American Lecithin Co., Inc.—For Multiple Sclerosis Vitamin A Research	1,025.00
Mr. and Mrs. Walter W. Naumburg—For non-budgetary needs of the Laboratory	1,000.00
Mrs. Levy Mayer—In memory of Walter A. Hirsch—For leukemia research	1,000.00
Carried Forward	$68,888.27

BEQUESTS AND DONATIONS FOR SPECIAL PURPOSES DURING YEAR 1940

(Continued)

Brought Forward	$68,888.27
Frank Altschul—For Cardiograph Department Non-Budgetary Research Fund (through The Greater New York Fund)	1,000.00
Mount Sinai Hospital Research Foundation, Inc.—For venom research	850.00
Mark and William Bernstein—For Bacteriology Research	800.00
John Wyeth & Brother, Inc.—For study of intestinal secretions	700.00
John Wyeth & Brother, Inc.—For study of the continuous drip treatment of peptic ulcer	600.00
Louis Chiron—For special needs of the surgical group in urology	500.00
Dazian Foundation for Medical Research—For studies on secretions of para-sympathetic substance	500.00
Dazian Foundation for Medical Research—For study of the chemical and physiological characteristics of intestinal secretions	500.00
Mrs. Charles Altschul—For cardio-vascular research	500.00
American Medical Association—To investigate the influence of nutrition and drugs on the cardiac output in coronary occlusion	500.00
"A Friend"—For Dr. Joseph Brettauer Fellowship Fund (part payment toward a $1,200 grant)	500.00
Emergency Committee in Aid of Displaced Foreign Medical Scientists—Stipend for Dr. Erich Kuznitzky	500.00
Anonymous—For cardio-vascular research	500.00
Mrs. Louis J. Grumbach—For support of cancer research of Dr. Richard Lewisohn	500.00
Max J. Shapiro—For support of neurology research	500.00
Mrs. Walter A. Hirsch—In memory of Walter A. Hirsch— Toward costs of Blood Plasma Project	300.00
American Medical Association—For Bacterial Endocarditis Animal Research	250.00
Dr. M. Davidson—For Research Fund	250.00
Philip J. Goodhart—For cardio-vascular research	200.00
Dr. Samuel M. Peck—For Venom Research	179.36
Dr. Samuel M. Peck—For Vitamin A and Carotene Research	150.00
Dr. Louis Chargin—For Vitamin A and Carotene Research	150.00
Arthur Lorsch—For Medical Conference expenses	150.00
Greater New York Chapter of the National Foundation for Infantile Paralysis, Inc.—For the care of Infantile Paralysis	146.40
Jean Goldwurm—For research purposes	135.00
Mrs. Charles Klingenstein—To commemorate an anniversary— For Hospital Bulletin Fund	125.00
Carried Forward	$79,874.03

73

BEQUESTS AND DONATIONS FOR SPECIAL PURPOSES DURING YEAR 1940

(Continued)

Brought Forward	$79,874.03
Mrs. Charles Klingenstein—For Staff Loan and Relief Fund	100.00
Mrs. Arthur Lehman—For cardio-vascular research	100.00
I. Magnin & Co. Employees of New York Office—As an expression of esteem and affection in celebration of the 70th birthday of E. John Magnin—For non-budgetary purposes	100.00
Mrs. Kurt Semon—For exhibit expenses	100.00
Howard M. Ernst—For non-budgetary purposes	100.00
Anonymous—In appreciation of Dr. Leon Ginzburg—For Staff Loan and Relief Fund	100.00
Mrs. Waldemar Kops—For trees	100.00
Associated Alumni of The Mount Sinai Hospital—For Library Fund	100.00
Edwin C. Vogel—For tree	50.00
Mrs. Isaac Friedenheit—In memory of her son, Myron G. Friedenheit's birthday—For Research Fund	50.00
Mrs. Henry L. Lambert—For tree	50.00
Benjamin Mordecai—For tree	50.00
Carl H. Pforzheimer, Jr.—For tree	50.00
George B. Bernheim—For tree	50.00
Dr. Irving Somach—For cardio-vascular research	50.00
Dr. Rudolph Kramer—For Staff Loan and Relief Fund	50.00
Chevra-Kadisha—For Research Fund	38.00
Walter W. Kohn—In memory of Mr. Charles Klingenstein's birthday—For Staff Loan and Relief Fund	25.00
George E. Coleman—For non-budgetary purposes	25.00
Mrs. Richard Hirsch—In honor of Mr. Charles Klingenstein's birthday—For Staff Loan and Relief Fund	25.00
Mr. and Mrs. Richard Hirsch—In memory of Mr. Charles Klingenstein—For Staff Loan and Relief Fund	25.00
Mrs. Henry Frank—In celebration of Mr. Henry Frank's seventy-fifth birthday—For children's treat	25.00
Dr. Joseph Laval—For repair of projector	25.00
First New Sandez Society—For Research Fund	25.00
Mrs. Max Danziger—"As a birthday treat to the children"	25.00
Dr. Henry Reiss—For Research Fund	25.00
Miss Grace M. Mayer—In memory of Dr. Leo Kessel—For Research Fund	10.00
Total	$81,347.03

DONATIONS DURING YEAR 1940

The Workmen's Circle	$300.00
Mrs. Jean C. Sheehan—In appreciation of the care given by the Hospital to her son	100.00
Miss Elsie Strauss—Toward the support of the free work at the Hospital	50.00
Dr. Joseph Laval	50.00
Maxwell J. Hoffman	25.00
Mrs. Emil Berolzheimer	25.00
George J. Dorfman	25.00
The Misses Albert	10.00
Mr. and Mrs. Edwin de Lima—In memory of Mr. Morton L. Adler	10.00
Walter Littwitz	10.00
Mr. J. Bendien—In memory of Mr. Theodore Goldberg and Mr. Oscar Lambert	10.00
Mrs. John S. Schulte—In memory of Master Jonathan Walter Fried—To be used for purposes in connection with Children's Pavilion	10.00
Miss Evelyn Rosenfeld—In memory of Mr. William Schreiber—To be used for Children's Ward	10.00
Nathan Kaufman	10.00
Mrs. Chas. A. Wimpfheimer—In memory of Mrs. Daisy Strauss	10.00
Central Synagogue	10.00
Mrs. Albert Weiler	10.00
William Schwartz	10.00
Miscellaneous donations	36.00
Total	$721.00

ENDOWMENTS FOR SPECIAL PURPOSES

Mr. and Mrs. Charles Klingenstein Fund............................$114,000.00
Established by Mr. and Mrs. Charles Klingenstein; income
to be used for non-budgetary purposes as determined
annually by the Board of Trustees.

Benjamin Altman Fund.. 100,000.00
Established by provision in the will of Benjamin Altman;
one-half of the income to be utilized to defray expenses of
the Neurological Department, the remainder for the general
purposes of the institution.

**Marjorie Walter Goodhart and Florence Henrietta Walter
Children's Clinic Endowment**.................................... 100,000.00
Founded by their parents, Florence B. and William I.
Walter; income to be used for the purposes of Children's
Clinic.

**Marjorie Walter Goodhart and Florence Henrietta Walter
Memorial Fund** 25,000.00
Established by provision in the will of Miss Rosie Bern-
heimer; income to be applied towards the running expenses
of the Children's Clinic.

Babette Lehman Fund 100,000.00
Founded by Mrs. Babette Lehman; income to be utilized
for the advancement of preventive medicine.

Louis W. Neustadter Fund.. 100,000.00
Founded by provision in the will of Mrs. Henry Neustadter;
distribution of income to be made annually on the 16th day
of March, a portion to needy and indigent patients in the
Hospital on that date, the remainder for the general purposes
of the Hospital.

Mount Sinai Hospital Fund for Medical Education............... 50,000.00
Joseph F. and Zillah Cullman contributed $25,000.00 as a
nucleus of said fund, and $25,000.00 contributed by the
estate of Henry P. Goldschmidt; the income to be used to
defray expenses arising out of clinical lectures, demonstrations and conferences, and for cognate purposes.

Alfred A. and Ruth M. Cook Fund................................... 50,000.00
Founded by Alfred A. and Ruth M. Cook; income to be
applied to special experimental work in the Social Service
Department.

Florette and Ernst Rosenfeld Foundation............................ 50,000.00
Founded by Florette and Ernst Rosenfeld; for the estab-
lishment and special support of a Department of Radium
and Radiotherapy.

Dr. Isador Abrahamson Neurological Fund....................... 50,000.00
Established by provision in the will of Stella Heidelberg
Abrahamson; the income from this fund to be used for
Fellowships for research work and study in the field of
neurology and psychiatry.

George Blumenthal, Jr. Fellowship Fund........................... 45,000.00
Founded by Mrs. Florence Blumenthal; income to be applied
to the maintenance of two Fellowships in Pathology.

Helen B. Millhauser Fund 37,000.00

ENDOWMENTS FOR SPECIAL PURPOSES
(Continued)

Etta C. Lorsch Memorial Fund.. $34,000.00
Established by provision in the will of Etta C. Lorsch
($10,000); by members of the Board of the Social Ser-
vice Auxiliary ($10,000.00); and by many of her friends
($4,370.00); the sum of $10,000.00 was added by provision
in the will of William N. Cohen; income to be disbursed
by the Social Service Auxiliary for the special country care
of children.

Jacob Mayer Fund.. 30,000.00
Founded in memory of Jacob Mayer for equipping and
maintaining a pneumonia room.

Harriet Meyer Memorial Fund.. 25,000.00
Founded by Eugene Meyer; income to be used for experi-
mental work in the Social Service Department.

Alice Goldschmidt Sachs Endowment Fund............................. 25,000.00
Established by provision in the will of Alice Goldschmidt
Sachs; income to be used for medical education.

Moritz Rosenthal Fellowship Fund.. 25,000.00
Established by provision in the will of Moritz Rosenthal;
income to be used for medical, surgical, clinical or
laboratory Fellowships as granted to men selected by the
Board of Trustees.

Ambulance Fund 20,000.00
Established by Murry Guggenheim; income to be applied
toward the maintenance of the ambulance service.

Murry Guggenheim Scholarship Fund.................................... 20,000.00
Founded by Murry Guggenheim; income to provide medals
and twelve scholarships of $100 each annually to nurses of
The Mount Sinai Hospital School of Nursing.

Moritz Warburg Social Service Fund..................................... 20,000.00
Founded by Felix M. and Paul M. Warburg; income to be
applied to the work of the Social Service Department.

Emanuel Van Raalte Endowment Fund for Medical
Education 20,000.00
Legacy; income to be used for medical education.

Minnie Kastor Memorial Fund.. 19,775.00
Founded by Alfred B. Kastor as a tribute to the memory
of his mother; income to be used for psychiatric work
through the service of a Fellow in psychiatry.

Charles Klingenstein Fellowship Fund.................................... 18,000.00
Established by Mrs. Charles Klingenstein; income to be
used for Fellowship in any clinical or laboratory department
of the Hospital as determined by the Board of Trustees.

Robert and John Kaufmann Vacation Fund............................. 11,000.00
Founded by Max Kaufmann; income to be used for
providing vacations, preferably for crippled children.

Theodor Escherich Fellowship Fund...................................... 10,000.00
Founded by Edward S. Steinam; income to be applied
to the maintenance of a Fellowship in Pathology.

Moses Heineman Fellowship Fund... 10,000.00
Founded by Moses Heineman; income to be applied to the
maintenance of a Fellowship in Pathology.

Dr. Henry Koplik Fund.. $10,000.00
Established by provision in the will of Dr. Henry Koplik; income to be disbursed by the Social Service Department and devoted solely to the care of infants and children, whose parents are unable to pay ward fees.

Eugene Meyer, Jr. Fellowship Fund................................. 10,000.00
Founded by Eugene Meyer, Jr.; income to be applied to the maintenance of a Fellowship in Pathology.

William Henry Welch Lecture Fund.............................. · 10,000.00
Established by Dr. Emanuel Libman; income to be used to provide lectures to be named after Dr. William Henry Welch of Johns Hopkins University.

Emil Wolff Social Service Fund...................................... 10,000.00
Established by Emil Wolff; income to be applied to the work of the Social Service Department.

Library Funds 7,200.00
Dr. Abraham Jacobi Library Fund of $5,000.00 established by the Board of Trustees to commemorate the eightieth birthday of Dr. Abraham Jacobi; income to be applied to the purchase of books for the Hospital Library.

Dr. Fred S. Mandlebaum Memorial Fund of $2,200.00 contributed by many of his friends; income to be applied to the purchase of books for the Hospital Library.

Charles and Camilla Altschul Fund for Nursing in Wards.... 5,000.00
Founded by Charles and Camilla Altschul; to defray the expense of special nursing in the wards.

Isaac C. Bishop Fund.. 5,000.00
Established by provision in the will of Morris Bishop; income to be used for the relief, care and benefit of poor patients suffering from cancer.

Edward Gamaliel Janeway Lecture Fund....................... 5,000.00
Founded by Edward S. Steinam; income to be utilized to bring important investigators to Mount Sinai Hospital, to present the result of their work.

Fannie C. Korn Fund... 5,000.00
Founded by Mrs. Fannie C. Korn—In Memory of Henry Korn; for the establishing and maintaining of a splint and apparatus room for the Orthopedic Service.

Mount Sinai Hospital Alumni Fund................................. 4,400.00
Donation of Dr. H. F. L. Ziegel; income, and if necessary, capital, to be expended in defraying part or all of the cost of caring in private rooms of the Hospital for members of the Associated Alumni of Mount Sinai Hospital, the expenditures for any one case not to exceed $200.

Morris Littman Social Service Fund.............................. 3,000.00
Established by provision in the will of Morris Littman; income to be applied to the work of the Social Service Department.

MEDICAL RESEARCH FUNDS

The Abraham and Amelia Meyers Memorial Fund.....................$227,000.00
Established by provision in the will of Amelia Meyers; income to be used in the furtherance of medical and scientific research.

S. S. Prince Research Fund... 100,000.00
Established by provision in the will of S. S. Prince; income to be used for research work.

Henry and Emma Rosenwald Foundation................................... 100,000.00
Established by provision in the will of Mrs. Emma Rosenwald; income to be used for research work. If such work becomes impracticable or inadvisable, the income is to be used for any other purpose designated by the Trustees.

Kops Foundation for Pathological Research............................. 70,000.00
Income to be used from time to time for special work in the Pathological Department, under the direction of the Board of Trustees, preference to be given to research.

The Lorsch-Sachs Endowment Fund for the Promotion of Medical Research 60,000.00
Created by Josephine Lorsch, Nellie and Harry Sachs in memory of Albert Lorsch, Jenny and Sigmund Lorsch; income to be used for the study of some promising scientific problems especially for research work bearing upon the origin and cure of cancer.

Max Nathan Laboratory Fund... 30,000.00
Established by his wife and daughters; income to be used primarily towards the payment of salaries in the Laboratory Research Department.

Eugene Littauer Research Fund.. 25,000.00
Founded by Eugene Littauer in memory of Nathan Littauer; income to be used for medical research work.

William N. Cohen Research Fund... 25,000.00
Established by provision in the will of William N. Cohen; income to be used for research work.

Elias Asiel Research Fund.. 21,000.00
Founded by Irma A. Bloomingdale and Nelson I. Asiel; income of which is to be applied to the payment of salaries or fellowships in the research work of the Pathological Department.

Eugene Strauss Endowment Fund for Medical Research...... 20,000.00
Established by provision in the will of Charles Strauss; income to be used for medical research.

Carried Forward $678,000.00

MEDICAL RESEARCH FUNDS

(Continued)

Brought Forward $678,000.00

Morris J. and Carrie Hirsch Fund.................................... 12,500.00
Established by Walter A. and Steven J. Hirsch in memory
of their parents ($10,000.00); and donation ($2,500.00) from
Mr. and Mrs. Steven J. Hirsch in memory of Walter A.
Hirsch; income to be devoted to work in connection with
the study of cancer.

Rosie Bernheimer Memorial Fund....................................... 10,000.00
Established by provision in the will of Miss Rosie Bern-
heimer; income to be used for clinical research work.

Morris Fatman Medical Research Fund.......................... 10,000.00
Founded by Morris Fatman in memory of Solomon A.
Fatman.

Etta C. and Arthur Lorsch Fund...................................... 10,000.00
Founded by Etta C. and Arthur Lorsch; income to be devoted
to Laboratory research work.

Elsie and Walter W. Naumburg Fund............................ 10,000.00 .
Established by Mr. and Mrs. Walter W. Naumburg; income
to be used exclusively for Chemical Research at Mount Sinai
Hospital.

Virginia I. Stern Fund.. 10,000.00
Legacy; income to be used for medical research work.

**Herman Younker Fund for Clinical and Pathological
Research** 10,000.00
Established by Mrs. Herman Younker; income to be used
exclusively for clinical and pathological research.

Joel E. Hyams Fund.. 10,000.00
Established by provision in the will of Rosalie Hyams;
income to be devoted to research work in cancer.

Leo L. Doblin Endowment Fund for Research Work........... 9,250.00
Legacy; income to be used solely for research work in the
pathological laboratory (On account of $10,000.00 legacy).

Arthur E. Frank Medical Research Fund............................ 7,500.00
Established by provision in the will and in memory of
Arthur E. Frank; the income from this fund is to be
devoted to Laboratory research work, preferably in connection with the study and cure of cancer.

Florentine S. Sutro Research Fund................................... 5,000.00
Legacy; income to be used for research work.

Total $782,250.00

80

ENDOWMENT FUNDS

The Jacob Newman Fund...$319,000.00

The Bella Stiefel Fund 50,000.00

The Carrie M. and Gustav Blumenthal Fund.... 35,000.00

The George and Florence Blumenthal Fund...... 30,000.00

The Philip J. and Hattie L. Goodhart Fund........ 30,000.00

The Ellin P. and James Speyer Fund...................... 30,000.00

The Annie C. and Charles A. Wimpfheimer Fund 30,000.00

The Murry and Leonie Guggenheim Fund............ 25,000.00

The Tillie S. and Alfred Jaretzki Fund................. 25,000.00

The Adolph and Emma Lewisohn Fund................... 20,000.00

The Edward Oppenheimer Fund.............................. 20,000.00

The Estelle and Hugo Blumenthal Fund............ 15,000.00

The Elias and Lina Meyer Asiel Fund.................. 10,000.00

The John A. and Henrietta Cook Fund.................. 10,000.00

The David L. and Carrie F. Einstein Fund............ 10,000.00

The Paul and Miriam H. Gottheil Fund.............. 10,000.00

The Albert N. Hallgarten Fund.............................. 10,000.00

The Henry and Rosa Lehman Fund...................... 10,000.00

The Albert A. Levi Fund.. 10,000.00

The Eugene and Harriet Meyer Fund.................... 10,000.00

The Henry and Josephine Morgenthau Fund...... 10,000.00

The Rosalie and Max Nathan Fund...................... 10,000.00

The Mr. and Mrs. Sam S. Steiner Fund.................. 10,000.00

The Isaac and Virginia Stern Fund...................... 10,000.00

The Alexandre and Julie Weill Fund.................... 10,000.00

$759,000.00

financial pi

The cost of operating the Hospital was $ 2,269,247

These operating costs were exclusive of costs of research, post-graduate medical education and other activities not directly connected with maintenance of the Hospital.

Approximately $1,300,000 was used for salaries and wages. This sum, of course, does not include the value of the services given gratis to the sick poor by our unpaid professional staff.

To meet part of these costs patients paid to the Hospital only . $ 1,109,883

Receipts from other miscellaneous sources amounted to . . . . $ 9,545

The difference is the total philanthropic expense for the year, or $ 1,149,819

Grants from Federation, the United Hospital Fund, the Greater New York Fund and the City, supplied the Hospital with a total of $ 1,000,639

Income from endowment funds, donations, etc., amounted to . $ 59,811

Leaving the Hospital with a final
net shortage or deficit of . .$ 89,369
This deficit added to other deficits
since the depression years beginning with 1930, has now reached
a total of . . . .$ 1,796,193

The large deficits of the past eleven years could
have been avoided only by curtailing in
quantity or quality, or both, the services
rendered by the Hospital to the sick poor
of the City. Because these services are urgently
needed, it has been the policy of the Board of
Trustees to maintain them as long as possible,
and the deficits have been met out of the
limited capital funds of the Hospital.

Such capital funds were expected to provide
income for maintenance purposes and the
depletion of these funds to keep the Hospital
going has correspondingly reduced such
income. There is obviously a limit to this
constant drain on the Hospital's reserves.

Due to this serious depletion of income, the
Hospital urgently appeals for increased capital
donations so that it may continue to serve
adequately and efficiently all who need its care.

TREASURER'S REPORT

STATEMENT OF CURRENT RECEIPTS

FOR THE YEAR ENDED DECEMBER 31st, 1940

HOSPITAL:

Payments of Patients:

Private Pavilion Patients	$617,689.08	
Semi-Private Pavilion Patients	308,503.89	
Ward Patients	122,745.72	
Ward Patients treated under Workmen's Compensation Act	5,973.63	
Out-Patient Department Patients	51,070.11	
Total		$1,105,982.43

Payments by:

City of New York for Part Maintenance of Free Ward Patients and for Custodians		193,033.04

Contributions:

Federation for the Support of Jewish Philanthropic Societies	$261,428.57	
Associated Hospital Service of New York for deferred liability in Semi-Private and Ward cases, returned to Federation which adjusted this sum in its 1939 accounting	2,771.51	
	264,200.08	
Greater New York Fund (through Federaton)	41,626.00	
United Hospital Fund	63,873.03	
Donations	721.00	
Total		370,420.11

Income from Investments:

Permanent Fund	9,624.67	
Endowment Fund	29,520.46	
Other Special Funds for Budgetary Purposes	17,270.08	
Total		56,415.21
Total Budgetary Receipts (Hospital)		1,725,850.79

SCHOOL OF NURSING:

From Federation for the Support of Jewish Philanthropic Societies	297,430.83	
From Other Sources for Budgetary Purposes	10,244.92	
Total Budgetary Receipts (School of Nursing)		307,675.75
Carried Forward		2,033,526.54

Brought Forward $2,033,526.54

SOCIAL SERVICE AUXILIARY:
From Federation for the Support of Jewish
 Philanthropic Societies $100,772.50
From United Hospital Fund 10,175.00
Greater New York Fund (through Federation)
 as part of United Hospital Fund...................   6,925.00
From Other Sources for Budgetary Purposes....   5,875.21

 Total Budgetary Receipts (Social Service
  Auxiliary) 123,747.71

LADIES' AUXILIARY:
From Federation for the Support of Jewish
 Philanthropic Societies 22,604.00

 Total Receipts for Budgetary Purposes
  (Four Societies) 2,179,878.25
Appropriations from Principal and/or Income
 of Special Funds for Stated NonBudgetary
 Purposes (per contra) 129,347.71

 Total Receipts (Budgetary and Non-
  Budgetary) (Four Societies) $2,309,225.96

*Taken from Permanent Fund to meet 1940 Deficits
from Budgetary Operations:*
Hospital *$1,239.74*
School of Nursing *74,570.98*
Ladies' Auxiliary *1,455.29*

 Total from Permanent Fund for 1940 Deficits   *77,266.01*

*Taken from Social Service Auxiliary Special
Account for 1940 Deficit*.........................   *12,103.05*

 **Total taken from Capital to meet the 1940
 Deficits from Operations**........................   **$89,369.06**

STATEMENT OF CURRENT DISBURSEMENTS
FOR THE YEAR ENDED DECEMBER 31st, 1940

HOSPITAL:

Administration:

Salaries and Wages of Officers and Clerks	$100,485.26	
Telephone Wages	12,001.68	
Salaries of Custodians	9,165.47	
Pensions	3,720.00	
Telephone Service	23,164.76	
Stationery and Printing	5,727.12	
Miscellaneous	828.48	
Total Administration		$155,092.77

Professional Care of Patients:

Salaries and Wages:

Physicians	47,025.98	
Nurses	26,423.00	
Druggists	13,917.86	
Orderlies	57,882.80	
Follow-up and Clinical Secretaries	22,481.89	
Medical and Surgical Supplies	171,157.56	
Total Professional Care of Patients		338,889.09

*Out-Patient Department:

Salaries and Wages	39,911.25	
Stationery and Printing	2,152.66	
Supplies	4,496.72	
Total Out-Patient Department		46,560.63

Radiograph Department:

Salaries and Wages	27,666.86	
Supplies	34,149.69	
Total Radiograph Department		61,816.55

Radiotherapy Department:

Salaries and Wages	8,142.48	
Supplies	1,776.38	
Radium	35.12	
Total Radiotherapy Department		9,953.98
Carried Forward		$612,313.02

*The items included under this heading are those which are chargeable directly and exclusively to the Out-Patient Department. The actual cost of conducting the Out-Patient Department, including the proportion of other expenses properly chargeable to it, is $396,649.

Brought Forward		$612,313.02
Electro-cardiograph Department:		
Salaries and Wages	$2,100.87	
Supplies	1,554.77	
Total Electro-cardiograph Department		3,655.64
Department of Laboratories:		
Salaries and Wages	87,829.46	
Supplies	25,756.38	
Total Department of Laboratories		113,585.84
Provisions		353,689.58
Dietary Department:		
Salaries and Wages	100,463.25	
Supplies	11,296.79	
Total Dietary Department		111,760.04
Housekeeping Department:		
Salaries and Wages	85,272.45	
Furniture and Housefurnishings	26,934.45	
Crockery and Silverware	6,675.19	
Dry Goods	6,149.46	
Beds and Bedding	6,234.87	
Total Housekeeping Department		131,266.42
Laundry Department:		
Salaries and Wages	44,949.53	
Supplies	10,279.49	
Total Laundry Department		55,229.02
General House and Property Expenses:		
Salaries and Wages	109,001.44	
Renewals and Repairs	92,697.42	
Light, Heat and Power	71,065.11	
Total General House and Property Expenses		272,763.97
Insurance		19,464.49
Carried Forward		$1,673,728.02

Brought Forward $1,673,728.02

Auditing and Accounting:

Salaries and Wages $38,627.83
Sundries 7,140.34
Stationery and Printing 1,904.12
Postage 3,696.38
Lettering of Tablets 228.75
Awards to House Staff 600.00
Annual Report 1,165.09

Total Auditing and Accounting...................... 53,362.51

Total Budgetary Disbursements (Hospital) 1,727,090.53

School of Nursing—Total Budgetary Disbursements 382,246.73
Social Service—Total Budgetary Disbursements...... 135,850.76
Ladies' Auxiliary—Total Budgetary Disbursements 24,059.29

Total Disbursements for Budgetary Pur-
poses (Four Societies) 2,269,247.31
Disbursements from Principal and/or Income of
Special Funds for Stated Non-Budgetary Pur-
poses (per contra) 129,347.71

Total Disbursements (Budgetary and Non-
Budgetary) (Four Societies) $2,398,595.02

PERMANENT FUND AND OTHER ENDOWMENTS
OF WARDS, ROOMS AND BEDS

Received for Endowment of Wards, Rooms and Beds................. $3,224,616.93
Cash and Securities on Hand.. 979,288.40

*Deficit in Permanent Fund, December 31, 1940...................... $2,245,328.53

* This amount has been borrowed from the Permanent Fund mostly to
provide for Deficits in current expenses and in part for payment of real
estate acquired for Hospital purposes. It is hoped that unrestricted donations and legacies, to enable repayment of this loan, will be received within
a reasonable period of time.

COMPARATIVE STATEMENT OF STATISTICS

For the Year Ended December 31st, 1940
And the Year Ended December 31st, 1939

HOSPITAL PATIENTS
GENERAL WARDS AND PRIVATE ROOMS

	1940	1939
Patients in hospital at beginning of year [1]	607	634
Patients admitted during year [2]	16,668	16,354
Total number of patients treated in hospital during year (Emergency Ward not included)	17,275	16,988
Remaining in hospital at end of year [1]	637	607
Patients treated in Emergency Room (not admitted) [3]	21,807	19,713
Total number of patients admitted since the hospital was founded [2]	467,268	450,600

Patients discharged during year:		
Well or Improved	13,636	13,359
Unimproved	2,269	2,223
Died	733	799
Total [2]	16,638	16,381

Maximum number of patients on any one day [1]	731	733
Minimum number of patients on any one day [1]	543	402
Average number of patients per day	647	636
Average hospital days per patient	13.7	13.7
Mortality rate for the year (all deaths including those which occurred on day of admission)	4.2	4.6

Distribution of days of hospital care for the year:	No. of Days	%	No. of Days	%
General Wards—free to patients	116,454	49.17	127,206	54.76
General Wards—part free to patients	43,095	18.19	27,251	11.73
Semi-Private Pavilion patients	41,207	17.40	42,170	18.16
Private Pavilion patients	36,095	15.24	35,665	15.35
Total	236,851		232,292	
Maintenance days (patients and employees included)	701,150		684,143	

1 Midnight Census.

2 Excludes internal transfers between private, semi-private and ward services.

3 Includes Emergency Dental Treatments reported also in Hospital Dental Statistics. These must be added to O. P. D. Statistics to give complete record of out-patient services.

COMPARATIVE STATEMENT OF STATISTICS
(Continued)

	1940		1939	
	Patients Treated	%	Patients Treated	%
Percentage of total number of patients treated in various divisions:				
General Wards	11,949	67.93	11,893	68.51
Semi-Private Rooms	2,816	16.01	2,662	15.33
Private Rooms	2,826	16.06	2,805	16.16
Total [4]	17,591		17,360	

	1940	1939
Disposition of applications received during the year:		
Admitted to General Wards as free to patients	9,055	9,252
Admitted to General Wards as part free to patients	2,480	2,207
Admitted to Semi-Private Rooms at rates below cost	2,703	2,540
Admitted o Private Rooms	2,746	2,727
Not admitted for various reasons (ward applications)	4,305	4,770
Total Applications	21,289	21,496
Reasons for non-admission to Wards:		
Offered admission but refused by applicant	72	82
Referred to District Staff for care	293	346
Lack of room—referred elsewhere	356	291
Out of Borough—no room	124	146
Able to pay for private care	18	53
Minor ailments	2,480	2,439
Chronic incurable diseases [5]	423	757
Alcoholism [5]	36	51
Contagious diseases [5]	140	102
Infectious diseases [5]	72	131
Pregnancy [5]	32	54
Disturbing mental disorders	259	318
Total	4,305	4,770

DISTRICT MEDICAL SERVICE

	1940	1939
Applicants for admission visited at home	197	259
Patients cared for at home	95	130
Total number of patients visited	260	346
Total number of visits made by physicians	292	387
Analysis of total visits made by physicians:		
Admission to hosiptal recommended	70	102
Admitted (included in general hospital statistics)	70	102
Referred to other institutions	39	26
Not at home when doctor called	6	14
Minor ailments—treated at home	39	35
Unsuitable for hospital admission	107	162
Referred to Out-Patient Department	28	38
Patients ceased before arrival	—	2
Not found at given address	3	8

4 Not adjusted for 316 internal transfers (1940) between private, semi-private and ward services.
5 Referred to appropriate hospital.

COMPARATIVE STATEMENT OF STATISTICS
(Continued)
OUT-PATIENT DEPARTMENT STATISTICS

	1940	1939
Total visits [6]	357,567	345,093
Total prescriptions	166,991	146,397
Patients new in year	10,281	10,157
Patients from past years	19,378	21,292
Total individuals	29,659	31,449
Out-Patient Department days	304	302
Daily average prescriptions	549	485
Daily average consultations	1,176	1,143
Average daily attendance of physicians	199	198
Average daily attendance of nurses	25	24
Average daily attendance of volunteer aids	33	33
Maximum consultations on any one day	1,508	1,456
Maximum prescriptions on any one day	884	899

ANALYSIS OF CONSULTATIONS

Name of Clinic	Morning Session	Afternoon Session	1940 Total	1939 Total
Internal Medicine	10,426	31,486	41,912	38,921
Minor Medical	183	366	549	580
Basal Metabolism	1,367	—	1,367	1,377
Gastro-Enterology	9,031	—	9,031	8.374
Diabetic	9,129	—	9,129	8,920
Adult Cardiac	4,766	2,582	7,348	7,015
Adult Asthma	14,558	—	14,558	12,569
Chest	1,655	—	1,655	1,421
Hematology	—	8,804	8,804	7,902
Blood Bank	—	2,135	2.135	2,052
Plasma for Britain Project	—	2,856	2,856	
Neurology and Psychiatry	6,339	7,157	13,496	11,240
Dermatology	9,427	14,858	24,285	25,368
Arseno-Therapy	—	1,434	1,434	1,907
Surgical	14,575	10,376	24,951	25,513
Breast	—	244	244	226
Genito-Urinary	5,273	1,883	7,156	6,491
Rectal	4,555	—	4,555	4,206
Gynecological	9,003	12,156	21,159	22,128
Ear, Nose and Throat	2,731	16,690	19,421	19,404
Eye	4,366	12.550	16,916	15,331
Thrombo-Angiitis Obliterans	9,999	273	10,272	11,363
Orthopedic	840	13,309	14,149	14,242
Children's Medical	8,871	11,567	20.438	20,427
Children's Asthma	—	10,325	10,325	9,869
Children's Cardiac	1,292	—	1,292	1,476
Children's Health	—	2,206	2.206	2,200
Dental	8,811	6,180	14,991	15,563
Physical Therapy	13,718	11,393	25,111	25,378
Radiotherapy	6,073	6,811	12,884	11,988
Roentgenology	5,161	—	5,161	4,857
Electrocardiography	1,722	—	1,722	1.493
Occupational Therapy	1,190	—	1,190	1,233
Nutrition	—	4,865	4,865	4,059
Total Consultations	165,061	192,506	357.567	345.093

[6] This figure does not include emergency visits by out-patients in accident and emergency room outside of regular clinic hours. Inclusive total is 374,383 for 1940 and 364,806 for 1939.

COMPARATIVE STATEMENT OF STATISTICS
(Continued)

DEPARTMENT OF LABORATORIES
Examinations in Central Laboratory

	1940	1939
Bacteriology:		
Blood Groupings	8,473	6,648
Nose and Throat Cultures	129	99
Blood Cultures	1,892	1,558
Pus Cultures, etc.	8,361	6,527
Post Mortem Cultures	101	123
Special Anaerobic Cultures	255	185
Bacteriophage Cultures	14	7
Loewenstein Cultures	4	4
Plasma Bank Cultures	391	——
Staphylococcus Pathogenicity	2,993	2,642
Streptococcus Pathogenicity	450	461
Pneumococcus Typings	533	678
Neufeld Tests	429	547
Vaccines	91	84
Bacteriophage Tests	8	7
Guinea Pig Inoculations	479	338
Miscellaneous Animal Inoculations	80	51
Widal Reactions	344	241
Wasserman Tests	11,882	10,866
Kahn Tests	3,983	3,265
Kahn Tests—Plasma Bank	2,366	——
Agglutination Reactions	633	506
Complement Fixation Tests	72	102
Precipitation Tests	368	420
Colloidal Gold Tests	992	854
Globulin Determinations	951	802
Heterophile Reactions	394	281
Cell Counts	1	4
Miscellaneous Tests	401	207
Total	47,070	37,507

Surgical Pathology and Morbid Anatomy:		
Examinations of Operative Specimens	6,711	6,031
Post-Mortem Examinations	341	344

COMPARATIVE STATEMENT OF STATISTICS

(Continued)

DEPARTMENT OF LABORATORIES—(Continued)
Examinations in Central Laboratory—(Continued)

	1940	1939
Chemistry:		
Complete Blood Chemistry	643	818
Partial Blood Chemistry	10,953	10,921
Urine Chemistry	95	173
Gastro-Intestinal Contents	79	68
Examinations for Heavy Metals	109	81
Functional Tests	3,017	2,534
Examinations for Spinal Fluid	1,211	1,080
Miscellaneous Tests	251	182
Total	16,358	15,857
Hematology:		
Blood Counts	674	566
Blood Volumes	44	22
Fragility of Red Cells	34	38
Congo Red Tests	39	21
Sedimentation Tests	220	259
Hematocrit Determinations	56	78
Heterophile Reactions	—	2
Bone Marrow Examinations	214	168
Formalin Tests	9	8
Reticulocyte Counts	269	180
Prothrombin Tests	340	—
Miscellaneous Tests	28	164
Total	1,927	1,506
Endocrinology:		
Aschheim-Zondek Tests	249	287
Frank-Goldberger Tests—Blood	134	258
Frank-Goldberger Tests—Urine	563	569
Pituitary Blood Tests	3	9
Pituitary Urine Tests	728	437
Pituitary Blood Serum	26	177
Estrogenic Substance and Gonadotropic Hormone Tests	691	609
Total	2,394	2,346
Blood Bank:		
Volunteer Donors for Wards [7]	2,135	2,052
Transfusions Given with Stored Blood	1,984	1,910
Volunteer Donors for Britain [7]	2,856	—

[7] Included in O. P. D. Statistics.

COMPARATIVE STATEMENT OF STATISTICS

(Continued)

Laboratory for Routine Clinical Microscopy in Private Pavilion, Semi-Private Pavilion and Out-Patient Department

	1940			1939		
	PRIV. PAV.	SEMI-PRIV. PAV.	O.P.D.[8]	PRIV. PAV.	SEMI-PRIV. PAV.	O.P.D.[8]
Routine Urines	12,953	14,155	5,943	10,537	12,401	6,138
Phenolsulphonphthalein Tests....	24	34	6	26	27	4
Blood Counts	4,728	4,530	3,727	3,707	3,617	3,142
Feces	348	392	642	343	422	541
Sputa	68	135	409	47	136	420
Smears	11	25	1,298	33	15	1,174
Gastric Contents	66	80	——	53	96	——
Spinal Fluids	40	50	77	60	44	——
Blood Sugars	——	——	666	——	——	687
Quantitative Urines	76	58	264	31	53	415
Galactose Tests	4	——	2	4	——	2
Sedimentation Tests	——	——	730	——	——	659
Concentration Tests	4	26	126	17	20	88
Janney Tests	5	4	173	3	5	171
Miscellaneous Tests	23	37	32	15	37	68
Total	18,350	19,526	14,095	14,876	16,873	13,509

Laboratory for Routine Clinical Microscopy in Wards[9]

	First Medical Service		Second Medical Service	
	1940	1939	1940	1939
Routine Urines	12,240	12,014	12,580	11,151
Phenolsulphonphthalein Tests	17	15	34	6
Blood Counts	4,234	3,847	4,161	3,267
Feces	2,400	2,900	2,369	2,194
Sputa	328	399	181	249
Smears	138	153	100	119
Gastric Contents	212	141	255	239
Spinal Fluids	7	18	45	29
Galactose Tests	127	157	131	115
Concentration Tests	141	92	195	124
Janney Tests	51	39	92	60
Miscellaneous Tests	70	89	126	183
Total	19,965	19,864	20,269	17,736

8 Does not include clinical microscopy examinations in individual clinics by members of visiting medical staff.

9 Does not include clinical microscopy examinations in Surgical Services and Medical and Surgical Specialties, performed by members of House Staff.

94

COMPARATIVE STATEMENT OF STATISTICS
(Continued)

Clinic Laboratories in Out-Patient Department

Urinalysis:	1940		1939
Genito-Urinary	3,684		2,729
Gynecological	1,422		619
Medical	3,964		3,539
Diabetic	9,762		9,026
Children's	1,901		1,527
		20,733	17,440
Tuberculin Tests	2,179		3,240
Dark Field Examinations	40		39
Smears:			
Genito-Urinary	3,379		2,729
Gynecological	5,767		4,016
		9,146	6,745
Gastric Analysis	920		985
Total		**33,018**	**28,449**

LABORATORY FOR BASAL METABOLISM
(Hospital Laboratory) [10]

	1940	1939
Private Patients	69	70
Semi-Private Patients	179	175
Ward Patients	1,545	1,154
Nurses	71	32
Total	**1,864**	**1,431**
Maximum number of examinations on any one day	13	11

DEPARTMENT OF RADIOLOGY

Radiography:	1940	1939
Number of Examinations	24,189	23,152
Number of Plates Taken	73,151	66,451
Number of Fluoroscopic Examinations	7,814	7,576
Radiotherapy:		
Number of New Patients	579	562
Number of Visits (old and new patients) [11]	13,398	13,516
Number of Treatments (old and new patients)	10,654	8,618

Radiotherapy Treatments:

		P.P.	SEMI-P.P.	WARD	O.P.D.	TOTAL
High Frequency	1940	0	0	0	8	8
	1939	1	0	1	17	19
Radium	1940	0	0	25	13	38
	1939	0	1	35	8	44
Superficial Therapy	1940	2	2	19	1,441	1,464
	1939	2	6	24	1,327	1,359
Deep Therapy	1940	211	183	1,414	7,336	9,144
	1939	185	277	1,424	5,284	7,170
Total	1940	213	185	1,458	8,798	10,654
	1939	188	284	1,484	6,636	8,592

10 O. P. D. examinations reported in O. P. D. Statistics.
11 Includes 12,884 Visits in 1940 and 11,988 Visits in 1939, which were reported in O. P. D. Consultations.

COMPARATIVE STATEMENT OF STATISTICS
(Continued)

DEPARTMENT OF PHYSIOTHERAPY
(Hospital)

	1940	1939
Massage	1,279	988
Exercise	1,015	705
Gymnasium Treatments	2,290	2,204
Low Tension Currents	335	406
Hydrotherapy	2,860	2,990
Diathermia	78	64
Hyperthermia	527	525
Short Wave	868	1,446
Ultra-Violet	1,816	1,712
Photothermia (Infra-Red Lamp)	3,014	2,710
Thermo Hood	1,052	1,047
Total number of treatments for year	15,134	14,797
Maximum number on any one day	65	40

DENTAL DEPARTMENT
(Hospital)

	1940	1939[12]
Number of Patients	3,472	2,508
Number of Visits[13]	4,628	3,557
Diagnostic Procedures:		
X-Rays:		
Number of Patients	3,413	2,161
Number of Films	11,683	9,370
Cultures	31	31
Specimens for Pathology	38	6
Total Number of Treatments	3,934	3,045
Extractions	2,376	1,493
Oral Surgery	187	91
Fillings	142	134
Prophylaxis	99	60
Minor Care	1,084	1,239
Mechanical Work	11	8
Fractures	35	20
Patients Examined on Wards:		
Number Examined	1,949	1,397
Number Referred to Department	438	413
Maximum number on any one day	28	23

12 Figures for 1939 recast in order to show figures comparable with 1940.
13 This includes 3,119 emergency ward visits in 1940 and 2,261 in 1939.

COMPARATIVE STATEMENT OF STATISTICS

(Continued)

DENTAL DEPARTMENT

(Out-Patient Department)

	1940	1939
Extractions	1,639	1,615
Fillings	1,532	1,357
Orthodontia	571	601
Oral Surgery	222	229
Mechanical Work	3,219	3,574
Root Canal Therapy	93	99
Pyorrhea Treatments	241	267
X-Ray Examinations	1,285	1,224
Cultures	54	35
Fractures	37	77
Other Treatments	3,138	3,305
	12,031	12,383
Examinations only	3,591	3,425
Total number of services for year	15,622	15,808
Total number of visits [14]	14,991	15,563
Maximum number of visits on any one day	90	95

ELECTROCARDIOGRAPH DEPARTMENT

	1940	1939
Electrocardiographic Examinations:		
Private Patients	184	184
Semi-Private Patients	125	163
Ward Patients	5,159	4,591
Out-Patients[15]	1,722	1,493
Heart Sound Examinations [16]	109	—
Total number of examinations	7,299	6,431
Maximum number on any one day	34	38

ELECTRO-ENCEPHALOGRAPHY LABORATORY

	1940	1939
Electro-Encephalograms	550	124

CONSULTATION SERVICE

	1940	1939
Patients admitted	3,098	2,829
Referring doctors	624	635

14 Included in O. P. D. Consultations.
15 Included in O. P. D. Consultations—Morning Session.
16 Beginning August 1, 1940.

COMPARATIVE STATEMENT OF STATISTICS

(Continued)

FOLLOW-UP CLINICS

REPORT FOR 1940

	No. of Clinic Sessions	No. of Appointments Given	Appointments Kept 17	Cases Closed	Referred for Further Treatment	Referred for Readmission
Medical	82	2,750	2,153	269	427	66
Surgical	130	7,143	5,330	562	746	262
Gynecological	48	3,158	2,289	300	287	59
Orthopedic	24	1,095	840	96	162	48
Pediatric	42	963	702	58	81	10
Neurological	23	855	553	73	19	24
Ear, Nose and Throat	16	1,337	819	162	40	65
Eye	11	405	303	37	70	24
Radiotherapy	86	1,774	1.471	9	147	26
Physiotherapy	11	118	67	9	5	—
Hematology	10	104	72	9	2	—
Total	483	19,702	14,599	1,584	1,986	584

17 Included in O. P. D. Consultations .

98

REPORT OF THE COMMITTEE ON
OUT-PATIENT DEPARTMENT

In 1940, the sixty-eighth year of service of the Out-Patient Department was completed, leaving behind its record of accomplishment and of service. Over 29,000 persons of all ages, colors, races and creeds have passed through its doors to receive the healing ministrations of its doctors, nurses and social workers, and to benefit by the latest aids of medical science, fortified by human sympathy and understanding. Our community obligations have been discharged to the full extent of our facilities. Professional services have directly benefited thousands and indirectly benefited many thousands more. Potential wage-earners have in many cases been restored to useful activities; others, unable to continue in former occupations because of physical infirmities, have been rehabilitated in less strenuous pursuits; cardiac, asthmatic and other chronically-afflicted children and adults have been guided in ways of living useful and happy lives within their capacities; early diagnosis, segregation and intensive case-findings have protected countless friends, relatives and other contacts of patients with transmissible diseases; in short, the facilities of modern preventive and curative medical science have been placed at the disposal of those whose limited financial resources have made it impossible to secure them on their own account.

Every applicant for clinic admission underwent a thorough but sympathetic inquiry in order to exclude as recipients of charitable services those who were not truly medically indigent. In addition, those patients who had attended the clinic for some time were re-investigated in order to determine whether improved financial circumstances warranted the reference of any of these patients to a private physician. Numerical limitations were placed on new admissions in order to prevent the clinics from becoming overcrowded and allowing mere mass of numbers to become the criterion of accomplishment rather than quality of medical service rendered. Indeed, it unfortunately became necessary on occasion during the year to discontinue altogether new admissions to certain clinics because the physical capacity of these clinics, consistent with individualization of treatment, had been reached. In spite of this, however, 29,659 individuals were admitted for treatment in the more than 50 separate clinics of the Out-Patient

Department, of which number 10,281 came for the first time in 1940 and 19,378 continued their treatment begun in previous years. These 29,659 persons, plus those who came to the Blood Bank, made a total of 357,567 visits during the year, the largest number in the history of the institution and one of the largest attendances of voluntary hospital out-patient departments anywhere in the United States. A high average of nearly 12 visits per patient during the year was attained, indicative of the excellence of the medical care given and the recognition by each patient of the importance of medical care. 166,991 prescriptions were compounded during the year for clinic patients, representing an average of 549 prescriptions a day, an increase of more than 14% over the previous year.

To make all this possible, 761 individual physicians came to the clinics. An average of 199 attended the clinics each day and gave freely and willingly of their time and service. They were ably assisted by 64 lay volunteer workers who relieved them of non-clinical routines, thus allowing more time for examination and treatment of patients. To these physicians and volunteers for their services, the Out-Patient Department Committee is grateful.

In constant attendance in the clinics were 10 graduate and 15 student nurses, the latter adding to the training received in the wards of the Hospital in the care of the bedridden patient, the knowledge of the medical, social and nursing problems confronting the ambulatory patient. To transform the medical advice given to the patients regarding personal care, diet, school and business activities, home life, etc., into concrete realities, trained social workers were attached to many clinics. It is difficult to provide a yardstick for the value of the services rendered by these social workers, yet the improvement of the results of medical care rendered in our clinics today over that of 20 years ago is in large measure due to more adequate understanding of the social and economic problems facing clinic patients in relation to their medical symptoms and the solution of many of these problems through the efforts of the social workers.

The activities of the clinics of the Out-Patient Department were closely co-ordinated with those of the other Hospital departments—wards, accident room, and follow-up clinics—so that continuous observation and treatment of the patient was maintained at all times. In addition, constant inter-clinic consultative refers were made, with the physician who saw the patient originally in the parent clinic remaining in personal charge of the entire case, affording the advantages of specialty consultations while maintaining a single physician in direct charge of every patient. Intimate supervision was offered to the clinical assistants by the clinic chiefs whose duty it was to review every new case and to teach and guide the assistants in the more complicated diagnostic and therapeutic problems.

Thus the unlimited educational opportunities represented by the wealth of the clinical material seen in the clinics were utilized to their fullest extent. Frequent conferences were held, attended by physicians, nurses and social workers, at which interesting cases were reported by the clinical assistants and discussed by the entire staff. Those untrained in the preparation and presentation of case reports were encouraged to take advantage of these opportunities for broadening their professional experiences and capacities. Opportunity was also given to many foreign physicians who, dispossessed and repudiated by the countries whose scientific reputations they helped build, transferred their allegiance to this country where they hoped to establish themselves as useful members of a community to whose welfare and advancement they might contribute. The physicians were trained in American methods of diagnosis and therapy, as well as the language, habits and customs of their newly adopted land. A number of these physicians have already left us to settle in and be assimilated by other communities in need of medical men.

The clinics were also used for teaching purposes in the postgraduate courses offered by the Mount Sinai Hospital in collaboration with the College of Physicians and Surgeons of Columbia University. A total of 329 students from 13 states and 7 foreign countries were enrolled. Part of the training course of every student nurse consisted, in 1940, of a period of 8 weeks spent in the various OPD clinics, under the guidance of a teaching nurse-supervisor who, by formal lectures, conferences and discussions, augmented the practical knowledge obtained by the student nurses in the clinics.

In addition to the numerous health and educational benefits already listed, many specific contributions were made by the clinic physicians in the form of scientific undertakings; among these were research studies in male and female sex hormones and techniques in bio-assay, investigation into the problem of differentiation of organic and functional angina pectoris, ascillometric studies in patients with coronary-artery disease, clinical research in new procedures in radiation therapy, extensive work in vascular allergy, arthritis, peptic ulcer and ulcerative colitis, vitamins, insulin, obesity and malnutrition, and many other subjects.

Several changes were made during the year, necessitated by the expansion of activities in various clinic departments. In an effort to control the serious complicating infections of the lower extremities to which diabetic patients are subject, a graduate podiatrist was added to the diabetic clinic staff. The nutrition group of the Metabolism clinic was moved to larger quarters in order to care for an increasing number of patients needing diatetic management.

The psychiatric clinic, hard-pressed for additional facilities to satisfy the demands made upon its services, introduced the so-called "double-session days," in which, instead of one group of physicians attending each morning, two groups attended, one from 9:00 A. M. to 10:30 A. M., and the other from 10:30 A. M. to noon. Thus twice as many physicians could serve the clinic and more patients be treated. An additional psychiatrist was also made available to the general medical clinics so that psychiatric consultations might be promptly available in evaluating the mental components of the patients' symptomatologies.

To further the efforts of the clinic physicians, nurses and social workers in educating clinic patients in personal hygiene, proper diet and exercise, prevention of the spread of contagious disease, etc., appropriate pamphlets on these topics have been secured from various public-health agencies and are being distributed to the patients in the OPD.

In 1940, co-operation with the Central Tabulating Bureau of the New York City Department of Health was begun. This is a project to centralize all statistics on venereal disease, in a more intensive effort to control this illness, and to this project Mount Sinai Hospital lent its full co-operation.

During the year, the radiotherapy follow-up clinic of gynecological patients was moved from the regular follow-up department to the gynecology clinic in the OPD so that the superior facilities for gynecologic examinations present in the clinic might be available to the radiotherapy department.

I cannot close this report without repeating my thanks to those whose efforts made these accomplishments of the OPD in 1940 possible.

Respectfully submitted,

LEONARD A. HOCKSTADER,
Chairman.

REPORT OF COMMITTEE ON LABORATORIES

LABORATORY OF BACTERIOLOGY

A large part of the work of this laboratory is considered routine bacteriology, the various activities of which can be conveniently classified under the following sub-headings:

(a) Bacteriology proper, the purpose of which is to isolate and identify bacteria and viruses in patients.

(b) Serology, which is concerned with the immunological methods and identification of bacteria; serological methods of diagnosis of syphilis (Wassermanns and Kahns) and other diseases such as infectious mononucleosis, gonorrhea, typhoid, dysentery, etc.; and identification of human blood groups.

There has been a decided increase in the amount of routine in 1940. The increase in serology is due to several reasons. A small portion could be accounted for by the Blood-Plasma-for-Britain project. The major portion of the increase may be attributed to (a) the addition of new serological tests for diagnosis of disease; (b) the continuous but advantageous introduction of new serological methods as a help to routine bacteriology; (c) the augmented demand for Wassermann and Kahn tests necessitated by the New York State Laws requiring syphilis tests in pregnancy and for marriage licenses; (d) the organization of the Blood Bank. The greater burden placed on the technicians engaged in Wassermann and Kahn tests is thus far being carried satisfactorily, but it is questionable whether more work can be added without enlarging the present facilities.

There is a striking difference between the volume of work done for the wards on one hand, and for private and semi-private patients on the other hand, as is frequently pointed out by the administrative officers of the Hospital. The main cause appears to be the attempt of the physicians in charge of private cases to reduce the hospital costs to their patients as much as possible; also, the fact that most private cases are surgical in nature, which may be responsible for a somewhat smaller need for some of the bacteriological tests.

During the latter part of 1940, the services of the junior intern were discontinued in the house staff organization and the duties taken over by a full-time technician. To provide for the night emergency services, an experienced physician, usually a former member of the house satff, was permitted to reside in the Hospital and required to serve on every third night and every third weekend with the regular residents or interns in pathology and bacteriology. This scheme has resulted in an improvement in service since, in the past, the work of the junior, changing every month, was not always uniform.

A working unit-time scheme was developed to indicate how much time was spent in 1940 on the performance of each test listed. With this information in mind, it was possible to determine whether the amount of work involved was jutified by the usefulness of a test. Thus, it was seen that the time devoted to blood culture work is considerable. However, the results are positive in a high percentage of cases, and therefore, in spite of the burden to the department, it is considered important to continue the present method.

During the past years, persistent attempts have been made to train in bacteriology young physicians interested primarily in clinical medicine, surgery, and special laboratory methods, with the ultimate purpose of securing later their services at "liaison officers." Thus far satisfactory results were obtained from the faithful efforts of a number of physicians. The usefulness of this service consists in the interpretation of laboratory findings to the clinical staff; actual work in the wards with certain laboratory methods carried out best in proximity to the patients; supervision of special means of collection of specimens not infrequently necessary to preserve their full values; and also the service of pointing out to the laboratory staff the needs of the clinicians.

Since the use of the animals is an essential prerequisite for much of the work done in the laboratories, there is a constant demand for the facilities of the single animal room. The room with its present facilities is an uncomfortably overcrowded place and one which is overburdened. These factors lead in turn to difficulty in allocating the time of use of the room among some of the workers. A new plan will be tried in the hope that it will meet more satisfactorily the needs of the staff within the present limited space.

The work in the animal room does not represent all the activities with animals. An adjacent small room is used continuously for injections of small animals, inoculations of infectious materials, tumor-transplants, animal post-mortem examinations, etc. Not infrequently as many as ten people may be found working at the same time in the small room, all of them requiring the service of helpers simultaneously. Through many locally built ingenious devices, the helpers manage to fill the essential needs and to keep nearly everyone satisfied. This situation, however, is very unsatisfactory and is bound to reflect upon the accuracy and quality of the work done under such conditions. The need for improvement is great but no real improvement is possible without providing for greater space.

It is impossible in a brief report to give a detailed description of the activities of all professional workers who were connected with the laboratory of bacteriology during 1940, as (1) voluntary assistants; (2) research assistants; (3) fellows; (4) observers; (5) those having appointments in other departments who spent nevertheless a part of their time in the laboratory of bacteriology; (6) members of the visiting staff of the Hospital who work in the laboratory, and finally (7) non-appointees who have collaborated with the laboratory without actually working in it.

However, the activities of these members may be described briefly as (a) routine duties in the central bacteriological laboratories and in the annex, (b) routine "liaison," (c) research directly pertaining to clinical problems and representing an outgrowth of routine work in bacteriology and serology, and (d) laboratory research.

In order to set forth some criteria for the evaluation of the above activities, an attempt has been made, wherever possible, to appraise the workers on the basis of training, conscientiousness, successes and failures, with due consideration of the underlying causes, and on the basis of their findings to decide on those who, in the opinion of the Department, should be further encouraged. In the summary which will follow, a few only are selected for mention.

One worker for five years has engaged in an interesting approach to fundamental problems of the physiology of the skin. Clearcut physico-chemical laws determining the diffusion of foreign substances into the skin were experimentally and mathematically developed, assuming that the fate of a substance injected into the skin is conditioned by the same relationships as the diffusion of the substance through some inanimate membrane having the same gradient of permeability as the skin. By this analogy it was found that the electrical charge of the substance injected into the skin plays a very important role in the diffusion. Successful attempts which followed eliminated the method of injection for the introduction of foreign substances under or into the skin. The material may be merely placed on a small portion of the skin. Following the application of a mild electric current there occurs a rapid diffusion of the substance into the skin, the so-called iontophoresis. When colored particles are thus introduced, the rate and area of diffusion are made obvious almost instantaneously. After the basic principles had been established, the work was extended into the field of allergy where abnormal relationships may be assumed to exist. This phase of the studies carries interesting practical implications which may improve the prophylactic treatment of hay fever.

Advantage was taken of a recently described apparatus of Tiselius for electrophoresis, which finds wide application in many biological investigations. Thus far it has been possible to isolate a major constituent of ragweed which is unpigmented, a highly skin-reactive producing hay fever fraction as well as other fractions the role of which remains to be determined. Immunological studies made by means of certain physiological methods of Dale became necessary to ascertain the role and connection between the fractions obtained by the method of Tiselius. This phase of the work is being carried on in collaboration with the Department of Physics of the College of Physicians and Surgeons.

The holder of the Moritz Rosenthal Fellowship has been intensely interested in immunological problems with special reference to the phenomenon of local skin reactivity. He is actively engaged in observations, which he hopes to complete during 1941, on the relation of the toxins of diphtheria to the phenomenon. Recently, incidentally to other investigations, he made the interesting original observation on the production of a hemorrhagic reaction in the conjunctiva of rabbits following the intravenous injection of toxic filtrates potent in the elicitation of the phenomenon of local skin reactivity. He also noted that the reaction of the conjunctiva was absent in rabbits developing the positive phenomenon. The non-specific protective effect of the phenomenon of local skin reactivity upon various infections (anthrax, vaccinia virus, etc.) has been previously observed by a number of investigators. The findings seem to offer a possible approach to the elucidation of the mechanism of this protection against infections. Furthermore, also parallel to other observations, there seems to arise a possibility to produce a local phenomenon in the sciatic nerve. This finding may have an interesting practical bearing on our understanding of the cause of certain types of inflammation of this nerve.

There has always remained in the minds of medical investigators, an open question as to the fate of poisons (toxins and viruses) in the animal and human body afflicted by infectious diseases. When toxins and most of the viruses enter the body they produce no effect during the so-called incubation period preceding for some days the specific symptoms. The supervening clinical picture is almost always the same in a given disease. During the incubation period, and in many instances even during the disease, it is impossible to demonstrate the presence of the toxins or the viruses in the blood, and in some diseases, even in the diseased organs themselves. The problem of determining how these disease-producing agents reach the susceptible organs and trace their fate in the organs has remained unexplained, although it has attracted many investigators (in case of tetanus, several researches dealing with this problem date back to 1888).

It always has seemed to the bacteriologist that it may prove of utmost importance to find out the route in the host taken by the invading agents and the manner of the invasion. Because of the constancy of the duration of the incubation period and the symptomatology, he made the assumption that the mode of transportation of disease-producing agents to the organs of the host in each disease are rigidly predetermined. For lack of facilities and special apparatus, he has only recently started the work on the problem, reasoning as follows:

In order to obtain a constant and regular effect, the toxins and viruses must take advantage of some regular means of transport to the cells, tissues, and organs, i. e., a means which under conditions of normal function invariably comes into intimate contact with all the vital parts of the body of the hosts. It then occurred to him that hemoglobin may be utilized by toxins and viruses to serve this purpose. Hemoglobin, the red pigment of the blood, is the most vital agent of life since it makes respiration of the cells possible by making oxygen, with which it enters into combination, available to the tissues, and also by removing carbon dioxide to the outside. Since a number of chemicals are known to attach themselves easily to hemoglobin, the question was asked whether, like oxygen, the toxins and viruses do not also become attached to the hemoglobin and thus, in a constant and regular manner, come into intimate contact with the host. In order to prove this contention a number of experiments were performed on tetanus, which showed that, following special precautions, almost the entire amount of the tetanus toxin injected subcutaneously into a guinea-pig may be recovered in association with the hemoglobin during the stages of the active disease.

Similarly startling results were obtained with toxins of other diseases, like diphtheria, typhoid, meningococcus, and also possibly infantile paralysis, herpes, and small-pox viruses. Thus, it became obvious at the early stage of the work that one was dealing with a fundamental principle governing the transportation of disease agents to the organs—the points of their attack. In following up the findings, two alternative plans presented themselves; (a) to begin the application of the principle found to various diseases with a view to utilizing the new possibilities for practical preventive and therapeutic purposes which could be approached with comparative ease; (b) to devote all the attention on the laws underlying the principle in order to establish first a firm basis for future investigation. One of these had to be selected for immediate pursuance. Although the first alternative appeared attractive, efforts were concentrated on the investigations of the fundamental laws, and progress has thus far been made, which is considered of value for all the investigations to follow and most essential for bringing convincing and unquestionable proof to the contention.

The present organization of the laboratory offers opportunities for many future objectives of which the following are a few:

A. Constant progress is being attained in bacteriological and immunological research by numerous investigators, having the ultimate purpose of diagnosis and treatment of disease. Modern bacteriological and immunological routine cannot therefore exist independently of research. In view of the fact that this laboratory has carried out incessant scientific investigations on various phases of bacteriology and immunology, it has become possible to develop a modern standard of clinical bacteriological investigations which may develop still further and bear more fruit provided this trend is continued.

B. It has also been long realized that modern clinical sciences, which intend to keep pace with the present trends, require that at least some members possess the understanding of bacteriology and immunology in the broad sense. Endeavors, therefore, have always been made to train clinicians in bacteriology and immunology and maintain their connection with this department for as long a period of time thereafter as possible. These clinicians could then bring to the wards the laboratory point of view and in exchange call to the attention of the laboratories the clinical tasks.

C. Research having for its goal the ultimate attainments in treatment and diagnosis of diseases will always remain essential in a medical institution of high standard. The past work of the laboratory has laid a foundation to certain already widely recognized novel traits which, if further supported, may express themselves in the establishment of a department of immunology in which the physiological sciences could be appropriated as a new tool for future investigations on infectious diseases, i. e., laboratory of immuno-physiology. Certain physical facilities, mostly in the nature of physical, chemical and physiological equipment ordinarily neglected in bacteriological and immunological studies, have been acquired and put to use. The efforts already made suggest that encouraging opportunities may exist in this direction.

LABORATORY OF CHEMISTRY

The laboratory has continued in its greatly varied services with unabating activity. The number of routine specimens in chemistry, clinical microscopy and endocrinology has run roughly parallel with the activity of the clinical services and private pavilions, but specific increases, especially in clinical microscopy, will be noticed from the statistics reported elsewhere. These are due to the increased application of chemo-therapeutic measures.

The groups interested in endocrinology and gastro-enterology have offered numerous scientific contributions, and at the same time have served as the backbone for the training of others in their respective clinical fields, by conferences, seminars and consultations.

The endocrine laboratory, in addition to increased routine work, has completed a standard test for male sex hormone of great practicality, replacing the capon by the inexpensive one-day-old chick. Gonadotropic and estrogenic tests for the female hormones, greatly improved and fully standardized in this laboratory, are gaining general favor. Research work in connection with the gynecological services dealt with the value of implantation therapy for the prevention and alleviation of menopause and postoperative symptoms. The effect of hormones and drugs on the mobility of the Fallopian tubes was studied extensively. The sex hormones in adrenal cortical tumor and virilism were investigated.

The gastro-enterology research group continued its investigation of fundamental physiological problems of moment to the corresponding medical and surgical services, as well as of clinical researches concerning surgical vagotomy and the drip treatment for peptic ulcer. A long range study of the effects of various inflammatory and carcinogenic agents applied to the stomach mucosa in experimental animals was initiated in collaboration with the National Cancer Institute of the United States Public Health Service.

The pharmacological laboratory has built an ingenious kymographion for the registration of brain temperature with an accuracy of 1/100 of a degree, and studies of the effects of drugs have been completed, others being in progress.

The work of the chemical laboratory, in collaboration with numerous members of the medical and neurological services, has been integrated to great advantage, during 1940. Two fields stand out, in which the usefulness of the existing space facilities was increased by the correlation of related problems with each other.

These fields are the vitamins and the filtrable constituents of the blood. As to the former, the receipt of extramural funds has permitted the purchase of a fluorescence photometer for the chemical determination of the Vitamin B complex. The study of the "fertility vitamin" (tocopherol) in the treatment of amyotrophic lateral sclerosis (a form of paralysis considered incurable) and the metabolism of lipoids and carotenoids in special reference to the "seeing vitamin" A complex in multiple sclerosis has yielded novel and encouraging results, which are followed through and correlated with Vitamin B studies of the diabetic group. This group has evolved a test for the objective estimation and laboratory confirmation of clinical Vitamin B1 deficiencies. This work has led to the introduction of a fat-tolerance test, which is also used for the study of fat resorption in the presence of lecithin and bile acids. Very gratifying results in these coordinated vitamin studies issued from the therapeutic application of Vitamin A by the dermatologists in otherwise untractable thickening of the skin (hyperkeratosis). It will be merely a question of time and the provision of more laboratory facilities for the workers to throw open their experiences with vitamin determinations to the routine use of the Hospital.

The second field mentioned above, that of the filtrable blood constituents, has been represented by studies of the magnesium in hypothyroidism, complementing the laboratory's previous work in Graves' disease. Another outgrowth of these studies is a salt-and-water-retention test in diseases of the adrenal gland and in conjunction with their hormonal treatment. The study of diffusible and non-diffusible iodine in the blood strikes in a parallel direction. Improvements in the technique of ultra-filtrable uric acid in gout and certain hepatic conditions are in progress. Observations of hibernation in woodchucks, gophers and turtles are preliminaries to the study of blood electrolytes at lowered body temperature and during sleep.

Investigations of acetyl choline esterase, an enzyme important in the transmission of nerve impulses, have been resumed and are nearing the stage of clinical application. Other enzymes under investigation include the oxidases of the skin and the white blood corpuscles with a view to the toxic effect of certain drugs. Finally, the enzyme carbonic anhydrase has been studied in lower animals at the Bermuda Biological Station. This work has opened new views for the seemingly remote problem of the influence of sulfanilamide therapy on respiration. Synthesis of sulfanyl derivatives has been continued in the organic chemistry laboratory. Another contribution to chemotherapy was the study of the behavior of arsenic in the blood in a group of patients treated for primary lues by the intravenous-arsenic-drip method.

The more than 100 methods used in the routine laboratory have been summarized in the form of a book recently published by the assistant chemist under the title of "Manual of Clinical Chemistry." The physiological chemistry seminar has continued its monthly sessions in 1939-40 and 1940-41 with an attendance often in excess of 100. Subjects of clinical interest were discussed by guests from various colleges and by members of the laboratory staff. The associate pharmacologist of the Hospital functioned as an adviser to the clinical services in many questions of therapy; he also gave lectures on toxicology. Members of the staff have presented papers and participated in discussions at local and national meetings too numerous for listing.

LABORATORY OF PATHOLOGY

During the year 1940, 54 fellows, research and voluntary assistants worked in the laboratories of morbid anatomy, surgical pathology, neuropathology, hematology, and the subdivisions of ophthalmopathology, otopathology, laryngopathology, and dermopathology.

The routine work of the departments comprised 341 postmortem examinations; neuropathology—111 examinations of the central nervous system; surgical pathology—6,711 examinations of operative specimens; hematology—1,927 examinations.

The work, both routine as well as investigative, was carefully supervised by the senior pathlogists. It is this constant supervision which was the main source of the training in pathology offered by the laboratory. It was supplemented by the weekly microscopic seminars at which the current material was freely discussed. Monthly journal club meetings were continued during the year at which the current medical literature was reviewed and discussed.

Sight was not lost of the truth that training in pathology is of value to the trainee only if there is correlation with the practical problems of medicine and surgery. That this type of post-graduate training in pathology is appreciated seems shown by the increasing number of applicants for appointments. As further evidence of the value attached by other hospitals to this educational service is the increasing demand for those trained here.

The weekly clinico-pathologic conferences in the Blumenthal Auditorium were conducted as heretofore with an average attendance of well over 350, not only of physicians affiliated with the hospital, but also many from the metropolitan area. The presentation of the pathologic material has become more instructive through the use of color pictures which reproduce the natural color of the specimens much better than the prepared materials which had been demonstrated in the past.

Formal courses were given as part of the Hospital's program of post-graduate teaching under the auspices of Columbia University. These covered diseases of the nervous and circulatory systems, the gastro-intestinal tract and the liver and bile ducts. Laboratory courses were also given in ophthalmopathology and otopathology. An exhibit on the circulation of the eye, illustrated by many color photomicrographs and tables, was given at the annual meeting of the American Medical Association in New York City and received honorable mention. A number of lectures and demonstrations were given by members of the staff.

By invitation, members of the laboratory of morbid anatomy participated in the exhibit of the American Medical Association, with demonstrations and discussions using color photographs illustrating autopsy material. Three lectures on the pathology of tuberculosis were given to the sophomore class of the College of Physicians and Surgeons, and a lecture on lymphosarcomatosis to the student body of Long Island Medical College, all at the invitation of the respective professors of pathology. The first memorial address for deceased staff members of the Cook County Hospital in Chicago was also delivered by the Hospital pathologist in May at the invitation of the trustees and faculty of the Graduate School. Lectures on neuroanatomy were given by other staff members in conjunction with the Graduate School of New York University, and lectures on neuro-syphilis in New Jersey in conjunction with the New Jersey State Board of Health.

The results of the reasearch activity of the department is shown by the number of publications which appeared during the year in medical journals. The list is too long to be given in its entirety but may be mentioned briefly.

The cancer group has continued its investigations of the effect of concentrated spleen extract on malignant neoplasms in mice. It has added to the line of its research the use of yeast extract. The successful treatment of spontaneous breast carcinoma is most interesting because heretofore such tumors have been consistently resistent to any form of indirect therapy. The presentation of the group's result at the annual meeting of the American Association for Cancer Research in Pittsburgh attracted great interest and favorable comment. The acting director of the Institute for Cancer Research of Columbia University has carried out a series of experiments and has fully corroborated the results. The hospital group is attempting to isolate the active principle of the spleen and yeast extracts and is now beginning to transfer its investigations from small to larger laboratory animals.

Other investigators in the laboratory have shown that vascular contraction in shock, originally described as affecting the vessels of the gastro-intestinal tract, is also manifest in the kidneys where it causes acute ischemic necrosis. This is an extension of their work which has indicated the significance of the vasomotor component of homeostasis as a mechanism for causing organic tissue changes.

Still others have described an unusual granuloma of the bone, simulating primary neoplasm, a clinico-pathologic entity which had not yet been fully recognized.

It is evident that the research program of the laboratory of pathology pivots around the morphologic aspect of human disease. The material from the operating room and autopsy table continues to offer problems worthwhile of study, especially in correlation with questions of clinical interest. In spite of the advanced state of morphologic research, its potentialities have not yet been exhausted and even today an intense application to the tissue changes in human disease will bear significant results. Thus in the last year studies have been completed of autopsy material of lupus erythematosus and observations have been made which throw new light on a hitherto rather obscure morbid entity. Unfortunately, pathologic anatomy can establish only certain facts. The explanation of their cause requires other methods, particularly the introduction of experiments.

This report would not be complete if it did not indicate that the facilities of the laboratory are not adequate for the accomplishment of its task. Lack of technical personnel, and particularly lack of space, prevents a full utilization of the opportunities, and consequently our contributions fall short of the desired goal.

OFFICERS AND DIRECTORS OF THE MOUNT SINAI HOSPITAL SCHOOL OF NURSING

REPORT OF THE MOUNT SINAI HOSPITAL SCHOOL OF NURSING

To the Board of Trustees of The Mount Sinai Hospital:

Gentlemen :

The School of Nursing was founded in 1881, just sixty years ago. These have been full, useful years, whose main course has been shaped by the desire of the Board of Directors to keep apace with trends in nursing education, and to offer the students a sound educational program. It has likewise been our aim to help the individual student to develop abilities to make a satisfactory adjustment to all aspects of her professional environment in the practice of nursing, as well as to the non-professional aspects of her living. Some of the means for attaining these goals have been: improvement in the method of selecting students; higher entrance academic requirements; revisions in the curriculum, and an increase in the number of hours devoted to theoretical subjects; shorter working hours for students; improvement in housing and in the health program; improvements in library, teaching facilities and records; a development of student responsibility through participation in student government; more emphasis on extra-curricular activities; provision for scholarship and loan funds; more full-time teachers on our staff; provision for faculty members to take advanced academic and professional courses; increase in general staff nurses so that students would not carry the responsibility of the nursing service.

All of the changing practices, through the sixty years, are reflected in our work and progress during the year just passed. Although the achievement is unspectacular, it is nevertheless real. Our curriculum now includes 1,275 hours of instruction, including ward teaching, and 5,570 hours of nursing practice, which is a highly satisfactory balance between hours spent in the classroom and those devoted to practice in the various divisions of the hospital.

During 1940, improvements were made in the rotation of students through the various clinical divisions in order to better correlate our instruction and technical practice. An adjustment in the night duty plan was made which now limits night duty assignments to second and third year students, and at the same time reduced the number of weeks spent on night duty. A greater emphasis has been placed on health teaching throughout the entire curriculum.

There have been three resignations from the faculty. Miss Clare Skaling, class of 1931, senior nursing arts instructor, resigned in September in order to complete work for her master's degree at Teachers College. Miss Blanche Gubersky, assistant nursing arts instructor, was promoted to the senior position, and Miss Sylvia Barker, head nurse, was appointed to the assistant's post.

Miss Elizabeth Clanton, class of 1931, senior science instructor, resigned in order to accept another position, and Miss Myrtle Larsen, junior science instructor, also resigned. Miss Frances Sell, B.S., class of 1936, returned to the school to succeed Miss Clanton, while Mrs. Mayzie Rich, B.S., Strong Memorial Hospital, University of Rochester, was appointed to succeed Miss Larsen.

During the year, 112 new students were enrolled in the school. Eighty-one of this group received the cap of the school after completing the preliminary term. Six accepted students withdrew from the school during the year: one for personal reasons, two because of ill health, and three because of inability to meet scholarship standards.

We are pleased to report that there has been no serious illness in our student group, although the daily average of students off duty due to illness was seven. Annual physical examinations, as well as annual pulmonary x-rays were carried out as usual. We are deeply grateful to our school doctors and consultants for their services, and the care which they have given so generously to the students and graduate staff.

As usual, many social and recreational activities have been enjoyed by the students. Sports, dances, dramatics, teas and musicals have been given. The senior class play, "Comedy of Errors," was presented to the students and friends of the school on December 13th and 14th. Committees of the Student Association have been very active and most of the recreational activities have been planned by the committees in cooperation with faculty advisors.

During the first three days of April our school was surveyed by two representatives of the Accrediting Committee of the National League of Nursing Education. We are pleased to report that we have been accredited by this national organization, and that the name of our school will appear on the first list of schools to be accredited on a national basis.

In October, a number of graduate nurses were added to our general duty staff in order to reduce the time on duty of head nurses and general staff nurses to a 48-hour week, and enable us to grant a full day off duty each week. Many of our graduate nurses who had asked permission to live outside the residence were granted this privilege because we were unable to accommodate the increased number of nurses now employed.

Fourteen of our graduates have enrolled for advanced courses at Teachers College or New York University. Several have already done considerable work on the master's degree level with the expectation of earning that degree in the near future. The school is fortunate in having the Emil Berolzheimer Fund which can be used for higher education of our graduates.

The Alumnae Association, which now has a membership of 790, has had a very active and progressive year. Many outstanding speakers, including doctors from the hospital staff, have participated in the programs presented at the monthly meetings of the Association. Special invitations have been graciously extended to the student nurses, who have become very much interested in the work of the Alumnae Association.

The Registry for special nursing has had a very active year, with an increase of 394 calls over the previous year. The total number of nurses enrolled on the Registry was approximately 470. The registrars received 8,781 calls: 7,320 were for patients in the hospital, and 1,461 were for patients outside of the institution. Thirty-one calls were received for which it was not possible to secure a nurse from our list, and it was necessary to refer the calls to another professional registry.

We are pleased to announce that Mrs. Louis Loeb and Mr. Seymour Dribben were elected members of the School of Nursing Board.

A class of over fifty students will be admitted in February of 1941, one of the largest classes we have ever accepted at this time of the year. This has been deemed advisable due to world conditions.

The year ends with the following staff of graduate and student nurses:

Principal, School of Nursing and Superintendent of Nurses	1
Assistant Principal	1
Assistant Superintendent of Nurses	1
Instructors	10
Supervisors	11
Head Nurses	78
Graduate Nurses for General Staff Nursing	161
Student Nurses	210
Total	473

We extend grateful thanks to Dr. Joseph Turner, Director of the Hospital, for his support and valuable assistance at all times.

The Board of the School gratefully acknowledges the untiring devotion and efforts of the faculty and staff, under the inspiring leadership of Miss Grace A. Warman, the Principal of the School and Superintendent of Nurses.

We look forward to the coming year with confidence. Public attention is now focused upon nursing education more than ever before, due in part to the increasing influence of the nurse in community life and to the speed up of our national defense program. We shall continue to give our best efforts to educating young women for the practice of nursing and to maintaining our school in its present position of excellence and leadership.

HUGO BLUMENTHAL,
President.

SPECIAL FUNDS OF THE MOUNT SINAI HOSPITAL SCHOOL OF NURSING

Albert W. Scholle Memorial Fund.. $40,000.00
Founded by William and Frederic Scholle as a tribute to
the memory of their father; income to be used to provide vacations and recreation for nurses and students of
the School of Nursing.

Estelle and Hugo Blumenthal Scholarship and Graduation
Fund 35,000.00
Founded by Estelle and Hugo Blumenthal to provide an
annual scholarship to the student of the graduating class
chosen for special fitness to advance in the profession of
nursing by taking a Post Graduate course at Columbia
University. This fund also provides a prize of $15.00
to each graduating student.

Emil Berolzheimer Memorial Fund.. 20,000.00
Founded by Mrs. Emil Berolzheimer in memory of her
husband, Emil Berolzheimer; the income to be used for
higher education of nurses.

Murry Guggenheim Scholarship Fund....................................... 20,000.00
Established in 1905 by Murry Guggenheim; income to
provide annually twelve scholarship awards of $100.00
each to students who have shown exceptional ability
during the year.

Jacques D. Wimpfheimer Memorial Fund................................. 10,000.00
Founded by Charles A. Wimpfheimer in memory of his son,
Jacques D. Wimpfheimer. Any student requiring financial
assistance during training may call upon this fund.

Charles A. Wimpfheimer Emergency Relief Fund.................... 2,500.00
Established by Charles A. Wimpfheimer; income and, if
necessary, principal not to exceed $100.00 in any one year
to be used for the relief of members of the Alumnae
Association.

Lillie Stern Scholle Pleasure Fund... 9,000.00
Founded by Albert W. Scholle; the income to be used
largely to defray the expenses of parties, dances and social
gatherings of the students.

Mr. and Mrs. Sam S. Steiner Fund... 5,000.00
Founded by Mr. and Mrs. Sam S. Steiner in memory of
their beloved son, William J. H. Steiner; the income to be
used for the relief of needy graduate nurses of the School.

Carrie M. and Gustav Blumenthal Graduating Class Prize
Fund 5,000.00
Established by provision in the will of Gustav Blumenthal;
income to be distributed annually as a prize or prizes among
the graduating class in such manner as the Directors may
from time to time deem advisable.

SPECIAL FUNDS OF THE MOUNT SINAI HOSPITAL
SCHOOL OF NURSING
(Continued)

Kalman and Harriet r. Haas Fund.. $3,000.00
> Founded by Kalman Haas; the income to be used for
> the general purposes of the School.

Carrie Untermeyer Fund.. 2,600.00
> Founded by Mrs. Carrie Untermeyer; to establish an
> award of $100.00 annually to the student graduating who
> has the best record for kindness and proficiency in actual
> bedside nursing.

Solomon and Betty Loeb Fund.. 2,500.00
> Founded by Solomon Loeb; income to provide annual
> prizes to students.

Educational Fund 2,500.00
> Founded by Mrs. Berthold Levi in memory of Berthold Levi;
> the income to be used for higher education of students.

Mr. and Mrs. Morris Fatman Relief Fund for Graduate Nurses 2,500.00
> Founded by Mr. and Mrs. Morris Fatman; income to be
> used for the relief of graduate nurses.

Eugene Meyer, Jr. Library Fund.. 2,000.00
> Founded by Eugene Meyer, Jr.; the income to be used to
> supply books and magazines for the school library.

Amy C. and Fred H. Greenebaum Fund.. 2,000.00
> Established by Mr. and Mrs. Fred H. Greenebaum; income
> to be used for an annual award to the most deserving
> student nurse in any class.

Isabella Freedman Fund.. 1,500.00
> Established by Mrs. Isabella Freedman; the income to be
> used for one or two awards to students in the graduating
> class who have shown marked ability, proficiency and
> interest in their work.

Daniel Kops Prize Fund.. 1,000.00
> Founded by Employees of the House of Kops in memory
> of Daniel Kops; the income to be applied to the awarding
> of a prize to the nurse who holds the best record for bedside
> nursing and kindness to patients.

Pension Fund Mount Sinai Alumnae Association. Approx. 180,000.00
> Established to provide pensions to nurses after many years
> of service.

REPORT OF THE
MOUNT SINAI HOSPITAL SCHOOL OF NURSING

TREASURER'S REPORT

Statement of Disbursements and Receipts for the Year Ended
December 31st, 1940

Disbursements:

Payroll:

Student Nurses	$13,603.92
Graduate Nurses	260,230.56
Office Assistants	9,281.61
Housekeeping	34,827.92
Attendants	29,351.89
Tuition	17,206.67
Postage	247.47
Sundries	871.08
Stationery and Printing	1,634.27
Household Supplies	3,690.21
Telephone	1,843.30
Advertising	1,890.00
Books	2,087.64
Uniforms	4,345.65
Graduation Exercises	1,134.54

Total Disbursements $382,246.73

Receipts from:

Federation	$297,430.83
Matriculation Fees	5,410.00
Registry Fees	4,047.00
Sundry Receipts	87.92
Permanent Fund Income	585.00
Haas Fund Income	115.00

Total Receipts   307,675.75

Deficit *   **$74,570.98**

---

* *Taken from Permanent Fund of Hospital.*

SOCIAL SERVICE AUXILIARY OF THE MOUNT SINAI HOSPITAL

COMMITTEE

Mrs. Alfred A. Cook ....*President*
Mrs. Myron I. Borg ....*Vice-President*
Mrs. Henry S. Glazier ....*Treasurer*
Mrs. Siegfried F. Hartman ....*Assistant Treasurer*
Mrs. Robert M. Benjamin ....*Secretary*

Mrs. Julian S. Bach, Jr.	Mrs. Herbert H. Lehman
Mrs. George Backer	Mrs. Louis M. Loeb
Mrs. Paul Baerwald	Mrs. George W. Naumburg
Mrs. Robert E. Binger	Mrs. Carl H. Pforzheimer, Jr.
Mrs. Robert G. Blumenthal	Mrs. Moritz Rosenthal
Mrs. Arthur J. Cohen	Mrs. Philip A. Roth
Mrs. Leonard A. Cohn	Miss Edith Sachs
Mrs. Frederick L. Ehrman	Mrs. William D. Scholle
Mrs. Frederick M. Heimerdinger	Mrs. Henry Siegbert
Mrs. Marco F. Hellman	*Mrs. E. L. Smith
Mrs. Walter A. Hirsch	Mrs. Albert Stern
Miss Angie Jacobson	Mrs. Roger W. Straus
Mrs. Alan H. Kempner	Mrs. Irwin Untermyer

Mrs. Frank L. Weil

* Deceased.

STANDING COMMITTEES

Mrs. Frederick M. Heimerdinger............*Cardiac Clinics*
Mrs. Philip A. Roth................................*Children's Health*
Mrs. Arthur J. Cohen, *Chairman*
Mrs. Robert M. Benjamin ⎬ ......*Children's Social Service*
Mrs. Frederick L. Ehrman
Mrs. Paul Baerwald, *Chairman*
Mrs. William D. Scholle ⎬ ......*Clothing*
  Associate Chairman
Mrs. George W. Naumburg....................*Employment*
Mrs. Julian S. Bach, Jr......................*Library*
Mrs. Louis M. Loeb ⎬ ......*Medical Clinics* / ......*Medical Wards*
Mrs. Walter A. Hirsch..........................*Neustadter Home*
Mrs. Henry Siegbert, *Chairman*
Mrs. Robert M. Benjamin
Mrs. Henry S. Glazier ⎬ ......*Nominating*
Mrs. Walter A. Hirsch
Mrs. Moritz Rosenthal
Mrs. Leonard A. Cohn ....*Occupational Therapy—In-Patient*
Mrs. Irwin Untermyer ....*Orthopedic Clinics*
Mrs. Frank L. Weil ....*Volunteers*
Miss Edith Sachs, *Chairman* ⎬ ....*Workshop*
Mrs. Robert E. Binger

CONFERENCE COMMITTEE

MRS. ALFRED A. COOK ....*Chairman*

DR. ISRAEL S. WECHSLER	MRS. ARTHUR J. COHEN
DR. ALFRED E. FISCHER	MRS. LEONARD A. COHN
DR. EDWARD B. GREENSPAN	MRS. WALTER A. HIRSCH
DR. LAWRENCE S. KUBIE	MRS. LOUIS M. LOEB
DR. WILLIAM H. MENCHER	MRS. FRANK L. WEIL

DR. HERMAN ZAZEELA
DR. JOSEPH TURNER *(ex-officio)*
MRS. FANNY L. MENDELSOHN *(ex-officio)*

VOLUNTEERS

MRS. FRANK L. WEIL...*Chairman*
MRS. ROBERT H. KRIDEL..*Assistant Chairman*

MISS BEATRICE ALPERN	MISS PEGGY FILER
MRS. HARRY ANGELO	MRS. ALFRED FISCHER
MRS. HAROLD BARNETT	MISS IRENE ELISE FISCHER
MRS. IRVING BARON	MRS. ARTHUR FLASH
MRS. ROBERT BARSTOW	MISS JEAN FRANK
MRS. JOSEPH BAUMANN	MISS REGINA B. FRANKENBERG
MISS CHARLOTTE BEEKMAN	MISS DORIS FREEMAN
MISS EILEEN BERMAN	MRS. SARA FRENKEL
MRS. I. J. BERNHEIM	MISS CHARLOTTE FRIEDMAN
MRS. GEORGE S. BICKWIT	MR. JOSEPH LEWIS FRIEDMAN
MRS. ADOLPH BLANK	MRS. HENRY J. FRIENDLY
MISS SUSANNE BLEECKER	MRS. GUS FULD
MRS. DAVID BLOCK	MRS. JOSEPH GAINES
MISS ELLAN BORENFREUND	MRS. VICTOR GETTNER
MRS. WILLIAM BRATTER	MISS BERNICE GLASER
MISS SELMA CHUCK	MISS BABETTE GLUCKMAN
MISS GERTRUDE COHEN	MRS. SAM GOLDSMITH
MRS. PETER A. COHN	MRS. JACOB GRAY
MISS BETTE CROCKETT	MISS MARION GREENBERG
MISS FLORENCE DALY	MISS HELEN HAAS
MRS. DAVID S. DAVIDSON	MISS IRMA J. HENRY
MRS. CHARLES DEITSCH	MRS. ROBERT HERZOG
MRS. BERNARD DENZER	MISS MURIEL C. HESS
MRS. HENRY DOUBILET	MRS. PHILIP HETTLEMAN
MRS. WALTER A. DREYFOUS	MRS. MARTIN HIRSCHFELD
MRS. GEORGE C. ENGEL	MISS JANET HOCHSTADTER
MRS. WILLIAM ERDMANN	MRS. ASCHER HOLZMAN
MRS. MILDRED FALK	MISS ELAINE HOLZMAN
MISS EDITH FELDBRAU	MR. HANS JELINEK
MISS DORIS FELDMAN	MISS GRACE JEROME
MRS. SIGMUND FEUCHTWANGER	MISS RUTH KAHN
MRS. SAMPSON R. FIELD	MISS SHIRLEY KAPLAN

VOLUNTEERS—(Continued)

Miss Mildred Kassvan
Miss Alma Katz
Mrs. Jerome Katz
Mrs. Ruby Katz
Mrs. Herbert M. Kaufman
Mrs. Brandon Keibel
Mrs. Roger King
Miss Doris Jane Kleinman
Mrs. Charles Klingenstein
Mrs. Henry Klingenstein
Miss Muriel Klubock
Mrs. Samuel Kolesky
Miss Alice Kreindler
Miss Ruth Kreis
Mrs. Robert H. Kridel
Mrs. Abraham Landesman
Mrs. Edwin Lane
Mrs. Percy W. Lansburgh
Mrs. Sidney. D. Leader
Mrs. Phillip Leavitt
Mrs. William Lehman
Mrs. Benjamin Linde
Mrs. David Lippman
Mrs. Irving Lowenstein
Mr. Boris Magasanik
Mrs. Sol Mann
Mrs. Arthur Marcus
Mrs. Mortimer Marcus
Mrs. Zelda B. Marcus
Mrs. Carl L. Marek
Mrs. Herbert Meyer
Mrs. Jerome Meyer
Mrs. Arnold B. Milgrim
Miss Rosalind Jessica Mindlin
Mrs. Gustave Minton
Miss Rhoda Lucille Mintz
Miss Phyllis Moskowitz
Mrs. Louis Napoleon
Mrs. Cyrus H. Nathan
Mrs. Monroe Newberger
Mrs. Louis Olden
Mrs. Julius Palleri
Mrs. Nathan A. Perilman
Mrs. Fred Perlberg
Mrs. Emil Peterson
Miss Jane Poll
Mr. Milton Sax Rafale

Miss Lia Rein
Miss Jessie Resnik
Mrs. Gertrude Rhodes
Miss Rhoda Robinson
Miss Shirley Robinson
Miss Pearl Rogalsky
Mrs. Irwin Rome
Miss Ann Rosenthal
Mr. Robert Rosenthal
Mrs. Leon Rothschild
Mrs. Abraham Rotwein
Mr. Abraham Austin Salmon
Mrs. W. Schlossman
Miss Barbara Scofield
Miss Muriel Seligman
Mrs. Gregory Shwartzman
Miss Sadie Siegel
Miss Zelda Silverman
Mrs. Norman Silverstein
Mrs. Herbert J. Simon
Mrs. Harry Singer
Miss Rita Slavitt
Miss Charlotte Slonin
Miss Edna Stein
Mrs. Laurence B. Stein
Mrs. William H. Stein
Mr. Irving D. Steinhardt
Miss Nancy Stern
Miss Anne Stubblefield
Mrs. Edward Sulzberger
Mrs. Irving Taylor
Mrs. Ann Tishman
Mrs. Abraham Topkis
Mrs. Daniel Trotzky
Miss Edith Tuchman
Mr. Louis B. Turner
Miss Mildred Walton
Mrs. John Wasserman
Mrs. Beatrice F. Weil
Mrs. Leopold Weil
Mrs. Jacob Weinstein
Mrs. Max Weintraub
Mrs. Robert M. Werblow
Mrs. Leroy Whitelaw
Mrs. Nancy Ruth Widerman
Mrs. Eli Winkler
Miss Jean M. Wood

Miss Muriel Zinoroy

REPORT OF THE SOCIAL SERVICE DEPARTMENT

The Social Service Department has completed another year of service, and I have the honor to present the report for 1940. Financial resources did not permit any expansion of our program and therefore, with a few minor exceptions, we were restricted to following the pattern of organization of the past few years. We realize that there still exists an unequal distribution of case load among the workers which can be remedied only by making changes in our intake policies or by additional social service assistance.

As the United Hospital Fund requested uniform statistics from all Social Service Departments, it was again necessary to change our method of counting cases and it is therefore impossible to make a comparison between the volume of work in 1939 and that in 1940. During the past year the department cared for 8,324 new cases and 2,796 reopened and recurrent cases. We held 228,992 interviews in the Hospital and 13,601 interviews outside the Hospital. 6,461 patients were referred to various community organizations and we sent 9,993 reports to cooperating agencies. These statistics do not include the very large number of patients who received slight services, but due to the necessity of lessening the clerical work of the staff, no record of the number was made.

The work on the Adult Wards was considerably hampered by several changes in our staff personnel. This was particularly regrettable, because the demands for intensive social case work on these services were greatly increased by the assignment of more psychiatrists to the ward services. The findings of the psychiatrists receive serious consideration at the joint conferences of the house staff and the social workers. The consultations with the psychiatrists have been of great value, not only in working through an evaluation of the problems and potentialities for treatment in the particular cases under consideration, but also because they have been helpful to the worker in treating other cases more adequately. We had hoped to be able to add another worker to cover the Neurological Wards and Clinics, but as this was not possible, the burden of this service was assumed by the psychiatric social workers.

On the Children's Services, particularly in the clinics, the doctors continued to find serious physical and social maladjustments, many of which needed intensive and time-consuming case work treatment. Supervision of diet and nutrition continues to be an important part of our work with the children, and the need for the extension of the Nutrition Clinic service is evident. At present the dietitian in the Out-Patient Department is available to a selected group of adults, but only in a few cases can she be consulted by the social workers in the Children's Division.

The workers responsible for the morning and afternoon Adult Medical Clinics and the numerous special clinics have great difficulty in attempting to serve the many patients referred by the physicians. During the past four years, Mrs. Louis M. Loeb has closely followed the progress of a group of thirty young diabetic patients in the clinic, in the home and at school. These patients are from fourteen to twenty-five years of age. All have been given intelligence tests during the past year and some achievement and vocational tests as well, to assist them in making their educational and vocational plans. We hope to continue to follow this group in future years to determine the progress they may make.

The administrator of the Out-Patient Department has been extremely helpful in systematizing certain routine duties of the orthopedic workers, enabling them to give more time to the patients. Intensive case work service was required for a group of scleroderma cases in the Thrombo-Angiitis Obliterans Clinic, and awareness of the needs of these patients has enabled the worker to achieve some excellent results.

In August, the Venereal Disease Division of the Department of Health installed a Central Tabulating Unit System in the Luetic Clinic. Progress cards supplied by the Department of Health are checked and returned to them by the head nurse after each visit of the patient to the clinic and by the social workers after each interview and home visit. We believe that eventually this new system will save time by eliminating clerical work incidental to following up cases, and thus enable the workers to accept more patients from the Skin Clinic.

In the Genito-Urinary Clinic, all male patients with acute gonorrheal infections are interviewed by the social worker, and in order to assure continued attendance, a follow-up system similar to the one in the Luetic Clinic has been instituted. Particularly distressing are the problems of the group of older men, many of whom suffer from chronic bladder and kidney diseases. This group, although small in number, presents innumerable difficulties and taxes the worker's ingenuity. An understanding worker, however, can do much to help make their living conditions more tolerable.

We secured convalescent care for 2,290 patients during the past year, 120 more than in 1939. Of this number, 814 were sent to the Neustadter Home for Convalescents, one of the very few homes that accommodates both men and women and admits patients who require nursing care and special diets. An increase in the number of children for whom the doctors recommend long periods of convalescence made it necessary for us to take an additional bed from the Speedwell Society, so that we have again a total of three beds. The cost of our convalescent care program, notwithstanding the free and low-cost vacancies which we were able to obtain, remained high, but the physical and mental improvements brought about by this service justify the expense.

The meager facilities for children with heart disease were still further reduced by the closing of several convalescent homes. However, the Convalescent Home for Hebrew Children is taking a few cardiacs, giving them the regimen of a cardiac home. If this project is successful, we shall have another resource for children from five to twelve years of age. One of the branches of the Protestant Episcopal City Mission, which accepted men for convalescent care, was also closed, curtailing still further facilities for male convalescents.

Four hundred eighty-two boys and girls were sent to summer vacation homes, 70 more than last year. We were able to care for more of our colored children, having been fortunate in securing a few additional vacancies for them. However, there is need for better provisions for colored children of all ages, particularly for boys from 11 to 16.

There are many unmet needs in the community at present and we continue to be seriously handicapped by the lack of adequate provisions for chronic patients, and facilities for dental services, and we stress again the importance of more convalescent homes for cardiacs, and convalescent and vacation homes for adolescent boys and girls, from 16 to 21.

Regular conferences held by the members of our staff continued to offer them the opportunity to discuss topics of interest. This year the subject of recording was chosen as the staff project. Under the leadership of one of our supervisors, it is being considered from many angles, and we anticipate some constructive suggestions for improving our record system.

A few of our workers were again given scholarships, enabling them to take courses and participate in several institutes during the year. One of our supervisors attended the National Conference of Social Work in Grand Rapids, Michigan, from which she brought back interesting and stimulating reports to the other members of the staff and to the Social Service Committee.

We continued to cooperate with the School of Nursing, giving every student four weeks experience in the department, as well as assisting the nurses with case studies and acquainting them with the social aspects of illness.

An increasing number of doctors are conferring at regular intervals wtih the social workers assigned to them. The growing participation on the part of the doctors in the work of the department was noticeable at the two meetings of the Conference Committee on Social Service held during the year. At one of the departmental conferences held by the doctors, the program was devoted to medical social work. Our director, Mrs. Louis Mendelsohn, gave a short history of the growth and work of the department, and the workers discussed the subject of charting and the relationship between doctors and social workers.

As in the past, we have made extensive use of many community resources, which have given us their fullest cooperation in our efforts to render valuable services to our patients. Our relationship with the various public relief agencies remains an active one, requiring innumerable conferences on joint cases, and the Works Progress Administration Housekeeping Service has continued to fill a vital need.

In caring for our refugee clients, we worked closely with the National Refugee Service on the many intricate problems presented by these hard-pressed people. One question, which frequently needs to be clarified for these patients, is that of resettlement, and it is in this sphere that the medical social worker can often be of greatest service. Planning for chronic patients is, no doubt, the most difficult problem we face in dealing with this group.

We have made increasing use during the last few years of the Volunteer Motor Corps Service of the American Red Cross, which provided transportation for a number of our patients, so as to enable them to come to the clinics for treatment.

The Occupational Therapy Department took care of 1,809 patients, 327 of whom were able to come to our Workshop, making a total of 1,301 visits. The increase over the previous year of 125 patients and 464 visits proves the growing demand for functional work for patients. Requests for this type of work are constantly being received from the medical staff, but we cannot accept additional referrals until we are permitted to add another professional Occupational Therapist to our staff. It is interesting to note that 3.932 articles were made by the patients during 1940. The total cost of the materials for these articles was $459.27, which was considerably less than we spent in 1939, thanks to the many generous donations of materials received from friends. During this, the third year of our experiment in reconditioning toys, approximately 2,400 toys were renovated. 377 of these were given to the children throughout the year, and the remainder of 2,023 distributed during the holiday season.

The Social Service Workroom enrolled 20 new female and 9 new male patients. Many of those who received their original experience and training there are now gainfully employed. We realize more and more the benefits our patients derive through this activity, and the important role it plays in their rehabilitation. The annual sale, which was held in November, was again very successful. During the greater part of the year, the shop was kept busy filling orders for private individuals and for one of the leading specialty shops in the city. A considerable amount of sewing and knitting for the American Red Cross and Bundles for Britain was undertaken by the patients. A depot was established for the distribution of wool to graduate nurses and to Hospital employees who were interested in knitting for various war relief organizations. Some of the wool was generously donated by Miss Edith Sachs.

One hundred thirty-four volunteers served in the Hospital during the year. An assistant was appointed in the fall to help the Chairman of the Committee on Volunteers, Mrs. Frank L. Weil, in the supervision of this work. We were fortunate in securing a number of capable young women, mainly college girls, as substitutes during the summer months. Many of our volunteers gave additional time to the Blood Plasma project, and a new group was enrolled for this service to assist wherever lay workers could be used. Two more volunteers were assigned to the kindergarten this year, to instruct the children of school age, who are hospitalized for a long time. We are most grateful to the many volunteers who have served the Hospital faithfully, particularly to those who have been with us for a period of years.

It was with deep regret that we accepted the resignation of Mrs. William de Young Kay, who so ably reorganized our Library, and we welcomed to our Board Mrs. Julian S. Bach, Jr., who has assumed the supervision of this service. Mrs. George W. Naumburg has assisted one of the supervisors with our employment project. In connection with this work, she visited many employment agencies and interviewed some of our clients who were experiencing difficulty in obtaining employment. Through her efforts, 21 patients or members of their families were placed during the last three months of the year. Mrs. Irwin Untermyer and Mrs. Marco F. Hellman visited the various settlements and health agencies situated near the Hospital to make a study of the resources for the teaching of simple home economics and hygiene. As a result of the interest created by their survey, a class in home economics was established in one of the nearby settlement houses which some of our patients attended.

With regret we record the death of Mrs. Max J. Breitenbach to whose generosity extending over a long period of years not only we, but the many mothers and children for whom she provided summer care, are so deeply indebted.

The Federation for the Support of Jewish Philanthropic Societies and the United Hospital Fund have given us the financial assistance necessary to carry on much of our work, and we are most appreciative of their support. The members of our Board have served on committees of both these organizations and have taken an active part in their fund raising campaigns.

The professional staff of the Hospital has continued to give the lay group the same splendid cooperation as they have offered for many past years and to all who have worked together so effectively for the welfare of the patients and who have been so helpful in the work of the Social Service Department, I wish to give expression to my gratitude and thanks.

Respectfully submitted,

RUTH M. COOK,

President of the Social Service Auxiliary.

THE MOUNT SINAI SOCIAL SERVICE AUXILIARY

REPORT OF THE TREASURER
For Year Ended December 31st, 1940
REGULAR ACCOUNT
DISBURSEMENTS

Appliances	$13,485.24	
Extra Nourishment, Special Diets, etc.	1,080.97	
Boarding	20.05	
Convalescent Care	14,556.05	
Relief	2,621.94	
Shoes, Clothing, etc.	2,616.91	
Transportation	2,668.37	
Medication	735.46	
Education and Recreation Supplies	858.48	
Salaries	94,599.13	
Workers' Expenses	565.83	
Office Supplies (Including Stationery, Printing and Postage)	1,913.74	
Affiliation Dues	58.50	
Magazines and Newspapers	63.14	
Sundries	6.95	
Total Disbursements		$135,850.76

RECEIPTS

Federation	$100,772.50	
Greater New York Fund (Through Federation as part of United Hospital Fund grant)	6,925.00	
United Hospital Fund	10,175.00	
Income from Investments	1,974.99	
Refunds from Patients, etc.	3,900.22	
Total Receipts		123,747.71
Deficit *		*$12,103.05*

* *Taken from Non-budgetary Special Accounts of Social Service Auxiliary (See below under Special Account).*

SPECIAL ACCOUNT

Balance, January 1st, 1940	$17,482.19	

RECEIPTS

Donations, etc., 1940	13,073.28	
Appropriation from Principal and Income of Special Funds	4,863.74	
Interest on Bank Acceptances	119.72	
Total Credits		$35,538.93

DISBURSEMENTS

Special Accounts	$5,474.29	
Summer Work	5,893.00	
Transferred to Regular Account for 1940 Deficit	*12,103.05*	
Total Disbursements		23,470.34
Balance, December 31st, 1940		$12,068.59

DONATIONS FOR SPECIAL ACCOUNTS

Anonymous	$750.00
Anonymous (In Memory of Mr. Dudley Sicher)	10.00
Bach, Mrs. Julian S. (In Memory of Mr. Samuel A. Sicher)	5.00
Bach, Mrs. Julian S. (In Memory of Mrs. Maimie Cohn)	5.00
Bach, Mrs. Julian S. (In Memory of Mr. Percy W. Lansburgh)	5.00
Bach, Mrs. Julian S. (In Memory of Mr. Joseph Koshland)	5.00
Bach, Mrs. Julian S. (In Memory of Mr. Fred H. Greene)	5.00
Bach, Mrs. Julian S., Jr.	15.00
Baerwald, Mrs. Paul	550.00
Benjamin, Mrs. Robert M.	100.00
Binger, Mrs. Robert E.	100.00
Blumenthal, Mr. George (For Special Non-budgetary Purposes)	507.50
Blumenthal, Mrs. Gustav (In Memory of Mrs. Daisy Strauss)	5.00
Blumenthal, Mrs. Robert G.	275.00
Bogdish, Miss Molly	10.00
Borg, Mrs Myron I.	25.00
Breitenbach, Mrs. Max J. (In Memory of Mr. Max J. Breitenbach)	1,000.00
Cohen, Mr. and Mrs. Arthur J. (For Special Non-Budgetary Purposes)	1,000.00
Cohen, Mrs. Arthur J.	550.00
Cohn, Mrs. Leonard A.	525.00
Cohn, Mrs. Leonard A. (For Special Designated Purpose)	125.00
Cohn, Mrs. Leeonard A. (In Memory of Mr. Joseph Koshland)	10.00
Cohn, Mrs. Leonard A. (In Memory of Mr. Albert J. Erdmann)	5.00
Cohn, Mr. and Mrs. Leonard A. (In Memory of Mr. Percy W. Lansburgh)	10.00
Cohn, Mr. and Mrs. Leonard A. (In Memory of Mr. Fred H. Greene)	25.00
Cohn, Mr. and Mrs. Leonard A. (In Memory of Mr. Harry Bronner)	10.00
Cook, Mrs. Alfred A.	1,050.00
Davis, Miss Hannah (In Memory of Parents, Edward and Elisa Davis)	15.00
Ehrman, Mrs. Frederick L.	100.00
Elsinger, Mrs. W. H. (For Special Designated Purpose)	125.00
Elsinger, Mrs. W. H. (In Memory of Mrs. Maimie Cohn)	5.00
Elsinger, Mrs. W. H. (In Memory of Mr. Lawrence W. Mack)	5.00
Galinger, Mrs. George W. (In Memory of Mrs. Sophie Colp)	5.00
Glazier, Mrs. Henry S.	1,075.00
Goodeve, Mr. & Mrs. Lindsay M.	140.00
Goldman, Mr. Herman (For Special Non-Budgetary Purpose)	25.00
Hartman, Mr. and Mrs. Siegfried F.	325.00
Hartman, Mr. Siegfried F. (In Memory of Mr. Max Schwarz)	10.00
Carried Forward	$8,512.50

DONATIONS FOR SPECIAL ACCOUNTS

(Continued)

Brought Forward	$8,512.50
Hartman, Mr. Siegfried F. (In Memory of Mr. Siegfried Schleissner)	3.00
Heimerdinger, Mrs. Frederick M.	225.00
Hellman, Mrs. Marco F.	110.00
Hilb, Mrs. Hannah	30.00
Hirsch, Mr. Richard (In Memory of Mrs. Max J. Breitenbach)	25.00
Hirsch, Mr. Steven J. (In Memory of Mr. Walter A. Hirsch)	100.00
Hirsch, Mrs. Walter A.	625.00
Hirsch, Mrs. Walter A. (In Memory of Mr. Walter A. Hirsch)	100.00
Israel, Mr. and Mrs. Charles (In Memory of Mr. Morton L. Adler)	10.00
Jacobson, Miss Angie (In Memory of Mr. Samuel A. Sicher)	10.00
Jacobson, Miss Angie (In Memory of Mr. Albert J. Erdmann)	5.00
Jacobson, Miss Angie (In Memory of Mr. Fred H. Greene)	5.00
Joseph, Mr. and Mrs. D. S. (In Memory of Mr. Max Steuer)	5.00
Joseph, Mr. and Mrs. D. S. (In Memory of Miss Olivia Leventritt)	5.00
Kay, Mrs. William de Young	50.00
Kempner, Mrs. Alan H.	275.00
Klingenstein, Mrs. Charles (In Memory of Mr. Ernst Rosenfeld)	10.00
Kops, Mr. and Mrs. Waldemar (In Memory of Mr. Max Schwarz)	10.00
Kops, Mr. and Mrs. Waldemar (In Memory of Mrs. Jennie Gumpert)	10.00
Kops, Mr. and Mrs. Waldemar (In Memory of Mr. Richard F. Erental)	10.00
Kops, Mr. and Mrs. Waldemar (In Memory of Mr. Milton Lipscher)	10.00
Kops, Mr. and Mrs. Waldemar (In Memory of Mr. Frederick Greenbaum)	10.00
Kops, Mrs. Max and Family (In Memory of Mr. A. N. Gitterman)	10.00
Kops, Mrs. Max and Family (In Memory of Mr. Richard F. Erental)	10.00
Kops, Mr. Max, Jr. (In Memory of Mr. Israel Brozan)	5.00
Lehman, Mrs. Herbert H.	1,020.00
Loeb, Mrs. Louis M.	175.00
Mayer, Mr. Robert H. (In Memory of Mr. Walter A. Hirsch)	20.00
Mendelsohn, Mr. Louis. (In Memory of Mr. Arthur C. Mendelsohn)	15.00
Meyer, Mr. and Mrs. Carl (In Memory of Mr. Walter A. Hirsch)	50.00
Naumburg, Mrs. George W.	620.00
Pforzheimer, Mrs. Carl H., Jr.	110.00
Pforzheimer, Mrs. Carl H., Jr. (For Non-Budgetary Purposes)	20.00
Carried Forward	$12,210.50

DONATIONS FOR SPECIAL ACCOUNTS

(Continued)

Brought Forward $12,210.50
Rapaport Fund, Meyer (In Memory of Mr. Meyer Rapaport).... 50.00
Rosenthal, Mrs. Moritz 530.00
Roth, Mrs. Annie (In Memory of Mrs. Max J. Breitenbach)...... 50.00
Sachs, Miss Edith 275.00
Saks, Mrs. Horace A. (In Memory of Mr. Percy W. Lansburgh) 10.00
Schamberg, Mrs. Lucile (In Memory of Mr. Percy W. Lansburgh) 5.00
Scholle, Mrs. William D. 250.00
Sidenberg, Mrs. George M. (In Memory of Mr. Percy W. Lansburgh) 5.00
Siegbert, Mrs. Henry 210.00
Som, Dr. Max L. 15.00
Stern, Mrs. Albert 125.00
Straus, Mrs. Roger W. 250.00
Stroock, Mrs. Stephen J. (In Memory of Mrs. Mamie Cohn).... 10.00
Untermyer, Mrs. Irwin 275.00
Wallerstein, Mrs. Leo (For Special Designated Purpose)............ 100.00
Weil, Mrs. Frank L. 110.00
Weil, Mrs. Leon 50.00
Wyle, Mr. and Mrs. Milton (In Memory of Mrs. Mamie Cohn) 10.00
Patients' Refunds, etc. 390.28

Total $14,930.78

DONORS OF CLOTHING

Abel, Mrs. Harold
Abrahams, Mrs. A. I.
Academy of the New York Assn.
  for Jewish Children, The
Anfanger, Dr. Ludwig Anger
Astro, Mrs. Ralph
Bach, Miss Agnes
Bach, Miss Bianca
Bach, Miss Florine
Bach, Mrs. Milton J.
Baerwald, Mrs. Herman F.
Baerwald, Mrs. Paul
Ballin, Mrs. Greta
Becker, Mrs. Herman
Benjamin, Mrs. Robert M.
Bernhard, Mr. Henry
Bernheim, Mrs. Mortimer
Bernstein, Mrs. Louis
Bess-Edna Company
Binger, Mrs. Robert E.
Bixer, Mrs. Herman
Blum, Mrs. Robert
Blumenthal, Mr. George
Blumkin, Mrs. Abraham J.
Blun, Mrs. Edwin
Breidner, Mrs. Joseph
Byk, Mrs. Paul M.
Chuck, Miss Selma
Cohen, Mrs. Arthur J.
Cohen, Miss Florence
Cohen, Mrs. George W.
Cohen, Mrs. Samuel
Cohn, Mrs. Leonard A.
Cohn, Mrs. Peter A.
Cook, Mr. and Mrs. Alfred A.
Cook, Miss Madeleine R.
Cuming, Mrs. Alice
Deitsch, Mrs. Charles
DeMenasce, Mrs. Elinor
Dillenberg, Mrs. D. Alan
Dreyfous, Mrs. Walter
Ehrman, Mrs. Frederick L.
Elias, Mrs. Henry H.
Engel, Mrs. George C.
Engel, Miss Jean
Erdmann, Mrs. William
Falk, Mrs. Myron S., Jr.
Fischer, Dr. Alfred E.
Forman, Mrs. Abraham
Forsch, Mrs. Albert

Forsch, Mrs. Sidney
Frank, Dr. Robert T.
Frankenheimer, Miss Ida
Frankenheimer, Miss Rose
Frankenthaler, Mrs. Alfred
Friend, Miss Alice J.
Gabriner, Mr. Arthur
Glazier, Mrs. Henry S.
Glazier, Mrs. William S.
Goldsmith, Mrs. S. M.
Gottheil, Mrs. Paul
Greenhall, Mrs. A. Frank
Hamann, Miss Elsa
Hamershlag, Mrs. Joseph
Hartman, Mrs. Siegfried F.
Heilbron, Mrs. Ralph
Heimerdinger, Mrs. B.
Heimerdinger, Mrs. Joseph E.
Hellman, Mrs. Marco F.
Heming, Mrs. Charles E.
Hendricks, Mrs. Henry S.
Herrman, Mrs. A.
Herzheim, Mrs. M.
Herzog, Mr. Oscar M.
Hessberg, Mrs. Lena
Heyman, Mrs. David M.
Hirsch, Mrs. Walter A.
Hochschild, Mrs. Walter
Hyman, Dr. and Mrs. Abraham
Hyman, Mrs. Charles J.
Ittleson, Mrs. Henry, Jr.
Jackson, Mrs. Milton J.
Jacobs, Mrs. Samuel E.
James Monroe Women's Relief Corps
  (Through Mrs. Pauline Isaacs)
Katzive, Dr. Julius A.
Kavish, Mr. Isaac
Kay, Mrs. William de Young
Kempner, Mrs. Alan H.
Kempner, Mrs. S. Marshall
Keschner, Dr. Harold W.
Klaif, Mrs. Pearl (In memory of
  Mr. Max Klaif)
Klein, S.
Klieger, Dr. and Mrs. Israel Stanley
Klingenstein, Mrs. Charles
Kohnstamm, Mrs. Lothair S.
Kridel, Mr. William
Kronish, Miss Esther
Lambert, Dr. Robert K.

DONORS OF CLOTHING—(Continued)

Landesman, Mrs. Abraham
Leader, Dr. Sidney D.
Leavitt, Mr. Ezra G.
Leavitt, Mrs. Philip B.
Leslie, Dr. Harold N.
Leventritt, Mrs. Edgar M.
Levinson, Mrs. Jesse W.
Levy, Mrs. Charles
Levy, Mrs. Martin
Liebman, Mrs. Charles J.
Liebman, Mrs. Thomas
Liebmann, Mrs. Samuel
Lipnick, Miss Florence (In memory
  of Mrs. Anna Lipnick)
Lippmann, Mr. David
Loeb, Mrs. Carl M.
Loeb, Mrs. Carl M., Jr.
Loeb, Mrs. Henry
Loeb, Mrs. Louis M.
Loew, Mrs. Edgar
Long, Mrs. Louis
Lowenstein, Mrs. Irving
Markowitz, Mrs. M.
Mayer, Mrs. Jonas
McElroy, Mrs. E. B.
Megali, Miss Marie
Mendelsohn, Mr. Louis
Mernick, Mrs. Joseph
Meyer, Mrs. Emil R.
Minrath, Mrs. William R.
Moolten, Dr. Sylvan E.
Morgenthau, Mrs. Eugene
Mount Sinai School of Nursing
Neaman, Mrs. Pearson E.
Needlework Guild of America
Palchik, Mrs. Louis
Paymer, Miss Adell
Peterson, Mrs. Eugene
Pforzheimer, Mrs. Carl H., Jr.
Picker, Mrs. Eugene
Prince, Mrs. Leo M.
Rains, Mrs. S. E.
Rand Stores, The
Ravitz, Mrs. M. L.

Rosenthal, Mrs. John
Rosenthal, Mr. Leon
Rosner, Mrs. Charles
Rothschild, Mrs. Fred W.
Sachs, Dr. Bernard
Sachs, Miss Edith
Sachs, Mrs. Samuel
Salomon, Mrs. Edward
Sansiper, Mrs. Rose
Scharff, Mrs. Maurice R.
Schneider, Mrs. Meyer
Scholle, Mrs. William D.
Schubart, Mrs. I. O.
Schubart, Mrs. William Howard
Schwartzchild, Mrs. Fritz
Seligman, Mr. Milton
Siegel, Miss Sadie
Silverblatt, Miss Bessie
Simon, Dr. Bernard
Sinai, Miss Mollie
Slazenger, Mrs. F. L.
Somach, Dr. and Mrs. Irving
Spingarn, Mrs. Arthur B.
Spinner, Mrs. Julia
Squire, Dr. and Mrs. Jack
Stachelberg, Mrs. Charles (In mem-
  ory of Mr. Harry Bronner)
Stern, Mrs. I. Foster
Straus, Mrs. Roger W.
Strauss, Mrs. Jacob
Sulzberger, Miss Anne
Trace, Mrs. Meyer
Ullmann, Mrs. Albert
Ulmann, Estate of Mr. James
Unger, Mrs. Abraham
Vogel, Mrs. Edwin
Weil, Mrs. Frank L.
Weil, Mr. George L.
Werblow, Mrs. Robert M.
Wimpfheimer, Mr. Harold D.
Wolf, Mr. Julian
Yankauer, Mrs. Walter D.
Zamkin, Dr. and Mrs. Harry O.

GIFTS OF ARTICLES

TOYS AND GAMES

Abrahams, Mr. and Mrs. A. I.
Adelman, Mrs. J.
Albarelli, Miss Angela
Albarelli, Mr. Joseph
Applebaum, Miss Sylvia
Arnheimer, Mrs. H. Irving
Arnstein, Mrs. Alexander E.
Arnstein, Miss Joan
Arnstein, Miss Lynn
Arnstein, Miss Sandra
Atlas, Mrs. David
Baker, Mrs. Herman
Beck, Miss Edith
Beir, Mr. Bertram S.
Benjamin, Mrs. Robert M.
Berolzheimer, Mrs. Alfred C.
Bickwit, Mrs. George S.
Blum, Mrs. Robert
Blum, Mrs. Samuel
Blumenthal, Mrs. George
Bratter, Mrs. William J.
Brunner, Dr. Martha
Burd, Mrs. Clara
Cahn, Mrs. William M., Jr.
Cimiotti, Mrs. G.
Cohn, Mrs. Leonard A.
Cohn, Mrs. Peter A.
Cook, Mrs. Alfred A.
Cowen, Mrs. Arthur, Jr.
Dalton School
Dammann, Mrs. Richard W.
Dannenberg, Mrs. Mannie
Danziger, Mrs. Frederick S.
Danziger, Mrs. Max
Dreifus, Mrs. Charles, Jr.
Elias, Mrs. Henry H.
Engel, Mrs. George C.
Engel, Mrs. Irving M.
Falk, Mrs. Myron S., Jr.
Feuchtwanger, Mr. & Mrs. Sigmund
Fischer, Dr. Alfred E.
Frankenthaler, Mrs. Alfred
Fried, Mrs. Walter J.
Gabriner, Mr. Arthur
Gerson, Mrs. David
Gimbel, Mrs. Louis S., Jr.

Glazier, Mrs. William S.
Goldsmith, Mrs. James A., Jr.
Good Cheer Doll Group (Through
  Mrs. H. Edwards)
Goodman, Mrs. Andrew
Goodman, Mrs. David D.
Gottlieb, Mrs. Leo
Greene, Mrs. Fred H.
Harteveld, Mrs. Henry H.
Hecht, Mrs. George J.
Heilbron, Mrs. Ralph
Heming, Mrs. Charles E.
Heyman, Mrs. David M.
Heyman, Mrs. Jacob
Hirsch, Mrs. C.
Hirsch, Mrs. Steven J.
Hochschild, Mrs. Walter
Hyman, Mrs. Charles J.
Ittleson, Mrs. Henry, Jr.
Jacobi, Miss Ellen
Jacobs, Mrs. Robert A.
Kahn, Mrs. Elliot M.
Kay, Mrs. William de Young
Kempner, Mrs. S. Marshall
Keschner, Dr. Harold W.
Klee, Mrs. David
Landesman, Mrs. Abraham
Lehman, Mr. Robert
Leiter, Mrs. H. Evans
Lenander, Mrs. F.
Levison, Mrs. Jesse W.
Levy, Mrs. Ben C.
Levy, Mrs. Robert J.
Liebman, Mrs. Thomas
Loeb, Mrs. Carl M., Jr.
Loeb, Mrs. Louis M.
Loeb, Miss Suzanne
Marcuse, Mrs. James E.
Martin, Mrs. Herbert S.
Maybaum, Miss Dorothy
Meyer, Mrs. Maurice, Jr.
Minton, Mrs. Lucy Sperry
Moses, Mrs. John H.
Newman, Mrs. J. Kiefer, Jr.
Nordeman, Mr. Jacques C.
Oppenheimer, Mr. and Mrs. Jerome H.

TOYS AND GAMES—(Continued)

Perilman, Mrs. Nathan A.
Pforzheimer, Mrs. Carl H., Jr.
Pollak, Mrs. Maurice
Reckford, Mrs. Joseph S.
Rifkind, Mr. Simon H.
Rose, Mrs. Oscar
Rosenthal, Mrs. Charles S.
Rosenthal, Mrs. Daniel D.
Rosenthal, Mrs. John
Rosenwald, Mr. James B.
Rosner, Mrs. Charles
Sadowsky, Mrs. Jack P.
Salfeld, Mrs. Henry
Schafner, Master Eliot
Schneer, Mrs. Mary
Scholle, Mrs. William D.
Schwab, Miss Diane
Sidenberg, Mrs. George M.
Sidenberg, Mr. Henry

Skutch, Mrs. Ira
Spindler, Mrs. Jack
Stern, Mrs. B. Albert
Stern, Mrs. George A.
Sulzberger, Miss Anne
Sulzberger, Mrs. David H.
Tamm, Mrs. George L.
Taussig, Mrs. Charles W.
Trachtenberg, Mrs. Harold B.
Vogel, Mrs. Edwin C.
Von Hoeoler, Baroness
Wallerstein, Master George
Weil, Mrs. Frank L.
Weil, Mrs. Walter L.
Wood, Mr. George
Works Progress Administration
(Toy Shop)
Yankauer, Mrs. Walter D.
Zuckerman, Mrs. Paul S.

BOOKS AND MAGAZINES

Abraham, Mrs. Otto
Adler, Mrs. Jerome C.
Adler, Mrs. Paul
Adsit, Mrs. P. B.
Albarelli, Miss Angela
Albert, Mrs. S. S.
Alkus, Mrs. I. Jack
American Red Cross
Anna's Hats
Arnheim, Dr. Ernest E.
Arnoff, Mrs. Ellis
Arnold, Mrs. Stella M.
Aronsohn, Mrs. Nat H.
Arnstein, Mr. Alexander E.
Arrow, Mrs. Harry I.
Astro, Mrs. Ralph
Atlas, Mrs. David
Auster, Mrs. Rose
Bach, Mrs. Julian S., Jr.
Bach, Mrs. Milton J.
Backer, Mrs. George
Backner, Mr. Lester
Baerwald, Mrs. Paul
Baker, Mrs. Herman
Bastian, Dr. Carlisle C.
Baumann, Miss Rose

Berenstein, Dr. Harry
Bernheim, Mrs. Isaac J.
Bernheim, Mr. Leonard Henly
Bernheim, Mrs. Mortimer
Bernheim, Mrs. Sidney
Berolzheimer, Mrs. Alfred C.
Berolzheimer, Mrs. Edwin M.
Bickwit, Miss Barbara
Bilsky, Miss Ruth
Binger, Mrs. Robert E.
Blum, Mrs. Robert
Blumenthal, Mrs. Robert G.
Blun, Mrs. Edwin
Boorstein, Mrs. Pauline
Bratter, Mrs. William J.
Brisk, Mrs. Charles S.
Broom, Mrs. Martin M.
Browning, Mrs. S. Pearce, Jr.
Brunner, Dr. Martha
Brussel, Mrs. Herbert S.
Buchman, Miss Helen
Bullowa, Mrs. Arthur M.
Byk, Mrs. Paul M.
Camasser, Mr. Harry
Cogan, Mrs. Alan D.
Cohen, Mrs. Arthur J.

BOOKS AND MAGAZINES—(Continued)

Cohen, Mrs. George W.
Cohn, Mrs. Leonard A.
Cohn, Mrs. Peter A.
Collier, Master Frederic
Collier, Master Gilman
Colp, Mrs. Ralph
Cook, Mrs. Alfred A.
Costume Novelties, Inc. (Through Mr. B. L. Solomon)
Cullman, Mrs. Joseph F., Jr.
Cuming, Mrs. Alice T.
Dammann, Mrs. Richard W.
Danowsky, Rabbi Dr. Joseph
Danziger, Mrs. Max
Deitsch, Mrs. Charles
Dickson, Mrs. Leonard
Donenfeld, Mr. Harry
Ehre, Dr. Samuel
Einstein, Mr. Julius
Elias, Mrs. Henry H.
Eliasoph, Dr. Benjamin
Falk, Mrs. Myron S., Jr.
Farmer, Mrs. Alfred Sheridan
Fechheimer, Mr. S. M.
Fidanque, Mrs. Benjamin D.
Finkenberg, Mrs. I.
Fishman, Mrs. Louis D.
Forsch, Mrs. Albert
Frank, Mrs. D.
Frank, Mrs. Henry
Frank, Miss Jean
Frank, Mr. Nathan
Frank, Dr. Robert T.
Frankenthaler, Mrs. George
Freeman, Miss Lois
Friedenheit, Master Arthur
Friedman, Mrs. Julius B.
Friedlander, Miss Mary Ellen
Friedlander, Master Charles
Friedlander, Mr. Marcus S.
Fuerst, Mrs. William F.
Fuhs, Mrs. Arnold L.
Furchgott, Mrs. Leo
Galinger, Mrs. George W.
Garfunkel, Mr. J. H.
Garlock, Dr. John H.
Geiss, Mr. Lawrence
General Printing Ink (Through Mr. Herbert Kaufman)
Genn, Mrs. G. H.

Geyer, Cornell and Newell
Gilbert, Mr. Eli
Glazier, Mrs. Henry S.
Gluck, Miss Mildred K.
Goldsmith, Mrs. Arthur J.
Goldsmith, Mrs. Elsie Borg
Goldsmith, Dr. J.
Goodman, Mrs. Edwin
Goodman, Mrs. Maurice
Gottheil, Mrs. Paul
Greene, Mrs. Fred H.
Greenhut, Mrs. B. J.
Greenspan, Mr. George
Greenwald, Mr. Leo
Groupp, Mrs. Bertha
Gubkin, Mr. I.
Guilden, Mrs. Ira
Guinzburg, Mrs. Harold A.
Guinzburg, Mrs. Mary C.
Gutman, Mr. John
Halle, Mrs. H. J.
Hanson, Mrs. Edward C.
Harkavy, Dr. Edward E.
Hartman, Mrs. Siegfried F.
Heilberg, Miss Frieda
Heimerdinger, Mrs. Frederick M.
Heimerdinger, Mrs. Joseph E.
Hellman, Mrs. Marco F.
Heming, Mrs. Charles E.
Hendricks, Mrs. Henry S.
Henshel, Mr. Harry D.
Herald Tribune, New York
Herkimer, Miss E.
Herschel, Mrs. Maurice B.
Hess, Miss Muriel
Heyman, Mrs. David M.
Heymann, Mrs. Jacob
Hirsch, Mrs. Laurence M.
Hirsch, Mrs. Steven J.
Hirsch, Mrs. Walter A.
Hirschfield, Mr. Benjamin Lewis
Hochschild, Mrs. Walter
Hospital Service Plan of Technical Publicity Assn., Inc.
Hunter, Mrs. Frances
Hunter, Mrs. George
Isaacs, Miss Deborah
Isaacs, Mrs. Myron S.
Isaacs, Mr. P. N.
Israel, Mrs. A. C.

BOOKS AND MAGAZINES—(Continued)

Jacobi, Miss Ellen
Jaffee, Mrs. Hattie A.
James Monroe Women's Relief Corps (Through Miss Pauline Isaacs)
Kahn, Miss Barbara
Kaskel, Mrs. Max
Kaskor, Mr. Adolph
Kaufman, Mrs. Elkin S.
Kaufman, Mr. Robert
Kaye, Mrs. Harold
Kempner, Mrs. Alan H.
King, Miss Edith
Klee, Mrs. David
Kleeman, Mr. and Mrs. Max E.
Klein, Miss Frances
Klein, Dr. Joseph
Klein, Dr. Samuel H.
Klingenstein, Mrs. Charles
Klingenstein, Mrs. Joseph
Kohnstamm, Mrs. Lothair S.
Kralovie, Miss Florence
Kridel, Mrs. Robert H.
Kriendler, Mrs. Robert I.
Kubie, Dr. Lawrence S.
Kulick, Dr. Bernard
Kulick, Dr. Morton
Kutner, Mr. Adolph
Lamport, Mrs. Samuel C.
Landesman, Mrs. Abraham
Langer, Mr. and Mrs. Harry
Langley, Master Neil
Lansburgh, Mrs. Percy W.
Lasker, Mr. Bernard
Latz, Mrs. Hattie S.
Laval, Dr. Joseph
Lavine, Mr. Jack
Leavitt, Mr. Ezra G.
Leavitt, Mrs. Philip B.
Leggett, Francis H. and Company
Lehman, Mrs. Irving
Lehman, Mr. Robert
Leiter, Mrs. H. Evans
Levy, Mrs. Benjamin J.
Levy, Mrs. Charles
Levy, Mrs. Edward B.
Levy, Mrs. Joseph A.
Levy, Mrs. L. Napoleon

Levy, Mrs. Robert J.
Lewengood, Mrs. Abraham
Liebman, Mrs. Charles J.
Liebmann, Mrs. Samuel
Liebowitz, Mrs. Harry H.
Lilienthal, Dr. Howard
Lippmann, Mrs. David
Lippmann, Dr. Robert K.
Liszt, Mrs. Max
Loeb, Mrs. Carl M., Jr.
Loeb, Mrs. Louis M.
Loeb, Mrs. Morris
Loeb, Mrs. Otto S.
Loeb, Mrs. Richard
Long, Mrs. Louis
Lorsch, Mr. Henry
Mack, Mrs. Walter S.
Magnin, Mrs. Stella
Mair, Mr. Hugh
Manges, Dr. Morris
Markowitz, Mrs. M.
Marks, Mrs. Minray J.
Martin, Mrs. Herbert S.
May, Mrs. Henry
Meinhard, Mrs. Leo I.
Mendelsohn, Mrs. Louis
Meyer, Mrs. Jerome
Meyer, Mrs. Maurice, Jr.
Miller, Miss Belle
Mintz, Dr. Maurice E.
Mitchell, Mrs. Harold M.
Moolten, Dr. Sylvan E.
Mordecai, Mr. Benjamin
Moreland, Mrs. Andrew
Morgenthau, Mrs. Henry
Morris, Mrs. S. Fred
Moschcowitz, Mrs. Paul
Nathan, Mrs. Cyrus H.
Neaman, Mrs. Pearson E.
New, Mrs. Sidney
New York Journal and American
Newton Elkin Shoe Company
Norton, Mrs. John
Olden, Mrs. Louis
Oppenheim, Mrs. Charles, Jr.
Oppenheimer, Dr. B. S.
Oppenheimer, Mr. Julius
Ottinger, Mrs. Simon

BOOKS AND MAGAZINES—(Continued)

Parker, Mrs. Alfred P.
Parris, Mr. David
Peterson, Mrs. Eugene
Philips, Mrs. Herman
Picker, Mrs. Eugene
Pollak, Mrs. Maurice
Posner, Mr. Edwin
Putzel, Mr. Norman
Rains, Mr. and Mrs. S. E.
Reis, Mrs. Arthur M.
Reubens, Mrs. Raymond
Rhodes, Mr. Harold S.
Riley, Mrs. Gilbert H.
Rittmaster, Mrs. David H.
Roe, Mrs. I. J.
Roos, Dr. Alan
Rose, Mrs. Oscar
Rosenberg, Mr. Alex
Rosenthal, Mrs. Daniel D.
Rosenstein, Mrs. Henry
Rosovsky, Miss Rebecca
Rossbach, Mrs. Max J.
Sachs, Miss Edith
Sachs, Mrs. Samuel
Samuels, Mrs. Florence L.
Samuels, Mrs. Morris
Schaffner, Dr. Bertram
Schafner, Master Eliot
Scheuer, Mr. Jacob H.
Schlivek, Mrs. Kaufman
Scholle, Mrs. William D.
Schreiber, Mrs. William
Schulman, Mrs. Louis
Schulte, Mrs. John S.
Schulte, Mrs. Joseph M.
Schwabacher, Mrs. Herman
Sender, Dr. Fanny
Shamp, Miss May
Shapiro, Mrs. B. J.
Shire, Mr. Harold W.
Sidenberg, Mrs. Henry
Siegfried, Mrs. Charles M.
Simon, Mrs. Sol
Sittenfield, Mrs. M. J.
Slotnick, Mr. S.
Sobel, Mrs. Joseph
Solomon, Mr. Julius
Spencer, Mrs. Harold

Spingarn, Mrs. Arthur B.
Spiro, Mr. Abraham I.
Springer, Miss Bessie
Stern, Mr. Carl J.
Stern, Dr. Leo
Stern, Mrs. Samuel
Stettenheim, Mrs. I. M.
Stettiner, Mrs. Herman
Stora, Master Gerald
Stoller, Mrs. M.
Stralem, Mrs. Donald S.
Straus, Mrs. Hugh Grant, Jr.
Strauss, Mrs. Maurice J.
Strauss, Mrs. Nathan
Stroock, Mrs. Stephen J.
Sulzberger, Mrs. Arthur Hays
Tausaι.l, Mrs. Felix
Taylor, Mrs. G.
Trent, Mrs. Edwin
Turner, Dr. Joseph
Untermyer, Mrs. Irwin
Untermyer, Miss Louise
Upton, Mr. John
Van Raalte, Mr. Jim
Van Raalte, Mr. Tom
Van Raalte, Mrs. Z. A.
Waldman, Miss Jane
Warburg, Mr. Edwin M. M.
Watsky, Dr. Ralph W.
Watters, Mrs. Leon L.
Weil, Mrs. Arthur W.
Weil, Mrs. Leon
Weil, Mrs. Theodore
Weiler, Master John
Weinberg, Miss Carrie
Weinstein, Mr. B.
Wexler, Mrs. Celia
Wheeler, Miss Lilian R.
White, Mrs. Edward E.
Willheim, Mrs. William
Williams, Mrs. Leonard
Wimpfheimer, Mrs. Charles A.
Wimpfheimer, Mr. Harold D.
Wimpfheimer, Dr. Seymour
Wise, Mrs. Edmond E.
Wood, Mrs. M. E.
Wylie, Mrs. Milton
Zuckerman, Mrs. Henry

FLOWERS AND PLANTS

Abrahams, Mrs. A. I.
Bayer, Mr. Milton
Behr, Mr. Adolph (Florist)
Beir, Mrs. Bertram S.
Berolzheimer, Mrs. Edwin M.
Bogdish, Miss Mollie (In honor of Mrs. Tobias May)
Brentano, Mrs. Simon
Bronstein, Mrs. Herman
Congregation Emanu-El Temple (Confirmation Class)
Congregation Emanu-El Temple (Women's Auxiliary)
Congregation Rodeph Sholom Temple (Confirmation Class)
Cook Mrs. Alfred A.
Danziger, Mrs. Charles
Danziger, Mrs. Max
Dix, Mr. Jacob J.
Ehrman, Mrs. Frederick L.
Frank, Mrs. Laurence
Gardner, Mrs. Edwin S.
Gruntal, Mrs. Herman
Goldman, Mrs. A.
Goldstein, Miss Leila
Hart, Henry Inc. (Florist)
Hebrew Day Nursery (Junior Matrons of the Auxiliary)
Hess, Miss Caryl L.
Hess, Mr. Herman M.
Hoffman, Mrs. Norbert
Holmes, Mr. Duncan A. (Through Dr. Harold T. Hyman)
Hughes, Miss Edythe (In memory of Mrs. Catherine Waters Hughes)
Hutcheson, Mr. Ernest
Ickelheimer, Mrs. Henry R.
Jacoby, Dr. J. Ralph (In memory of Dr. George Jacoby)
Jacoby, Mr. Stephen
Kalter, Mrs. Max

Kislik, Mrs. Anna F.
Knights of Pythias (Columbus Lodge)
Klingenstein, Mrs. Charles
Lamport, Mrs. Arthur M.
Langner, Miss Claire
Lasker, Mr. Bernard
Lehman, Mr. Robert
Leidesdorf, Mr. and Mrs. Samuel D.
Levi, Mrs. Arthur D.
Levy, Mrs. Max
Long, Mrs. W. H. (Florist)
Martini, Mrs. Werner
Mintz, Dr. and Mrs. Nathan
Mt. Neboh Sisterhood
Murray, Miss Beatrice F.
Neugass, Mrs. Ludwig
Oestricher, Mrs. Sophie
Pforzheimer, Mrs. Carl H., Jr.
Rapaport, Mrs. Meyer
Rittenberg, Miss Anne
Rittenberg, Miss Lillian
Rosenberg, Mrs. Nathaniel
Samuels, Mr. Samuel
Schloss, Mr. Jerome
Schoenfeld, Dr. Dudley D.
Shalita, Dr. Benjamin G.
Standard Wholesale Florist
Steuer, Mrs. Max D.
Stone, Mr. and Mrs. Joseph
Temple Emanu-El Religious School
Thornton, Miss Mabel
Untermeyer, Miss Jean S.
Vander Poel, Mr. William H.
Wallach, Mr. Harry K.
Weil, Mrs. Arthur W.
Weil, Mrs. Leon
Wise, Mr. Jacob B.
Wolff, Mr. Max
Zimmerman, Mr. Jack
Zuckerman, Mrs. Henry

ICE CREAM, CANDY AND CAKE

Albert, Miss Violet
Arnheimer, Mrs. H. Irving
Blackstone, Mrs. Alex
Bloom, Mrs. Hannah

Bluhm, Mr. Leo H.
Blumenthal, Mrs. George
Cook, Mrs. Alfred A.
Congregation Emanu-El Temple

ICE CREAM, CANDY AND CAKE (Continued)

Danziger, Mrs. Max
Frank, Mrs. Henry
Fried, Mrs. E.
Friedman, Mrs. David
Goldstein, Master Bobby
Hahlo, Mrs. Hugo H. (In honor of Miss Virginia E. Adler)
Henry, Miss Irma J.
Jacobi, Miss Ellen
Jewish War Veterans of United States (Metropolitan Post)
Kasse, Mrs. Sidney
Keimowitz, Miss Edith
Klauber, Master William
Landesman, Mrs. Abraham
Lasker, Mr. Bernard
Levine, Miss Barbara Joyce
Levinsohn, Mrs. Sophie G.

Lewis, Master Peter
Lobel, Mr. Benjamin
Locke, Miss Gladys Carol
Loeb, Miss Suzanne
Mendelsohn, Mrs. Louis (In memory of Mrs. Jennie Breitenbach)
Mendelsohn, Mr. and Mrs. Louis (In memory of Mr. Arthur C. Mendelsohn)
Moss, Mrs. Charles B.
Pollack, Mrs. Herbert
Rosenfeld, Mr. Harry
Schulte, Mrs. Joseph M.
Siegel, Miss Sadie
Vigard, Mrs. Abel A.
Willstatter, Mrs. Alfred
Wyler, Mrs. Sigmund

MISCELLANEOUS DONATIONS

Allan, Miss Sheila (Studio Club, Young Women's Christian Association)
Arnold, Mr. Oscar M.
Arnstein, Mr. Leo
Aronsohn, Mrs. Nat H.
Baerwald, Mrs. Paul
Bergmann, Mr. Milan
Berolzheimer, Mrs. Alfred C.
Berolzheimer, Mrs. Edwin M.
Bick, Dr. Edgar M.
Blumenthal, Mrs. Robert G.
Borg, Mrs. Myron I.
Buchman, Miss Helen
Chargin, Dr. Louis
Cohen, Mrs. George W.
Cohen, Mrs. Samuel
Cohn, Mrs. Leonard A.
Conried, Mrs. Richard
Cook, Mrs. Alfred A.
Dammann, Mrs. Richard W.
Davis, Mr. Arthur
Davis, Miss Hannah
Dreyfus, Mrs. Raoul
Drucker, Miss Marie S.
Dunham, Miss Ella P.

Einstein, Miss Bella
Eising, Mrs. Edwin B.
Elishewitz, Mrs. Jacob
Elsinger, Mrs. W. H.
Englander, Mrs. Ben B.
Federation Thrift Shop
Fisher, Miss E.
Fisher, Mrs. Jessie
Forsch, Mrs. Sidney
Frankenheimer, Miss Ida
Frankenheimer, Miss Rose
Franklin, Mrs. Emil
Free Milk Fund for Babies
Friedenheit, Mrs. Isaac
Gabriner, Mr. Arthur
Gimbel, Mr. Adam L.
Gimbel, Mr. Bruce A.
Ginsberg & Horan Company
Goldman, Mrs. Fannie
Goldman, Mrs. L.
Goldmark, Mr. Godfrey
Goodkind, Mrs. Louis W.
Gottheil, Mrs. Paul
Great Atlantic & Pacific Tea Company, The
Gruntal, Mrs. Herman

MISCELLANEOUS DONATIONS—(Continued)

Guggenheim, Mrs. Daniel
Gutnik, Mrs. Henriette
Haas, Miss Marion F.
Harlow, Mr. Arthur H.
Hartman, Mrs. Siegfried F.
Heimerdinger, Mrs. Joseph E.
Heming, Mrs. Charles E.
Henry, Mrs. Charles I.
Herald Tribune, New York
Heyman ,Mrs. David M.
Hirsch, Mrs. Walter A.
Hirschfield, Mr. Mortr
Hochschild, Mrs. Walter
Home for Aged and Infirm Hebrews
    of New York, The
Horowitz, Mrs. Gussie
Hydeman, Mrs. Edwin M.
Hyman, Dr. and Mrs. Abraham
Israel, Mrs. Charles
Jacobi, Mr. Lester
Kaufman, Mr. and Mrs. Myer L.
Keller, Miss Ruth
Klingenstein, Mrs. Charles
Kohnstamm, Master Dick
Kohnstamm, Mrs. Lothair S.
Kops, Mr. Waldemar
Kridel, Mr. William
Kubie, Dr. Lawrence S.
Lambert, Dr. Robert K.
Landesman, Mrs. Abraham
Lee, Mr. George
Levy, Mrs. Ben C.
Lieberman, Mrs. Charles Joseph
Loeb, Mrs. Louis M.
Longman, Mrs. Horace
Luria, Mr. Max
Maass, Mr. Herbert M.
Minton, Mrs. Lucy Sperry
Moses, Miss Leila Tyndall
Myers, Master Richard
Neumeyer, Mrs. G. H.
Newman, Miss Rose
O'Brien, Mrs. John

Oppenheimer, Dr. B. S.
Pforzheimer, Mrs. Carl H., Jr.
Pinto, Mrs. Joseph
Pollack, Dr. Herbert
Powel, Miss Lilly
Raiss, Mrs. Albert
Reig, Mrs. Ben
Reutlinger, Mr. Jack (Through
    Dr. Herman Zazeela)
Rosenberg, Mr. Samuel (Through
    Mr. Louis Schneiderman)
Rosenstein, Mrs. Henry
Rosner, Mrs. Charles
Rosovsky, Miss Rebecca
Ryan, Miss Edith
Sachs, Miss Jane
Sacks, Mr. Dudley
St. John's Guild Floating Hospital
Schein, Dr. Albert J.
Schlossberg, Mr. Alfred
Seagram Distillers Corporation
Selig, Dr. Seth
Stettiner, Mrs. H.
Siegbert, Mrs. Henry
Silberg, Mr. Robert H.
Silverman, Miss Betty
Silverstein, Mr. Leo
Solomon, Mrs. A.
Stag, Mrs. Sam
Straus, Mrs. Roger W.
Strauss, Mr. Bertram (Through
    Dr. Edgar M. Bick)
Stroheim & Romann
Sufrin, Mrs. Oscar J.
Talbot, Mrs. Elizabeth M.
Temple Emanu-El
Wacht, Mr. William W.
Watters, Dr. Leon L.
Weil, Mrs. Frank L.
Weil, Mrs. Walter L.
Wise, Mrs. Edmond E.
Wyle, Mrs. Milton

CONTRIBUTIONS TO ABRAHAM JACOBI LIBRARY

American College of Dentists
Arnheim, Dr. Ernest E.
Associated Alumni of The Mount
   Sinai Hospital
Barnett, Dr. Roy
Beck, Dr. David
Bick, Dr. Edgar M.
Bishop, Dr. Louis Faugeres, Jr.
Boas, Dr. Ernst P.
Brezin, Dr. David
Brooklyn Hospital
Collegiate Press, Menasha, Wisconsin
Colp, Dr. Ralph
Corn Products Refining Company
"Dental Digest"
Dental Items of Interest Publishing
   Co., Inc.
Fishberg, Dr. Arthur M.
Frank, Dr. Maxwell S.
Friesner, Dr. I.
Garlock, Dr. John H.
Globus, Dr. Joseph H.
Gross, Dr. Sidney W.
Hartman, Mr. Irving
Hebrew Medical Journal
Hirsch, Dr. I. Seth
Hochstadter, Mr. Walter
Hyman, Dr. Abraham

Jewish Hospital of Brooklyn
Kahn, Dr. Samuel
Klemperer, Dr. Paul
Kohn, Dr. Jerome L.
Kubie, Dr. Lawrence S.
Levy, Mrs. I. H.
Licht, Dr. Sidney
Lilienthal, Dr. Howard
Manges, Dr. Morris
Master, Dr. Arthur M.
Mayo Clinic
Mead, Johnson and Company
Modern Dentists
Montefiore Hospital
Moschcowitz, Dr. Eli
Neuhof, Dr. Harold
New York Academy of Medicine
New York Medical College and
   Flower Hospital
"New York Medical Week"
Pollack, Dr. Herbert
Sea View Hospital
Steinitz, Dr. Ernst
Surgeon General's Office, U. S. Army
   Medical Library
Turner, Dr. Joseph
Vineberg, Dr. Hiram

REPORT OF
THE MOUNT SINAI HOSPITAL
LADIES' AUXILIARY SOCIETY

OFFICERS

MRS. LEOPOLD BERNHEIMER ....President
MRS. OSCAR ROSE ....Treasurer
MRS. JOSEPH A. ARNOLD ....Secretary

To the Board of Trustees of The Mount Sinai Hospital:

Gentlemen:

I note the passing of another year and that the time is at hand at which to make my yearly report of our Society's activities. My sincere regret is that my health, during the past year, did not permit me to attend the weekly meetings at which our ladies gave such splended and enthusiastic service to the worthy cause. Our thanks are due to them and my personal appreciation must find expression through this report.

Since I last addressed you, I have noticed the passing of several of our most ardent workers, and their loss is sorely felt by all of us.

Respectfully submitted,

MRS. LEOPOLD BERNHEIMER,

President.

TREASURER'S REPORT

Statement of Disbursements and Receipts for the Year Ended
December 31st, 1940

DISBURSEMENTS

Linens and Bedding	$18,457.54	
Wearing Apparel	5,601.75	
Total Disbursements		$24,059.29

RECEIPTS

From Federation for the Support of Jewish Philanthropic Societies	22,604.00
Deficit *	*$1,455.29*

* *Taken from Permanent Fund of Hospital.*

REPORT OF NEUSTADTER HOME

The affiliation between the Neustadter Home and the Mount Sinai Hospital completed its fourth year in 1940. This affiliation has continued to influence favorably the management of the Neustadter Home and has proved to be of benefit to both societies. The Home has benefited by the use of the Hospital's medical, administrative, executive, purchasing and other services, and the Hospital has benefited by having an improved convalescent service available to many patients who previously could not receive such care. The Home has become more and more the convalescent department of the Hospital and most of the Home's guests are now referred to it by the Hospital.

During 1940 a total of 841 convalescents was admitted; 522 female and 319 male. This represents an increase of 44 patients over the previous year, most of the increase being represented in male patients. The total number of patient days was 19,040, a substantial increase over the previous year's total of 17,713. The average length of stay was a fraction over 22 days, and the average gain in weight of the Home's guests was between 4 and 5 pounds. The cost of each meal prepared was just over 18 cents.

The personnel of the Home continues to number 30, of whom 12, including the visiting doctor, are members of the professional staff, and 18 are classified among the maintenance staff.

The Home has continued to progress in its physical appearance and condition. The principal improvement was the installation of an automatic elevator, making it possible to admit sicker patients for convalescence and to accommodate them on the second floor. Hitherto many of these patients could not be admitted because of their inability to climb the stairs. The living rooms on the second floor have also been put to greater use by the guests since the installation of the elevator. Another improvement was the installation of storm windows and a more effective heating plant unit in the men's recreation room in the basement, thus making this room comfortable and usable throughout the year. Many advances and improvements were made in the conduct of the dietary service and in the activities of the occupational-therapy and recreation departments.

Dr. Herman Zazeela, the staff physician, has completed a six months' statistical analysis of the work with the Neustadter patients. The following are a few salient and important factors worthy of mention:

1. Vitamin preparations are being prescribed more and more for the patients. This is in line with the recently accepted theories and findings of research workers in the fields of vitamin deficiency. The study indicates that the use of these vitamins will probably increase in the future.

2. Closer co-operation has been possible with the various follow-up clinics at the Hospital. Increased opportunities have been provided to permit the clinician who treated a patient during the acute illness to observe its progress during the various stages of convalescence and to advise in the further care and treatment of the convalescent. This has been particularly noticeable in patients suffering from chest ailments who must stay at the Home for several months. It is now possible to arrange for two, three and four visits to the follow-up clinic of the Hospital for continued observation, including x-ray examination, and in this way to plot a course of continued treatment and eventual discharge.

3. Better co-ordination in the matter of exchange of records and medical notes has been effected with the help of Dr. George Baehr.

4. The analysis goes into many details of the types of patients who have been accepted during the six months' period, their length of stay, their weight gains, the types of diets used; and even though patients have been admitted who are sicker at the time of admission than had been the case before, the nursing service has been able to cope with these needs with even greater efficiency.

A new development in 1940 was the beginning of routine inspection visits by groups of student nurses from the Mount Sinai Hospital School of Nursing. The visits were aimed to acquaint the nurses with the character of the service and to observe the work of the Home in the convalescent care of patients, many of whom they had nursed previously in the wards of the Hospital. The result has been a greater interest on the part of the nurses in convalescent care and the visualization of what convalescent care really involves.

The fact that no set period has been fixed for convalescence but that the patients' conditions determine the length of stay, the emphasis on special diets when indicated on clinical grounds, the pleasant atmosphere of the Home, the thorough treatment, and the minimum amount of restrictive institutional regulations, are, we believe, important factors in our continued progress. An indication of our progress is the growing evidence that the physicians at the Hospital are more conscious of our convalescent service and of its value, and are referring to us more patients who can benefit by proper convalescent care. That our guests have been pleased by their experience seems indicated by the many unsolicited letters of favorable and grateful comments sent to us by patients.

During the past year, $54,804.89 was spent for the routine budgetary activities of the Home. To meet these expenditures, $39,761 was available from income from the Neustadter Foundation. Grants were received from the Greater New York Fund in the amount of $1,736, and from the United Hospital Fund in the amount of $3,348. The Board of the Neustadter Home is grateful to these agencies for this support. Payments in part made by some patients for their care amounted to $1,675. The net budgetary deficit for the year was $15,043.54, which is less by $811.47 than the budgetary deficit of 1939.

This report would be incomplete without an expression of the sincere gratitude of the Board and of myself to those who have contributed to this work. Special thanks are extended to Miss Helen Butler, our Superintendent, and to the loyal and devoted staff of the Home; to Dr. Herman Zazeela, our capable medical officer; to the Mount Sinai Hospital's administration and particularly to Dr. Joseph Turner; to Mrs. Mendelsohn, Miss Hallahan, Miss Henderson, and Mr. Cubberley; to Mr. Sidney Goldstone who continues to give us his expert advice in building matters; and to all others who have given so freely of their time and efforts in making more and better convalescent care available to those that need it. I should be ungrateful if I did not also express my own thanks to the Board for its splendid co-operation throughout the year, and for making my part of the work so pleasant and satisfying.

Respectfully submitted,

HORTENSE M. HIRSCH,
President.

Dedicated Buildings

CHILDREN'S PAVILION

ERECTED IN LOVING REMEMBRANCE OF

LEWIS EINSTEIN

AND

MILLY EINSTEIN FALK

BY

HENRY L. EINSTEIN

1921

PRIVATE PAVILION

DEDICATED TO THE MEMORY OF

MEYER AND BARBARA GUGGENHEIM

BY THEIR CHILDREN

1920

Dedicated Buildings

OUT-PATIENT BUILDING

DEDICATED TO THE MEMORY OF

MAYER LEHMAN

BY HIS CHILDREN

1904

ADOLPH LEWISOHN PATHOLOGICAL AND LABORATORY BUILDING

DONATED BY

ADOLPH LEWISOHN

1904 - 1922

Dedicated Buildings

AUDITORIUM

DEDICATED TO THE
MEMORY OF

GEORGE BLUMENTHAL, JR.

BY

FLORENCE AND GEORGE BLUMENTHAL

1920

LABORATORY BUILDING

DEDICATED TO THE MEMORY OF

ABRAHAM AND AMELIA
MEYERS

1938

Dedicated Buildings

CHILDREN'S CLINIC

DEDICATED TO THE MEMORY OF

FLORENCE HENRIETTA WALTER

AND

MARJORIE WALTER GOODHART

BY THEIR PARENTS

FLORENCE B. AND WILLIAM I. WALTER

1916 - 1923

Endowment of Wards

THE
CHARLES A. WIMPFHEIMER WARDS
FOR
SURGICAL TREATMENT
OF
DISEASES OF STOMACH AND INTESTINES
FOUNDED BY
CHARLES A. WIMPFHEIMER
1916

THE ADOLPH BERNHEIMER
MEMORIAL WARD

———

FOUNDED BY HIS DAUGHTER ROSIE
FEBRUARY 16TH, 1897

THE MRS. ADOLPH BERNHEIMER
MEMORIAL WARD

———

FOUNDED BY HER DAUGHTERS
ROSIE BERNHEIMER AND FLORENCE B. WALTER
FEBRUARY 16TH, 1916

Endowment of Wards

MAIN OPERATING ROOM

DEDICATED TO THE MEMORY OF

ISAAC AND BABETTE BLUMENTHAL

BY

ALFRED, GUSTAV, HUGO, BENJAMIN
AND GEORGE BLUMENTHAL

1904

GENITO-URINARY WARD

DEDICATED TO THE MEMORY OF

JOEL GOLDENBERG

BY PROVISION IN HIS WILL

1904

THE SIMON ROTHSCHILD WARD

IN PERPETUITY

1905

Endowment of Wards

THE EMANUEL LEHMAN MEMORIAL WARD

DEDICATED FEBRUARY 15TH, 1911

———

FOUNDED BY

MRS. SIGMUND LEHMAN, MRS. EVELYN L. EHRICH,
MR. PHILIP LEHMAN

THE

JOSEPH AND SOPHIA SACHS MEMORIAL WARDS

———

DEDICATED TO THE MEMORY OF THEIR PARENTS BY

SAMUEL AND HARRY SACHS

1913

THE ELIAS WARD

———

IN THIS WARD BEDS WERE ENDOWED:
THREE BEDS IN MEMORY OF RAPHAEL ELIAS
THREE BEDS IN MEMORY OF SARAH ELIAS
THREE BEDS IN MEMORY OF ROBERT F. ELIAS
THREE BEDS IN MEMORY OF HENRY F. ELIAS

ALL FOUNDED BY THE PROVISION OF THE WILL OF
HENRY F. ELIAS

1928

Endowment of Wards

THE ALFRED AND HANNAH BLUMENTHAL WARD

FOUNDED 1922

THE LOUIS N. KRAMER MEMORIAL

FOUNDED BY PROVISION
OF HIS WILL

1930

Endowment of Rooms

DEDICATED TO THE
MEMORY OF
LINA MEYER ASIEL
BY
ELIAS ASIEL
1904

THE EDWARD LAUTERBACH ROOM
DEDICATED IN PERPETUITY
BY THE
BOARD OF TRUSTEES
OF
THE MOUNT SINAI HOSPITAL
IN GRATEFUL RECOGNITION OF HIS
EMINENT SERVICES
1904

DEDICATED BY
DISTRICT GRAND LODGE No. 1
INDEPENDENT ORDER
FREE SONS OF ISRAEL
M. SAMUEL STERN, GRAND MASTER
1901
FOUR BEDS

DEDICATED FOR THE BENEFIT OF
THE ALUMNAE
OF THE
MOUNT SINAI HOSPITAL SCHOOL OF NURSING
BY
MRS. MAX NATHAN
1904

Endowment of Rooms

DEDICATED TO THE ALUMNAE OF

THE MOUNT SINAI HOSPITAL
SCHOOL OF NURSING

BY

MR. AND MRS. CHARLES KLINGENSTEIN

1931

IN MEMORY OF

ISAAC STRAUSS
1825-1876

ENDOWED BY HIS SON

CHARLES STRAUSS

1934

IN MEMORY OF

HENRIETTA STRAUSS
1819-1893

ENDOWED BY HER SON

CHARLES STRAUSS

1934

THE JACOB AND HENRIETTA
SNEUDAIRA ROOM

FOUNDED BY PROVISION IN THE WILL OF

MOSES J. SNEUDAIRA

1935

Tablets

ERECTED IN X-RAY MUSEUM

IN MEMORY OF

BERTHA WEHLE NAUMBURG

FOUNDED BY HER SON

WALTER W. NAUMBURG

MARCH 3RD, 1922

ERECTED IN RADIO-THERAPY
DEPARTMENT

DEPARTMENT OF
RADIUM AND RADIO-THERAPY

FLORETTE AND ERNST ROSENFELD
FOUNDATION

1923

ERECTED IN X-RAY DEPARTMENT

EQUIPPED BY

LOUISA AND SAMUEL SACHS

IN MEMORY OF THEIR DAUGHTER

ELLA SACHS PLOTZ

1923

ERECTED IN THE MAIN HALL

IN GRATEFUL RECOGNITION AND REMEMBRANCE
OF THE
GENEROSITY AND SERVICES OF

SIDNEY S. PRINCE

TRUSTEE AND OFFICER
OF
THE MOUNT SINAI HOSPITAL

1929

Tablets

ERECTED IN OUT-PATIENT
DEPARTMENT

OUT-PATIENT DEPARTMENT DENTAL CLINIC
EQUIPPED AND SUPPORTED BY
DAVID A. SCHULTE
1925

ERECTED IN PATHOLOGICAL
LECTURE HALL

DEDICATED TO THE MEMORY OF
ISAAC AND SARAH ERDMANN
1925

ERECTED IN LABORATORY
NORTH BUILDING

ERECTED BY
CHARLES A. WIMPFHEIMER
A MOST GENEROUS FRIEND OF THE HOSPITAL
1926

ERECTED IN SOCIAL SERVICE
DEPARTMENT

IN LOVING MEMORY OF
ETTA COHEN LORSCH
1928

Perpetual Beds

In Memory of
Louis W. Neustadter
Dedicated by his wife
1873

In Memory of
Daniel Joseph Jaffe
Dedicated by the family
1874

In Memory of
Isaac Dittenhoefer
Dedicated by
Abram J. Dittenhoefer
1874

In Memory of
Lewis Einstein
1875

In Memory of
Katy White
Wife of J. L. Englehart
Niece of Jonas and Yette Heller
1875

In Memory of
Mary Rosenbaum
By her husband,
Sigmund D. Rosenbaum
1876

Endowed in Memory of
Lazarus Hallgarten
1876

In Memory of
Martin and Joseph Bachrach
Beloved sons of
Samuel and Babette Bachrach
1877

In Memory of our beloved mother
Mina Schafer
Wife of Mayer Schafer
1878

In Memory of
Benjamin Nathan
Dedicated by will of his wife
1879

Dedicated by
Sarah Heinemann
1879

In Memory of
Abraham Scholle
1880

In Memory of
Leonora Wormser
Vice-President of the Ladies' Auxiliary
Society
Wife of Simon Wormser
1880

In Memory of
Nathan Blun
Endowed by his children
1880

In Memory of
Mary S. Sahlein
Wife of William Sahlein
1881

In Memory of
William Sahlein
1881

In Memory of
David Wallerstein
1881

In Memory of
Harris Aronson
1881

In Memory of
Arnold Uhlman
Dedicated by the family
1883

In Memory of
Joseph Reckendorfer
Dedicated by his wife
1883

In Memory of
Isaac and Ida Meyer
Dedicated by their children
1883

Perpetual Beds

In Memory of
Herman Friedlander
Dedicated by his family
1883

In Memory of
Nathan Asiel
Dedicated by his family
1883

In Memory of our beloved brother
Siegmund Spingarn
1884

In Memory of
Emanuel Hoffman
Dedicated by the family
1884

In Memory of
Adolph Hallgarten
1885

In Memory of
Siphra Stern
Dedicated by her children
1887

In Memory of
Benjamin F. Meyer
Dedicated by his brother
1887

In Memory of
Jonas Heller
Dedicated by the family
1887

In Memory of
Henry Herrman
Endowed by Esther Herrman
1889

In Memory of
Henryette Mortimer
and Edward Rosenfeld
Dedicated by the husband and father
1889

In Memory of
Maurie E. Ansbacher
Dedicated by
Adolph B. and Frances E. Ansbacher
1889

In Memory of
Sidney Speyer
Dedicated by his brother
James Speyer
1890

In Memory of
Nathan Littauer
1891

Dedicated to the Memory of
Hirsch Wallach and
Bienchen Wallach
By their son, Isaac Wallach
1891

Endowed in Memory of
Louise Littauer
Daughter of Nathan and Harriet Littauer
1891

In Memory of
Rosa Veit
1892

To the Memory of
Sophia Roth
Dedicated by her husband
Ludwig Roth
1892

In Memory of
Bernard L. and Fanny Tim
Endowed by Louis and Solomon Tim
1892

In Memory of
Sigmund Robertson
Dedicated by the family
1892

Perpetual Beds

In Memory of
Grace A. L. Cullman
Dedicated by her husband
1892

In Memory of
Esther Asiel
Dedicated by her son
1892

Dedicated to the Memory of
Moses Wasserman
1893

In Memory of
Dr. Joseph Mainzer
Dedicated by his brother
1893

In Memory of
Johanna Fatman
Dedicated by S. A. Fatman
1893

In Memory of
**Sylvester Brush
and Sarah, His Wife**
Dedicated by their children
1893

In Memory of
Jesse Seligman
Dedicated by the family
1894

In Memory of our beloved mother
Babette Scholle
1894

Dedicated to the Memory of
Albert S. Rosenbaum
1894

In Memory of
Israel D. and Henrietta Walter
Dedicated by their son
William I. Walter
1894

In Memory of
Isaac Bernheimer
1894

In Memory of
Moritz Josephthal
Dedicated by his widow
1895

To the Memory of
Leopold Boscowitz
Dedicated by his brothers and sisters
1837—1895

In Memory of her beloved son
Joseph Louis Myers
Dedicated by Louisa Myers
1895

In Memory of
Adolph T. Scholle
Dedicated by his father
1895

In Memory of
Adolph Bernheimer
Dedicated by his daughter
Miss Rosie Bernheimer
1895

In Memory of
Bertha Morris
Dedicated by her relatives
1896

Founded by and in Memory of
David Wallach
Chicago, Ill.
1896

In Memory of
Mayer Goldsmith
Dedicated by his widow
1896

169

Perpetual Beds

In Memory of
Mathilda Oppenheimer
Dedicated by her husband
1897

In Memory of
Bernard Mainzer
Dedicated by the family
1897

Dedicated by Antoinette Mayer
In Memory of her son
Carl Theodor Mayer
1897

In Memory of
Adelaide Ballin King
Dedicated by her husband
1897

In Memory of
Mariane Ickelheimer
Dedicated by Mrs. Julie Heidelbach
1897

In Memory of
Julius L. Goldenberg
Dedicated by his mother
·1897

In Memory of
Bernard Cohen
1897

In Memory of
S. J. Spiegelberg
A former Director of this Institution
1898

In Memory of
Elias Jacobs
Dedicated by his wife
1898

Dedicated by
Mr. and Mrs. George Blumenthal
1898

The Rosalie Nathan
Perpetual Bed
Dedicated to the Cause of Humanity
1899

In Memory of
Martin H. Lehmaier
1899

Dedicated to the Memory of
Lydia Wolff
Wife of Abraham Wolff
1900

Dedicated to the Memory of
Abraham Wolff
1900

In Memory of
David Marks
Dedicated by his wife
1900

In Memory of
Louise Hoffman
Dedicated by her children
1900

Housman Memorial Beds
Dedicated by Arthur A. Housman
(Two Beds)
1900

In Memory of
Robert Graham Dun
1900

In Memory of
**His Wife, Bertha,
and Daughter, Sophie**
Dedicated by David Kohn
1900

Perpetual Beds

In Memory of My Beloved Parents
Simon and Rosetta S. Bernheimer
Dedicated by Jacob S. Bernheimer
1900

In Memory of
Henrietta Rubens
Dedicated by her husband
Charles Rubens, Paris
1901

In Memory of
Lazarus and Babette Morgenthau
Dedicated by Henry Morgenthau
1901

In Memory of
Edward B. Simon
Dedicated by his wife
1901

In Memory of
Josiah L. Webster
Dedicated by C. B. Webster
1901

In Memory of
Joseph Kaufman
Founded by provision in his will
1901

In Memory of
Emanuel Lauer
Dedicated by his daughters
Carrie Lehman and Sophie Goodhart
1901

In Memory of
Bernard and Henrietta Heineman
Dedicated by their son
Moses Heineman
1901

In Memory of
Marx and Sophie Hornthal
Dedicated by their children
1901

In Memory of
Moses Bruhl
Dedicated by his wife and daughters
1901

In Memory of
Moritz and Ernestine Cohn
Dedicated by their children
1901

In Memory of
Betty Loeb
Dedicated by her husband
Solomon Loeb
1902

In Memory of
Elizabeth Jeffries Garvey
Dedicated by Andrew Jeffries Garvey
(Two Beds)
1902

In Memory of
Louis and Yetta Stix
1902

In Memory of
Theodore G. Weil
1902

Two Beds
The Jacob Rubino Beds
1902

In Memory of
Fanny Myers
Dedicated by David E. Sicher
1902

In Memory of
Jacob S. Bernheimer
Dedicated by his wife and children
1902

Perpetual Beds

In Memory of
Bernard Baruch
Endowed by his grandson
1902

Dedicated by
The Hebrew Mutual Benefit Society
To Commemorate Its Seventy-fifth Anniversary
1902

In Memory of
Rachel V. and Charles Sternbach
Dedicated by their son
Sidney M. Sternbach
1903

In Memory of
Florentine Weinberg
Dedicated by Philip Weinberg
1903

In Memory of
Clara Wertheim
Dedicated by Henry P. Wertheim
1903

Dedicated to the Memory of
Jacob Bookman
1903

In Memory of
Edward J. King
Dedicated by his wife
Rosalie King
1904

In Memory of
Marcus L. Stieglitz
Dedicated by his wife
Sarah Stieglitz
1904

In Memory of
Joseph Freedman
Dedicated by his son
Andrew Freedman
1904

In Memory of
Simon Borg
Dedicated by his wife
Cecelia Borg
1905

In Memory of
Ruth M. Gross
By her parents
Morris and Carrie L. Gross
1905

In Memory of
Hannah Vogel
Dedicated by her husband
William Vogel
1905

In Memory of
M. S. Mork
Dedicated by his wife
Minnie Mork
1905

Dedicated by
Mr. and Mrs. Eugene Meyer
1905

In Memory of
Joseph B. Bloomingdale
1905

In Memory of
Adolph Herrmann
Founded by provision in his will
1906

Endowed by Emma B. Hendricks
In memory of her sons
Edgar Hendricks
Henry H. Hendricks
and Clifford B. Hendricks
1906

Endowed by Emma B. Hendricks
In Memory of her Husband
Joshua Hendricks
1906

Perpetual Beds

In Memory of
Bennett and Sarah B. King
1906

In Memory of
Samuel E. and Mary Halle
Endowed by Jacques S. Halle
1906

In Memory of
Cecelia Borg
Dedicated by her children
1906

**The Lyman C. and Hattie
Bloomingdale Perpetual Bed**
1906

In Memory of
Walter A. Schiffer
Dedicated by his wife
1907

In Memory of
Isaac Wallach
Founded by provision in his will
1907

In Memory of
Louis Josephthal
Founded by provision in his will
1907

In Memory of
Isabella Arnold Bernheimer
Dedicated by her children
1907

In Memory of
Hedwig Rosenbaum
By her husband
Sigmund D. Rosenbaum
1908

**The Leopold Laderer
Caroline Laderer and
Samuel L. Laderer
Perpetual Bed**
1908

In Memory of
Emily Lazarus
Founded by provision in the will of
Amelia B. Lazarus
1908

In Memory of
Simon W. Glazier
Dedicated by his wife and children
1908

In Memory of
Isaac S. and Sarah Erdmann
1909

The Ernest Ehrmann Bed
Founded by provision in his will
1909

In Memory of
Solomon Herzog
Founded by Edward N. Herzog
1909

In Memory of
Arthur A. Housman
Founded by provision in his will
(Two Beds)
1909

In Memory of
Abraham B. Frank
Dedicated by his wife
1909

In Memory of
Leopold Gusthal
Dedicated by his sisters
1909

In Memory of
Gustav Bernheim
Dedicated by his wife and children
1909

173

Perpetual Beds

In Memory of
Mary Mayer
Founded by David Mayer
1910

In Memory of
Therese Josephthal
Founded by provision in her will
1910

In Memory of
Edward A. and Bertha R. Price
Founded by Julie Price Erdman
1910

In Memory of
Dr. Joseph Schnetter
Founded by provision in his will
(Three Beds)
1910

In Memory of
Bertha Horn
Founded by provision in the will of
Michael Horn
1910

In Memory of
Rev. Dr. Gustave Gottheil
Rabbi, Temple Emanu-El
1873-1899
Founded by Paul Gottheil
1910

In Memory of
Dr. Herman Baerwald
Founded by Paul Baerwald
1910

In Memory of
Valentine and Fanny Loewi
Dedicated by the family
1911

In Memory of
Edna Saks Levy
Dedicated by Mr. and Mrs. Andrew Saks
1911

The Emma Rosenwald Bed
Founded by provision in her will
1911

In Memory of
Henry Rosenwald
Founded by Mrs. Henry Rosenwald
1911

In Memory of
**Allen L. Mordecai
and Kate Mordecai**
Dedicated by their children
1911

In Memory of
Alexander L. Kaufmann
Founded by provision in his will
1911

In Memory of
Julius Ehrmann
Founded by provision in the will of
Mathilda Ehrmann
1912

In Memory of
James and Amelia Strauss
Founded by provision in the will
of their son, Nathan F. Strauss
1912

In Memory of
Dr. Max Herzog
Founded by
Mr. and Mrs. Abram N. Stein
1912

In Memory of
Dr. Wolfgang Mack
1808-1883
Founded by provision in the will of
Jacob W. Mack
1912

Perpetual Beds

In Memory of
Jacob Wolfgang Mack
1845-1912
Dedicated by Jennie and Ella Heyman
1912

In Memory of
Luise Mack
1808-1887
Founded by provision in the will of
Jacob W. Mack
1912

In Memory of
Mathilda Ehrmann
Founded by provision in her will
1912

In Memory of
Florence Henrietta Walter
Dedicated by her aunt
Rosie Bernheimer
1913

In Memory of
Marcus and Bertha Goldman
1913

In Memory of
Lewis S. Levy
Founded by provision in his will
1914

In Memory of
Mary Levy
Founded by provision in the will of
Lewis S. Levy
1914

In Memory of
Julius and Fanny Robertson
Founded by provision in his will
1915

In Memory of
Maurice and Mathilde Seligmann
Dedicated by
George and Arthur Seligmann
1915

In Memory of
Erwin Beit Von Speyer
Founded by his uncle
James Speyer
1915

In Memory of
Max and Nina Herzog
Dedicated by their daughter
Bella H. Kaufmann
1915

In Memory of
Samuel and Helene Prince
Dedicated by their children
1915

In Memory of
Leonard S. Prince
Dedicated by his father and mother
December 23, 1915

In Memory of
Madge N. Haas
1915

In Memory of
David, Gustave B. and Charles Calman
Founded by provision in the will of
Emma Calman
1915

In Memory of
Tillie Hochschild
1916

Perpetual Beds

In Memory of
Mrs. Samuel H. Spingarn
Endowed by provision in the will of
Samuel H. Spingarn
1916

In Memory of
Samuel H. Spingarn
Endowed by provision in his will
1916

In Memory of
Henrietta Bondy
Founded by her son
Emil C. Bondy
1916

In Memory of
Jacob and Rosina Erdmann
Founded by Albert J. Erdmann
1916

In Memory of
Charles Bondy
Founded by his son
Emil C. Bondy
1916

In Memory of
Karl Schwabach
Founded by his uncle
James Speyer
1917

In Memory of
**Henry and Rosalie
Klingenstein**
Dedicated by their son
Charles Klingenstein
1917

In Memory of his Parents
Josephine and David Salzer
Dedicated by Leopold Salzer
1917

In Memory of
Mrs. Isaac Wallach
Founded by provision in her will
1917

In Memory of
Johanna and Rosalie Moses
Dedicated by their sister
Julia R. Ballerstein
1917

In Memory of
Bernhard Stern
Dedicated by his brother
Benjamin Stern
1917

In Memory of
Amelia Heidelberg
Dedicated by Isaac N. Heidelberg
1917

In Memory of
Rachel H. Pfeiffer
Founded by provision in her will
1917

In Memory of
Belle Glazier Bernheimer
Founded by provision in her will
1917

In Memory of
Charles E. Schafer
Endowed by his wife
1917

Endowed by
Mr. and Mrs. Philip J. Goodhart
1918

In Memory of
Theresa and Joseph Fox
1918

In Memory of their Parents
Louise and Leopold Salzer
Dedicated by their children
(Two Beds)
1918

176

Perpetual Beds

In Memory of
Joshua Rothblatt
Dedicated by his parents
Bernard and Ida Rothblatt
1919

In Celebration of the
Ninetieth Birthday of
Max Nathan
April 15, 1919
Presented by his daughter
Irma N. Straus

In Memory of
Meyer H. Lehman
Dedicated by his sisters
Mrs. Harriet Weil
and Mrs. Bertha Rosenheim
1919

In Memory of
Julius Lewisohn
London, England
Dedicated by his son
1919

In Memory of
William Klingenstein
of London, England
Dedicated by his nephew
Charles Klingenstein
1919

In Memory of
Emma and Albert Kaskel
Founded by provision in the will of
Emma H. Kaskel
1919

In Memory of
**Mayer Lehman and
Babette Lehman**
Dedicated
(Two Beds)
1919

Dedicated to
The Clara de Hirsch Home
By Dr. Josephine Walter
1919

The Louis M. Sonnenberg Bed
Founded by provision in his will
1919

In Memory of
Alan Harry Simon
Dedicated by
Mr. and Mrs. Harry G. Simon
1919

In Memory of
Ferdinand A. Straus
Dedicated by his son
Lionel F. Straus
1919

In Memory of
Henry Bendheim
Dedicated by his brother
Adolph D. Bendheim
1919

In Memory of
Levi Bamberger
Founded by Albert and Clara Blum
1919

The Three
J. D. Wendel Beds
Endowed in Memory of the Former
Tenants of John D. Wendel
1919

In Memory of
Sara Sonnenberg Beck
Dedicated by Martin Beck
1919

In Memory of
Aron Weil
Dedicated by his wife
Dora Weil
1919

Perpetual Beds

In Memory of his Parents
Vitus and Fanny Lambert
Dedicated by their son
August V. Lambert
1920

In Memory of
Oscar M. Leiser
Founded by provision in his will
1920

In Memory of
Edith Stine Schiffer
Founded by her husband
Jack W. Schiffer
1920

In Memory of
Mayer and Babette Lehman
Dedicated by
Mr. and Mrs. Morris Fatman
1920

In Memory of
Alphons Lewis
Founded by provision in his will
1920

In Memory of
David Lehman
Dedicated by his sisters
Mrs. Harriet Weil and
Mrs. Bertha Rosenheim
1920

In Memory of
Matilda Ollendorff
Dedicated by her husband
1920

In Memory of
Marjorie Walter Goodhart
Founded by her aunt
Rosie Bernheimer
October 19, 1920

In Celebration of the
Seventy-fifth birthday of
Frances M. Fechheimer
September 4, 1920
Dedicated by her son
Sam M. Fechheimer

Dedicated by
Mr. and Mrs. Henry Budge
1920

In Memory of
Max J. Breitenbach
Dedicated by his wife and children
1920

In Memory of
Aaron and Johanna Fatman
Dedicated by
Mr. and Mrs. Morris Fatman
1920

In Memory of
Aline Bernheim
Founded by her sons
George B. and Alfred L. Bernheim
1921

In Memory of
Ellin Prince Speyer
Founded by her husband
James Speyer
1921

In Memory of
Arnold and Fannie Falk
Dedicated by Myron S. Falk
and K. George Falk
1921

In Memory of
Rosalie, Fannie, Charles, Simon and Joseph Lederer
Founded by provision in the will of
Charlotte Lederer
1921

Perpetual Beds

In memory of her parents
Samuel and Bella Haas
Founded by Mrs. Dudley D. Sicher

In Memory of
Henry and Hanna Herrmann
Dedicated by their son
Frederick Herrmann
1921

In Memory of
Jacob L. and Sophie Kops
Dedicated by their children
1921

In Memory of
Esther Wyman
Founded by provision in her will
1921

In Memory of
Sydney Michael Hyman
Dedicated by his parents
Michael and Rose Hyman
1921

In Memory of
Clara Glazier
Founded by provision in her will
1922

In Memory of
Carrie Rapp and Samuel Rapp
Founded by provision in the will of
Samuel Rapp
1922

In Memory of
**David James King and
Adelaide Ballin King**
Dedicated by their daughter
Louise King Reckford
1922

In Memory of
Caroline Bookman
Founded by provision in her will
1922

In Memory of
Dorothea Haas Weiler
Founded by provision in the will of
her son
Charles H. Weiler
1923

In Memory of
Jacob H. Semel
Founded by provision in his will
1923

In Memory of
Marks Weiler
Founded by provision in the will of
his son
Charles H. Weiler
1923

In Memory of
**Morris S. Barnet
and
Alvina Barnet**
Dedicated by Morris S. Barnet
(Two Beds)

Dedicated by
Addie W. Kahn
1923

In Memory of
Walter J. Rose
Dedicated by his mother
1924

In Memory of
**Gabriel Mayer
Antoinette Mayer
Otto L. Mayer**
Founded by provision in the will of
Otto L. Mayer
1924

Endowed by
Abraham Erlanger
1924

Perpetual Beds

Founded by
Charles Hendricks
1924

The Ella Hellman Bed
Founded by provision in her will
1924

In Memory of
Solomon C. Guggenheimer
March 24th, 1924

In Memory of
Jacob Wertheim
Dedicated by his wife
Emma Stern Wertheim
1925

In Memory of
Louis S. Frankenheimer
Dedicated by
Ida and Rose Frankenheimer
1925

In Memory of
Pauline Mayers
Endowed by her husband
Morris Mayers
1925

In Memory of
Elkan and Bertha Naumburg
Dedicated by their son
Walter W. Naumburg
1926

In Memory of
Siegfried W. Mayer
Founded by provision in his will
1926

In Memory of
Samuel Baumann
Dedicated by his wife
Henrietta Baumann
1926

In Memory of
Henrietta Rawitser
Dedicated by her daughter
Theresa V. Rawitser
1926

In Memory of
Morris Rossin
Dedicated by his wife
Martha S. Rossin
1927

In Memory of
Lewis Schoolhouse
Endowed by
Joseph Runsheim
1927

Dedicated to their friends
George and Florence Blumenthal
By
Edmond and Suzanne King Bruwaert
1927

In Memory of
Samuel J. and Esther Gans
Dedicated by their son
Simeon C. Gans
1927

Endowed by
Mr. and Mrs. Albert E. Goodhart
1927

In Memory of
Arthur E. Frank
1927

In Memory of
Solomon Friedman and Amelia G. Friedman
1928

In Memory of
Samuel Bachrach and Babette Bachrach
1928

Perpetual Beds

In Memory of
Richard M. Homberg
Founded by provision in the will
of his mother
Florence N. Homberger
1928

In Memory of
Isaac N. Heidelberg
Dedicated by his daughters
1928

In Memory of
William Vogel
Dedicated by his sons
Harry Wm. and Bernard Wm. Vogel
1928

In Memory of
Herman Rawitser
Dedicated by his wife
Theresa V. Rawitser
1929

In Memory of
Al and Minnie Hayman
Founded by provision in the will of
Minnie Hayman
(Two Beds)
1929

In Memory of
Ada Heidelberg Strauss
Dedicated by her husband
Seymour A. Strauss
1929

The Rebecca Friedlander Bed
Founded by provision in her will
1929

In Memory of
Heinemann and Rosa Vogelstein
Dedicated by their children
1929

In Memory of
Mayer Mayer and Fanny Mayer
Beloved Father and Mother of
Bernhard Mayer
1929

In Memory of
Mary Small Einstein
Dedicated by her husband
I. D. Einstein
1930

In Memory of
Henry Stern and Mathilda Stern
Dedicated by their son
Meyer Stern
1930

The Selina E. Summerfield Bed
Founded by provision in her will
1931

In Memory of
Lucy Herzfeld
Dedicated by
Felix and Ida Herzfeld
1932

In Memory of
Richard and Matilda Sidenberg
1932

In Memory of
Henry Block
Bequest of
Alice A. Kohler
1932

The Fred H. Greenebaum Bed
Founded by provision in his will
1933

Perpetual Beds

In Memory of
Jacob Hirsh
Dedicated by his wife
Julia Hirsh
1927
and
In Memory of
Julia Hirsh
Dedicated by her children
(Two Beds)
1933

In Memory of
Heyman and Martha Pincus
Founded by provision in the will of
Martha Pincus
1933

In Memory of
Adolph
Charlotte and Mary Arber
Founded by provision in the will of
Adolph Arber
1933

In Memory of
Ludwig and Rebecca Dreyfuss
Founded by provision in the will of
Ludwig Dreyfuss
(Two Beds)
1934

Dedicated in memory of
William Hyams
and Emma Hyams
1935

In Memory of
Sarah King
1935

In Memory of
Myron Goldsmith Friedenheit
Born, September 7, 1898
Died, January 15, 1936
Dedicated by his parents

In Memory of
Elizabeth P. Hewes
Founded by provision in her will
1936

The Straus Memorial Beds
In Memory of
Lionel F. Straus
Dedicated by his wife, May H. Straus
(Two Beds)
1937

In Memory of
Nathan and Ella Necarsulmer
Bequeathed by their daughter
Helena Necarsulmer
1937

In Memory of
Ralph J. Jacobs
Founded by provision in his will
1937

In Memory of
Virginia Guinzburg Kleinert
1937

In Memory of
Ellen Ida Cardozo
Provided in the will of
Benjamin N. Cardozo
1938

To the Memory of
Adolph F. Hochstadter
and Rosa H. Hochstadter
Endowed by their son
Edwin A. Hochstadter
(Two Beds)
1940

Perpetual Beds

Children's Pavilion

In Memory of
Henry L. Einstein
Founded by Cecilia Einstein
1922

In Memory of
Sol H. Kohn
Dedicated by Lillie V. Kohn
1922

Founded by
Benjamin Mordecai
1922

In Memory of
Nellie M. Rice
(Two Beds)
1922

In Memory of
Robert Reis
Dedicated by Sarah Reis
1922

In Memory of
Carrie Wormser
Founded by provision in the will of
her daughter, Julia Seligman
(Four Beds)
1922

In Memory of
Constance Davis Mordecai
Founded by Benjamin Mordecai
(Two Beds)
1923

Dedicated by
Dr. A. V. Moschcowitz
To commemorate the marriage of his
daughter, Frances Ethel Frowenfeld
1923

In Memory of
Joseph and Babet Semel
Founded by provision in the will of
Mrs. George Heyman
1924

In Memory of
George and Hannah Heyman
Founded by provision in the will of
Hannah Heyman
1924

Endowed by
Cecilia Einstein
1924

In Memory of
William Frankenheimer
Dedicated by
Ida and Rose Frankenheimer
1925

In Memory of
Abraham Leipzig
Founded by provision in his will
1925

In Memory of
Adolph Frank Hochstadter
Endowed by Rosa Hayman Hochstadter
1926

In Memory of
Rosa Hayman Hochstadter
Founded by provision in her will
1926

In Memory of
Solomon and Amalia Bondy
Founded by provision in the will of
Maurice S. Bondy
1926

In Memory of
Babette Rothschild
Dedicated by her daughter
Ida R. Cullman
1926

Marx Rothschild
Dedicated by his daughter
Ida R. Cullman
1926

In Memory of
Charles and Mary Weisberger
1926

Perpetual Beds

Children's Pavilion

The Aaron Bachrach
and Jennie Bachrach Bed
1927

In Memory of
Marcus Loew
Dedicated by Caroline Loew
1928

The Peter F. Meyer Beds
Founded by provision in his will
(Five Beds)
1929

In Memory of
Samuel and Hattie Binswanger
1929

The Adelaide F. Pfeiffer Bed
Founded by provision in her will
1929

Ludwig Ulmann
In memory of his brother
Bernard Ulmann
1930

In Memory of
Agnes C. Rice
Founded by provision in her will
1930

In Memory of
Laura Rossman
Dedicated by will of Selma Rossman
1932

In Memory of
Robert Rossman
Dedicated by will of Selma Rossman
1932

In Memory of
Simon and Lucy Drukker
Dedicated by the will of their daughter
Jeannette D. Beaumont
1933

In Memory of
Elias Kempner
Founded by provision in his will
1933

In Memory of
Louis B. G. Garland
Dedicated by his parents
Edward S. Garland and
Lillian B. Garland
1933

The Samuel and Isabella
Kritzman Beds
Founded by provision in the will of
Isabella Kritzman
(Five Beds)
1935

In Memory of
Herman Loevy
Dedicated by
Edwin F. Young
(Two Beds)
1936

In Loving Memory of
Frances Clayton Moses
Dedicated by her aunt
Catherine Sampson
1936

In Memory of
Lena Kemp
Founded by provision in her will
1937

In Memory of
Celia and Solomon
Oppenheimer
Founded by provision in the will of
Solomon Oppenheimer
1938

In Memory of
Louise Renskorf
Provided in the will of her mother
Millie H. Renskorf
1938

To the Memory of
Al Hayman and Minnie Hayman
Endowed by their nephew
Edwin A. Hochstadter
(Two Beds)
1941

184

Memorial Beds

In Memory of
Emanuel de Castro
Dedicated by Margaret D. Plant
1902

In Memory of
Joseph E. Heimerdinger
Dedicated by his brother and sisters
1904

In Memory of
Samuel R. and Jane Jacobs
Dedicated by their children
1904

In Memory of
Babetta Adelsberger
Dedicated by her daughter
Mrs. Emanuel M. Gattle
1905

In Memory of
Samuel Adelsberger
Dedicated by his daughter
Mrs. Emanuel M. Gattle
1905

In Memory of
Isaac A. and Sarah J. Singer
Dedicated by a son
1906

In Memory of Our Beloved Son
Max Reutlinger
Dedicated by
Mr. and Mrs. Emanuel Reutlinger
1908

The Charles Mayer Bed
Founded by Max W. Mayer
January 18, 1909

In Memory of
Sigmund Neustadt
Dedicated by Mrs. Agnes Neustadt
1909

Dedicated by Max Loewenstein
In Memory of
Edward I. Loewenstein
Died July 20, 1912

In Memory of
Seligman and Therese Oppenheimer
Dedicated by their children
1913

In Memory of
Michaelis H. Ziegel
Founded by his son
H. F. L. Ziegel
1913

In Memory of My Beloved Mother
Fannie Mandelbaum
and My Beloved Brother
Max Mandelbaum
Bella Del Monte
1914

In Memory of
Henry Liebmann
Dedicated by his wife
Emma Liebmann
1915

The Pauline, Jacob and Edward S. Bamberger Bed
1915

In Memory of
Edward C. Heymann
Dedicated by his parents
Chas. E. and Helen R. Heymann
1915

In Memory of
Richard Limburg
Dedicated by Mrs. Clara L. Limburg
1916

Frederick Jacobi Memorial Bed
Endowed by Flora and Frederick Jacobi
1916

Memorial Beds

In Memory of
Mayer and Yette Katzenberg
Dedicated by their children
1916

In Memory of
Rachel Kaufmann
Dedicated by her husband
Gustav Kaufmann
1918

In Memory of
Mr. and Mrs. Emanuel S. Kuh
Dedicated by their daughter
Nellie Kuh
1918

In Memory of
Nathan Cohen
Founded by his parents
Mr. and Mrs. Isaac Cohen
1921

In Memory of
Alfred Frank
Dedicated by his brothers and sisters
1923

In Memory of
George and Rose Epstein
and Their Son David
1927

In Memory of
Morris Woititz
and Frances S. Woititz
1937

In Memory of
Levi and Sarah Goldenberg
Founded by their daughter
Helen B. Chaim
1938

In Memory of
Their Beloved Father and Mother
Aaron and Amy H. Coleman
By:
Constance Coleman and
Janet C. Dillenberg
1940

In Memory of
Evelyn Tanenbaum
Provided in the will of
Moses Tanenbaum
1940

Life Beds

Founded by
Mrs. DeWitt J. Seligman
1882

Founded by
Ethel F. Seligman
Daughter of
Mr. and Mrs. DeWitt J. Seligman
1897

Dedicated to
Elsie Nathan
1902

The May S. Harlow nee Stern
Life Bed
Founded by her April 28, 1904

The Lucile M. S. van Heukelom
Life Bed
Founded November 24, 1904

The Helen Fox Life Bed
Founded by Henry Morgenthau
April 7, 1906

Founded by
A Friend
1907

In Memory of
Joseph Dannenberg
of Macon, Georgia

The Dr. Manges Life Bed
Founded by a Friend of The Hospital
1912

In Memory of
Fannie Behrens Wolfe
and Solomon Baird Wolfe, M.D.

In Memory of
Max Weil
Dedicated by his wife
1914

In Memory of
Joseph Honig
Founded by Louise H. Mandelbaum
1916

In Memory of
Isidore Jackson
Dedicated by his wife and son
September 14, 1920

In Memory of
Leonard M.
Dedicated by his parents
Alexander and Rose M. Joseph
1920

In Memory of
Morris Goldstein and
Pauline Goldstein
Endowed by their children
1921

Endowed by
Francois Kleinberger
1921

In Honor of
Minnie Kastor
Endowed by her husband,
Adolph Kastor
1922

In Memory of
Benjamin Ehrlich
Endowed by his wife
Fannie Ehrlich
1929

In Memory of
Julius Kaufmann
Endowed by his wife
Emma H. Kaufmann
1930

Founded by
Pauline F. Baerwald
March 26, 1931

Dedicated to Humanity by
Solomon and Dora Shapiro
(Nee Monness)
1932

In Memory of
Clara L. Limburg
Dedicated by her children
1935

Previous to 1867		
	Judah Touro	$20,000 00
1867	Jacob Abrahams	5,000 00
1869	Benjamin Nathan	10,000 00
	Joseph Fatman	10,000 00
1872	Dr. S. Abrahams (1872-1873)	14,020 00
1876	Lewis Philips	11,711 51
1879	Michael Reese	25,000 00
1882	Simeon Abrahams	10,980 00
1883	Mrs. Judith Einstein	5,000 00
1885	Julius Hallgarten	10,000 00
1886	Miss Sarah Burr (1886-1893)	54,900 00
1888	Isaac Hoechster	5,000 00
1889	Henry Herrman	5,000 00
	William Meyer (1889-1891)	12,252 34
1891	Daniel B. Fayerweather (1891-1897)	9,933 03
1893	Joseph Rosenberg (1893-1926)	9,995 54
	Abraham Kuhn	5,000 00
1895	Adolph Bernheimer	5,000 00
1897	Mayer Lehman	17,958 00
1902	Andrew J. Garvey (1902-1939)	15,283 65
	Jacob F. Cullman	10,000 00
1903	Julius Beer	10,000 00
	Adolph Openhym	5,000 00
1904	Solomon Loeb	10,000 00
1905	Simon Rothschild	50,000 00
	Salomon Rothfeld	5,000 00
	Meyer Guggenheim	20,000 00
1906	Frederick Uhlmann	5,000 00
	Mathilde C. Weil (1906-1907)	12,144 99
1907	Emanuel Walter	7,500 00
	Marx W. Mendel	16,044 10
1908	Amelia B. Lazarus (1908-1909)	29,995 76
1910	Adolph Kerbs	5,000 00
	Emanuel Einstein	9,525 00
	Chas. Rubens	5,695 00
	Ludwig Stettheimer (1910-1913)	24,748 39
	Rosa Schreiber	6,267 74
	Margaret J. P. Graves	10,000 00
1911	John Stemme	5,000 00
	Charles E. Tilford (1911-1940)	152,083 38
	Martin Herman	5,000 00

188

1912	Jacob Small (1912-1929)	$14,864 30
	Andrew Saks	5,000 00
	Moses Weinman	5,000 00
	Samuel Lilienthal	14,762 08
1913	John J. Clancy (1913-1914)	25,000 00
	Ernst Thalmann	10,000 00
	Benjamin Guggenheim	10,000 00
	William Scholle	10,000 00
	Nathan Herrmann	5,000 00
1914	Lewis S. Levy (1914-1916)	16,343 74
1915	Constant Mayer	13,948 09
	David E. Sicher	10,000 00
	Jacob Langeloth	5,000 00
	Moses Lowenstein	5,000 00
1916	Andrew Freedman	5,000 00
	Solomon Wolf (1916-1917)	11,860 18
	Amelia Lavanburg (1916-1917)	10,175 84
	Emil Bondy	10,000 00
	Herman N. Walter	5,000 00
1917	J. S. Halle	5,000 00
	Rachel H. Pfeiffer	15,000 00
	Esther Schlesinger	22,002 42
1918	Meyer H. Lehman	25,000 00
1919	Kalman Haas	10,000 00
	Benjamin Blumenthal	15,000 00
	Henry J. Duveen	5,000 00
	Margaret Olivia Sage (1919-1921)	100,000 00
1920	Joseph Frank	447,374 70
	Pearl Weinman	7,065 85
	Isaac N. Seligman	5,000 00
	Babette Lehman	5,000 00
	Julius Kayser	10,000 00
	Baruch Kaufman	14,250 00
1921	William Salomon	10,000 00
1922	Adolph D. Bendheim	5,000 00
	Mary Helen Finch	5,000 00
	Julia Seligman (1922-1936)	12,682 29
1923	Morris S. Barnet	35,000 00
	Eleanor von Koppenfels	25,000 00
1924	Jacob Rossbach	5,000 00

1925	Eugene Meyer	$10,000	00
	Emily A. Watson	24,998	20
	Emanuel Spiegelberg	5,000	00
	Michael Dreicer	10,000	00
1926	Emil Wolff	29,794	12
	Adolph Boskowitz	20,000	00
	Solomon A. Fatman	20,000	00
	Louis S. Stroock	5,000	00
	Albert Lorsch	5,000	00
	Harriet Weil	5,000	00
	Morris J. Hirsch	5,000	00
	Lewis Schoolhouse	5,000	00
	Jonathan Nathan (1926-1933)	5,130	89
1927	Alexander Herman (1927-1928)	100,000	00
	Lottie Estelle Mayer (1927-1928)	33,461	87
	Sophie W. Low	8,457	47
	Charles Altschul	7,500	00
	Mortimer H. Heyman	5,000	00
	Morris Weinstein	5,000	00
	Harry Mayer	5,000	00
1928	Al Hayman	25,000	00
	Aline Myers	15,027	87
	Morris Rossin	10,000	00
	Isaac J. Bernheim	5,000	00
	Marmaduke Richardson	5,000	00
1929	Simon R. Weil (1929-1934)	156,468	28
	Michael P. Rich	20,000	00
	Emma Blumenberg—In memory of her brothers, Marc A. and Louis Blumenberg (1929-1930)	12,473	66
	Harriet F. Haas	10,000	00
	Harmon W. Hendricks	10,000	00
1930	Harry H. Meyer (1930-1940)	206,703	49
	Betsy S. Korminsky	5,000	00
	Pauline Myers	5,000	00
	Louis C. Raegner	5,000	00
1931	Julius Marcus	19,185	83
	Louis Marshall (1931-1937)	11,581	27
	William Hartfield (1931-1936)	10,061	59
	Alfred M. Heinsheimer	5,000	00
	Frieda Wimpfheimer	5,000	00
1933	Isaac Marx	7,500	00

1934	Rudolph J. Schaefer (1934-1937)	$64,845 88
	Ludwig Dreyfuss	25,000 00
	Benjamin Stern (1934-1937)	25,000 00
1935	Bertha Weinman—For the Moses Weinman Memorial Fund (1935-1936)	1,471,431 49
	Joseph Runsheim (1935-1937)	17,872 25
	Lawrence Pike (1935-1940)	4,156 66
1936	Edward J. King—For the Edward J. King and Jennie I. King Memorial Fund (1936-1940)	1,636,294 37
	Isa Nordlinger (1936-1937)	9,199 21
	Augustus W. Openhym (1936-1940)	37,604 21
	Louise C. Colten	2,800 29
	Abraham Cohn	2,622 65
	Henry F. Wolff	2,503 47
1937	Marco Fleishman—For the Rosetta and Marco Fleishman Memorial Fund (1937-1938)	743,829 95
	Carrie L. Lehman	10,000 00
	Henry Ollesheimer (1937-1939)	10,020 98
	Ephraim B. Levy	5,000 00
	Leah Simpson	5,000 00
	Jacob W. Gutman	2,500 00
	Henry Jacoby (1937-1938)	2,732 30
	Joseph N. Frank (1937-1940)	438 06
1938	Henry W. Putnam	50,000 00
	Bettie Meierhoff	36,543 07
	Harry J. D. Plaut	5,107 50
	Charles S. Erlanger	5,000 00
	Emanuel Felsenheld (1938-1940)	2,500 00
1940	James Ulmann	50,000 00
	Amalia F. Morse	15,000 00
	Ida Meyer	14,813 35
	Fannie H. Cox	9,377 34
	Alfred A. Kohn	1,000 00
	Bertha Y. Lambert	1,000 00
	Susman J. Valk	250 00
	Edward A. Weiss	100 00

LIFE MEMBERS

HARRY CONTENT ....111 Broadway

ABRAM I. ELKUS..40 Wall Street

MRS. E. B. HART..2111 Madison Avenue

SAMUEL A. LEWIS..7 Warren Street

MRS. J. S. MENKEN......................................104 East 79th Street

ARTHUR MEYER....................71 Fitzjohn Avenue, London, N. W.

WALTER W. NAUMBURG................................121 East 64th Street

MRS. FLORENCE S. ROBERTS....................Hotel Villa Del Arroyo,
Pasadena, Cal.

JAMES SPEYER..24 Pine Street

MRS. ALBERT D. STEIN

ISADOR M. STETTENHEIM..17 Cedar Street

195

197

SUPERINTENDENTS AND DIRECTORS SINCE 1855

Superintendents—Directors#

*1855-1866 JULIUS RAYMOND
*1867-1875 G. SCHWARZBAUM
*1876-1878 LEOPOLD B. SIMON
*1879-1892 THEODORE HADEL
*1892-1899 LEOPOLD MINZESHEIMER
*1899-1904 S. L. FATMAN
1904-1928 S. S. GOLDWATER, M.D.
1928-   JOSEPH TURNER, M.D.

Associate Director

1927-1928 JOSEPH TURNER, M.D.

Assistant Superintendents—Assistant Directors#

*1892-1892 LEOPOLD MINZESHEIMER
*1896-1902 GUSTAVE ABRAMS
*1903-1904 SOLON J. RIESER
1903-1904 S. S. GOLDWATER, M.D.
1906-1908 SIDNEY E. GOLDSTEIN
*1908-1909 D. M. BLOOM, M.D.
1910-1915 H. J. MOSS, M.D.
1914-1915 A. J. BELLER, M.D.
1915-1916 EMANUEL GIDDINGS, M.D.
1916-1920 HERMAN SMITH, M.D.
*1918-1919 SIMON TANNENBAUM, M.D.
1920-1922 LEOPOLD BRAHDY, M.D.
1920-1926 E. M. BLUESTONE, M.D.
1922-1927 JOSEPH TURNER, M.D.
1925-1927 J. J. GOLUB, M.D.
1927-1937 STEPHEN MANHEIMER, M.D.
1927-1934 LOUIS MILLER, JR.
1934-1941 J. A. KATZIVE, M.D.
1935-1939 JANDON SCHWARZ, M.D.
1937-1938 M. A. GREEN, M.D.
1938-   MAXWELL S. FRANK, M.D.
1940-   MORRIS H. KREEGER, M.D.
1941-   DAVID H. ROSS, M.D.

Title changed to Director and Assistant Director in 1917.
* Deceased

GRADUATES OF THE HOUSE STAFF

PRIOR TO 1884

*Deceased

*Mark Blumenthal
*F. Tilden Brown
*R. M. Cramer
*R. B. Coleman
D. H. Davison
*Wm. L. Estes
*Benson M. Feldman
*Albert Fridenberg
*O. Froelich

Alfred Meyer
*J. R. Nilsen
R. Offenbach
*S. Rapp
J. M. Rice
*J. Rudisch
*John Van Der Poel
Julius Weiss

SURGEONS

1884 *James L. Shiland
      *Walter Hitchcock
1885 *J. Clark Steward
      *Herman J. Schiff

1886 *F. C. Husson
      *Alfred N. Strouse
1887 *William H. Wilmer
      *H. S. Stark
1888 Guy C. Rich
      Howard Lilienthal
1889 L. J. Ladin
      Geo. B. Cowell
1890 Samuel L. Weber
      A. D. Mewborn
1891 *Southgate Leigh
      David B. Lovell
1892 *Edwin C. Sternberger

1893 Geo. L. Brodhead
      *S. M. Brickner
1894 Martin W. Ware
      Thomas T. Tuttle
1895 Charles A. Elsberg
      *Nathan Breiter
      *J. Ralston Lattimore
1896 Albert A. Berg
      *William H. Luckett
1897 Charles Goodman
      J. B. Morrison
1898 *Harry Rodman
      *Walter M. Brickner
1899 Sidney Ulfelder
      *L. W. Allen
1900 Leo B. Meyer
      Eugene H. Eising

PHYSICIANS

1884 Edward Burns
      Charles H. May
1885 Arthur B. Coffin
      *Josephine Walter
      *Charles F. Mason
1886 *E. L. H. Swift
      *Edward J. Ware
1887 Charles G. Giddings
      *Abraham Korn
1888 *E. H. Walsh
      *H. E. Sanderson
1889 *Simon D. Elsner
      G. L. Nicholas
1890 R. H. Cunningham
      *Max Jackson
1891 *Fred S. Mandlebaum
      *H. P. Palmer
1892 *E. C. Levy
      Percy H. Fridenberg
1893 Henry A. Cone

1894 *W. Jarvis Barlow

1895 *Sidney Yankauer

1896 Emanuel Libman
      William P. Loth
1897 Herman B. Baruch
      Sidney V. Haas
1898 Louis Hauswirth

1899 William G. Eckstein
      A. F. Foord
1900 Israel Strauss

199

GRADUATES OF THE HOUSE STAFF

(Continued)

SURGEONS	PHYSICIANS
1901 M. Thorner Truman Abbe	1901 *I. W. Becker Herman Schwarz
1902 *Edwin Beer Major G. Seelig	1902 *Edward A. Aronson Milton Gerschel
1903 *Meyer M. Stark Robert T. Frank Eli Moschcowitz	1903 *Herbert L. Celler *Alfred Fabian Hess David Kramer
1904 D. Lee Hischler Albert G. Swift Fred H. MacCarthy C. F. Jellinghaus	1904 Bernard S. Oppenheimer Arthur Bookman *H. F. L. Ziegel Louis Bauman
1905 Sol. Hyman Isadore Seff William J. Haber Horace Leiter	1905 Geo. W. T. Mills *Samuel Feldstein *Gustav A. Fried *Leo Kessel
1906 C. Morris Hathaway Milton Bodenheimer Ernest Sachs Solomon Wiener	1906 Julius J. Hertz Jesse G. M. Bullowa Julian J. Meyer Max Taschman
1907 Orville H. Schell Eben Alexander, Jr. Aims R. Chamberlain Harold Neuhof	1907 Alfred E. Cohn *Louis Jacobs *Louis G. Kaempfer *Walter J. Highman
1908 John C. A. Gerster Abraham Hyman Isidor C. Rubin	1908 *Jacob Wisansky Abraham E. Jaffin Albert A. Epstein Max Scheer
1909 Howard E. Lindeman Herbert D. Manley *Charles Ryttenberg Fred. G. Oppenheimer	1909 Abraham Sophian Joseph Rosenthal *Maurice T. Munker Murray H. Bass
1910 Abraham O. Wilensky Benjamin F. May George Baehr Samuel H. Geist	1910 Bernard H. Eliasberg Burrill B. Crohn *Milton Hahn Richard H. Hoffmann
1911 Louis Greenberg Philip Liebling Irving Simons Leo Mayer	1911 Harry Wessler Nathaniel Barnett *H. W. Emsheimer Hiram Olsan
1912 Herman Jaffe Sidney Cohn Isidor Kross Julius Blum	1912 Salo N. Weber *Morris H. Kahn *Abraham Zingher Meyer Rosensohn
1913 Abraham J. Beller Oscar Baumann Jesse D. Schwartz Ira Cohen	1913 *Alexander Hofheimer Jacob Sachs Edward Mahler Daniel Poll

SURGEONS		PHYSICIANS	
1914	Hyman R. Miller C. Koenigsberger Edward Bleier Abraham Strauss	1914	Arthur S. Rosenfeld Maurice F. Lautman John L. Kantor Louis H. Levy
1915	Ralph M. Bruckheimer Sol. Shlimbaum Paul W. Aschner *John F. Grattan	1915	A. I. Loewenthal David Beck Louis G. Shapiro Jacob Piller
1916	Joseph A. Landy Nathan Rosenthal Adolf A. Weiss Waldemar R. Metz	1916	Willard D. Mayer Lester J. Unger Ernst P. Boas Joseph Harkavy
1917	Harry C. Saltzstein David M. Natanson Max D. Mayer Leo Edelman	1917	Harry Plotz Charles G. Giddings, Jr. Louis Berman William Rosenson
1918	*Eugene Klein Louis Carp Samuel Kahn Julius Gottesman Leopold Brahdy Lewis T. Mann	1918	Joseph Felsen William Friedman Max Harrison Reuben Steinholz Harold T. Hyman Louis Hausman
1919	Herman Sharlit Morris Brooks Morris A. Goldberger Emanuel Salwen Joseph A. Lazarus Barney M. Kully Henry S. Fischer Jerome M. Ziegler	1919	Jerome L. Kohn Asher Winkelstein Edward Hollander Irving R. Roth Abraham Kardiner Kaufman Wallach
1920	Leo J. Hahn Rudolph Kramer Samuel Hirshfeld Max Schneider *Harold L. Meierhof Nathan Sobel	1920	Ira M. Olsan Charles Green Leo Loewe Philip Finkle Edward Lehman Harry D. Pasachoff
1921	Laurence Jones William Harris Martin A. Furman Leonard M. Lyons Sylvan D. Manheim Joseph B. Stenbuck	1921	Morris J. Lavine Saul A. Ritter *Benj. B. Eichner Philip Astrowe Frederic D. Zeman Alton M. Amsterdam
1922	Joseph M. Marcus Samuel Silbert Percy Klingenstein Joseph S. Somberg Henry Milch Samuel Gaines	1922	Nathan Muskin Sydney C. Feinberg Samuel Z. Levine David Gaberman David Soletsky Leon Ginzburg

SURGEONS	PHYSICIANS
1923 Benj. N. Berg	**1923** Samuel Rosen
Julian B. Herrmann	Samuel Rosenfeld
Arthur H. Aufses	Arthur M. Master
Louis Kleinfeld	Louis Hodes
Saul S. Samuels	Philip Cohen
Edwin A. Seidman	William S. Collens
1924 Seth Selig	**1924** Roland I. Grausman
David Warshaw	Alfred M. Goltman
Seymour Wimpfheimer	Coleman B. Rabin
Sidney Friedman	Ephraim Shorr
Elias L. Stern	Robert K. Lambert
Gordon D. Oppenheimer	David Ball
1925 Robert K. Lippmann	**1925** Leon Goldsmith
Edward A. Horowitz	Benj. Eliasoph
Robert H. Feldman	Richard M. Brickner
Martin Schreiber	Harold A. Abramson
Leon Ginzburg	Alfred E. Fischer
Irving A. Frisch	Harry I. Weinstock
1926 *A. Philip Zemansky, Jr.	**1926** Harry Schwartz
Edward O. Finestone	J. Lester Kobacker
Mayer E. Ross	Nathan Cherwin
Edward J. Bassen	Harry S. Mackler
Samuel Mufson	Joseph Laval
Clarence K. Weil	David Wexler
1927 Ernest E. Arnheim	**1927** Abraham L. Goldwyn
Walter F. Welton	William J. Bearman
Hyman Rosenfeld	Ameil Glass
Arthur S. W. Touroff	Milton J. Matzner
1928 Moses Swick	**1928** Jacob E. Holzman
Abraham Firestone	Elmer S. Gais
Sidney Grossman	Abraham L. Kornzweig
William H. Mencher	*John Cohen
1929 William Leifer	**1929** Samuel H. Averbuck
Sidney Hirsch	Joseph Uttal
Monroe A. Rosenbloom	Herman Zazeela
Robert L. Craig	Alfred Romanoff
1930 Lester R. Tuchman	**1930** Solomon Silver
Ameil Glass	Samuel Melamed
Isidore Schapiro	William J. Hochbaum
William L. Ferber	Shirley H. Baron
1931 Maurice M. Berck	**1931** Sylvan E. Moolten
Lyon Steine	Arthur Schifrin
Borris A. Kornblith	*Herbert M. Klein
Herbert S. Talbot	Rose Spiegel
1932 Samuel H. Klein	**1932** Arthur R. Sohval
Erwin K. Gutmann	Robert V. Sager
Joseph A. Gaines	Albert B. Newman
William Sheinfeld	William M. Hitzig

202

GRADUATES OF THE HOUSE STAFF

(Continued)

	SURGEONS		PHYSICIANS
1933	Perry S. Horenstein	1933	Herman S. Roth
	H. Evans Leiter		Frederick Bridge
	Abraham J. Gitlitz		Jacob E. Stern
	Alexander H. Rosenthal		Saul W. Jarcho
1934	Meyer Abrahams	1934	Hyman Levy
	Sidney Rosenburg		Harry L. Jaffe
	Jacob S. Goltman		Abraham Penner
	Leonard J. Druckerman		Frederick H. Theodore
1935	Albert J. Schein	1935	D. Alfred Dantes
	Emanuel Klempner		Israel Schiller
	Edward E. Jemerin		Sheppard Siegal
	Herman J. Meisel		Benjamin Rubin
1936	Irving A. Sarot	1936	Milton Mendlowitz
	Paul Kaufman		Henry Dolger
	Sidney M. Silverstone		Morton W. Willis
	Alan N. Leslie		Morris F. Steinberg
1937	Gabriel P. Seley	1937	Samuel Nisnewitz
	Leon G. Berman		Edward R. Schlesinger
	Herman R. Nayer		Sidney L. Penner
	Ralph W. Flax		Eugene Somkin
	Robert C. Elitzik		Edgar A. Baron
	Nathan Mintz		Morton Yohalem
1938	Julius L. Weissberg	1938	Max Ellenberg
	Vernon A. Weinstein		Samuel C. Bukantz
	Abner Kurtin		S. Zelig Sorkin
	Sylvan Bloomfield		Robert A. Newburger
	Leonard S. Bases		Ralph E. Moloshok
	Leon N. Greene		Sydney G. Margolin
1939	Nathan Adelman	1939	Milton Landowne
	Joseph M. Szilagyi		Irving A. Beck
	Emanuel Wachtel		Irving Solomon
	Samuel Diener		Herman Anfanger
	Alexander Thomas		Sidney Cohen
	Bernard S. Wolf		Emanuel B. Schoenbach
1940	Elliott S. Hurwitt	1940	Daniel Stats
	Bernard E. Simon		Clifford L. Spingarn
	Gerson J. Lesnick		Arthur W. Seligmann, Jr.
	Herbert M. Katzin		Mary C. Tyson
	Rudolph E. Drosd		Alvin J. Gordon
	William I. Glass		Samuel S. Dorrance
1941	Leon M. Arnold	1941	Selvan Davison
	David Miller		George L. Engel

ONE-YEAR INTERNS AND EXTERNS

1898	L. A. S. Bodine	1913	S. Aronowitz
	W. M. Lazard		Oscar L. Levin
1899	E. A. Rosenberg		A. Levy
	E. D. Lederman		*Marcus A. Rothschild
	*A. W. Roff		M. Lobsenz
1900	Edward J. Miller		H. L. Sherman
	*Chas. E. Rosenwasser		S. Genovese
	J. Howard Staub	1914	C. G. Ratner
1901	Leon Bandler		*J. S. Meltzer
	*Eugene P. Bernstein		W. Rosen
1902	S. S. Goldwater		A. Unger
1906	Kaufman Schlivek		T. Halpern
	*Isadore Goldstein		D. H. Bluestone
	William Branower		A. Mendelson
	Isadore Kaufman	1915	J. Sinkowitz
1907	B. Rein		D. Kronman
	Edgar D. Oppenheimer		I. Pelzman
	P. Fiaschi		J. Haimann
	Jerome S. Leopold		I. W. Jacobs
1908	*Wm. I. Wallach		A. Brody
	M. Reuben	1916	*J. L. Furst
	M. C. Pease, Jr.		M. A. Sager
	Michael Barsky		*J. A. Rosenberg
1909	H. C. Fleming		Joseph Reiss
	E. W. Abramowitz		I. Rosen
	Wm. Lapatnikoff		L. L. Roth
	E. M. Carson	1917	M. Varzahbedian
	I. Shapiro		*H. Martinson
	Jacob Roemer		A. Jerskey
1910	Charles Gluck		J. Rosenfeld
	Mark Cohen		Louis Nahum
	Jerome Zuckerman		J. J. Wiener
	Charles Gottlieb		B. E. Strode
	Ralph H. Goss	1918	A. Altschul
1911	D. Tannenbaum		Samuel K. Levy
	Arthur J. Bendick		Leon Antell
	*J. J. Fabian		W. Sellinger
	*Hugo Blum		M. J. Radin
	William Thalhimer		Max Dobrin
	Clarence Brown		Jacob Branower
1912	Harry G. Goldman	1920	*Harold Rypins
	Saul Levy		D. S. Dann
	Harold A. Cohen	1923	S. S. Lichtman
	Samuel Wetchler	1924	M. Biederman
	*Samuel Silverman		M. L. Guttmacher
	Abraham J. Newman		Max Brahdy
	Carl C. Franken		Isabel Beck

* Deceased.

ONE-YEAR INTERNS AND EXTERNS
(Continued)

1925 Wm. B. Rose
Julius Kavee
Gertrude Felshin

1926 Emanuel W. Benjamin
Eli Y. Shorr

1927 Harry Weiss
Sidney D. Leader
Paul S. Roland
Walter Bromberg
Ben. Z. Steine
Hudythe M. Levin
Moses R. Buchman
S. I. Kooperstein
Herman Slass

1928 Murray A. Last
P. Goolker
William Chester
J. Fuhrman Heinrich
Isabel Globus
S. P. Carp
Sidney D. Leader
Harry Rosenwasser
Harry Feld

1929 George Frumkes
Michael C. Kemelhor
Louis Schneider
Saul Miller
Bernard S. Brody
Marcy L. Sussman
David Beres

1930 Harold A. Abel
Charles K. Friedberg
Harry Keil
Clement H. Golden
Henry A. Baron
Sidney Housman
Charles Sutro
Herbert Lampert
Nathan H. Sachs

1931 Hyman Lieber
Edward B. Greenspan
Harry Yarnis

1931 Henry Peskin
Robert H. Abrahamson
Ralph T. Levin
Max L. Som
Bernard Amsterdam

1932 David R. Levine
Bernard Amsterdam
Samuel A. Feldman
Sidney E. Lenke
Irving Kowaloff
Alice I. Bernheim
*Charles J. Sage
Carl Zelson
F. J. de Frume

1933 Benjamin Allen
Bension Calef
Simon Dack
Edward Greenberger
Harold W. Keschner
Arnold Treitman
Fred R. Schechter
Robert Ullman
L Oscar Weisman

1934 Meyer Emanuel
Ralph W. Flax
Sidney L. Gottlieb
David Littauer
M. Edward Hipsh
Charles W. Rieber
Louis M. Rosati
Jandon Schwarz

1935 Albert D. Kistin
Vernon A. Weinstein
Morris M. Kessler
William Finkelstein
Herman I. Kantor
Jean Pakter
William Epstein
M. Edward Hipsh
Samuel B. Weiner

1936 Simon H. Nagler
Samuel M. Bloom
Max Ellenberg
Jean Pakter

INTERNS IN PATHOLOGY

1911	Daniel Poll	1929	Reuben Cares
1912	Louis H. Levy		Harry Moskowitz
1913	Paul W. Aschner	1930	Harold A. Aaron
1914	Harry Plotz		Victor H. Kugel
1915	William Rosenson	1931	Sidney E. Lenke
1916	Julius Gottesman		Jacob S. Goltman
1917	Lewis T. Mann	1932	Sidney Licht
1918	Martin Vorhaus	1933	Milton Mendlowitz
1919	Maurice Rashbaum		Irving A. Sarot
1920	Percy Klingenstein	1934	Leon G. Berman
1921	Saul S. Samuels		*Milton Steiner
1922	Sol. S. Lichtman	1935	Samuel C. Bukantz
1923	Martin Schreiber		Nathan Mintz
1924	Lionel S. Auster	1936	Nathan S. Hiatt
	Clarence K. Weil		Joseph M. Szilagyi
1925	Abraham Firestone	1937	Alexander Thomas
1926	William Leifer		Bernard S. Wolf
	Alfred Romanoff	1938	Tibor J. Greenwalt
1927	Irving Nachamie		Daniel Luger
	S. David Glusker	1939	Roy N. Barnett
1928	Henry H. Lichtenberg		Merrill P. Haas
	Arthur Schifrin	1940	Robert Landesman
			Irving G. Kroop

INTERNS, EXTERNS AND RESIDENTS IN RADIOLOGY

1921	Sidney H. Levy	1930	Isidore Klein
1922	Rubin Lavine		Saul J. Tamarkin
	Barnett P. Freedman	1931	Harry Herscher
1923	Harry S. Olin	1932	Simon Shulman
	Harry Gross		Louis E. Zaretski
1924	Irving Schwartz		Gerald J. Bernath
	Max Newer	1933	Mitchell Burdick
1925	Jacob R. Freid		Gayland L. Hagelshaw
	Nathaniel H. Robin	1934	Israel Kirsh
	Emanuel J. Wexler		Edward D. Sherman
1926	William Snow	1936	Irving I. Cowan
	Sol. Taubin		Joseph Jellen
1927	Albert Kean		Benjamin Copleman
	Samuel Poplack	1937	Max Schenck
	Samuel Sinberg		Marston T. Woodruff
1928	Carye-Belle Henle	1938	Arnold Bachman
	Benjamin J. Sax		Robert J. Ruby
	Emanuel W. Benjamin	1939	Lester Freedman
1929	Myer E. Golan	1940	Jack H. Levy
	Charles Lipsky		Nathan Rudner
	Samuel Richman		

* Deceased.

RESIDENT STAFF

PRIVATE AND SEMI-PRIVATE PAVILIONS

SURGEONS	PHYSICIANS
1905 Albert G. Swift	
1906 Edwin A. Riesenfeld	
1907 Milton Bodenheimer	
1908 Wm. Branower	1908 Julius Kaunitz
1909 Eben Alexander, Jr.	1909 J. Russell Verbrycke
Harold Neuhof	
1910 Abraham E. Jaffin	1910 *Jacob Wisansky
1911 J. C. Wooldridge	1911 Joseph Rosenthal
1912 J. Irving Fort	1912 Oris S. Warr
A. O. Wilensky	
1913 J. W. Brennan	1913 A. B. James
J. E. King	
1914 A. J. Beller	1914 B. M. Dear
H. E. Schorr	*Morris H. Kahn
1915 Jesse D. Schwartz	1915 Edward Mahler
1916 *H. S. Marcley	1916 Joseph D. Kelley
Edward Bleier	
1917 Sol Shlimbaum	1917 Joseph Reiss
J. Ramsay Crawford	
Joseph A. Landy	
1918 Adolf A. Weiss	1918 Joseph Rosenfeld
David M. Natanson	
1919 Max D. Mayer	1919 Hubert Mann
G. D. Von Deylen	
Milton S. Fine	
1920 Wm. A. Flick	1920 Louis Sacks
Thomas J. Sullivan	
Joseph Lazarus	
1921 Arnold Messing	1921 Selian Hebald
Paul S. Lowenstein	
1922 Joseph Heyman	1922 A. Isaacman
L. W. Pritchett	
1923 Benjamin Kogut	1923 Stanley S. Myers
Edward Lorentzen	
Samuel Gaines	
1924 Seymour F. Wilhelm	1924 Bernard Appel
Ernst Springer	
Abram A. Weiss	
A. J. Sparks	
Elias Rubin (10 months)	

---

* Deceased.

RESIDENT STAFF

PRIVATE AND SEMI-PRIVATE PAVILIONS
(Continued)

SURGEONS	PHYSICIANS
1925 Franklin I. Harris	1925 Samuel Schindelhelm
George S. Lachman	
Elias L. Stern	
Nathaniel H. Blumenkranz	
1926 Norman F. Laskey	
Samuel Hochman	
Edward O. Finestone	
1927 Joseph M. Frehling	1927 Abraham M. Schaefer
M. Lester Levy	
C. D. Moore	
1928 Harold W. Goldberg	1928 Henry Z. Goldstein
Edward Jacobs	
Myron A. Sallick	
David Sloane	
1929 Jacob J. Enkelis	1929 Max E. Panitch
Samuel S. Hanflig	
Robert I. Hiller	
Bernard D. Kulick	
1930 Samuel Imboden	1930 Bernard S. Brody
Samuel P. Suffin	
Eske H. Windsberg	
1931 Sidney Rosenburg	1931 Harold A. Abel
Henry A. Baron	
Lyon Steine	
1932 David A. Susnow	1932 Harry Yarnis
Joseph Tomarkin	
Erwin K. Gutmann	
Meyer Corff	
1933 Joseph Tartakoff	1933 Frank A. Bassen
Robert Turell	
Perry S. Horenstein	
1934 H. Evans Leiter	
Robert H. Abrahamson	
Arthur J. Harris	
1935 Meyer Abrahams	1935 Abraham Penner
Zachary R. Cottler	
Albert M. Schwartz	
Jerome Gross	
Anthony Kohn .	
Leonard J. Druckerman	
1936 Leo H. Pollock	
Seebert J. Goldowsky	
Edward E. Jemerin	1936 Samuel Baer
Irwin P. Train	

RESIDENT STAFF

PRIVATE AND SEMI-PRIVATE PAVILIONS
(Continued)

SURGEONS	PHYSICIANS
1937 Ernest D. Bloomenthal	1937 David E. Scheinberg
Aaron Prigot	William Finkelstein
Meyer L. Goldman	Albert Cornell
Louis Scheman	
Leon M. Caplan	
Sigmund A. Siegel	
Gabriel P. Seley	
1938 Julian A. Jarman	1938 Herman G. Helpern
Philip Cooper	Philip M. Gottlieb
Ralph W. Flax	
Lawrence Essenson	
Benjamin Gitlitz	
H. Earle Tucker	
1939 Arthur Gladstone	1939 Milton H. Adelman
Sylvan Bloomfield	Morris H. Kreeger
Vernon A. Weinstein	
Leon N. Greene	
Robert W. Mann	
Jerome S. Coles	
1940 Leon J. Taubenhaus	1940 William Kaufman
Nathaniel C. Schlossmann	Martin A. Zionts
Bernard Friedman	
Earl M. Edison	
Albert S. Lyons	
1941 Marvin P. Rhodes	

RESIDENT STAFF

WARD SERVICES

Neurology
1924	William Malamud
	David Rothschild
1925	M. Weinstock Bergman
	David I. Arbuse
1926	Herman G. Selinsky
1927	Sol W. Ginsburg
	Jacob J. Kasanin
1928	Lewis J. Doshay
	Walter Bromberg
1929	William Berman
	Isabel Globus
1930	P. Goolker
	Lewis H. Loeser
1931	Paul Sloane
	Bernard S. Brody
1932	William Schick
	Samuel A. Sandler
	Louis Levenstim
1933	Daniel E. Schneider
	Jacob H. Friedman
1934	Abraham Blau
	Morris B. Bender
1935	Norman Reider
1936	Sidney Tarachow
	Norman A. Levy
1937	Morris M. Kessler
	Laurence M. Weinberger
	Jerome E. Alderman
1938	Mark G. Kanzer
	Edwin A. Weinstein
1939	Eugene P. Mindlin
	Hyman E. Yaskin
1940	Bertram Schaffner
	Sydney G. Margolin

Pediatrics
1924	Philip Cohen
	Alfred Nathans
1925	E. Gordon Stoloff
	Isabel Beck
1926	Samuel Karelitz
	Samuel J. Levin
1927	Alfred E. Fischer
	Gustave F. Weinfeld
1928	Abbot L. Winograd
	Harry S. Mackler
1929	Moses R. Buchman
	Sidney D. Leader
1930	David Beres
	Peter Vogel
1931	Jacob L. Rothstein
	A. E. Cohen
1932	George J. Ginandes.
	Albert A. Rosenberg
1933	Martin L. Stein
	Carl Zelson
1934	Louise Rauh
1935	Jacob Brem
	Samuel Ehre
1936	Howard C. Leopold
	Sidney Blumenthal
1937	Arthur Lesser
	Samuel B. Weiner
	Jean Pakter
1938	Howard G. Rapaport
	David B. Davis
1939	Victor L. Szanton
	Jacob Danciger
1940	Herschel J. Kaufman
	Arnold Widerman

Oto-Laryngology
1924	Louis Kleinfeld
1925	Samuel Rosen
1927	Joseph G. Druss
1928	Irving B. Goldman
1929	Ben Z. Steine
1930	Harry Rosenwasser
1931	Joseph L. Goldman
1932	William J. Hochbaum
1933	Max L. Som

Gynecology
1924	Arthur Katzenstein
	Karl Polifka
1925	Morris R. Matus
	Seymour Wimpfheimer
1926	Howard A. Power
	Edward A. Horowitz
1927	Frank Spielman
1928	Jacques D. Soifer
	Alan F. Guttmacher
1929	Oscar Glassman
1930	Benj. E. Urdan
	Maurice Feresten
1931	Irving Nachamie
	Mervin A. Henschel
1932	Phineas Bernstein
	Henry A. Baron
1933	Joseph A. Gaines

RESIDENT STAFF

WARD SERVICES
(Continued)

Oto-Laryngology
1934 Eugene R. Snyder

1935 Benj. I. Allen

1937 A. H. Neffson

1938 Lester L. Coleman

1939 Samuel M. Bloom

1940 Michael S. Zeman

Gynecology
1934 Sidney N. Mendelsohn
     U. J. Salmon
1935 Robert Turell
     H. Melvin Radman
1936 Emanuel Klempner
1937 Robert I. Walter
     Norman Margolius
     Herbert F. Newman
1938 Arthur M. Davids
     Phoenix M. Sales
1939 Nathan Mintz
     Jack Squire
1940 Norbert B. Reicher
     Irving L. Frank

Ophthalmology
1928 David Wexler
1929 Robert K. Lambert
1930 Murray A. Last
1931 Saul Miller
1932 Herman I. Weiss
1933 Samuel L. Saltzman
1934 Abraham L. Kornzweig

1935 Nathan S. Rubin
1936 Frederick H. Theodore
1937 Jacob Goldsmith
1938 Frank M. Green
1939 Louis C. Ravin
1940 Herman K. Goldberg

Orthopedics
1938 Samuel R. Rubert

1939 Otto Lehmann

1940 Alvin M. Arkin

INTERNS IN DENTISTRY
1933 Marvin G. Freid
     Herbert L. Goodfleish
1934 Henry I. Cohen
     Harry A. Suslow
1935 Louis Kroll
1936 Robert S. Gilbert
     Manuel Gottlieb

1937 Ben Pine
     Robert W. Slutzky
1938 Robert S. Hess
     Lee R. Kulick
1939 Manuel Burness
     Alfred R. Shepard
1940 Lester H. Sablow
     Henry Ellison

ADMITTING PHYSICIANS
1908-1911	Max Rosenberg	1928	Elmer S. Gais
1912-1913	*Herbert W. Emsheimer	1929	Samuel H. Averbuck
1914-1915	Daniel Poll	1930	Herman Zazeela
1916	David Beck	1931	Isidore Schapiro
1917-1918	Joseph Harkavy	1931-1933	Rose Spiegel
1919	Asher Winkelstein	1934	Herman S. Roth
1920-1921	Philip Finkle	1935	Hyman Levy
1922	Leon Ginzburg	1936	D. Alfred Dantes
1923	Arthur M. Master	1937	Alan N. Leslie
1924	Coleman B. Rabin	1938	Herman I. Kantor
1925-1927	Lewis E. Persoff	1939	Julius L. Weissberg
1928	Sidney Grossman	1940	Irving Solomon

* Deceased.